Tilman Riemenschneider

◆

Master Sculptor
of the
Late Middle Ages

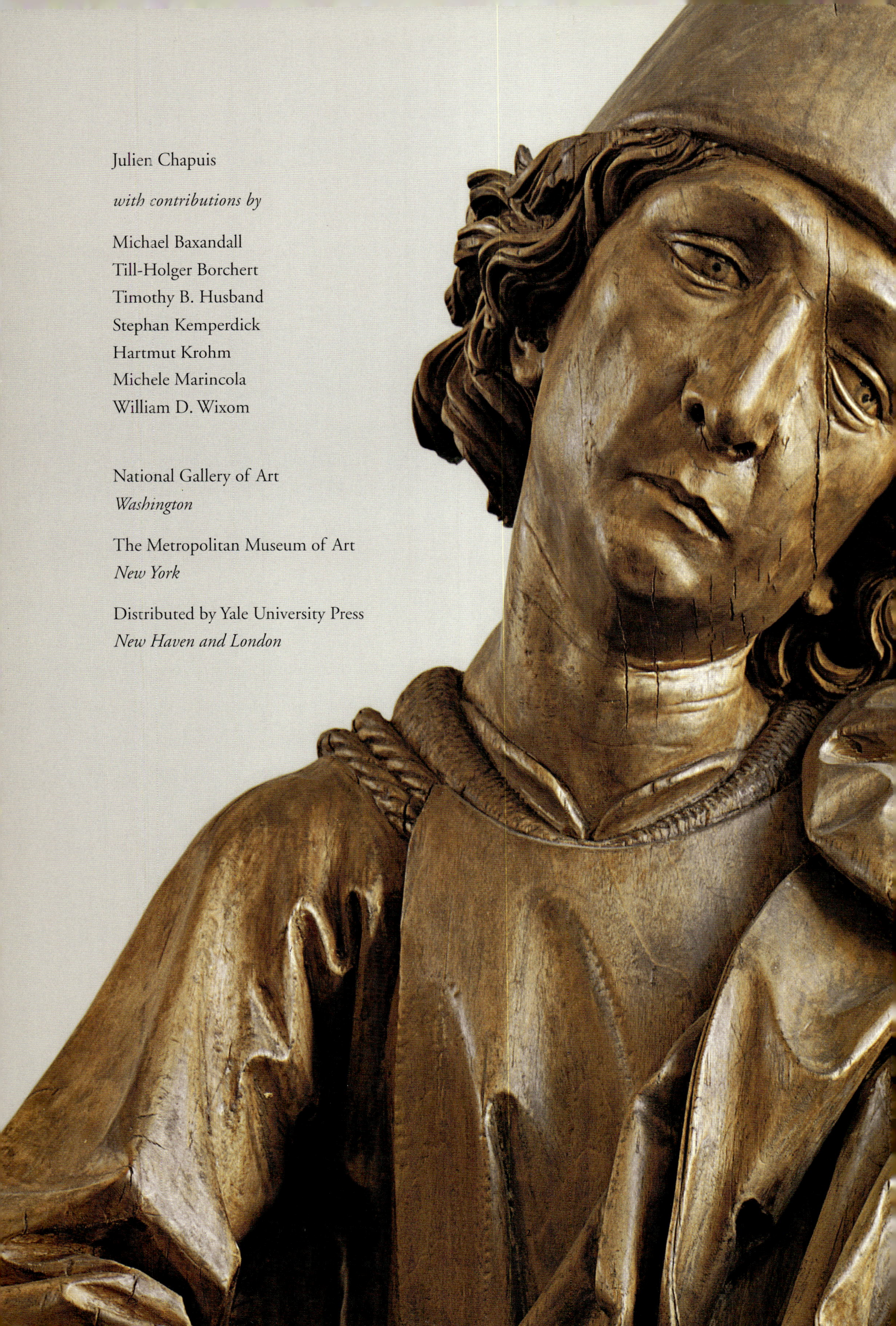

Julien Chapuis

with contributions by

Michael Baxandall
Till-Holger Borchert
Timothy B. Husband
Stephan Kemperdick
Hartmut Krohm
Michele Marincola
William D. Wixom

National Gallery of Art
Washington

The Metropolitan Museum of Art
New York

Distributed by Yale University Press
New Haven and London

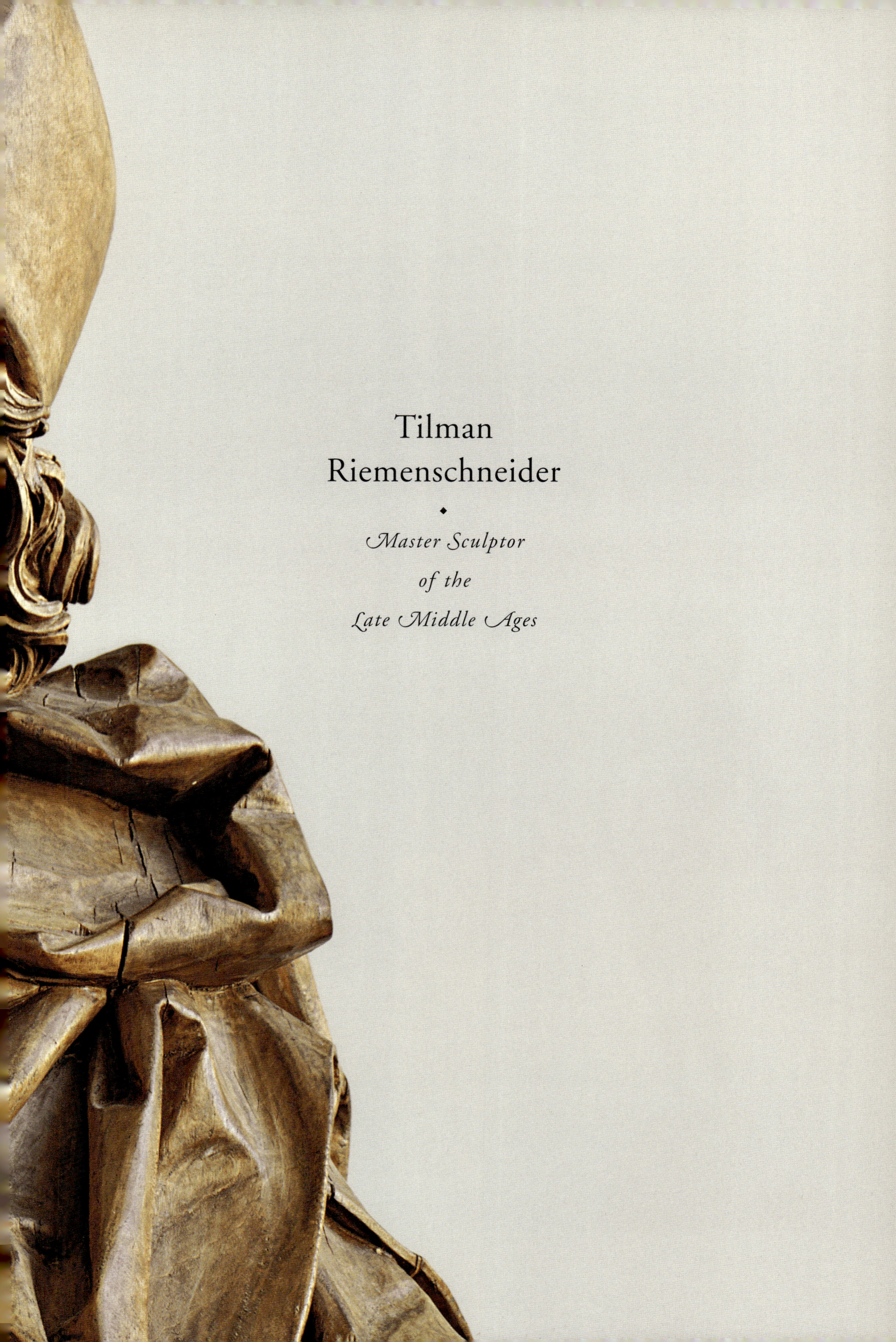

Tilman Riemenschneider

Master Sculptor
of the
Late Middle Ages

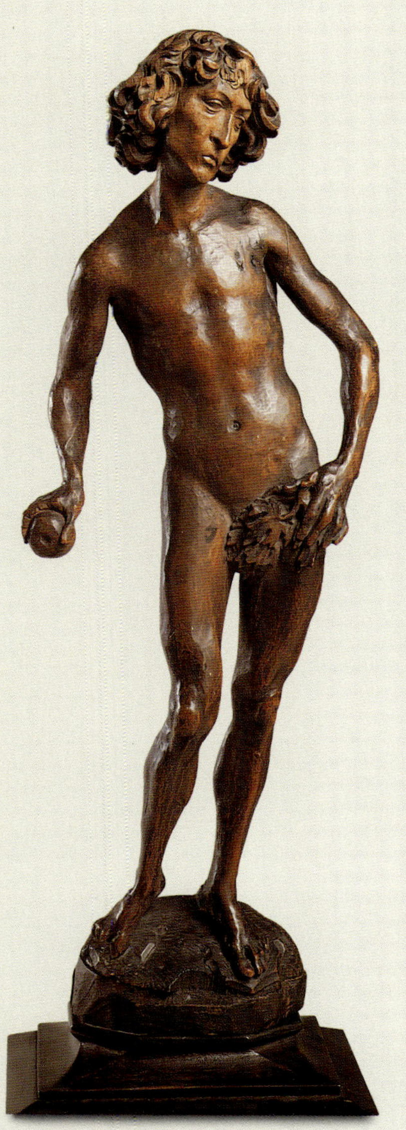

In New York the exhibition
is made possible in part
by Bayerische Landesbank

Additional support for the exhibition in
Washington and for the catalogue comes
from the Samuel H. Kress Foundation
and The Circle of the National Gallery
of Art

Support for the catalogue in New York
has been provided by the Doris Duke
Fund for Publications

The exhibition is organized by the
National Gallery of Art, Washington,
and The Metropolitan Museum of
Art, New York

An indemnity has been granted by the
Federal Council on the Arts and the
Humanities

• *Exhibition Dates* •
National Gallery of Art, Washington,
3 October 1999–9 January 2000

The Metropolitan Museum of Art,
New York, 7 February–14 May 2000

This book has been produced by the
Editors Office, National Gallery of Art,
Washington

Editor-in-chief, Frances P. Smyth
Edited by Tam Curry Bryfogle
Translations by Ulrike Mills
Designed by Margaret Bauer

Primary photography by Bruce M. White
Calligraphy by Julian Waters
Index by Elaine Luthy

Typeset in Adobe Garamond by Duke
and Company, Devon, Pennsylvania
Printed on 150 gsm Burgo Larius demi-
matt by Arnoldo Mondadori Editore,
Verona, Italy

Clothbound books distributed by
Yale University Press, New Haven and
London

• *Library of Congress
Cataloging-in-Publication Data* •

Riemenschneider, Tilman, d. 1531.
Tilman Riemenschneider: master sculp-
tor of the late Middle Ages / Julien
Chapuis; with contributions by Michael
Baxandall…[et al.].
     p.   cm.
Catalogue of an exhibition held at the
National Gallery of Art, Washington, DC,
3 October 1999–9 January 2000 and
The Metropolitan Museum of Art, New
York, NY, 7 February–14 May 2000.
Includes bibliographical references and
index.

ISBN 0-300-08162-6 (hardcover)
ISBN 0-89468-244-X (softcover)

1. Riemenschneider, Tilman, d. 1531,
Exhibitions. 1. Chapuis, Julien.
11. Baxandall, Michael. 111. National
Gallery of Art (US). 1V. Metropolitan
Museum of Art (New York, NY).
V. Title.

NB588.R5A4 1999
730'.92 — DC21   99-25450

Cover: *Virgin and Child on the Crescent
Moon* (detail), c. 1495, Museum für
Angewandte Kunst, Cologne, Sammlung
Wilhelm Clemens (cat. 16)

Back cover: *Assumption of the Virgin*
altarpiece (detail), c. 1505-1510, Herrgottskirche, Creglingen

Title page: *Saint Luke* from the predella
of the Münnerstadt altarpiece (detail),
1490–1492, Staatliche Museen zu Berlin,
Skulpturensammlung (cat. 13 C)

Copyright page: *Adam*, 1495–1505,
Kunsthistorisches Museum, Vienna,
Kunstkammer (cat. 20)

Page 8: Apostles in the *Assumption of the
Virgin* altarpiece (detail), c. 1505–1510,
Herrgottskirche, Creglingen

Page 13: *Lamentation* (detail), 1519–1523,
Pfarrkirche, Maidbronn

• Contents •

*S*triking a rare balance between formal elegance and expressive strength, the sculpture of Tilman Riemenschneider stands solidly anchored in the late Gothic tradition while also reflecting emerging humanist concerns. The present exhibition brings together many of the sculptor's finest works from throughout his career, including elements from altarpieces, cult figures, objects of private devotion, models, and sculpture with a secular function. We have also been able to reunite here for the first time several works that once belonged to the same ensembles but have long since been dispersed to different collections.

Riemenschneider, active in Würzburg from around 1483 until 1531, was one of the first sculptors to abandon polychromy on occasion, making a conscious aesthetic decision to leave visible his favored material, limewood. The dramatic change can be appreciated here in the contrast between his monochrome wood sculpture and several figures that have retained much of their original polychromy. His mastery of other materials is illustrated by exquisite works in alabaster and sandstone. The inclusion of a few particularly fine works by Riemenschneider's most important predecessors and contemporaries—such as Niclaus Gerhaert von Leiden, Michel Erhart, and Veit Stoss—allows his achievement to be viewed in its proper artistic context.

The exhibition and its accompanying catalogue have been organized and overseen by Julien Chapuis, assistant curator in the department of medieval art and The Cloisters at The Metropolitan Museum of Art. His intelligence, keen eye, and commitment to the highest scholarly and aesthetic standards have ensured an exemplary presentation of the works.

The Metropolitan Museum is grateful for Bayerische Landesbank's generous support of the exhibition in New York, especially for the kind assistance of Alfred H. Lehner, Chairman of the Board of Management; Dr. Eberhard Zinn, Member of the Board of Management; and Wilfried Freudenberger, Senior Executive Vice President and General Manager of Bayerische Landesbank in New York.

Our profound thanks go to the many lenders who have been willing to part with important works in their care to make possible this groundbreaking exhibition. Colleagues in European and American museums as well as churches and private collectors have responded with great generosity to our requests. We are also grateful to Dr. Edmund Stoiber, MdL, Minister President of the Free State of Bavaria, and to the Embassy of the Federal Republic of Germany in Washington.

Earl A. Powell III
Director, National Gallery of Art

Philippe de Montebello
Director, The Metropolitan Museum of Art

Bayerisches Nationalmuseum, Munich

City of Nuremberg

The Cleveland Museum of Art

Dumbarton Oaks, Washington, DC

Germanisches Nationalmuseum, Nuremberg

Governing Body of the Lutheran Church of Saint James, Nuremberg

Hessisches Landesmuseum, Darmstadt

Historisches Museum, Frankfurt am Main

Kunsthistorisches Museum, Vienna

Kunstsammlungen Böttcherstrasse, Bremen

Mainfränkisches Museum, Würzburg

S. Mehringer, Munich

The Metropolitan Museum of Art, New York

The Montreal Museum of Fine Arts

Musée du Louvre, Paris

Museum für Angewandte Kunst, Cologne

Museum für Kunst und Gewerbe, Hamburg

Museum of Fine Arts, Boston

National Gallery of Art, Washington

The Nelson-Atkins Museum of Art, Kansas City

North Carolina Museum of Art, Raleigh

Parish of Saint James, Grosslangheim

Parish of Saints Peter and Paul, Grossostheim

Private Collections

Rijksmuseum, Amsterdam

Spencer Museum of Art, The University of Kansas, Lawrence

Staatliche Museen zu Berlin, Skulpturensammlung

Stiftsmuseum der Stadt Aschaffenburg

The Victoria and Albert Museum, London

Württembergisches Landesmuseum, Stuttgart

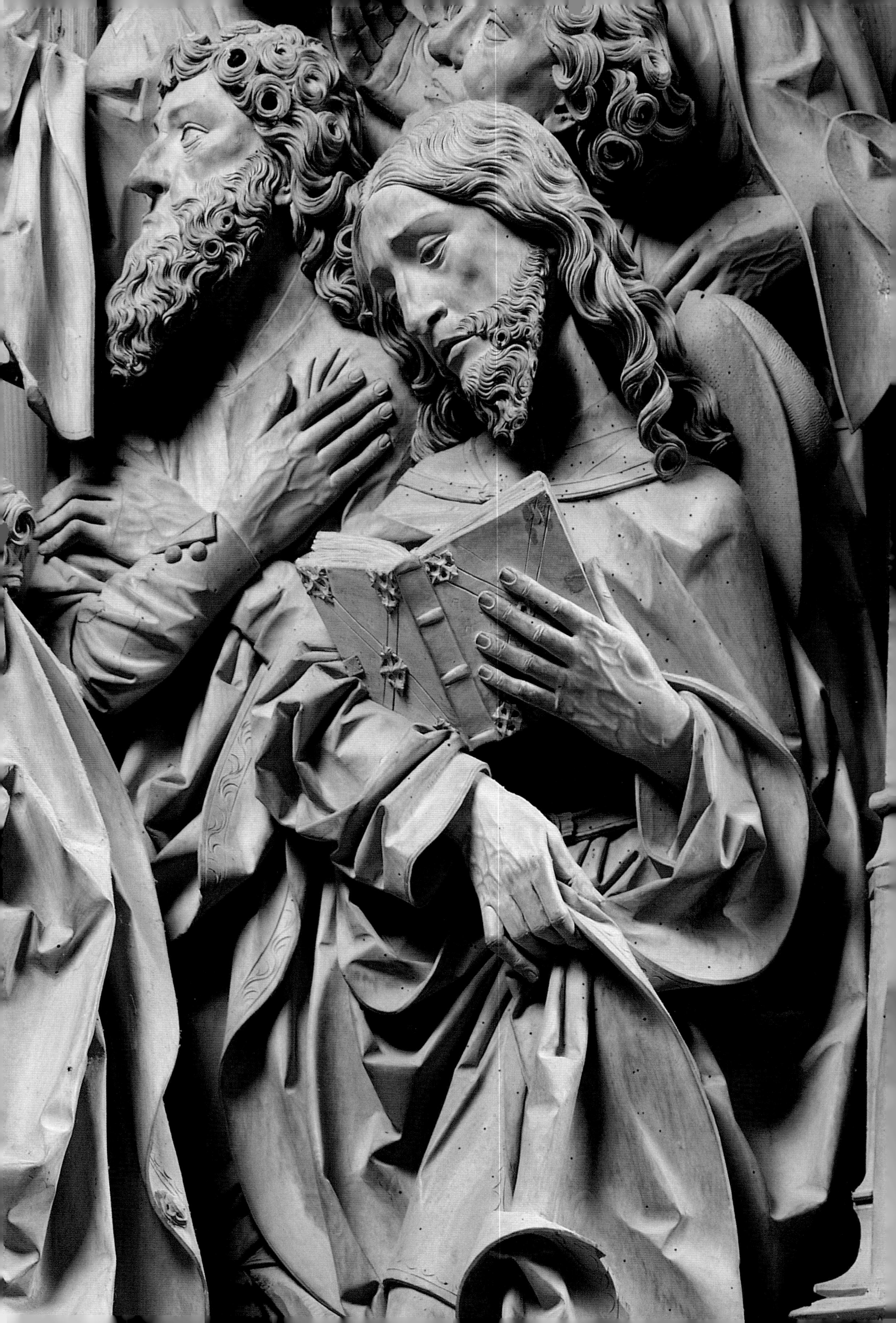

The exhibition *Tilman Riemenschneider: Master Sculptor of the Late Middle Ages* has been three years in the making. The idea originated in 1996, while I was a Samuel H. Kress Fellow at the Center for Advanced Study in the Visual Arts at the National Gallery of Art in Washington. It has taken shape since my move to The Metropolitan Museum of Art in 1997. I am extremely grateful to the directors of both institutions, Earl A. Powell III and Philippe de Montebello, for their trust and for their unflagging commitment to the exhibition.

While all of my colleagues at lending institutions have been exceedingly helpful, Hartmut Krohm, chief curator at the Skulpturensammlung of the Staatliche Museen zu Berlin, must be singled out for his extraordinary support of the project. He was not only willing to lend an unprecedented twelve key works from his museum but was instrumental in securing major loans from other institutions. The undisputed expert on Riemenschneider, Dr. Krohm wrote an essay and several entries for the catalogue, offered a critical reading of the object texts, and provided countless photographs as well as invaluable advice. I am also indebted to Arne Effenberger, director of the Skulpturensammlung, for agreeing to this exceptionally generous loan.

My heartfelt gratitude goes to the keepers of Riemenschneider's works in other collections: Reinhold Baumstark and Rainer Kahsnitz at the Bayerisches National-museum, Munich; Alan Borg, Paul Williamson, and Norbert Jopek at the Victoria and Albert Museum, London; Guy Cogeval and Hilliard Goldfarb at the Montreal Museum of Fine Arts; Sybille Ebert-Schifferer, Ina Busch, Theo Jülich, and Moritz Woelk at the Hessisches Landesmuseum, Darmstadt; Diane de Grazia and Stephen Fliegel at the Cleveland Museum of Art; Ulrich Grossmann, Renate Eikelmann, and Frank Matthias Kammel at the Germanisches Nationalmuseum, Nuremberg; Volker Himme-lein and Heribert Meurer at the Württembergisches Landesmuseum, Stuttgart; Wil-helm Hornbostel and Bernhard Heitmann at the Museum für Kunst und Gewerbe, Hamburg; Ingrid Jenderko-Sichelschmidt at the Stiftsmuseum der Stadt Aschaffen-burg; Edward Keenan and James Carder at Dumbarton Oaks, Washington, DC; Rainer Koch and Kurt Wettengl at the Historisches Museum, Frankfurt am Main; Ronald de Leeuw, Jan Piet Filedt Kok, Reinier Baarsen, and Frits Scholten at the Rijksmuseum, Amsterdam; Manfred Leithe-Jasper and Helmut Trnek at the Kunsthistorisches Mu-seum, Vienna; Father Alkuin Mahr of the Parish of Saints Peter and Paul, Grossostheim; Adolf Mehringer at S. Mehringer, Munich; Father Petro Müller of the Parish of Saint James, Grosslangheim; Andrea Norris and Susan Earle at the Spencer Museum of Art,

Lawrence, Kansas; Malcolm Rogers, Anne Poulet, and Jeffrey Munger at the Museum of Fine Arts, Boston; Pierre Rosenberg, Jean-René Gaborit, and Sophie Guillot de Suduiraut at the Musée du Louvre, Paris; Brigitte Tietzel and Gerhard Dietrich at the Museum für Angewandte Kunst, Cologne; Hans-Peter Trenschel and Claudia Lichte at the Mainfränkisches Museum, Würzburg; Marc Wilson and Roger Ward at the Nelson-Atkins Museum of Art, Kansas City; and Lawrence J. Wheeler, David Steel, and Dennis Weller at the North Carolina Museum of Art, Raleigh. The sudden deaths of Maria Anczykowski, director of the Kunstsammlungen Böttcherstrasse, Bremen, and Robert Bergman, director of the Cleveland Museum of Art, prevented them from seeing the exhibition, which they supported with generosity. I am also deeply grateful to those lenders who wish to remain anonymous, as well as to several individuals whose help in securing loans was essential: His Excellency Paul-Werner Scheele, Bishop of Würzburg; Jürgen Lenssen, Kunstreferent for the Diocese of Würzburg; Michael Petzet, Generalkonservator, Bayerisches Landesamt für Denkmalpflege; Florian Eitle; and Larry Putterman.

Conservators in many institutions examined sculptures, made them available for study, treated and prepared them for transport, and answered many queries. I would like to thank in particular Rodrigue Bédard in Montreal, Bruce Christman in Cleveland, Isabelle Garachon in Amsterdam, Kathleen Garland in Kansas City, Cordula Kähler in Frankfurt am Main, Stephanie Kleidt in Würzburg, Frédéric Lebas in Hamburg, Erwin Mayer and Axel Treptau in Munich, Hans-Werner Nett in Cologne, Arnulf von Ulmann in Nuremberg, Hans Westhoff in Stuttgart, and Adelheid Wiesmann-Emmerling in Darmstadt. Special appreciation is due to Bodo Buczynski in Berlin and Eike Oellermann in Heroldsberg for their generous advice.

The following individuals have contributed, in different ways, to the success of this exhibition: Herbert Beck, Anthony Blumka, Elisabeth-Charlotte Bollert, Babette Buller, Erwin Emmerling, Nina Gockerell, Heide Grape-Albers, Carina Greven, Walter Haberland, Tilman Kossatz, Dietrich Kötzsche, Rolf Kreib, Elaine Luthy, Liliane Masschelein-Kleiner, Peter Mookhoek, Hélène Mund, Nicholas Penny, Richard Pettit, Helmut Ricke, Gerald Stiebel, Cyriel Stroo, and David Wille.

The catalogue, which aims at balanced yet diverse presentations of Riemenschneider, results from the collaboration of its authors, to whom I am extremely grateful. Some of them are mentioned elsewhere in this preface. More than anyone else, Michael Baxandall has changed the way we approach German sculpture; his essay invites us to reflect on the nature of representation and the act of perception. Till Borchert and Stephan Kemperdick, in addition to contributing excellent texts, have been true friends.

Much of the appeal of the book derives from its magnificent new photography, most of which is by Bruce White. I would like to thank him and the institutions that facilitated his work, in particular the Diocese of Würzburg, the governing bodies of the churches in Aub, Creglingen, Grosslangheim, Grossostheim, Grünsfeld, Hassfurt, Maidbronn, Münnerstadt, Rothenburg, Steinach, and Volkach, as well as several of the museums listed above.

This handsome volume reflects the vision of Frances P. Smyth, editor-in-chief of the National Gallery, and the tireless dedication of her staff. I was privileged to work with a superb editor, Tam Curry Bryfogle, who brought elegance and precision to the text, and with Margaret Bauer, whose lucid and intelligent design does full justice to Riemenschneider's sculpture. Ulrike Mills contributed excellent translations and reviewed the entire project. Sara Sanders-Buell gathered illustrations, while Mariah Shay and Karen Kretzer provided administrative and budget support. It was a pleasure to be part of their team.

Many other employees at the National Gallery gave the exhibition their full support. I am especially grateful to Alan Shestack, deputy director, for his continuing interest. Kathleen McCleery Wagner, Jessica Stewart, and Jennifer Cipriano, in the exhibitions department headed by D. Dodge Thompson, assumed the herculean task of orchestrating the loans and ensuring the effective collaboration of all parties involved. I am most grateful to them, as I am to Jonathan Walz for his efficiency and kindness. The design department headed by Mark Leithauser, with Donna Kwederis and William Bowser, created an evocative installation, while Gordon Anson provided sensitive lighting. Mervin Richard offered crucial advice on the packing and display of the sculpture. Sally Freitag and Hunter Hollins ensured the smooth transport of objects. I am grateful to John Hand, who acted as curatorial liaison, for his guidance and friendship over the years. On several occasions I was received with hospitality by conservators Shelley Sturman and Judy Ozone. I would also like to thank Susan Arensberg, William Breazeale, Ted Dalziel, Elon Danziger, Gregory Jecmen, Andrew Krieger, Kathleen Lane, Douglas Lewis, Alison Luchs, Melissa McCracken, Henry A. Millon, Gregg Most, Therese O'Malley, Ruth Philbrick, Margaret Porta, Andrew Robison, Chris Vogel, Gary Webber, Jeffrey Weiss, and Nancy Yeide.

Throughout the various stages of this project, I have received invaluable assistance from colleagues at The Metropolitan Museum of Art. For her guidance and commitment to this exhibition, I am deeply grateful to Mahrukh Tarapor. I would also like to express my sincere appreciation to Doralynn Pines, Kent Lydecker, and Harold Holzer. The tenacity of Emily Rafferty, Lynne Winter, and Sarah Higby secured essential funding. Ashton Hawkins, Sharon Cott, and Stephanie Basta offered expert counsel. Linda

Sylling solved countless logistical problems. For his support on editorial matters, I am greatly indebted to John O'Neill. Herbert Moskowitz and Aileen Chuk supervised all registrarial matters with diplomacy. It was a pleasure to work with Daniel Bradley Kershaw, who conceived the elegant exhibition design, and with Zack Zanolli, who deserves praise for his sophisticated lighting. Jack Soultanian provided important advice. I also wish to extend thanks to Maryan Ainsworth, Barbara Bridgers, Keith Christiansen, Joseph Coscia, Jeff Daly, Pete Dandridge, Martha Deese, James Draper, Tony Frantz, Sophia Geronimus, George Goldner, Constance Harper, Ann Lucke, Esther Morales, Christopher Noey, Nadine Orenstein, Gwen Roginsky, Kenneth Soehner, Richard Stone, Sian Wetherill, George Wheeler, Ari Wiseman, and Egle Zygas.

This exhibition would not have been possible without the backing of my colleagues in the department of medieval art and The Cloisters, who often took on extra duties to afford me the time to bring this project to completion. To William D. Wixom and Peter Barnet, retired and present department heads, I am grateful for advice and understanding. I would like to thank my fellow curators Barbara Boehm, Helen Evans, and Charles Little for their support. I am also indebted to Christine Brennan, Keith Glutting, Lauren Jackson-Beck, Deirdre Larkin, Theo Margelony, Thom Morin, Paige North, José Ortiz, Mary Shepard, Tom Vinton, and Ann Webster. Christina Alphonso deserves special thanks for her efficiency and patience. The enterprise has benefited from the perspicacity of four research assistants, Susanne Reece, Christine Kitzlinger, Brian Gallagher, and especially Elaine Barella. I owe much to conservator Michele Marincola for her dedication, knowledge, and kindness. She wrote an insightful essay for the catalogue and reviewed many of the texts. Over the past two and a half years I have been engaged in a continuous dialogue with Timothy Husband, who not only contributed entries to the catalogue but offered guidance on all things essential; this exhibition would not be what it is without him.

Throughout my work on this project, I received encouragement, constructive criticism, and good humor from many friends. Katey Brown is first among them. I am also grateful to Peter Antony, Tom Armentrout, Truus van Bueren, Anne van Buren, Joe Carpenter, Jesús Escobar, Molly Faries, Carter Foster, Eileen Fry, Kevin Gepford, Steve Godeke, Nicholas Haylett, Ursula Held, Eric Lee, Philippe Lorentz, Catherine Metzger, Beth Miller, Karel Nat, Mark Newbanks, Ted Porter, Sebastian Preuss, William Priester, Annette Rupprecht, Stephen Saitas, Renato Salazar, John Sare, Thijs Tromp, Karin Wester, and Scott Westrem. Finally, I wish to thank my parents for their steadfast support.

Julien Chapuis

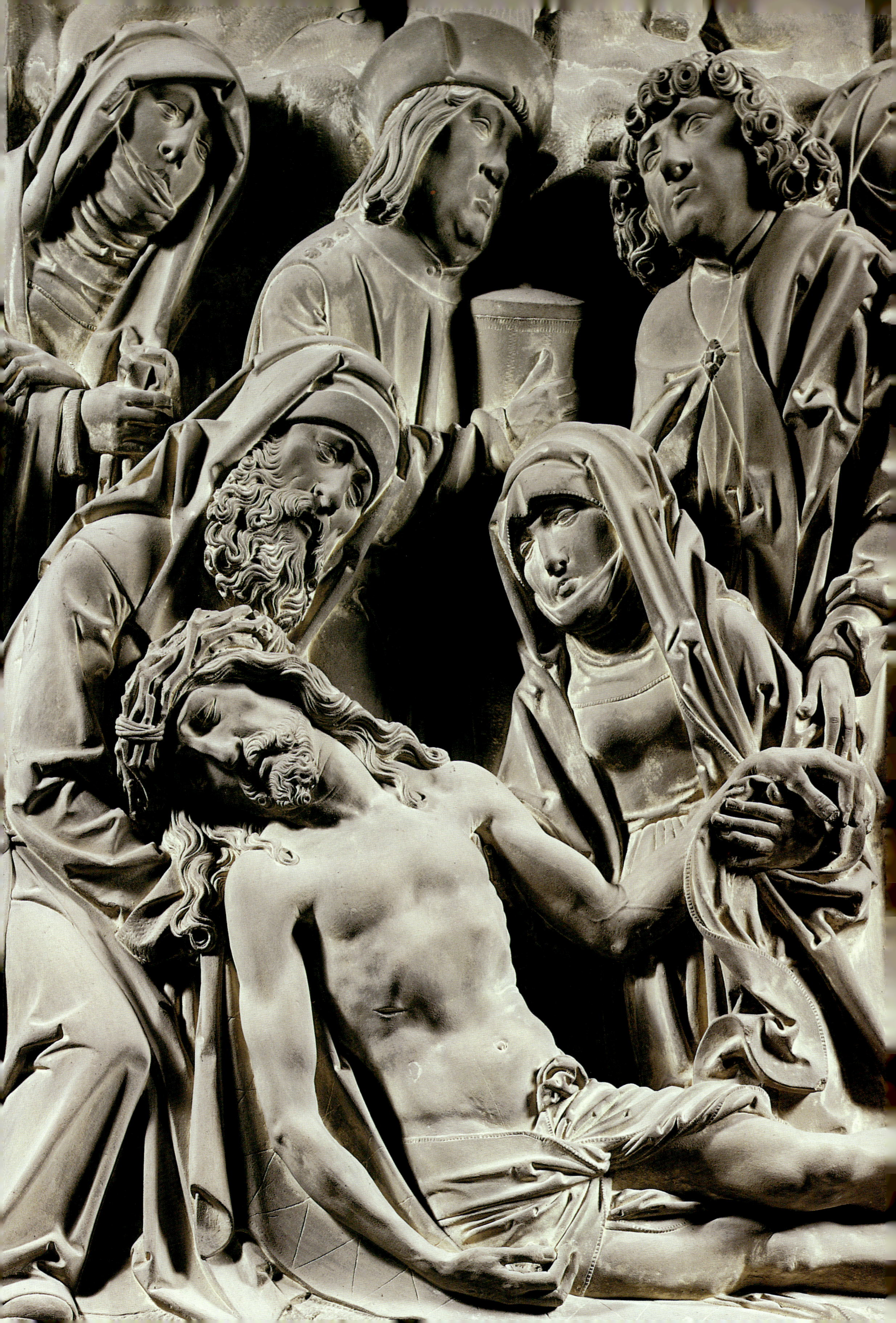

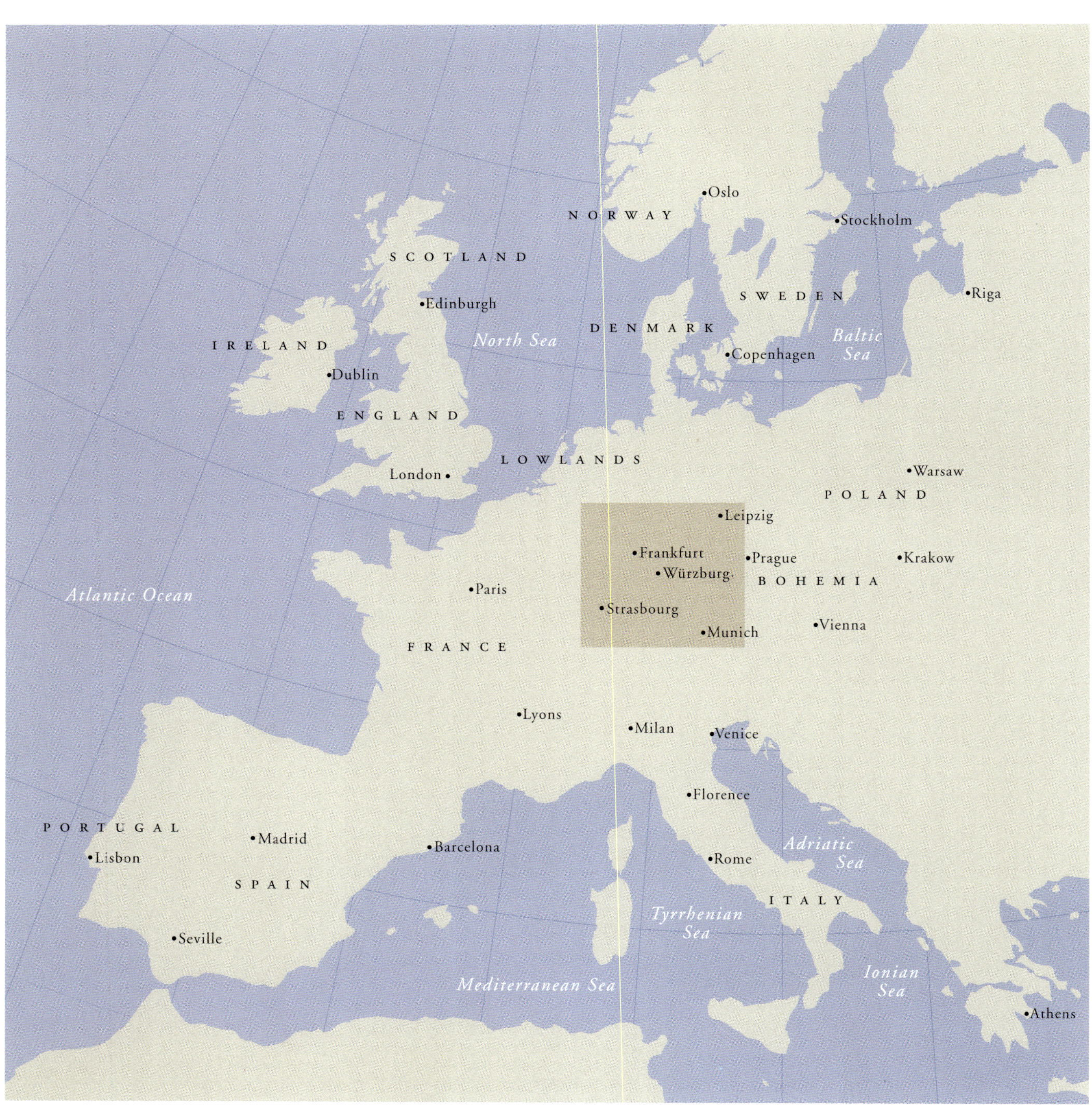

NORWAY
Oslo
Stockholm
SWEDEN
Riga
SCOTLAND
Edinburgh
IRELAND
North Sea
DENMARK
Baltic Sea
Dublin
Copenhagen
ENGLAND
LOWLANDS
Warsaw
London
POLAND
Leipzig
Frankfurt
Prague
Krakow
Würzburg
BOHEMIA
Paris
Strasbourg
Atlantic Ocean
Munich
Vienna
FRANCE
Lyons
Milan
Venice
Florence
PORTUGAL
Madrid
Adriatic Sea
Lisbon
Barcelona
Rome
SPAIN
ITALY
Tyrrhenian Sea
Seville
Ionian Sea
Mediterranean Sea
Athens

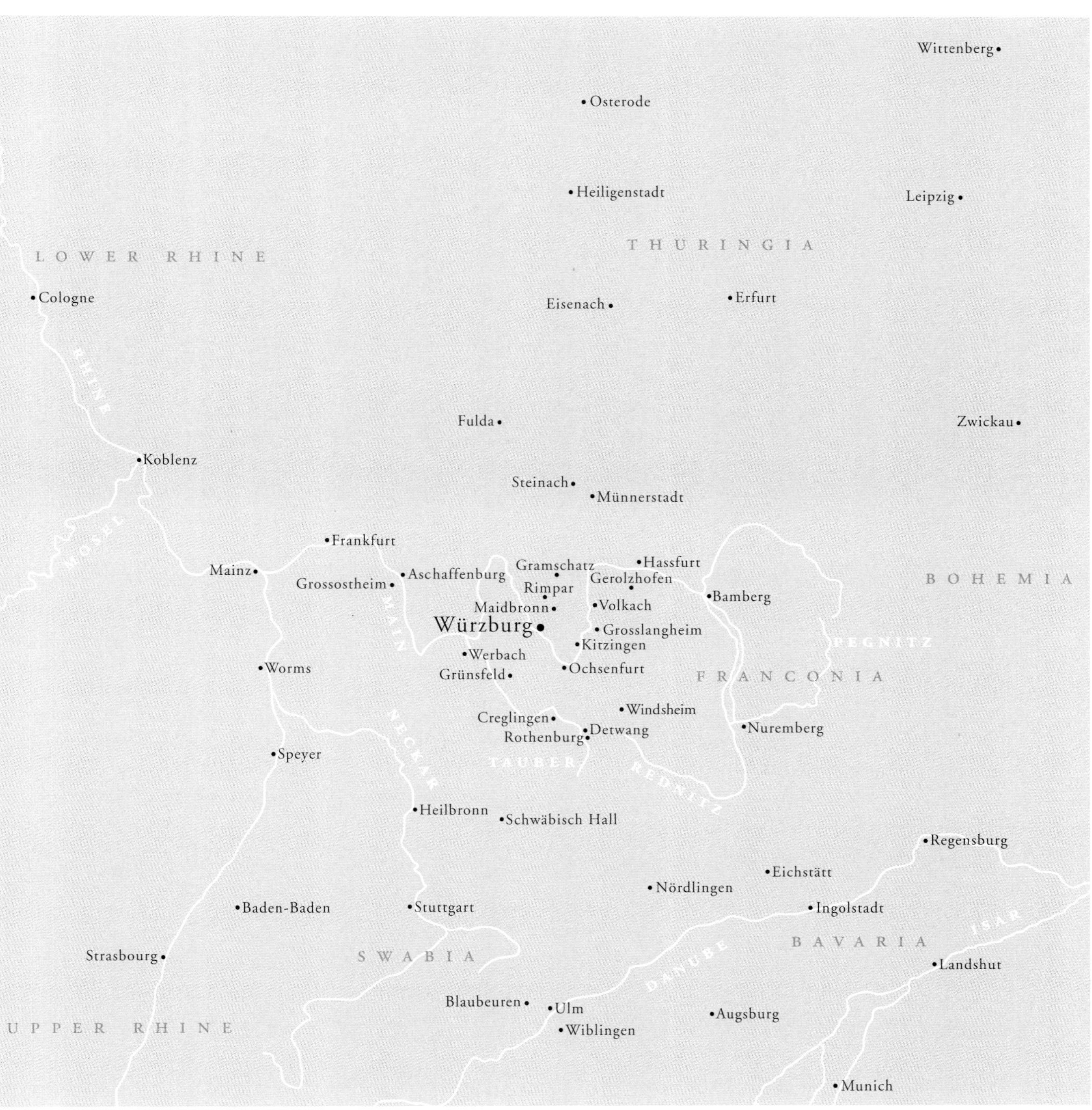

Sites relevant to the study of Riemenschneider's oeuvre

⁕ c. 1460 ⁕
Tilman Riemenschneider born
in Heiligenstadt im Eichsfeld.

⁕ c. 1465 ⁕
Tilman Riemenschneider
the Elder, the sculptor's father,
moves with his family to
Osterode am Harz, where he
becomes master of the mint.

⁕ 1479 ⁕
A Tilman Riemenschneider
abandons his position as curate of the altar of Saint Anne
in the church of Stift Haug
in Würzburg. It is not clear
whether this is the young
sculptor or another person.

⁕ 1483 ⁕
Riemenschneider finds em-
ployment as a journeyman
in a workshop in Würzburg,
where he joins the Saint
Luke's brotherhood.

⁕ 1485 ⁕
Marries Anna Schmidt, née
Uchenhofer (d. 1494), acquires
citizenship, and becomes a
master. His workshop is located
in the house "zum Wolmanns-
ziechlein."

⁕ 1490 ⁕
Signs a contract on 26 June
with the municipal council of
Münnerstadt for an altarpiece
for the church of Mary Magdalen; the altarpiece is erected
in September 1492 (cat. 13).

⁕ 1491 ⁕
Signs a contract on 5 May
with the municipal council of
Würzburg for sandstone figures of Adam and Eve for the
south portal of the Marienkapelle; the figures are installed
in September 1493.

⁕ 1494 ⁕
On 7 April the municipal
council of Windsheim com-
missions sculpture, including a
Crucifixion, for the high altar
of the parish church of Saint
Kilian. The encasement had
been provided by a Nuremberg
joiner. The figures are delivered
in 1496–1497 (destroyed by
fire in 1730).

⁕ 1496 ⁕
Signs a contract on 21 October
with Lorenz von Bibra, prince-
bishop of Würzburg, for the
funerary monument of his
predecessor, Rudolf von Scherenberg (ruled 1466–1495),
which is installed in Würzburg
Cathedral in 1499. The city
council of Rothenburg commissions a now-lost Marian
altarpiece for the Jakobskirche
from a Würzburg sculptor,
probably Riemenschneider.

⁕ 1497 ⁕
Riemenschneider marries Anna
Rappolt (d. 1506 or 1507).

⁕ 1499 ⁕
Signs a contract on 19 August
for the tomb of Emperor
Heinrich II and Empress Kunigunde in Bamberg Cathedral;
the monument is completed
and installed in September 1513.

⁕ 1499–1500 ⁕
Produces a Crucifixion group
for the choir beam in the
church of Saint Kilian in
Windsheim (destroyed by
fire in 1730).

⁕ c. 1500 ⁕
Riemenschneider and his shop
begin carving a cycle of sandstone figures of Christ, John
the Baptist, and the apostles
for the buttresses of the Marienkapelle in Würzburg, which
are installed in late 1506.

⁕ 1501 ⁕
Signs a contract on 15 April
with the Rothenburg municipal council for the *Holy Blood*
altarpiece in the Jakobskirche.
The encasement had been
commissioned in 1499 from
the Rothenburg joiner Erhart
Harschner. The figures are
delivered in installments in
1502, 1504, and early 1505.

⁕ 1504 ⁕
Elected to the Würzburg city
council.

⁕ 1505 ⁕
Among the delegates of the
municipal council to greet
Emperor Maximilian on his
visit to Würzburg. The municipal council of Rothenburg
commissions a Saint Anne
altarpiece for its Marienkapelle,
of which fragments may still
exist (cat. 30); the retable is
installed in 1506.

• 1505/1506 •
A sculptor from Würzburg,
presumably Riemenschneider,
carves a crucifix for the castle
chapel in Wittenberg, commissioned by Prince-Elector
Friedrich the Wise (the sculpture is destroyed by fire in
1760).

• 1506 •
Riemenschneider makes a table
for the Würzburg city hall.

• 1507/1508–1509/1510 •
Receives payments for an
All Saints retable for the high
altar of the church of the
Dominican nuns in Rothen-
burg; figures from that altarpiece may still exist (cat. 32).

• 1508 •
Marries Margarete Wurzbach
(d. around 1520).

• 1508–1510 •
Works on the decoration of
the high altar of Würzburg
Cathedral, which is still incomplete in 1519; the altarpiece is
dismantled in 1701.

• 1509 •
First elected to the Upper
Council in Würzburg. His
retable of *Christ and the
Apostles,* commissioned by
Elisabeth Bachknapp, is in-
stalled in the church of
Saint Kilian in Windsheim.

• 1514 •
Serves a second term on the
Upper Council. Receives a
commission for a small altar-
piece, no longer extant, for the
Frickenhausen parish church.

• 1514 or 1515 •
Delivers a canopy for the
bronze baptismal font of the
Ochsenfurt parish church
(canopy destroyed in 1674).

• 1516 •
Delivers a crucifix for the
Steinach parish church.

• 1518 •
Elected to the Upper Council
for a third term.

• 1520 •
Signs an estate settlement
with his children. Marries his
fourth wife, a woman named
Margarete (surname unknown).

• 1520 or 1522 •
Funerary monument of Prince-
Bishop Lorenz von Bibra
(ruled 1495–1519) is erected in
Würzburg Cathedral.

• 1520–1521 •
Riemenschneider is mayor of
Würzburg.

• 1521–1522 •
Serves as mayor emeritus and a
member of the Upper Council.

• 1521–1522 •
Works on the *Virgin of the
Rosary* for the pilgrimage
church at Volkach.

• 1525 •
During the Peasants' Revolt,
Würzburg opposes Prince-
Bishop Konrad von Thüngen
(ruled 1519–1530). The city
surrenders on 7 June and asks
the prince-bishop for forgiveness. Riemenschneider, as
a member of the municipal
council, is arrested, questioned,
and tortured. He is released
from the Marienberg fortress
on 8 August. A portion of his
estate is confiscated.

• 1526 •
Sandstone relief of the *Lamentation* is erected in the
church of the Cistercian
nuns at Maidbronn.

• 1527 •
Riemenschneider carries out
restoration work on altarpieces
that had been damaged during the Peasants' Revolt in the
church of the Benedictine
nuns in Kitzingen.

• 1531 •
Dies in Würzburg on 7 July
and is buried in the cathedral
cemetery, between the cathedral and the Neumünster;
his tombstone is unearthed
during street work in 1822.

Adapted from Tilman Riemenschneider. Frühe Werke *[exh.
cat., Mainfränkisches Museum
Würzburg] (Regensburg, 1981),
20–21.*

Dimensions are given in centimeters followed by inches in parentheses. Height precedes width, which precedes depth.

Captions throughout the publication and headings to object entries in the *Catalogue of the Exhibition* assume, unless otherwise specified, that a sculpture has been produced under Riemenschneider's direct supervision, if not by his own hand.

Bibliographical references have been abbreviated throughout the catalogue entries, with full citations provided at the back of the book. References to exhibition catalogues are abbreviated using the city of the exhibition's first showing and the date of publication.

The woodcut reproduced on the divider pages of this catalogue shows the medieval city of Würzburg. The cathedral, depicted in the center foreground, houses Riemenschneider's funerary monuments to Rudolf von Scherenberg and Lorenz von Bibra. His figures of Adam and Eve, his monument to Konrad von Schaumberg, as well as his series of apostles were commissioned for the Marienkapelle, in the middle distance to the right. The sculptor was imprisoned in the Marienberg Fortress, at the top of the rise to the left, following the Peasants' Revolt of 1525. The woodcut is from Hartmann Schedel's *Liber Chronicarum,* published by Anton Koberger in Nuremberg in 1493 (National Gallery of Art, Washington, Gift of Paul Mellon, in Honor of the 50th Anniversary of the National Gallery of Art).

Recognizing Riemenschneider   *Julien Chapuis*

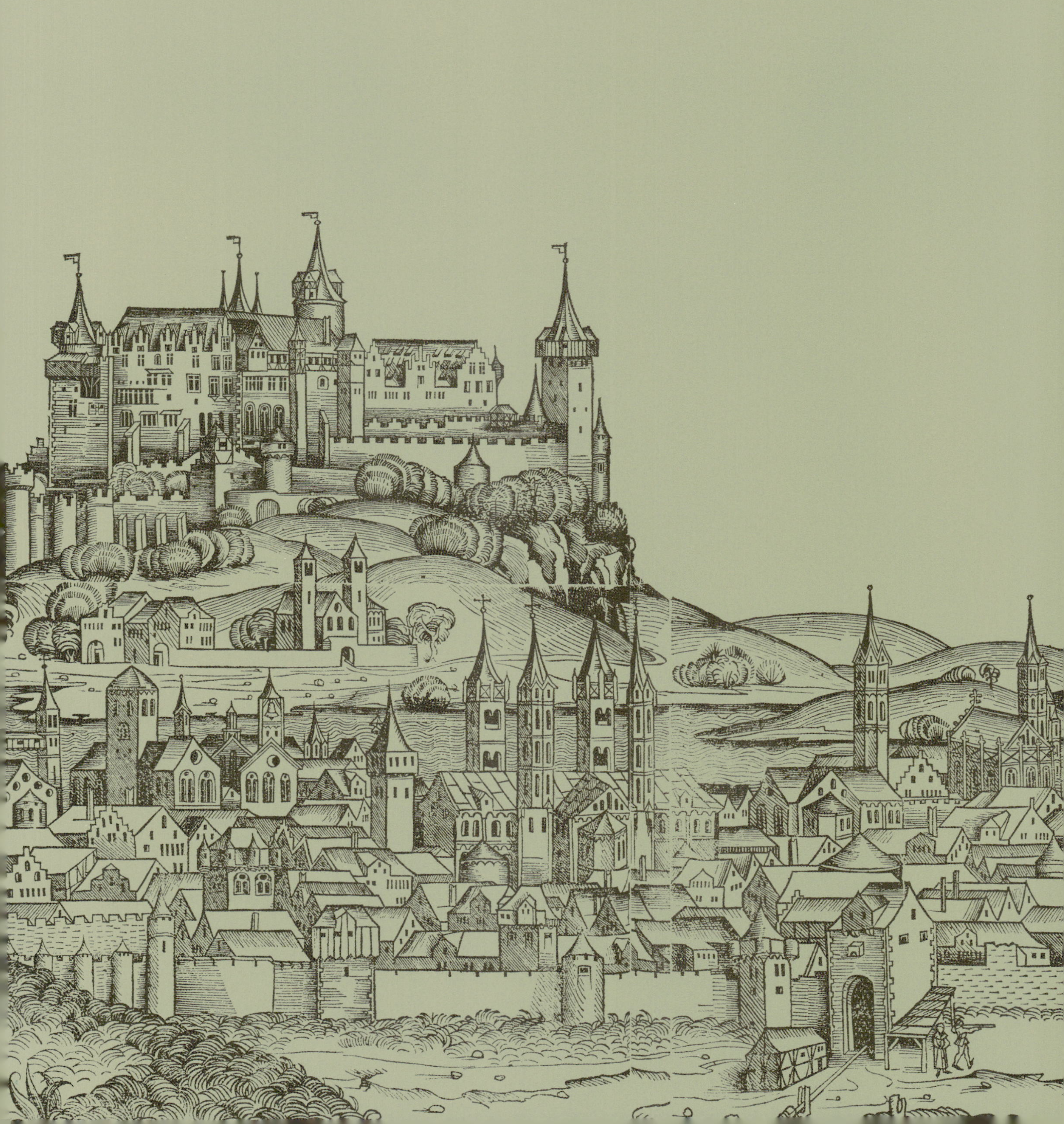

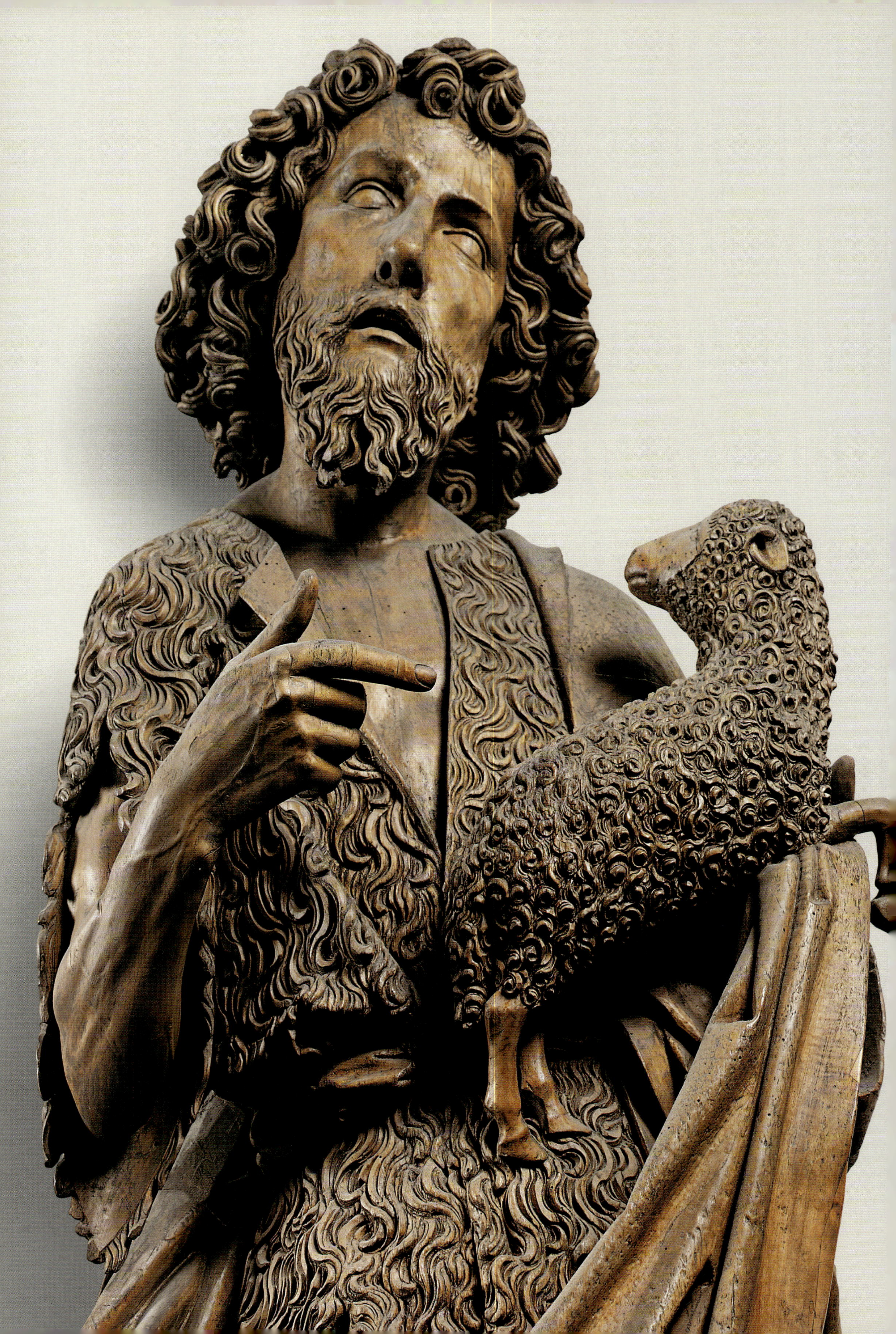

IGH ON AN OTHERWISE unadorned plaster wall in the parish church of Hassfurt, a small town on the river Main some twenty miles northeast of Würzburg, stands a haunting limewood sculpture of transfixing eloquence (fig. 1). Generally held to be an early work (c. 1490), this figure representing Saint John the Baptist is a paradigm of Tilman Riemenschneider's sculptural genius. It is also an ideal sculpture with which to begin a discussion of Riemenschneider's oeuvre, because it allows mention of some of the major issues involved in its study. ❦ His lips parted as if to speak, John points to the lamb that rests its back hooves at his waist and turns its head to face him. Known as the one who baptized Jesus in the river Jordan, John seems to call out, "Behold, the Lamb of God, who takes away the sin of the world!" (John 1:29). In an ancient gesture of deference, he holds the lamb through the cloth of his mantle, not daring direct contact. Riemenschneider's prophet conveys a sense of high drama, which is in keeping with his solemn message of repentance and redemption. As one who lived in the wilderness and sustained himself on locusts and wild honey, he wears a garment of camel's hair with a leather girdle around his waist (Matthew 3:1–4; Mark 1:6; Luke 3:2). His lean face and wide-open eyes, encircled by a mass of curly hair, convey intense inspiration and suggest that spiritual sustenance supersedes the physical. His visionary expression and the precariousness of his stance, with his forward left foot turned out, evoke his description in the Gospels as the "voice of one crying in the wilderness." The salient muscles, veins, and tendons in his right arm underscore the seriousness of his quest. The pointing finger, inclination of the head, and broad upward sweep of drapery all lead the viewer's eye to the lamb.

Detail of *Saint John the Baptist* (fig. 1), c. 1490, Pfarrkirche, Hassfurt

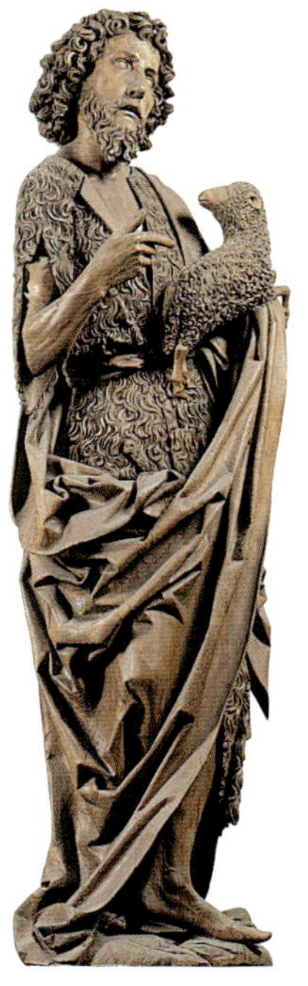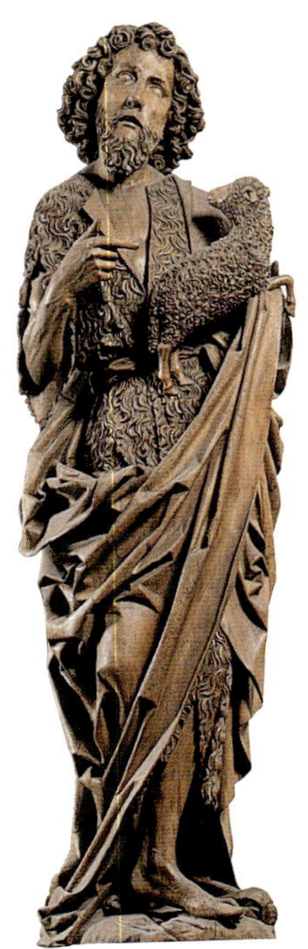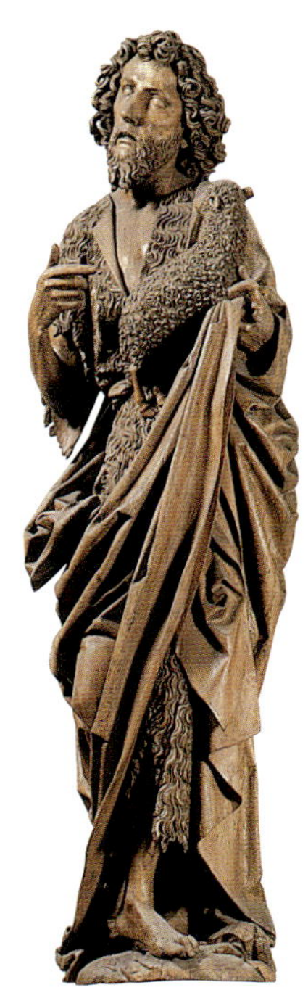

Alternate views of *Saint John the Baptist,* c. 1490, limewood, Pfarrkirche, Hassfurt

John the Baptist is perceived in Christian thought to be the link between the Old and the New Testaments. As the last and greatest of the prophets, he immediately precedes Christ. For a late medieval sculptor embarking on a depiction of John the Baptist, few elements were predetermined beyond his costume, his meager diet, and his holding a lamb and pointing to it, a detail dictated by centuries-old tradition. Riemenschneider's figure was to be installed in a church, and its intended viewers would have heard the passage from John 1:29 countless times, because the words are pronounced by the priest at Mass after the consecration of the Eucharist. Thus the sculptor could reasonably assume that his audience would, consciously or intuitively, perceive an image of John the Baptist as a reference to the central tenet of the Christian faith. How effectively this was communicated and elicited a pious response was entirely a function of the artist's creative skills. Certain conventionalized formal means, such as the costume, physical appearance, attributes, and even compositional and iconographic formulas, were of course at his disposal. Variations of a familiar solution frequently proved expedient. But in more inventive hands the site, scale, source of light, and viewer's approach dictated how carefully surfaces were manipulated, how mass and voids were modulated, and how forms were modeled to enhance the play of light. Exceptionally, highly innovative solutions brought profound emotive value to the subject.

Knowing the scriptural basis for the sculpture, we perceive it to be a moving depiction of John the Baptist and therefore effective as a focus for veneration. The figure also engages us in other experiential ways. We quickly become aware of the attention lavished on details. Riemenschneider differentiated among four kinds of hair, for instance, each of varying density and curliness, and he accurately observed and rendered the bone and musculature of John's right arm. Forgetting for a moment that we are looking at a piece of limewood, we recognize in it elements derived from our immediate realm of experience. Equally important, the sculpture makes us aware of our own physicality, of our being and moving in space before it. Standing in front of the figure, we unconsciously compare it to our own bodies and realize that it is life-size. Although unfinished in the back, as is true of most of Riemenschneider's carvings, the sculpture is remarkably spatial. The drapery, arranged in deep, angular furrows that catch shadows and create a rich contrast of light and dark, suggests the body underneath yet does not precisely define it. It also encourages the viewer to move around from the left to the right of the figure, following the generous upward sweep of the mantle. The three most important thematic elements of the composition—John's open mouth, his pointing gesture, and the lamb itself—remain legible from a wide vantage. Indeed the *Saint John* is entirely coherent when seen in full profile from either side.

Riemenschneider employs other means to unite the space of the sculpture with that of the viewer. Although the figure stands on a grassy patch that serves as a base and thus is separated from the world in which it functions, Riemenschneider allows a fold of drapery to fall over the edge of the base, into the space of the viewer, which blurs this boundary.[1] The conceit dramatically intensifies the immediacy of the sculpture as an object of veneration.

The Hassfurt *Saint John* allows mention of two additional issues that are central to the study of Riemenschneider's work. First, recent technical findings suggest that the figure was not originally painted, as had hitherto been customary, but that the viewer was meant to see the work uncolored.[2] The significance of monochromy, a subject of considerable debate surrounding Riemenschneider's oeuvre, is discussed at length elsewhere in this catalogue. Second, the sculpture is no longer seen in its original context. The church at Hassfurt contains five figures by Riemenschneider and his workshop, of which the *Saint John* is clearly the best, and they may once have been combined in one large or several smaller altarpieces.[3] In the course of centuries the figures were separated, a fate shared by most of the artist's creations.

Because so many of Riemenschneider's works have been altered over time or removed from their original settings and remain undocumented, it is from the objects themselves that we must take our clues. Scrutinizing their surfaces, we gain insights into their original appearance and changes they have undergone. On another level, understanding the conceptual structure of the works allows us to draw conclusions as

1. This effect is unfortunately weakened by a modern console, which is broader than the original base.

2. The sculpture was restored in 1990–1991 by Erwin Mayer and Regina Becker of the Bayerisches Landesamt für Denkmalpflege. There are apparently no traces of an original polychromy on the surface. I am grateful to Mr. Mayer for discussing this unpublished information with me.

3. See *Tilman Riemenschneider. Frühe Werke* [exh. cat., Mainfränkisches Museum Würzburg] (Regensburg, 1981), 170–176 and 332–335.

to their intended placement. When creating a sculpture, Riemenschneider often considered its installation, whether against a column, high on a wall, or in the shrine of an altarpiece, and introduced optical corrections. For example, he might elongate the proportions of a figure meant to be installed above eye level so that the anatomy would remain coherent when seen in strong foreshortening (see cat. 28). Riemenschneider's most accomplished works invite us to join a dialogue on the nature of representation and, through their expressiveness, cause us to reflect on more universal human issues.

• *The Sculptor's Life and Oeuvre* •

Little is known about Riemenschneider's early life, other than that he was born in about 1460 in Heiligenstadt in Thuringia and that in 1465 his father, also called Tilman, moved with his family to Osterode am Harz, where he became master of the mint. It was possibly through his uncle Nikolaus that Riemenschneider was first drawn to Würzburg. With degrees in both canon law and secular law, the uncle had a wide sphere of influence. He enjoyed direct access to Prince-Bishop Rudolf von Scherenberg and held various offices in Würzburg: he was vicar of the cathedral, financial administrator of the diocese, and imperial notary. In 1479 a Tilman Riemenschneider from the diocese of Mainz left his position as curate, or assistant to the parish priest, in the church of Stift Haug in Würzburg. The name was common, however, and it is unclear whether this man was the young sculptor or another person.[4]

4. Justus Bier, "Riemenschneider's Helpers in Need," *The Metropolitan Museum of Art Bulletin* 21 (1963), 323–324; see also Würzburg 1981, 20; Walter Prochaska, "Zur Herkunft Tilman Riemenschneiders aus Heiligenstadt im Eichsfeld," in Würzburg 1981, 385–388; and Erik Soder von Güldenstubbe, *Kulturelles Leben im Würzburg der Riemenschneiderzeit* (Berlin, 1981), 3–4 (supplement to Würzburg 1981).

In the absence of documentary evidence, it is only by comparing Riemenschneider's works with the production of other regions that art historians have been able to discern where he might have been trained. It was common for artists in northern Europe to travel long distances: they could be apprenticed to a master in one city and wander for a few years after completing their training, seeking temporary employment as journeymen in different areas. The mobility of sculptors, painters, glaziers, goldsmiths, and illuminators resulted in artistic cross-fertilization and a rapid dissemination of styles across vast regions. Several of the greatest artists of the fifteenth century traveled widely, synthesizing different artistic currents. Claus Sluter, the revolutionary sculptor from around 1400, left his native Haarlem in Holland to enter the service of Philip the Bold, duke of Burgundy, in Dijon. The engraver and painter Martin Schongauer, who was born in Colmar, south of Strasbourg, and spent most of his active life there, was enrolled for a year at the university of Leipzig. His profound knowledge of the art of Rogier van der Weyden strongly suggests that he spent time in the south Lowlands. Hans Memling, often considered the epitome of fifteenth-century painting in Bruges, came from the region of Würzburg, and his art combines features from central Germany with the formal language of Rogier. Niclaus Gerhaert von Leiden, arguably the one artist from whom Riemenschneider learned most, was probably a native of Holland. Active in Strasbourg, he was called to Wiener Neustadt by Emperor Friedrich III in 1467 to carve his tomb; major monuments of his art are found in Trier, Nördlingen, and Baden-Baden.

As Hartmut Krohm argues in his essay for this catalogue, it is most probably in Strasbourg and Ulm that Riemenschneider received his apprenticeship. An early work such as the alabaster *Saint Barbara* (cat. 4) exhibits a volumetric treatment of forms, an almost kinetic conception of sculpture, and drapery that suggests as much as it conceals the body underneath. These features presuppose the direct knowledge of a work such as the Dangolsheim *Virgin and Child,* attributed to Niclaus Gerhaert (Krohm essay, fig. 2). Both the Nuremberg *Fragment from an Adoration* and the Cleveland *Saint Jerome* (cats. 9 and 11) reveal Riemenschneider's indebtedness to Michel Erhart and the sculpture of Ulm (see also cat. 12). The third factor in the equation of the genesis of Riemenschneider's style is his intimate knowledge of the engraved production of Martin Schongauer, through which, indirectly, he absorbed lessons in the formal elegance and restrained pathos of Rogier van der Weyden.

Riemenschneider settled in Würzburg in 1483, joined the Saint Luke brotherhood of painters, sculptors, and glaziers, and found employment as a journeyman in an unspecified workshop. Two years later, in 1485, he married Anna Schmidt, the widow of a goldsmith, became a burgher of Würzburg, and acquired the title of master, which allowed him to employ both apprentices and journeymen and to sell works under his own name. Possibly helped by connections established in Würzburg through his uncle, but certainly by the virtuosity of his early sculpture, his workshop rapidly grew into one of the most prolific in Franconia, and he received commissions from ecclesiastical and municipal authorities in Würzburg and other towns in the vicinity as well as in cities outside the diocese, such as Bamberg and Wittenberg.

A *Passion* altarpiece that Riemenschneider produced shortly after 1485 for a church in Rothenburg (probably that of the Franciscans) gives a measure of his creative powers at the beginning of his career.[5] Although the retable has been dismantled, the two groups originally flanking the Crucifixion in the central shrine reveal the exceptionally high quality of the work (fig. 2). In its expression of pathos the relief of the *Mourning Women and Saint John* calls to mind a painting such as Rogier's *Descent from the Cross* in the Prado. A detail such as John's head reveals the superb sculptural execution, particularly evident in the treatment of the hair. It also shows how much the polychromy—unusually well preserved—adds to the drama and immediacy of the work.

The altarpiece must have established Riemenschneider as the leading sculptor of the region. It was the first of several commissions for Rothenburg. In 1496 the local

5. On the *Passion* altarpiece, see Würzburg 1981, 23–72; and Rainer Kahsnitz, *Tilman Riemenschneider. Zwei Figurengruppen unter dem Kreuz Christi,* Bayerisches Nationalmuseum (Munich, 1997).

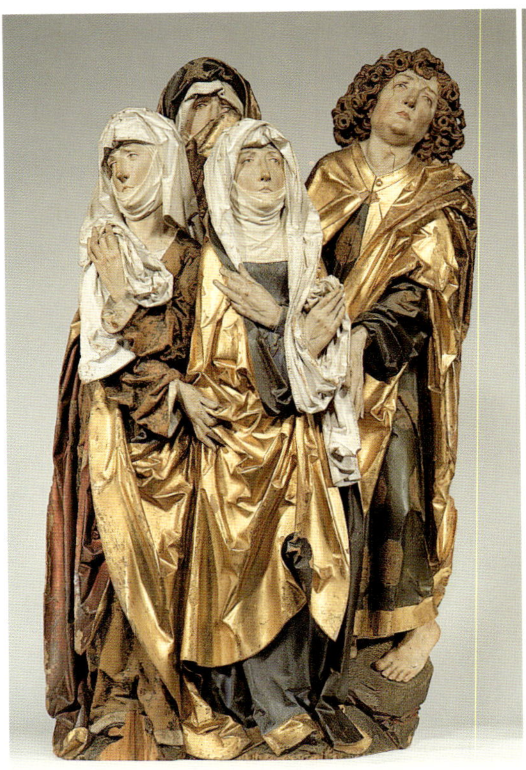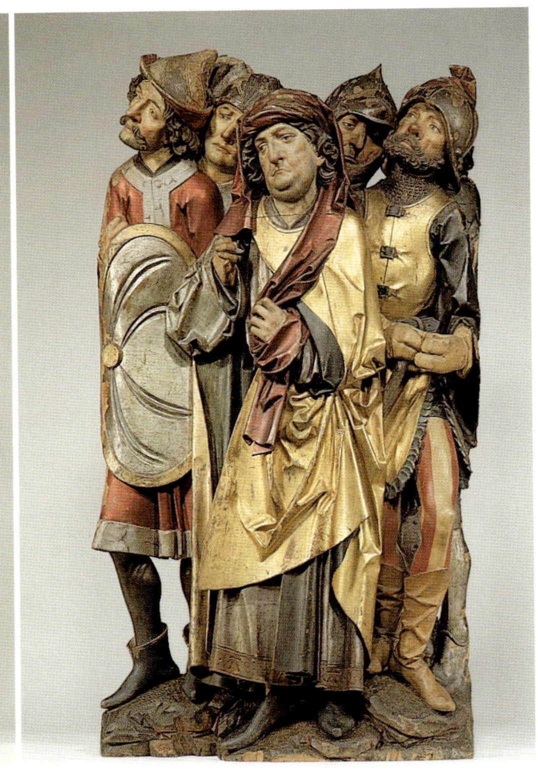

2.

Mourning Women and Saint John and *Caiaphas and His Soldiers* from a *Passion* altarpiece for a church in Rothenburg,
c. 1485–1490, limewood with original polychromy, Bayerisches Nationalmuseum, Munich

municipal council commissioned a Marian altarpiece, now lost, for the Jakobskirche
from a Würzburg sculptor, probably Riemenschneider. For the west choir of the same
church Riemenschneider in 1501–1504 produced the sculptural elements for the *Holy
Blood* altarpiece, one of his major works, which is discussed at some length below. He
delivered a *Saint Anne* altarpiece in 1506 for the Marienkapelle (see cat. 30) and received payments in 1506–1510 for an *All Saints* retable for the high altar of the church
of the Dominican nuns (see cat. 32). A *Crucifixion* altarpiece, now in Detwang (cat.
33, fig. 2), was moved in 1653 from Rothenburg.[6]

 From the beginning of his career Riemenschneider demonstrated his proficiency
in a variety of materials. Among his earliest works are engaging carvings in alabaster
(cats. 2 and 4), a medium he used for at least the first twenty years. After 1487 he showed
his ease at carving sandstone in the funerary monument of Eberhard von Grumbach
in Rimpar (cat. 18, fig. 1), for which the arms and legs are entirely freestanding. Early
masterpieces in this material are the over-life-size *Adam* and *Eve,* commissioned in 1491
by the municipal council of Würzburg and installed on either side of the south portal
of the Marienkapelle in 1493 (fig. 3; and Krohm essay, fig. 5). Their exquisite work-
manship is apparent in the extremely subtle, almost sensual treatment of surfaces. That

6. Kahsnitz 1997, 31–32.

26

Riemenschneider could carve such large figures out of this brittle material, stand them on completely undercut legs, and convey a sense that they are hovering, weightless, above us is nothing short of a tour de force. Riemenschneider was working at the same time on a monumental limewood altarpiece for which he had signed a contract with

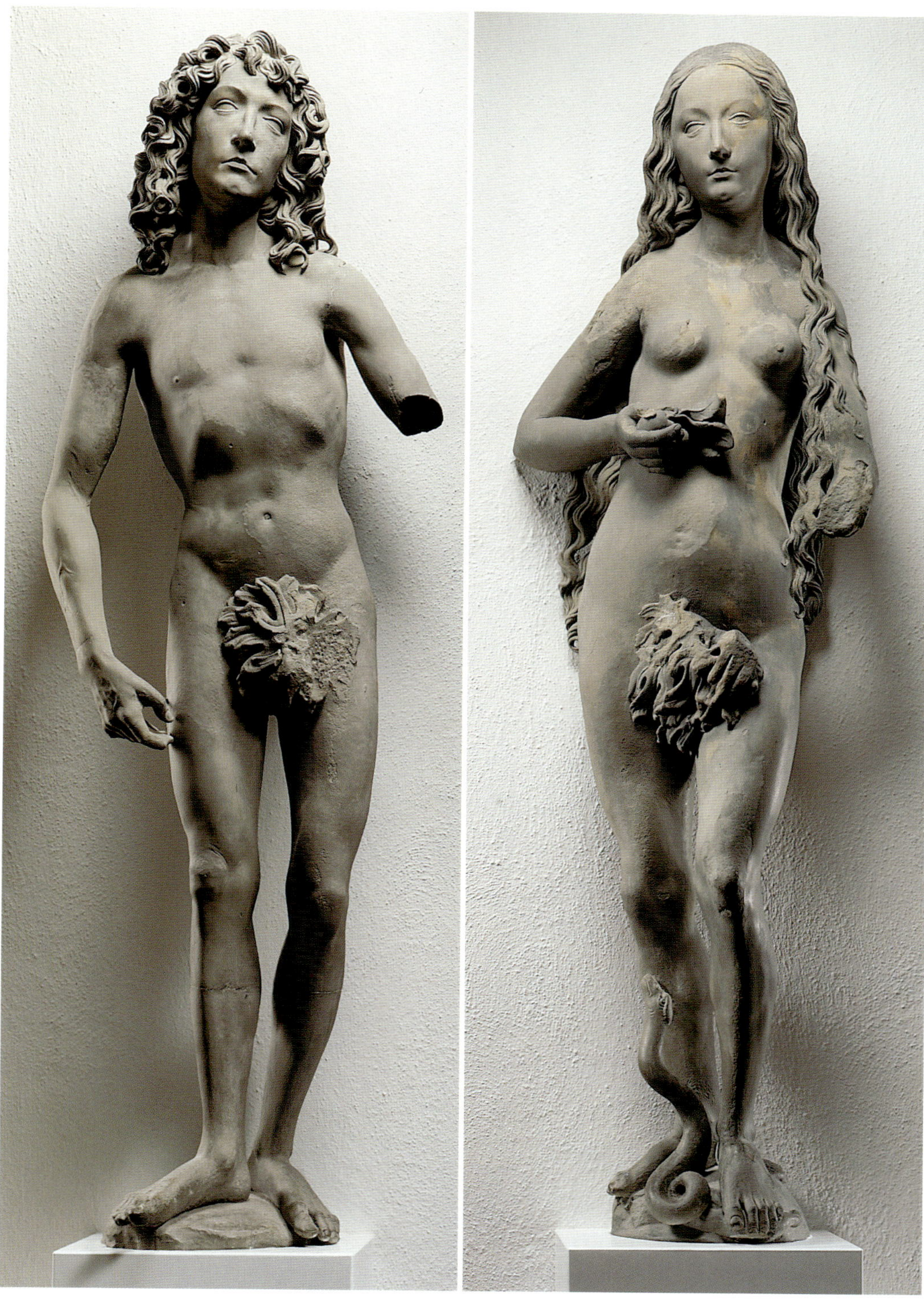

3.

Adam and *Eve* from the south portal of the Marienkapelle in Würzburg, 1491–1493, sandstone, Mainfränkisches Museum, Würzburg

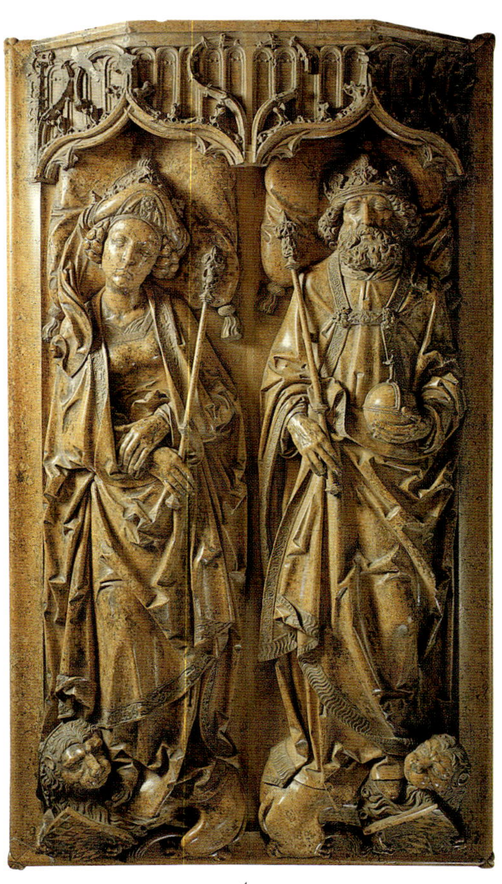

Tomb of Heinrich II and Kunigunde (view from the top), dedicated 1513, Solnhofen stone,
Bamberg Cathedral

the municipal council of Münnerstadt in 1490 (see cat. 13). He erected the retable, uncolored, in 1492 in the choir of the church of Mary Magdalen.

His next important commission came from Prince-Bishop Lorenz von Bibra, who instructed Riemenschneider in 1496 to carve the funerary monument of his predecessor, Rudolf von Scherenberg (Kemperdick essay, fig. 1), who had died in the previous year. Carved of pinkish marble with a sandstone framework and installed in Würzburg Cathedral in 1499, the memorial is one of the high points in Riemenschneider's oeuvre. A striking physiognomy, the elderly man towers over us. A prince of the church in full episcopal regalia, he is also distinguished by his sword as a worldly ruler, the duke of Franconia. The sculpture is remarkable for its sensitive treatment of surfaces and its integration of figure and architecture.

In 1499 the bishop and cathedral chapter of Bamberg commissioned from Riemenschneider a new tomb for the patron saints of the diocese, Emperor Heinrich II (d. 1024) and his wife Kunigunde (d. 1033) (fig. 4). Known as the *Kaisergrab,* the monument stands in the east end of the nave of Bamberg Cathedral. Although apparently the effigies of the imperial couple and five reliefs with scenes from their lives were executed mostly in the early years of the sixteenth century, the monument was not dedicated until 1513.[7] Made of yellow grayish Solnhofen stone,[8] an extremely fine limestone particularly suited for detailed carving, the quality of its execution is very high. The agreed-upon payment, at least 307 guilders, was also more than twice what Riemenschneider received for the Münnerstadt altarpiece.[9]

On 15 April 1501 Riemenschneider signed a contract with the municipal council of Rothenburg for the execution of sculpture for the *Holy Blood* altarpiece in the Jakobs-kirche (fig. 5). The figures were delivered in installments in 1502, 1504, and 1505. The central shrine includes Riemenschneider's rendering of the Last Supper, flanked by the Entry into Jerusalem and the Agony in the Garden on the wings. The predella contains two angels with instruments of the Passion on either side of a crucifix. The *Gesprenge,* or superstructure, holds the figures of the Virgin and Gabriel, forming an Annunciation, with the Man of Sorrows at the top. The Jakobskirche was a pilgrimage church, and the altarpiece was designed as a gigantic monstrance for the display of the relic of the Holy Blood, housed in an earlier cross held by two angels in the superstructure.[10]

Like the Münnerstadt retable of 1490–1492, the *Holy Blood* altarpiece was delivered without polychromy. The only touches of color are the irises and pupils of the eyes, painted black, and the touches of red applied to the lips and wounds. After their installation, the figures received a translucent lightly pigmented layer—still preserved though somewhat darkened—which gives the wood the color of amber. At the other end of the nave, in the east choir, stands Friedrich Herlin's altarpiece of 1466, which combines fully polychrome figures in the shrine and paintings on the wings (Krohm essay, fig. 3). The contrast between the two works is striking. It would certainly have been obvious to pilgrims who walked in procession around the church. Until the erection of the organ in the west choir, both retables could be seen from almost anywhere in the nave simply by turning around. The implications of monochromy have prompted heated debate and are discussed from different vantage points in this catalogue by Hartmut Krohm, Michael Baxandall, and Michele Marincola. The degree to which the absence of color reduces the immediacy of a sculpture is evident when one compares the head of Saint John from the *Passion* altarpiece with those of the figures in the central shrine of the *Holy Blood* altarpiece (see figs. 2 and 6). We instantly recognize the reddish paint around John's eyes as a sign that he has been weeping, and we empathize with him. This emotional appeal is more difficult to achieve without color.

Despite the limitations imposed by the idiom of monochromy, Riemenschneider found other means, also borrowed from our immediate realm of experience, to engage us in his altarpiece. The retable is site-specific. The open predella allows a view of the masonry of the choir. The back of the shrine, behind the figures, is open through a

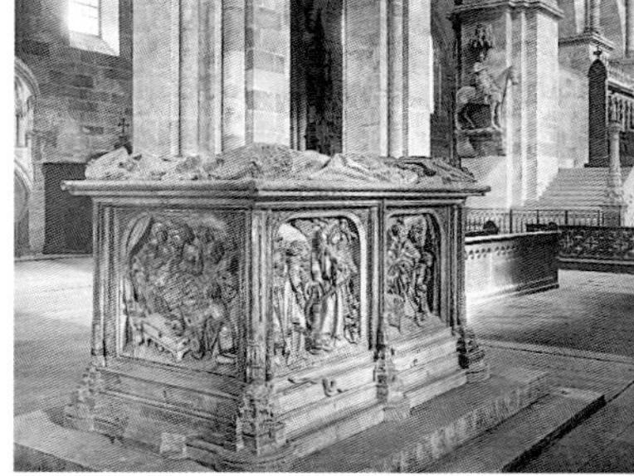

Tomb of Heinrich II and Kunigunde in situ, Bamberg Cathedral

7. Iris Kalden, *Tilman Riemenscheider. Werkstattleiter in Würzburg* (Ammersbek bei Hamburg, 1990), 114.

8. Würzburg 1981, 351.

9. On the *Kaisergrab,* see especially Kalden 1990, 53–57, 76–77, and 113–116.

10. Susanne Reece is preparing a dissertation for Ohio State University on the *Holy Blood* altarpiece in relation to pilgrimages to the Jakobskirche

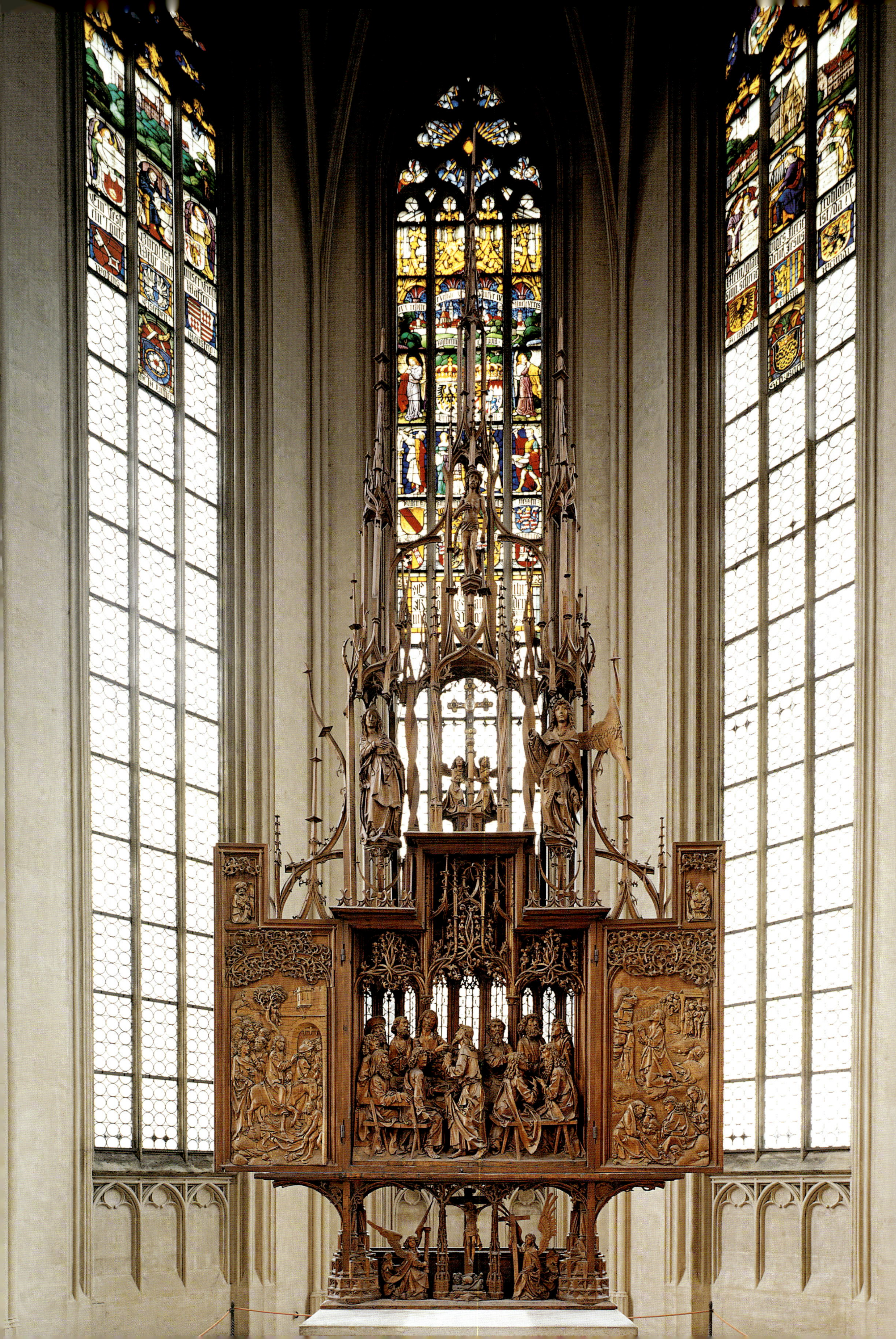

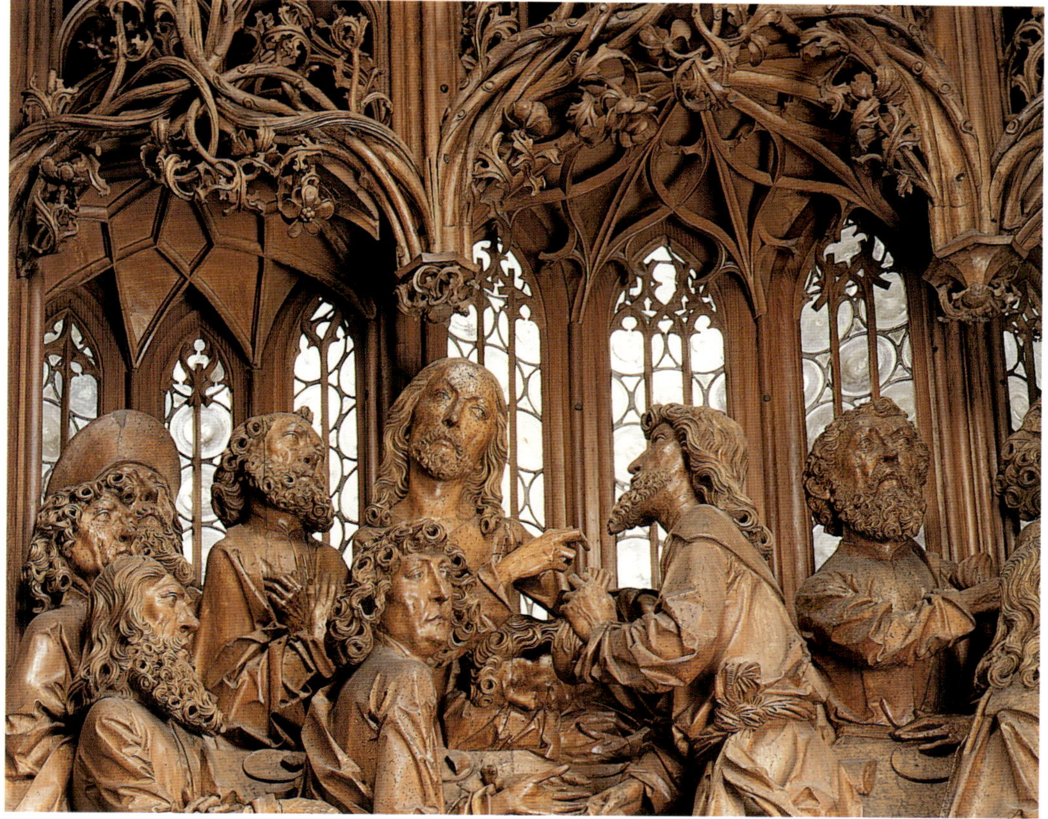

6.

Detail of the *Holy Blood* altarpiece, showing the central shrine with its ribbed vaulting and circular-paned glass windows

series of glazed lancet windows that resemble both in form and in tracery the architectural windows of the choir. Although the present-day grisaille glass in the choir dates from the nineteenth century, it appears that originally the windows were filled with small circular panes of heavy clear glass *(Butzenscheiben)* like the ones at the back of the altarpiece (fig. 6).[11] The ribbed vaulting above the Last Supper in the shrine follows, at least in part, the same pattern as the structural vaulting in the choir above. Standing before the altarpiece, we realize that the scene takes place in a space that is very much like the architectural space in which we stand. These clues are subtler than those offered by paint, yet they allow an actualization of the scene in question by placing it in an identifiable setting.

The unification of the space of the sculpture with that of the viewer reveals an intense reflection on the nature of representation, which is made all the more acute by the inclusion of the relic in the superstructure. Riemenschneider's sculpted group offers a visualization of the Last Supper. The relic above it is its proof positive: it establishes a direct link between the viewer and the event. The presence of the relic believed to contain the blood of Christ confirms the viewers' impression that the Last Supper is actually taking place before them in Rothenburg.

11. Christof Trepesch, *Studien zur Dunkelgestaltung in der deutschen spätgotischen Skulptur* (Frankfurt, 1994), 266–267.

5.

Holy Blood altarpiece in situ, 1501–1505, limewood, Jakobskirche, Rothenburg

Opening the back of the altarpiece allowed the sculptor to take full advantage of changes in natural light in the choir, so as to put various elements into focus at different times of day. With the light coming mainly from the left in the morning, it is mostly the front row of figures that emerges, while the back row stays in shadow. Later Judas becomes increasingly isolated. Afternoon light enters from the choir windows and through the windows at the back of the shrine, bringing the figures at the back into view.[12] The use of light as a creative element is particularly obvious if one stands before the altarpiece on a day when the wind moves clouds rapidly in front of the sun, causing the light to change and the figures to seem to come to life.

Presumably shortly after completing the *Holy Blood* altarpiece, Riemenschneider embarked on the creation of his only other retable to have survived virtually intact (fig. 7). Equally ambitious, this monochrome altarpiece is not documented but is generally dated about 1505–1510. The small Herrgottskirche in Creglingen, in the Tauber valley, was built in the fourteenth century in a field where a peasant found an intact eucharistic host while plowing. Riemenschneider's retable stands on an original altar, not in the choir, but in the middle of the church's nave, on the precise spot of the miraculous discovery. The central shrine contains the *Assumption of the Virgin,* witnessed by the apostles, flanked by the Visitation and the Annunciation on the left wing, and the Nativity and the Presentation in the Temple on the right wing. The Coronation of the Virgin is depicted in a chapel-like structure above the corpus, while the Man of Sorrows crowns the *Gesprenge.* The predella is divided into three compartments, with the Adoration of the Magi at one side and Christ and the Doctors on the other side of a niche with angels holding a cloth, presumably for the placement of a monstrance containing the miraculous host. The Creglingen altarpiece, like that in Rothenburg, combined narrative representations with an actual relic. And like the *Holy Blood* altarpiece, the back of the *Assumption* shrine is pierced by lancet windows (unglazed here), which unify the space of the retable with that of the church.

Riemenschneider used natural light to its full advantage in Creglingen to create what might be called chiaroscuro sculpture. The altarpiece receives far less light than the one in Rothenburg, mainly through two narrow lateral windows as well as through the windows of the east choir and an oculus in the west wall. Inside the church the eye grows accustomed to darkness and sees the figures slowly take form. The quality of execution in the central sculpture is superb. The apostles are widely differentiated in their postures, physiognomies, and reactions. The draperies contain rich contrasts between florid and quiet passages, which create a complex play of light and dark. It has been argued that the development of graphic arts in Germany in the fifteenth century paved the way for the acceptance of uncolored sculpture.[13] And indeed, standing

12. For an eloquent description of this phenomenon, see Michael Baxandall, *The Limewood Sculptors of Renaissance Germany* (New Haven and London, 1980), 189–190.

13. Würzburg 1981, 154.

7.
Assumption of the Virgin altarpiece in situ, c. 1505–1510, limewood, Herrgottskirche, Creglingen

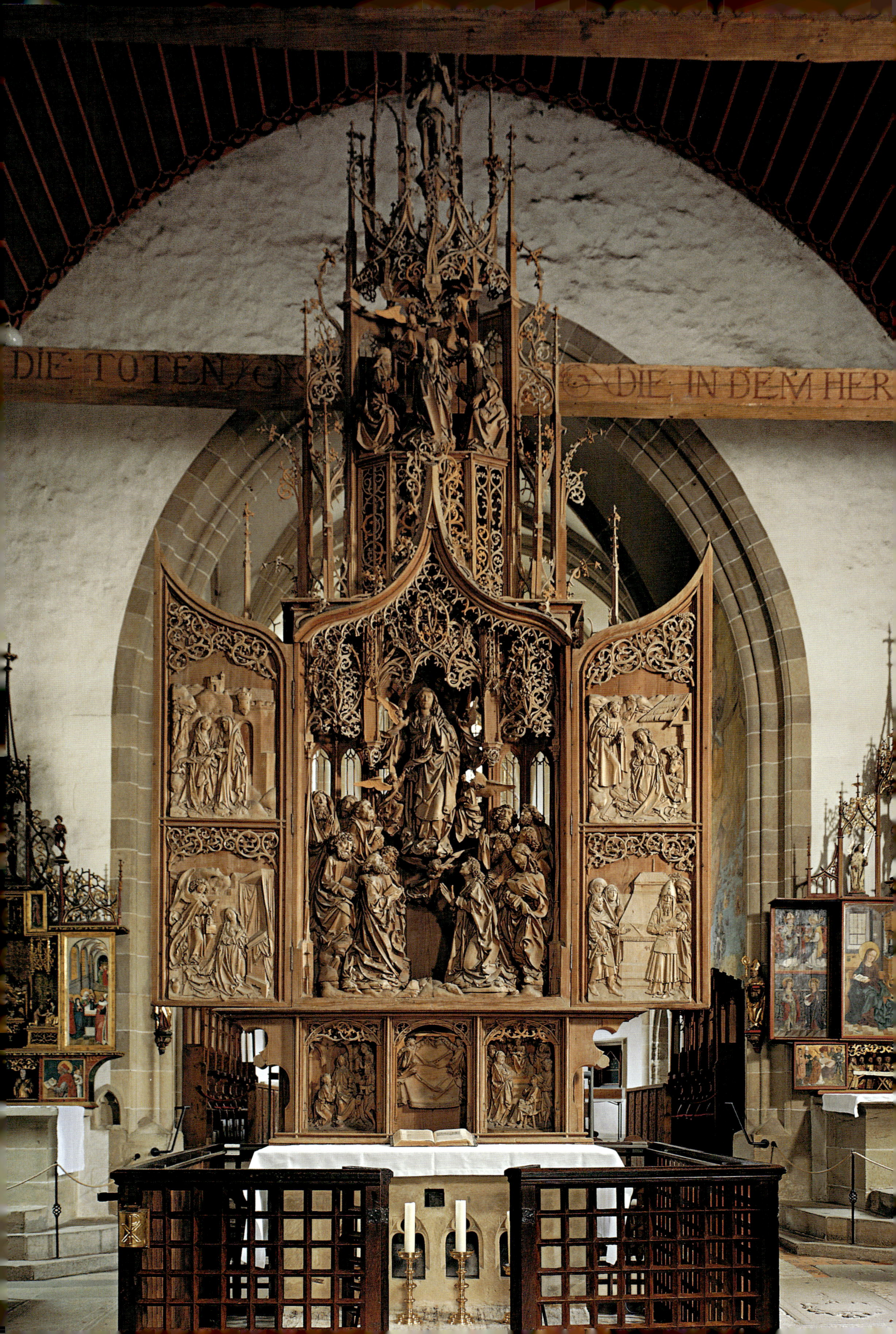
DIE TOTEN
DIE IN DEM HER

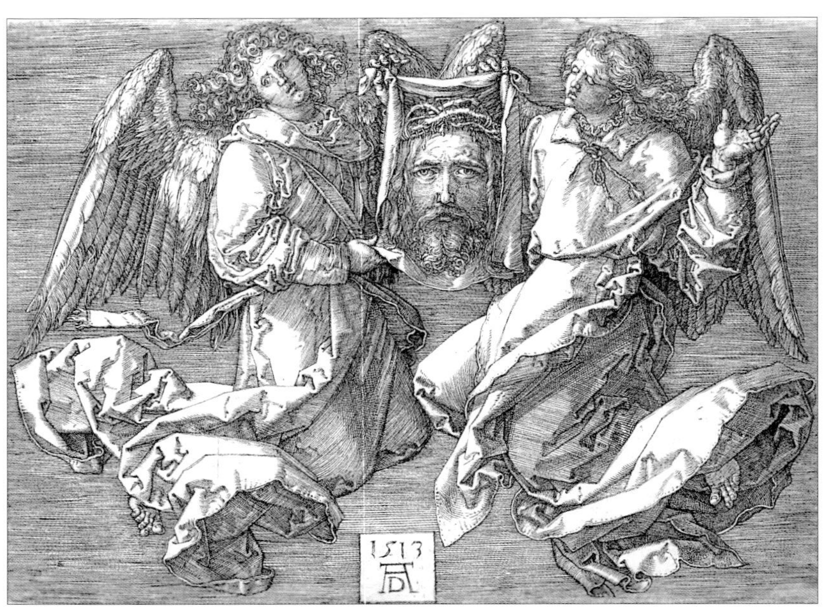

8.

Albrecht Dürer, *Sudarium Held by Two Angels,* 1513, engraving, National Gallery of Art, Washington, Rosenwald Collection

before the Creglingen altarpiece, we are reminded of the rich tonal range of Dürer's engravings, such as his 1513 *Sudarium Held by Two Angels* (fig. 8).

As Riemenschneider had carved the funerary monument of Rudolf von Scherenberg, so he carved that of his successor, Lorenz von Bibra, between 1515 and 1522 (Kemperdick essay, fig. 2). The younger bishop, who died in 1519, did not live to see the work to completion. Bibra has a slightly less imposing presence than does Scherenberg. Although intended to receive a Gothic framework, the red marble effigy is flanked by classicizing columns that support an arch. Chubby putti, instead of lions and robed angels, hold the armorial shields; and more putti—possibly of later date—frolic amid garlands at the top. This unique instance of Italianate motifs in Riemenschneider's oeuvre may reflect the wish of Bibra himself, who in 1518 attended the diet *(Reichstag)* in Augsburg, a city that had adopted the Renaissance vocabulary more readily than had Würzburg.[14]

The masterpiece of Riemenschneider's late career is his sandstone *Lamentation* relief in the church of Cistercian nuns in Maidbronn, carved between 1519 and 1523 (fig. 9). The relief integrates ten figures into an organic whole, in which foreground and background flow effortlessly into one another. The pyramidal composition establishes the cohesion of the work. Compared with earlier sculpture, an abstraction has taken place. The faces are less individualized than in the Creglingen altarpiece, for example. The draperies are simplified, revealing more legible bodies through the fabric. Anecdotal details have been banished to create a grand calligraphy of forms. As Hart-

14. Kalden 1990, 47–48.

mut Krohm points out elsewhere in this catalogue, the degree of abstraction in Christ's body is characteristic of Riemenschneider's treatment of sandstone and is found already in his *Adam* and *Eve* of 1491–1493.

According to an inscription later added to the relief, the *Lamentation* was erected in 1526 in the church in Maidbronn as a monument to the victory over the Peasants' Revolt of 1525.[15] This has a particularly ironic resonance, since it was precisely Riemenschneider's stance during the Peasants' Revolt that abruptly ended his career. The sculptor had been a respected member of Würzburg society. He was elected to the municipal council on several occasions; in 1505 he was among the councillors to receive Emperor Maximilian on his visit to Würzburg; he served as mayor in 1520–1521. The Peasants' Revolt of 1525, which was particularly violent in Franconia, was aimed at the Catholic nobility. Konrad von Thüngen, prince-bishop of Würzburg from 1519 until 1530, in-

15. Würzburg 1981, 21.

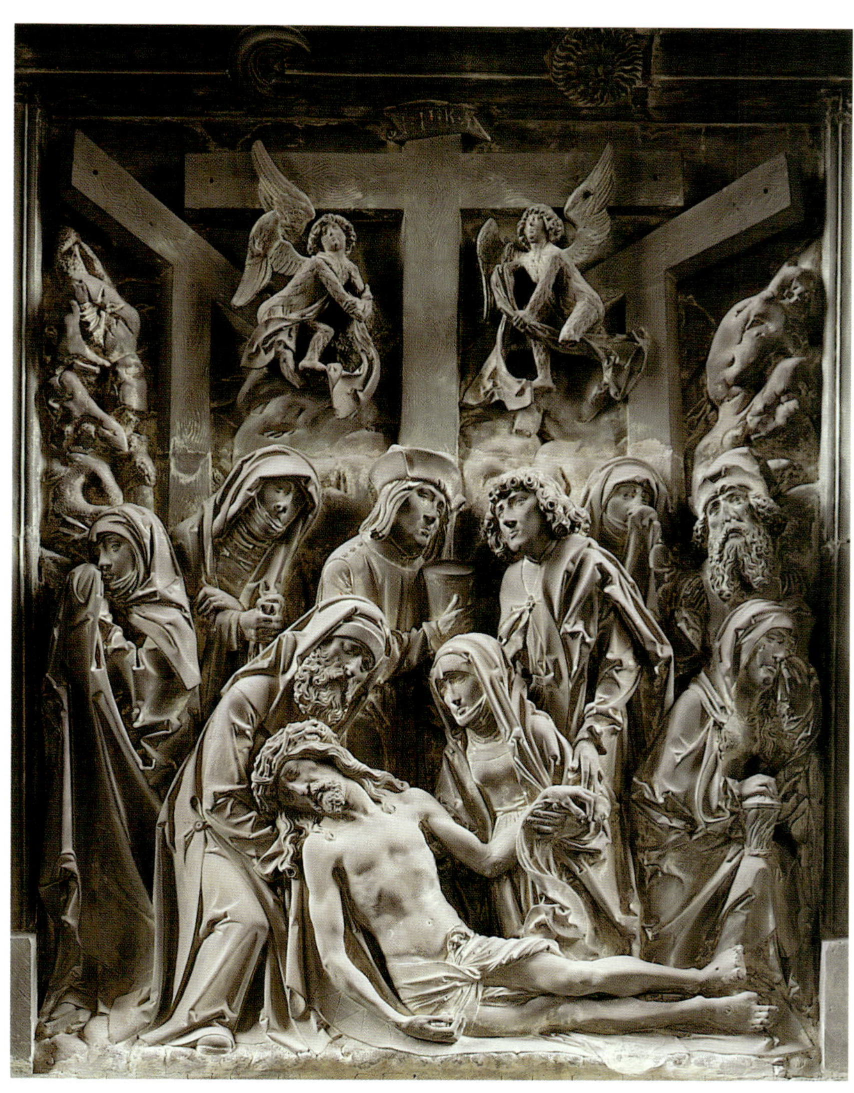

9.

Lamentation, 1519-1523, sandstone, Pfarrkirche, Maidbronn

tended to gather all the troops of his principality in the city and to use it as the center of his defense against the peasants. The municipal council, including Riemenschneider, opposed its lord and refused to allow his troops to enter Würzburg. On 7 June 1525, after the revolt was finally crushed, Riemenschneider was dismissed from the council. Accused of fomenting rebellion, he was jailed in the Marienberg Fortress for two months and apparently tortured.[16] Whether Riemenschneider had the interests of the peasants at heart or, more likely, opposed the prince-bishop in an attempt to maintain Würzburg's independence from feudal control, his political stance has greatly colored the way his oeuvre came to be interpreted over time. His fall from grace with the prince-bishop meant virtually the end of his career. The only mention of work after 1525 is for some minor repair he carried out in 1527 on altarpieces in the church of the Benedictine nuns in Kitzingen[17]—for which he had carved his early *Anna Selbdritt* (cat. 15). No sculpture by him can be proven to have been created between the Peasants' Revolt and his death in 1531.

• *The Study of Riemenschneider* •

The present-day emphasis on originality and authenticity is partly rooted in the nineteenth-century notion of the artist as a lonely creator. The cult of the genius, which glorified individuals as diverse as Canova, Beethoven, Delacroix, or Rodin, did much to promote this idea, as did the solitary careers of painters such as Constable or Cézanne, who spent years revisiting the same motifs in search of new formal solutions. In addition, the actual or perceived monetary value of art has exacerbated the obsession with the "autograph work." Recent changes in attribution usually find mention in the media only when they have a bearing on the price of the works in question.[18]

This attitude stands in marked contrast with the practice of late medieval workshops. It is instructive in this regard to consider Albrecht Dürer's letters from 1507 to 1509 to the Frankfurt banker Jakob Heller, who had commissioned a large altarpiece of a Coronation of the Virgin from the Nuremberg painter. Since the patron and the artist lived in different cities, their negotiations, which would otherwise have been carried out orally, are recorded in writing. On two occasions Dürer promised exceptionally *(sonderlich)* to paint the central panel with his own hand,[19] which implies that this was not current practice. Indeed, several artists worked together on the wings of the retable: in his letter of 19 March 1508 Dürer informed Heller that he left the underpainting of the shutters to collaborators.[20] In addition, his letter of 28 August 1507 tells that a preparer applied the ground layer and the gilding to the central panel.[21] In Dürer's view the principle of "being by one's own hand" *(Eigenhändigkeit)* governed only the creative parts of the production process. The letters also reveal that, unless specified otherwise,

16. Bier 1963, 325; Würzburg 1981, 21.

17. Würzburg 1981, 21.

18. In the 1980s, for example, curators at the Gemäldegalerie in Berlin concluded that the technique of the *Man with the Golden Helmet*, one of the stars of the museum's Rembrandt collection, was difficult to reconcile with that of the master and thus the painting must be by a talented follower.

19. Letters of 19 March 1508 and 24 August 1508 published in Hans Rupprich, *Dürer. Schriftlicher Nachlass* (Berlin, 1956), 1:65–66.

20. Rupprich 1956, 65.

21. Letter of 28 August 1507, in Rupprich 1956, 64.

both patrons and artists understood a work of art to be the product of a collaborative effort; the nature of the collaboration could certainly vary.

Like Dürer, Riemenschneider ran a prolific workshop. For a period of at least forty years, from his becoming a master in 1485 to his involvement in the Peasants' Revolt in 1525, Riemenschneider taught apprentices and employed journeymen. Documents reveal that he trained at least twelve pupils.[22] Although the Würzburg regulations do not specify how an apprentice would be taught, it can be surmised that by observing and imitating the work of other members of the shop, one would gradually learn all steps of the craft. In the first months one's role was probably restricted to menial duties, such as keeping the workshop clean, learning the rudiments of handling the sculptor's tools, and hollowing the back of figures to prevent them from cracking. After repeated practice an apprentice might be entrusted with more important stages in the production process, such as roughing in the general form of a figure. Depending on his ability, he may eventually have become responsible for the entire execution of a sculpture. Skilled apprentices could evidently produce salable work on their own, but the statutes of the painters' corporation at Tournai would levy a fine on those who made and sold a work without their master's knowledge.[23] This would appear to reflect common practice.

The second category of collaborators consisted of the journeymen, probably paid by the day, about whom much less is known because they are seldom mentioned in documents. They were almost certainly fully trained sculptors who simply could not afford the title of master. It is fair to assume that Riemenschneider entrusted these able craftsmen with the production of entire figures; the degree to which he delegated aspects of the production must have varied. He probably employed several assistants when working on major commissions concurrently, as was the case in the first five years of the sixteenth century when he was responsible for the imperial tomb in Bamberg, a series of sandstone apostles for the Marienkapelle, and the Rothenburg *Holy Blood* altarpiece. Likewise, Riemenschneider must have relied more heavily on journeymen and apprentices in his periods of direct involvement in municipal government: in 1504, 1509, 1514, and 1518, when he was a councillor; or in 1521–1522, when he was mayor of Würzburg.

Attempting to distinguish Riemenschneider's autograph works from those of his assistants is a futile task, given the collaborative nature of late medieval workshops. By definition, members of a workshop were fluent in the stylistic idiom of the master. Apprentices learned all steps of the craft from the master himself, and they necessarily adopted his repertoire of facial types, hands, and drapery patterns. Since they were not allowed to sell work under their own names, journeymen had to adapt their styles to agree with those of their masters. Some scholars have nonetheless scrutinized the

22. Kalden 1990, 36.

23. Lorne Campbell, "Early Netherlandish Painters and Their Workshops," in Dominique Hollanders-Favart and Roger van Schoute, eds., *Le dessin sous-jacent dans la peinture. Colloque III: Le problème Maitre de Flémalle-van der Weyden* (Louvain-la-Neuve, 1981), 43–61, esp. 47.

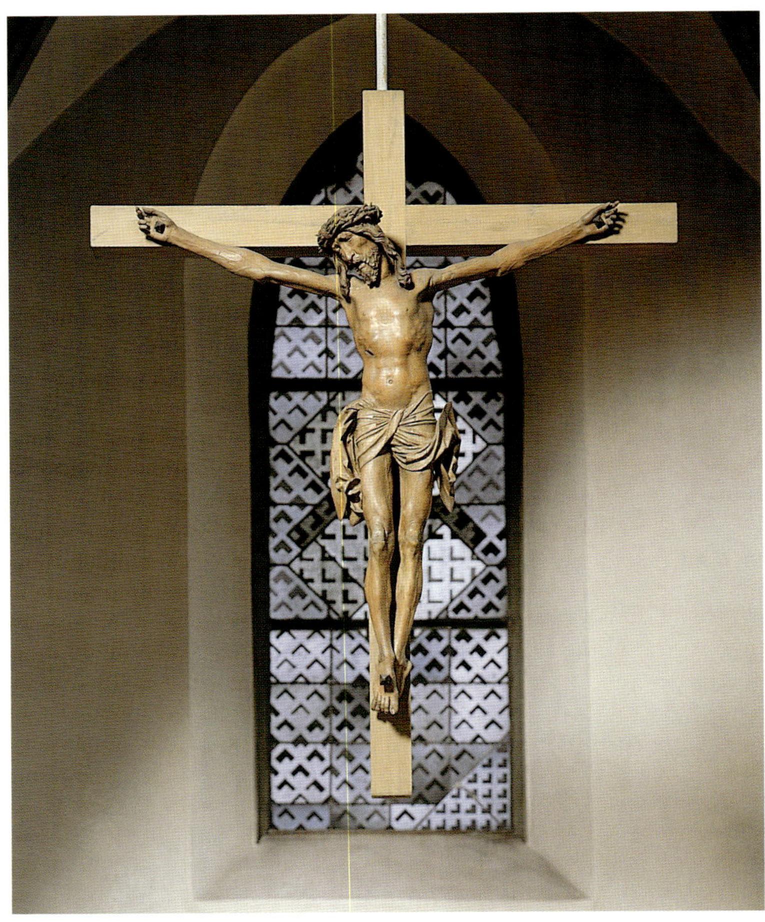

Crucifix, 1516, limewood, Pfarrkirche, Steinach

24. Kalden 1990, 101–143.

25. Justus Bier, *Tilman Riemenschneider. Die späten Werke in Holz* (Vienna, 1978), 125.

surface of figures in an attempt to distinguish among members of the workshop—one author has counted as many as twenty-six assistants between 1490 and 1524.[24]

A major obstacle to distinguishing hands is that no single sculpture can be proven to be entirely autograph and thereby function as a touchstone for the attribution of other works. This is true even of the *Crucifix* at Steinach (fig. 10), which contained a slip of parchment stating that "in the year of our Lord 1516 this figure was carved by master Tilman, councillor in Würzburg."[25] The sculpture is arguably the best crucifix in Riemenschneider's oeuvre. The anatomy is carefully observed, and the treatment of surfaces is superb, even in the back. The elongated, slender limbs and the tense musculature of the abdomen convey an affecting sense of exhaustion. Like several of Riemenschneider's finest works, this one captures the most emotionally charged moment: the very instant of Christ's death. His eyes are not entirely shut, and his mouth is open, as if to gasp for air. A light breeze seems to cause the loincloth to flutter slightly, reinforcing the impression of the last minutes of life. Given the exquisite quality of the sculpture, the inscription would appear to confirm its status as a fully autograph

Riemenschneider, but it can only be taken to certify that the work was created in the master's shop under his supervision, not that Riemenschneider alone was responsible for its execution.

The art historian then has to confront a fairly large number of figures that share a similar formal language and yet are of uneven quality. Of course, quality is a subjective notion, and our definition of it differs from that of the late Middle Ages. The concept is used throughout this catalogue to describe works that combine intelligence in sculptural conception, an expressive rendering of their given subjects, and a subtle, differentiated treatment of surfaces. The Hassfurt *Saint John* possesses all three characteristics to an exceptional degree, as do the Cleveland *Saint Jerome,* the *Noli me Tangere* from the Münnerstadt altarpiece, the sandstone *Anna Selbdritt* from Würzburg, the Berlin *Saint Matthias,* and the images of the *Virgin and Child* in Cologne and at Dumbarton Oaks (cats. 11, 13 F, 15, 16, 24, and 45). Although it is tempting to regard these works as fully autograph, we cannot necessarily equate conceptual and formal excellence with execution by the master himself. It is conceivable that the workshop at times employed assistants whose virtuosity equaled that of the master. Three of Riemenschneider's contemporaries illustrate the point. Leonardo da Vinci far surpassed Verrocchio, in whose household in Florence he lived in the 1470s. The same is true of Albrecht Dürer, who trained with the Nuremberg painter Michael Wolgemut from 1486 until 1490. The situation was apparently no different in sculpture. It has been argued that the best figures of the monumental Calvary group in the minster of Lübeck are not by Bernt Notke himself, but by an assistant named Eggert Suarte.[26] Yet one fact is certain: in all periods of its forty-odd years of activity Riemenschneider's shop produced works of the highest quality. This suggests that Riemenschneider, the one person who was in the shop throughout these years, supervised all aspects of its production closely to maintain its level of excellence and that he had the lion's share in the execution of these works.

It is useful to refer again to Dürer's letters to Jakob Heller in order to appreciate some of the criteria that defined quality in the late Middle Ages. Dürer recognizes a hierarchy based on the price paid for a commission and distinguishes between accomplished painting, common painting, and peasant pictures *(kleiblen, gmaine gmäll,* and *Bauerntafeln).* The latter is clearly a derogatory term used to describe coarse paintings in rural churches, but the distinction between accomplished and common painting is dependent on the amount of labor required. Dürer writes that he would have produced many more pictures in a year had he practiced only common painting; at the same time, one cannot earn a living from accomplished painting alone.[27] While the Heller altarpiece occupied him for many months, Dürer proudly declared that *Christ*

26. Eike Oellermann, "Bernt Notkes Werk, dessen Geschichte und Restaurierung," in *Triumphkreuz im Dom zu Lübeck. Ein Meisterwerk Bernt Notkes* (Wiesbaden, 1977), 56. For a different interpretation, see Hartmut Krohm, "Notke, Bernt," in *Neue deutsche Biographie* (Berlin, 1999), 19:359–361.

27. Letter of 26 August 1509, in Rupprich 1956, 72.

among the Doctors, a painting now in the Thyssen-Bornemisza collection, was completed in five days.[28] His letters to Heller put into words a practice that was also current in sculpture. The contract of 1493 for Adam Kraft's tabernacle in the Lorenzkirche in Nuremberg specifies that the artist must lavish care on the central portion of the structure but that he must not make the foot or the spire too refined because people seldom look at them.[29]

The principle of a hierarchy of execution based on the price and intended placement of a commissioned work also governed the production of Riemenschneider's shop. The sculptor was paid almost as much for the sandstone *Adam* and *Eve* alone (see fig. 3), which were to flank the south portal of the Marienkapelle, as for the figures of Christ, John the Baptist, and the twelve apostles of equal size that he provided later for the buttresses of the same building.[30] As figures central to the overall sculptural program, the *Adam* and *Eve* had to be perfectly legible from the ground. The apostles, by contrast, were to be installed much higher, and their treatment of surface is accordingly much coarser (see cat. 24, fig. 1; and cat. 31, fig. 2). The difference in quality between the two groups is striking, and, to employ Dürer's terminology, it seems to illustrate the distinction between accomplished and common sculpture.

A second problem faced by the art historian is the establishment of a chronology of Riemenschneider's oeuvre. So few works are securely dated, yet their study allows the following generalizations about the evolution of the style practiced by Riemenschneider and his shop. The early datable figures, such as the *Mary Magdalen* and *Saint Elizabeth* from the 1490–1492 Münnerstadt altarpiece (cat. 13, figs. 1 and 2) and the 1491–1493 *Eve* from the Marienkapelle, exhibit a strongly volumetric treatment and invite approach from a variety of viewpoints. The figures of the *Holy Blood* altarpiece of 1501–1504 do not have the same sculptural mass. A comparison of the Münnerstadt *Saint Matthew* (cat. 13A) with the bearded apostle in the right foreground of the *Holy Blood* altarpiece (cat. 23, fig. 1), both figures turned to the side with one hand raised, makes this point quite clearly. The Münnerstadt Matthew sits obliquely, his right knee on the axis of the sculpture; his mantle has fallen off his right shoulder and surrounds his body, unifying front and back. The Rothenburg apostle is held almost entirely in a plane; his cloak has fallen off his shoulder, but this detail functions as a linear rather than a spatial device and does not convincingly surround the body in space.

The draperies in both the *Holy Blood* altarpiece and the retable of *Christ and the Apostles* from Windsheim, created before 1509 (cat. 40, fig. 1), have also been comparatively simplified. While in Münnerstadt deep furrows catch shadows and create sharp contrasts of light and dark, here shorter, shallower angular folds contrast with surrounding flat or curved areas of fabric. The effect is on the whole less volumetric and

28. The cartellino in the lower left corner bears the date, Dürer's monogram, and the inscription "opus qui[n]que dierum."

29. Hans Huth, *Künstler und Werkstatt der Spätgotik* (Augsburg, 1923), 56.

30. While Riemenschneider and the municipal council agreed that he would be paid 120 guilders for the *Adam* and *Eve,* the sculptor was to receive 10 guilders per figure for the later commission; see Hanswernfried Muth, *Tilman Riemenschneider. Die Werke des Bildschnitzers und Bildhauers, seiner Werkstatt und seines Umkreises,* Mainfränkisches Museum (Würzburg, 1982), 29, 52.

more calligraphic. Dated works from the end of Riemenschneider's career—the funerary monument of Lorenz von Bibra of 1515–1522, the Maidbronn *Lamentation* of 1519–1523, and the Volkach *Virgin of the Rosary* of 1521–1522—show an even greater simplification of forms. While the draperies of the *Holy Blood* altarpiece exhibit the fractures typical of a heavily starched fabric, garments in the later works bend supplely, in fewer, rounded folds, and seem to be made of a more substantial material, such as thick wool or leather. The early works invite the mobility of the viewer on a wide arc; the late works, characterized by a planar treatment, are essentially intended for frontal viewing.

Although Riemenschneider often adapted his sculptural means to the specific function and placement of his commissioned works, a comparison of two dated monumental figures still in situ confirms the validity of the development sketched above. Even though the 1490–1492 Münnerstadt *Saint Elizabeth* (cat. 13, fig. 2) was made to stand in the central shrine of a retable, where the carpentry, tracery, and other figures would have prevented the viewer from moving freely around her, she has a much stronger sculptural mass and spatial presence than the 1521–1522 *Virgin of the Rosary* in Volkach (cat. 45, fig. 1). Her arms push the mantle away from her body, revealing the space around it and giving the sculpture width as well as depth. The volumes of the face are emphasized by the powerful mass of the headdress. The Volkach Virgin, by contrast, hangs from an arch in front of a church choir, a setting that paradoxically allows a much greater mobility of the viewer (since churches did not have pews in the Middle Ages). Yet the sculpture is conceived for a single, frontal vantage point. The arms are held close to the body, and the drapery and the face have been compressed into series of planes.

Constructing a chronology of Riemenschneider's oeuvre around the few documented extant works is both aided and hampered by the evident use of models in the shop, a point well illustrated by the retable from the Johanneskapelle in Gerolzhofen (fig. 11).[31] The central shrine of this altarpiece houses a sculpture of the Virgin and child flanked by Saint John the Baptist on the left and by a Saint Sebastian on the right that replaces the original Saint Wolfgang. The compositions of three of the reliefs in the wings are based on engraved sources, and the latest, the *Beheading of Saint John,* relies on Lucas van Leiden's 1512–1513 engraving, thus establishing a *terminus post quem* for the retable.[32] On the other hand, the figure of John the Baptist in the central shrine repeats, with a few variations, the composition of the Hassfurt *Saint John,* thought to date from about 1490.[33] The Virgin follows a compositional type formulated by Riemenschneider in about 1500, which retained currency in the workshop until about 1520 (see cat. 28). Thus the date of the Gerolzhofen altarpiece, clouded by the use of models for the figures in the central shrine, is clarified only by a shutter relief dependent on a graphic source of known date.

31. The altarpiece was commissioned for the Johanneskapelle in Gerolzhofen, a building that had been remodeled by Bishop Lorenz von Bibra in 1497; see Theodor Müller, *Die Bildwerke in Holz, Ton und Stein von der Mitte des 15. bis gegen Mitte des 16. Jahrhunderts,* Bayerisches Nationalmuseum (Munich, 1959), 157.

32. *The Baptism of Christ* on the left is based on an engraving by Schongauer; *The Presentation of John the Baptist's Head to Herod* follows Dürer's woodcut of 1511 (Kalden 1990, 58–59).

33. See Würzburg 1981, 175.

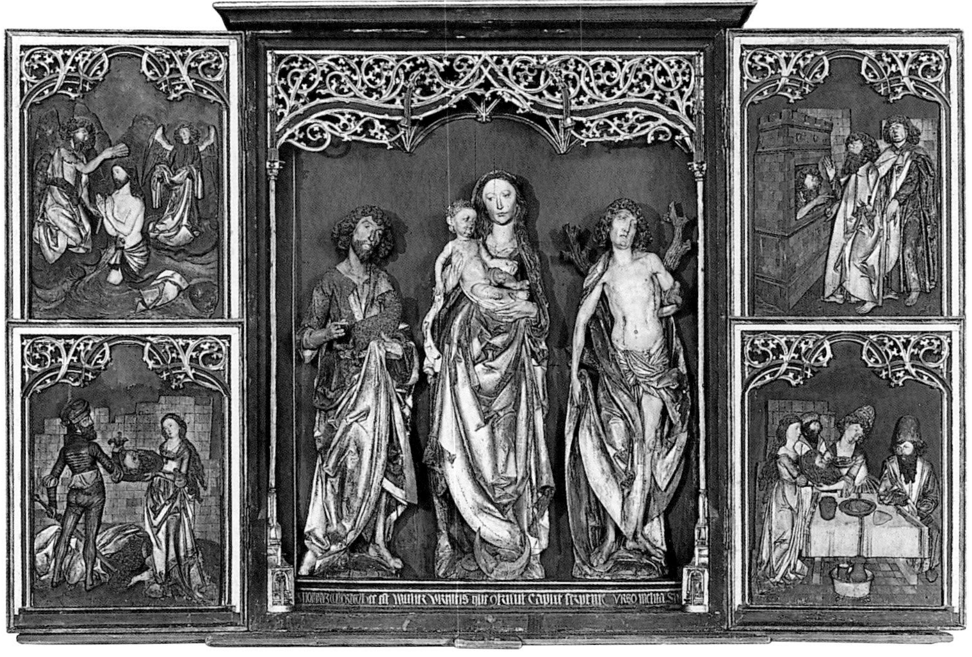

11.

Saint John the Baptist altarpiece from Gerolzhofen, c. 1513–1515, limewood with ancient polychromy,
Bayerisches Nationalmuseum, Munich

The recurrence of a composition many years after a sculpture left the workshop implies that visual records were kept for reference. While some of these may have been drawings, others were necessarily three-dimensional, since designs were repeated from different vantages (compare front and side views of cats. 16 and 22). The use of sculptural models would have allowed the production of popular images without the direct participation of the master. This seems most evident in Riemenschneider's depictions of the Virgin and child, which largely fall into four compositional types.[34] Since models were most likely shown to prospective clients, it is not unreasonable to suggest that these were highly finished works intended to convey the sculptural conception to best effect and to aid in securing a commission. Detailed execution would also have given assistants clear guidelines for the composition to be replicated. Only a handful of sculpture can be considered models by Riemenschneider. The identifying criteria, admittedly subjective, are a relatively early date, superior quality compared to other variants of the same composition, and small size, which would have saved room in the workshop.[35]

Riemenschneider and his workshop, as we have seen, also relied on prints—often engravings by Martin Schongauer—as points of departure for reliefs and figural sculpture. Widely circulated, Schongauer's compositions rapidly entered the visual vernacular and achieved iconic status. The relationship of the sculpture to the engraving varies from case to case. The superb *Noli me Tangere* from Münnerstadt is a complete reformulation of Schongauer's composition, conveying a keener sense of drama (cat.

34. Holger Simon, *Der Creglinger Marienaltar von Tilman Riemenschneider* (Berlin, 1998), 176–179.

35. Kalden 1990, 89–90.

13 F, and cat. 13, fig. 6). The relief is a considered and innovative response to a creation of Riemenschneider's much-admired predecessor. By contrast, the Gerolzhofen *Baptism of Christ* repeats almost literally Schongauer's print of the same subject (cat. 27, fig. 1). It would seem that Riemenschneider here simply instructed one of his assistants to enlarge the engraving sculpturally to the specified dimensions of the altarpiece shutter. This workshop praxis, which allowed the production of both masterpieces and routine work, calls to mind Dürer's remark to Heller that one cannot make a living from accomplished art alone; it was essential for an artist's livelihood to manufacture works more expediently as well.

• *Epilogue* •

Riemenschneider died in 1531, three years after Albrecht Dürer. Even though the two artists have at times enjoyed equal popularity in the public domain, especially in Germany, they traveled different paths. To be sure, Dürer was trained and steeped in the artistic and visual culture of southern Germany. The organization of his workshop in Nuremberg followed the model current in northern Europe at the time. Dürer's enormous graphic production is unimaginable without Martin Schongauer's engravings, which he admired as much as Riemenschneider did; he journeyed to Colmar in 1492, only to hear that the older master had died the previous year. Yet Dürer was thoroughly convinced of his own place in a new generation. He went to Italy on two occasions, absorbed the lessons of Renaissance painters such as Mantegna and Bellini, studied antique sculpture and architecture, and read the treatises of both antique and modern theoreticians, such as Euclid and Alberti. The first artist in northern Europe to leave a theoretical as well as an artistic oeuvre, Dürer wrote extensively on subjects such as the rendering of the human figure, systems of proportion, and one-point perspective. His work profoundly affected the course of German art in the sixteenth century. Dürer clearly envied the independence of Italian artists; while the Venetians treated him like a gentleman, he felt sufficiently demeaned in Nuremberg to refer to himself as a parasite.[36]

Riemenschneider's genius lay in his endowing existing indigenous traditions with new life. This applies to different aspects of his art, such as his use of compositions by other artists and his exploration of the nascent medium of monochromy. In two reliefs from the Münnerstadt altarpiece (cat. 13 E−F) he took graphic renderings of similar subjects as starting points for the general arrangement of his figures but, reformulating them entirely, reached a new level of psychological depth. Transcending the limitations of monochrome sculpture, he created works that are emotionally charged despite the absence of paint. Like a set designer, he fully exploited the potential of light as a creative medium that brings sculpture to life, almost in a painterly way.

36. Letter of 13? October 1506 from Venice to Willibald Pirckheimer, cited in translation in Wolfgang Stechow, *Northern Renaissance Art 1400–1600: Sources and Documents* (Evanston, 1966), 91.

The evolution of Riemenschneider's formal language defies simple explanation. His works reveal his keen understanding of Christian doctrine, and Riemenschneider was certainly aware of contemporary concerns within the Church on the abuse of images. Both Erasmus and Luther, for example, acknowledged the usefulness of images in teaching the illiterate, but they warned against the inherent danger of idolatry: pious veneration gave way to idolatry when images ceased to function as aids toward a higher form of spirituality and became themselves objects of adoration.[37] It is tempting to see Riemenschneider's increasing flattening of forms as an attempt to reduce the corporeality—and thus the presence—of his figures and to emphasize their character as man-made images. At the same time, artists often lean toward an abstraction of form in their late work and achieve a synthesis encapsulating the very essence of their art.

Works from different periods throughout Riemenschneider's career show that the formal lessons of his predecessors remained a constant. A late work like the grand *Virgin and Child* at Dumbarton Oaks illustrates the influence of Niclaus Gerhaert von Leiden (compare cats. 6 and 45) just as compellingly as an early work like the Hassfurt *Saint John.* Both use the conceit of drapery falling over the edge of the base to unite the world of the sculpture with that of viewer. Although highly stylized, the late work contains details based on an observation of nature, such as the Virgin's left thumb pressing into the child's thigh, another motif derived from Gerhaert, which also underscores the theological dogma of Christ as God made flesh.

Equally important, Rogier van der Weyden's influence, by way of Schongauer's engravings, can be felt throughout Riemenschneider's career. The late Maidbronn *Lamentation* conveys a very different pathos than the early *Passion* altarpiece from Rothenburg. While the *Passion* reliefs achieve an individualization of particulars, the *Lamentation* relief can best be characterized as a distillation of effects. In its expressive faces, its use of color, its emphatic gestures underscored by dramatic drapery passages, the early work calls out for an immediate emotional response. Its polar opposite is found in the idealized visages, restrained poses, and simplified draperies of the Maidbronn relief. Reduced to bare essentials, the latter expresses a quiet sorrow that enjoins meditation instead. Riemenschneider's best works, regardless of their date, depend on the active participation of the viewer. The dialogue they invite will not leave us unaffected.

37. David Freedberg, "Art and Iconoclasm, 1525–1580: The Case of the Northern Netherlands," in *Kunst voor de beeldenstorm* [exh. cat., Rijksmuseum] (Amsterdam, 1986), 69–84, esp. 69–70.

I owe much to Till Borchert, Katey Brown, Timothy Husband, Stephan Kemperdick, Hartmut Krohm, Michele Marincola, and William D. Wixom for their critical reading of the text.

The Sources of Riemenschneider's Art   *Hartmut Krohm*

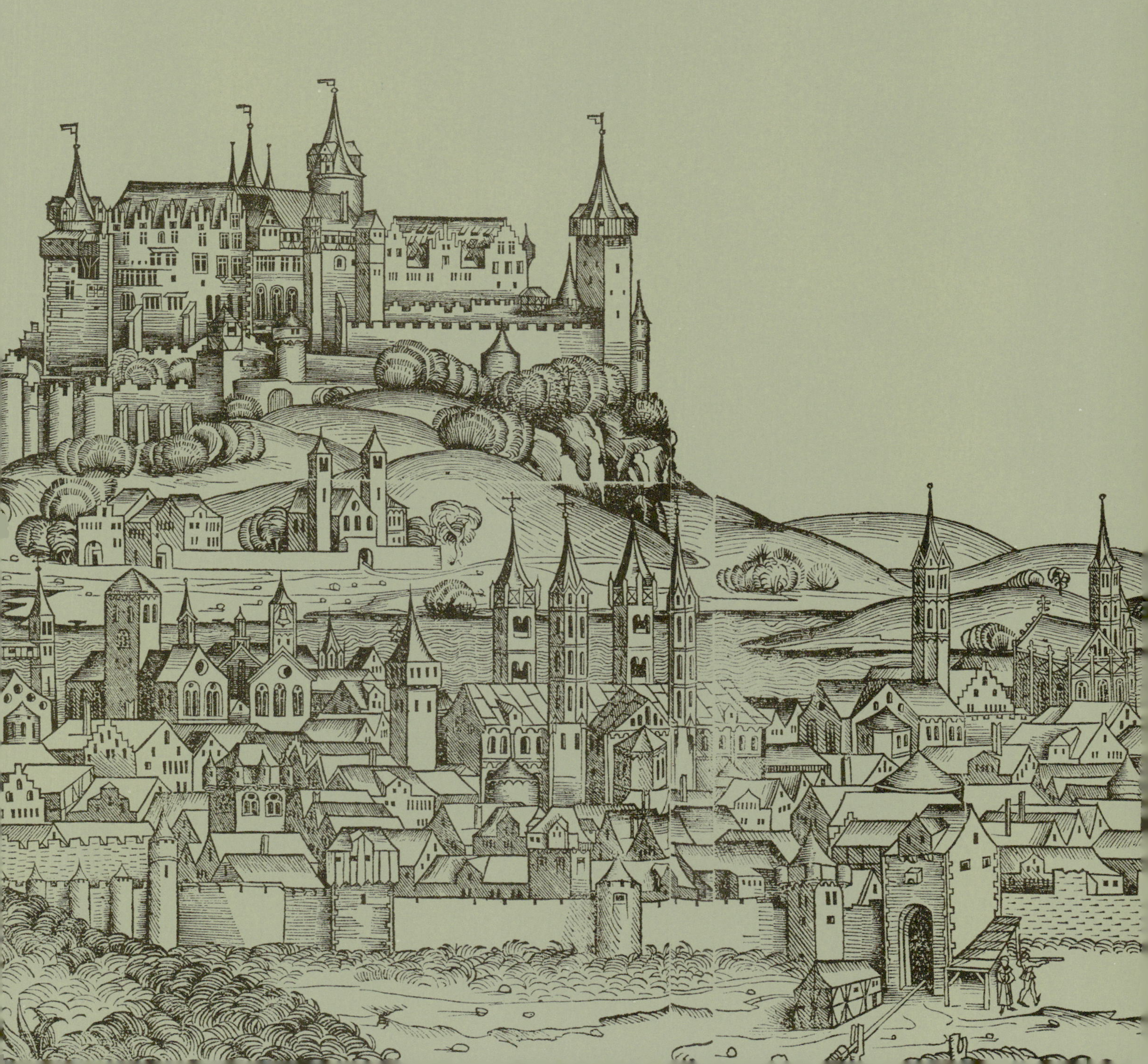

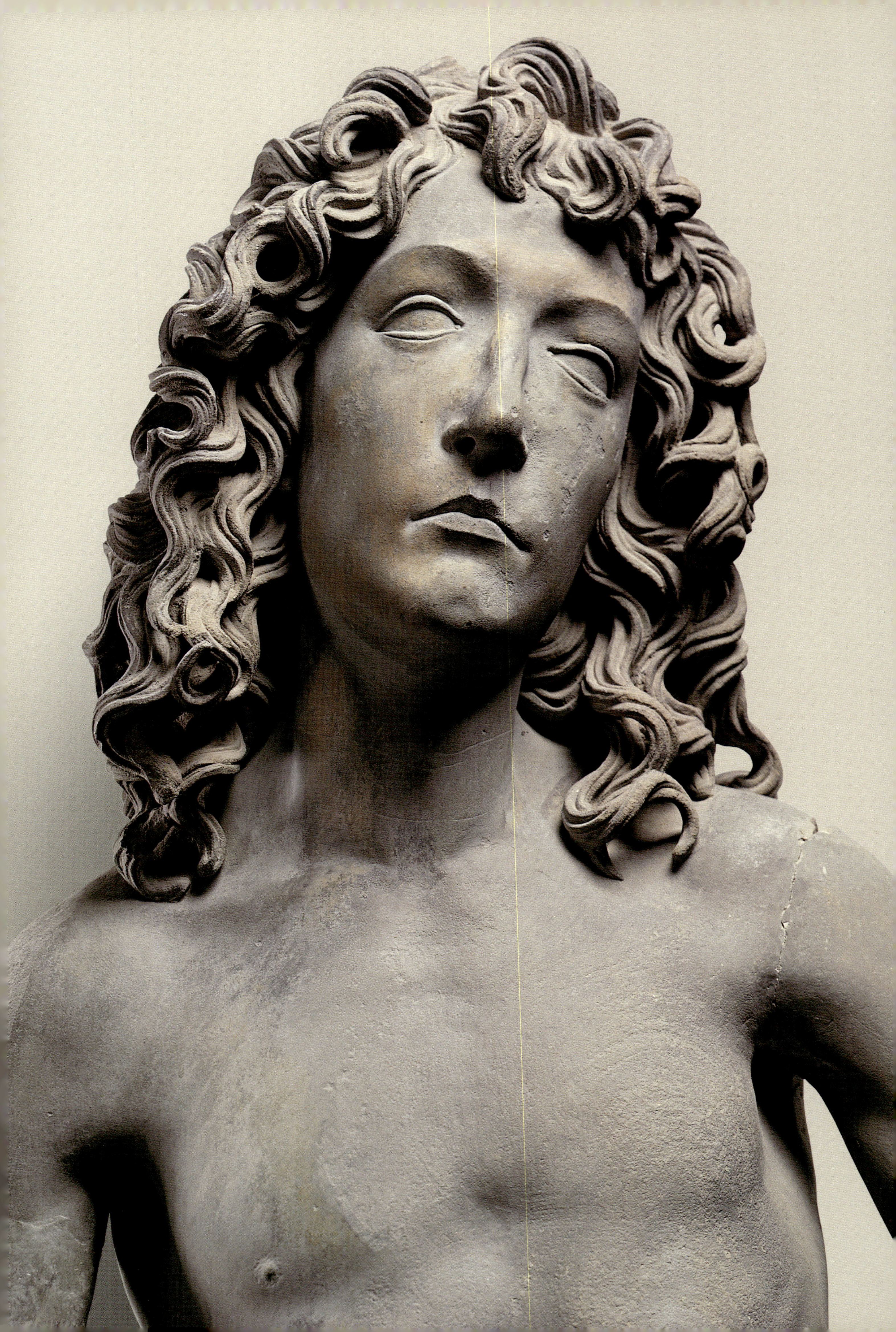

ℰCCLESIASTICAL DECORATION, especially for winged altarpieces, was in great demand in the fifteenth and early sixteenth centuries, and sculpture workshops flourished in southern Germany as never before. Among the creative talents active at the time, several individuals stand out, including Hans Multscher, Niclaus Gerhaert von Leiden, Veit Stoss, and Tilman Riemenschneider. The term "late Gothic" does not do justice to their art. Although technically master craftsmen, they were able to attain a much higher artistic level by studying masterpieces in their field. The importance of journeymen's travels and artistic interaction thus becomes obvious. This mobility resulted not only in greater specialization but in a new artistic consciousness.

The cities of Erfurt, Strasbourg, and Ulm have been named as places where Riemenschneider may have journeyed and come into contact with art that could have been significant for his own development. It has also been suggested that he may even have traveled to the Lowlands, as did many German artists during this period. This essay examines the validity of these hypotheses. ℂ Turning first to the region of Thuringia in central Germany, Erfurt enjoyed a thriving economy in the fourteenth and fifteenth centuries as well as an intellectual community centered on its university. In view of its geographic proximity to Riemenschneider's birthplace, Heiligenstadt, Erfurt would appear to have been the likely place where the sculptor received his training, although ultimately this assumption does not bear out.[1] Erfurt was the closest center of any art historical significance. In addition, the region around Heiligenstadt, like Erfurt, was subject to the bishopric

1. Edwin Redslob, "Erfurt als künstlerische Heimat Tilman Riemenschneiders," in *Festschrift Friedrich Winkler,* ed. Hans Möhle (Berlin, 1959), 171–179.

Detail of *Adam,* 1491–1493, Mainfränkisches Museum, Würzburg (Chapuis essay, fig. 3)

of Mainz. As a result of the "Feud over the Bishopric of Mainz," a conflict arising from the selection of a successor to the archbishop, Riemenschneider's parents had to leave Heiligenstadt around 1465. They moved to the town of Osterode in the Harz Mountains (in the Guelphian dukedom of Grubenhagen), but their connections to Erfurt could well have continued and prompted them to send their son there for his apprenticeship. Drawing precise conclusions about an artist's formative years, however, is extremely difficult, unless he trained with one of the most influential masters of the time. The young Albrecht Dürer, for example, learned his craft from Michael Wolgemut, a competent if not gifted Nuremberg master, but actually adopted little of artistic significance from him.

In the fourteenth century Erfurt achieved prominence in sculpture, which declined over the course of the fifteenth century, despite great productivity. Isolated examples of remarkable sculpture from that time include an alabaster relief of Saint Michael in the Sankt Severikirche (cat. 3, fig. 1) and a set of wooden angels on a baptismal font, both of 1467. Together with other works in alabaster scattered throughout central Germany, the relief may have been produced by an Erfurt workshop, which apparently ceased to function by the end of the 1460s.[2]

Even if Riemenschneider was not directly influenced by sculpture from Erfurt, as the current scholarly consensus suggests, the provenance of some of his works may nevertheless indicate ties to the city. These are small, easily transportable works in alabaster, intended for private devotion, such as the *Saint Jerome* in Cleveland and the *Virgin Annunciate* in the Louvre (cats. 11 and 21). Both works are said to have once belonged to the Benedictine abbey church of Saint Peter in Erfurt.

Of greatest importance for the development of Riemenschneider's style were the two leading artistic centers in southwest Germany, the imperial cities of Strasbourg and Ulm. Because of the construction of its cathedral, Strasbourg had been in a unique position since the thirteenth century to provide receptive journeymen stonemasons with the chance to study stone sculpture in its highest artistic forms—only major French cathedrals offered a similar opportunity. Shortly after the middle of the fifteenth century the Netherlander Niclaus Gerhaert von Leiden added new brilliance to Strasbourg's reputation as a showcase for exceptional stone sculpture, despite his brief stay of only a few years.[3] In 1460 Strasbourg followed the example of Ulm, its main artistic rival, by inviting Gerhaert to decorate the portal and façade of its newly constructed chancellery, just as Ulm had commissioned Hans Multscher, another sculptor trained mostly in France, to design the ceremonial window on the west side of its town hall in 1427.

A distinguishing characteristic of Niclaus Gerhaert's figural style is dimensionality. Whether sacred or profane, his sculpture appears to be alive. Within given spatial

2. About the group of related alabaster works from central Germany in Erfurt, Magdeburg, and Halberstadt, see Norbert Jopek, *Studien zur deutschen Alabasterplastik des 15. Jahrhunderts,* Manuskripte zur Kunstwissenschaft in der Wernerschen Verlagsgesellschaft, vol. 21 (Worms, 1988), 68–86.

3. About Niclaus Gerhaert von Leiden, see Otto Wertheimer, *Nicolaus Gerhaert. Seine Kunst und seine Wirkung* (Berlin, 1929); Roland Recht, *Nicolas de Leyde et la sculpture à Strasbourg (1460–1525)* (Strasbourg, 1987); Hartmut Krohm, "Zuschreibungen an Niclaus Gerhaert von Leyden. Eine noch längst nicht abgeschlossene Diskussion," in *Skulptur in Süddeutschland 1400–1525. Festschrift für Alfred Schädler,* ed. Rainer Kahsnitz and Peter Volk (Munich and Berlin, 1998), 109–128; Susanne Schreiber, "Studien zum bildhauerischen Werk des Niclaus von Leiden" (dissertation, Technische Universität, Berlin, 1996).

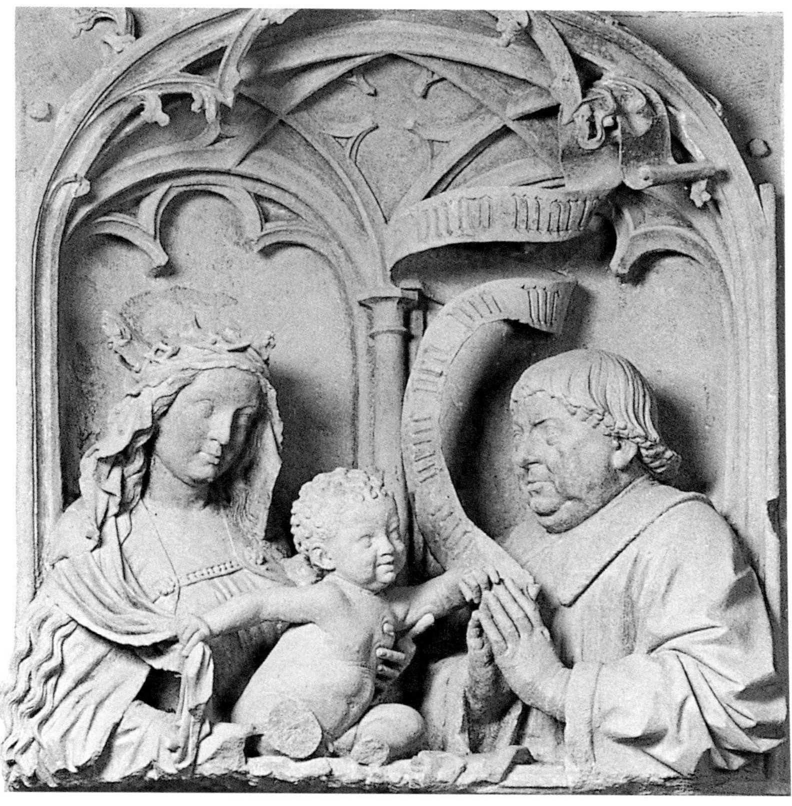

1.

Niclaus Gerhaert von Leiden, *Epitaph of a Canon*, 1464, sandstone, Cathédrale Notre-Dame, Strasbourg, Chapel of Saint John the Baptist

limitations, these highly cerebral works achieve an unprecedented dynamic. The observer is challenged to visualize the body itself, which remains largely hidden beneath several layers of clothing, from the outside inward. The movement that animates the figure is implied and can only be imagined, yet it defines the overall composition down to the last detail of an exceedingly complex structure. Gerhaert's guiding principle is the veiling and unveiling in the mind's eye. The spatial presence of Gerhaert's works would remain unequaled, although his formal inventions inspired artists in the most disparate locations, especially in Vienna, where he was active from 1467 until his death in 1473. A final attempt to emulate Gerhaert's formal conception can be seen in the *Annunciation* and the cycle of apostles in the parish church of Wiener Neustadt.[4]

Friedrich III, who reigned from 1440 to 1493, was evidently one of Gerhaert's most important patrons. The sculptor's mode of representation must have corresponded with the emperor's concept of piety. Friedrich also promoted artists who worked in the sculptural tradition established by Gerhaert, offering them commissions in the eastern regions of the empire. Gerhaert's work follows an artistic path that can be traced to creations of earlier periods, from the paintings of Jan van Eyck to the works of Burgundian court sculptor Claus Sluter. Gerhaert's figures have a visionary quality

4. Karl Oettinger, *Lorenz Luchsperger. Der Meister der Wiener Neustädter Domapostel,* Forschungen zur deutschen Kunstgeschichte, vol. 12 (Berlin, 1935).

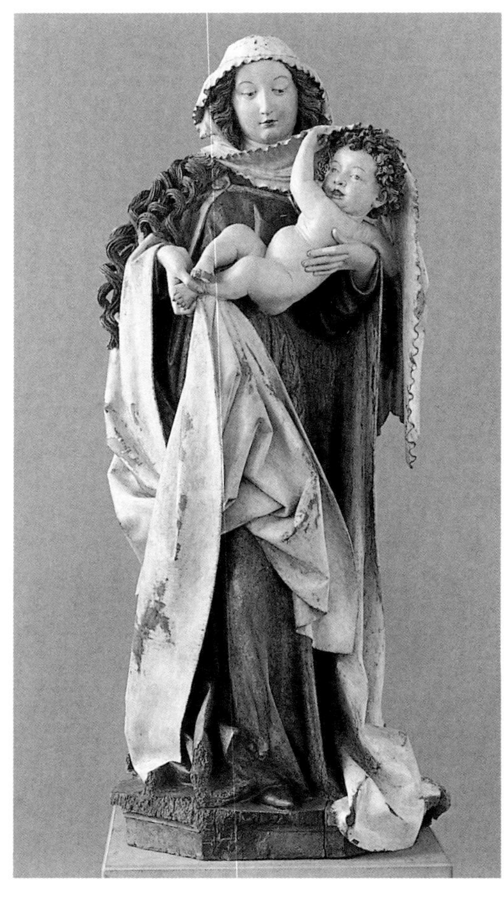

2.

Attributed to Niclaus Gerhaert von Leiden, *Virgin and Child* from Dangolsheim, c. 1460–1465, walnut with original
polychromy, Staatliche Museen zu Berlin, Skulpturensammlung

5. A similar work, although in very low relief, is the highly deteriorated epitaph of the Strasbourg archbishop Albrecht of Bavaria in Saverne, Alsace. Compare Recht 1987, fig. 287.

6. Petra Krutisch, "Die Beurteilung der Dangolsheimer Muttergottes in der kunst-wissenschaftlichen Literatur," in *Die Dangolsheimer Muttergottes nach ihrer Restaurierung* [exh. cat., Staatliche Museen, Skulpturensammlung] (Berlin, 1989), 25–36; Krohm in Kahsnitz and Volk 1998, 109–111.

that seems to transcend the earthly realm. At the same time, the "physical" immediacy that Van Eyck established between his patrons Nicolas Rolin or Joris van der Paele, for example, and the object of their devotion—the Virgin—finds its sculptural equivalent in Gerhaert's *Epitaph of a Canon* from the chapel of Saint John the Baptist in Strasbourg Cathedral (fig. 1). This visual conceit may have been perceived as too "daring" and was seldom repeated.[5]

Especially in Riemenschneider's early work we encounter figural types that can be traced to Gerhaert's creations, such as the Dangolsheim *Virgin and Child* in Berlin (fig. 2)[6] or the high altar retable of the Sankt Georgskirche in Nördlingen (see cat. 5, fig. 2). The tendency in his work was toward a gradual synthesis of Gerhaert's understanding of form, which Riemenschneider used to great effect, for instance, in the architectural context of the canopy figures above *Adam* and *Eve* (see fig. 5). Riemenschneider's conception of art in intellectual terms, however, was based only to a limited degree on Sluter, Van Eyck, or Gerhaert. The Würzburg sculptor was much closer to the ascetic vision of a Rogier van der Weyden or a Martin Schongauer.

Gerhaert's expressive style became muted in the works of his immediate followers, as can be detected in Strasbourg as early as the 1460s, when Gerhaert in fact resided there. The change is apparent in the *Nativity* formerly in the Spetz collection in Colmar, now in the Rijksmuseum, Amsterdam. Around 1466 the same sculptor executed the crucifix and angels in the high altar retable of the Jakobskirche in Rothenburg, which bears the signature of the Nördlingen painter Friedrich Herlin (fig. 3). This sculptor was also employed by the emperor, carving the saints in the chapel of the Viennese Hofburg; immediately afterward he began work on the foremost retable created under the rule of the Hungarian king, Matthias Corvinus, that in the Sankt Elisabethkirche in Kaschau (Košice).[7] The slender, delicate limbs and precisely carved features of his figures indicate a range of expression that became characteristic of Riemenschneider's art barely fifteen years later.

Among the most engaging figural works in late Gothic sculpture are those attributed to the Master of the Amsterdam Nativity. These objects are intended for intimate viewing, much more so than Gerhaert's work, and they encourage contemplation. This is also the case with the small applewood Virgin (cat. 7), produced in Strasbourg around 1470 and showing the influence of Gerhaert's figural style, especially in its reserved quality. Like Riemenschneider's *Saint Barbara* (cat. 4), this composition is based on contrasts and is reminiscent of works such as the Dangolsheim Virgin. Along with the vitality derived from Gerhaert's work, the serious, pensive expression of the small figure

7. Hartmut Krohm, "Bemerkungen zur kunstgeschichtlichen Problematik des Herlin-Retabels in Rothenburg o. T.," *Jahrbuch der Berliner Museen,* new series 33 (1991), 185–208; Hartmut Scholz, "Hans Wild und Hans Kamensetzer. Hypotheken der Ulmer und Strassburger Kunstgeschichte des Spätmittelalters," *Jahrbuch der Berliner Museen,* new series 36 (1994), 93–140; Kaliopi Chamonikolasová, "Nicolaus Gerhaert of Leyden in the Moravian Context," *Wiener Jahrbuch für Kunstgeschichte* 49 (1995), 61–84.

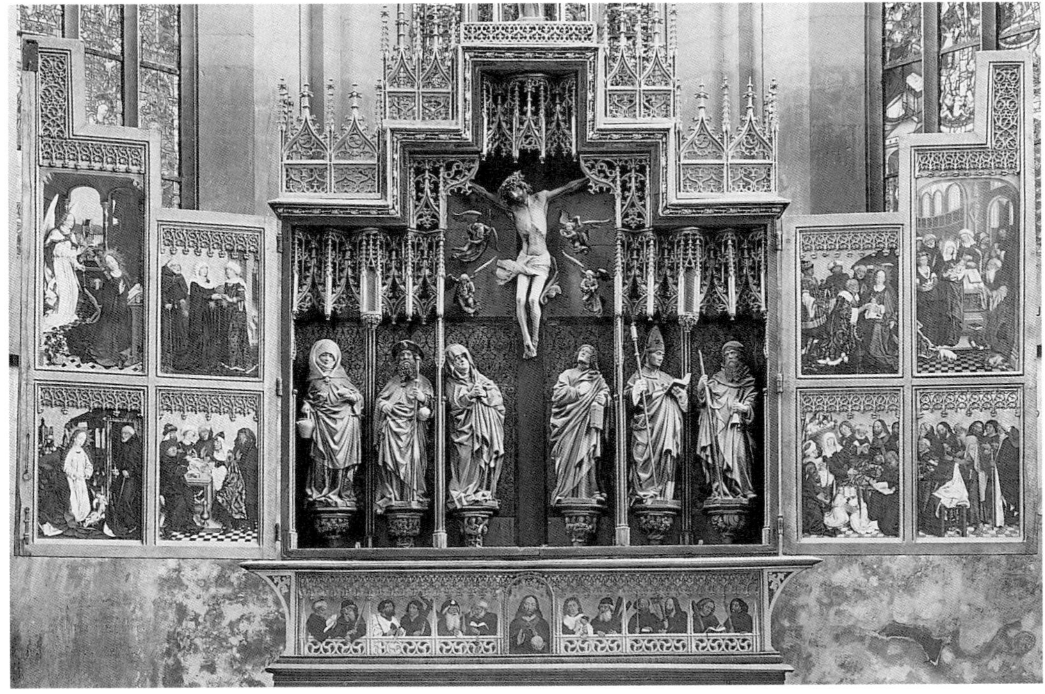

3.

High altar retable signed by Friedrich Herlin, 1466, Jakobskirche, Rothenburg

of Mary and the vulnerability of the child radiate a calm that is characteristic for Riemenschneider as well. This peaceful air also influences the manner in which the viewer approaches the statuette and facilitates the grasp of its essence. Features that elicit pious and meditative contemplation are accentuated.

It is not by accident that the most striking aspect of the applewood *Virgin and Child,* the mother's protective gesture over the torso of the child, appears, raised to a remarkable level of artistic expression, in a contemporary work: a small engraving by Martin Schongauer (fig. 4).[8] The miniature quality of the printed image indicates that it was intended for a similar devotional purpose as the applewood Virgin, whose face clearly shows traces of wear from frequent handling. Schongauer's engraving demands focused attention, and an intimate relationship between the image and the viewer ensues.

Developments in Strasbourg art aimed at devotional practices may have been important for Riemenschneider. His contact with the graphic work of Martin Schongauer, also active in the Upper Rhine region at this time—in Colmar, Alsace—was influential. The formal repertoire of Niclaus Gerhaert on Riemenschneider's early work is equally evident in some of the figures in the Münnerstadt altarpiece of 1490–1492 (cat. 13) or in the statues in the parish church of Hassfurt (Chapuis essay, fig. 1) completed by Riemenschneider and his workshop.[9] Another sculpture that deserves special attention in this context is the Virgin attributed to the young Riemenschneider by Alfred Schädler in 1981 (cat. 1).[10] In addition, the Virgin from Wasserliesch (cat. 14, fig. 1) apparently served as a link between Gerhaert's school and Riemenschneider.[11]

In connection with the *Adam* and *Eve* of 1491–1493 for the south portal of the Marienkapelle in Würzburg, it appears that the design has its roots in Strasbourg, both in the cathedral and its sculptural ornament, as well as in the art of Gerhaert. It is striking that two groups of small figures—the Annunciation and Christ appearing to Mary Magdalen—Riemenschneider mounted on the canopies above *Adam* and *Eve* (fig. 5) exhibit Gerhaert's principle of core and shell. This comes into play especially when one considers the visual accessibility of these figures from different vantages. The principle is applied to promote contextual clarification: thus the Virgin's cloak is open, exposing her body, which will receive Christ.[12]

Strasbourg was probably the city that brought Riemenschneider in touch not only with sculpture by Gerhaert but also with Netherlandish art. At the same time he came to know the inventions of Rogier van der Weyden through Schongauer's engravings. Speculation that Riemenschneider traveled to the Lowlands as a journeyman sculptor cannot be confirmed.[13] Yet one must account for his close connection to Rogier's formal tradition, which reaches well beyond the epigonic dispersion of this art in Germany and is less apparent in singular motifs than as a general approach.

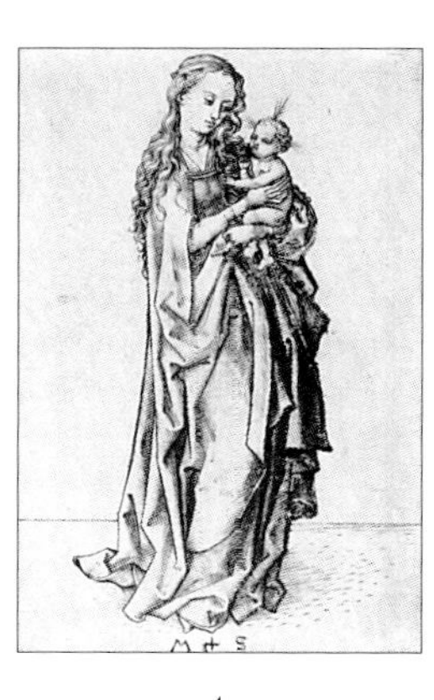

4.
Martin Schongauer,
Virgin and Child,
c. 1475–1480, engraving,
Staatliche Museen zu
Berlin, Kupferstichkabinett

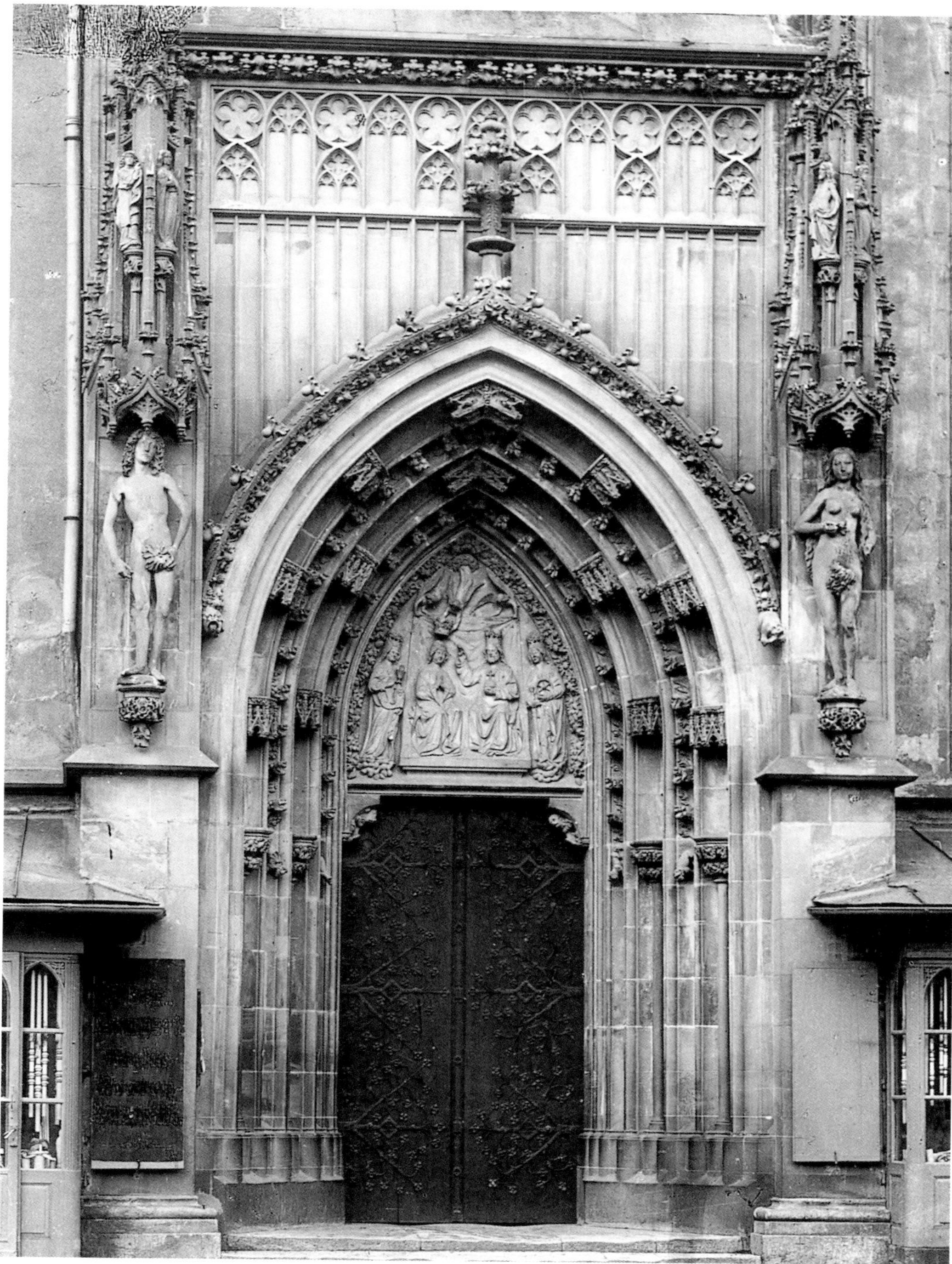

5.

South portal of the Marienkapelle in Würzburg showing Riemenschneider's *Adam* and *Eve* in situ.
Photographed before 1894

Netherlandish sources, or at least sources influenced by Netherlandish art, seem to be most evident in Riemenschneider's early *Passion* altarpiece—completed just after 1485 for a church in Rothenburg but now dispersed—particularly in the figural groups for the shrine and predella of the retable.[14] The reliefs recently acquired by the Bay-erisches Nationalmuseum in Munich (Chapuis essay, fig. 2) may derive from two

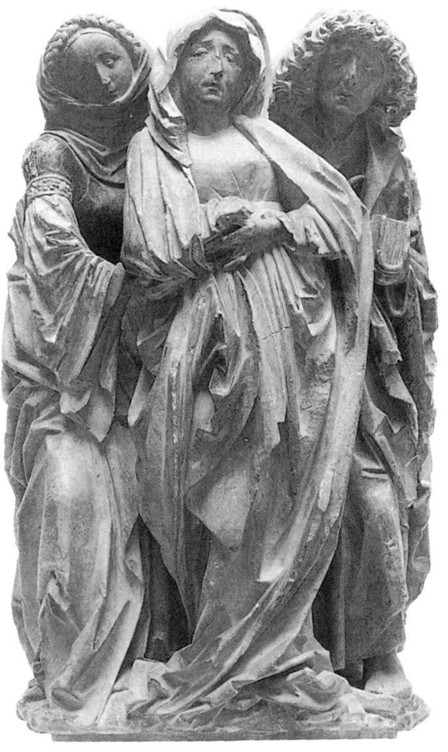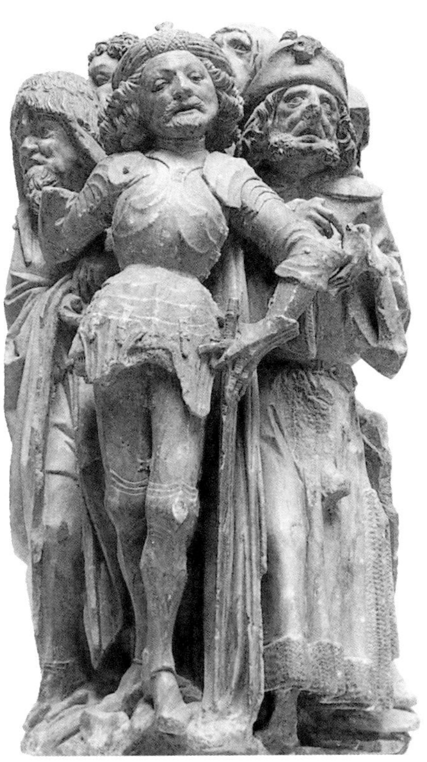

6.

Strasbourg, two groups from a Crucifixion, c. 1470, alabaster, Musée de l'Oeuvre
Notre-Dame, Strasbourg

alabaster groups in the Musée de l'Oeuvre Notre-Dame in Strasbourg from around 1470 (fig. 6).[15] Yet the main features of the putative models have been reformulated here in the language of a Rogier van der Weyden or a Martin Schongauer. The mourning figures from the *Passion* altarpiece reveal in their quiet attentiveness and subtle gestures a proximity to compositions by Rogier, such as his grand *Descent from the Cross* of the 1430s from Louvain, now in Madrid. This observation should in no way minimize the significance of the alabasters in Strasbourg.[16] They were probably once part of a larger, much-noted ensemble of figures installed in Strasbourg Cathedral, several of which appear to have been reused to repair the pulpit in the cathedral, perhaps in 1616/1617. The importance of these works becomes clear in connection with the stylistic development of the Strasbourg sculptor Nicolas Hagenower.[17] Further, the figure of a bishop saint (fig. 7), which apparently belonged in the same context and is now located in a niche at the foot of the cathedral pulpit, is striking in its treatment of the chasuble, which is held before the body like a shield. This sleeveless vestment and the individualized facial features may suggest, perhaps unjustly, the influence of Niclaus Gerhaert. Certainly the exemplary force of the bishop's figure should not be underestimated. The piece may have inspired the drapery pattern of Veit Stoss' effigy of King Kasimir IV of Poland in Krakow. It may also have influenced Riemenschneider.[18]

54

The fame and early appreciation of this sculpture in Strasbourg is supported by the existence of a drawing by an artist active in Strasbourg known as the Master of the Drapery Studies.[19]

The *Mourning Women* relief from the predella of the *Passion* altarpiece (fig. 8) bears some resemblance to a *Lamentation* completed in 1501 by Nicolas Hagenower for the high altar of Strasbourg Cathedral (fig. 9).[20] Both groups can probably be traced to the same (Netherlandish?) source — a sculpture, painting, or drawing that artists may have been able to view in Strasbourg. This connection may confirm that Riemenschneider was able to acquire a knowledge of Netherlandish art in Strasbourg, which was so receptive to art from the West.[21]

Next to Strasbourg, Ulm was the most important sculptural center in southern Germany at this time. The city possessed a number of masterworks from the previous generation, which must have attracted journeymen artisans from many regions. Among these were sculpture by Hans Multscher (d. 1466/1467) as well as projects undertaken in the 1460s and hitherto unequaled in their scope, such as the decoration of the chancel, tabernacle (c. 1465/1470), sedile, choir stalls, and high altar of Ulm Minster. The stalls and high altar were executed between 1467 and 1481 under master joiner Jörg Syrlin the Elder. With the decoration of the choir and the vaulting of the church, Ulm offered

19. For this drawing in the Berlin Kupferstichkabinett, see Michael Roth, "'Strassburger Fenster' in Ulm und ihr künstlerisches Umfeld," in *Bilder aus Licht und Farbe. Meisterwerke spätgotischer Glasmalerei* [exh. cat., Ulmer Museum] (Ulm, 1995), 217–219, no. 72.

20. See Recht 1987, 263–264.

21. As illustrated in the "Molsheimer Reliefs" from the former high altar retable in Strasbourg's charterhouse, which may have been created in Brussels.

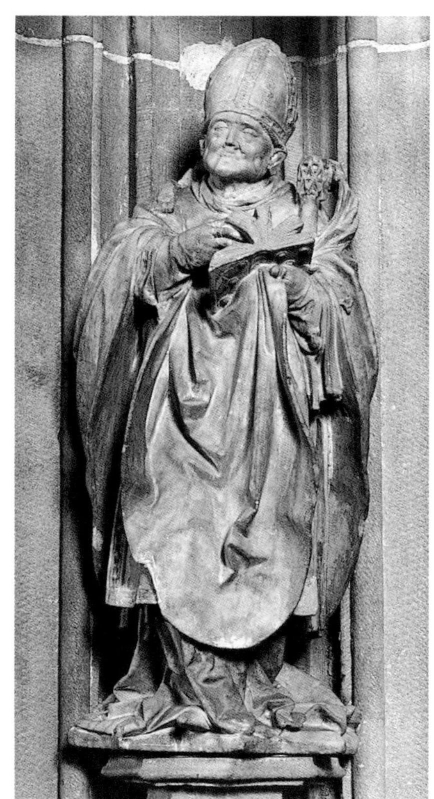

7.

Strasbourg, *Standing Bishop Saint*, c. 1470, alabaster, Cathédrale Notre-Dame, Strasbourg

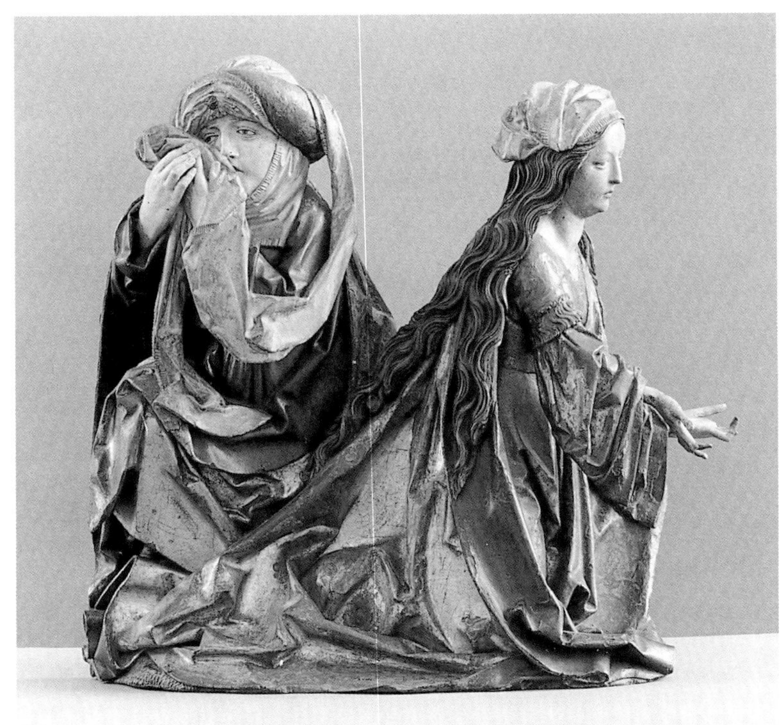

8.

Mourning Women from the predella of a *Passion* altarpiece, c. 1485–1490, limewood with original polychromy,
Staatliche Museen zu Berlin, Skulpturensammlung

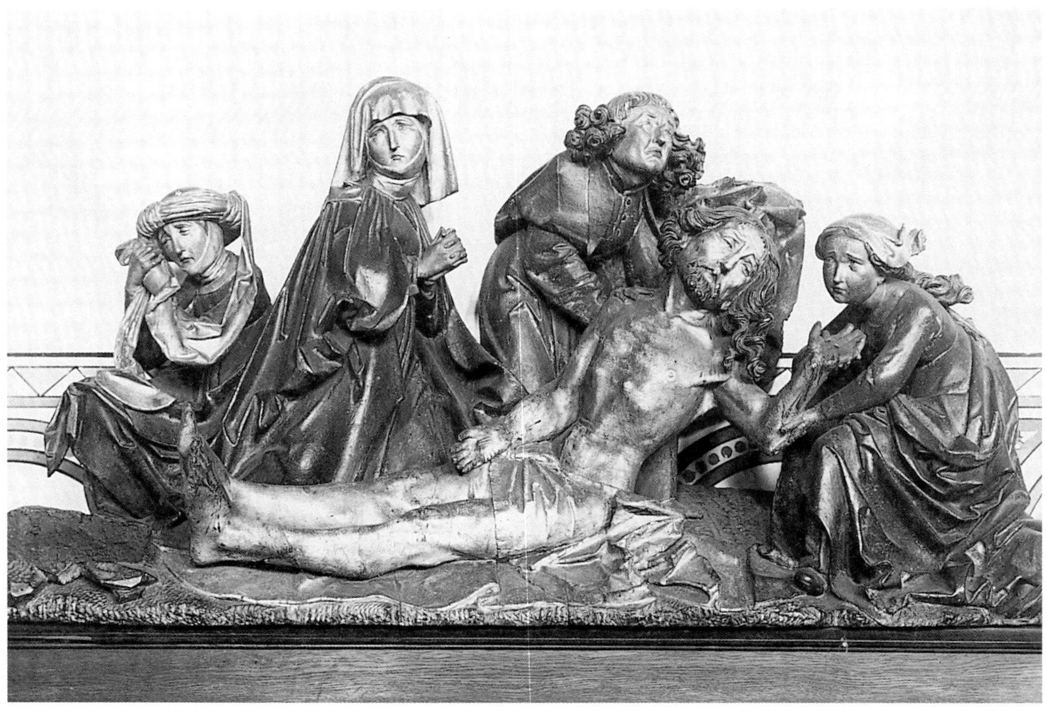

9.

Nicolas Hagenower, *Lamentation* from the predella of the high altar retable in Strasbourg Cathedral, 1501, limewood with
polychromy, Collège Saint-Etienne, Strasbourg

a monument whose dimensions at that time rivaled those of the great French cathedrals. Only the large western tower of the church, begun in 1392 by Ulrich von Ensingen, was left unfinished owing to structural problems.

The most accomplished sculptor active in Ulm after the death of Hans Multscher was unquestionably Michel Erhart, to whom Wolfgang Deutsch first ascribed the famous busts of philosophers and sibyls in the choir stalls of Ulm Minster (see cat. 12, fig. 2).[22] This attribution has been gaining acceptance recently.[23] The key points in Deutsch's argument are the figures in a retable Erhart appears to have completed in 1494 for the high altar of the Benedictine monastery church in Blaubeuren near Ulm (cat. 12, fig. 1), and a crucifix in the parish church of Sankt Michael, Schwäbisch Hall, also from 1494 (see fig. 11).

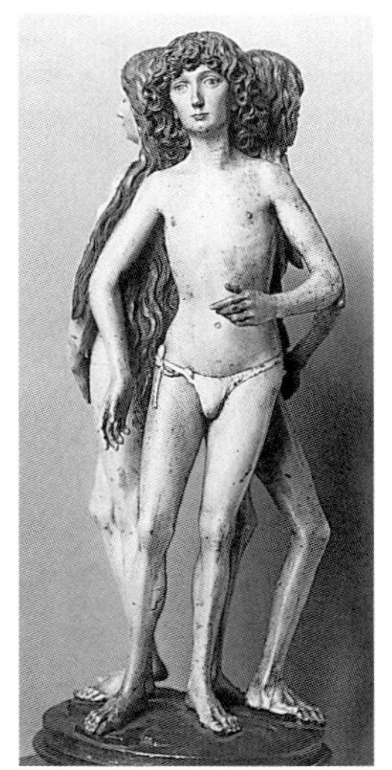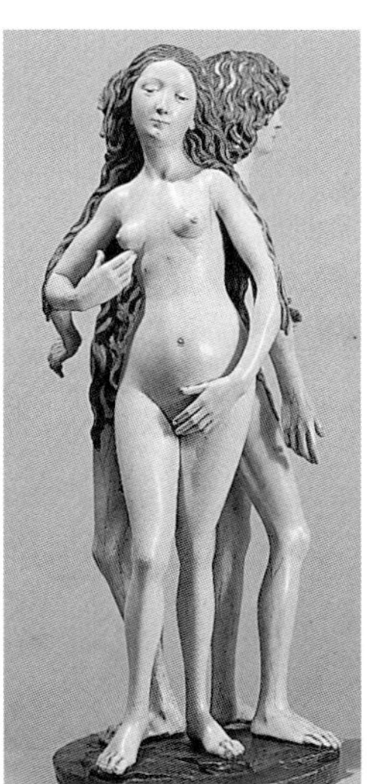

10.

Attributed to Michel Erhart, *Vanitas* (two views), c. 1480, limewood with original polychromy, Kunsthistorisches Museum, Vienna, Kunstkammer

The loincloth on the crucifix is signed by Erhart, making this the only work that can be conclusively attributed to the artist.[24] Two related works of first-rate quality, a *Seated Virgin and Child* in Berlin (cat. 12) and a three-figure *Vanitas* group in Vienna (fig. 10) of a youth with an old and a young woman all standing back to back, have been attributed to Gregor Erhart, the son of Michel Erhart. Gregor was active from about 1495 to 1525 in the rich city of Augsburg. Under closer inspection, however, the two works shed more light on sculpture ascribed to the father than on that of the son, and they offer possibilities for comparison with works by Riemenschneider as well.[25]

Pursuing questions of attribution with respect to Michel and Gregor Erhart would lead the current discussion too far astray. Yet if we assume a date of around 1480 for the *Vanitas* in Vienna, with the father as the more likely creator, we have a more appropriate context for understanding the work. The young woman in this composition is a typical late Gothic figure, with finely formed limbs and a delicate physique. Her appearance is determined above all by the ornamental stylization of her contours, which harmonize well with her overall gestural expression. As a female nude, the figure is not far removed from an engraving of the Assumption of Mary Magdalen by Master E. S. dated in the 1460s.[26] A life-size Mary Magdalen in the Louvre, whose composition and proportions clearly show the influence of Albrecht Dürer, is probably by Gregor Erhart.[27] Taking into consideration the pronounced physicality and temporal character of the latter, it is hard to imagine that the same artist could have produced the *Vanitas,* a work so deeply indebted to formal concepts of the late Gothic. The *Vanitas* could have served as a model for Riemenschneider's *Adam* and *Eve* from the Marienkapelle in Würzburg, which also evince a sensual treatment of idealized beauty.

22. Wolfgang Deutsch, "Der ehemalige Hochaltar und das Chorgestühl, zur Syrlin- und zur Bildhauerfrage," in *600 Jahre Ulmer Münster,* ed. Hans Eugen Specker and Reinhard Wortmann (Ulm, 1977), 242–322.

23. David Gropp, *Das Ulmer Chorgestühl und Jörg Syrlin der Ältere,* Neue Forschungen zur deutschen Kunstgeschichte, vol. 4 (Berlin, 1999).

24. Deutsch's "Michel Erhart und sein Verhältnis zu Gregor Erhart und Syrlin dem Älteren" of 1969 remains unpublished. For an overview, see Anja Broschek, *Michel Erhart* (Berlin and New York, 1973).

25. See Deutsch 1969, 178–183; Heribert Meurer in *Hans Multscher* [exh. cat., Ulmer Museum] (Ulm, 1997), 421–422.

26. Holm Bevers, ed., *Meister E. S. Ein oberrheinischer Kupferstecher der Spätgotik* [exh. cat., Staatliche Graphische Sammlung] (Berlin, 1987), 69, fig. 80.

27. Alfred Schädler, "Gregor Erharts 'La Belle Allemande' im Louvre," *Aachener Kunstblätter* (1994), 365–376.

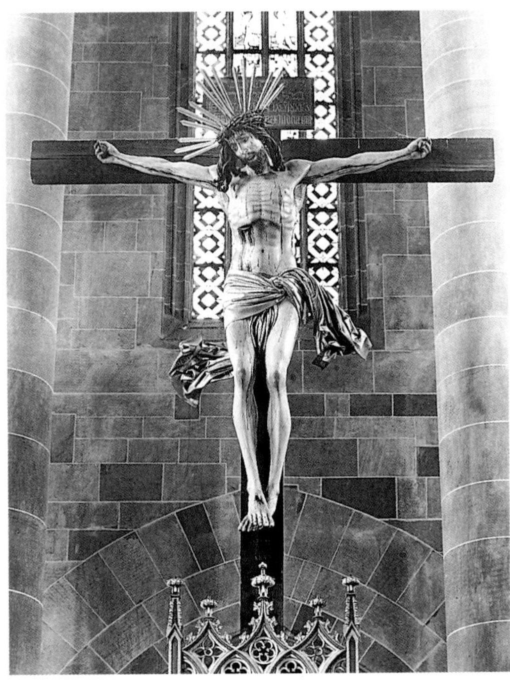

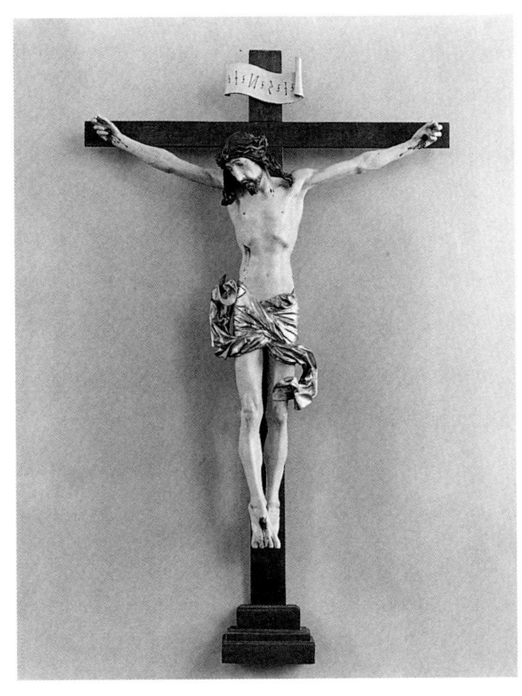

11.

Michel Erhart, *Crucifix*, 1494, limewood with
original polychromy, Stadtpfarrkirche Sankt Michael,
Schwäbisch Hall

12.

Crucifix, c. 1485–1490, limewood with modern polychromy,
Pfarrkirche Sankt Matthäus, Heroldsberg

The *Seated Virgin* in Berlin (cat. 12), which can probably also be attributed to
Michel Erhart and dated around 1480, is again a work that appears to be rooted in the
sculptural tradition of Niclaus Gerhaert. For comparison, two works now in Vienna,
a *Virgin* and *Saint James the Greater,* both exhibit the influence of Strasbourg.[28] Characteristic for each work is the complex arrangement of folds in the clothing, dictated by
the underlying structure of the body. The seated Virgin's legs are crossed at the ankles,
with her knees apart to give the reclining Christ child a broad surface on which to lie.
The distinctive way in which the artist has used the mother's body and the folds of
her dress to create this resting place for the child indicates an intimate understanding
of Gerhaert's figurative concepts. The Berlin Virgin could well have inspired Riemenschneider's *Saint Matthew* from Münnerstadt (cat. 13 A) or the *Saint Anthony* for the
Ursulinenkirche in Würzburg, an early workshop piece lost to fire during World War II.[29]
If we follow this line of reasoning, however, we could also argue that Riemenschneider's creative impulses may have come from sculptural designs developed in the Upper
Rhine region.

Crucifixes play a major role in the oeuvres of both Riemenschneider and Michel
Erhart, and the two artists share a similar vision of Christ's suffering. A 1505 / 1506 commission from the prince-elector Friedrich the Wise for the castle chapel in Wittenberg
indicates how highly Riemenschneider's work must have been regarded. Likewise, two

58

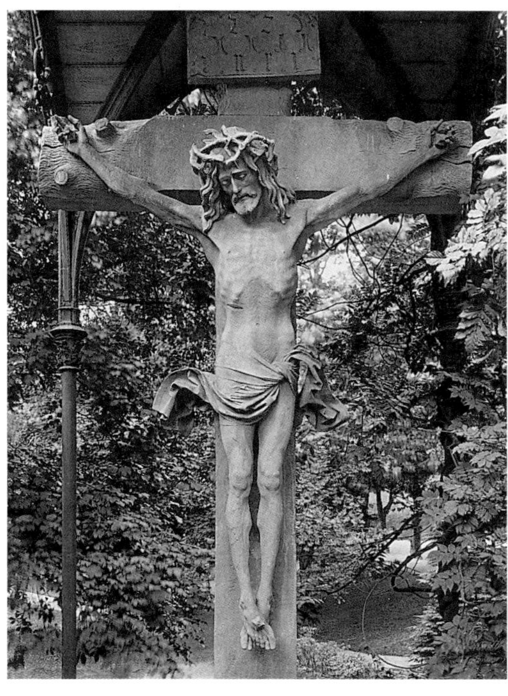

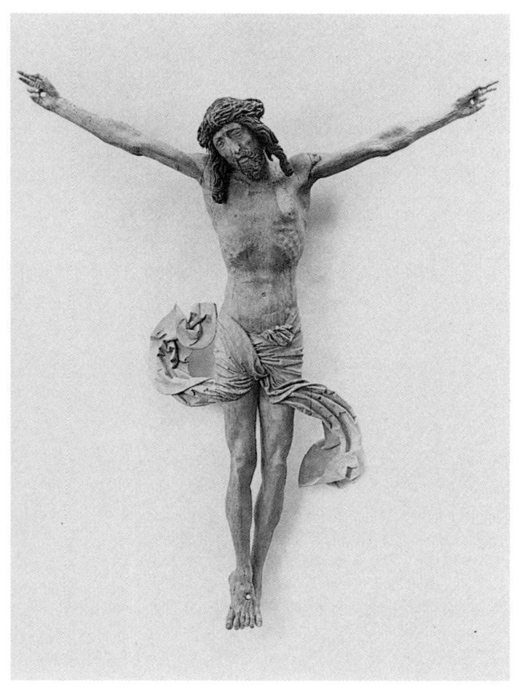

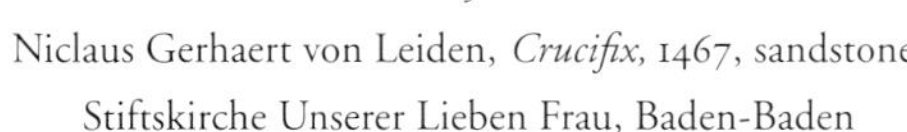

13.

Niclaus Gerhaert von Leiden, *Crucifix,* 1467, sandstone,
Stiftskirche Unserer Lieben Frau, Baden-Baden

14.

Crucifix, c. 1495, limewood, Pfarrkirche Sankt
Nikolaus, Eisingen

of Erhart's crucifixes were commissioned for churches far from Ulm: Sankt Michael
in Schwäbisch Hall, signed and dated 1494 (fig. 11); and Sankt Martin in Landshut,
completed in 1495. Riemenschneider scholarship lacks consensus on the attribution
and dating of specific works,[30] and it seems important to clarify the date of the Heroldsberg *Crucifix* (fig. 12), a work of especially high quality. Certain distinctive features
suggest that it once belonged to the *Passion* altarpiece from Rothenburg, one of the
artist's earliest creations.[31]

Riemenschneider scholars frequently stress the importance of Niclaus Gerhaert's
famous stone *Crucifix* of 1467 in Baden-Baden (fig. 13). Riemenschneider's *Crucifix*
in Eisingen near Würzburg (fig. 14), a work of relatively large proportions, shows some
affinity with Gerhaert's work, but to only a limited degree. Gerhaert is interested in
anatomical detail and tends to enhance athletic features, thus emphasizing the humanity of God's son. Riemenschneider's more abstracted representations (see also cat. 33
and Chapuis essay, fig. 10) evoke different associations. His crucifixes are distinguished
above all by a fine, graceful rendering of the limbs. The face of Christ is usually narrow with sunken cheeks, framed by lively, twirling, ornamental curls of hair. These
features evidence a nobility undiminished by suffering. The refined physical features
elicit empathy, and the forlorn facial expression, reflecting distress over the sins of mankind, manifests psychic pain.

30. For dates of works of art,
see Justus Bier, *Tilmann Riemenschneider. Die späten Werke in
Holz* (Vienna, 1978), 67–82; see
also Alfred Schädler, "Zu Tilman
Riemenschneiders Kruzifixen,"
Artibus et historiae 24 (1991),
37–51.

31. Hartmut Krohm and Andrea
Kleberger in Würzburg 1981,
56–66; Kahsnitz 1997, 71–72.

The superb quality of Riemenschneider's stone sculpture suggests that he regarded this material more highly than wood. His few works in alabaster (cats. 2, 4, 11, 21), the figures of *Adam* and *Eve* from the Marienkapelle (Chapuis essay, fig. 3), the *Anna Selbdritt* in the Mainfränkisches Museum (cat. 15), the monument to Rudolf von Scherenberg in Würzburg Cathedral (Kemperdick essay, fig. 1), and finally the *Kaisergrab* in Bamberg Cathedral and the *Lamentation* relief in Maidbronn (Chapuis essay, figs. 4 and 9) represent the peak of Riemenschneider's artistic achievement.

Equal command of wood and stone sculpture was a rarity among artists of the late fifteenth and early sixteenth centuries, yet nearly all of the great sculptors of the time possessed such mastery, including Hans Multscher, Niclaus Gerhaert, and Veit Stoss. Stone sculpture often achieves its best effect in an innovative architectural context, as Multscher's town hall window in Ulm, Gerhaert's portal façade of the Strasbourg chancellery (no longer extant), and Adam Kraft's tabernacle in the Lorenzkirche in Nuremberg all bear eloquent witness. Niclaus Gerhaert's gravestone in Wiener Neustadt commemorates the artist as a "master craftsman and builder," referring to his work on the cathedral or the chancellery. He and presumably all the artists named here, including Riemenschneider, received training in the building trades. It was apparently the only method by which sculptors could learn the art of stone carving. Stonemasonry requires many of the skills expected of a stone sculptor, which far exceeded those needed to execute the functional framing of a structure and often involved the optimal use of elaborate architectural forms in the presentation of figural sculpture.

Because Riemenschneider appears to have been well acquainted with the art of Niclaus Gerhaert and most likely traveled and worked as a journeyman sculptor in the Upper Rhine region, it is possible that he received his training in the art of stonemasonry in Strasbourg. This could have taken place in a workshop such as that connected with the construction and maintenance of the cathedral, but there is no definitive evidence to support this theory.

We can also assume that Riemenschneider intensively studied sculptural art from widely varying contexts as well as from earlier periods, even though no obvious repetition of motifs is evident. His precise, sensual treatment of surfaces, especially of exposed flesh, so animates the stone that it virtually appears to be skin. He strove for and achieved astounding mimetic effects. Essentially similar intentions can be found in the works of Niclaus Gerhaert, yet these yield a different meaning than that found in Riemenschneider's work. In the *Epitaph of a Canon* (see fig. 1) Gerhaert faithfully reproduces the coarse, callused skin of his subject (similar to Claus Sluter's earlier treatment of the prophets on the *Well of Moses* in Champmol). Gerhaert consciously dispensed with a polished treatment, allowing the visible tool marks to determine the final impression. Similarly, in his tomb of Archbishop Jakob von Sierck in Trier the hatchwork left by Gerhaert's toothed chisel endows the robe with the texture of fabric and enhances the dynamic play of light and shadow over the stone's surface.

Riemenschneider worked in a completely different, highly abstracted manner. His representations improve on nature. *Adam* and *Eve* from the Würzburg Marienkapelle, who in their flawlessness seem to have regained the state of grace, are created with the stone's surface and the sublime effects of light particularly in mind. The figure of Christ in the *Lamentation* relief in Maidbronn conveys the impression of a body transfigured, ethereally transformed.

Late in the fifteenth century sculptors elsewhere in southern Germany attempted to achieve these effects with completely smooth surfaces. The 1492 epitaph by Adam Kraft for the Schreyer and Landauer families (Sankt Sebalduskirche, Nuremberg), completed the same year as the Münnerstadt altarpiece (cat. 13), is a notable example. Even if these parallels cannot be drawn too closely, sculpture from the Strasbourg school of around 1480 could have influenced Kraft as well as Riemenschneider. At this time works were produced in Strasbourg—probably by the cathedral workshop—that were clearly indebted to Gerhaert in form and composition but whose handling exhibits entirely new techniques and principles. Major examples are the sandstone figures on the cathedral's pulpit, completed in 1484/1485 by the architect Hans Hammer, and the *Anna Selbdritt* (cat. 8), originally from Alsace and now in Berlin. The exquisite surface of the latter approximates Riemenschneider's stone sculpture while distancing it from that of Niclaus Gerhaert, even though it is closely related conceptually.

The unusual sensuality of the *Adam* and *Eve* or of the Maidbronn figure of Christ elevates the viewer's reflections from the transcendent beauty of the temporal to that of the spiritual realm. This perceptual process toward a heightened awareness also applies to Riemenschneider's effigies of Eberhard von Grumbach in Rimpar and of Konrad von Schaumberg in the Würzburg Marienkapelle (cat. 18, figs. 1 and 2), which, despite the realistically rendered armor, seem to hover in space. This abstracted sensuality, conveying such spiritual concepts as sanctity, culminated in stone sculpture around 1500. Its direct antecedent is found in Bohemian sculpture of the late fourteenth century, especially the so-called Beautiful Madonnas (*Schöne Madonnen*).

Adam and *Eve,* originally mounted on decorative columns flanking the south portal of the Würzburg Marienkapelle (see fig. 5), and the monument to Rudolf von Scherenberg are major examples of figural works that achieved their full effect in a larger architectural context. This particular mode of figural presentation was influenced by Upper Rhenish formal concepts. The *Adam* and *Eve,* with their contours standing

32. For details about the figures, platform, and canopy, see Justus Bier, *Tilman Riemenschneider. Die frühen Werke* (Würzburg, 1925), 71.

33. This aspect of the *Adam and Eve* is explored at length in Hubert Schrade, *Tilman Riemenschneider* (Heidelberg, 1927), 9–16.

34. See Justus Bier, "Riemenschneider's Use of Graphic Sources," *Gazette des Beaux-Arts* 99, no. 50 (1957), 203–222; Hartmut Krohm, "Der Schongauersche Bildgedanke des *Noli me tangere* aus Münnerstadt," in *Flügelaltäre des späten Mittelalters*, ed. Hartmut Krohm and Eike Oellermann (Berlin, 1992), 84–102.

out against the smooth background of the pillars, appeared to be floating. Tall canopies accentuated their vertical pull.[32]

The viewer experiences *Adam* and *Eve* in a state of paradisiacal beauty, before the fall from grace. The larger programmatic context and architectural framework of the portal reinforced the perception that the first man and woman have been redeemed by their Creator. At this moment the divine plan of salvation reaches its completion in the triumph of the Church, symbolized by the Coronation of the Virgin on the portal's tympanum, which dates to the early fifteenth century. A predominant feature of the *Adam* and *Eve* is their wistful facial expressions, so typical of Riemenschneider, which convey a sense of melancholy that transcends the Middle Ages and anticipates later periods. The pain incurring from the original sin knells like a distant memory, and suffering is presented as a means of purification.[33] This is also true of the evangelists in Münnerstadt (cat. 13A–D). Their faces reflect a central theme in Riemenschneider's work: original sin precedes redemption.

• *Martin Schongauer and New Forms of Representation* •

Riemenschneider's artistic activity immediately followed the first great achievements in engraving, a medium developed around 1440 from the techniques of goldsmiths. Compared with the woodcut, which came into use fifty years earlier primarily to disseminate "popular" devotional images, engraving was viewed as an important innovation. Even taking into account the oeuvre of the artist identified as Master E. S., who evidently worked in Strasbourg in the 1460s, and granting him a greater creative role than is generally assumed, there is no doubt about the prominence of the Colmar printmaker Martin Schongauer as a master in this new art form. By significantly expanding the expressive range of engraving, Schongauer made a crucial contribution toward the flourishing of the graphic arts in the time of Dürer.

Schongauer's engravings, which show a high degree of abstraction appropriate for the medium, reflect his understanding of the art of Rogier van der Weyden. Rogier's goal was a novel, empathetic presentation of religious subjects, and Schongauer's engravings partake of Rogier's spirituality. These images enjoin a meditative process through which their meaning, expressed in a sublime language, can be gradually comprehended. This aspect of Schongauer's work is most apparent in his Passion series, especially in the varied psychological content.

Schongauer's reformative bent, striving for greater spirituality in his art, coincided with that of Riemenschneider, who was deeply indebted to the Colmar artist from the very beginning.[34] In some instances the direct adoption of graphic works can be confirmed, as in the wings of the Detwang altarpiece, where assistants dutifully replicated

Schongauer's inventions. Riemenschneider himself created more freely interpretative renderings that elaborate on Schongauer's concepts. We see this most clearly in comparing the *Noli me Tangere* relief from the Münnerstadt altarpiece with Schongauer's earlier print of the subject (cat. 13 F, and cat. 13, fig. 6). Riemenschneider follows Schongauer in portraying Mary Magdalen and Christ reaching toward one another to establish a spiritual connection, though no physical contact is made. Gesture and details of the clothing are influenced by the print, as is the compositional unity. It was unusual around 1500 for the reliefs on the wings of a large-scale altarpiece such as that in Münnerstadt to encourage intensive observation, even eliciting a meditative state in the viewer. Riemenschneider's carved images are so subtly detailed and conceived that their nuances can only be grasped after prolonged contemplation.

Riemenschneider's monochrome altarpieces create effects that simulate those of the graphic arts. Dispensing with color required a rigorous, consistent process of abstraction, resulting in a sharper formal focus. These images rely on the complex interaction of light and shadow on their surfaces. Especially in rendering the folds in the garments, whether carved or drawn, Riemenschneider and Schongauer reached common ground; while carving emphasizes the linear arrangement of folds, engraving underscores the relieflike shapes of a specific drapery motif. The expressiveness of stylized garments contribute to a forceful rendering of subjects in Riemenschneider's work: in the Münnerstadt *Noli me Tangere,* for example, the drapery patterns comment eloquently on the interaction of Christ and Mary Magdalen. Likewise, the restlessness in the folds of the seated evangelists from the predella of the same altarpiece (cat. 13 A – D) conveys the impression of ecstatic agitation.

• *The Nonpolychromed Retable: Preliminary or Final Form?* •

Riemenschneider's Münnerstadt altarpiece of 1490–1492 was considered the earliest monochrome retable until the publication in 1992 of Eike Oellermann's technical findings that identified the high altar retable of 1483 in the parish church of Sankt Martin in Lorch am Rhein as a monochrome work (fig. 15).[35] Since then an archival discovery by Gerhard Weilandt has moved this date even further back and has established yet another, earlier work: the high altar retable of Ulm Minster, which has vanished without a remnant. It was erected between 1474 and 1481 under the direction of Jörg Syrlin the Elder, with the substantial collaboration of Michel Erhart.[36] It is doubtful whether the phenomenon of dispensing with color in carved wooden altarpieces can be reliably retraced much further, unless one takes into consideration grisaille or similar techniques in paintings or in altarpieces with partly painted alabaster figures or reliefs.

35. Krohm and Oellermann 1992, 9–22.

36. Gerhard Weilandt, "Ein archivalischer Neufund zur Fassung des Hochaltarretabels im Ulmer Münster," *Ulm und Oberschwaben* 49 (1994), 51–61; Gerhard Weilandt, "Der wiederaufgefundene Vertrag Jörg Syrlins des Älteren über das Hochaltarretabel des Ulmer Münsters. Zum Erscheinungsbild des frühesten holzsichtigen Retabels," *Zeitschrift für Kunstgeschichte* 59 (1996), 437–460.

37. Wolfgang Deutsch, "Die Konstanzer Bildschnitzer der Spätgotik und ihr Verhältnis zu Niclaus Gerhaert," *Schriften des Vereins für Geschichte des Bodensees und seiner Umgebung* 81 (1963), 11–129, see esp. 127–128.

38. See Jörg Rosenfeld, "Niclaus Gerhaert von Leiden in Strassburg," *Jahrbuch der Staatlichen Kunstsammlungen in Baden-Württemberg* 32 (1995), 13–32.

39. For nonpolychromed retables, see Jürgen Michler, "Die holzsichtigen Skulpturen auf der Stuttgarter Weckmann-Ausstellung *Meisterwerke Massenhaft*," *Kunstchronik* 47 (1994), 412–418; Hartmut Boockmann, "Bemerkungen zu den nichtpolychromierten Holzbildwerken des ausgehenden Mittelalters," *Zeitschrift für Kunstgeschichte* 57 (1994), 330–335; Hartmut Krohm, "Das Bordesholmer Retabel des Hans Brüggemann. Bemerkungen zur Forschungssituation," in *Der Bordesholmer Altar des Hans Brüggemann. Werk und Wirkung*, ed. Uwe Albrecht et al. (Berlin, 1996), 9–21, esp. 18–19; Barbara Rommé, "Holzsichtigkeit und Fassung. Zwei nebeneinander bestehende Phänomene in der Skulptur des ausgehenden Mittelalters und der frühen Neuzeit," in *Gegen den Strom. Meisterwerke niederrheinischer Skulptur in Zeiten der Reformation* [exh. cat., Suermondt-Ludwig-Museum] (Aachen, 1996), 97–111; Georg Habenicht, "Anmerkungen zum ungefassten Zustand des sogenannten Bamberger Altars," *Zeitschrift für Kunstgeschichte* 60 (1997), 482–513; see also notes 35 and 36 above.

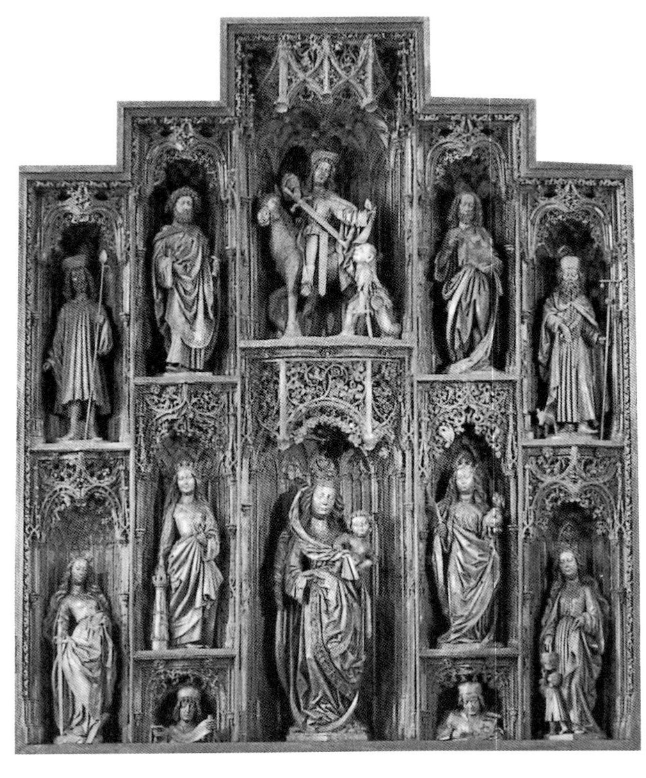

15.

Middle Rhenish, shrine of the high altar retable, 1483, Pfarrkirche Sankt Martin, Lorch am Rhein

Wolfgang Deutsch's hypothesis that the 1466 altarpiece of the cathedral in Constance, with carvings by Niclaus Gerhaert, was in fact nonpolychromed may not be so far off the mark.[37] Deutsch considered the omission of color to be the type of artistic innovation attributable to the Netherlander. He also wondered if the altarpiece in Constance—which, like that in Ulm, fell victim to the iconoclasm of the Reformation—may have had other features seen later, such as fenestrations in the back of the shrine, like those that appear in Riemenschneider's retables in both Rothenburg and Creglingen (Chapuis essay, figs. 5 and 7). Deutsch's argument cannot be dismissed as idle speculation, for the altarpiece in Lorch is closely related to creations by Gerhaert and his school.[38] It fits within a sculptural context that encompasses other nonpolychromed examples, such as Hans Syfer's Heilbronn altarpiece of 1498 and Christoph von Urach's retable in Besigheim, as well as polychromed altarpieces such as that by Nicolas Hagenower formerly in Strasbourg Cathedral. Polychromed and nonpolychromed retables stand side by side within a narrowly defined sculptural tradition; later works seem to delineate a separation between these two categories of finishing techniques, a discussion that must be pursued elsewhere.

Documents pertaining to the Münnerstadt altarpiece confirm that in 1504/1505 Veit Stoss applied color to Riemenschneider's work. The practice of adding polychromy to wooden sculpture at a later stage was not unique and casts doubt on whether sculpture without color and gilding was intended to remain that way. Riemenschneider's preference for nonpolychromed sculpture was by no means limited to wooden altarpieces but also applied to stone carvings, such as the *Lamentation* in Maidbronn and other figures in an architectural context. And yet it has been repeatedly argued that the "unfinished" retable is a consequence of the Reformation.[39] Monochrome finishing in many variations was an established aspect of fourteenth- and fifteenth-century German art, originally derived from Italy. In light of this tradition, it is difficult to assume the existence of a dictum in the period around 1500—an era of great change with respect to the understanding and practice of art—according to which every altarpiece would have to be finished in color.[40]

It seems important in this regard to return to an essay by Johannes Taubert published in 1969.[41] Taubert correctly saw the nonpolychromed retable as closely related to polychromed work. He wanted to clarify that the absence of color did not necessarily mean a new aesthetic philosophy, but a qualitative change in the conventional mode of representation. Using the same logic, we can also explain one aspect of this phenomenon: how artists compensated for the lack of color, with its range of expressive possibilities, by substituting other surface treatments, including punch work or translucent, sometimes pigmented glazes. For such decoration the term "monochrome" is appropriate,[42] and the monochrome approach is central to this discussion of nonpolychromed altarpieces.

Current investigations into the significance of monochromy are inconclusive, especially with regard to the role of the retable as a vehicle of religious meaning. Other more abstract expressions were being developed in the graphic arts in search of a new visualization of Christian beliefs. Riemenschneider's altarpieces should be seen in this context. The deliberate rejection of color may reflect an asceticism, the apparent preference for "poverty," which is admittedly balanced by a variety of other decoration.

Taubert's intent was to define surface treatments as a phenomenon that could be interpreted art historically, while the tendency today is to focus on their technological aspects.[43] The phrase "visibility of the wood" *(Holzsichtigkeit)* has come into play over the last several years in German scholarship, for instance, emphasizing technique and the aesthetics of the material.[44] Erich Hubala argues against this evaluation and returns to Taubert's views: "Riemenschneider took care that we would not see the limewood but rather the figure, namely the image and not the raw material."[45]

Among prior nonpolychromed altarpieces that may have exercised influence on Riemenschneider's art, the Lorch retable displays variety in its figures and ornament to create a more complex form. It is similar in this respect to a retable now in Kefer-

40. See Jürgen Michler, "Materialsichtigkeit, Monochromie, Grisaille in der Gotik," in *Denkmalkunde und Denkmalpflege. Wissen und Wirken. Festschrift für Heinrich Magirius zum 60. Geburtstag am 1. Februar 1994* (Dresden, 1995), 197–221.

41. Johannes Taubert, "Zur Oberflächenbehandlung der sogenannten ungefassten spätgotischen Holzplastik," in *Farbige Skulpturen. Bedeutung, Fassung, Restaurierung* (repr. Munich, 1978), 73–88.

42. Hartmut Krohm and Eike Oellermann, "Der ehemalige Münnerstädter Magdalenenaltar von Tilman Riemenschneider und seine Geschichte. Forschungsergebnisse zur monochromen Oberflächengestalt," *Zeitschrift des Deutschen Vereins für Kunstwissenschaft* 34 (1980), 16–99, esp. 68–70; Eike Oellermann, "Erkenntnisse zur ursprünglichen Oberflächengestalt des Münnerstädter Magdalenenaltars—Möglichkeiten einer Rekonstruktion," in Würzburg 1981, 318–322, esp. 318–319.

43. See Hartmut Krohm, "Technologischer Befund und Strukturanalyse," in *Figur und Raum. Mittelalterliche Holzbildwerke im historischen und kunstgeographischen Kontext*, ed. Uwe Albrecht and Jan von Bonsdorff (Berlin, 1995), 282–288.

44. Also see essays by Hans Westhoff and Heribert Meurer in *Meisterwerke Massenhaft. Die Bildhauerwerkstatt des Niklaus Weckmann und die Malerei in Ulm um 1500* [exh. cat., Württembergisches Landesmuseum] (Stuttgart, 1993), 135–145, 147–151.

45. Erich Hubala, "Besprechung der Ausstellung *Tilman Riemenschneider. Frühe Werke*," *Das Münster* 35 (1982), 226–231, esp. 229.

markt, Austria, which was apparently created in Passau somewhat earlier and may have been originally polychromed. Regardless of whether the Lorch retable can be traced to earlier sources in the Upper Rhine region, it is an unusually harmonious composition that is enhanced by the lively interaction of light and shadow produced by sunlight, which changes with the time of day. Only recently has scholarship focused critical attention on how late medieval sculptors used light as a creative factor.[46] Despite unresolved questions, the Lorch retable is a good example of certain formal concerns that we encounter again, magnified, in Riemenschneider's work.

In the case of the altarpiece in Ulm, a large preliminary drawing from 1474 preserved in Stuttgart (Kemperdick essay, fig. 3) gives only a remote impression of the final work.[47] But the choir stalls (cat. 12, fig. 2) and their elaborate nonpolychromed carvings, still intact today, are a major component in the church's original decoration. The grand artistic intention behind the design—not only its unusual size but also the innovative and prominently placed busts on the sides of the stalls—allows some idea of the overall concept of the high altar retable. There are many indications that the scale and quality of this ensemble exerted a lasting influence on subsequent altarpieces.

• The Intellectual Environment: Patrons and Clients •

Riemenschneider's uncle Nikolaus may have played a role in the sculptor's decision to settle in Würzburg. He served as *procurator fisci* for Prince-Bishop Rudolf von Scherenberg, who ruled the diocese of Würzburg from 1466 to 1495. In light of this connection, it is conceivable that the prominent bishop was a patron of Riemenschneider's, perhaps even his intellectual mentor. Scherenberg aspired to comprehensive reform in his diocese that would affect all relevant spheres of political and spiritual life. His own objectives certainly found an echo in Riemenschneider's art, which aimed to communicate in emotionally accessible terms the message of salvation. This new rendering of Christian imagery rapidly became popular and instituted stylistic conventions that left the artist little room for variation; as a result, the dating of individual works, especially the Virgins and crucifixes, is impeded. Riemenschneider's unity of formal expression sought "truth" in representation. The images should therefore be free of arbitrary, accidental, and artificial elaboration.

We can assume that the evocative content of Riemenschneider's early work led to his rapid progress as the most sought-after sculptor within a large region that had a considerable demand for religious art. Particularly notable is the role of the Middle Franconian imperial city of Rothenburg, which was open to different artistic currents in the fifteenth century. According to recent research, the sculptor's first commission for a large altarpiece came shortly after 1485 from a church in Rothenburg, probably that of the Franciscans.[48] He and other sculptors in his circle received a steady stream of orders for sculpture from churches in and around Rothenburg. Indeed, that city appears to have followed Würzburg in adopting Riemenschneider's artistic conception as its guiding impetus. Here and elsewhere in central and northern Germany at the beginning of the sixteenth century the sculptor's style spread dramatically. Other artists working in his tradition included Peter Breuer of Zwickau, the best known but not the primary pupil of Riemenschneider; a workshop established around 1510 in Magdeburg, first discussed by Justus Bier; the Master of the Prenzlau Altarpiece in the Uckermark, who worked in Lübeck (see cat. 36, fig. 2); and the outstanding sculptor Franz Maidburg, whose activity has been documented in Upper Saxony and in the Rhineland.[49]

One of the most important findings of the research project on Riemenschneider's early career carried out from 1977 to 1981 under the auspices of the Berlin museums was that since the mid-1480s the young sculptor from Würzburg had worked on occasion with the Franciscan painter Martin Schwarz of Rothenburg. The *Passion* altarpiece, long known under the misleading name "Wiblingen Retable," confirms this collaboration.[50] Riemenschneider, whose conception of art had been shaped by Martin Schongauer, apparently shared the same spiritual beliefs as Schwarz, who had also been influenced by the master from Colmar. The self-restraint characteristic of this school allowed few departures from sacrosanct imagery. This appears to reflect a new understanding of religious images within certain circles. With regard to Riemenschneider, a question arises here on which research has not even begun: to what degree pious subjects, portrayed so tangibly in Schongauer's paintings and engravings, were circulated by the mendicant orders. Riemenschneider's first contact with Schongauer's art must have preceded his collaborative efforts with Martin Schwarz, for the sculptor's work is more directly aligned with Schongauer's. Yet it is possible that the Franciscan brother paved the way in Rothenburg for the sculptor from Würzburg.

The significance of Rothenburg for Riemenschneider's early development can hardly be overstated, although next to nothing is known about his clients or the spiritual climate of this imperial city at the time. The *Holy Blood* altarpiece in the Jakobskirche (Chapuis essay, fig. 5) is one of the highest artistic achievements among monochrome retables. Pilgrimages to this church that focused on the relic of the blood of Christ led to high expectations for the ambitious project, and the commission included a first-rate joiner, Erhard Harschner.[51] Martin Schwarz was also named as an arbiter in Riemenschneider's contract for the *Holy Blood* altarpiece—and this, in the case of an altarpiece not intended to be painted (further evidence of the changing artistic consciousness around 1500).[52]

48. See Würzburg 1981, 24–32; Eike Oellermann and Karin Oellermann, "Das Detwanger Retabel und sein Detail," in *Der Detwanger Altar von Tilman Riemenschneider* (Wiesbaden, 1996), 13–44, esp. 39–43; Kahsnitz 1997.

49. For the workshop in Madgeburg, see Justus Bier, "Neue Beiträge zur Riemenschneider-Forschung," pt. 1, *Mainfränkisches Jahrbuch für Geschichte und Kunst* 6 (1954), 129–139; for Maidburg, see Anton Legner, "Das Sakramentshäuschen im Kölner Domchor," in *Verschwundenes Inventarium. Der Skulpturenfund im Kölner Domchor* [exh. cat. Schnütgen-Museum und Dombauverwaltung des Metropolitankapitels] (Cologne, 1984), 61–78.

50. See note 48 above; see also Eike Oellermann, "Die Bedeutung des Malers Martinus Schwarz im Frühwerk Riemenschneiders," in Würzburg 1981, 285–302; Hartmut Krohm, *Die Rothenburger Passion im Reichsstadtmuseum Rothenburg ob der Tauber* (Rothenburg, 1985); Kristine Scherer, *Martin Schwarz. Ein Maler in Rothenburg ob der Tauber um 1500*, Beiträge zur Kunstwissenschaft, vol. 47 (Munich, 1992).

51. Eike Oellermann, "Der Beitrag des Schreiners zum spätgotischen Schnitzaltar," *Zeitschrift für Kunsttechnologie und Konservierung* 9 (1995), 170–180. Harschner may also have worked on the *Assumption of the Virgin* altarpiece in Creglingen (Chapuis essay, fig. 7).

52. Devotional writings of the time may give insights into the artist's work. See Ewald M. Vetter, "Riemenschneiders Magdalenenaltar im Spiegel mittelalterlicher Frömmigkeit," *Würzburger Diözesangeschichtsblätter* 55 (1993), 111–142; and Ewald M. Vetter, "Geschichte, Ikonographie und Deutung des Retabels," in *Der Detwanger Altar von Tilman Riemenschneider* (Wiesbaden, 1996), esp. 90–91.

53. Bier 1957, 101–102.

54. See Erik Soder von Güldenstubbe, *Kulturelles Leben
im Würzburg der Riemen-
schneiderzeit* (Berlin, 1981)
(supplement to Würzburg 1981).

Translation by Ulrike Mills.

Riemenschneider's early commissions in Rothenburg are even more remarkable considering that his first concern would surely have been to establish himself in Würzburg, his new home. Yet the motivation behind the patronage he enjoyed in both places was probably the same. Of primary interest is his relationship with Rudolf von Scherenberg, whose virtues are extolled in the inscription on Riemenschneider's 1496–1499 monument to the bishop in Würzburg Cathedral.[53] He is praised as the virtuous and wise prince and religious leader, duke of Franconia and bishop of Würzburg, who laid a secure foundation for both his worldly and his spiritual reigns and promoted peace with all the means at his disposal. He attained an old age through exemplary conduct and the virtue of moderation. Riemenschneider's rendering of the bishop, which accentuates his asceticism, cannot be considered a true portrait but a reflection of the spiritual power that allowed the prelate to surpass his own limitations.

Riemenschneider created a monument that transcended tradition. In the figure of the prince-bishop we see the God-given, singular power of virtue, the wisdom to govern, and the will to reform. This final attribute was directed not only at institutions but at the spiritual life of the times—Rudolf von Scherenberg was the second Kilian, the embodiment of the apostle of the Franconians. The late Gothic tracery on the Scherenberg monument enhances the symbolic value of the ascendant movement implied in the sculpture. The framing device is markedly different from that surrounding the monument to Scherenberg's successor, Lorenz von Bibra, also sculpted in Riemenschneider's workshop, which functions merely as a border.

Riemenschneider secured the contract for the design and execution of the Scherenberg monument right after the prince-bishop's death in 1495. When the young sculptor set up his workshop in Würzburg in 1485, the bishop was already quite old.[54] It is worth considering whether the conception of the work was not determined with Scherenberg at an earlier date, since it appears to correspond precisely with the image the bishop himself had of his mission. The Scherenberg monument seems an appropriate conclusion to this essay, as it arguably represents the pinnacle of Riemenschneider's artistic achievement and also dramatically underscores the fact that the artist's development, probably from its very beginnings, was indebted to a particular spiritual constellation that had many far-reaching implications and associations.

A Sculptor in Würzburg   *Stephan Kemperdick*

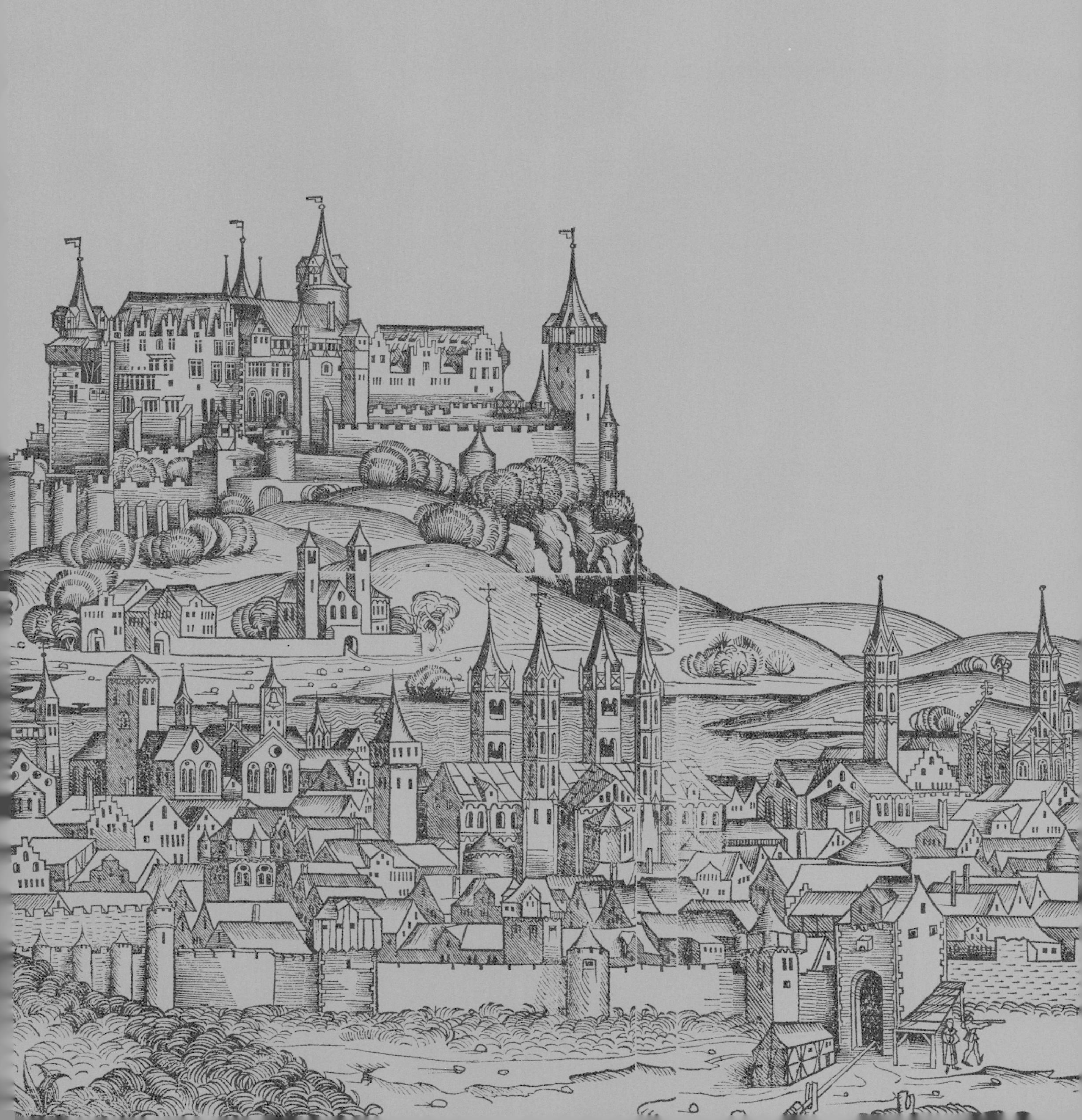

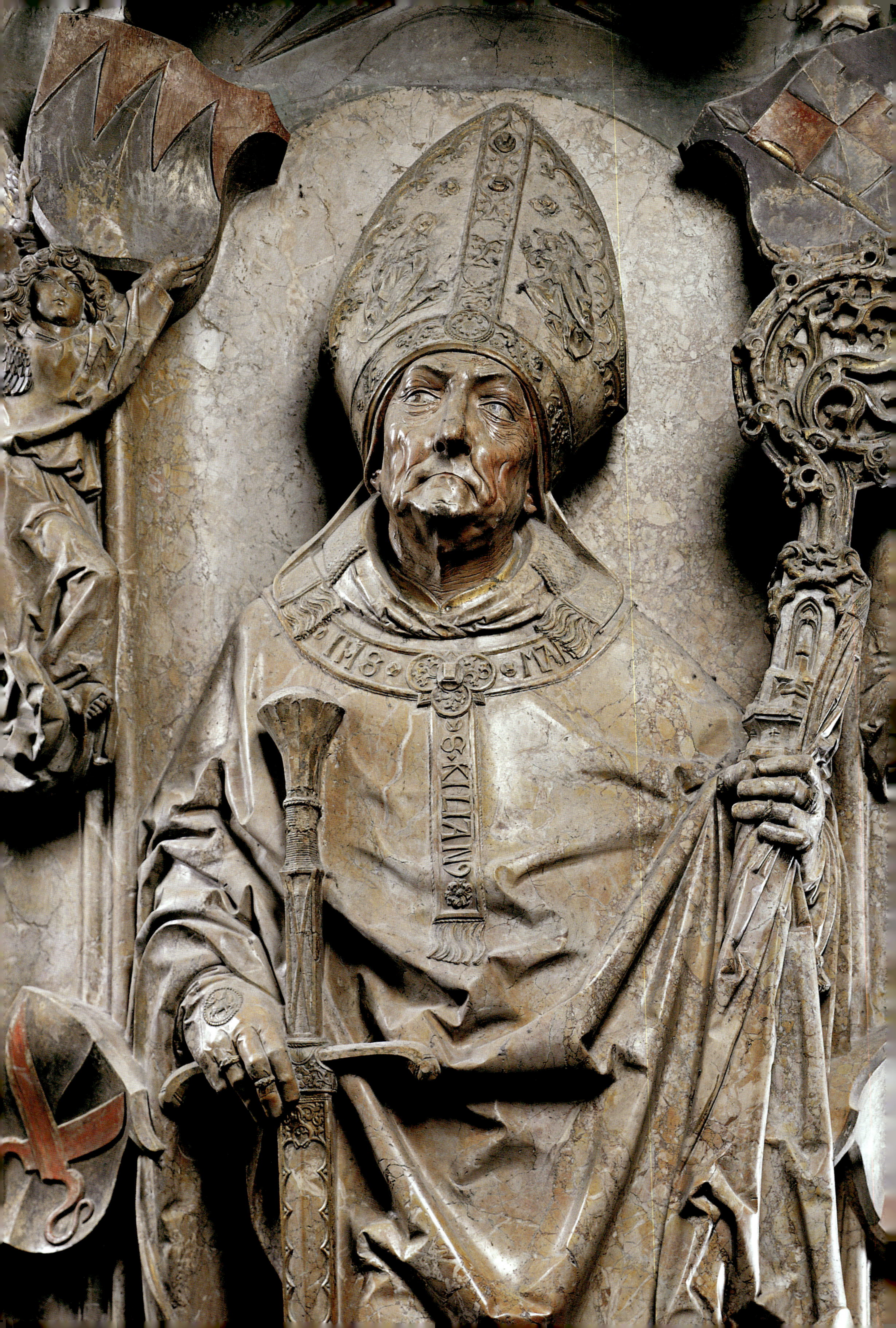
IHS · MA
S · KILIANVS

ÜRZBURG, THE CITY where Tilman Riemenschneider ran his workshop for more than forty-five years, drew much of its character during the late Middle Ages from its designation as a bishopric. As a commercial center it had only regional significance; its main product and the only export commodity worth mentioning in terms of quantity was wine, cultivated at this time as a near monoculture.[1] With a population of approximately 6,000 to 7,000, Würzburg was much smaller than two other centers of wood carving at the time: Nuremberg (located in Franconia, as is Würzburg), which had a population of almost 30,000 and was the third largest city in the empire; and the Swabian metropolis of Ulm, which had about 17,000 inhabitants. Würzburg also lagged behind the other two cities economically, and this partly had to do with political differences. Nuremberg and Ulm were both free imperial cities, which were self-governing and otherwise obligated only to the emperor, whereas most other towns in the empire were under a regional ruler. A prince-bishop ruled in Würzburg, serving not only as the spiritual sovereign of the diocese but also as secular leader of the principality, the so-called *Hochstift*—a clearly smaller region that was not congruent with the diocese. ⁑ From about 1250 on, this subordinate status of Würzburg produced continuous conflicts over the centuries, with the city resisting the rule of the bishop. Many of these conflicts became violent, fueled by hostilities toward the bishop and clergy over economic inequalities. The clergy were exempt from contributions to the tax base of Würzburg. Under the protection of the city they could conduct business without paying taxes or customs, thus they represented unfair competition for the secular merchants and traders. Further-

1. Concerning Würzburg see Hannelore Götz, *Würzburg im 16. Jahrhundert* (Würzburg, 1986); Harald Hirsch, "Quellen und Untersuchungen zur städtischen Verwaltung und zur Sozialstruktur in Würzburg unter Bischof Gottfried IV. Schenk von Limburg, 1445–1455," *Mainfränkisches Jahrbuch für Geschichte und Kunst* 36 (1984), 49–135; Karl Trüdinger, *Stadt und Kirche im spätmittelalterlichen Würzburg* (Stuttgart, 1978).

Detail of the *Monument to Rudolf von Scherenberg* (fig. 1), 1496–1499, Würzburg Cathedral

more, the clergy removed taxable property from the municipal tax base through purchases of land and other real estate. Such privileges were opposed primarily by the professional guilds, thirty-seven of which were known in the year 1373, and this opposition led the bishop to outlaw the guilds repeatedly. Their political force came to an end with the battle of Bergtheim in 1400, in which the troops of Bishop Gerhard von Schwarzenburg decisively crushed the forces mobilized by the city. Also as a consequence of this defeat the city had to pay high reparations for the next forty years or so, which prompted many of Würzburg's patricians to move to surrounding imperial cities.

The conflicts between Würzburg and its bishop were not eliminated through these developments, although they subsided in the second half of the fifteenth century under the firm rule of Prince-Bishop Rudolf von Scherenberg (1466–1495). This energetic man succeeded in restoring the sorely neglected finances of his territories and was able to redeem nearly all of the lands that had been mortgaged by his predecessors.[2] He promoted the economy by establishing fairs and issued numerous laws to regulate commerce. Thus he was for the most part in agreement with the city, which experienced an economic resurgence at this time. Bishop Rudolf also later attempted to reform the clergy and in 1479 invited the first printers from Strasbourg to take up their profession in Würzburg. After his death at about age ninety-five, he was remembered as a strong but pious and just ruler.

The citizens of Würzburg, despite their defeat in 1400, continued to participate to a certain degree in the government of the city, primarily through its two councils. The municipal, or lower, council has been documented from the middle of the thirteenth century, and at the end of the Middle Ages it comprised twenty-four councillors, who annually elected two mayors from their own ranks. The jurisdiction of this council was limited, however, and pertained primarily to administrative tasks. New members could be proposed by the council only in a list of six candidates, from which either the bishop or the cathedral chapter (in alternation as of 1495) selected the new councillor. Of greater importance was the episcopal, or upper, council, first recorded toward the end of the thirteenth century. In 1499 it consisted of four members from the cathedral chapter and three canons from the collegiate churches on the one side, and seven citizens on the other: three councillors from the lower council, one representative each from the three leading trade groups—vintners, bakers, and butchers—and one representative of the city's craftsmen and artisans. The composition of this upper council ensured a balance between the citizenry and the clergy, though a special administrator of the bishop cast the determining vote in the case of a tie. The upper council regulated craftsmen, defining their bylaws and setting their measurement standards and wages. This council was also responsible for the police force and judicial matters.

2. Alfred Wendehorst, *Bistum Würzburg. 3. Die Bischofsreihe von 1455 bis 1617*, Germania Sacra, new series 13 (Berlin and New York, 1978), 20–51.

Access to membership on the city council was not open to all adult inhabitants of Würzburg, even though the only explicit requirements for candidacy were resident status and a good reputation. But not everyone living in the city was a citizen: one had to be born in lawful wedlock and usually had to pay a special fee to become a citizen. In addition, the status conferred certain rights, but also obligations such as the payment of taxes and guard duty. And, in fact, those who did have access to council membership belonged to the upper levels of society. They had connections with the high clergy, with senior associates of the bishop and the cathedral chapter, and with the nobility in the surrounding areas. Although craftsmen were often found among the councillors, these men were especially respected and wealthy representatives of their occupation. Members of the lower social strata, which made up the majority of the population—including minor craftsmen, maids, or day laborers—did not have a place on the city council.

Tilman Riemenschneider, who apparently arrived in Würzburg as a trained sculptor and, together with two other "painter's journeymen," took an oath of allegiance to the two mayors of the city on 7 December 1483, spent the next fourteen months as a journeyman in an unknown workshop without being a citizen.[3] He received his citizenship, free of charge, on 28 February 1485 and was now referred to as a *Bildschnitzer* (wood-carver). By this time he may have been married to Anna, the widow of a goldsmith,[4] and it has been proposed that this might explain why he was given free citizenship, although there is no proof for this supposition. Such gifts have been documented in several German cities, and Gerhard Weilandt has confirmed that the very few persons who received free citizenship in the city of Ulm were highly qualified artisans and artists.[5] The purpose of the privilege was apparently to attract just such specialists when they were needed by the community. Possibly this was the case with Riemenschneider, since there were only two other sculptors documented in Würzburg at the time: Michael Weiss and Ulrich Hagenfurter, who died in 1500 and 1494, respectively, and from whom no works are known.[6] The bishop's city and diocese would obviously have had a demand for sculpture. Riemenschneider may indeed have come to Würzburg, where his family already had connections, with the expectation of favorable employment.[7] In any case, his wife brought to the marriage her departed husband's estate, "zum Wolfmannsziechlein," where Riemenschneider was to work from then on. It seems unlikely that the sculptor would also have taken over the deceased goldsmith's workshop,[8] since the tools and working space he needed would have been quite different.

Riemenschneider experienced rapid social advancement in the years following his arrival in Würzburg, accompanied by the acquisition of wealth and his appoint-

3. Iris Kalden, *Tilman Riemenschneider. Werkstattleiter in Würzburg* (Ammersbek bei Hamburg, 1990), 13–15; Georg Anton Weber, *Til Riemenschneider. Sein Leben und Wirken* (Regensburg, 1911), 13–16.

4. Kalden 1990, 13–14; Weber 1911, 15.

5. Gerhard Weilandt, "Die Ulmer Künstler und ihre Zunft," in *Meisterwerke Massenhaft. Die Bildhauerwerkstaat des Niklaus Weckmann und die Malerei in Ulm um 1500* [exh. cat., Württembergisches Landesmuseum] (Stuttgart, 1993), 372.

6. Justus Bier, *Tilmann Riemenschneider. Die späten Werke in Holz* (Vienna, 1978), 62–63; P. Paulus Weissenberger, "Die Künstlergilde St. Lukas in Würzburg," *Archiv des historischen Vereins von Unterfranken und Aschaffenburg* 70 (1936), 207.

7. Erik Soder von Güldenstubbe, "Kulturelles Leben im Würzburg der Riemenschneiderzeit," in *Tilman Riemenschneider. Frühe Werke* [exh. cat., Mainfränkisches Museum Würzburg] (Regensburg, 1981), 3–6.

8. As is assumed in Kalden 1990, 13–14.

ment to several offices. In 1504 he became a member of the city's lower council for the first time, and beginning in 1505 he served in various capacities, including as keeper of the Marienkapelle, a prestigious position that involved the financial administration of this municipal chapel. For a time he was also in charge of taxation, the most important office in the lower council.[9] In November 1520 Riemenschneider's activity on the council was finally crowned by his election as mayor, a position that was filled anew each year. Between 1509 and 1522 he was appointed to the upper council four times, each time for one year of service, which was also considered to be a high social distinction. Since the sculptor had been appointed by the cathedral chapter to oversee its vineyards from 1507 to 1519, he also enjoyed its protection, social prestige, immunity in civil court cases, and other advantages.[10]

Riemenschneider's social and economic situation before the Peasants' Revolt of 1525 was thus that of a wealthy and respected artisan who had ascended to the upper levels of Würzburg's secular society and had connections within the highest circles of the church. Among those who commissioned works from him were the city council of Würzburg, which ordered sculpture for the exterior of the Marienkapelle (see Chapuis essay, fig. 3), and the city councils of Münnerstadt and Rothenburg on the Tauber. The ecclesiastical authorities in Würzburg were equally significant clients: the chapter of the cathedral instructed him to produce so essential a monument as its new high altar, and the Prince-Bishop Lorenz von Bibra ordered from Riemenschneider his own impressive funerary monument and that of his predecessor, Rudolf von Scherenberg (figs. 1 and 2). Finally the bishop and chapter of Bamberg Cathedral commissioned from him the elaborate official tomb for the founders and patron saints of Bamberg, Emperor Heinrich and his wife, Kunigunde.[11]

During the late Middle Ages it was not uncommon for artists in Germany and the Lowlands to enjoy a respected position and moderate wealth, for they belonged to a relatively small group of artisans who provided expensive products that were important to the upper classes. Certain masters among these artisans also attained high office. In addition to Riemenschneider, there was a painter, Johann Wagenknecht, in Würzburg at this time who became a member of the city council in 1516 and was elected mayor in 1525, having apparently conducted himself agreeably during the Peasants' Revolt. In 1516 Wagenknecht painted the crucifix that Riemenschneider had carved for the church in Steinach (Chapuis essay, fig. 10), as is inscribed on a slip of parchment found inside the sculpture—which also mentions that both Riemenschneider and Wagenknecht were members of the Würzburg city council.[12] The key to social advancement was the master's standing as a respected craftsman, not as an artist, a role that did not yet have any special status in society. At the same time, the creation of

9. See Kalden 1990, 17–29.

10. August Amrhein, "Die Würzburger Zivilgerichte erster Instanz, I. Teil," *Archiv des historischen Vereins für Unterfranken und Aschaffenburg* 56 (1914), 129–132.

11. See Kalden 1990, 47–78.

12. Weissenberger 1936, no. 30; Bier 1978, 125.

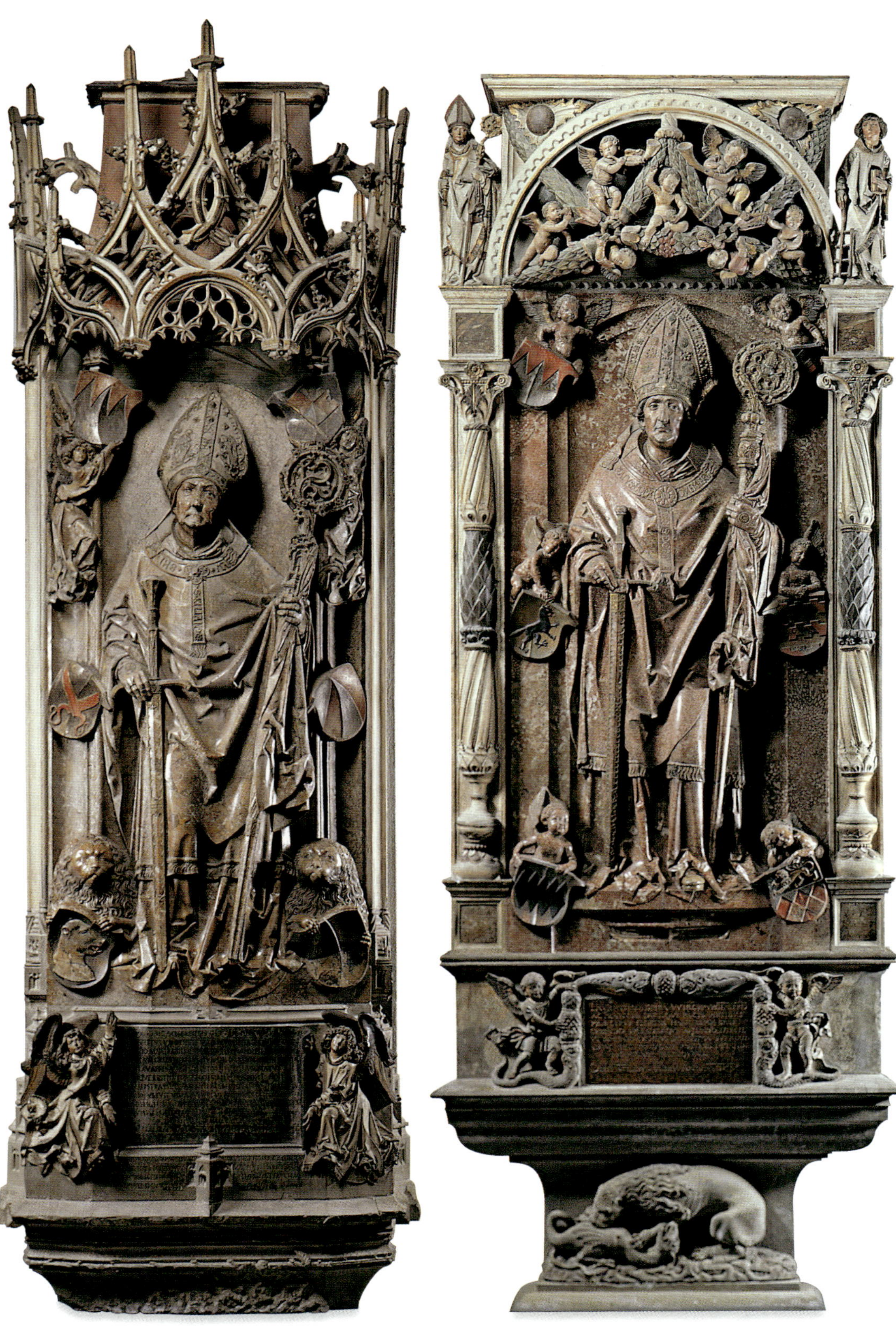

1.
Monument to Rudolf von Scherenberg, 1496–1499, marble
and limestone, Würzburg Cathedral

2.
Monument to Lorenz von Bibra, 1515–1522, marble
and limestone, Würzburg Cathedral

major works seems to have promoted both the professional and social reputations of an artist. In the case of Riemenschneider, his election to the city council by the cathedral chapter followed his execution of the impressive Scherenberg memorial.

Artists during the late Middle Ages in Germany and in the Burgundian Lowlands were generally highly specialized craftsmen bound in relatively rigid organizations.[13] In many towns, guilds provided this structure as well as political cohesiveness, experiencing their greatest development in the fourteenth century. An individual guild often encompassed several unrelated professions, such as painters and shopkeepers in Ulm, for instance. Even in cities like Würzburg, where guilds were not officially sanctioned, the crafts were organized in structures similar to those of guilds and had their own rules and regulations. These guidelines were not always set down in writing; and when they were, they were often at a late stage in their development and remained less than comprehensive in scope. Fundamental rules were based on tradition and were well known among the craftsmen; written documentation usually occurred in response to grievances and conflict. Around 1500, when times began to grow more difficult, craftsmen increasingly attempted to adjust to the changing social and economic conditions by writing down their statutes. Generally, the function of the guilds and crafts was to equalize opportunities and conditions for all master craftsmen, to control detrimental internal competition and prevent outside competition, and to ensure "honor" and a certain standard both in production and in the training of apprentices.

In Würzburg the collective craft (*Handwerk*) of glaziers (including stained-glass painters), panel painters, and sculptors first received a statute of formation from the upper council in 1470, in response to demands made by the craftsmen themselves. In this particular craft the sculptors were by far the smallest group: among the sixty-three master craftsmen recorded on the list from 1470 until 1522 (when Riemenschneider's son Georg became a master), there were only eight sculptors, compared with twenty-eight glaziers and twenty-seven painters.[14] Furthermore, it appears that the sculptors were listed among the painters. Apparently in Würzburg these two crafts were not always rigorously differentiated and were often carried out in the same workshop.[15] Johann Wagenknecht, the painter mentioned above, received his training in the workshop of the sculptor Ulrich Hagenfurter and later became the teaching master of the sculptor Georg Mor.[16] In light of this, the description of Riemenschneider as a "painter's journeyman" on his arrival in Würzburg does not conclusively identify the kind of workshop he entered; it would not necessarily have been exclusively a sculptor's workshop.[17]

The glaziers' and painters' statute of 1470 confirms that each year two sworn master craftsmen—one glazier and one painter—should oversee the work of the craft

13. The most comprehensive treatment of this subject is still Hans Huth, *Künstler und Werkstatt der Spätgotik* (1923; Darmstadt, 1967).

14. Weissenberger 1936, 208–214; Wilhelm Rolfs, *Die Grünewald-Legende* (Leipzig, 1923), 115–116.

15. Concerning the relationship of painters to sculptors, see also Max Hasse, "Maler, Bildschnitzer und Vergolder in den Zünften des späten Mittelalters," *Jahrbuch der Hamburger Kunstsammlungen* 21 (1976), 31–42.

16. Rolfs 1923, 115–116.

17. He would certainly have been allowed to work in a painter's workshop such as that of the painter Simon, who was first mentioned in 1470, died before 1501, and was married to an Anna Riemenschneyderin (Rolfs 1923, 114–117).

and be accountable to the upper council.[18] It contains a number of guidelines concerning the kinds of materials to be used by painters and glaziers as well as rules for arbitrating disputes among members and determining penalties for offenses. It also ordains that anyone in the craft who takes an apprentice from outside the city must have him swear allegiance to the two mayors of Würzburg within fourteen days. And any outsider who wanted to establish himself as a master craftsman in the city had to prove that he was born in lawful wedlock (an important requirement, also found in craft statutes of other cities, which guaranteed the "honor" of the craft) and had to become a citizen and enter the craft after paying two guilders for candles.[19] Riemenschneider followed these regulations with his journeyman's pledge in 1483 and his acquisition of citizenship in 1485.

The last two paragraphs of the statute concern the Saint Luke brotherhood, the officially sanctioned organization for painters and glaziers. Such brotherhoods were widespread in the late Middle Ages, usually bound to a certain profession, and they were primarily religious in nature. In typical fashion the Saint Luke brotherhood in Würzburg required members to attend meetings — penalties were prescribed for absence as well as for insulting a brother — and it provided for regular Mass and for funeral services for departed members.

Many guidelines concerning the operation of a craft are assumed in the statute without being explicitly stated, such as the basic categories of master, journeyman, and apprentice. Masters were independent craftsmen, who alone could accept commissions and work on their own; journeymen and apprentices were strictly subordinate. Apprentices usually lived with their masters, which meant that the master had to have a wife and a household. With his first marriage Riemenschneider thus fulfilled one of the basic requirements for becoming a master.

We can assume that in Würzburg, as in other cities, an apprentice or his parents paid the master a premium, though the statute of 1470 spells out only a fee of a half guilder and two pounds of wax for the brotherhood at the beginning of an apprenticeship. The length of such training was likewise not defined in the statute, though a period of at least four years was set in 1496 for painters and sculptors in Ulm, the longest of all apprenticeships in that city.[20] This aspect of apprenticeship was not regulated in Würzburg until 1543, when grievances and very different economic conditions dictated that training last at least two years.[21] Around 1500 the practices regarding apprenticeships in Würzburg were presumably similar to those in Ulm.

Historical records document the names of twelve apprentices in Riemenschneider's workshop, employed in succession, we assume, over the workshop's forty-odd-year operation. If the apprenticeships were evenly distributed over this period, and if we

18. Stephanie Kleidt, "Die Lukasbruderschaft in Würzburg am Ende des Mittelalters," in *Lucas Cranach. Ein Maler-Unternehmer aus Franken* [exh. cat., Haus der Bayerischen Geschichte] (Augsburg, 1994), 124–130; Weissenberger 1936, 182–185; Hermann Hoffmann, *Würzburger Polizeisätze*, Veröffentlichungen der Gesellschaft für Fränkische Geschichte, vol. 10, ser. 5 (Würzburg, 1955), 136–139.

19. Proof of legitimate birth is again required in an addendum to the statute from 1488, together with a pledge of adherence to all sections of the statute.

20. Weilandt in Stuttgart 1993, 376–378.

21. Weissenberger 1936, 190.

allow for brief overlaps in tenure, as permitted in Ulm at this time, the average length of training for Riemenschneider's apprentices was around four years.[22] Many of his pupils came from other cities in southern Germany; one of the first even came from as far away as Cologne.[23] A later career can be attributed to only a very few, among them Peter Dell the Elder.[24]

Apprentices generally began their training at around age fourteen, and when they finished, it was customary to embark on a period of travel as journeymen. These travels were seldom required, but they were probably the rule and had the effect of expanding the journeyman's knowledge and disseminating styles across regions.[25] They also tended to lead journeymen to other cities for the rest of their careers. Riemenschneider arrived in Würzburg already trained as a journeyman, who had apparently become acquainted during his travels with the art of wood carving as practiced in Ulm and in the Upper Rhine area.[26] Of course, not every journeyman became a master, since this last step undoubtedly necessitated a certain start-up capital. In Würzburg the obstacles to becoming a master craftsman appear to have been set so high that the need for a qualifying masterpiece (*Meisterstück*) was not established until 1571, whereas it had been introduced in some other cities as early as the fifteenth century. This test of skill required by the guilds could also serve as a means of limiting the number of master craftsmen allowed to settle in one place.[27]

Journeymen as a group were very poorly documented at this time. They appear to have been quite numerous but enjoyed few rights. In Würzburg there were no limits to the number of journeymen one could hire, and Riemenschneider appears to have employed many. They cannot be identified through written records, but scholars have relied on stylistic means to suggest that as many as twenty-six journeymen may have worked with Riemenschneider between 1490 and 1524.[28] It is difficult to delineate clearly the styles of journeymen sculptors because they were expected to work in a style as close as possible to that of the master to ensure a degree of uniformity in pieces produced by the workshop. (This practice endured long past the Middle Ages and was, for example, still followed in Rembrandt's studio.[29]) Some of Riemenschneider's success can be attributed to his development of a style of sculpting that he was able to pass on to his assistants,[30] allowing him to produce and sell a great number of works at relatively favorable prices.[31] He had the largest and most efficient workshop for wood and stone sculpture in the Würzburg vicinity. Other sculptors in the area—a few of whom are identifiable by name, but not by a recognizable oeuvre—did not present any serious competition.[32]

Although large, important sculptural compositions were almost always commissioned, some of the objects created in the workshops of artists at this time were des-

22. Kalden 1990, 33–38; Hasse 1976, 36.

23. For a list of these apprentices see Kalden 1990, 35–36; two of them came from the nearby town of Mergentheim; Wilhelm from Cologne was dismissed as dishonest *(unredlich)*.

24. Kalden 1990, 37–38.

25. In Krakow two years of travel were required for a journeyman (Huth 1967, 89 n. 14). Albrecht Dürer reports that his father traveled as a journeyman in the Lowlands before 1455; see *Albrecht Dürer. Schriften und Briefe* (Leipzig, 1989), 47.

26. Hartmut Krohm, "Zu Methode und Ergebnissen des Forschungsprojekts. Das Problem der künstlerischen Herkunft," in Würzburg 1981, 7–19.

27. Weissenberger 1936, 191; concerning the *Meisterstück* see Huth 1967, 14–16; and Michael Baxandall, *The Lime-wood Sculptors of Renaissance Germany* (New Haven and London, 1980), 111–116.

28. Kalden 1990, 101–143.

29. *Rembrandt: The Master and His Shop* [exh. cat., Gemäldegalerie, Staatliche Museen zu Berlin] (Munich, 1991).

30. Baxandall 1980, 180–186.

31. For a list of works and prices see Baxandall 1980, 73; this list does not, however, account for the high costs of polychromy, which would not have been carried out by Riemenschneider.

32. The list of sculptors in the Saint Luke brotherhood up to about 1520 included Weiss, Hagenfurter, Gilg Haller (d. 1500), Wolf Reuss (who became master in 1509), Georg Mor (still living in 1537), and Hans Hartz (who became master in 1520). See Rolfs 1923, 116.

tined for the open market. We do not know how sizeable the market was for ready-made art, but it seems to have been considerable in both the Lowlands and Germany from at least the fifteenth century on.[33] The Nuremberg artist Veit Stoss, a contemporary of Riemenschneider's and a very distinguished sculptor (see cats. 25 and 35), sold his products at fairs and maintained a sales stand in the city.[34] In Würzburg in 1513 it was stipulated that glaziers from outside the city could offer their wares for sale only on a few days of the year;[35] thus we can assume that a market for ready-made works of art existed there. Consequently, it seems likely that Riemenschneider's shop produced pieces of sculpture for this market—perhaps some of the smaller surviving works that drew on the popular iconography of crucifixes and the Virgin and child.

Of much greater importance, both artistically and financially, were the large commissions, which often required the participation of several independent master craftsmen. Depending on the specifics of each contract, such a collaborative team could comprise a wood-carver, a joiner, and a painter (if, as in the case of Riemenschneider, the sculptor's workshop did not paint the objects carved there). A patron either could engage different masters individually or could negotiate a contract with one master, who would subcontract parts of the project to other craftsmen.[36] For the *Holy Blood* altarpiece in Rothenburg the shrine encasement was commissioned separately from the local joiner Erhard Harschner before the contract for Riemenschneider's work was settled. Contracts usually followed a certain pattern, whether they covered an entire project or just a part: they named the parties involved, described the work, and defined the delivery date as well as the payment and terms of payment. It was also customary in such documents to include the possibility of a bonus for a product that turned out especially well. Like many master craftsmen, Riemenschneider usually earned premiums for exceptional results, even when he was late, sometimes very late, in completing his work.[37] Tardiness in the delivery of commissioned artworks appears to have been quite common at this time and was seldom penalized.

It seems as if the design of a commissioned work could be determined in various ways, with the artist playing different roles. The patron generally defined the iconography, based on the function of the piece. With respect to the actual appearance of the work, however, the contract was often rather general. In many cases reference is made to a presentation drawing (*Visierung*), of which very few originals from this period survive, none from Riemenschneider's commissions. Some presentation drawings were quite refined and detailed, conveying a concrete view of the final piece— such as the drawing for the high altar retable of Ulm Minster from 1474 (fig. 3)[38]—while others were mere sketches, giving only an approximation.[39] We can assume that most often the drawings were from the hand of the artist, as was probably the case with

33. Illustrated in a well-known painting of a sculptor's or painter's workshop by Konrad Witz from Basel, c. 1440; also, concerning the open market for art, see Weilandt in Stuttgart 1993, 382–383; Lorne Campbell, "The Art Market in the Southern Netherlands in the Fifteenth Century," *Burlington Magazine* 118 (1976), 188–198; and Huth 1967, 19–20.

34. Baxandall 1980, 102.

35. According to an addendum to the statute for craftsmen (Weissenberger 1936, 186).

36. Baxandall 1980, 102–106; Huth 1967, 85–86.

37. This was the case with his *Adam* and *Eve* figures commissioned in Würzburg; concerning the original contracts and documents see Justus Bier, *Tilmann Riemenschneider*, 4 vols. (Würzburg, Augsburg, Vienna, 1925–1978).

38. Gerhard Weilandt, "Der wiedergefundene Vertrag Jörg Syrlins des Älteren über das Hochaltarretabel des Ulmer Münsters. Zum Erscheinungsbild des frühesten holzsichtigen Retabels," *Zeitschrift für Kunstgeschichte* 59 (1994), 437–460. This huge, 2.31-meter-high drawing is extremely unusual in its detail. Contrary to the assumption in scholarly literature, it is probably not from the hand of Jörg Syrlin the Elder, whose name appears on the reverse side. The preserved contract speaks of a "visier ime fürgehalten," which means a drawing that *was presented to* Syrlin. For the actual text see Weilandt 1993, 437.

39. Huth 1967, 40–49.

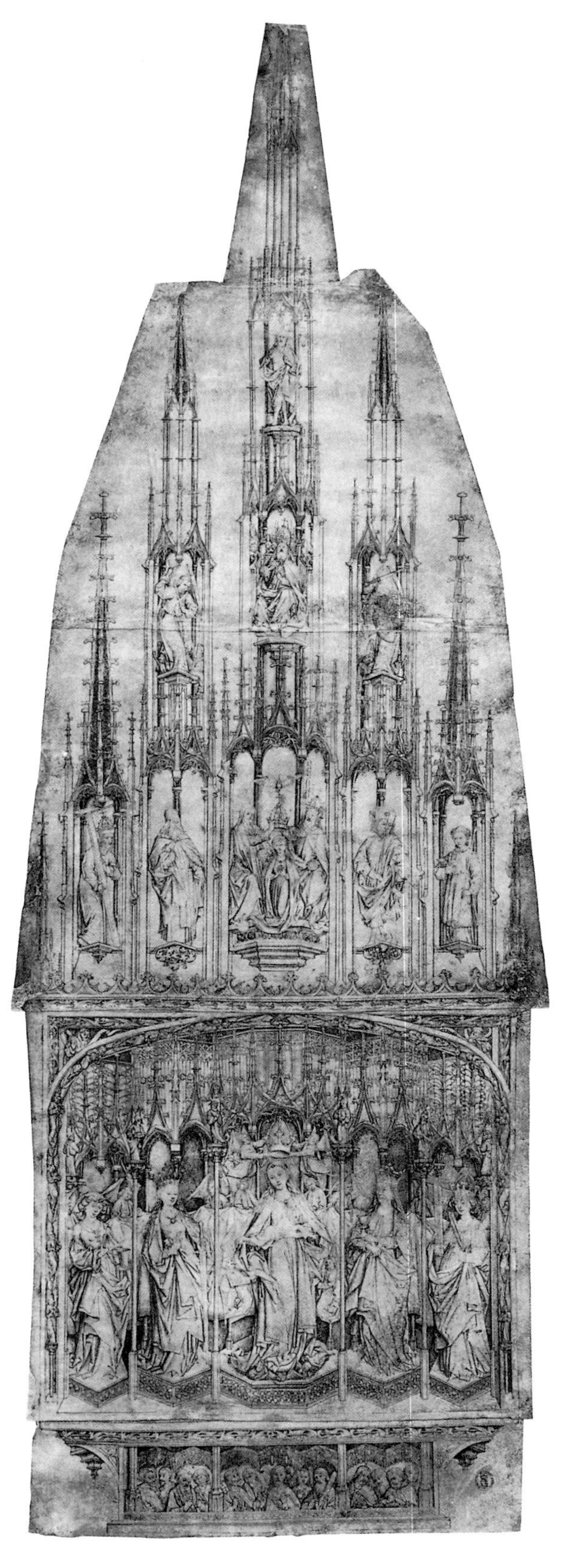

3.

Presentation drawing for the high altar retable of Ulm Minster, 1474, Württembergisches Landesmuseum, Stuttgart

Riemenschneider's contract for the altarpiece in Münnerstadt (see cat. 13).[40] Others were supplied to the artist, as was apparently the case with Riemenschneider's commission for the Scherenberg monument; here the design was meant to follow that of earlier bishops' memorials.[41]

The question of who designed the *Holy Blood* altarpiece in Rothenburg (see Chapuis essay, fig. 5) is more problematic, for Riemenschneider sculpted the figures, but Harschner had earlier received the commission for the shrine encasement. The sculptor's scene of the Last Supper represents a novel treatment of the theme and harmonizes well with the chapel-like architecture of the shrine, which was unusual for its time.[42] Thus it seems likely that Riemenschneider consulted both with Harschner regarding the overall design of the altarpiece and with the patron regarding the iconography. In the case of the statues of *Adam* and *Eve* for the Marienkapelle in Würzburg (Chapuis essay, fig. 3), it appears to have been Riemenschneider himself who suggested a new treatment of the theme. At the end of 1492 — a year and a half after the work was commissioned and several months after the original delivery date had passed — the city council of Würzburg decided by majority vote that Adam could be sculpted without a beard; this approval was evidently necessary for Riemenschneider to carry out his design.[43] Here and probably in most other cases we can assume that the actual representation of the subject, which was often a traditional motif, was left up to the artist — with the proviso that, should the need arise, the design could be reviewed by the patron.

Unusually detailed instructions exist for the desired appearance of the figures in Riemenschneider's commission for the altarpiece in Münnerstadt — detail that may or may not have been incorporated into the now-lost presentation drawing for the retable. Yet Riemenschneider neglected to follow many of the specifications in the contract.[44] Presumably those who commissioned the altarpiece made very few revisions, and it seems unlikely that Riemenschneider would have even thought to seek approval for the numerous small changes he made. Some contracts from this period even included provisions for the master craftsman to portray more, if necessary, than the contract specified.[45]

A master's reputation rested not on his ability to follow the obvious dictates of a particular iconographic theme but on his approach to creative challenges and on his artistic style.[46] The trend toward more individual artistic expression is clear in the decision that the Strasbourg painters guild made in 1516 to require candidates for the title of master to design their *Meisterstück* "freely," without models.[47] The modern image of the artistic genius had not yet established itself north of the Alps,[48] and yet some artists were already widely or even internationally known. This was true of the great

40. See reproductions of the contracts for Michael Pacher's altarpiece in Mondsee in Huth 1967, 115; concerning the retable in Münnerstadt, see Würzburg 1981, 115–166; and Kalden 1990, 64–66.

41. Kalden 1990, 67–73.

42. There are different assumptions regarding the author of the design of this altarpiece: see Kalden 1990, 50–53, 64–66; and Barbara Welzel, "Tilman Riemenschneider und das Bildprogramm des Heiligblut-Altares in Rothenburg o. T.," in *Flügelaltäre des späten Mittelalters,* ed. Hartmut Krohm and Eike Oellermann (Berlin, 1992), 199–210.

43. Würzburg 1981, 243.

44. Justus Bier, *Tilmann Riemenschneider. Die frühen Werke* (Würzburg, 1925), 92–99.

45. See the contracts with Hans Stettheimer from 1453 and Michael Pacher from 1471 in Huth 1967, 111, 115.

46. On this matter see especially Baxandall 1980.

47. Hans Rott, *Quellen und Forschungen zur Kunstgeschichte im XV. und XVI. Jahrhundert,* vol. 3 (Stuttgart, 1936), 220.

48. Even the Italian artists of this period were also bound for the most part by firmly established, guildlike organizations; see Anabel Thomas, *The Painter's Practice in Renaissance Tuscany* (Cambridge, 1995).

Netherlandish painters above all, although most belonged to guilds and had to work in accordance with contracts, just as minor wood-carvers did. A number of German artists also enjoyed a notoriety beyond their particular regions: for instance, the young Albrecht Dürer during his travels as a journeyman wanted to seek out the engraver and painter Martin Schongauer; and in 1467 Emperor Friedrich III summoned Niclaus Gerhaert from Strasbourg to Wiener Neustadt to design his tomb. Work by the Nuremberg sculptor Veit Stoss, too, was exported to places as far away as Portugal. And while Riemenschneider produced sculpture almost exclusively for the diocese of Würzburg and the surrounding areas,[49] his work was also in demand beyond Franconia. The elector Friedrich the Wise instructed him in 1505 to produce a large crucifix for the castle church in distant Wittenberg.[50] As the elector also employed Lucas Cranach the Elder and ordered works by Dürer and Hans Burgkmair, this commission testifies to Riemenschneider's considerable reputation, as does the fact that his artistic style was imitated by a number of minor sculptors in northern and central Germany.[51]

Riemenschneider created a distinctive formal language: his figural compositions and facial types are easily remembered, and they were surely recognized and valued by his contemporaries. The importance of an idiosyncratic style is evident from the interest focused on certain artists from this period. It is also articulated by the Strasbourg preacher Johannes Geiler von Kayserberg, noting that "anyone who passes a pleasing altarpiece sees right away which master has done it, and says: Hirtz did it" (his example being the painter Hans Hirtz, who was active around the middle of the fifteenth century).[52] Artists began to be distinguished from artisans, even though they worked under similar conditions. Around 1520 the sculptors of Strasbourg presented their case for artistic recognition by citing the reputations of well-known predecessors like Niclaus Gerhaert or Hans Jöuch, who had already been active around 1430, artists whose "fame was known to emperors and princes" and who had contributed to the fame of the city.[53] Yet the modern notion of the artist who rises far above ordinary craftsmen, and values himself as such, can only be recognized north of the Alps with the advent of Albrecht Dürer. Only about ten years younger than Riemenschneider, Dürer clearly belonged to a new generation and era.[54]

49. Jörg Rasmussen, "'…far stupire il mondo.' Zur Verbreitung der Kunst des Veit Stoss," in *Veit Stoss. Die Vorträge des Nürnberger Symposions* (Munich, 1985), 107–122.

50. Justus Bier, *Tilmann Riemenschneider. Die reifen Werke* (Augsburg, 1930), 6, 167–168. The sculptor in question is identified only as "the master of Würzburg," but he is surely identical with Riemenschneider; the whereabouts of the crucifix is unknown.

51. See references in Kalden 1990, 38 n. 127.

52. *Evangelia in usslegung* (Strasbourg, 1517); cited in Rott 1936, 194.

53. Rott 1936, 268–269; also Baxandall 1980, 118.

54. Fedja Anzelewsky, *Albrecht Dürer. Das malerische Werk*, 2 vols., 2nd ed. (Berlin, 1990), 15–17. Translation by Richard Pettit.

The Perception of Riemenschneider *Michael Baxandall*

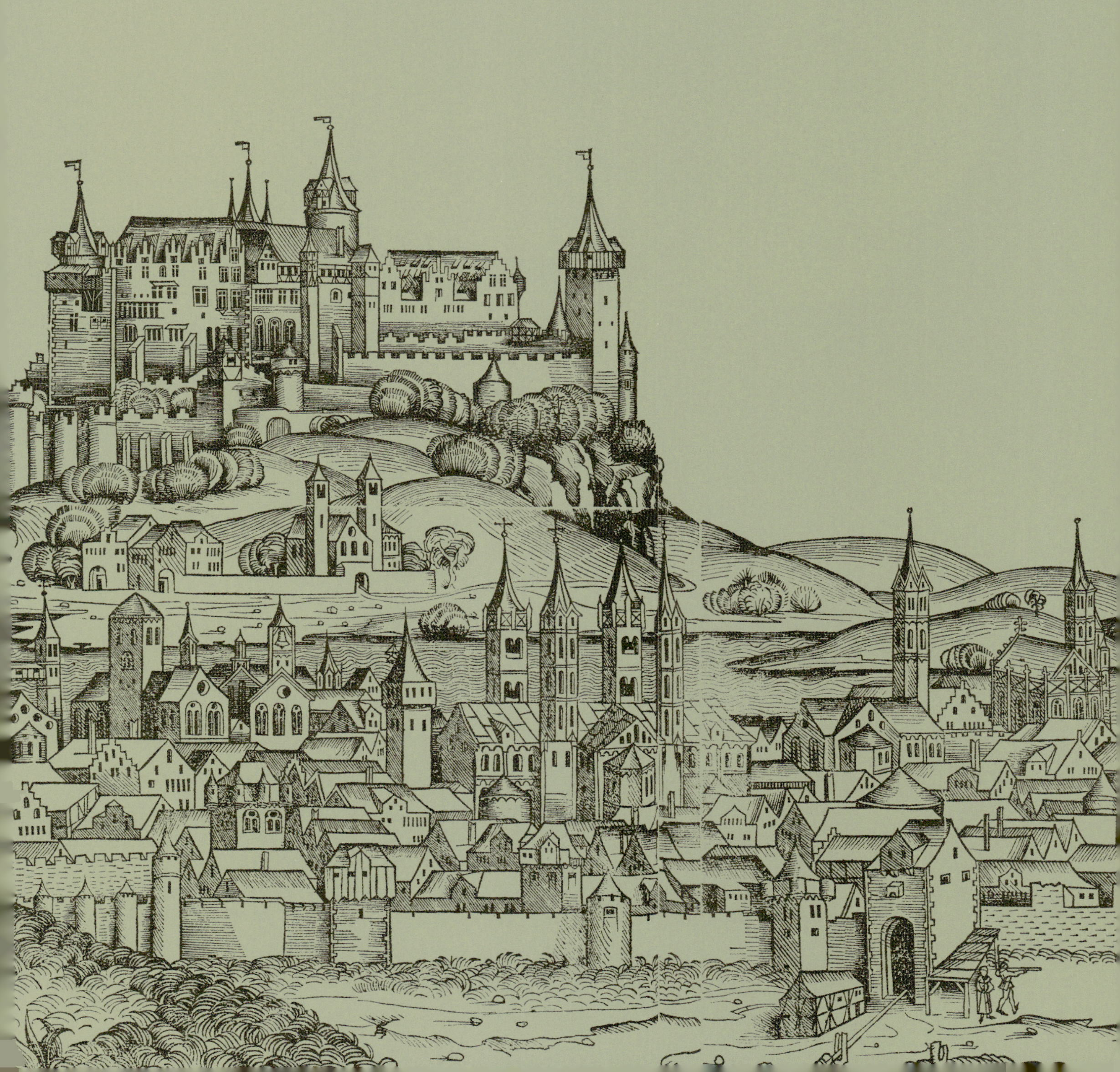

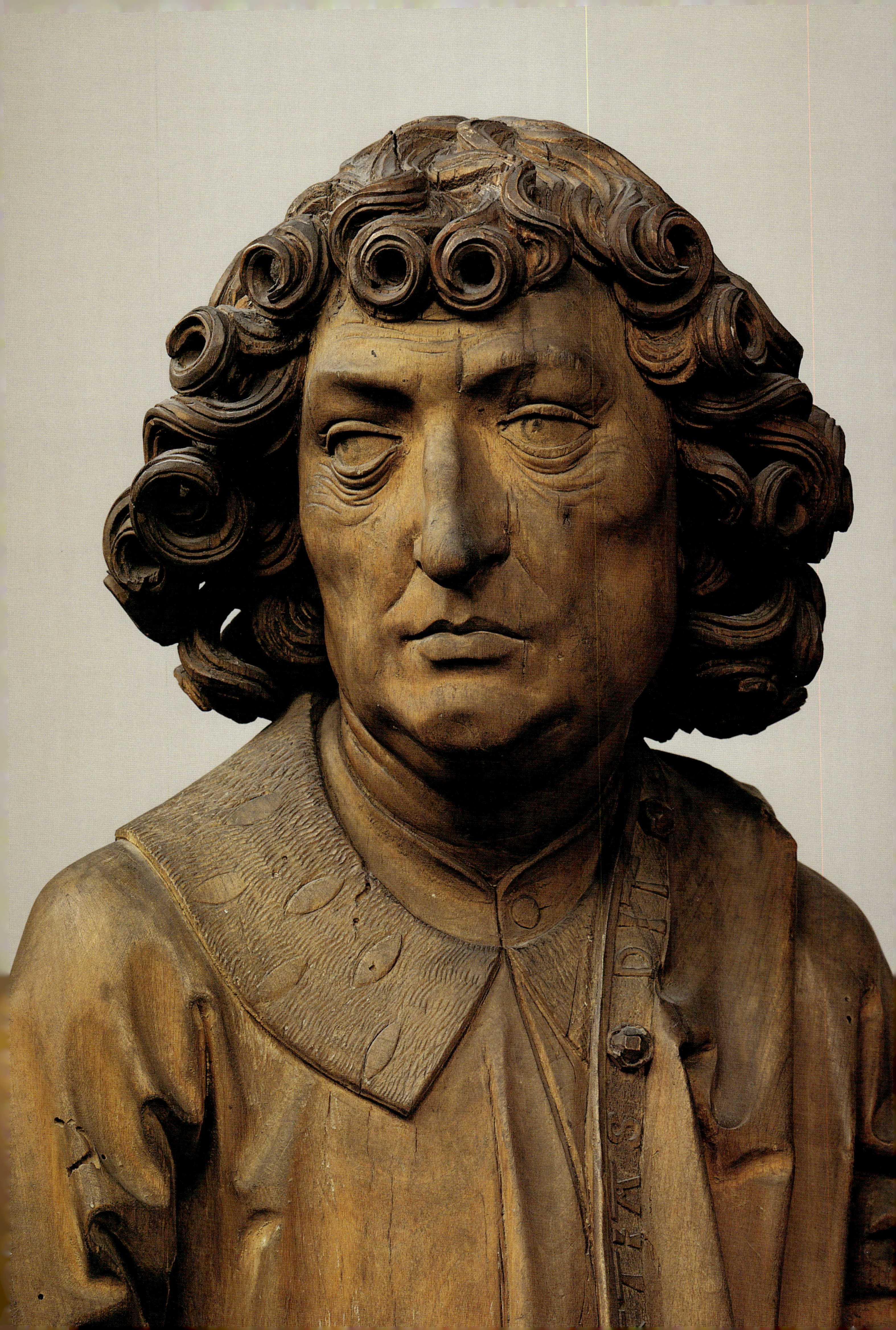

TILMAN RIEMENSCHNEIDER made many different kinds of sculpture. He worked in various materials—alabaster, a strange mottled reddish German marble, a fine yellowish limestone, gray and greenish gray sandstone, and most of all in the wood of the linden or lime tree. He made some freestanding figures, a fair number of reliefs, and many figures that are designed to stand against walls or in retable shrines and thus are fully modeled in the front but not behind. He made some works that narrate stories and many others that represent the figures of sacred persons in a more absolute way. He made both sculpture that was fully colored and sculpture that was not. This last—particularly his development of monochrome wood sculpture—is a crux. ❡ Another preliminary point about Riemenschneider's sculpture is that it is quite plentiful. His workshop seems to have been relatively large for the period; and his prices, when known, seem to have been relatively low. It may seem paradoxical that, although his work involved strategies for large-scale production—delegation of the physical work, simplification of process, and repetition of such standard features as eyes, hands, and hair—the best of it is unusually subtle and refined. But this is not really a paradox. Delegation, and the need to communicate his wishes to assistants, suggests a radical and reflective analysis of the potentialities of his art. The simplification of production implies a discreet economy and tact in his use of his medium. And if component features such as eyes and hair are repetitious, as they certainly are, at least they reveal an acquired assurance about just how they work and how they can be delicately applied. In effect, Riemenschneider made use of his circumstances to exalt the sculptor's process.

With all of this, Riemenschneider raises questions of how we look at sculpture, and perhaps also how we *should* look at it, if we want to get the sort of experience it was designed to give. Especially with respect to the standing figure, how do we perceive Riemenschneider's sculpture?

The most basic and important operation in the act of visual perception is to locate the edges of things. Our eyes register an array of light values and discontinuities, and our minds interpret these as the surfaces and edges of objects, partly by projecting schematized knowledge of possible objects into the array of light. Within these object edges a second basis of vision is the modeling of surfaces by light and shade. Such object perception is what our visual system has primarily evolved to achieve. But looking at a sculpture by Riemenschneider—or anything we might consider a work of art— is not the normal use of perception. Out of aesthetic or devotional or even casual interest, we are likely to continue to inspect the sculpture long after the first moment's basic visual act, long after having identified it as a wood or stone figure of a woman or man in a certain attitude. That identification will usually have happened within the first second of looking at the sculpture, but we go on looking.

Still, the equipment with which we continue to scan the sculpture—the visual system—is largely the same equipment that was evolved for and used in the basic act of vision. Edges are primary. But now they are available for the artifice of the sculptor, who can manipulate them in all sorts of other ways.

In Riemenschneider's culture an important aspect of sculpture is what one may call the "arc of address." Statues were not usually truly freestanding but stood in niches in shrines. They were designed to present themselves toward the front, but not to a single point in front. Most of them do not have just one optimum angle of view— which would make them less effective as devotional objects (and as sculpture)—but offer themselves over a sector, the arc of address. They do this by representing poses with implications of address in more than one direction.

The Virgin's head in the *Virgin and Child* from Dumbarton Oaks (fig. 1) looks toward our right, but her right knee and foot can suggest movement a little to our left; and the presence of the Christ child allows address, through his head and outstretched arms, sharply to our left. This bears on the possible edges of the statue, since a view from the direction addressed by the Virgin's head—a movement presenting the figure in one character—will offer a silhouette or outline different from a view from the direction addressed by the movement of her right leg. Each angle of view has its own combination of movement and outline, a different encounter of different character.

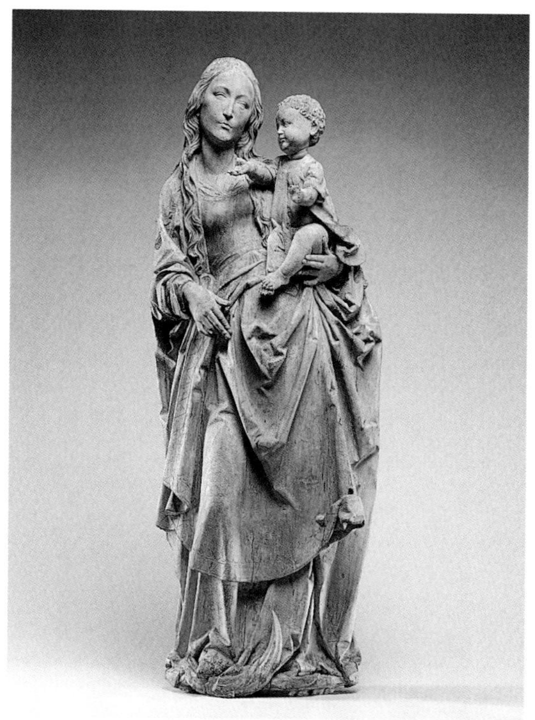

Virgin and Child on the Crescent Moon (cat. 45), 1521, limewood, Dumbarton Oaks, Washington, DC, House Collection

At first, representational statues of human beings like Riemenschneider's may seem less full of optical artifice than, say, images of human beings depicted on a flat surface. They may seem to be more like a replica or model; they do not seem to re-duce three dimensions to two dimensions, after all, which is the basic feat of pictorial representation and the origin of many of its resources. But it is worth thinking of the sculptor's strange project in another way—of the sculptor as having to achieve in a third dimension many of the pictorial things a picture has to do in only two dimensions.

Where a picture usually delineates the edge of an object just once, with one out-line representing one angle of view, the *Virgin and Child* has to establish and coordi-nate as many delineations or outlines as there are angles of view of itself. It is, in this sense, multidimensional drawing, but instead of drawn lines the sculptor uses the sur-faces of his wood or stone. The visible surface of one angle of view is the silhouette of another angle of view, and vice versa. The surfaces of the figures are not just mod-eled envelopes of volumes but also devices to present a changing series of edges, when we change our positions and our angles of view.

Riemenschneider's manipulation of such edges or outlines is not patently ener-getic. The real edges of the *Virgin and Child* do not alter in a dramatic way when we move within the arc of address. The drama of edges depends in part on a second basis of vision, the modeling of forms by light and shade.

Most of Riemenschneider's sculpture stood in churches and was submitted, in the course of the day and the year, to varied kinds of light from different directions: morning and evening light, directed light on bright days and diffused light on cloudy days, light reflected from the surfaces of other things, light refracted through irregular glass, sometimes multiple flickering candle lights. Riemenschneider was accustomed to providing objects that would function in many lights. Any part of the surface of a sculpture may take on a relative brightness from the following primary conditions of illumination:

• Direct light, ranging from full light on a surface that faces a light source perpendicular to itself to less-than-full light on surfaces otherwise angled to the light source.
• Full or "deep" self-shadow on the surfaces of a solid not accessible to the light, the solid blocking light to itself.
• Projected or cast shadow, where light is kept from a surface not by its own solid support but by some other form, *including other parts of the same object,* interposing itself between that surface and the light.
• Light reflected from facing surfaces, which will be less focused than direct light owing to scattering and weaker owing to absorption.
• Luster, concentrated reflections of the light source itself, particularly on shiny curved surfaces.

Diffused light—light reflected and re-reflected from the whole ambience—will soften and compose the contrasts of these conditions to a greater or lesser degree. An intricate and overlapping array of all of them is part of any Riemenschneider carving.

In the Munich *Saint Barbara* (fig. 2), for instance, the dominant lighting is direct, coming from the left in this reproduction, and much of the surface brightness varies according to its angle to the light. But there is self-shadow on the right side of the figure as seen here—on the turbanlike headdress, shoulder, and hip obviously—and, on a smaller scale, on the right side of many drapery folds. Only diffused reflected light from the ambience lets us see within this self-shadow. There is also projected shadow, not just that cast by the chalice on Saint Barbara's body but that overlapping and extending the self-shadow on the left edge of the cloak. In contrast, concentrations of luster highlight her temple, nose, breasts, and fingers.

It is worth distinguishing between the five conditions of illumination because each has systematic peculiarities.

• Surfaces open to direct light are those with full *modeling,* since their brightness varies according to the angle at which the light falls on them: illumination of a surface is proportional to the cosine of the angle of the light's incidence upon it.

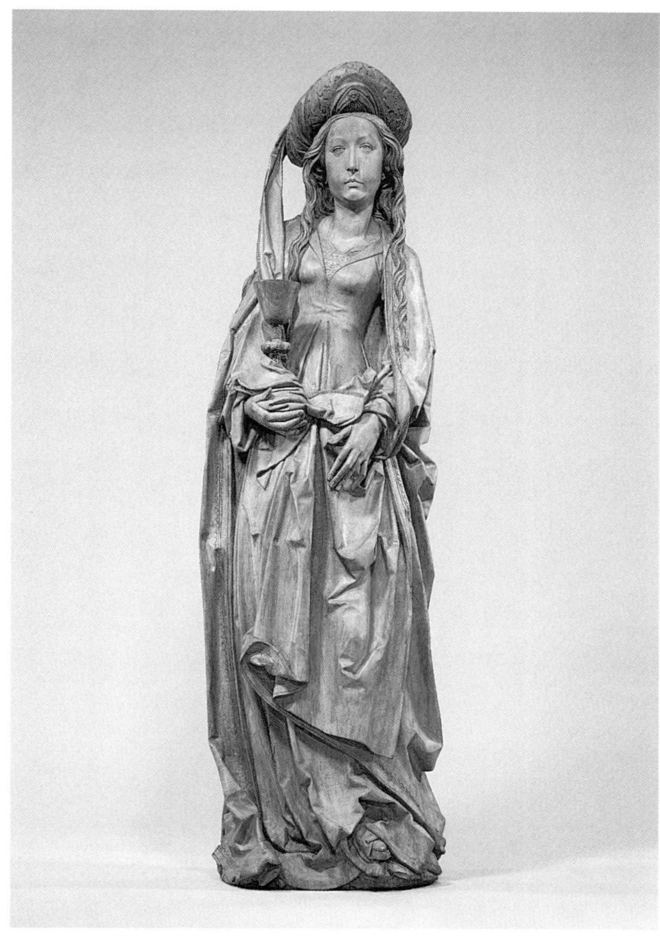

Saint Barbara, c. 1510, limewood, Bayerisches Nationalmuseum, Munich

• Surfaces where a solid is self-shadowing have no such modeling gradient. Self-shadow is the *same value* all over.

• Surfaces in cast shadow are *not as dark* as those in self-shadow because they tend — owing to the intrinsic geometry of normal solids — to face other surfaces that throw immediately reflected light.

• Reflected light brings a subdued element of differentiation and even modeling into most shadows. It also picks up and transmits the *color* of the reflecting surface.

• Luster is outside the system: its *location is relative* to the position of the beholder, moving on the surface according to the angle of view as a normal direct highlight does not.

All this means that selectively different formal organizations are created by different lightings, not just different codings of the same organization. Since direct light produces graded modeling and self-shadow does not, shifting the light source from one side of an object to the other does not reverse the light-to-dark coding to dark-to-light. It selects a new organization.

In our basic perception of the world, reading forms from this sort of array is probably less powerful than reading objects from their characteristic edges. But light and shade can be used in sculpture to create suborganizations and counterorganizations, emphases and special effects, many of them occasional and dependent on particular lighting. We may consider some of the surfaces, especially those toward the front of the figure, not just as simple replications of folds and kinks in fabric but as devices designed to interfere with different kinds of light.

Riemenschneider cannot have planned all the possible lighting patterns on his surfaces, of course, but his huge production must have given him ample experience of the actual surface arrangements that led to what pleased or satisfied him. From this, no doubt, he could work more intuitively.

• Surfaces and the Internalization of Edges •

One way that has been recommended for thinking about surface forms of sculpture is as a relation between "fruit" forms—rounded, expansive, burgeoning—and "crystal" forms, which present straight ridges and facets:[1] both can be either positive or negatively void, and one of them can underlie or insert local episodes in the other. This does not in fact quite match the surface character of Riemenschneider. But, thinking in this style and taking the *Virgin and Child* and *Saint Barbara* (figs. 1 and 2) as examples, what dialectic of what forms would suggest his structural habit? There seem to be three main scales of plastic-cum-lighting event here.

1. Philip Rawson, *Sculpture* (Philadelphia, 1997), 96–97.

• The largest is a gently curved and usually vertical ridge or shallow depression, hardly a "fruit" form but generous enough, corresponding to an accented thigh or some fall of cloth, and lending itself to definition by direct light.
• Around and sometimes encroaching on these are linear systems of smaller-scale and much steeper ridges, almost rodlike at their crests, often somewhat off-vertical and articulated in relation to each other rather than to anything beneath. They tend to catch both direct light and luster.
• Smaller yet, local flurries of kink and buckle are not really "crystal" forms but have a certain negative, faceted stiffness, commenting on the intersections and dynamics of the rodlike ridges.

Such is the goodwill toward representation installed in us by vision's object-identifying mission that we are disposed to accept all this as drapery and a body beneath.

In much of this sculpture the lighting brings us back to edges in a remarkable way. Often the most intense concentration of light is an edge of drapery. The sharply rounded edge and the polished and lacquered wood catch and stabilize luster, which

90

is otherwise more mobile, shifting on surfaces in response to movement by the beholder. To a slightly lesser degree the rodlike ridges do the same, enabling a sort of linear drawing with light. Indeed, such sculpture shares some characteristics with the contemporary mode of drawing on toned paper with white lead. This introduces a secondary realm of linear edges into the interior of the figure, often more assertive than the outlines. Yet this strange calligraphy cannot be read absolutely. How we take it, what meaning we derive from the dance on which it leads our eye and our attention, depends on a complex sense of the figure as a human presence, both Riemenschneider's presence and the Virgin's or Saint Barbara's presence.

• *The Unresolved Figure* •

The perception of edges and of light and shade is preliminary to acknowledging that a sculpture is a representation of a human being. Summary recognition comes very early and develops along with our exploration of the artifice of edges and lights that sustains the representation. How does the sculpture augment, control, and complicate the sense we develop of these humanities?

It is common for late Gothic standing figures of Riemenschneider's time to be posed in a spiraling, counterpoised attitude, suggestive of a lounging elegance, a stationary saunter. This has much to do with defining the "arc of address." Many of Riemenschneider's figures have a specialized variation of this attitude, in which it is hard to know quite what coherent bodily movement the stance could capture. Usually differences in representational effect derive from various angles of view; often the effect is to direct a range of local movements out toward several points in the arc of address.

With Riemenschneider the accumulative character of the attitude is uneasy, a sort of overall wince, almost as if the figure is unable to find a pose. It is nothing like the later mannerist double-helical serpentine figure. Perhaps we lack terms and concepts for such attitudes and would find it helpful to borrow terms of the culture itself. With sculpture particularly in mind, Albrecht Dürer—sixty miles away in Nuremberg and toward the end of Riemenschneider's life—categorized six possible types of standing pose, providing linear diagram notations for them (fig. 3): bent, curved, turned, wound, either stretched or compacted, and thrust *(gebogen, gekruppt, gewandt, gewunden, gestreckt/gekrupft, geschoben)*. No single type entirely covers the attitude of any of Riemenschneider's more evolved figures, but trying to use the terms may sharpen our sense of the attitudes' complexity. For instance, we might see the Dumbarton Oaks *Virgin and Child* (fig. 1) as modulating from a mildly thrust position below into a wound/bent position above.

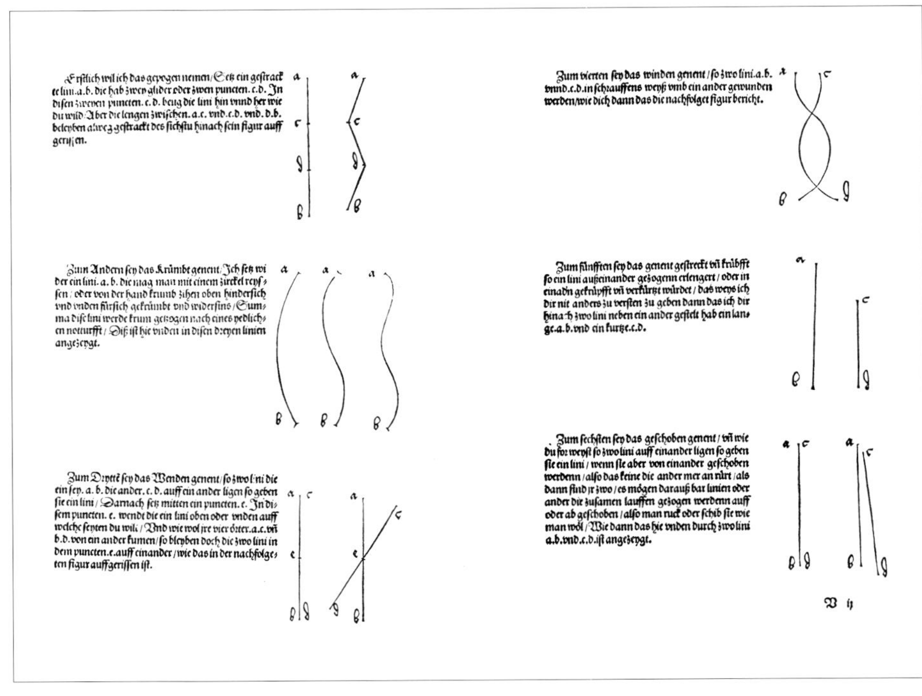

3.

Albrecht Dürer's diagram of six attitudes of the human figure: bent, curved, turned, wound, stretched or compacted, thrust. From *Vier Bücher von menschlicher Proportion* (Nuremberg, 1528), v 1 b.–v 2 a

Our somatic response to statues, our sense of them with our own bodies, can combine various elements: empathy, an internal reaction to another's bearing toward us, an instinct to circle for an encompassing overview or visual grasp. How we respond to the unwillingness of Riemenschneider's figures to resolve into a coherent attitude will depend on what experience and knowledge we bring to them. These are pre-Reformation saints; no amount of scholarship will teach late twentieth-century viewers how to *feel* about their sufferings and their powers better than the strangeness of the figures themselves. Some affect or feeling is registered in their unquiet attitudes, and the quality becomes clearer as we move with respect to these figures.

• *The Approach from Below* •

We look at sculpture while moving laterally — that is, across the arc of address — but also while moving toward it. Sculptors can make use of this in various ways. Leonardo da Vinci,[2] another contemporary of Riemenschneider's, pointed out that the closer we come to most solids, the less we see of them; this makes possible interesting changes in object edge. What is more determinative for Riemenschneider's figures is that they were usually set in stations higher than floor level, sometimes considerably higher. Thus the closer we approach a figure, the lower our angle of view becomes (see fig. 4). Medieval and Renaissance sculpture is full of evidence that sculptors very consciously

2. *The Literary Works of Leonardo da Vinci*, ed. Jean-Paul Richter, 3d rev. ed. (London and New York, 1970), 85.

took low viewpoint into account. There are the odd hunched shoulders and protruding heads of so many Gothic statues. There is also Giorgio Vasari's story of the trick
Donatello played on the cloth guild at Florence, persuading them he had reworked
his figure of Saint Mark simply by putting it up into its intended station at Orsan-
michele. A lower angle of view alters relationships within a statue.

Riemenschneider habitually manipulated the effect of a low viewpoint. As we
approach any statue from below, the head and the hands, which are principal bearers
of human character, come into more compact relation to one another through foreshortening. Hands—of which Riemenschneider had a finite but eloquently flexed
repertory—become relatively closer to our eyes, while heads become relatively further
away. To compensate, Riemenschneider sometimes made his heads disproportionately
large for the bodies, with an almost doll-like effect in the level view (see cat. 23, fig. 1).
In the close, low view that was intended, an illusion of proportionality is achieved by
the greater distance of the head from the eye.

In normal visual experience we allow for greater distance and expect the farther
thing to appear relationally smaller. Yet this is not, nor is it meant to be, normal experience. Moreover, our assurance in matters of foreshortening depends on familiarity
with the angle of view, and we rarely encounter human figures from sharply below.
Thus Riemenschneider, like Mantegna in his *Dead Christ*,[3] can use the perceptual tol-
erance caused by unfamiliarity to smuggle in a more than naturally large head—which,
at another level of perception, still retains the emphasis of its real mass.

With Riemenschneider it is possible to feel that our approach to the figure has
made things seem right. Head and hands have come into more active relation; the
elaborate modeled patterning of the lower half of the figure is more present and plastic and positive. And it is our own act of approach that has produced this effect.

3. Most recently on this aspect
of Mantegna's *Dead Christ,*
see Robert L. Solso, *Cognition
and the Visual Arts* (Cambridge,
Mass., 1994), 185–186.

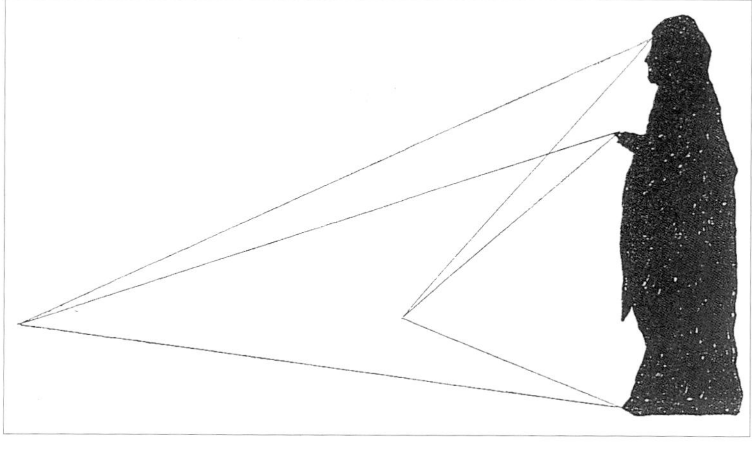

4.

Diagram of the progressive effects of foreshortening

Another, more local, manipulation by Riemenschneider in response to a low view-point concerns the set of the eyes. His handling of eyes is repetitious, based on a few variants of one effective formula in which the lids are framed by one or more crease-like grooves, the number depending on the subject's age. Often asymmetrical and downward sloping, the eyes have an obvious pathos, which actually increases as we approach from below, with a poignant, almost plangent effect, because the eyes are set wide apart at a receding angle to each other on the face. This may be seen as little more than a late Gothic trick of a rather facile kind, which Riemenschneider shares with other artists of the time, but he works it hard and well.

A delicate but relevant point to add here is that if a figure is not set high enough for us to experience the full approach-from-below effect a partial substitute would be to get down on our knees before it.

• Seeing the Wood •

What are we to make of Riemenschneider's crucial move from colored sculpture to monochrome sculpture (see especially cat. 13)? It is important to keep in mind that, though monochrome, the sculpture was not just bare wood: it was varnished with a unifying brown compound; and a few details, such as lips and the pupils of eyes, were still pigmented.[4] In addition, some of the intricate surface carving, such as the bro-cade pattern on *Saint Barbara's* headdress (fig. 2), shows continuity with elaborate polychrome techniques and tastes. Finally, various extrinsic considerations may have been in play at the time, possibly a shortage of money to pay for an ornate polychrome finishing. But these matters apart, what are the perceptual consequences of the new monochromy?

For us, more accustomed to seeing unpigmented sculpture, there is not as great a jolt of strangeness as there must have been in the 1490s. But a basic shift in experi-ence can still be appreciated. In polychrome sculpture we tend to see the statue as a surrogate person. In monochrome sculpture we see a figure in a worked material; we are more aware of the substance of the sculpture, and so of the work as represen-tation. We are, and must be, more active in our address to monochrome sculpture: we contribute more to the perception. We see it is wood, for example, and we know it is carving; we project the human figure into it more energetically and enjoy our part in the transaction. And since we ourselves have had much to do with creating the human being in the wood, our experience of it is stronger. Estrangement stimulates projection.

What are the implications of seeing sculpture specifically as wood? In a culture in which wood is an important material for life and work, the statue is associated with

4. Eike Oellermann, "Die Restaurierung des Heilig-Blut-Altares von Tilmann Riemen-schneider," *24. Bericht des Bayerischen Landesamtes für Denkmalpflege 1965* (1966), 75–85; Johannes Taubert, "Zur Oberflächengestalt der sogenann-ten ungefassten spätgotischen Holzplastik," *Städel-Jahrbuch* 1 (1967), 119–139, reprinted in Johannes Taubert, *Farbige Skulpturen* (Munich, 1978), 73–88; *Tilman Riemenschneider. Frühe Werke* [exh. cat., Main-fränkisches Museum: Würzburg] (Regensburg, 1981).

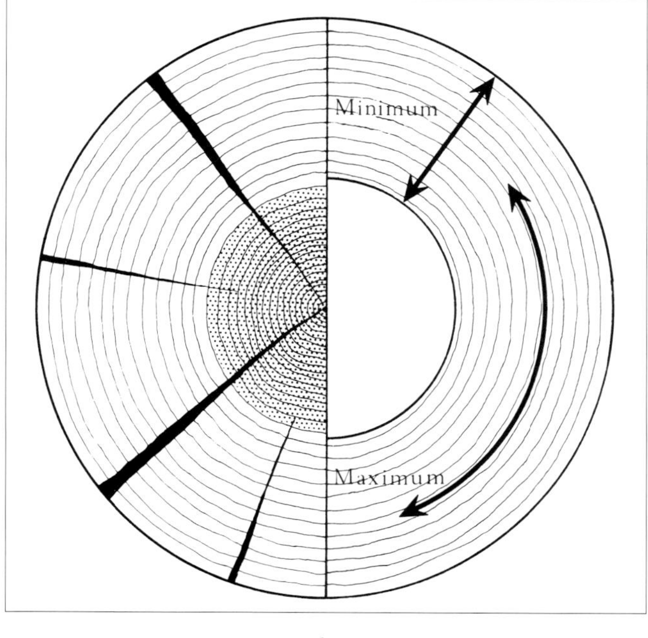
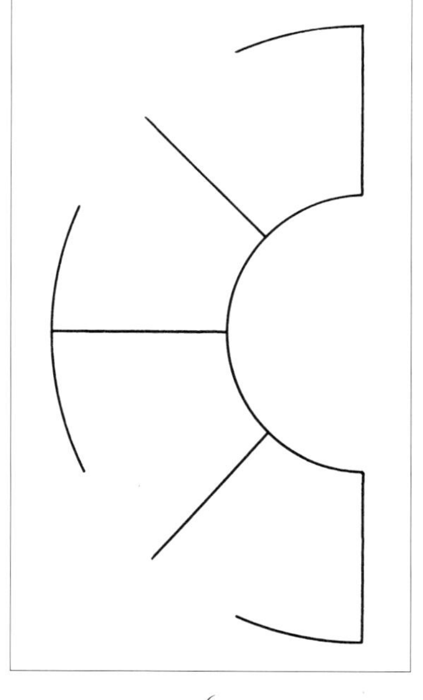

5.
Diagram of the internal strains in limewood and the
excavation of heartwood

6.
Diagram of the principle of
occupying volume

properties of the material that bear on its shape. To see the wood, we must first see the tree. The wood of a statue is a section of the trunk of a tree. At the center of a tree trunk is heartwood. This heartwood, if left in fine hardwoods such as limewood, may initiate rot or cause cracking in the outer wood through its refusal to shrink along with it. For a standing draped limewood figure, sculptors thus normally used C-section halves of the trunk with the heartwood removed at the back (see fig. 5).[5] It often helps to know this.

But time will cause cracking even in the C-section unless local forms are discreetly chosen to contract and expand coherently, both in themselves and in relation to the whole, as humidity changes. Wood sculpture must, as it were, be able to breathe; it must be able to shrink and swell without excessive internal strain. Coherence derives from the cell structure of the wood, a complex matter, but the dominant fact is that the wood shrinks more orbitally than radially, thus is liable to crack radially. This tension can be observed in the fine vertical — not horizontal — cracks that have, after half a millennium, appeared on the surface of some figures.

To sum it up crudely: large solid masses are risky, particularly in outer areas and horizontal shelflike flats; vertical radial forms are safe, as are annular forms if they are allowed to float freely (see fig. 6). Of course, no actual carving of a human figure could confine itself to a section like that in figure 6, which is simply a paradigm of a hidden syntax underlying sculpture in fine hardwoods such as limewood.[6]

5. Hubert Wilm, *Die gotische Holzfigur: Ihr Wesen und ihre Bedeutung,* 3d ed. (Stuttgart, 1942), 23–37; Arnulff von Ulmann, *Bildhauertechnik des Spätmittelalters und der Frührenaissance* (Darmstadt, 1984), 123–132; Hans Westhoff and Gerhard Weilandt, "Vom Baumstamm zum Bildwerk: Skulpturenschnitzerei in Ulm um 1500," in *Meisterwerke Massenhaft. Die Bildhauerwerkstatt des Niklaus Weckmann und die Malerei in Ulm um 1500* [exh. cat., Württembergisches Landesmuseum] (Stuttgart, 1993), 245–263.

6. Michael Baxandall, *The Limewood Sculptors of Renaissance Germany* (New Haven and London, 1980), 27–38.

Riemenschneider, unlike his peer Veit Stoss (compare figs. 7 and 8), did not habitually achieve effects or establish affect by an energetic display of athletic risk taking with this syntax. In fact, there are arguments for his early training having been more as a sculptor in stone and alabaster than in limewood. Whether from technical caution, then, or taste, or the exigencies of his large-scale production, or constraints imposed by the quality of the timber he had to use—or perhaps from all of them—he negotiated this side of wood sculpture warily.

He is clearly observant of the limewood syntax. Consider the forms of his *Saint Matthias* in Berlin (fig. 7) in relation to the diagram in figure 6: how the wood has been excavated to allow the larger forms of arms or drapery to move independently as integrally radial *or* orbital sections; how horizontal structures are few and small; and how the head has been shifted sideways out of the dangerous central heartwood axis. There seems to be a vertical radial/orbital matrix underlying the design.

Then consider how little any of this holds true in the quite different material conditions of the five-plank relief *Noli me Tangere* from Münnerstadt, where Riemenschneider was free to pursue suggestions from Martin Schongauer's copper engraving in all directions (see cat. 13 F, and cat. 13, fig. 6).

But, to borrow systematic terms of the period, Riemenschneider's way of working with limewood was "plain" not "ornate." This is an essential part of his character as an artist, and it is surely not fanciful to feel that something of it moves into our sense of his figures. Let us say, as a rough covering term, that they are "mild" in this respect.[7]

7. For "plain" *(blos)*, "ornate" *(zierlich)*, "mild" *(senft)* as systematically differentiated terms in Riemenschneider's culture, see Baxandall 1980, 143–163.

8. These and other anxieties about religious images in Riemenschneider's time are discussed in relation to the sculpture in Baxandall 1980, 50–78, but see, more recently, Bernhard Decker, "Reform within the Cult Image: The German Winged Altarpiece before the Reformation," in *The Altarpiece in the Renaissance*, ed. Peter Humfrey and Martin Kemp (Cambridge, 1990), 90–105; and Jörg Rosenfeld, "Die nichtpolychromierte Retabelskulptur als bildreformatorisches Phänomen im ausgehenden Mittelalter und in der beginnenden Neuzeit," in *Flügelaltäre des späten Mittelalters*, ed. Hartmut Krohm and Eike Oellermann (Berlin, 1992), 65–83.

• *Artifice and Humanity* •

We may see the statues here as art before we see them as religious images, but in their own culture they were devotional instruments first—which is not to say their artifice would not have been observed and valued. In Riemenschneider's time three principal functions for religious images had long been officially approved: to represent the matter of religion clearly; to engage our feelings for that matter; and to offer an image that could lodge in the memory. Through the lively visual sense, it was believed, the visual arts were apt to fill all three functions: they could be clear, moving, and memorable.

Three common worries concerned how religious sculpture might be misused: people might confuse images of saints with the saints themselves—idolatry; people might attend to showy materials or even showy skill more than to the subject matter represented; and people might take magnificent art as a glorification of the patron who had paid for it more than as a glorification of God and the holy persons it depicted.[8] The sculptor walked a narrow line, and so did the beholder. Riemenschneider, more than many sculptors, ensured that we negotiate it in a decent but positive way. The

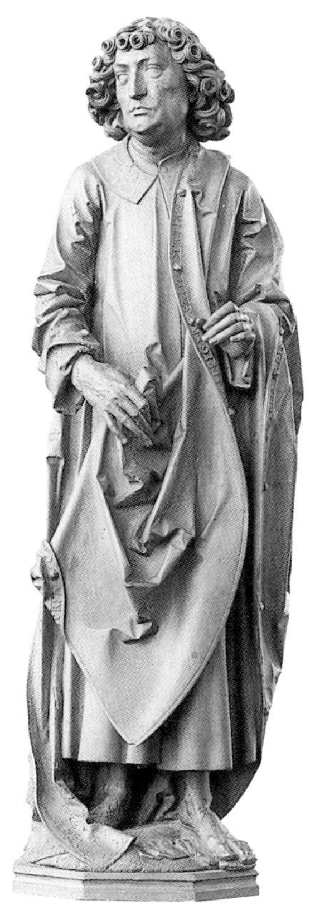
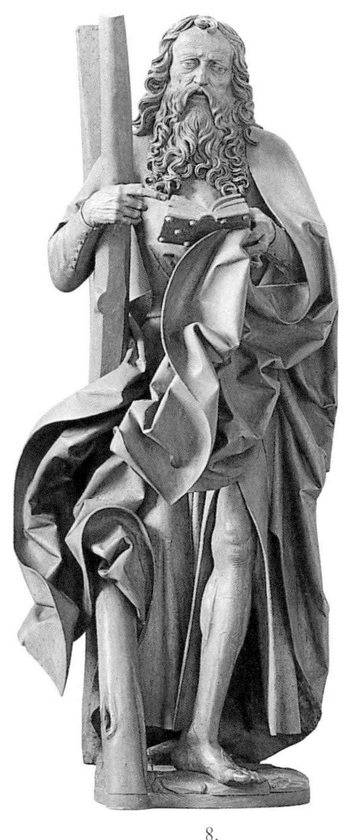

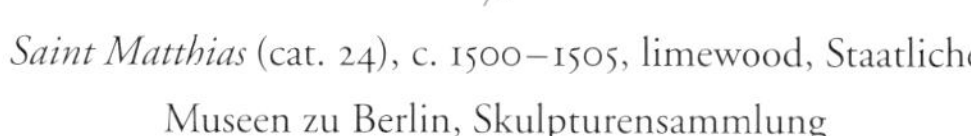

7.

Saint Matthias (cat. 24), c. 1500–1505, limewood, Staatliche
Museen zu Berlin, Skulpturensammlung

8.

Veit Stoss, *Saint Andrew,* c. 1510–1520, limewood,
Sebalduskirche, Nuremberg

monochromy that differentiated images of saints from the saints themselves, the appearance of plainness, and the increasingly modest material are all devotionally wholesome.

The humanity of Riemenschneider's figures is unquiet, responsive to approach and indeed demanding of it, yet "mild." This human quality is not just a certain replicated human look or physiognomy; to take it as only that sentimentalizes the work in an impoverishing way. Rather, the humanity is something installed in the process of our seeing the sculpture, in all the detail of our active experience of its artifice. We enact and live out the character of these figures in the style of our perception: the gait of our visual scanning, the manner of our locating edges, the mode of our ordering lights and darks, the developing balance of our attention, the pace and rhythm of our projecting and confirming, even the moving of ourselves around the sculpture.

So the worked lumps of wood or stone are permanent material supports for activity—activity by us. The intrinsic meaning of the sculpture lies in the qualities of the perceptual experience we derive from our activity. But that activity is substantially programmed by Riemenschneider. To apprehend the meaning, we will have been colluding with Riemenschneider's manipulation of us, and part of our perception may well be that Riemenschneider was, in a mild way, a very astute and controlling character indeed.

The Surfaces of Riemenschneider *Michele Marincola*

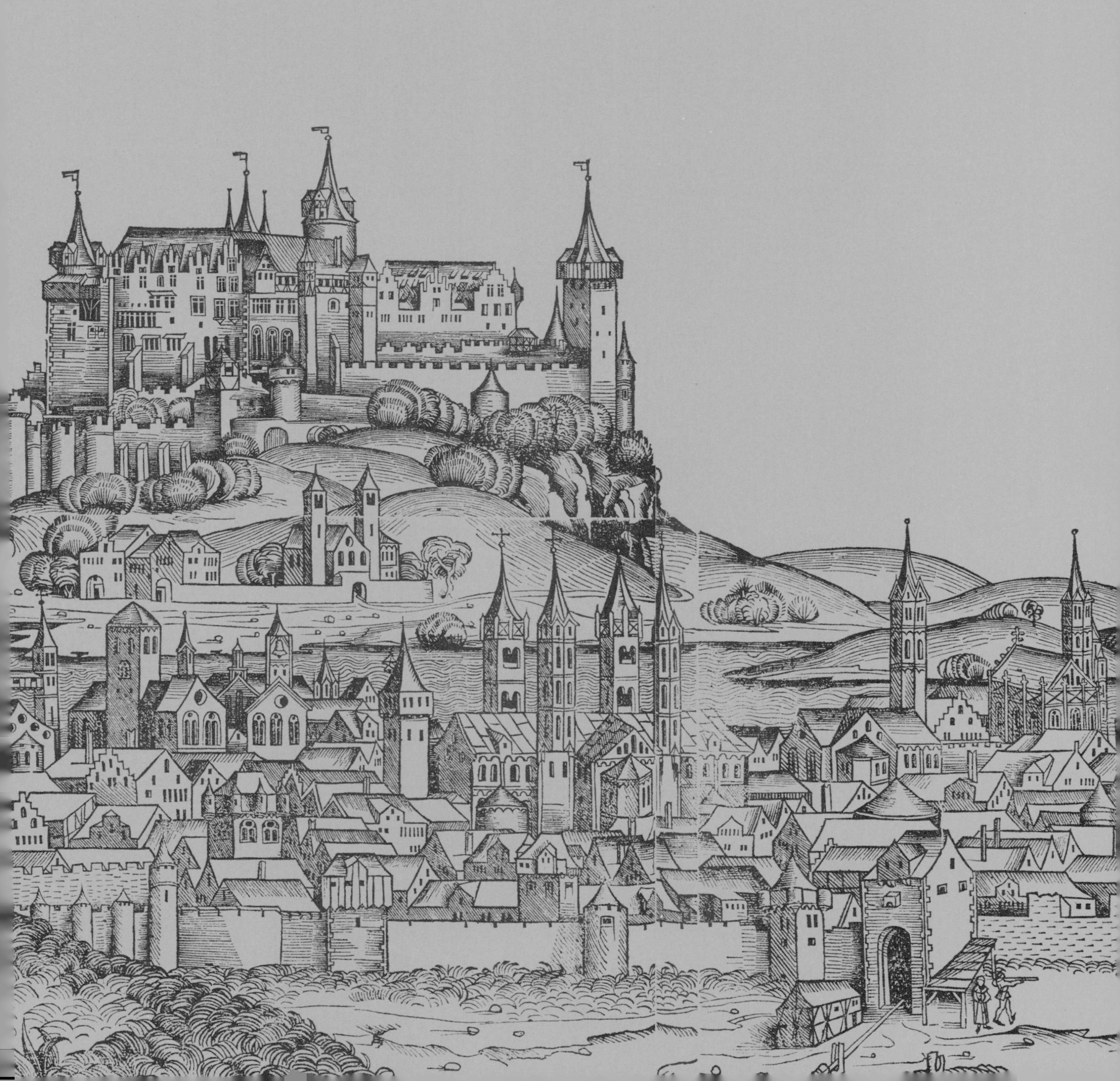

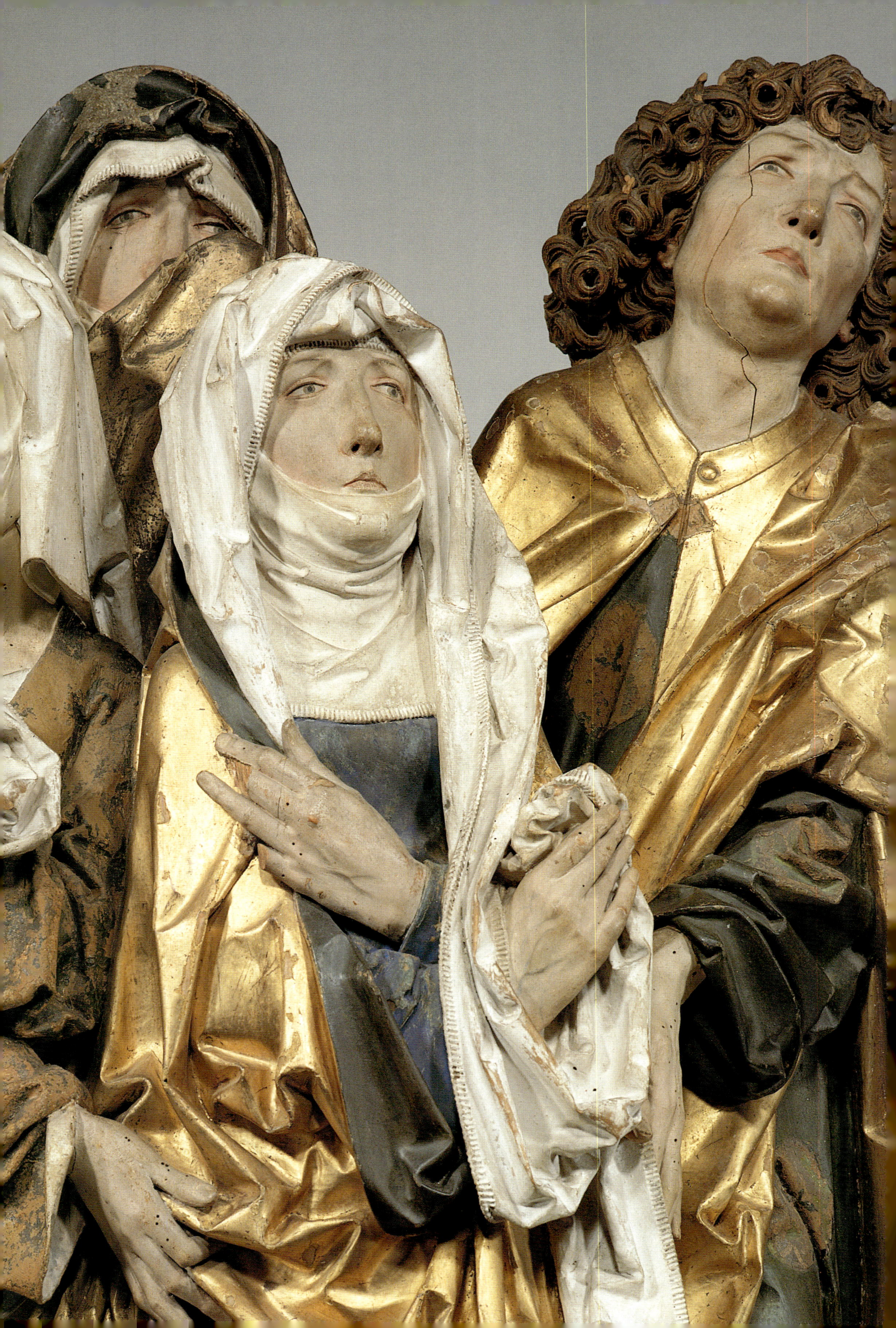

AN OVERWHELMING majority of objects in this exhibition catalogue are unpainted today, giving a deceptive impression of their original appearance and of medieval wooden sculpture in general. As is well known, most late Gothic sculpture, including many of the wooden figures by Tilman Riemenschneider and his workshop, was meant to be brightly colored, or polychromed; almost all, however, have experienced significant change over time. Polychrome sculpture was often repainted or even stripped of all of its decorative layers, revealing a surface that was never meant to be seen. But not all medieval sculpture was colorfully painted. Like several other sculptors of the period, Riemenschneider worked both in a traditional polychromatic style and in a technique known as monochromy, which is distinguished by a renunciation of naturalistic coloration. This essay examines the complexity of surface treatments on Riemenschneider's polychrome and monochrome sculpture and the changes they underwent in their subsequent histories. ❧ Although Riemenschneider worked with equal ease in wood and in stone[1] — including alabaster, marble, and sandstone — most of the works in this catalogue were carved in limewood, and my text consequently focuses on the sculptor's treatment of this material. Limewood, or linden *(Tilia cordata, T. platyphyllos),* is especially suitable for sculpture, since it shows no difference between spring and summer growth and has homogeneity in all directions, making it easier to carve than other woods, such as oak, with its pronounced ray structure. Limewood has a uniform, whitish gray to very pale red color, which deepens with age and exposure to light. Finished wood figures stood in shrines carved from a species of softwood, such as pine or spruce. Small-scale wooden

1. Bodo Buczynski and Artur Kratz, "Untersuchungen an Steinbildwerken Tilman Riemenschneiders," in *Tilman Riemenschneider. Frühe Werke* [exh. cat., Mainfränkisches Museum Würzburg] (Regensburg, 1981), 335–375.

2. See Thomas Brachert, "Fassung von Bildwerken," *Reallexikon zur deutschen Kunstgeschichte* (Munich, 1978–1979), 748–752.

3. Friedrich Kobler, "Fassung von Bildwerken II: Handwerk," *Reallexikon zur deutschen Kunstgeschichte* (Munich, 1981), 749.

4. Michael Baxandall, *The Limewood Sculptors of Renaissance Germany* (New Haven and London, 1980), 106; and Rainer Brandl, "Art or Craft?: Art and the Artist in Medieval Nuremberg," in *Gothic and Renaissance Art in Nuremberg 1300–1550* [exh. cat., The Metropolitan Museum of Art] (New York, 1986), 51–53.

sculpture, like the Vienna *Adam* (cat. 20), was fashioned from pearwood, an extremely fine grained material well suited to detail.

Who exactly painted these objects? The highly regulated guilds in medieval Europe dictated who had the right to paint sculpture, and this usually fell to painting studios, not sculpture workshops.[2] In fact, in the late Middle Ages the practical examination given to journeymen panel painters who applied for master status in certain cities included the task of painting sculpture *(Fassmalerei).*[3] Less frequently the sculptor was also the painter of the work, as was true with Veit Stoss' *Annunciation* in the Lorenzkirche in Nuremberg (fig. 1). This was possible because Stoss worked in a self-governed imperial city, where painting and sculpture were considered free arts and, though overseen by the city council, were not subject to guild regulations.[4] But neither Riemenschneider nor any member of his workshop executed the polychromy for the sculpture they carved. Thus Riemenschneider must have worked with a number of Franconian painters. A parchment inscription discovered in a cavity in the back of the *Crucifix* from Steinach (Chapuis essay, fig. 10) serves as a rare document of the division of labor between Riemenschneider and a painter, in this instance Johann Wagen-

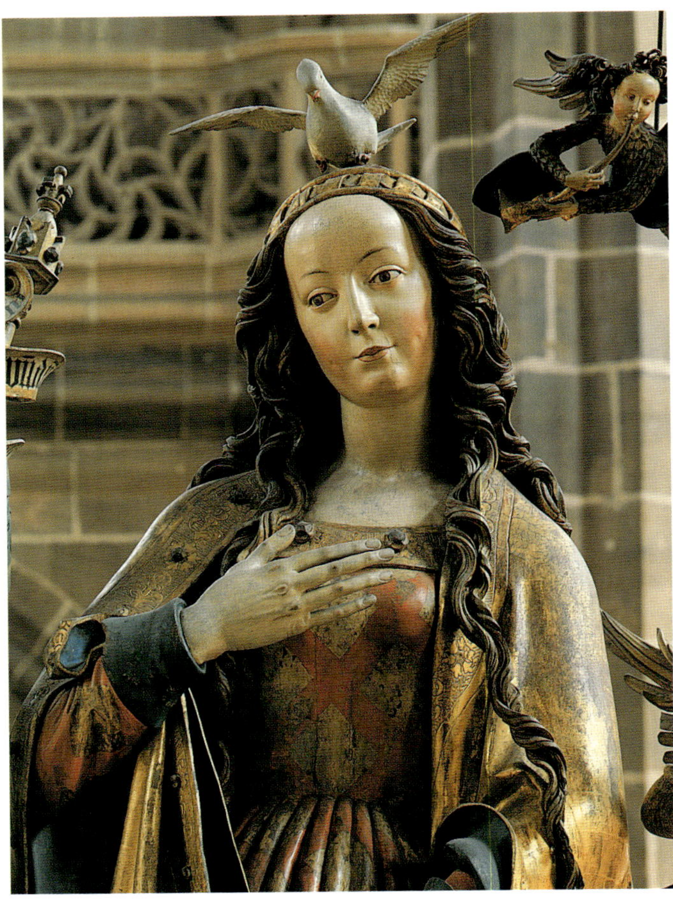

1.

Detail of the Virgin from Veit Stoss' *Annunciation,* 1518, limewood with original polychromy, Lorenzkirche, Nuremberg

knecht of Würzburg.[5] Similarities between details on panel paintings by Martin Schwarz (c. 1460–1511) and the same details on polychrome sculpture by Riemenschneider have led scholars to associate these two artists as well.[6] Schwarz, a monk in a Franciscan monastery in Rothenburg, was also master of an active painter's workshop in that city.

It is almost certainly the case that for retable sculpture intended to be left unpolychromed Riemenschneider and his workshop painted the eyes and lips directly on the wood surface. Exactly who finished the surfaces with transparent glazes is not recorded, but this important step was evidently completed on site once the sculpture was installed by the workshop within the shrine. The *Holy Blood* altarpiece in the Jakobskirche in Rothenburg (Chapuis essay, fig. 5) received its pigmented glaze after the installation of its figural sculpture, as is clear from the pooling of material at the juncture between figures and shrine.[7]

Between 1485 and 1490 Riemenschneider sculpted two extraordinarily well preserved painted figural groups from the Crucifixion scene of a *Passion* altarpiece now in the collection of the Bayerisches Nationalmuseum, Munich (Chapuis essay, fig. 2), which are among the most important extant early works by the artist.[8] The coloration is typical of late Gothic practice in southern Germany and, together with the painted decoration of the *Saint Stephen* and *Saint Lawrence* from the Cleveland Museum of Art and one of the female saints from Frankfurt (see cat. 32 A–D),[9] conveys a sense of the original appearance of Riemenschneider's polychrome works.

In contrast to Romanesque practice, Gothic sculptors usually finished the wood surface of their sculpture to a high degree, making the job of the painter that much easier, since less time had to be spent applying and carving ground layers.[10] Some preparation of the surface by the *Fassmaler* was nonetheless needed. Examination of the *Passion* altarpiece figures revealed that a glue sizing was first applied to the bare wood to close the pores and prevent paint media from penetrating the wood. Plant fibers (perhaps hemp) were adhered directly to the wood over joints and repairs to disguise join lines and to reduce the likelihood of cracks appearing later in paint layers. Patches of woven textile were used for the same purpose underneath the polychromy of the Cleveland Museum of Art's *Saint Lawrence*.[11] On top of these preparations came the white ground layer, a primary support for the metal leaf and paint. Late medieval ground layers typically consist of a white mineral pigment, usually chalk in northern Europe, bound with a water-soluble adhesive like animal glue. As on other south German late Gothic sculpture, the white ground layers seen on the Munich and Cleveland figures were unevenly applied—quite thickly under areas of gilding and quite thinly elsewhere. This was done for technical reasons, since burnishing gold leaf

5. See Justus Bier, *Tilmann Riemenschneider: Die späten Werke in Holz* (Vienna, 1978), 125.

6. Hartmut Krohm, "Martin Schwarz, der Fassmaler des Altares," and Eike Oellermann, "Die Bedeutung des Malers Martinus Schwarz im Frühwerk Riemenschneiders," in Würzburg 1981, 28–32 and 285–302.

7. See Eike Oellermann, "Die Restaurierung des Heilig-Blut-Altares von Tilman Riemenschneider," in 24. *Bericht des Bayerischen Landesamtes für Denkmalpflege 1965* (1966), 74–85, esp. 78.

8. Rainer Kahsnitz, *Tilman Riemenschneider. Zwei Figurengruppen unter dem Kreuz Christi*, Bayerisches Nationalmuseum (Munich, 1997). These works are the focus of a comprehensive technical examination by Axel Treptau, conservator, Bayerisches Nationalmuseum, Munich, and I am indebted to him for information included in this essay. A detailed technical publication is planned.

9. A preliminary technical study of the Cleveland saints was completed by the author in preparation for the exhibition. Thanks are due to Stephen Fliegel, assistant curator of medieval art, and to the staff of the conservation department, Cleveland Museum of Art. Technical information on the Frankfurt female saints is drawn from an examination report by Andrea Kleberger, completed in 1977.

10. Eike Oellermann, "Die spätgotische Skulptur und ihre Bemalung," in Würzburg 1981, 276.

11. Visible on the proper left sleeve of the white alb. This use of textile patches (*Kaschierungen*) is quite common for painted medieval sculpture. Also seen are pieces of recycled parchment and matted animal hair.

required a thicker ground as padding. On the other hand, a thick ground would obscure subtle finishing of the surface, thus areas of complex carving usually received a shallow preparation. The grassy knolls on which the Munich figures stand have a zigzag pattern *(Tremolierung),* and thin ground layers leave the deep carving visible. Final polishing of the ground was accomplished with fine abrasives and damp rags.[12]

The first areas completed after the application of ground layers were those to receive burnished metal leaf. The lavish use of gold leaf for draperies and shrine interiors is characteristic of late medieval polychromy. Late Gothic sculpture often exploited elaborate draperies, with numerous alternations between inner and outer sides of the garments. And by contrasting a burnished gold leaf outer side with a matte blue or enamel-like red lining, an artist heightened the legibility of these drapery patterns, particularly useful in the lighting conditions and viewing distances in churches. The *Fassmaler* might also choose from powdered gold, leaf or powdered silver, tin leaf, or a gold-silver laminate called *Zwischgold.*[13] Glazes applied over the various metals gave coloristic or textural effects and, in the case of silver, prevented tarnishing.[14] The leaf metal could be attached in a couple of ways. Laying the leaf on a ground of reddish clay and glue, called bole, allowed the metal to be burnished to a high gleam with an agate or a tooth. The outer sides of the cloaks of the *Passion* altarpiece figures, in excellent condition, shine with burnished gold leaf on a reddish brown bole, subtly textured with a silky wash of glue over the gold (see page 100).[15] Oil, or mordant, gilding produced a less metallic sheen, because the sticky, pigmented drying oil that attached the metal leaf did not permit burnishing. The preparatory layers, however, could be very thin and so would not mask detailed carving. The elaborate curls of the Cleveland saints are embellished in this fashion.[16]

The surfaces of the Munich, Frankfurt, and Cleveland figures bear generous amounts of silver leaf. While silver leaf was often used in the late Middle Ages in imitation of armor and weapons—as on the *Caiaphas* relief (fig. 2)—Riemenschneider's sculpture is noteworthy for the lavish application of this metal for the linings of the gilded robes. Red or green transparent glazes painted over the silver created a rich, enamel-like effect. Another metal leaf found on both the Munich and Cleveland figures is *Zwischgold,*[17] an extremely thin layer of gold beaten together with a thicker layer of silver leaf. The oxidation of the silver component of the laminate since the late fifteenth century makes this metal leaf appear dark today, but its original appearance was pale gold. *Zwischgold* broadened the palette of metallic color that the *Fassmaler* had at hand, and it was most likely used to create subtle differences from the gilded areas.[18] This may have been the intention in the hair of the Cleveland saints. The laminate also frequently appears in folds of gilded drapery hidden from direct view, as on the mantle

12. Elizabeth Krebs, Hans Westhoff, and Roland Hahn, "Werkzeuge und Materialien in den spätmittelalterlichen Werkstätten der Bildhauer, Schreiner und Maler," in *Meisterwerke Massenhaft. Die Bildhauerwerkstatt des Niklaus Weck- mann und die Malerei in Ulm um 1500* [exh. cat., Württembergisches Landesmuseum] (Stuttgart, 1993), 301–309.

13. See Thomas Brachert, "Die Techniken der polychromierten Holzskulptur," *Maltechnik-Restauro* (1972), 177–189.

14. That unprotected silver discolored was well known by Riemenschneider's day. See *On Divers Arts: The Treatise of Theophilus,* trans. John G. Hawthorne and Cyril Stanley Smith (Chicago, 1963), bk. 3, chap. 80, p. 158.

15. Kahsnitz 1997, 59.

16. Mark T. Wypyski, associate research scientist, Sherman Fairchild Center for Objects Conservation, The Metropolitan Museum of Art, identified *Zwischgold* on a ground pigmented with lead-tin yellow, using scanning electron microscopy/energy-dispersive spectroscopy (SEM/EDS).

17. Also called *Twistgold, gedeildes gold,* and *Gedeelt Golt;* see Hans Huth, *Künstler und Werkstatt der Spätgotik,* 2nd ed. (Darmstadt, 1967), 63.

18. Brachert 1972, 189.

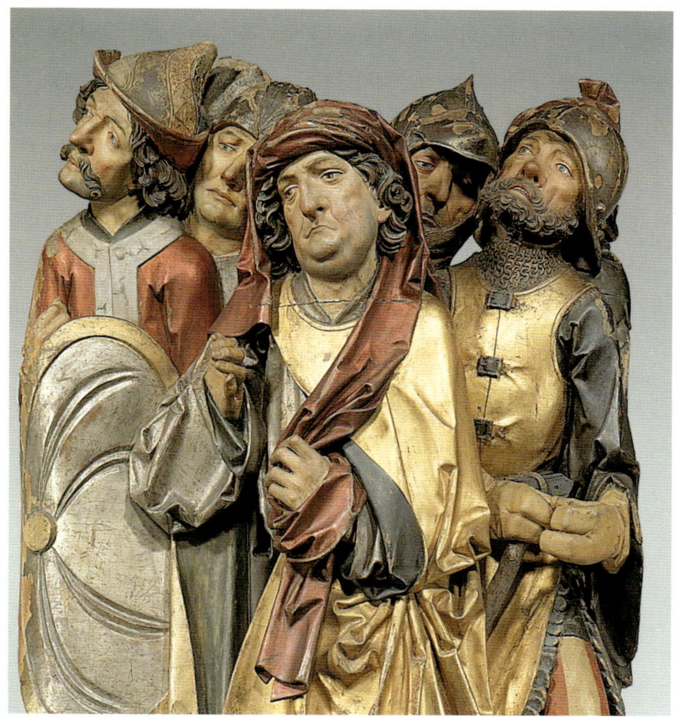

2.

Detail of *Caiaphas and His Soldiers*, c. 1485–1490, limewood with original polychromy,
Bayerisches Nationalmuseum, Munich (after treatment)

of the middle mourning woman in the Munich *Passion* relief, a figure mostly obscured by the Virgin and her companion (see page 100). This use suggests that an additional purpose was to save money, since the composite leaf was significantly less expensive than pure gold and darkened only over time. Its mention in medieval contracts in fact usually occurs in the context of its being forbidden as a substitute for real gold.[19]

Tin leaf in this period was a cheaper and more stable alternative to silver — or to gold, when glazed with yellow lake pigments. Tin also assumed an important role in the manufacture of prefabricated imitations of elaborate textile patterns called press brocades *(Pressbrokatapplikationen)*. To simulate costly Italian silks, a *Fassmaler* applied the low-relief press brocades to surfaces, either as contiguous sections in imitation of cut velvets or as patches on smooth-textured cloth (see fig. 1). These intricately detailed decorations can be difficult to appreciate today, for they are usually quite damaged because of the instability of the materials or misguided restoration. An artist made press brocades by pressing a piece of tin leaf into a wood or metal mold carved with the desired pattern, then backing it with a plastic fill material, either beeswax or a chalk-glue mixture.[20] He pulled the mass out of the mold, decorated the tin side further as desired with paint and gold leaf, and glued it to the painted surface of the sculpture. Since press-brocade molds seem to have belonged to the painter and to have been among the tools that remained in the workshop, they have been seen as a kind

19. See Huth 1967, 97–98 n. 116.

20. Fritz Buchenrieder, "Friedrich Herlins Nördlinger Hochaltar von 1462: Beschreibung der Fassung der Skulpturen, der Restaurierungsmassnahmen und Retuschen," in Johannes Taubert, *Farbige Skulpturen* (Munich, 1978), 158; Josephine A. Darrah, "White and Golden Tin Foil in Applied Relief Decoration," in *Looking Through Painting: The Study of Painting Techniques and Materials in Support of Art Historical Research*, ed. Erma Hermens (Baarn [The Netherlands] and London, 1998), esp. 60–77.

21. Thomas Brachert, "Press-brokatapplikationen, ein Hilfsmittel für die Stilkritik," *Jahresbericht des Schweizerischen Instituts für Kunstwissenschaft* (1963), 37–47; Oellermann in Würzburg 1981, 285–302; and Hans Westhoff et al., *Graviert, Gemalt, Gepresst: Spätgotische Retabelverzierungen in Schwaben,* Württembergisches Landesmuseum (Stuttgart, 1996), 26–28.

22. For a medieval recipe, see the *Liber Illuministerius* from Kloster Tegernsee, c. 1500, in Ernst Berger. *Quellen und Technik der Fresko-, Oel- und Tempera-Malerei des Mittelalters* (Munich, 1912), 182. There is also a recipe for press brocades (p. 196).

23. Identified by Mark T. Wypyski using SEM/EDS.

24. See also Robert Feller, "Barium Sulfate: Natural and Synthetic," in *Artists' Pigments: A Handbook of Their History and Characteristics,* vol. 1, ed. Robert Feller (Cambridge and Washington, DC, 1986), 47–64.

25. Cords noted by Annette Kollmann, private conservator, who completed an investigation of the figure in May 1998. Stephanie Kleidt, conservator, Mainfränkisches Museum, Würzburg, suggested the comparison with early sixteenth-century painting.

26. Oellermann in Würzburg 1981, 276–277.

of quasi signature for a specific artist.[21] Eike Oellermann has attributed the polychromy of the Munich figures to Martin Schwarz based on the similarity of its press-brocade patterns to those seen on his panel paintings.

Other materials applied to the surfaces of Riemenschneider's sculpture heighten the illusion of reality with three-dimensional effects. Stars or dots stamped out of gilded or silvered paper or parchment were sometimes affixed to the paint surface with animal glue.[22] The white alb of the Cleveland *Saint Lawrence,* for instance, was originally sprinkled with *Zwischgold*-covered paper dots.[23] Recent analysis has shown the white alb of the *Saint Stephen,* as well as the "gilded" dots with their fluted edges (fig. 3), to be the product of modern restoration. The metal leaf was identified as copper and zinc (brass), a common nineteenth-century substitute for gold leaf. And instead of the chalk white seen on *Saint Lawrence,* a mixture of lead white and barium sulfate was found on *Saint Stephen.* Barium sulfate was first distributed commercially between 1810 and 1820.[24]

The *Lüsterweibchen* from Ochsenfurt also bears traces of an applied ornament that imitated contemporary costume. Nearly covered by the early twentieth century overpaint, a few twisted fiber cords are still attached by tiny wooden dowels to the banded and puffed sleeves. These cords resembled those seen on the clothing of fashionably dressed women in paintings from the same period, where the black cording crossed over sections of white, puffed sleeves (see cat. 41).[25]

A distinctive feature of south German panel painting and polychrome sculpture in the second half of the fifteenth century is the use of pure color rather than pigments that have been mixed to obtain a desired hue.[26] Painters relied less on new materials than on a variety of techniques to create the increasingly illusionistic surfaces characteristic of the time. The choice of pigments was quite limited: opaque mineral reds such as vermilion and red lead, often with a translucent red glaze on top; mineral

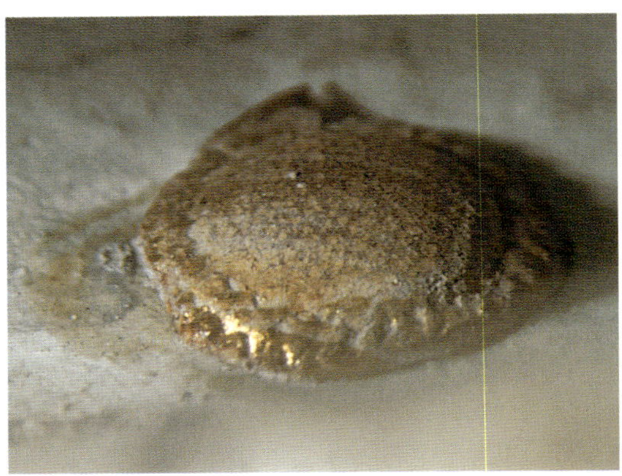

3.
Photomicrograph of nineteenth-century applied decoration on *Saint Stephen* (cat. 32A), The Cleveland Museum of Art

yellows including ochers and lead-tin yellow; copper greens and azurite blues, usually in two layers like the reds; brown ochers; black; and white, both lead white and chalk. Painters made their own paints in the workshop by adding pigments to various binding media, and these binders influenced the final appearance of the paint. Azurite and lead white, often bound in glue or gum, gave a very matte appearance, as in the blue and white layers of the Munich figures. To achieve an especially velvety texture, painters could scatter coarsely ground azurite on the surface of the wet glue. They could create lustrous effects by using linseed oil as the binder or by layering glazes over opaque colors or metal leaf. Glazes consist of mixtures of colorants, pine resin, and drying oils. Both inorganic and organic materials supplied color. Copper salts, for instance, tinted a translucent green glaze called copper resinate. The sources for red colorants to make translucent glazes were usually the same materials that provided dyestuffs for cloth in the Middle Ages. These dyes derive from the extracts of plants (such as madder root, *Rubia tinctorum*) or insects (like kermes, *Kermes vermilio* Planchon or lac, *Kerria lacca* Kerr) and are fixed onto a white substrate to form what is known as a lake pigment.[27] The colorant of the red glaze on the Munich reliefs has been identified as kermes.

Perhaps the most daring attempts at illusionism by south German *Fassmaler* involved painting faces. By exploiting the translucency, gloss, and malleability of oil paint, artists created strikingly lifelike images. They subtly blended the stubble of beards onto chins, particularly for mature men such as the Munich *Caiaphas* (see fig. 2). They even rendered facial hair plastically by pressing the wooden end of a brush into the still-soft paint. They painted tendrils of hair spilling onto foreheads, as seen on both the Cleveland and the Munich figures. Direct observation from nature is especially evident in the variations of skin tones. Artists imitated flesh tones by mixing white with red pigments; they reserved ruddier tones for male skin. The figure of Christ on the cross was depicted with green or blue tinges around the edges of red wounds to evoke in grisly fashion the pallor of dead flesh. Artists also rendered eyes in a startlingly naturalistic manner, in contrast to the earlier practice of simply painting them as flat circles of color. By the late fifteenth century artists were painting reflections in the eyes to suggest the surroundings of the sculpture. The way in which these reflections were depicted may be distinctive of a particular painter's workshop. The eyes of the *Saint Lawrence* (fig. 4), for instance, and also of the female saints in Frankfurt,[28] show two dots of white in a grayish brown iris balanced by a half-moon of white under the pupil. These are identical to eyes found on panel paintings by Martin Schwarz (fig. 5), suggesting that this painter or his workshop was responsible for the polychromy of the sculpture.[29] Yet the eyes of the figures in the Munich reliefs, whose polychromy is also attributed to Schwarz, are enlivened in a different way.[30]

27. Inken Stössel, *Rote Farblacke in der Malerei: Herstellung und Verwendung im deutschsprachigen Raum zwischen ca. 1400 und 1850* (Stuttgart, 1985); Jo Kirby, David Saunders, and John Cupitt, "Colorants and Colour Change," *Early Italian Paintings, Techniques and Analysis,* ed. Tonnie Bakkenist et al. (Maastricht [The Netherlands], 1997), 65–71.

28. First suggested by Andrea Kleberger; see Krohm in Würzburg 1981, 32 n. 5.

29. See also the eyes of the kings in the *Three Kings* panel of the Liebfrauen altarpiece in Rothenburg (Germanisches Nationalmuseum, Nuremberg).

30. An initial comparison of paint cross sections from the Munich and Cleveland sculpture revealed little similarity in painting technique.

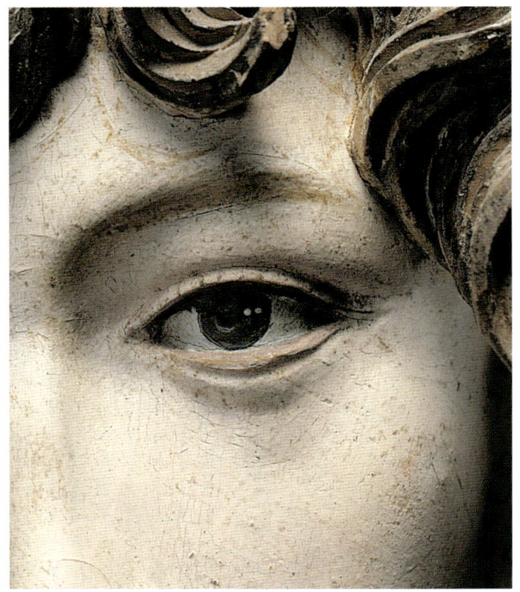
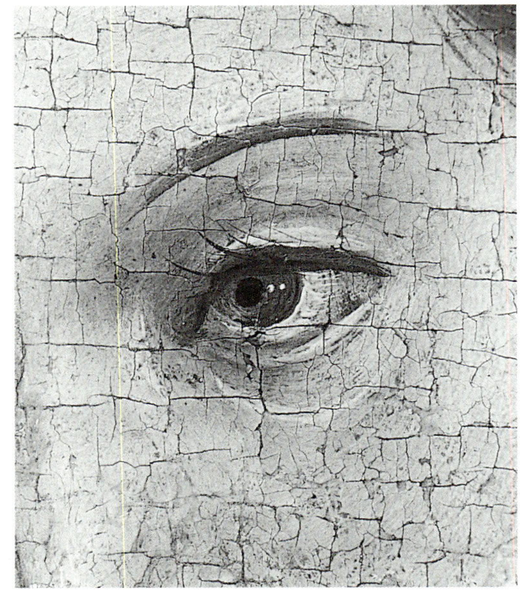

4.
Left eye of *Saint Lawrence* (cat. 32 D), The Cleveland
Museum of Art

5.
Left eye of Martin Schwarz' *Saint Apollonius*, c. 1485, panel
painting, Mainfränkisches Museum, Würzburg

31. Karl Bauer, "Der Marienaltar in der Hergottskirche bei
Creglingen," *Wirttembergisch
Franken. Zeitschrift des historischen Vereins für das Wirttembergische Franken* 6 (1863),
312–313. Till-Holger Borchert
brought this reference to
my notice.

32. Oellermann 1966, 75–85.

33. Taubert 1978, 73–88. Hans
Westhoff has proposed an alternate scheme based on regional
differences: "Holzsichtige
Skulpturen aus Ulm und Oberschwaben," in *Sculptures
médiévales allemandes: Conservation et restauration,* Colloquium,
Musée du Louvre (Paris, 1992),
393–418, esp. 402.

As early as 1863 Karl Bauer recognized that medieval altarpieces were occasionally left uncolored, when he described Riemenschneider's *Assumption of the Virgin*
altarpiece in Creglingen as unpainted (*unbemalt*) and compared it to his monochromatic
Holy Blood altarpiece in Rothenburg. Exactly what kind of surface the writer saw is
not clear, but he believed the *Assumption* altarpiece (Chapuis essay, fig. 7) had been intentionally finished without color.[31] Although since that time a number of scholars
have taken up the subject of Riemenschneider and monochromy, in 1966 Oellermann
was the first to publish the observation that the sculptor's surfaces were not left raw
but were finished with a translucent coating that allowed the wood to remain visible.[32]
In fact numerous late medieval south German sculptors practiced variant modes of
monochromy. Veit Stoss, Hans Leinberger, Niclaus Weckmann, Jörg Syrlin the Younger,
Daniel Mauch, and Henrik Douvermann, among others, all produced works that
rejected color in favor of an obvious wood finish, often in combination with rich surface elaboration.

Johannes Taubert has proposed the classification of monochromes in three categories: unpolychromed altarpieces, envisioned without color except for the eyes and
lips; half-painted, where flesh tones and garments are colored; and partly painted,
where color is restricted to backgrounds or attributes.[33] This terminology has led to
much debate in Germany. "Unpolychromed" describes what a work is not, not what
it is. But such works cannot be called "wood-colored," either, for they are not painted
to imitate a particular wood; nor can they be called "unpainted," for they are embel-

lished with limited amounts of color. They are simply not brightly colored. *Holzsichtig,* a term proposed by several German scholars, is perhaps most accurate. But the English translation—"that allows the wood to be seen"—is awkward. For the purposes of style, therefore, the term "monochromy" will be used in this text.[34]

New findings have augmented the significant research on Riemenschneider's monochrome sculpture undertaken in preparation for the seminal 1981 exhibition in Würzburg. It was thought, for instance, that Riemenschneider's 1490–1492 *Magdalen* altarpiece in Münnerstadt (see cat. 13) was the first monochrome retable created in south Germany. With the publication of the examination results of the sculpture over the high altar of 1483 in Sankt Martin in Lorch am Rhein, however, and the recent discovery of the 1474 contract for the shrine of the high altar in Ulm Minster (destroyed in 1531),[35] two earlier monochrome retables are recognized. Several well-documented works by Riemenschneider in addition to the Münnerstadt altarpiece also seem to have been conceived without polychromy: the *Holy Blood* altarpiece in Rothenburg, the *Assumption of the Virgin* altarpiece in Creglingen, the *Crucifixion* altarpiece now in Detwang (cat. 33, fig. 2), three groups created for the Windsheim parish church, and individual figures such as the *Crucifix* from Eisingen (Krohm essay, fig. 14). Additional works attributed to Riemenschneider or his workshop may originally have been monochromes, depending on technical readings described below.

A towering work presented almost entirely without color, the *Holy Blood* altarpiece in Rothenburg is so radical a departure from what came before that scholars are still grappling with its significance. Some believe that monochrome sculpture was made because master sculptors did not want their virtuoso carving obscured by a painter's work.[36] But it is likely that the choice of decorative mode lies at least partly with the patron. (Like most medieval artists, Riemenschneider had only limited control over many aspects of the contract, including central issues such as the iconographical program.) Other scholars believe that monochrome works represented a kind of revolution in style that must have its basis in pre-Reformation religious unrest.[37] Still others contend that monochromy did not exist as an artistic alternative but that unpolychromed works are actually only unfinished ones, that traditional painting had been intended but never carried out.[38] In fact we know that some sculptors purposefully rejected polychromy. Andreas Stoss, the son of sculptor Veit Stoss, left clear instructions that his father's last work, a monochrome altarpiece now in Bamberg, should remain unpainted.[39] Sometimes monochromy may be inferred from the presence of highly detailed surface decoration that would have been obscured by even a thin ground.[40] Yet no contemporary written document has been found that specifies monochromy for Riemenschneider's sculpture, and the surfaces of his works are seldom elaborately

34. The literature is extensive and includes important contributions by Taubert, Oellermann, and Westhoff. For a recent discussion see Barbara Rommé, "Holzsichtigkeit und Fassung," in *Gegen den Strom. Meisterwerke niederrheinischer Skulptur in Zeiten der Reformation* [exh. cat., Suermondt-Ludwig-Museum] (Aachen, 1996), 97–99.

35. Eike Oellermann, "Der Hochaltar in Sankt Martin zu Lorch am Rhein," in *Flügelaltäre des späten Mittelalters,* ed. Hartmut Krohm and Eike Oellermann (Berlin, 1992), 9–22. And Gerhard Weilandt, "Der wiederaufgefundene Vertrag Jörg Syrlins des Älteren über das Hochaltarretabel des Ulmer Münsters. Zum Erscheinungsbild des frühesten holzsichtigen Retabels," *Zeitschrift für Kunstgeschichte* 59 (1996), 437–460.

36. Huth 1967, 57–58; Taubert 1978, 74.

37. Jörg Rosenfeld, *Die nichtpolychromierte Retabelskulptur als bildreformerisches Phänomen im ausgehenden Mittelalter und in der beginnenden Neuzeit* (Ammersbek bei Hamburg, 1990); Jörg Rosenfeld, "Die nichtpolychromierte Retabelskulptur als bildreformerisches Phänomen im ausgehenden Mittelalter und in der beginnenden Neuzeit," in Krohm and Oellermann 1992, 65–83.

38. Hubert Wilm, *Die gotische Holzfigur,* 4th ed. (Stuttgart, 1944), 78; Walter Paatz, *Süddeutsche Schnitzaltäre der Spätgotik* (Heidelberg, 1963), 81; Hartmut Boockmann, "Bemerkungen zu den nichtpolychromierten Holzbildwerken des ausgehenden Mittelalters," *Zeitschrift für Kunstgeschichte* 57 (1994), 330–335.

39. R. Schaffer, *Andreas Stoss* (Breslau, 1926), 362; and Baxandall 1980, 48, 274.

40. See works by Leinberger or Douvermann, as discussed in Taubert 1978, 73–88.

textured. We are left, then, to deduce the original appearance from traces of materials or methods on the works themselves.

It is difficult to determine the original appearance of a work of art, and it is especially problematic to identify a sculpture as a monochrome. The transparent glazes central to the idea of monochromy consist of materials that are sensitive to common cleaning agents, thus are usually preserved only in traces, and these traces are often so altered by later treatments that any definitive statement is impossible. In the case of the Creglingen altarpiece, for example, a series of restoration campaigns stripped off the original glazes and impregnated the wood with materials meant to prevent insect attack.[41] These actions enormously complicate any scientific analysis that might take place. Monochrome glazes, even if present, may also be difficult to distinguish from wood sealant applied before ground and paint layers. In addition, the medieval sculptors' practice of painting the eyes directly on the wood during carving, perhaps as a working method to establish the gaze,[42] easily gives the mistaken impression of the finished eyes of a monochrome. Such eyes can be seen on Riemenschneider's *Saint George and the Dragon* (cat. 18), which was originally polychromed.

Our conception of Riemenschneider's monochromes is based on the present appearance of certain works, in particular the *Holy Blood* altarpiece, and on the analysis of components of the glaze. The *Holy Blood* altarpiece underwent a technical examination and treatment by Eike Oellermann in the early 1960s. Although the sculpture had been stained and waxed during routine housekeeping in the church, it was never brightly painted, and thus has existed as a monochrome for nearly five hundred years.

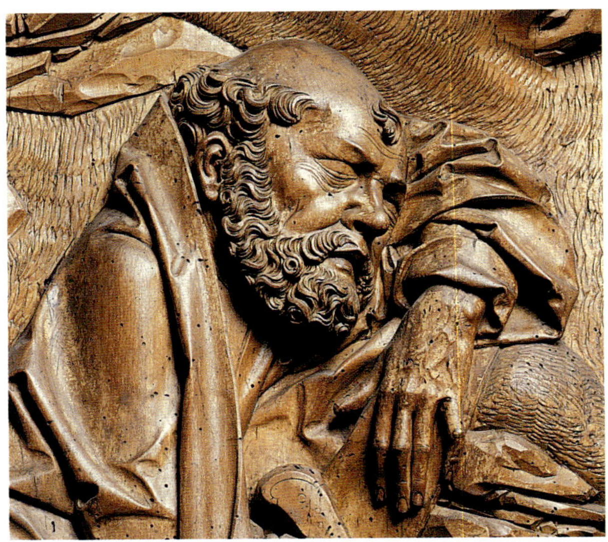

6.
Detail of Saint Peter with monochrome glaze missing from hand, *Holy Blood* altarpiece, 1500–1504, limewood, Jakobskirche, Rothenburg

Both the limewood figures and the shrine and foliate ornaments of spruce had originally been coated with a pigmented glaze made up of egg white and oils (egg tempera?) with ocher, charcoal, gypsum, and lead white (perhaps as a drying agent). This
glaze was found directly on the wood over the painted eyes and lips, and it appears to
have been applied in several layers in certain areas, perhaps to heighten the modeling
of the surface. The paler color of the limewood is visible in areas where the glaze is
missing (fig. 6). Lips were toned directly on the wood with madder lake, and the drops
of blood in the relief of *Christ on the Mount of Olives* were painted in vermilion and
lead-tin yellow. There was no trace of a dirt or dust layer beneath the pigmented glaze,
and later additions to the altarpiece bear no sign of the coating, indicating that the
glaze must have been applied shortly after the sculpting of the figures.[43]

Similar egg-based glazes have been identified on other works by Riemenschneider, including the Eisingen *Crucifix* and the Detwang *Crucifixion*.[44] A different glaz-
ing material seems to have been used on his Münnerstadt altarpiece. In an investigation of 1977/1978 traces of a pigmented surface coating were found on many of the
individual figures belonging to this retable. The glaze was described as consisting of a
protein (animal glue) and a tiny amount of oil, binding together black particles (charcoal), red or yellow oxides, and some lead white. Painted directly on the wood beneath
the glaze, the eyes (irises, pupils, folds of the eyes, and eyebrows) were rendered in
black, and the mouths in red. Elsewhere the glaze had penetrated deeply into the pores
of the wood and exhibited few characteristics of a discreet layer.[45]

Techniques available for media analysis have improved greatly since the 1960s
and 1970s,[46] and earlier analyses are currently being reevaluated. It is now thought that
the detection of a small amount of oil in the samples from the Münnerstadt and
Rothenburg altarpieces could be due to contamination from later treatments.[47] The
evidence nevertheless suggests that more than one type of quick-drying, translucent
material was applied to the raw surfaces of wood sculpture, including egg, animal glue,
and plant gums.[48] It also seems clear that the glazes were intentionally tinted with a
limited range of pigments, suggesting that these were standard additives. The consistency of the evidence argues against an accidental source for the pigments, such as a
dirty brush, which would have introduced a random number of materials. A translucent, pigmented glaze makes good sense for aesthetic and practical reasons: it gives a
finished appearance to the work, imparts a greater continuity to an altarpiece com-
posed of different species of woods,[49] and seals pores from dust particles.

Monochrome works by other medieval artists have coatings that consist chiefly
of animal glue without colorants,[50] though recent analysis of the coating on the altarpiece in Saint Martin at Lorch am Rhein suggests that a material similar to a penetrating

43. Oellermann 1966, 78.

44. See Ernst Metzl and Fritz
Buchenrieder, "Der Eisinger
Kruzifixus von Tilman Riemenschneider," *Jahrbuch der Bayerischen Denkmalpflege* 34 (1980),
89–110; and Eike Oellermann
and Karin Oellermann, "Das
Detwanger Retabel und sein
Detail," in *Der Detwanger Altar
von Tilman Riemenschneider*
(Wiesbaden, 1996), 13–44.

45. Oellermann in Würzburg
1981, 318.

46. See R. H. De Silva, "The
Problem of the Binding Medium
Particularly in Wall Paintings,"
Archaeometry 6 (1963), 56–64.

47. Personal communication,
Eike Oellermann, October 1998.
My sincere thanks are due to
Mr. Oellermann for his helpful
discussions during the prepara-
tion of this essay.

48. Michele Marincola, Jack
Soultanian, and Richard Newman, "Untersuchung eines
nichtpolychromierten Holzbildwerkes in The Cloisters:
Identifizierung einer ursprünglichen Oberfläche," *Zeitschrift
für Kunsttechnologie und Konservierung* 11 (1997), 238–248.

49. Limewood is typically pale
white in color, while spruce can
be much redder in tone; see
Oellermann 1966, 79–80; and
Taubert 1978, 77.

50. Hans Westhoff, "Holzsichtige
Skulptur aus der Werkstatt
des Niklaus Weckmann," in
Stuttgart 1993, 135–145. Myriam
Serck-Dewaide, "La Vierge à
l'Enfant de Berselius par Daniel
Mauch," in Louvre colloquium
1992, 385–389.

51. Oellermann 1992, 12. It is
not possible to be more exact
in describing this material,
since details of the completed
analysis are not given.

52. Taubert 1978, 89–96.

53. Taubert 1978, 74–75.

54. Round pieces of wood in
imitation of pearls were attached
either with glue or were stuck
on with tiny wooden pins (see
the Munich *Saint James* [cat. 31],
where only the pins remain).

55. A third figure from the
same group, the *Saint Elizabeth
of Hungary* (cat. 43 B), lacks
punch work decoration.

56. Another fragment from this
altarpiece, *Anne and Her Three
Husbands* (see cat. 36, fig. 1),
bears two different Maltese-
cross-shaped punch marks, used
with particular richness on the
edges and belts of the garments.

stain (perhaps based on plant extracts) was used to tint the surface of the wood, followed by a sealing layer of oil and protein.[51] More distinctive, as compared to Riemenschneider, is the complexity of decorative surface carving, particularly in the Ulm/Swabian, Lower Rhine, and Danube schools. The Castulus reliefs by Hans Leinberger, for example, are embellished by twenty-three different decorative punches.[52]

The rejection of color in figural sculpture results in a certain loss of naturalism, since verisimilitude is no longer possible in depicting human features or clothing. Taking the place of color is an increased exploration of texture. Ernst Willemsen noted close parallels between the use of color to distinguish sculptural form and the use of detailed surface carving on monochrome sculpture to differentiate flesh from drapery or figure from background.[53] Riemenschneider, like Stoss, was particularly adept at achieving this definition with a limited number of tools. In his *Noli me Tangere* relief from Münnerstadt (cat. 13 F) the richly patterned background of *tremoliert* landscape offers a dramatic contrast to the somber folds of drapery on the Magdalen and Christ.

Riemenschneider often finished drapery edges on both relief and three-dimensional sculpture with a running pattern of half-moon shapes carved into the wood with a chisel, sometimes augmented with applied wooden ornaments such as ersatz jewels[54] or, more rarely, with punch work. Unlike other artists of this genre, however, he only occasionally exploited tool marks for their coloristic effects. He evoked textiles with pattern, such as fine stippling in imitation of velvet. He decorated attributes and borders of garments with lines, vines, or diamonds cut into the wood with knives or chisels, combined with marks made by a shaped punch that was repeatedly struck into the wood. One female saint (fig. 7) preserves nine different tool marks, including three types of punches (a star, a flower, and a circle). A figure originally from the same altarpiece, the *Saint Catherine* (cat. 43 C), is similarly adorned with a combination of carved and punched work.[55] *Mary Salome and Zebedee,* a fragment of the *Holy Kinship* altarpiece (cat. 36 B), is ornamented with a Maltese-cross-shaped punch and carved half-moons.[56] The *Virgin and Child* from Dumbarton Oaks (cat. 45) bears faint impressions of a flower-shaped punch in the border of the Virgin's cloak.

The richness of the surface embellishment of these figures is comparable to the decoration of known monochromes by Riemenschneider. The Münnerstadt altarpiece displays five different patterns, including a circular punch on the bishop's miter in the reliefs; and the Creglingen altarpiece exhibits eight kinds of tool marks, including two punches—a Maltese cross and a circle (fig. 8). The punch had a long tradition of use in the decoration of areas of gilding on panel paintings and sculpture. Sometimes the blow of the mallet struck the punch so hard that it penetrated both gold and ground, leaving an impression in the wood below. These marks, when revealed by gilding losses,

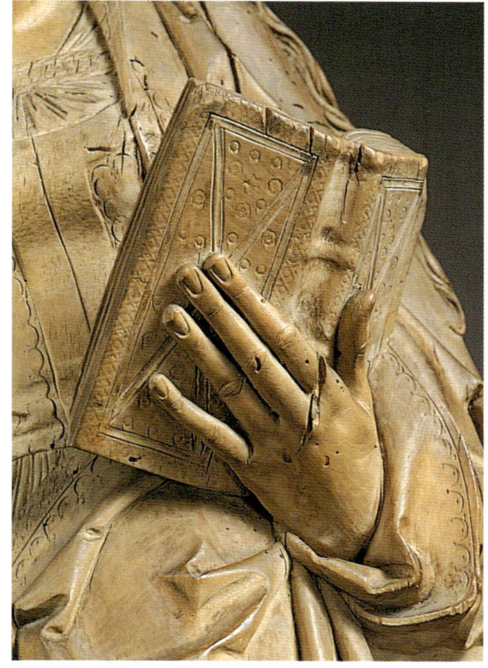

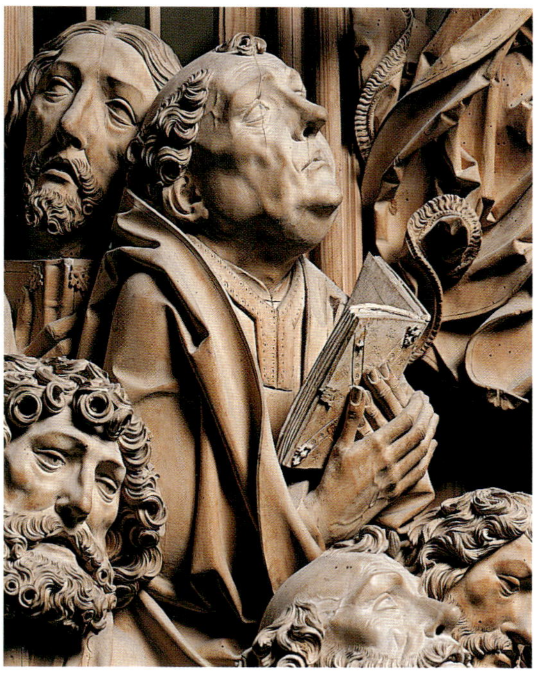

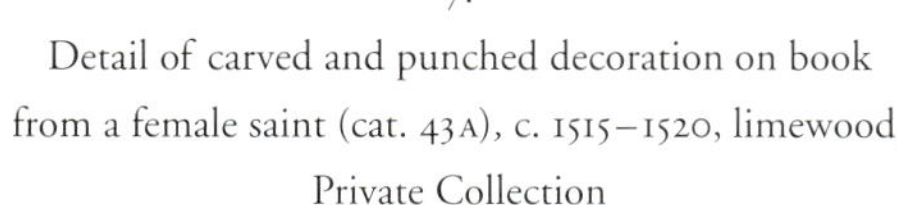

<table>
<tr><td align="center">7.
Detail of carved and punched decoration on book
from a female saint (cat. 43A), c. 1515–1520, limewood,
Private Collection</td><td align="center">8.
Detail of punched decoration from the Assumption of
the Virgin altarpiece, c. 1505–1510, limewood, Herrgottskirche,
Creglingen</td></tr>
</table>

may be confused with punch work applied on a monochrome surface. But only simple forms seem to leave a clear mark; more complex shapes like stars and rosettes do not make a distinct impression when struck through the usual thick ground.[57] For this reason, clear impressions from a shaped punch (particularly if it matches one seen on documented works) may be taken as an indication that the sculpture was originally a monochrome.

The best preserved of Riemenschneider's wooden sculpture, such as the Munich *Passion* figures, are those that have been largely protected from excessive light, humidity fluctuations, and insect attack. Paint can change in appearance, often radically, by darkening or bleaching, depending on its components and surrounding environment. Glazes are especially susceptible to discoloration: the copper resinate green applied over the silver leaf on the *Passion* figures is quite brown today, a typical change seen with this material.[58] The reds on these figures and on the Cleveland saints, however, are still brilliant, a somewhat unusual survival since red glazes will often fade with exposure to light. Monochromes also change. Although the *Holy Blood* altarpiece is probably close to its original appearance at the beginning of the sixteenth century, the oxidation of the wood and original coatings, as well as certain light-induced changes, have darkened the surface. We cannot in fact be certain of how this and other monochromes originally looked. And most of Riemenschneider's sculpture is considerably more altered in appearance than these well-preserved examples.

57. Taubert 1978, 89–96, esp. 93.

58. The most recent discussion of the phenomenon of copper resinate browning is by Renate Woudhuysen-Keller and Paul Woudhuysen, "'Copper Resinate' and Its Colour Changes," in Hermens 1998, 133–146. See note 20 above.

In addition, all of Riemenschneider's works have undergone restoration—many before the restorers recognized the existence of a transparent glaze. The *Assumption* altarpiece in Creglingen survived the iconoclasm of the Reformation only to have its original surface damaged through a series of misguided treatments. Although this altarpiece has never undergone a thorough technical examination, it is clear from its white and roughened surface that it has been harshly cleaned. On the backs of the figures numerous, faint inscriptions dating from 1550 to the present document the signatures of carpenters and painters who had evidently been hired to carry out restoration work; some had even written brief descriptions of their treatments.[59] The Detwang *Crucifixion* altarpiece bears a similar record in the hollowed reverse of the mourning women, where a pencil notation identifies "Franz Pauli aus Reichenhall 1896." Pauli, an artist active in several restorations in Rothenburg at the time, added neo-Gothic elements and made some repairs to the figures; he also applied a dark linseed oil varnish to the surface of the entire altarpiece, which has deteriorated into an opaque, blackish layer with a crusty, wrinkled finish. In applying such a varnish to monochrome wooden sculpture, the restorer probably had in mind many of the furnishings in the Jakobskirche in Rothenburg (including the *Holy Blood* altarpiece), which had all been restored with a dark oil varnish.[60] This taste for dark surfaces is in keeping with late nineteenth-century restoration practice in both monument offices and museums.

In contrast to panel paintings, sculpture was often repainted frequently, either because styles had changed and those responsible for the care of the works wanted to update the colors, or because the condition of the surface was damaged and restoration involved repainting. Overpainting sometimes closely followed the historical precedent. The *Saint Stephen* from Cleveland, for instance, received new polychromy that imitated that of the *Saint Lawrence* so nearly that it included "gilded" paper dots as part of the decoration. And Riemenschneider's *Mourning Virgin* in the collection of the Mainfränkisches Museum, Würzburg, has an overpaint of indeterminate date that is nevertheless sympathetic to the original scheme. The gray oil paint on the outer side of the cloak is probably an interpretation of the dirty original, as the grayish brown layer on the undergarment is evocative of a damaged or thinned azurite blue.[61]

Even a number of Riemenschneider's monochromes were painted at some point after their installation in a church. The most famous of these is the Münnerstadt altarpiece, delivered in 1492 as a monochrome and painted by Veit Stoss between 1504 and 1505 at the request of the town council. We do not know the reasons for the change, but the council had been contracting with a painter as early as 1497 "zu malen, zuuergulden vnd ausszufassen" (to paint, gild, and fully decorate) the altarpiece.[62] Later overpaint was removed in the course of restoration campaigns in this century, and the

---

59. See Simon 1998, 60.

60. Oellermann and Oellermann 1996, 15–16.

61. Oellermann and Oellermann, unpublished conservation treatment report, Mainfränkisches Museum Würzburg, 1998.

62. See Krohm and Oellermann 1992, 94; and Würzburg 1981, 117.

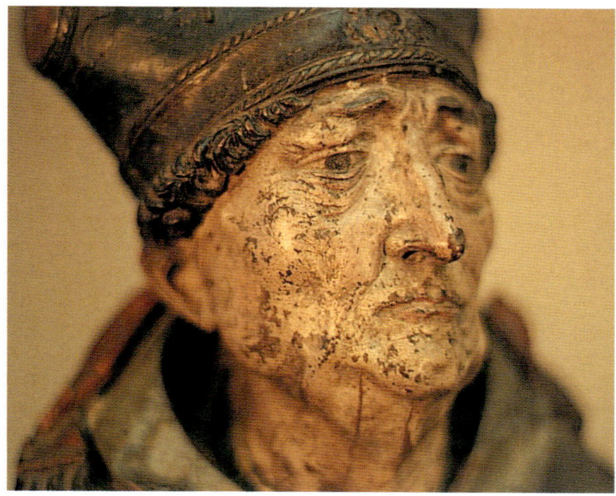

9.
Head of *Seated Bishop* (cat. 17), c. 1495, before
removal of modern overpaint, The Metropolitan Museum of Art,
New York, The Cloisters Collection

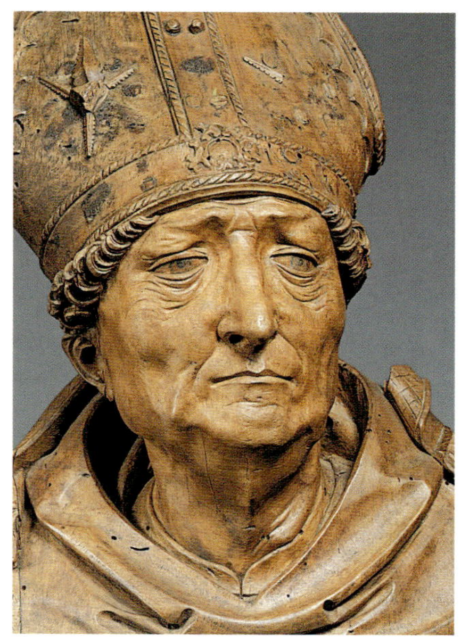

10.
Head of *Seated Bishop* after removal
of modern overpaint

figures were reinstalled on a new high altar in the church between 1978 and 1981.[63] The *Seated Bishop* from the Cloisters (cat. 17) had also been painted. When the sculpture entered the museum's collection in 1972, it still bore extensive passages of oil paint that were clearly post-Gothic in date: the repainting was coarsely executed and filled in losses and insect holes (fig. 9). The overpaint did protect traces of earlier layers, and conservator Rudolf Meyer found remains of a brown coating directly on the wood that could be an original monochrome glaze.[64] The delicate carving, particularly in the face, as well as certain technical details also suggested that the figure was probably originally monochromatic in finish.[65] On the basis of these findings, the oil paint was removed during treatment (fig. 10).

A host of sculpture was stripped of its original polychromy in the nineteenth century, often by immersion in lye (sodium hydroxide) or by applying a paste of a similar caustic solution. Although such chemical means are effective for paint removal, they also attack the wood fiber, stripping essential oils that lubricate and color the wood. Any alkali left behind will dessicate the wood, causing fine surface cracking (see fig. 7). Since chemical stripping leaves the surface of the wood raw and damaged, stains and waxes were often applied to restore color and shine, inviting a recleaning when these materials, in turn, darkened over time. The reasons for such aggressive action lie in a nineteenth-century antipathy toward color in sculpture, a consequence of neo-classical taste for "honesty toward the material"; this notion ennobled bare wood and rendered polychromy undesirable.[66] Many painted figures, such as the Berlin *Saint*

63. Würzburg 1981, 165–166.

64. Rudolf Meyer, unpublished conservation report, departmental files, The Cloisters, 1972. Surface treatments applied to saturate the wood after paint removal make an identification of the original layer difficult.

65. Charles E. von Nostitz, "Two Unpolychromed Riemenschneiders at The Cloisters," *Metropolitan Museum Journal* 10 (1975), 51–62.

66. Paul Philippot, "La Restauration des sculptures polychromes: introduction historique," *Restauratorenblätter* 18 (1998), 23–30.

67. Würzburg 1981, 170.

68. Rommé 1996, 97

I would like to thank my colleagues at The Metropolitan Museum of Art, Dr. George Wheeler and Dr. Julien Chapuis, for reading a first draft of this article and making suggestions.

George, had their original polychromy removed in an effort to bring the object closer to an ideal image. The *Saint John the Baptist* from Hassfurt (Chapuis essay, fig. 1) is documented as being stripped of its nonoriginal polychromy in 1889 for a different reason: the sculpture was to be given a new coat of paint, and the removal of older layers results in better attachment of the new paint to the wood.[67]

One of the challenges in examining Riemenschneider's sculpture today is to determine, when possible, if a figure was intended to be monochromatic or if original layers of polychromy have been removed. To determine whether the artist finished polychromes differently from monochromes, it is most important to consider his entire oeuvre,[68] but so few polychrome works exist that it is difficult to identify standard practice. In addition, his sculpture has undergone so much restoration that determining an original layer can prove a frustrating task. Nevertheless, certain details help distinguish one type from the other. The presence of aged, parallel scratches over old repairs in the surface of a work suggests that the sculpture was originally painted; such scratches gave increased purchase for the adhesion of a cloth patch over workshop repairs, areas that were then covered by layers of ground and paint. The *Saint Anne* from Munich (cat. 30) is an example. A dearth of detailed carving may indicate that a sculpture was meant to be painted, but this is not definitive, for Riemenschneider seldom gave his figures elaborately textured surfaces. Open insect channels running parallel to the surface identify a sculpture as having once been painted, since the beetles tunnel just below the ground layers, but such signs do not define *when* the paint was applied. Other details, such as painted eyes and lips and the insertion of wooden wedges into splits that opened during carving, are seen on both originally painted and monochrome sculpture. Good indications that the work may have been intended to be monochromatic are distinct punch marks—and a high level of detail in surface carving in general—and pigmented glazes found directly on the wood. With this in mind, a final suggestion is offered to the museum visitor, art historian, and art conservator: proceed not from theory but from the object. Each sculpture reveals its history in a few millimeters of depth, and the key to understanding lies in the accurate reading of that fragile surface. It is both sobering and exciting to know that for Riemenschneider, one of the most intensively studied sculptors of the medieval world, so many unanswered questions remain.

A Shifting Critical Fortune *Till-Holger Borchert*

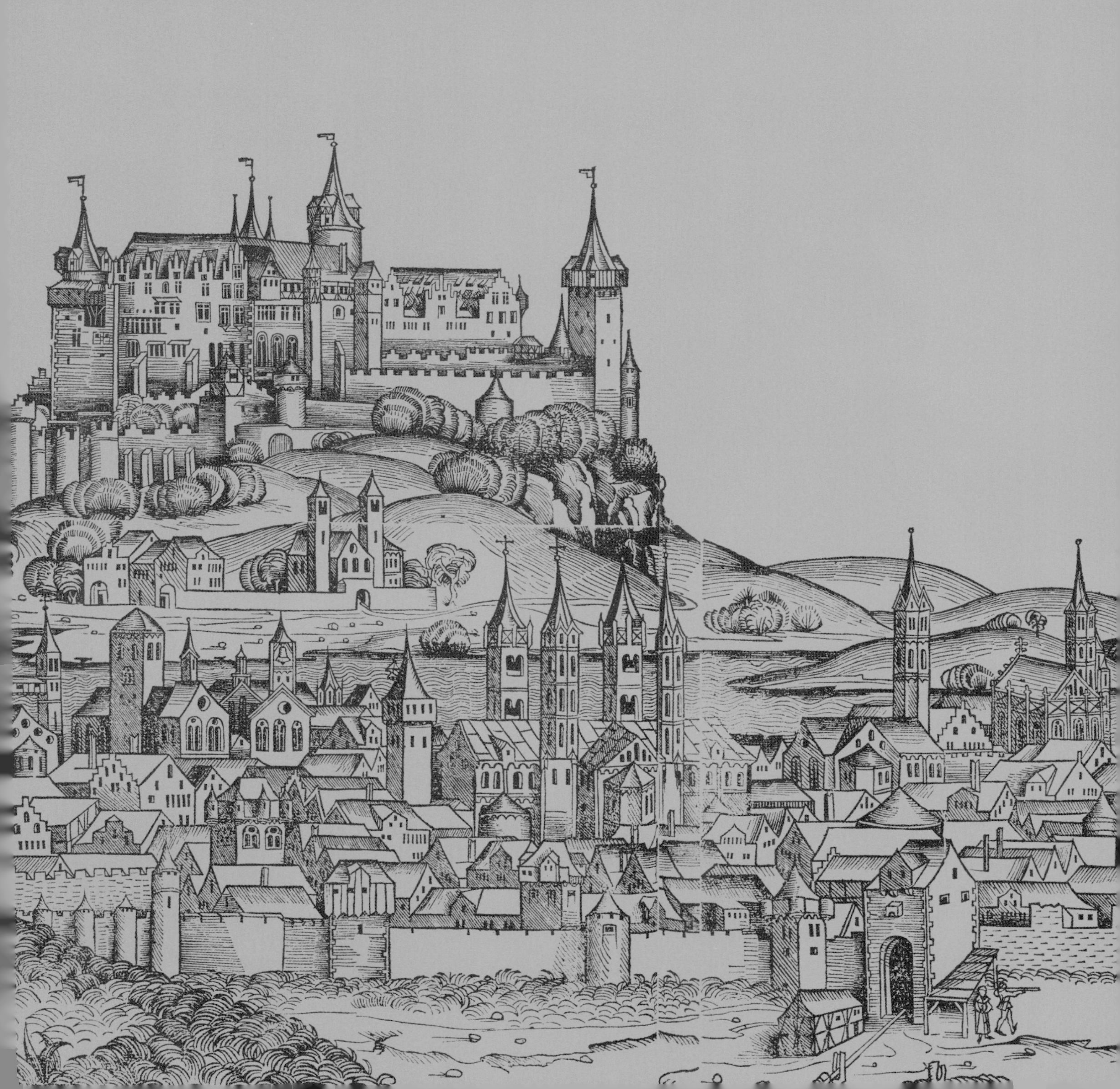

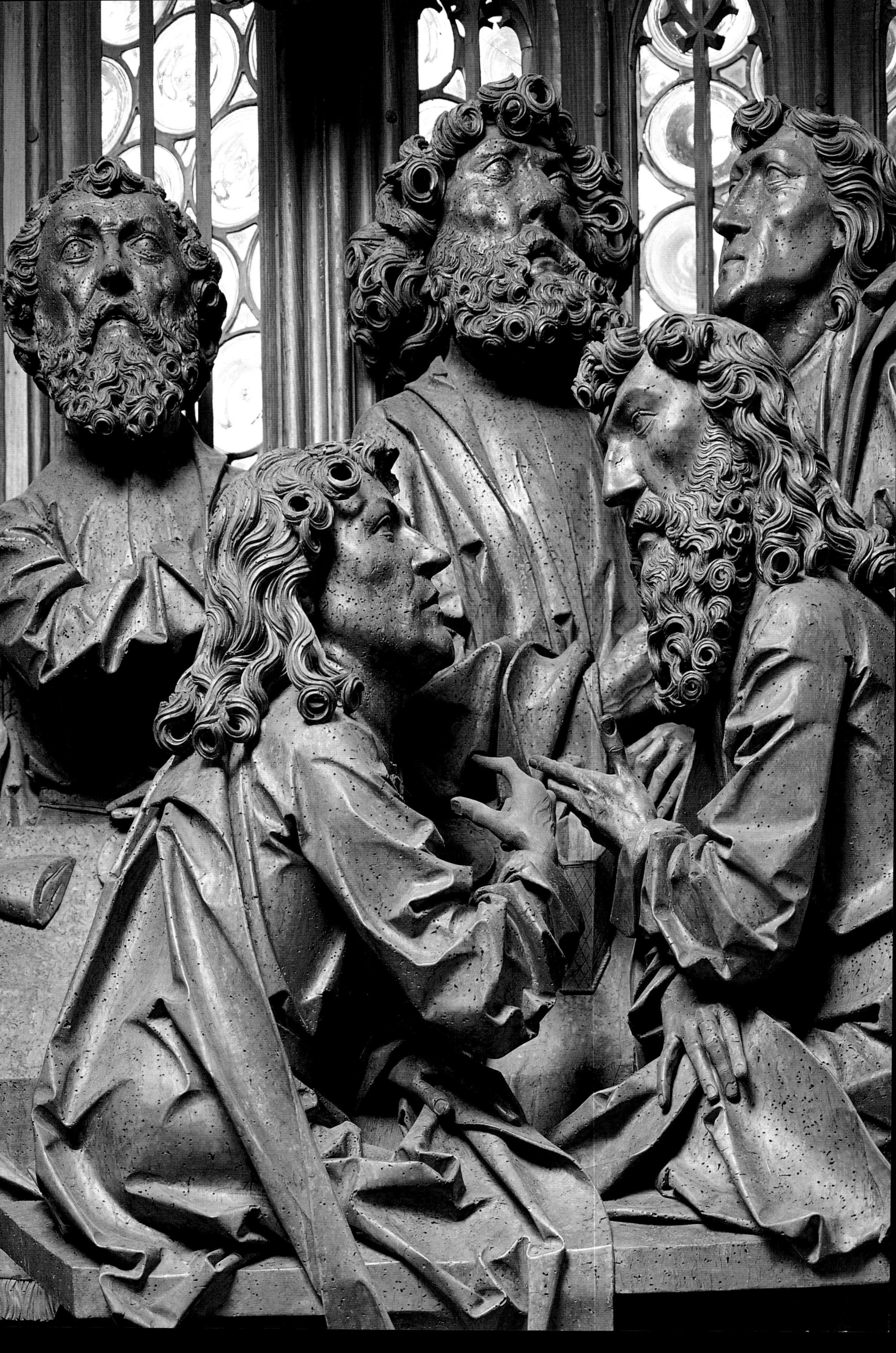

IN LATE NOVEMBER 1944 Thomas Mann, a Nobel Prize winner for literature and émigré from Nazi Germany living in exile in the United States, prepared a lecture "describing the German character and destiny" that he had agreed to deliver in February 1945. On 29 May 1945, shortly after the German surrender, Mann gave the speech "Germany and the Germans" to an American audience at the Library of Congress. The author intended to point out historical evidence for a German character trait that stood in the way of intellectual and political freedom. According to this premise, important intellectual movements, such as the Reformation or Romanticism, had often led to catastrophe in Germany. Mann explained this using the example of Martin Luther, who had called for intellectual freedom yet vehemently attacked concurrent demands by the Franconian peasants for political freedom. The Würzburg sculptor Tilman Riemenschneider, as introduced by Mann, represented a contrasting view. An accomplished artist who was equally successful in a civic career, he had even been elected to the office of mayor. Yet during the Peasants' Revolt, his conscience had forced him to "step out of the realm of the purely intellectual and aesthetic artist-citizen to become a fighter for freedom and justice. He sacrificed his own personal freedom and the quiet dignity of his existence for this cause, which was more important to him than art and peace of mind.... That too existed in Germany and always has."[1] ❦ The reference to Riemenschneider, which Mann used as a cautious attempt to win sympathy for the conquered enemy, was perceived with very different connotations when the speech was published in Germany shortly afterward. There the same passage could be interpreted as a rebuke for tacitly going along with the Third Reich or as an appeal for a

1. Thomas Mann, "Deutschland und die Deutschen" (1938–1945), in vol. 5 of *Essays,* ed. Hermann Kurzke and Stephan Stachorski (Frankfurt am Main, 1996), 260–281, 433–436; quotation on 268–269.

Detail of the Holy Blood altarpiece, 1500–1504, Jakobskirche, Rothenburg (Chapuis essay, fig. 5)

democratic future, for in Germany Riemenschneider's popularity was at that time surpassed only by Dürer's. Only one hundred years earlier, however, any references to the sculptor would have gone unrecognized, since the artist was then almost completely forgotten. He had been rediscovered only at the beginning of the nineteenth century.[2]

2. The list of literature about Riemenschneider's reception is brief: Hans-Christian Kirsch, *Tilmann Riemenschneider. Ein deutsches Schicksal* (Frankfurt am Main, 1983), 286–294; Vincent Mayr, "Der 'Deutsche Perugino,' Beobachtungen und Gedanken zum Riemenschneider-Bild im 19. und 20. Jahrhundert," *Musis et litteris. Festschrift für Bernhard Rupprich* (Munich, 1993), 423–434; and Hanswernfried Muth, "Die Wiederentdeckung Riemenschneiders: Zu den Anfängen der Riemenschneider-Forschung," *Viaticum Collegiale, Wegzehrung für Dr. Ernst-Günter Krenig zum Übergang in den sogenannten Ruhestand überreicht von seinen Freunden* (Würzburg, 1993), 93–98.

3. See Eduard Isophording, "Bekenntnisse und Erkenntnisse: Das Bild des Veit Stoss und seiner Kunst im 19. Jahrhundert," *Veit Stoss in Nürnberg,* ed. Rainer Kahsnitz [exh. cat., Germanisches Nationalmuseum, Nuremberg] (Munich, 1983), 81–82.

4. Universitätsbibliothek Jena, Ms.Sag.F.12; Ms.Bud.q.43; see Alfred Wendehorst, *Das Bistum Würzburg,* vol. 3, *Germania Sacra,* new series 13 (Berlin, 1978), 70.

5. Justus Bier, among others, assumed a reading mistake by Reinhardt; see *Tilmann Riemenschneider. Die späten Werke in Stein* (Vienna, 1973), 177 n. 1; and Muth 1993, 94.

6. See Lochner 1737, 2:288; and Ignatius Gropp, *Collectio novissima scriptorum et rerum Wirceburgensium,* 2 vols. (Würzburg, 1741–1744), 1:173.

7. Salver 1775, 375.

• *The Literary Tradition* •

The Nuremberg sculptors Veit Stoss, Adam Kraft, and Peter Vischer were already praised in Johann Neudörfer's contemporary *Nachrichten von Künstlern und Werkleuten* (1547), and this account was incorporated almost verbatim into Joachim von Sandrart's influential *Teutsche Akademie* (Nuremberg, 1675), which was used well into the early nineteenth century. Even Johann Heinrich Zedler's *Universal-Lexikon* (Leipzig, 1732–1750) followed Sandrart for its entries on Stoss and Vischer.[3] Riemenschneider was unknown at the time, his fame having faded shortly after his death in 1531. The only mention of him in sixteenth-century literature is in the description by Würzburg chronicler Johannes Reinhardt of the death of Bishop Lorenz von Bibra, since Riemenschneider had created the bishop's funerary monument: "the deceased received a magnificent stone, which had been made…by a world-famous artist…in Würzburg by the name of Dalo Alpino Schneider, who also created the effigy of Bishop Rudolf [von Scherenberg]" (see Kemperdick essay, figs. 1 and 2). The account by Reinhardt, long incorrectly attributed to the Würzburg historiographer Lorenz Fries, was published in Johann Peter von Ludewig's compendium, *Geschicht-Schreiber von dem Bischoffthum Wirtzburg* (Frankfurt am Main, 1713). Ludewig pointed out an alternate version of the name, "Dillmann Riemenschneider," which is also known from two episcopal records of the seventeenth century in which mention is made of "industriosum artificem Tilmannum Riemenschneider."[4]

In eighteenth-century literature Riemenschneider is therefore referred to as "Dalus Alpinus Schneider," following Reinhardt, but the origin and possible meaning of this version of the name are unknown.[5] When the Nuremberg antiquarian Jakob Hieronymus Lochner introduced a biography of Bishop Lorenz von Bibra in the second volume of his *Sammlung merkwürdiger Medaillen* (Nuremberg, 1737), he adopted the name of the sculptor from Ludewig.[6] Johann Octavian Salver, in his *Proben des hohen teutschen Reichs-Adels* (Würzburg, 1775), related only what he had learned from Reinhardt's chronicle (edited by Ludewig) about the memorial to the bishop and its artist: "A marble monument was placed on the pillar, created in the finest manner by the famous sculptor Dalo Alpino Schneider, who also worked on the monument for Bishop Rudolf" (depicted in the book; see fig. 1).[7] For the entry on Riemenschneider in the *Künstlerlexikon* (1763), Swiss scholar Johann Rudolf Füssli relied on Lochner's publication:

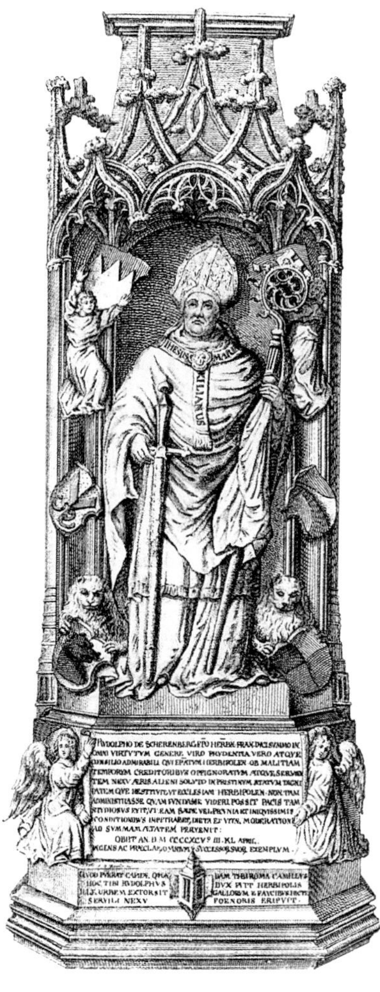

I.

Engraving of *Monument to Rudolf von Scherenberg* in Salver's book of 1775

"Schneider (Dalius Alpinus), a talented sculptor; made the monuments in a[nno] 1510 for the bishop of Würzburg, Laurentius von Bibra."[8]

• The Discovery of the Middle Ages •

The literature before 1800 conveyed little more than a mysterious version of Riemenschneider's name, taken mostly from older sources only remotely familiar with his work. This obvious disinterest in an aesthetic evaluation of Riemenschneider's art reflected the German taste of the eighteenth century, with its orientation toward France and Italy. The identification and acknowledgment of indigenous cultural roots in German medieval art occurred slowly. A monograph on Cranach prepared by Leipzig scholar Johann Heinrich Christ in 1726 is an especially early example of the awakening interest in German art, which was initially considered less for aesthetic than for historical reasons.[9] With Johann Wolfgang von Goethe's artistic assessment of the Gothic cathedral in Strasbourg in *Über deutsche Baukunst* (1772) and Johann Gottfried

8. Johann Rudolf Füssli, *Allgemeines Künstlerlexikon,* 2 vols. (Zurich, 1763–1767), 1:499, 2:250.

9. Johann Heinrich Christ, "Leben des berühmten Malers Lucas Cranach," *Acta erudita et curiosa, 1. Sammlung* (Nuremberg, 1726); see also Wilhelm Waetzold, *Deutsche Kunsthistoriker,* 2 vols., 3d ed. (Berlin, 1980), 1:45–46.

10. Waetzold 1980, 1:138–144, 146–151; Hans Belting, *Die Deutschen und ihre Kunst* (Munich, 1992), 15–21; Konrad Lotter, "Ästhetik des Nationalen. Entstehung und Entwicklung der nationalen Ästhetik in Deutschland 1770–1830," *Zeitschrift für Ästhetik und Allgemeine Kunstwissenschaft* 41 (1996), 205–232.

11. Walther D. Robson-Scott, "Wackenroder and the Middle Ages," *Modern Language Review* 50 (1955), 156–167; Silvio Vietta, "Vom Renaissance-Ideal zur deutschen Ideologie," *Romantik und Renaissance. Die Rezeption der italienischen Renaissance in der deutschen Romantik*, ed. Silvio Vietta (Stuttgart, 1994), 150–157.

12. Francis Haskell, *History and Its Images: Art and the Interpretation of the Past* (New Haven and London, 1993), 431–437; Ernst Behler, "Friedrich Schlegel und die Brüder Boisserée. Die Anfänge der Sammlung und ihr philosophischer Ausgangspunkt," *Kunst als Kulturgut. Die Bildersammlung der Brüder Boisserée—ein Schritt in der Begründung des Museums*, ed. Annemarie Guethmann-Siefert and Otto Pöggeler (Bonn, 1995), 30–41; Gerd-Helge Vogel, "Wirklichkeit und Wunschbild. Nürnberg, Albrecht Dürer und die Alten Meister in der Konzeption der Frühromantik," *Anzeiger des Germanischen Nationalmuseums* (1998), 11–24.

13. Christoph Gottlieb von Murr, *Merkwürdigkeiten der Fürstbischöflichen Residenzstadt Bamberg* (Nuremberg, 1799), 80–83.

14. *Acta Sanctorum* (Antwerp, July 1713), 3:714–720.

15. Joseph Heller, *Beschreibung der bischöflichen Gnadendenkmäler in der Domkirche zu Bamberg* (Nuremberg, 1827), 35–36; Paul Österreicher, "Über das Grabmal des Kaiserpaares Heinrich und Kunigunde zu Bamberg," *Neue Beiträge zur vaterländischen Geschichte, Geographie und Statistik* 1 (1831), 343–349.

Herder's *Von deutscher Art und Kunst* (1773), it became apparent that with the rediscovery of German art its ranking on the same level as French culture was also insinuated.[10]

The early Romantics continued in this vein. Wilhelm Heinrich Wackenroder's *Herzensergiessungen eines kunstliebenden Klosterbruders* (Berlin, 1796) talked about a brotherhood of Raphael and Dürer and presented a highly influential though idealized view of the Middle Ages.[11] In view of the Napoleonic occupation of large parts of Germany, and in the course of the rising patriotic movement during the Wars of Liberation, such ideas, which were especially promoted by Friedrich Schlegel and the Boisserée brothers, had a particular influence on the evaluation of German art of the Middle Ages. With the Wars of Liberation came an almost religious veneration of Dürer, accompanied by the mythical glorification of his hometown of Nuremberg as the paramount German art city.[12] The Romantic interest in German art of the past was deeply colored by patriotic convictions and was linked to calls for the foundation of a German nation-state. Painting and architecture received the greatest attention, but the identification and evaluation of late medieval sculpture was strongly affected as well.

The monument to Emperor Heinrich II and his wife, Kunigunde, in Bamberg Cathedral (Chapuis essay, fig. 4) provides a perfect example of the rising interest in medieval works of art after 1800. In 1799 Christoph Gottlieb von Murr still discussed the imperial grave exclusively from a historical perspective.[13] Artistic concerns were overshadowed by interest in the content of the relief sculpture. Murr relied on the *Acta Sanctorum,* in which the monument was depicted and which gave the date of completion as 1513.[14] Questions about the sculptor were of no interest to him.

The attribution to Riemenschneider was made only in 1827 by Joseph Heller, chair of the Bamberg art association. He had encountered the name "Thielemann Riemenschneider" on some account documents, and being familiar with the older literature on art, he recognized the identity of "Dalus Alpinus Schneider." In 1831 Paul Österreicher relinquished this version of the name in favor of "Riemenschneider," as indicated in the Bamberg sources.[15]

The imperial tomb received recognition in true artistic terms for the first time in 1842. Gustav Friedrich Waagen, director of the Berlin Gemäldegalerie and one of the most accomplished art connoisseurs of his time,[16] published the two-volume *Kunstwerke und Künstler in Deutschland* (Leipzig, 1843–1845), his most comprehensive study of German art. In the first part he discussed artistic monuments in the Harz Mountains and in Franconia; he had visited Bamberg, Nuremberg, and finally Würzburg in late summer of 1842. Having admired the interior of the Bamberg Cathedral, he praised the character and expression of the heads in the so-called Bamberg altarpiece by Veit

Stoss while criticizing its overall lack of formal harmony: "the loose principal movement of the garments…was disrupted by the many crinkled folds," which appeared "even more unpleasant in sculpture than in painting." But Waagen was enthusiastic about Riemenschneider: "By far the best sculpture in the cathedral is the tomb of Emperor Heinrich II and Kunigunde, which was created by the Würzburg sculptor Hans Thielemann Riemenschneider from 1499 to 1513….Without doubt the work belongs among the most outstanding pieces that German sculpture has to offer during that time. It would not surprise me if we found other works by the great master in other Franconian churches."[17]

When Waagen saw the *Holy Blood* altarpiece in Rothenburg shortly thereafter, however, he failed to recognize Riemenschneider's hand.[18] He also overlooked Riemenschneider's funerary monuments in the Würzburg Cathedral as well as the sculptural decorations on the nearby Marienkapelle. Since Waagen was evidently not familiar with the existing local research on Würzburg, his early appreciation of Riemenschneider was limited to the imperial tomb in Bamberg.

• *The Beginnings of Research on Riemenschneider: Würzburg* •

Riemenschneider was rediscovered in Würzburg by accident. During road construction in 1822 the former cathedral graveyard was found, and in it, the tombstone of the sculptor. It carried his likeness and the date of his death (fig. 2). The Würzburg local historian and publicist Carl Gottfried Scharold instigated the salvage operations and had the gravestone placed in the cloister of the cathedral. Scharold, whose civic employment had ended in 1814 with the absorption of Würzburg and the remainder of Franconia into the kingdom of Bavaria, had subsequently devoted his time to researching Würzburg history and art.[19] In 1818 Scharold described the origin and the interior of the Würzburg Marienkapelle. Documents in the city council archives proved Riemenschneider to be the sculptor of the stone statues of Adam and Eve and the apostles: "Thile Riemenschneider began to make those 14 figures…which are created entirely in the style of Albrecht Dürer."[20] This was the first mention of the sculptor after 1800.

The discovery of Riemenschneider's tombstone in 1822 was most likely a sensational event for Scharold. He later mentioned the incident frequently and emphasized his own contribution to the preservation of the stone, but it was probably only Heller's attribution of the Bamberg monument that motivated Scharold to investigate Riemenschneider more closely.[21] An important factor for his research was also the Historical Society of Lower Franconia and Aschaffenburg, of which Scharold was a cofounder in 1831. Like other historical societies in Bavaria, the Würzburg society was based on

16. For Waagen see Waetzold 1980, 2:29–45; and Gabriele Bickendorf, *Der Beginn der Kunstgeschichtsschreibung unter dem Paradigma "Geschichte." Gustav Waagens Frühschrift "Über Hubert und Jan van Eyck"* (Worms, 1985).

17. Waagen 1843, 1:87–88, also 82–84.

18. Waagen 1843–1845, 1:320.

19. See Scharold's handwritten biography, Staatsarchiv Würzburg, H.V.Ms.f.1345. For the biography see Leo Günther, "Karl Gottfried Scharold †1847," *Lebensläufe aus Franken* 4 (1930), 340–343.

20. Carl Gottfried Scharold, *Beyträge zur älteren und neueren Chronik von Würzburg* 1, no. 4 (1821), 44–45.

21. Muth 1993, 94.

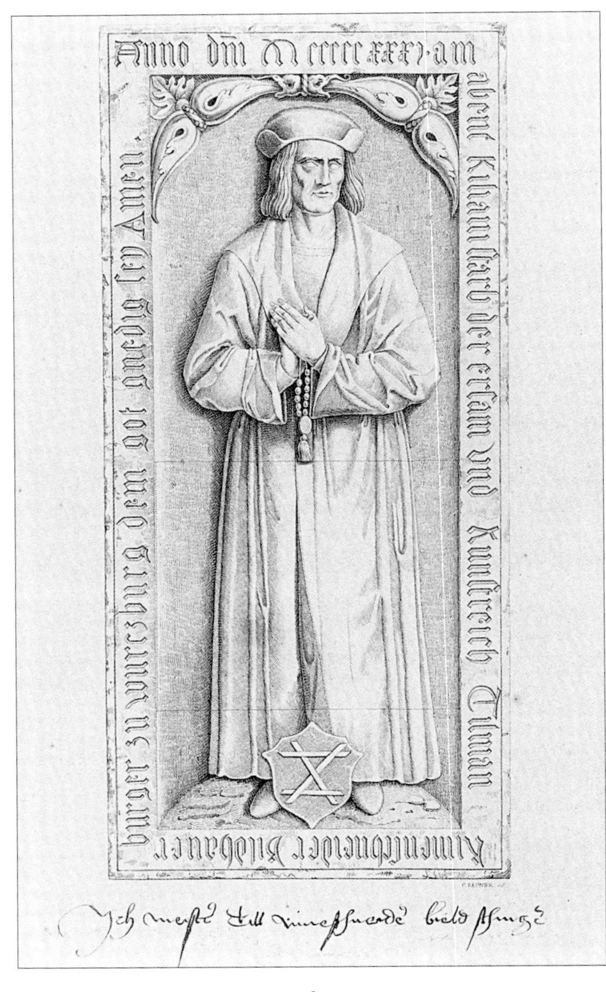

2.

Engraving of the tombstone of Riemenschneider illustrated in Carl Becker's monograph of 1849

22. For Bavarian art and cultural politics of that time, see "Vorwärts, vorwärts sollst du schauen…," *Geschichte, Politik und Kunst unter Ludwig I,* ed. Johannes Erichsen and Uwe Puschner (Munich, 1996). For historical societies in general, see *Deutsches Archiv zur Erforschung des Mittelalters* 13 (1957), 329–368. For Würzburg and Bavaria, see Siegfried Wenisch, "1831–1931. Der historische Verein von Unterfranken und Aschaffenburg: Ein Rückblick auf Werden und Wirken in 150 Jahren," *Mainfränkisches Jahrbuch* 33 (1981), 45–57; and Siegfried Wenisch, "König Ludwig I und die historischen Vereine in Bayern," in Erichsen and Puschner 1996, 323–330.

a cultural initiative by King Ludwig I. Following secularization, the Bavarian king attempted to prevent the threat to archives and works of art in abandoned churches, monasteries, and convents on a regional basis. The effort to preserve these monuments is mirrored in the bylaws of the society, according to which members were obligated to actively collect historical documents and works of art themselves or else to publish their research in the *Archiv des historischen Vereins,* edited by Scharold.[22]

In 1833 pastor Eugen Schön wrote about the history of Volkach in the *Archiv.* One document showed that the *Virgin of the Rosary* in the nearby pilgrimage church of Sankt Maria im Weingarten was created in 1522 by a "Master Dill" (cat. 45, fig. 1). Scharold, as the editor, gave an explanation in a footnote: "This master was Dill or Till (Dilmann) Riemenschneider, born in Osterode, who came to Würzburg as a sculptor in 1483 and became a citizen there and master of the Saint Luke guild of sculptors, panel painters, and stained-glass painters, and who died on the eve of Saint Kilian in 1531. He was a contemporary of Veit Stoss but almost surpassed him in talent." Scharold lists several works by the sculptor: the Würzburg bishops' effigies, the figures in the Marienkapelle, the Volkach *Virgin of the Rosary,* and *Anna Selbdritt* of the Kirchberg parish church as well as the Bamberg imperial tomb.[23]

In the following years Scharold examined additional works by Riemenschneider, and in 1844 he published an essay that also contained a description of the sculptor's life and work. The manuscript was among Scharold's collections for an encyclopedia of Franconian artists, which was part of his literary bequest, unpublished at his death in 1847.[24] For Scharold, Riemenschneider now belonged at the beginning of the blossoming of sculpture in Würzburg around 1500. Scharold recognized his sculpture as "works that are a fortunate imitation of the taste of the art school of that time, founded by Albrecht Dürer in Nuremberg, [and] for that reason are so well liked…by any lover of art and antiquities." That Riemenschneider's work had been held in high esteem, Scharold believed, was demonstrated by the numerous commissions he had received earlier; it was also obvious from the social rank of the sculptor: "His contemporaries, enchanted by the splendor of his works, seem almost to have fought over them. Convents, monasteries, and private citizens wanted to acquire works by the excellent master; and he was no less revered as a citizen.…The town awarded him the highest civic honor by making him mayor in 1521." The stark contrast to the artist's later reputation was no secret to Scharold. "Thilmann Riemenschneider deserved to have his name held in higher esteem because of the great mastery documented by his works. This would have happened, had he lived with and worked near the great artists of his time in Nuremberg."[25]

One hidden objective of Scharold's research on Riemenschneider may be revealed in this remark. Scharold was evidently interested in comparing the artistic heritage of his hometown with that of Nuremberg, which had then reached lofty dimensions. This may be the first glimpse of the claim that the artistic quality of the sculpture in both centers was equal; at the bottom of it was the traditional rivalry between the former Catholic bishops' residence, Würzburg, and the once-independent imperial city, Protestant Nuremberg.[26]

Following Waagen's description of the imperial tomb in Bamberg, Riemenschneider was not only recognized by local Franconian historians but gained attention outside the region. In *Handbuch der Kunstgeschichte* (Stuttgart, 1842) Franz Kugler pointed to the Bamberg monument and to Riemenschneider, whom he described as "a very remarkable, somewhat younger contemporary of Adam Kraft." Georg Kaspar Nagler's multivolume *Künstlerlexikon* (Munich, 1835–1852) followed suit.[27] When Jacob Burkhardt revised a second edition of Kugler's *Handbuch* in 1848, he already relied on Scharold's research concerning Riemenschneider's work in Würzburg, adding

23. Eugen Schön, "Historische Nachrichten über Volkach, besonders dessen kirchliche Verhältnisse," *Archiv des historischen Vereins für den Untermainkreis* 2 (1833), 87, note by Scharold.

24. Carl Gottfried Scharold, "Kleeblatt Alter Würzburger Künstler," *Archiv des historischen Vereins für Unterfranken und Aschaffenburg* 4 (1841), 144–153. See also the Scharold-Nachlass in the University library in Würzburg, M.ch.f.636, *Carl Gottfried Scharolds Collectionen zu einem fränkischen Künstlerlexikon,* fol. 300–302; archival and literary excerpts on Riemenschneider, fol. 38–50.

25. Scharold 1841, 152–153.

26. See Alfred Tausenpfund, "Von der Residenzstadt zur Kreishauptstadt," *Würzburg. Geschichte in Bilddokumenten,* ed. Alfred Wendehorst (Munich, 1981), 90–93.

27. Kugler 1842, 768; Nagler 1835–1852, 14:467.

the "masterfully and grandly executed marble monuments of two bishops [and] the austere and serious statues of the apostles on the Liebfrauenkirche."[28]

The first monograph on Riemenschneider was published in 1849, written by Carl Becker, a *Zollverein* customs inspector from Prussia who had chosen to retire in Würzburg in 1845. During military service in 1841 he had been in Paris, where he met Alexandre Lenoir, the director of the Musée des monuments français. The French scholar, who presented the art of the Middle Ages in his museum more persuasively than anyone before, had a lasting influence on Becker's interest in medieval art.[29] Becker's book on Riemenschneider was based on the careful study of the works over many years and on new source studies. Becker was able to add vital details to the sculptor's biography and illuminated for the first time Riemenschneider's role during the Peasants' Revolt, which would later fascinate Thomas Mann.

Even Becker was not immune to the political circumstances of his time, however. In 1848 Germany had undergone a revolution, with demands—forceful since the time of the Wars of Liberation—for voting privileges, the arming of the general population, and the founding of a nation-state. This revolution reflected the ideas of national liberalism in Germany, whose primary proponents were the educated elite; after initial successes it was soon suppressed.[30] It was not surprising that in 1849 Becker made Riemenschneider into a forerunner for civil liberty: "When the Peasants' Revolt broke out, not only the peasants but also the inhabitants of Würzburg tried to rid themselves of the yoke of church and aristocracy, among them Riemenschneider and the painter Philipp Dittmar, who were named as passionate fighters for religious and political freedom… [as] valiant, free-spirited *[freisinnig]* citizens" gathered in town against the bishop. Their defeat, Becker recognized, had serious consequences for Riemenschneider: he and eleven other councillors were excluded in 1525 from the city council as "revolutionaries," and he was apparently to execute no further sculpture.[31] Becker's use of the word *freisinnig,* which then unmistakably described political liberalism, must have triggered associations with the occurrences of the day.

The monograph was also a product of its time from an art historical point of view. Hardly any systematic research existed concerning the history of German sculpture; only works from Nuremberg had received close attention.[32] Riemenschneider, who, as Becker remarked, had been ignored by historiographic tradition, was thus almost entirely unknown. Becker intended "to vindicate the works by the excellent master" and award him the rank that, "based on his accomplishments, is his due without a doubt, next to his contemporaries Adam Kraft, Vischer, and others."[33] To accomplish this goal, Becker used engravings. By the standards of the time the publication was lavishly decorated, and the importance of these illustrations can hardly be over-

28. Kugler rev. ed. 1848, 804.

29. Carl Becker, *Leben und Werke des Bildhauers Tilmann Riemenschneider, eines fast unbekannten aber vortrefflichen Künstlers, am Ende des 15. und am Anfang des 16. Jahrhunderts* (Leipzig, 1849). For Becker, see *Das Germanische Nationalmuseum Nürnberg 1852–1977. Beiträge zu seiner Geschichte,* ed. Bernward Deneke and Rainer Kahsnitz (Munich, 1977), 1039. For Lenoir, see Haskell 1993, 236–252.

30. Rudolf Endres, "Franken und Bayern im Vormärz und in der Revolution von 1848/1849," "Vorwärts, vorwärts sollst du schauen…," in Erichsen and Puschner 1996, 199–217; Reinhard Rürup, *Deutschland im 19. Jahrhundert, 1815–1871* (Göttingen, 1984), 170–196.

31. Becker 1849, 4.

32. Isophording 1983, 83–86.

33. Becker 1849, 1–2.

estimated. Subtle shades of gray successfully conveyed the three-dimensional character of the sculpture (see fig. 3). Charles Regnier, the graphic artist responsible for the reproductions, had made the plates after designs by the Würzburg painter Franz Leinecker, who had rendered detailed drawings of seven works by Riemenschneider.[34]

Within the context of artistic evolution, Becker judged the Würzburg artist with reference to the sculpture of Nuremberg. He recognized a "close kinship to the great Nuremberg master Adam Kraft," but without interpreting it as a teacher-student relationship. For Becker, both artists had emerged from the same school, which he could not define. That Veit Stoss was not drawn as a comparison was doubtless because the known oeuvre of Riemenschneider then consisted mainly·of stone sculpture, major works as well as minor. Following Waagen, who was quoted extensively in the context of the Bamberg tomb, Becker stressed the "pure and simple beauty and the deepest

34. For Leinecker, see Thieme-Becker, 22:596.

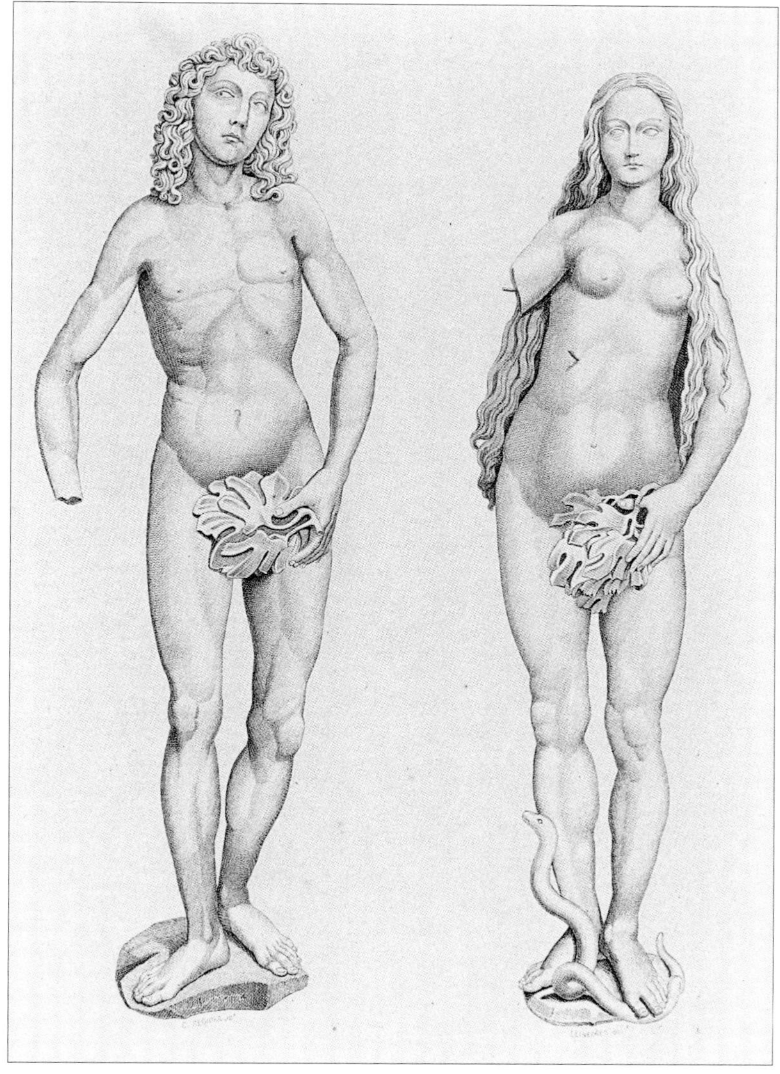

3.

Engraving of *Adam* and *Eve* illustrated in Carl Becker's Riemenschneider monograph of 1849

and noblest emotion" of the figures as well as the "melancholy expression of his heads, which are sometimes idealized." Becker perceived "no trace of the grimace that is often disturbingly present" in the sculpture of the time. Representations of the nude were based on "thorough study of nature," and the Würzburg portal statues of Adam and Eve reminded him of Jan van Eyck's Ghent altarpiece. Thus Riemenschneider seemed to confirm Kugler's observation that "sculpture in Germany during the first half of the sixteenth century generally achieved a higher level than painting and its development had rapidly advanced far ahead of it."[35]

Becker's list of works by the artist amounted to twenty pieces, a huge leap in quantity. Erring just as Scharold had, Becker occasionally picked up doubtful works from the "school" of Riemenschneider, as today's debates about attribution would have been strange to him: "The master's style…is so clearly visible in all his works that it is easy to recognize them…immediately."[36] Since Riemenschneider was generally considered a stone sculptor, the works newly attributed by Becker were almost exclusively works in marble and sandstone. The artistic development of the presumed stone sculptor seemed to Becker a coherent process, from the *Monument to Eberhard von Grumbach* in Rimpar to the Maidbronn *Lamentation*, whose figure of Nicodemus was believed to be a self-portrait of the sculptor (cat. 18, fig. 1; Chapuis essay, fig. 9).[37]

The scholarly importance of Becker's monograph on Riemenschneider was recognized instantly by early art historians. Kugler's review in the *Deutsches Kunstblatt* emphasized the illustrations, which offered "a completely satisfactory view of the direction and the artistic ability of the master," while his biography "gave a rare insight into the status of the German artists of that time, which was intricately linked to society."[38] Kugler did, however, complain that Riemenscheider's "importance in art historical terms was somewhat overstated." Becker's comparison of Riemenschneider with Kraft would rather reveal the "limitations" of the Würzburg sculptor, who "may be called more a charming than a great master." Kugler thereby fundamentally criticized the style of the early Romantics in evaluating medieval art in Germany, judging that they could no longer provide "full satisfaction" to the artistically "more mature need" of a professional art historian of Kugler's stature. Nevertheless, Riemenschneider was now established in German art history, next to Adam Kraft, as one of the most significant local stone sculptors of the time around 1500.

• *Riemenschneider's Carved Altarpieces* •

The carved wooden altarpieces on which Riemenschneider's reputation essentially rests today were considered anonymous until the end of the nineteenth century. The *Virgin of the Rosary* in the pilgrimage church near Volkach had already been safely attributed

35. Becker 1849, 5–6.

36. Becker 1849, 5–6.

37. Becker 1849, 16, and title vignette below the frontispiece. For Riemenschneider's self-portraits, see Corine Schleif, "Nicodemus and Sculptors: Self-Reflexivity in Works by Adam Kraft and Tilmann Riemenschneider," *Art Bulletin* 75 (1993), 599–626.

38. Franz Kugler, "Rezension zu Becker," *Deutsches Kunstblatt* 1 (1850), 25–26.

to the Würzburg sculptor since 1833. But even those carved tableaux known to the art historians of the early nineteenth century were plausibly attributed only after 1880. Ludwig Schorn had talked about Rothenburg's *Holy Blood* altarpiece (Chapuis essay, fig. 5) in his respected *Kunstblatt* in 1836. He regarded the fact that it had remained unpainted as an idiosyncrasy untypical for its time. He thought that it had probably been commissioned in 1474, and he believed it to be by Michael Wolgemut, who was considered the main representative of Nuremberg wooden sculpture, next to "the very original Veit Stoss." Schorn saw the *Holy Blood* altarpiece as a workshop piece, executed in the time between the presumably original works by Wolgemut and those by his successors, which had the distinction of "increasing ugliness."[39] Waagen, who had gone to see the Rothenburg altarpiece in 1842, counted the prominent composition among the "most ambitious works" of late medieval sculpture but was not yet thinking of Riemenschneider as its artist.[40]

A second carved wooden masterpiece by the artist was literally uncovered in 1833. In the Herrgottskirche in Creglingen, which became a funeral chapel after the Reformation, the original *Assumption of the Virgin* altarpiece had been nailed shut with boards and decorated with memorial plaques and flower wreaths. When these covers were removed in 1833 and the retable was opened, one of the most important carvings of the late Gothic reappeared (Chapuis essay, fig. 7) and soon sparked interest beyond the region.[41]

In 1862 Gottlieb Bunz discussed the altarpiece and considered an attribution to Riemenschneider, supported by the *Christliches Kunstblatt*.[42] The same year Karl Bauer contested this idea on stylistic grounds. He recognized similarities to the *Holy Blood* altarpiece and wanted to attribute both works to the same master, whose anonymity was for "all connoisseurs a challenge warranting further contemplation."[43] Both authors were in agreement about the artistic excellence of the *Assumption* altarpiece: "In technical respects the altarpiece shows a perfect mastery…and love in the execution…paired with knowledge of anatomy….The expressions of posture and face are especially dear and are true to nature and in character."[44]

The authors' defense of differing attributions was evidently related to the lack of polychromy. Bunz assumed that the sculpture was incomplete, while Bauer presumed aesthetic reasons: "Apparently our altarpiece has been executed…without coloring, and therefore it must have been meant to be seen in that way. This is all the more probable since the pupils of the figures have been indicated in a light brown."[45] Bauer made the comparison to the *Holy Blood* altarpiece, in which the wood was also visible, while Bunz' opposing thesis of an intended polychromy allowed a connection to the then-known oeuvre of Riemenschneider, namely the *Virgin of the Rosary*, which was then

39. Ludwig Schorn, "Beiträge zur Geschichte der deutschen Plastik," *Kunstblatt* 17 (1836), 11.

40. Waagen 1843–1845, 1:320.

41. *Mergentheimer Wochenblatt* 51 (1833), reprinted in Karl Bauer, "Der Marienaltar in der Herrgottskirche bei Creglingen," *Wirttembergisch Franken. Zeitschrift des historischen Vereins für das Wirttembergische Franken* 6 (1863), 304–310; Ottmar Schönuth, *Creglingen und seine Umgebungen* (Mergentheim, 1846), 54–55.

42. Gottlieb Bunz, "Ueber den Marien-Altar in der Herrgottskirche bei Creglingen," *Anzeiger für Kunde der deutschen Vorzeit,* new series 9 (1862), 239–240; Bauer 1863, 301; "Der Herrgottsaltar in der Creglinger Herrgottskirche," *Christliches Kunstblatt* (1863), 45–46.

43. Bauer 1863, 301–302.

44. Bunz 1862, 239–240; Bauer 1863, 302 n. 1, 312–313.

45. Bauer 1863, 312–313.

polychrome and illustrated in color in Becker. Only later did it become clear that these attributions were not mutually exclusive.

In 1882 Heinrich Weissbecker published conclusive archival documents in his study about the antiquities of Rothenburg, which proved that the *Holy Blood* altarpiece was in fact carved by Riemenschneider.[46] The find was introduced into the Riemenschneider literature in 1884 by Anton Weber, who presented further evidence in his Riemenschneider monograph. These documents now confirmed as well the sculptor's authorship of the Magdalen altarpiece in Münnerstadt (see cat. 13), which had by then been twice refurbished. Weber was also able to prove that Riemenschneider had created additional carved altarpieces for Rothenburg.[47] These important discoveries not only shed light on the hitherto unknown early career of the sculptor but also confirmed the attribution of the *Assumption* altarpiece in Creglingen. Riemenschneider was thus inducted into art history as a noteworthy sculptor.

Compared with Weber's study, Wilhelm Bode's richly illustrated *Geschichte der deutschen Plastik* (Berlin, 1885) was in some sense a setback for Riemenschneider. Even though he clearly outlined the artistic independence of Lower Franconian sculpture around 1500 from that of Nuremberg, Bode was skeptical about the Würzburg school. The prominent connoisseur doubted that the entire body of sculpture in Würzburg and its surrounding areas around 1500 could be by one single artist, considering its lack of stylistic unity. Bode was mistakenly convinced that he would be able to restore a separate "master of the Creglingen altar" as a precursor to Riemenschneider in Lower Franconia. His strongly defined "character…is…different from all contemporary Franconian and Swabian sculptors….Naturalism is a common feature for that time, but only a few German artists exercise it to the extent and with the seriousness that is maintained here." Bode assumed the main works by this anonymous artist were the carved altarpieces in Rothenburg, Detwang, and Creglingen. He believed that their sequence revealed the artistic development of their creator. The fact that the wood was visible in these works was seen as the strongest commonality; Bode was also aware of the color in the pupils on the Creglingen altarpiece. But the existence of two polychrome Virgins convinced him that the sculptor on occasion purposefully omitted color.[48]

By erroneously insisting on the existence of an anonymous artist, Bode also disputed that Riemenschneider was at that time the leading sculptor of Lower Franconia. The works by Riemenschneider that he accepted—essentially the oeuvre listed by Becker—indicated to Bode a continuous artistic decline. "In Riemenschneider's compositions the lack of an inner cohesion…[is] more pronounced than in the Master of the Creglingen altar….His talent suffices only to illustrate simple conditions, tenderness, quiet joy, or silent grief." But Bode thus acknowledged precisely the timelessness of Riemenschneider's works. "Those features that appeal directly to our modern sensibilities, the sometimes painfully melancholic and occasionally sensitive and sweet expressions, can be found in most portraits by the artist and give them a level of attraction that transcends the subjective, lively rendering of their outward appearance."[49] In this Bode singled out exactly those elements that had been considered characteristic of Riemenschneider since Waagen's evaluation. They had been the foundation for the sculptor's art historical reputation and, according to Wilhelm Lübke, had assured the "master a high rank in German sculpture."[50]

Lübke recognized Bode's contribution, despite the unfortunate error in attribution, as the first to demonstrate the artistic achievements of the retables in Creglingen and Rothenburg.[51] In that respect scholarship has since fully agreed with Bode's assessment. For the beginning of art historical scholarship and the popular admiration of Riemenschneider's altarpieces, Bode is therefore a strong influence along with Weber. Subsequently the view of the Würzburg artist's oeuvre changed so fundamentally that Georg Dehio in his *Geschichte der Deutschen Kunst* half a century later had to introduce his stone sculpture separately: "The popular idea of Riemenschneider is almost exclusively as a wood-carver."[52]

• *Paradigms of Riemenschneider Scholarship around 1900* •

Bode's study of German sculpture is important for additional reasons. The author had devised an order of specific time periods that would come to define the scholarship of late medieval art in Germany. In a chapter on the second blossoming of German sculpture Bode listed Riemenschneider, his predecessors, and his contemporaries for the first time under the heading "Renaissance." He based this on characteristics he thought had been realized in Italian sculpture and later in Northern sculpture as well. For Bode the Renaissance essentially resulted from an awakening interest in copying nature. In northern Europe this was achieved by direct observation, in Italy through the study of antiquity.[53]

This definition was only seemingly a break with the Romantic conception of the German Middle Ages. For Romantics, too, the interest in German art of the past was believed to stem from its similarities to Italy, although they accentuated religious content. In Bode's conception the dominant role of religion had been superseded by the observation of nature, and consequently formal considerations were preferred in discussions to the content of the works. Without doubt this reflected the secular tendencies that now dominated Prussian spiritual life, especially after the founding of the Reich in 1871. Moreover, instead of the differences between regional German art schools,

49. Bode 1885, 174.

50. Wilhelm Lübke, "Vorwort," in Carl Streit, *Tylmann Riemenschneider 1460–1531. Leben und Kunstwerke des fränkischen Bildschnitzers* (Berlin, 1888), 1:1–2.

51. Wilhelm Lübke, "Tilmann Riemenschneider," in *Wilhelm Lübke, Altes und Neues. Studien und Kritiken* (Breslau, 1891), 244–245.

52. Georg Dehio, *Geschichte der deutschen Kunst*, 4th ed. (Berlin, 1930), 2:261

53. Bode 1885, 111–115.

common factors were now stressed. After 1871 it became much more important to judge early German sculpture of the past in the wider context of European art.

Accordingly, the question arose in Riemenschneider scholarship as to the ways his art both still owed a debt to the Middle Ages and was already part of the concerns of the modern Renaissance. Weber, for instance, viewed Riemenschneider and the sculptors of his time as artists of the Middle Ages: "the Nordic art of that period still lacks the greater dignity of form that Italian art already knew to adopt….The distance to Italy can be seen most clearly at the beginning of the sixteenth century, when Northern art, as respectable as…its achievements appear, fails to participate in the great change that took place in Italy at that time." The respectable achievements he allowed Riemenschneider and German art were the ability to depict emotions and individuality of expression; they made up for the "lack of formal beauty."[54]

54. Weber 1888, 2.

55. Eduard Tönnies, *Leben und Werk des Würzburger Bildschnitzers Tilmann Riemenschneider 1468–1531* (Strasbourg, 1900), 2–3, 6.

56. See E. Schmidt-Volkmar, *Der Kulturkampf in Deutschland 1871–1890* (Göttingen, 1962).

57. Alfred Woltmann, *Die Deutsche Kunst und die Reformation* (Berlin, 1867); see Oskar Bätschmann and Pascal Griener, *Hans Holbein d. J.: Die Solothurner Madonna* (Basel, 1998), 142–143.

In referring to Bode's determination of time periods and his view of the Renaissance, Eduard Tönnies detected a pronounced change in the values represented by the work of Riemenschneider and his time. The old "typification of the arts" was now replaced by a highly individual relationship between the artist and nature. Tönnies believed therefore that individuality and the personal style of artists like Riemenschneider and Stoss became the preferred artistic ideal in Germany around 1500. To him this indicated a further synchronization between the German and the Italian Renaissance, although he did recognize that a sculptor such as Riemenschneider remained tied to the medieval system of crafts and stayed true to tradition in his subject matter: "The new…is the revival of old motifs, a documentation of nature study, and the psychological internalizing of the process. What he creates are real people…no longer idealized types….This facet of his art is what marks him as a modern man and an artist of the Renaissance, even though…he has not completely outgrown the Gothic."[55]

The arguments offered by scholarship around 1900 in designating a particular era for Riemenschneider can hardly be separated from the societal conflict known as culture war *(Kulturkampf),* which took place between the Prussian, Protestant-dominated empire and the Catholic Church after the founding of the Reich, and which poisoned intellectual life in the German empire for decades.[56] Scholarly investigations of German art and artists from around 1500 assumed the role of a sideshow, where ideological conflict was often played out.

The Holbein scholar Alfred Woltmann had already formulated the thesis in 1867 that Luther's Reformation was a genuine German cultural achievement, comparable to the Renaissance in Italy.[57] Woltmann's nationalistic concept of history took on a new meaning and provocative relevance in view of the clash between Protestantism and Catholicism. It not only denied the Reformation's iconoclasm, it attributed the foundation of an authentic German art, independent of foreign influences, to the impact of Luther and the Reformation.

In the Riemenschneider scholarship such ideas were important, since the sculptor was known to have opposed the Catholic bishop in 1525 while he was part of the city council of Würzburg, and he had taken the side of the rebelling peasants, who claimed allegiance to Luther. Depending on the denominational affiliation of the interpreter, this was seen as either symptomatic of Riemenschneider's reformatory sympathies or as a mistake, clearly not motivated by religious concerns but by the town citizens' wish for independence.

Tönnies, following Woltmann, praised the "great deed of liberation by Luther" and even went so far as to attribute democratic tendencies to German (Protestant) humanism, in contrast to Italy. He styled Riemenschneider a tragic figure, torn between Catholicism and the Reformation on the one hand and the late Gothic and the Renaissance on the other: "Fully and completely raised in the views of a time past, the master is caught in the storms of the new endeavors: his heart and intellect join them, but his artistic faculty is not able to follow."[58] On the Catholic side such views were disputed by Weber. In the first editions of his Riemenschneider study (1884, 1888) he had stated his belief that German art was deprived of its full bloom by the Reformation, which he compared to the "poisonous breath of the winter frost" or "gigantic blows of a hammer," which had "nailed the coffin of German art."[59] In the third edition of 1911 Weber had revised his text once more and sprinkled it with citations of political Catholicism: "The separation from Rome, the separation from the still-religious art of Italy became a misfortune for German art....The unified medieval culture was split …on the one hand into Protestants and Catholics, on the other into the uneducated and the classically schooled."[60] Weber strongly opposed those interpreters who wanted to see Riemenschneider as a Protestant. His counterthesis culminated in the observation that Riemenschneider had died a Catholic and, in observation of his faith, had been immortalized on his tombstone with a rosary in his hand. In the magazine *Der Katholik* Weber repeated his assertions in 1912.[61]

Despite differing models of development and intentions to use him as a confessional instrument, the art historical importance of the Würzburg sculptor was unquestioned in the years around 1900. Reducing Riemenschneider scholarship to concepts of historical development and the problem of his religious affiliation would result in a distorted picture. Scholarly interest was above all concerned with questions of attribution as well as with the chronology of his oeuvre and thus with his stylistic development, and art historical scholarship in the years before World War I made substantial progress in these areas.[62]

58. Tönnies 1900, 2–3, 65.

59. Weber 1888, 3; Anton Weber, *Til Riemenschneider. Sein Leben und Wirken,* 3d rev. ed. (Regensburg, 1911), 8. See also A. Streitberger, "Rezension zu Anton Weber," *Historisch-Politische Blätter für das katholische Deutschland* 102 (1888), 670–692.

60. Weber 1911, 8.

61. Weber 1911, 8; Anton Weber, "Das religiöse Bekenntnis Tilmann Riemenschneiders," *Der Katholik* 92/112 (1912), 457–459; Anton Weber, "Das religiöse Bekenntnis Tilmann Riemenschneiders," *Christliche Kunstblätter* 55 (1914), 99–101.

62. See Bier 1925, 5; see also Hartmut Krohm, "Zu Methode und Ergebnissen des Forschungsprojektes—das Problem der künstlerischen Herkunft," *Tilmann Riemenschneider. Frühe Werke,* 2nd rev. ed. [exh. cat., Mainfränkisches Museum Würzburg] (Berlin, 1982), 7–20.

Public museums in Germany also pursued these questions. They built collections of Riemenschneider's works in tandem with the growing scholarship and the increasing popularity of the artist. Significant additions were made by those museums that attempted to document the work of the Würzburg artist with the overall goal of a scholarly presentation of the body of German sculpture.[63] An advantage was that around the turn of the century prestigious private holdings of important works by Riemenschneider were dissolved.

Since 1890 Carl Streit had been in the process of selling his collection, which focused on the Würzburg workshop. The pieces were widely known, as Streit had published his holdings in 1875 and in a two-volume Riemenschneider monograph in 1888. The sculptor's oeuvre—hardly any distinction was made between originals, workshop, and school—was not only described but photomechanically reproduced at a previously unattainable level of quality, although the images were printed in reverse by mistake.[64] The collection of Wilhelm Sattler from Mainberg Castle near Schweinfurt had already been dispersed in 1887. Its importance lay in Sattler's earlier acquisition of the sculpture and reliefs from Riemenschneider's Magdalen altarpiece in Münnerstadt in the first decades of this century. Sattler also owned the bust of a bishop now in Washington (cat. 44).

With the dispersal of both private collections, first-rate works by Riemenschneider became available to augment the holdings of public museums, especially in Munich and Berlin.[65] Wilhelm Bode had purchased a polychrome *Virgin and Child* by the artist in 1882 for the newly established sculpture department of the museum in Berlin. In addition to earnest efforts to collect Italian Renaissance sculpture, he succeeded in the following years with further Riemenschneider acquisitions, evidently planning them systematically. He described the favorable conditions in the art market for late medieval German sculpture: "I had almost no serious competition.... A painted wooden figure could be purchased for a few hundred marks. If it carried the name of the preferred sculptor Riemenschneider, the German Perugino, the price would be double, perhaps triple."[66] In quick succession Bode purchased a fragment of an early *Passion* altarpiece from Rothenburg (Krohm essay, fig. 8) on the art market and secured four wooden saints in Kitzingen. But by 1887 he would consider himself lucky when he was able to buy at auction "original early masterpieces," Riemenschneider's evangelists from the predella of the Münnerstadt altarpiece (cat. 13A–D), for the sum of, as he later remembered, only 1,500 marks.[67]

From the same altarpiece the Berlin museum also acquired the relief of *Christ Appearing to Mary Magdalen* from the Sattler collection in 1901, while Benoit

63. Wilhelm Bode, "Die Entwicklung der öffentlichen Sammlungen der Kunst des Mittelalters und der Renaissance in Deutschland seit dem Krieg 1870/1871," *Deutsche Rundschau* 60 (1889), 129–138.

64. *Catalog der Kunst- und Antiquitätensammlung von Carl Streit in Würzburg* (Würzburg, 1875); Streit 1888. See also Lübke 1891, 238–246 (239–243 for person and collection).

65. See Theodor Müller, *Die Bildwerke in Holz, Ton und Stein von der Mitte des 15. bis gegen Mitte des 16. Jahrhunderts*, Bayerisches Nationalmuseum (Munich, 1959), vol. 13, pt. 2, pp. 83–94, nos. 132, 134–147, 149, 152. For the Mainfränkisches Museum in Würzburg, see Hanswernfried Muth, *Tilmann Riemenschneider. Die Werke des Bildschnitzers und Bildhauers, seiner Werkstatt und seines Umkreises*, Mainfränkisches Museum (Würzburg, 1982), 214–216, 236, 278.

66. Wilhelm von Bode, *Mein Leben*, ed. Thomas W. Gaethgens and Barbara Paul (Berlin, 1997), 167.

67. Bode 1997 ed., 199; see also Mayr 1993, 427–428.

Oppenheim, one of the few connoisseurs in Germany collecting independently of Bode, bought at auction the image of the *Christ in the House of Simon;* both reliefs (cat. 13 E–F) sold for 5,600 marks.[68] With determination and an exceptional eye for quality, Bode and his colleagues in Berlin continually expanded the department of German sculpture. The first catalogue of the collection in 1888 was succeeded in 1910 by a scholarly catalogue of German works, compiled with stringent and largely exemplary criteria by Wilhelm Vöge.[69]

The Riemenschneider collection in Berlin found its equal in the Bayerisches Nationalmuseum in Munich. The Nationalmuseum, founded in 1855, aimed for a collection of medieval arts and crafts of Bavaria. This was in addition to the "general inspection of sculptural monuments of the Middle Ages" devised in 1835, the inventory of which made important contributions to Riemenschneider scholarship. The Nationalmuseum had acquired Riemenschneider works long before Berlin had. In 1858 twelve seated apostles made of limewood, an alabaster *Annunciation,* and two statues of Saints Sebastian and Wolfgang from the collection of the Würzburg administrative counsel Martinengo arrived at the Nationalmuseum, acquired by the former commissioner of secularization at the beginning of the century.[70] The Munich collection grew considerably at this time. In 1890 several Riemenschneider works from the Streit collection were added (see cat. 31); and the collector presented the museum with a pair of angels from Münnerstadt in 1896. When the Sattler collection was auctioned, the Nationalmuseum acquired the Münnerstadt *Mary Magdalen* for 13,800 marks. Two additional pairs of angels entered the collection in 1911 and 1913, and the central *Assumption of Mary Magdalen* from the Münnerstadt altarpiece could finally be reconstructed in Munich. To offer a suitable presentation of its considerable collection, the Nationalmuseum even set up its own Riemenschneider chapel.[71]

Other German museums in Frankfurt, Darmstadt, and Hannover were mostly able to acquire representative single pieces, which came either from Franconia or from the art trade (see cats. 32 B–C and 33). The Germanisches Nationalmuseum in Nuremberg, whose bylaws stated that the focus of the collection was medieval and early modern art in Germany, was the only museum to compete, albeit not always successfully, with Berlin and Munich for Riemenschneider works (see cats. 9 and 43).[72]

The oldest Riemenschneider collection, however, belonged to Würzburg. It was begun in 1836 on the initiative of the Würzburg historical society. A statue of John the Evangelist came to the society at that time, and somewhat later a "xyloplast work by Riemenschneider" and the fragment of a Holy Kinship altarpiece were acquired.[73] Almost thirty pieces by the Riemenschneider workshop or school followed by the 1870s. The society accepted even those works whose conditions were precarious for its

68. Max J. Friedländer, *Erinnerungen und Aufzeichnungen* (Mainz and Berlin, 1967), 75; Muth 1982, 21.

69. Wilhelm Bode and Hugo von Tschudi, *Königliche Museen zu Berlin. Beschreibung der Bildwerke der christlichen Epochen* (Berlin, 1888), 92–94; Wilhelm Vöge, *Königliche Museen zu Berlin. Beschreibung der Bildwerke der christlichen Epochen, die deutschen Bildwerke und die der anderen cisalpinen Länder* (Berlin, 1910), 4:97–107, nos. 200–221.

70. Müller 1959, 83–94, nos. 129–157; Oskar Lenz, "Hundert Jahre Bayerisches Nationalmuseum," *Kunst und Kunsthandwerk, Meisterwerke im Bayerischen Nationalmuseum München. Festschrift zum hundertjährigen Bestehen des Museums 1855–1955,* ed. Theodor Müller (Munich, 1955), 7–27 (11 for the Martinengo collection); Weber 1884, 52–53.

71. *Führer durch das Bayerische Nationalmuseum* (Munich, 1913), 139–160, nos. 129–157 (room 16: Riemenschneider chapel); Lenz 1955, 26–28; Müller 1959, 83–94.

72. Heinz Stafski, "Die Skulpturensammlung," in Deneke and Kahsnitz 1977, 607–733.

73. Muth 1982, 16.

74. C. Heffner, *Die Sammlungen des historischen Vereins für Unterfranken und Aschaffenburg zu Würzburg* (Würzburg, 1875); Muth 1982, 16–17.

75. Muth 1982, 17–21.

76. Muth 1982, 21. Critiques and articles about the memorial exhibition are in Johann Konrad Eberlein, "Bibliographie zu Leben und Werk Tilman Riemenschneiders," *Beiträge zur fränkischen Kunstgeschichte* 3 (1998), 180–181.

77. Justus Bier, *Riemenschneider. Ein Gedenkbuch* (Würzburg, 1931); Bier 1925; Justus Bier, *Tilmann Riemenschneider. Die reifen Werke* (Augsburg, 1930); see *List of Displaced German Scholars* (London, 1936), 8; Bier 1973, 10; Hanswernfried Muth, "Justus Bier (1899–1990)," *Mainfränkisches Jahrbuch* 44 (1992), 7–13.

"Antiquarium." In 1894 the portal statues of Adam and Eve from the Marienkapelle came to the society's collection on long-term loan (Chapuis essay, fig. 3). By 1907 almost all the apostle figures from that edifice were there as well.[74] Würzburg followed the historical society's example by establishing a separate department for Riemenschneider's works in the city's art collections. The first piece listed was a table the sculptor had made for the town hall, followed by twenty additional works by 1913. Since its founding in 1893 the Franconian Society for Antiquities had also been successful in acquiring works by Würzburg's most famous sculptor, which were the main attraction in the society's exhibition of Franconian antiquities. After 1908 the three municipal collections were administered together, and acquisitions were made collectively. The Würzburg delegation gained Riemenschneider's *Anna Selbdritt* during the auction of the Sattler collection, bidding against Munich and Berlin, as well as two angels with candle prickets, considered workshop pieces.[75]

The Würzburg collections were combined in 1913 in the Franconian Luitpold Museum, which later became the Mainfränkisches Museum. The exhibition *Fränkische Altherthümer* marked the beginning of a tradition of exhibitions in Würzburg. In 1931 the Franconian Society for Antiquities organized the first exhibition of works by Riemenschneider in the new city museum, in a specially designed hall, on the occasion of the 400th anniversary of the artist's death.[76]

• Fractures and Lines •

For that exhibition a young art historian was hired to publish a memorial volume on the artist. Justus Bier had emerged in 1925 with a pioneering book about Riemenschneider's early work, and by 1930 he had submitted a second volume about the artist's mature work. The Franconian art historian, whose four-volume study about the sculptor is considered the standard of Riemenschneider scholarship to this day, had become director of the Kestner-Society in Hannover in 1929 after a stint as lecturer in adult education in Nuremberg, where he had devoted his efforts to the soon-to-be outlawed modern art. A Jew, he fled to the United States in 1936 to escape the Nazis. He taught at the University of Louisville in Kentucky from 1937, was director of the North Carolina Museum of Art in Raleigh from 1960 to 1970, and finished his groundbreaking study of Riemenschneider with two concluding volumes after he reached the status of "emeritus."[77]

In the Riemenschneider memorial volume Bier addressed the relationship between the art and the life of the sculptor: "Riemenschneider is one of those rare artists who attempt to achieve in their lives what they express in their work. As his sculpture is witness to the strong spiritual forces of the Reformation, his behavior in the confusion of the Peasants' Revolt shows that he was willing, without concern for his own existence, to join those who seemed to embody the Christian ideal that he had given living form in the figures of the apostles. What course did this life take, which can move us so profoundly through the unison of the intellectual expression in his work and his worldly fate?"[78]

Bier's question, aimed at the identity of artist and work, namely a psychological evaluation of the works of art, pointed to a consistent thread in the reception of Riemenschneider's work. It was important for the perception and interpretation of his sculpture, and it shaped the popular understanding of the sculptor in this century, as has the circulation of his work through the mass medium of photography.

Already in 1849 Becker had highlighted the circumstances of Riemenschneider's life during the Peasants' Revolt; he interpreted the artist's sympathies toward the peasants as a sign of his political progressiveness and saw the artist himself as a liberal precursor of civic freedom. Lübke had considered Riemenschneider in 1880 "one of the most respected men who were at the helm of the fight for religious and political freedom."[79] Around the turn of the century the supposedly symbiotic relationship between Riemenschneider's sculpture and his eventful biography was investigated. The basic idea that the life and work of an artist are intertwined has, of course, been familiar to art history since Vasari. During German Romanticism this idea had been used and elaborated in novels about artists. The authors and historians of German historicism, who still had ties to Romantic tradition, paid attention to the relationship between Riemenschneider's oeuvre and stylistic development and his rise and fall in society.

Tönnies and Weber in particular had investigated Riemenschneider's activities during the Peasants' Revolt and discovered that the former mayor had not only been removed from the city council but had also, on instructions from the bishop of Würzburg, been incarcerated in the fortress of Marienberg for weeks and even tortured. Riemenschneider's life showed startling similarities to the moving biography of the Nuremberg sculptor Veit Stoss, who had been bankrupted after a stellar career and had concluded his life cast out by society. The lives of both artists offered ample material for writers, who embellished recognized facts with fiction. While Stoss became the subject of a novel in the middle of the nineteenth century,[80] it took another fifty years before poets and writers focused on Riemenschneider, who had become generally known only in the mid-1880s. In 1899 Eduard Paulus published a poem about Riemenschneider with the subtitle *Ein Künstlerleben in 12 Gesängen* (An Artist's Life in Twelve Songs). The poem followed the life and work of the sculptor in the style of historicism, using Romantic cliches of the artist's existence or the ethos of the craftsman but also ideas from more recent scholarly literature, with an obviously more pointed

78. Bier 1931, 10.

79. Wilhelm Lübke, *Geschichte der Plastik von der ältesten Zeit bis zur Gegenwart*, vol. 2, 3d ed. (Leipzig, 1880), 729.

80. Isophording 1983, 92–94.

81. Eduard Paulus, *Tilmann Riemenschneider. Ein Künstlerleben in Zwölf Gesängen* (Stuttgart, 1899), 80.

82. Borowsky 1905, 71–90.

83. Weber 1911, 44.

84. Romain Rolland, *Das Gewissen Europas, Tagebuch der Kriegsjahre 1914–1919*, 3 vols., trans. Cornelia Lehmann (Berlin, 1983), 1:49–89, esp. 87; Werner Schivelbusch, *Eine Ruine im Krieg der Geister. Die Bibliothek von Löwen, August 1914– Mai 1940*, 2nd ed. (Frankfurt am Main, 1993), 25–50.

85. Lars Olof Larsson, "Nationalstil und Nationalismus in der Kunstgeschichte der 20er und 30er Jahre," *Kategorien und Methoden der deutschen Kunstgeschichte 1900–1930*, ed. Lorenz Dittmann (Stuttgart, 1985), 169–184; Belting 1992, 27; in general see Kurt Sontheimer, *Antidemokratisches Denken in der Weimarer Republik* (Munich, 1962).

focus. Here Riemenschneider's transition from the Gothic into the early Renaissance was addressed as well as Luther's influence on his work.[81] This should not simply be dismissed as an oversimplification of the available scholarship, since Ernst Borowsky evaluated the sculptor in similar terms in his *Lebensbilder des deutschen Humanismus* (Jena, 1905).[82] In 1911 Weber felt inclined to present arguments explicitly against Paulus; he must have assumed that his rendition of the life of the artist had been acknowledged by the public.[83]

The interest of educated society in German art of around 1500 had often grown hand in hand with issues of national unity and culture war. The wish to see these works could only now be accommodated through museum collections and new photomechanical methods of reproduction, and artists entered the public consciousness as historical personalities, with equal attention to their work. Dürer, Grünewald, Stoss, and Riemenschneider reached a level of popular recognition in the German empire comparable to Goethe or Beethoven. As national symbols they proved to the educated middle-class German that he belonged to a nation of at least as much cultural importance as the French and Italians. World War I—which the war propaganda of the Entente had made into a fight of European civilization against German barbarism after the German war crimes in Belgium—had intensified nationalism and led to an often hybrid sense of superiority. To German intellectuals, the war thus seemed to be a fight against the culture of their nation, and they therefore assured the world that they "would fight this battle as a *Kulturnation* to which the heritage of a Goethe, a Beethoven, a Kant is as sacred as its hearth and soil."[84]

The German defeat deeply shook the nation's sense of self-worth. The traumatic experience was sublimated not least in the art literature of the Weimar Republic, which had seamlessly succeeded the ruined empire.[85] Despite a serious scholarly ethic on which art historical research of facts and context continues to rely, and despite the multiplicity of interests, which reflected the pluralism of the society of the young republic, nationalistic aspects were all the more pronounced in the literature concerning German art of around 1500.

This must be kept in mind with regard to Georg Dehio, who continued his plan, begun in 1914, to write a "History of German Art" after the war. He produced a second volume in 1921, which dealt with German Gothic art up to the end of the rule of Emperor Maximilian I. Dehio considered especially sculpture from around 1500, in contrast to painting, "stylistically pure German and pure late Gothic." While Dehio wished to view Peter Vischer as "the German man in general, the symbol of the simple efficiency of our nation," Riemenschneider seemed to him to "make a concession to beauty, with ethical and artistic sincerity, which was unexpected for German art of that time."[86] Dehio had abandoned the European dimension of domestic art in favor of a cultural "separatism" of Germany, an idea first formulated by Kurt Gerstenberg in 1913 in a study, *Deutsche Sondergotik,* that received much attention during the upheaval of the world war.[87] Gerstenberg, influenced by Heinrich Wölfflin, Wilhelm Dilthey, and the psychology of nations espoused by Wilhelm Wundt, supported the thought that "each style, when considered for its content, contains not only the issue of history but also that of race."[88]

Gerstenberg relinquished such dogmas in an essay, already published during the Nazi regime, about a Netherlandish influence on Riemenschneider and in two popular illustrated monographs. The sculptor had long been considered a German artist, and special explanations about the national or racial character of his work were therefore unnecessary.[89] Illustrated books on Riemenschneider, published in 1933 by Theodor Demmler and Fritz Knapp before and just after the Nazis came to power, were equally noncommittal.[90] A nationalistic undercurrent is unmistakable, however, when Knapp writes about Riemenschneider that he "lacked the ambition to be anything but a German craftsman" and called his works "a piece of ur-Germanic humanity." Knapp may have had the traditional rivalry between the art of Würzburg and Nuremberg in mind, whose "sense of reality and…form" contained "certainly nothing ur-Germanic."[91]

The art literature of the Weimar Republic applied the thesis of German *Sonderweg,* or separatism, also to the general development of German sculpture from around 1500. Wilhelm Pinder's two-volume compendium *Die deutsche Plastik vom ausgehenden Mittelalter bis zum Ende der Renaissance* (Wildpark and Potsdam, 1924–1929) considered German sculpture "an exception in European art." Pinder believed that the era around 1500 was particularly defined by an autonomy of German sculpture: "All that is essential comes from inside, from the autonomous entelechy of German art." Pinder found little to praise in Riemenschneider. In comparison to the expressionist modernity of a Veit Stoss, Riemenschneider seemed to him "dried up" and "senile."[92] Pinder explained Riemenschneider's dominant influence on Würzburg sculpture as a phenomenon unrelated to his art: "Rarely have the more important masters had a greater effect on the destruction of the individuality of an entire artistic region than this gentle tyrant had on Lower Franconia." Pinder considered how structural analogies to Riemenschneider's art could be gleaned from topographic elements around the "sandstone city" Würzburg and may have promoted his influence on the region. He reiterated the recently developed concept of a "cultural topography," by which the geographic properties of a region shaped the character of its inhabitants, and thereby the essence of local artistic tradition.[93]

86. Dehio 1930, 252, 260.

87. Kurt Gerstenberg, *Die deutsche Sondergotik* (1913; 2nd ed. Darmstadt, 1969). The contemporary relevance of the book was already recognized by Hans Tietze, "Rezension zu K. Gerstenberg," *Kunstgeschichtliche Anzeigen* (1913), 52.

88. Heinrich Wölfflin, *Kunstgeschichtliche Grundbegriffe,* 5th ed. (Munich, 1921), 6; Wilhelm Dilthey, *Der Aufbau der geschichtlichen Welt in den Geisteswissenschaften* (Berlin, 1910); Wilhelm Wundt, *Völkerpsychologie. Eine Untersuchung der Entwicklungsgesetze von Sprache, Mythos und Sitte,* 10 vols. (1900–1920); Gerstenberg 1969, 9, 132–135.

89. Kurt Gerstenberg, "Riemenschneider und der niederländische Realismus," *Zeitschrift des Deutschen Vereins für Kunstwissenschaft* 1 (1934), 37–48; Kurt Gerstenberg, *Tilmann Riemenschneider im Taubertal* (Leipzig, 1939); Kurt Gerstenberg, *Tilmann Riemenschneider* (Vienna, 1941).

90. Theodor Demmler, *Tilmann Riemenschneider* (Berlin, 1923); Theodor Demmler, *Die Meisterwerke Tilmann Riemenschneiders* (Berlin, 1936); Fritz Knapp, *Riemenschneider und Würzburg* (Paderborn, 1931); Fritz Knapp, *Riemenschneider* (Leipzig and Bielefeld, 1935).

91. Knapp 1935, 7, 9.

92. Pinder 1924–1929, 2:396, 414. See also Willibald Sauerländer, "Vorwort," *Veit Stoss. Die Vorträge des Nürnberger Symposions* (Munich, 1985), 6–8. For the problem of expressionist conditioning in the critical reception, see Rainer Hausherr, "Texte über die Pietà Röttgen," *Bonner Jahrbücher* 165 (1965), 145–154; Gerhard Renda, "Nun schauen wir euch anders an," *Studien zur Gotikrezeption im deutschen Expressionismus* (Erlangen-Nuremberg, 1990).

93. Pinder 1924–1929, 2:414–415. Paul Piper, *Kunstgeographie. Versuch einer Grundlegung* (Berlin, 1936). For the history of terms and methods see Rainer Hausherr, "Kunstgeographie-Aufgaben, Grenzen, Möglichkeiten," *Rheinische Vierteljahresblätter* 34 (1970), 158–171.

94. Bier's essays are listed in Eberlein 1998, :98–199, nos. 281, 285, 287, 288, 332, 333; Hubert Schrade, *Tilmann Riemenschneider* (Heidelberg, 1927).

95. Pinder 1935, 6–7.

96. Pinder 1935, 199–206, esp. 205.

97. Sauerländer 1985, 6.

Essays by Justus Bier, published before his emigration, about Riemenschneider's origin and artistic heritage also dealt with this idea, as did Hubert Schrade's monograph of 1927.[94] The Lower Franconian literature about Riemenschneider gratefully made use of the concept of cultural topography as well. The art historical resonance of Würzburg, as asserted by Knapp, could be documented not only historically but also in topographic-folkloristic terms.

These key ideas of the Weimar Republic about German art history—the national character of art, the concept of German separatism, and the notion of cultural topography—were an invitation to abuse after Hitler came to power, not least because of their references to the psychology of nations and to biological theories on race, and they increasingly became a tool for Nazi ideology. While many art historians lost their lives on ethnic, religious, or political grounds or were forced into exile, there was no lack of attempts to come to terms with the Nazis or to gain their favor.

Pinder now thought it a historical necessity to rewrite the history of German art in the foreword to the first volume of his popular book, *Vom Wesen und Werden deutscher Formen* (Leipzig, 1935).[95] With his foreword to the third volume, *Die Kunst der Dürerzeit* (Leipzig, 1939), he became one of the intellectual arsonists of Nazism. "This book appears before a Germany that is once again forced to fight for its life and challenged to even greater victory.…The author, who is no longer able to participate personally in this second great war, hopes for a small consolation from this minor contribution to the fortification of the German nation: that its perusal may, in a small way, serve to inspire action."

With respect to German sculpture, Pinder's book represented only a minor revision of his 1924–1929 volumes. Riemenschneider, probably as a concession to his popularity, was now much more positively evaluated. The Creglingen altarpiece now revealed to Pinder an exemplary sense of devotion, which he celebrated as "one of the best traits of a nation that produced a Goethe."[96]

Examples of Riemenschneider's critical reception in the art historical literature of the Weimar Republic and the Third Reich give the impression that his work was not appropriated on an individual basis, but solely within the interpretive context of the entire development of German sculpture. In contrast to Riemenschneider, Veit Stoss and his unbending character seemed ideally suited for Nazi ideological purposes; the power of expression in his works was associated by Pinder with "readiness to fight." Stoss was also much more immediately connected with the historic perspective that the Nazis used for legitimation as a citizen of Nuremberg, a city in which the National-sozialistische Deutsche Arbeiter Partei (N S D A P) not accidentally convened the Reichsparty.[97] Riemenschneider's art was so popular that there was interest in appropriating this artist as well. Books on Riemenschneider by Reitzenstein, Gerstenberg, or Knapp were dutifully announced and reviewed in the party publication *Die Kunst im Dritten Reich*. That the Nazis intended to profit from the sculptor's popularity is especially obvious since the NSDAP's publishing house in Berlin produced a novel on Riemenschneider by Paul Johannes Arnold in 1938. It demonstrates a fascist veneration of heroes and artists that is seldom found to such a degree in German scholarly publications of that time. With this novel, reprinted in 1943 in an edition of 42,000 copies, and joined by the similarly heroic Riemenschneider novel *Die grosse Unruhe* by Felix Bielstein (Hamburg, 1943), ideological views and concepts of the world were conveyed much more successfully than in dry scholarly prose. The parallels between life and art, which had marked Riemenschneider's reception since Romanticism and had already prompted attempts to use him as a propagandistic tool during the empire, were trivialized and purposely abused by the Nazi ideologues: chances were that the distorted picture of the artist himself was to obscure his work.

One publication, which appeared in Switzerland in 1936, not in Nazi Germany, and which was pronounced the history of an intellectual viewpoint, was no less partial in its representation of the artist. In Karl Heinrich Stein's *Tilmann Riemenschneider im Bauernkrieg* (Zurich, 1936) the sculptor's resistance to authority presented a hidden appeal to resist Nazi terror. Thomas Mann, to whom the author dedicated the book in 1937, recognized this and used it in 1944 as a model for the Riemenschneider passage in his American speech "Germany and the Germans."[98]

Thomas Mann's view of Riemenschneider is that personality, which was completely separate from his work, has its own reception. When Justus Bier organized his retrospective of Riemenschneider's works in 1962, he reprinted Thomas Mann's passage as a matter of course in the catalogue. As an emigrant and scholarly expert, he must have enjoyed presenting his beloved Würzburg artist to American viewers in the words of Thomas Mann, as an example for "the other Germany."[99]

When Mann was quoted on the jacket copy of a book on Riemenschneider published in communist East Germany, where very different definitions existed for democracy and freedom, it became clear that even this interpretation was not immune from ideologically motivated reinterpretations by a totalitarian state. Riemenschneider was perceived not only as an artist who had accepted personal consequences for his convictions of freedom and justice; like many of his contemporaries, he was made into a representative of the socialists' "early civic revolution" and therefore an early forerunner of German socialism.[100]

In view of Riemenschneider's reception since the early nineteenth century, as represented here, one might perhaps detect a certain significance in the fact that during

98. Mann 1996, 268–269, 433–434.

99. *Sculptures of Tilmann Riemenschneider* [exh. cat., North Carolina Museum of Art] (Raleigh, 1962), frontispiece.

100. Edith Fründt, *Tilmann Riemenschneider* (Berlin, 1973).

Translation by Ulrike Mills.

the past few years very fundamental impulses for the scholarship of German sculpture from around 1500 have emanated from one study. In Michael Baxandall's *Limewood Sculptors of Renaissance Germany* (New Haven and London, 1980) the art history of that era is no longer described as a history of German artists, or of formal categories, but, from the distance of the European viewpoint, as a structural history.

Riemenschneider in America   *William D. Wixom*

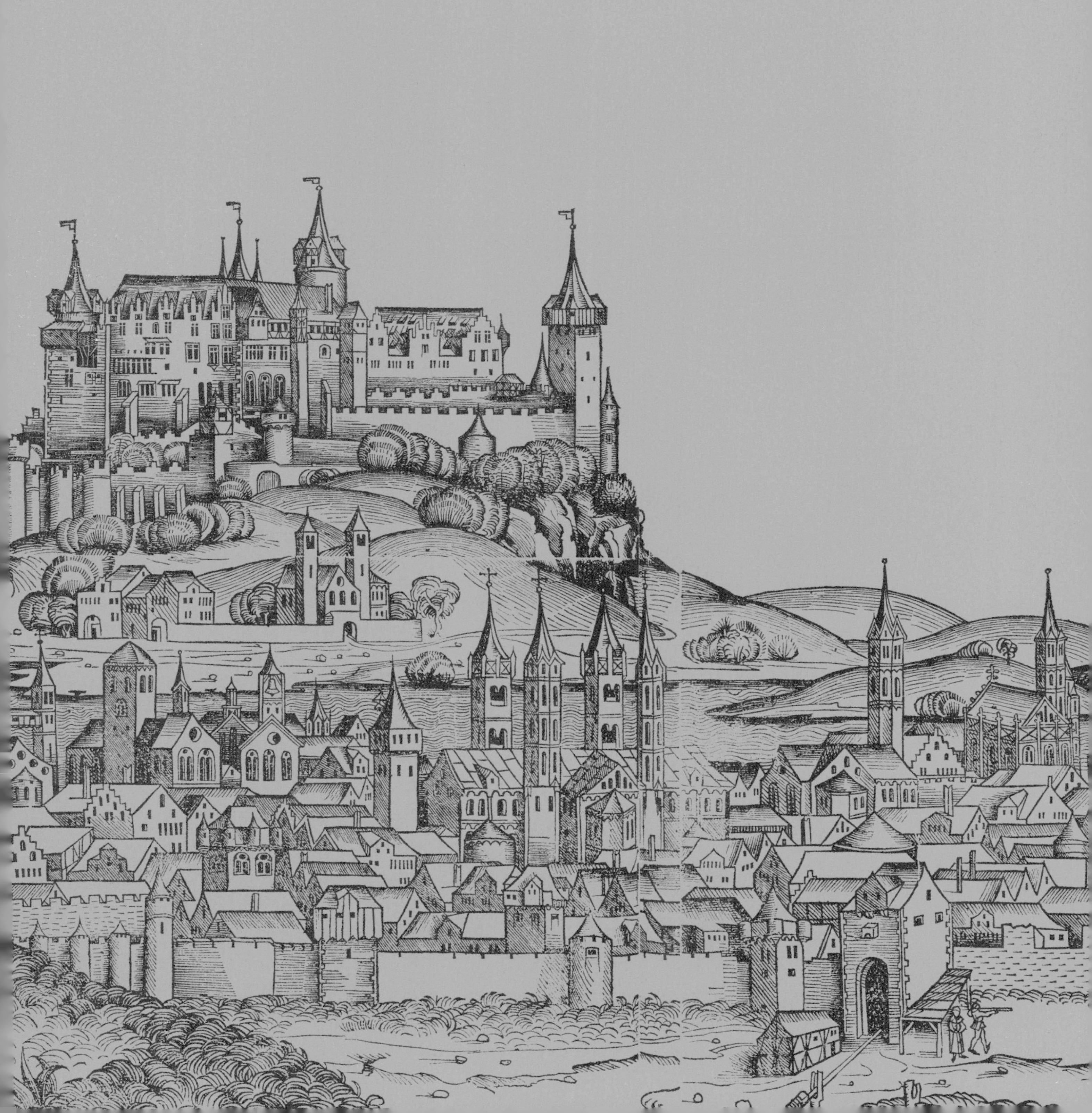

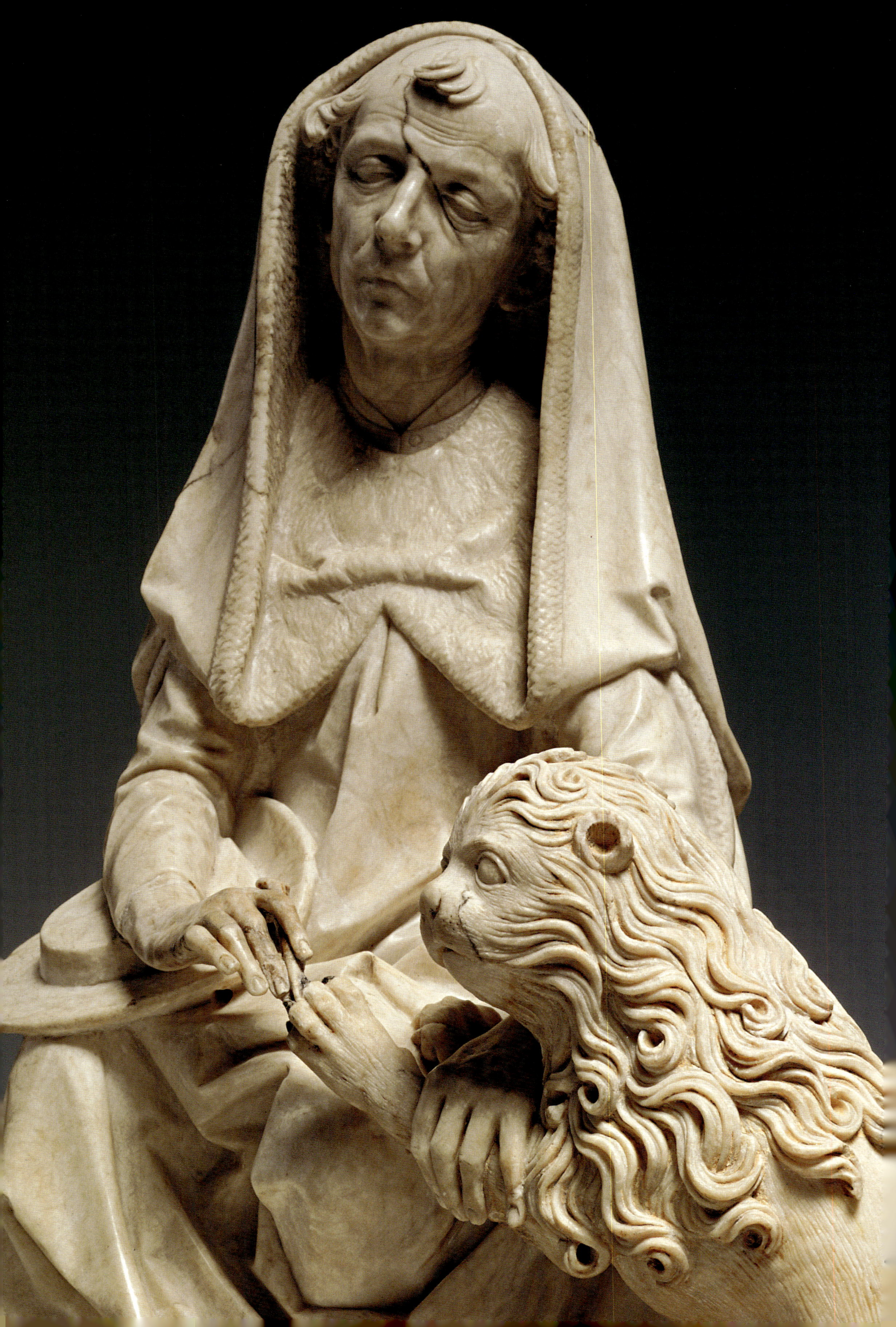

WENTY-FOUR EXAMPLES of sculpture by or attributed to Tilman Riemenschneider, his workshop, or followers can be seen today in the United States and Canada.[1] All but three are in public collections. Outside Germany, this is the largest assemblage of works representing a single major German sculptor of the late Gothic period. How can this phenomenon be explained? ℭ One approach is to review in summary fashion the surprisingly rich results of North American institutional collecting in the broader field of German late Gothic sculpture, in which the works by Riemenschneider have taken a significant place. The fledgling Metropolitan Museum began acquiring such pieces in 1885, and by the 1920s other museums as well as dealers and private collectors had begun to pursue this interest. The accompanying tabulation, a kind of timeline, chronicles the best and most notable examples in American collections. This impressive panorama is not widely known, either here or abroad.[2] ℭ William R. Valentiner (1880–1958), a scholar of wide-ranging taste and training (under Henry Thode, Cornelis Hofstede de Groot, and Wilhelm von Bode), served as curator of decorative arts at the Metropolitan Museum of Art from 1907 until 1914.[3] At the time he was also advising New York collectors such as the banker Henry Goldman (1857–1937),[4] whose *Bishop Saint* by Riemenschneider is now in the collection of the National Gallery of Art, Washington. Valentiner's appointment at the Metropolitan resulted from a request by the financier-collector J. Pierpont Morgan (1837–1913) for someone "capable of arranging for display the Hoentschel Collection, which he had acquired in Paris." In fulfilling this function and others, Valentiner came to know Morgan's catholic taste as well as his idiosyncrasies.[5] Morgan, serving in time

1. Alphabetically by location: Atlanta, The High Museum of Art, *Saint Andrew*; Baltimore, The Walters Art Gallery, *Anna Selbdritt*; Boston, Museum of Fine Arts, *Virgin and Child*, cat. 14; Cambridge, MA, Busch-Reisinger Museum, *Saint Anthony*; The Cleveland Museum of Art, *Saint Jerome with the Lion*, *Saint Stephen* and *Saint Lawrence*, cats. 11, 32 A, D; The Detroit Institute of Arts, *Virgin and Child*; Kansas City, The Nelson-Atkins Museum of Art, *Mourning Virgin*, cat. 34; Lawrence, Kansas, Spencer Museum of Art, *Virgin and Child*, cat. 22; The Minneapolis Institute of Arts, *Beheading of Saint John the Baptist* and *Presentation of the Head of Saint John the Baptist to Herod*; The Montreal Museum of Fine Arts, *Saint Sebastian*, cat. 39 A; New York, The Metropolitan Museum of Art, The Cloisters Collection, *Seated Bishop* and *Saints Christopher, Eustace, and Erasmus (Three Helper Saints)*, cats. 17, 23; *Standing Bishop*; New York, Private Collections, *Female Saint* and *Saint Catherine*, cat. 43 A, C; *Saint Sebastian*; Oberlin, Allen Memorial Art Museum, *Bust of Saint Urban*; Providence, Rhode Island School of Design, *Pietà*; Raleigh, North Carolina Museum of Art, *Female Saint*, cat. 10; Washington, DC, Dumbarton Oaks, *Virgin and Child on the Crescent Moon*, cat. 45; Washington, DC, National Gallery of Art, *Bishop Saint*, cat. 44.

2. For a broad survey that includes Gothic sculpture for all of Europe and England, see *Gothic Sculpture in America*, vol. 1, *The New England Museums*, ed. Dorothy Gillerman (New York and London, 1989); and the review, with important corrections, by Paul Williamson in *Burlington Magazine* 132, no. 1047 (June 1990), 418–419.

3. See Margaret Sterne, *The Passionate Eye: The Life of William R. Valentiner* (Detroit, 1980), 86–110.

4. Sterne 1980, 135 n. 304.

5. Sterne 1980, 90–95.

Saint Jerome with the Lion (cat. 11), 1490–1495, The Cleveland Museum of Art

6. *J. Pierpont Morgan Collector,* ed. Linda Horvitz Roth [exh. cat., Wadsworth Atheneum] (Hartford, 1987), 26–57, 205; Aaron Rottner, "J. P. Morgan and the Middle Ages," in *Medieval Art in America: Patterns of Collecting, 1800–1940* [exh. cat., Palmer Museum of Art, The Pennsylvania State University] (University Park, 1996), 115–126.

7. See Cornelius C. Vermeule III, Walter Cahn, and Rollin van N. Hadley, *Sculpture in the Isabella Stewart Gardner Museum* (Boston, 1977), 85–103, nos. 112–135; and Hilliard T. Goldfarb, *The Isabella Stewart Gardner Museum* (New Haven and London, 1995), 3–21, 134–139.

8. See William M. Milliken, *Born under the Sign of Libra* (Cleveland, 1977), 29–31; Sherman E. Lee, "William Mathewson Milliken on His 85th Year," *Bulletin of the Cleveland Museum of Art* 61 (December 1974), 319–320; Sherman E. Lee and William D. Wixom, "In Memoriam, William Mathewson Milliken, 1889–1978," *Bulletin of the Cleveland Museum of Art* 65 (April 1978), 110.

9. *Handbook of the Benjamin Altman Collection,* 2nd ed. (New York, 1928), no. 60. Unrelatable today to the works by Tilman Riemenschneider or by his two sculptor sons, Jörg and Hans, this long-ignored bust awaits thorough study. Certainly there is no three-dimensional comparison in importance with the star of German art in the Altman Collection, Albrecht Dürer's painting of the *Virgin and Child with Saint Anne,* 1519. See Kurt Löcher in *Gothic and Renaissance Art in Nuremberg 1300–1550* [exh. cat., The Metropolitan Museum of Art] (New York, 1986), 326–328, no. 144.

10. Germain Seligman, *Merchants of Art: 1880–1960* (New York, 1961), 71–74, 76.

as benefactor, trustee, and president of the Metropolitan, was one of the most intense, omnivorous, yet perceptive collectors America has ever experienced.[6] His early travel in Europe and his education in Switzerland and Germany (two years at the University of Göttingen) were part of the foundation of his artistic interests and culture. His first loans of German late Gothic sculpture came to the Metropolitan in 1908. Also in 1908 another early collector, the flamboyant and energetic Isabella Stewart Gardner (1840–1924), opened her home and collection in Boston to the public, with several works of German late Gothic sculpture displayed in the "Chapel" and the "Gothic Room" on the third floor of her pseudo-Venetian palace.[7]

In 1914 William M. Milliken (1889–1978) became an assistant and then an assistant curator of decorative arts at the Metropolitan Museum, serving in these capacities until 1917.[8] The bequest of Benjamin Altman (1840–1913) came to the Metropolitan in 1914, including a wood *Portrait of a Young Man* with traces of polychromy, "by Hans Tilman Riemenschneider," a curious conflation of the father's name with that of one of his sons.[9] During Milliken's tenure the Metropolitan in 1916 also acquired nearly a dozen examples of German late Gothic sculpture as the gift of J. Pierpont Morgan through his son. Many of these were from the Georges Hoentschel collection, sold to Morgan in installments through his principal dealer, Jacques Seligmann (1858–1923).[10] Morgan made most of his art purchases during the last decade and a half of his life. Three of his premier acquisitions had been put on display along with his first loans to the Metropolitan. One of these, a reliquary bust by Hans Multscher, was purchased after Morgan's death—along with a selection of Morgan's old master paintings, French furniture, and Renaissance bronzes—by industrialist Henry Clay Frick (1849–1919)[11] through Joseph Duveen. In 1917 the Metropolitan acquired nine more German late Gothic works as gifts of J. Pierpont Morgan.

The acquisition of sculpture in this field continued outside New York in the 1920s, with one purchase for the Smith College Museum and several for the Detroit Institute of Arts on the advice of William Valentiner, who was director there from 1924 to 1945.[12] Valentiner had been invited to Detroit by Ralph Harman Booth (1873–1931), president of the Detroit Arts Commission, and had traveled to Europe with him in 1922 to select works for the institute.[13] In the early 1930s the Paris collection of Edmond Foulc was sold to the Philadelphia Museum of Art, then under the directorship of the imposing and scholarly Fiske Kimball (1888–1955), with Francis Henry Taylor (1903–1957) as curator.[14] The bequest of Michael Friedsam (1858–1931) to the Metropolitan in 1931 included two examples of German late Gothic sculpture. Friedsam, president of B. Altman & Co., favored early French and German paintings.[15] In 1932 the Busch-Reisinger Museum in Cambridge, Massachusetts, and the Wadsworth

Atheneum, Hartford, with A. Everett Austin Jr. as its enterprising director from 1927 to 1946, began collecting in the field. Between 1937 and 1939 Robert Woods Bliss (1875–1962) and his wife, the distinguished founders of the Dumbarton Oaks Collection, and William Milliken, indefatigable director of the Cleveland Museum of Art from 1930 to 1958, acquired major works by master sculptors of the German late Gothic.

In the 1940s the Kress Foundation, the Art Institute of Chicago, and the Minneapolis Institute of Arts as well as other major institutions began to acquire sculpture of the period, either directly or indirectly from such prominent collectors as Henry Goldman, William Randolph Hearst (1863–1951), Otto H. Kahn (1867–1934), and Alastair B. Martin, all of New York, as well as from prominent New York dealers such as Rosenberg and Stiebel, H. Schaeffer Gallery, Blumka Gallery, and Brummer Gallery. A bequest to the Metropolitan Museum from investment banker George Blumenthal (1858–1941) included seven examples of German late Gothic sculpture. A slight man with delicate hands, Blumenthal is said to have had an acute sense for the tactile. Also in 1941 Frieda Schiff Warburg (d. 1958), widow of the German-born investment banker and philanthropist Felix M. Warburg (1871–1937), made gifts to the Busch-Reisinger Museum and to the Museum of Fine Arts, Boston.[16] A sale of works from the collection of newspaper baron William Randolph Hearst took place in 1941 at Gimbel Brothers, the New York department store. Hearst, often indiscriminate as a collector, could also on occasion acquire a masterpiece, such as Niclaus Gerhaert von Leiden's *Reliquary Bust of Saint Margaret of Alexandria*, c. 1465, later purchased by the Art Institute of Chicago. A number of Detroit area collectors joined William Valentiner, still director of the Detroit Institute of Arts, in acquiring several significant works in 1943. In 1944 the Samuel H. Kress Foundation purchased its first work by Riemenschneider, initiating a series of acquisitions of German late Gothic sculpture that it continued until 1962.[17] Alastair Martin, who is an intensely private and imaginative collector, made a generous gift to the Metropolitan Museum in 1948.[18] This was the *Holy Family* relief, later identified as being by Niclaus Weckmann.

In the 1950s a number of museums were able to add important works of German late Gothic sculpture to their collections. Purchases came through major dealers such as the Blumka Gallery, Mathias Komor, and Rosenberg and Stiebel in New York, John Hunt in Dublin, and Henri Heilbronner in Munich. Gifts came from the private collections of dealer Dikran Kélékian in New York as well as Mrs. Russell C. Veit and Joseph Pulitzer. Institutions that acquired works from these various dealers and collectors included the Cleveland Museum of Art, the Spencer Museum of Art at the University of Kansas, the Wadsworth Atheneum, the Jewett Art Center at Wellesley College, and the High Museum of Art in Atlanta. Sherman E. Lee, who had received

11. See Martha Frick Symington Sanger, *Henry Clay Frick* (New York, 1998), 363–364; and John Pope-Hennessy with Anthony F. Radcliff, *The Frick Collection: An Illustrated Catalogue*, vol. 1 (New York, 1970), xxv–xxvi.

12. Sterne 1980, 140–141, 159.

13. Booth became an important collector and donor. Some of the best paintings in his collection, including two portraits by Lucas Cranach the Elder, were given to the National Gallery of Art, Washington, by his widow in 1953.

14. *The Pennsylvania Museum Bulletin* 15 (February 1930), 3–63, and (April 1930), 4–9; David Dubon, "Masterpieces of the Renaissance Collection," *Apollo* xcx (July 1974), 18. Francis Henry Taylor later became director of the Metropolitan Museum of Art.

15. See *Les Donateurs du Louvre* (Paris, 1989), 211; and Louis Réau, "Une Collection de Primitifs français en Amérique," *Gazette des Beaux-Arts* (January 1926), 1–15.

16. Ron Chernow, *The Warburgs: The Twentieth-Century Odyssey of a Remarkable Jewish Family* (New York, 1993). Felix Warburg's grand neo-Gothic home, now the Jewish Museum, is on upper Fifth Avenue in New York, and what is known of his collection seems to consist of medieval and Renaissance art, especially early prints; see Dorothy Limouze and Susan D. Kuretsky, *The Felix M. Warburg Print Collection: The Legacy of Discernment* (Poughkeepsie, 1995).

17. Ulrich Middeldorf, *Sculptures from the Samuel H. Kress Collection: European Schools, XIV–XIX Century* (London, 1975), 123–128.

18. For an overview of the range of Martin's collecting, see *The Guennol Collection*, 3 vols. (New York, 1975, 1982, 1991).

his early training at the Detroit Institute of Arts under the directorship of William Valentiner, succeeded William Milliken as director of the Cleveland Museum in 1958. Building on Milliken's earlier interest in European sculpture, he supported the acquisition of two works by Riemenschneider — *Saint Stephen* and *Saint Lawrence* (cat. 32 A, D). At the same time James J. Rorimer (1905–1966), director of the Cloisters from 1949 to 1955 and of the Metropolitan Museum itself until 1966, began to acquire key German works to offset the French and Spanish dominance at the Cloisters.

Again in the 1960s museums added significant works to their sculpture collections. Major dealers such as Rosenberg and Stiebel, Edward R. Lubin, and Paul Drey, all of New York, were important sources, as were private collectors such as Dr. Siegfried J. Thannhauser (1885–1962) of Boston and the widow of Solomon R. Guggenheim (1861–1949) of New York. Justus Bier (1899–1990), director of the North Carolina Museum of Art in Raleigh from 1961 to 1970, acquired a sculpture by Riemenschneider in 1968.[19] Bier's erudite enthusiasm led to many firsts for his museum, including the acquisition of several sculpture to augment a strong paintings collection. The Nelson-Atkins Museum of Art also acquired a Riemenschneider at this time.

Fewer examples of important German late Gothic sculpture entered museum collections in the 1970s. Among them were three works by Tilman Riemenschneider or his workshop, one of which is the magnificent *Seated Bishop* acquired for the Cloisters Collection; another was purchased by the Montreal Museum of Fine Arts from the discerning German-born collector Lewis V. Randall (1893–1972). In the 1980s and 1990s the most significant acquisitions seem to have been made by the Metropolitan Museum. The collections of the Chicago bon vivant Thomas F. Flannery Jr. (1926–1980) and the Viennese Dr. Peter Hierzenberger were sold in London in 1983–1984.[20] By this time the Busch-Reisinger Museum had established itself as the only American museum collection to exhibit complete altarpieces, the preeminent format and context for German late Gothic sculpture.[21]

Several points stand out in this survey: the importance of museum professionals, the enterprise of art dealers (especially those in the United States), and the passion of private collectors. Each of these groups was dominated by either German-born individuals or persons steeped in German culture and art. Among the former, William Valentiner was instrumental in the early development of collections at the Metropolitan Museum and the Detroit Institute of Arts; Georg Swarzenski (1876–1957) and Hanns Swarzenski (1903–1985) helped shape the collection at the Museum of Fine Arts, Boston; and Justus Bier, at the North Carolina Museum of Art, mounted the first exhibition in the United States on the sculpture of Riemenschneider in 1962. Among American-born museum professionals, William Milliken traveled extensively in Ger-

19. See Inge Witt, "Justus Bier: Man of Vision," *North Carolina Museum of Art Bulletin* 12, no. 4 (1974), 9–27.

20. Sotheby Parke Bernet, 1–2 December 1983 and 3 April 1984, respectively.

21. See Peter Nesbit, "The Busch-Reisinger Museum and Its Tenth Decade: Reflections on Survival and Success," in *Harvard Art Museums: 100 Years of Collecting* (Cambridge, MA, 1996), 319–323, for the development and changes in connection with this important collection.

many in the 1930s and after World War II while he was director of the Cleveland Museum of Art, and James Rorimer, after his experiences in France and Germany at the close of World War II, made concerted efforts to add German sculpture to the Cloisters collection even though his own taste was primarily directed toward France. Charles Kuhn played a critical role in enriching the collections of the Busch-Reisinger Museum. The Swarzenskis and Bier had fled Nazi Germany because they were Jewish. They were not alone. Others who emigrated from Germany at this time included the dealers Leopold Blumka, A. S. and Paul Drey, Jacob Hirsch, Sammy Rosenberg, and Hans and Eric Stiebel.[22] American taste and knowledge gained enormously with the arrival of these individuals.

The most important private collector in America was J. Pierpont Morgan. The exhibitions of portions of his collections at the Metropolitan beginning in 1908 and continuing until after his death in 1913 as well as the gifts made in his name by his son in 1916 and 1917 had a tremendous impact on museum visitors and museum professionals alike. William Milliken, for one, worked on the Morgan collection from 1914 to 1917.[23] Even today "Morgan's individual acquisitions are important not only for their intrinsic aesthetic value and sheer bulk, but also for the preeminent and pivotal role they played in the development of America's taste for medieval art."[24]

European collections that were important sources for sculpture coming to America included those of Georges Hoentschel and Edmond Foulc in Paris, Dr. Richard Oertel and Georg Schuster in Munich, Catalina von Pannwitz in the Netherlands, and the Vienna Rothschilds. The taste of such foreign collectors, as well as the great, well-established museum collections abroad, must have influenced American preferences, not only that of Morgan but of Isabella Stewart Gardner, Benjamin Altman, Henry Walters (1848–1931), George Blumenthal, Felix M. Warburg, William Randolph Hearst, Henry Goldman, Solomon R. Guggenheim, Michael Friedsam, Lewis V. Randall, Mr. and Mrs. Robert Woods Bliss, Ralph Harman Booth, Thomas F. Flannery Jr., Richard B. Flagg,[25] Alastair B. Martin, and others.

The most discriminating of these individuals and the various institutions responsible for the phenomenal growth of American collections of German late Gothic sculpture sought and acquired outstanding examples in this field. Some of the works are by anonymous but gifted carvers, while others bear the names of several of the most distinguished masters, such as Niclaus Gerhaert von Leiden, Hans Leinberger, Hans Multscher, Nicolas Hagenower, Veit Stoss, and Niclaus Weckmann. It was in this setting that the availability of sculpture by Tilman Riemenschneider and his workshop struck a responsive chord.

22. See Helen Dudar, "The Blumka Tradition," *Connoisseur* (November 1983), 134–139; and *European Works of Art from the Private Collection and Gallery of the Blumka Estate* [sale cat., Sotheby's, New York, 9–10 January 1996]. See also *Affairs of Art: Rosenberg and Stiebel in America,* video film, New York, 1989.

23. Milliken 1977, 29–32.

24. Rottner 1996, 115.

25. *Medieval Art from Private Collections* [exh. cat., The Cloisters] (New York, 1968), no. 54.

Timeline of Selected
North American
Acquisitions of German
Late Gothic Sculpture

• 1880s and 1890s •

Swabia, possibly a pupil of Veit
Stoss, *Saint James the Greater,*
c. 1480, pine? with polychromy
and gilding, height 90 (35⅜),
The Metropolitan Museum
of Art, Gift of Charles Drake,
1885 (85.5.1).

(**1.**) Franconia, altarpiece with
scenes from the Life of the
Virgin and Holy Kinship,
dated 1548, wood with polychromy and painted wings
and predella within engaged
frame, height 82.2 (32⅜),
The Metropolitan Museum
of Art, Bequest of Mrs. A. M.
Minturn, 1890 (90.3.5). Illus.
Katharine Baetjer, *European
Paintings in The Metropolitan
Museum of Art by Artists Born
Before 1865: A Summary Catalogue* (New York, 1995), 229.

Saxony, *Holy Kinship* altarpiece,
c. 1510–1520, limewood? with
polychromy and gilding, height
155 (61), Isabella Stewart Gardner Museum, Boston, Pur-
chased in 1897 (S30n11). Illus.
Walter Cahn, *Sculpture in
the Isabella Stewart Gardner
Museum* (Boston, 1977), 93–95,
no. 122.

(**2.**) Upper Rhine or Swabia,
Saint Elizabeth of Hungary,
c. 1490, wood, height 119.5
(47), Isabella Stewart Gardner
Museum, Boston, Acquired
in 1893 (S30w11). Illus. Cahn
1977, 88, no. 116.

• 1910–1920 •

Franconia, *Bust of the Virgin
and Child,* early sixteenth
century, limewood, height
71.1 (28), The Metropolitan
Museum of Art, Hewitt Fund,
1911 (11.127.1). Illus. Joseph
Breck, *Catalogue of Romanesque, Gothic, and Renaissance
Sculpture* (New York, 1913),
234, no. 290.

Krakow, pupil of Veit Stoss,
The Baptism of Christ,
c. 1480–1490, limewood with
polychromy and gilding,
height 120.6 (47½), The Metropolitan Museum of Art,
Rogers Fund, 1912 (12.130.1).
Color illus. *Gothic and Renaissance Art in Nuremberg 1300–
1550* [exh. cat., The Metropolitan Museum of Art] (New
York, 1986), 236–237, no. 88.
(cat. 27)

Lower Saxony, Urban Master
of Hildesheim, *The Virgin and
Child, Saint Anne, and Saint
Emerentia,* c. 1515–1530, pine
with polychromy and gilding,
height 83.8 (33), The Metropolitan Museum of Art, Gift
of J. Pierpont Morgan, 1916
(16.32.208). Ex coll.: Georges
Hoentschel, Paris. See Gert van
der Osten, "Niederdeutsche
Bildwerke in Amerikanischen
Sammlungen," *Niederdeutsche
Beiträge zur Kunstgeschichte* 4
(1965), 101–108.

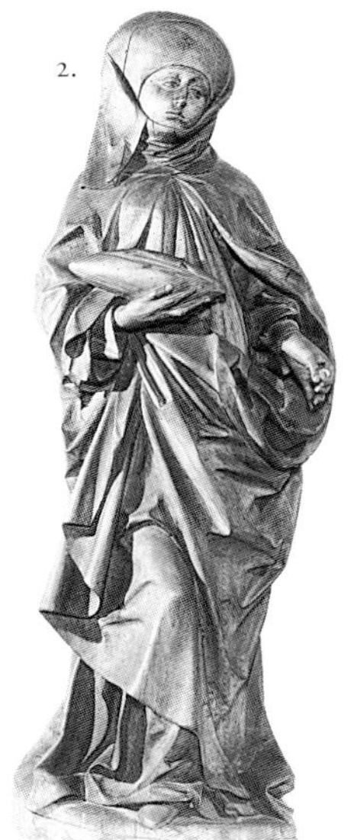

2.

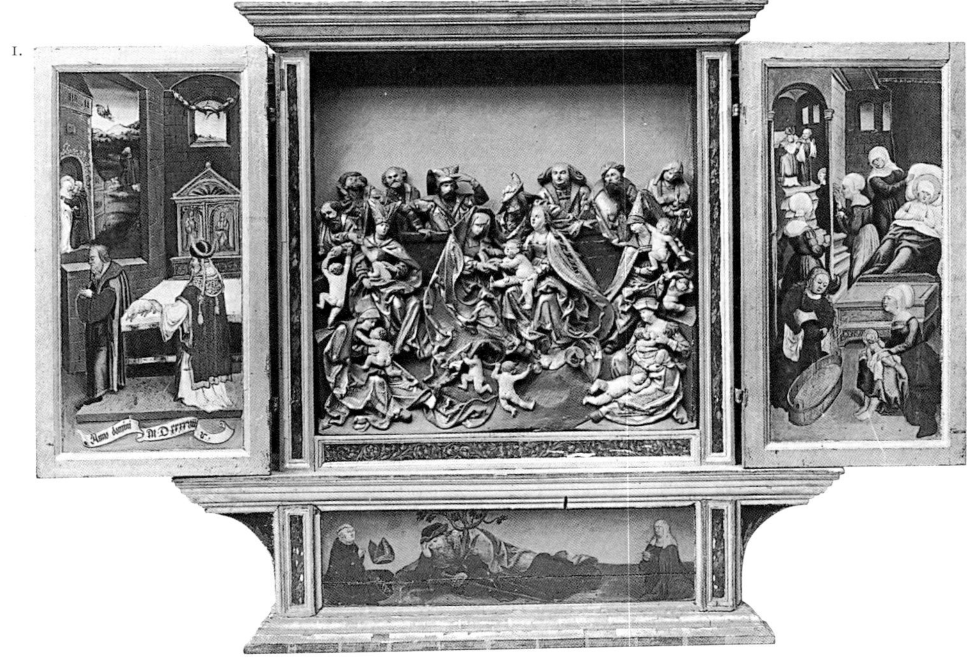

1.

Benedikt Dreyer (Lübeck,
active 1510–1530), *Meeting of
Saints Joachim and Anna at
The Golden Gate,* c. 1515–1520,
wood, height 55.7 (21⅞), The
Metropolitan Museum of Art,
Gift of J. Pierpont Morgan,
1916 (16.32.213). Formerly on
the high altar of the parish
church of Saint Michael in
Ledersdorf, near Düren.

(**3.**) Hans Multscher (Ulm,
c. 1400–1467), *Reliquary Bust
of Saint Catharine,* c. 1450,
copper alloy, height 32 (12⅝),
The Frick Collection, New
York (16.2.59). Ex coll.: [Dur-
lacher Brothers, London];*
J. Pierpont Morgan, London
and New York, 1910; [Duveen
Brothers, London]; Henry
Clay Frick (1849–1919), New
York, 1916. Wilhelm Bode's
attribution to Veit Stoss, now
abandoned, was repeated in
the *Guide for the Loan Exhibition of the J. Pierpont Morgan Collection* (New York, 1914),
illus. opp. 48. See also John
Pope-Hennessy, *The Frick
Collection* (New York, 1970),
3–7 (illus. in color); Jörg
Rosenfeld, "Unus Invenit-Alter
Fecit, Bronzebildwerke von
Hans Multscher?, eine nicht
ganz unproblematische Kunstgeschichte," in *Hans Multscher.
Bildhauer der Spätgotik in Ulm*
[exh. cat., Ulmer Museum]
(Ulm, 1997), 225–234, figs.
2–3, and n. 15.

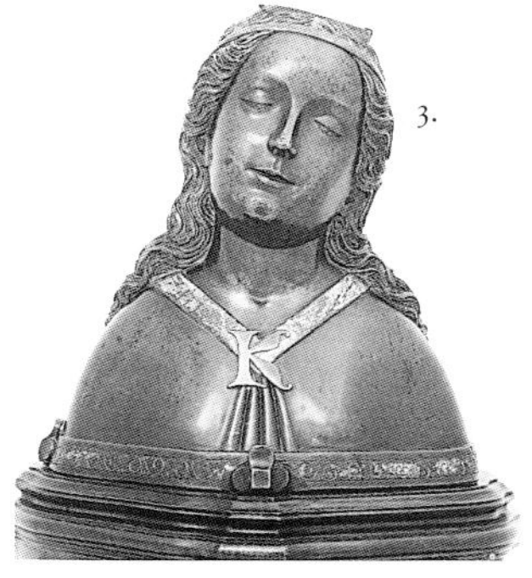

3.

(**4.**) Strasbourg, workshop of
Niclaus Gerhaert von Leiden,
*Reliquary Busts of Saints Cath-
erine and Barbara,* c. 1465,
basswood (limewood?) and ash,
respectively, both with polychromy, height 43.2 (17) each,
The Metropolitan Museum of
Art, Gift of J. Pierpont Morgan, 1917 (17.190.1734/1735).
From the Abbey Church of
Saints Peter and Paul, Wissembourg. Ex coll.: Victor Gay,
Paris; [sale, Drouot, 1909, lots
358, 359]; J. Pierpont Morgan,
London and New York, 1910.
Illus. Roland Recht, *Nicolas
de Leyde et la sculpture à Strasbourg (1460–1525)* (Strasbourg,
1987), 344, no. 1.10,11, pls. 35,
36; and Alfred Schädler, "Die
'Dürer' Madonna der ehemali-
gen Sammlung Rothschild in
Wien und Nicolaus Gerhaert,"
Städel Jahrbuch 10 (1983), 52.

• 1920s •

Franconia, circle of Veit Stoss,
Angel Bearing a Column, first
third of the sixteenth century,
limewood with traces of
polychromy, height 44.5 (17½),
Smith College Museum of
Art, Northampton, MA
(1920.26-1). Ex coll.: [Joseph
Brummer, New York]. Illus.
Gillerman 1989, 224–225,
no. 180.

Ulm, circle of Michel Erhart,
Virgin and Child, c. 1480,
limewood with traces of poly-
chromy, height 162.6 (64), The
Detroit Institute of Arts, Pur-
chased with funds from Ralph
Harman Booth (22.3). Ex coll.:
Abbey of Zwiefalten; anony-
mous dealer, Ochsenhausen;
Krupp collection, Essen; J. and
S. Goldschmidt, Frankfurt am
Main; Ralph Harman Booth,
Grosse Pointe, Michigan. Illus.
Peter Barnet, "Late Gothic
Wood Sculptures from Ulm,"
*Bulletin of the Detroit Institute
of Arts* 64, no. 4 (1989), 33–37,
figs. 7, 8.

Niclaus Weckmann (Ulm,
active 1481–1528), *Virgin and
Child,* 1510–1520, limewood
with polychromy and gild-
ing, height 100.3 (39½), The
Detroit Institute of Arts
(22.205). Illus. Barnet 1989,
36, 38–39, fig. 13.

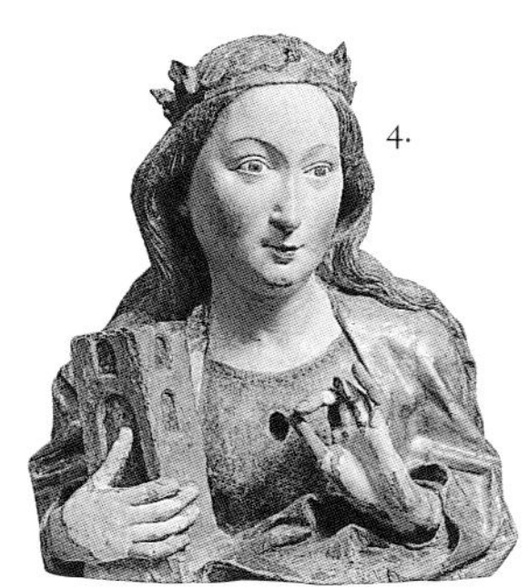

4.

• 1930s •

(**5.**) Master of Saint Benedict
(Hildesheim, active 1510–
1530), *Education of the Virgin,*
c. 1510–1515, wood with
polychromy, height 87 (34¼),
Philadelphia Museum of
Art, Gift of Elizabeth Malcolm Bowman in memory of
Wendell Phillips Bowman
(1930.1.163). Ex coll.: Edmond
Foulc, Paris. Illus. Gert von
der Osten and Horst Vey,
*Painting and Sculpture in Ger-
many and the Netherlands*
(Baltimore, 1969), 58, pl. 45.

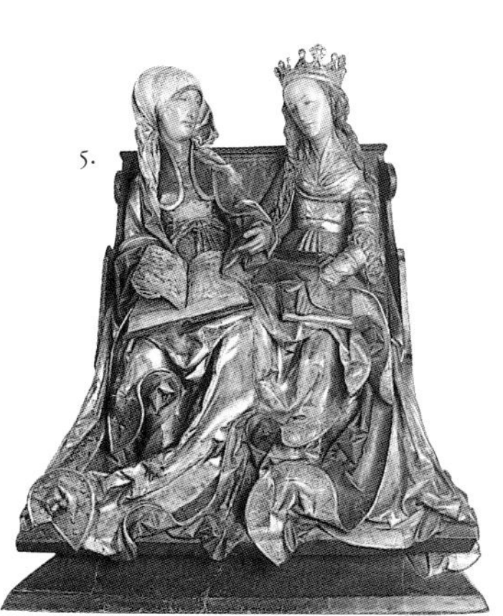

5.

Niclaus Weckmann (Ulm, active 1481–1528), *Saint Barbara* and *Saint Catherine,* limewood with traces of polychromy, height 98; 96 (38⅝; 37¾), Philadelphia Museum of Art, Gift of Elizabeth Malcolm Bowman in memory of Wendell Phillips Bowman (1930.1.167–168). Ex coll.: Edmond Foulc, Paris. Illus. Alfred Schädler, "Niclaus Weckmann. Bildhauer zu Ulm," *Münchner Jahrbuch der bildenden Kunst* 43 (1992), 68, figs. 22, 23.

Lower Rhine, *The Last Supper,* c. 1500, limestone relief, height 62.2 (24½), The Metropolitan Museum of Art, The Friedsam Collection, Bequest of Michael Friedsam, 1931 (32.100.143). Ex coll.: Emile Peres, Paris; [Kleinberger Galleries, New York]; Michael Friedsam, New York. Illus. *The Metropolitan Museum of Art Bulletin* 27, pt. 2 (1932), 54, no. 95; and Timothy B. Husband in *Decorative and Applied Art from Late Antiquity to Late Gothic* [exh. cat., Pushkin Museum] (Moscow and Leningrad, 1990), no. 74 (in Russian).

Franconia, influence of Veit Stoss; close to Master of the Schwabach High Altarpiece, *Saint Michael,* early sixteenth century, limewood? with polychromy and gilding, height 80 (31½), Wadsworth Atheneum, Hartford (1932.294). Ex coll.: [A. S. Drey, Munich(?)]. Illus. Gillerman 1989, 306, no. 230.

Thuringia, *Saint Anne* altarpiece, dated 1516, limewood with polychromy and gilding, height 120.6 (47½), Busch-Reisinger Museum, Cambridge, MA, Gift of Edna K. Loeb, 1932 (1932.65). Important as the third complete altarpiece to come to America. Ex coll.: Dr. Richard Oertel, Munich; [sale, Lepke, Berlin, 6–7 May 1913, no. 90, p. 26, pl. 58]. Illus. Charles L. Kuhn, *German and Netherlandish Sculpture 1280–1800: The Harvard Collections* (Cambridge, MA, 1965), 73, no. 28, pl. xxv; and Gillerman 1989, 207, no. 167.

Tilman Riemenschneider, *Virgin and Child on the Crescent Moon,* 1521, limewood, height 95.2 (37½), Dumbarton Oaks, Washington, DC, House Collection (5.37.06). Ex coll.: [said to have been acquired in Vienna around 1910 by Wilhelm Böhler, Munich]; [Siegfied Lämmle, Munich, before 1935]; [offered in the trade by Julius Böhler, H. Heilbronner, and Siegfried Lämmle, Munich, 1935]; [Richard H. Zinser, Stuttgart and Forest Hills, NY, 1935]; [Jacob Hirsch, New York]; purchased 13 February 1937 by Mr. and Mrs. Robert Woods Bliss, Washington, DC Dumbarton Oaks, Washington, DC, House Collection, since 1940. (cat. 45)

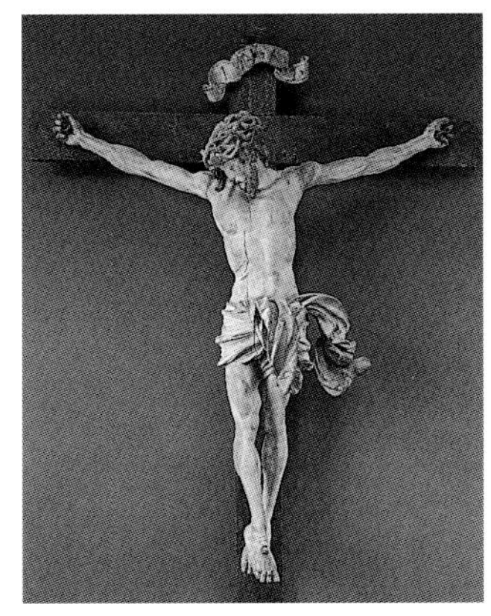

(**6.**) Hans Leinberger (Bavaria, active 1510–1530), *Corpus of Christ*, 1525–1530, limewood, height 118.1 (46½), The Cleveland Museum of Art, Purchase from the J. H. Wade Fund, 1938 (38.293). Ex coll.: Georg Schuster, Munich; [sale, Julius Böhler, Munich; 17–18 March 1938, lot 78]. William Milliken visited Landshut and other Leinberger sites for the first time in the early 1930s. Cover illus. William M. Milliken, *Bulletin of the Cleveland Museum of Art* 26, no. 4 (April 1939), 43–46; Milliken 1977, 116.

(**7.**) Master of Rabenden (Bavaria, active 1515–1520), *Pietà (Vesperbild),* c. 1515–1520, limewood with polychromy and gilding, height 89.1 (35), The Cleveland Museum of Art, Purchase from the J. H. Wade Fund, 1938 (38.294). Ex coll.: Georg Schuster, Munich; [sale, Julius Böhler, Munich, 17–18 March 1938, lot 94]. Frontispiece illus. Milliken 1939, 44–45.

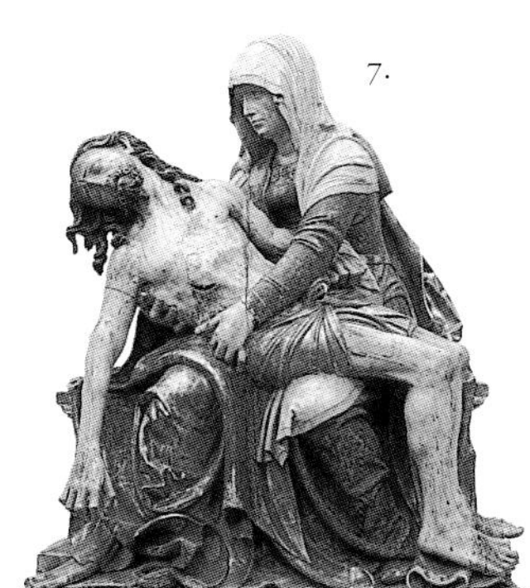

Veit Stoss (1477?–1533), *Mourning Virgin* from a Crucifixion group, c. 1500–1510, pearwood, height 31.4 (12⅜), The Cleveland Museum of Art, Purchase from the J. H. Wade Fund, 1939 (39.64). Ex coll.: Andreas Colli, Innsbruck (1933). (cat. 35)

Workshop of Tilman Riemenschneider, *Beheading of Saint John the Baptist* and *Presentation of the Head of Saint John the Baptist to Herod,* inscribed and dated 1519, white sandstone, height 104.8 (41¼) each, The Minneapolis Institute of Arts, The Edith Morrison Van Derlip Fund (39.14.1–2). Ex coll.: Satori; [Joseph Brummer, New York]. Illus. Justus Bier, "Two Stone Reliefs from Riemenschneider's Workshop in Minneapolis," *Gazette des Beaux-Arts,* ser. 6, no. 43 (March 1954), 165–178, 200–203, figs. 1a,b, 5a, 6a.

• 1940s •

Franconia, *Saint Catherine; Saint Barbara; Saint John the Evangelist;* and *Saint John the Baptist,* c. 1510, limewood with polychromy and gilding, height 109.2 to 114.3 (43 to 45), The Metropolitan Museum of Art, Bequest of George Blumenthal, 1941 (41.190.84–85/90–91). From a retable. Ex coll.: George and Florence Blumenthal, New York. Illus. Stella Rubinstein-Block, *Catalogue of the George and Florence Blumenthal Collection,* vol. 2 (New York, 1926), pls. XXII–XXIV.

Franconia, *Education of the Virgin,* c. 1510–1520, limewood with polychromy, height 83.8 (33), Busch-Reisinger Museum, Cambridge, MA, Gift of Mrs. Felix M. Warburg in memory of her husband (1941.35). Ex coll.: Felix M. Warburg, New York. Illus. Kuhn 1965, 69–70, no. 25, pls. XXII, XXIII.

Tilman Riemenschneider, *Virgin and Child on the Crescent Moon,* 1490s, limewood, height 120 (47¼), Museum of Fine Arts, Boston, Gift in memory of Felix M. Warburg, by his wife, Frieda Schiff Warburg (1941.653). Ex coll.: Felix M. Warburg, New York. (cat. 14)

Niclaus Gerhaert von Leiden (active 1460–1473), *Reliquary Bust of Saint Margaret of Alexandria,* c. 1465, walnut, height 50.8 (20), The Art Institute of Chicago, Lucy Maud Buckingham Collection (43.1001). From the Abbey Church of Saints Peter and Paul, Wissembourg. Ex coll.: Gavet (late 1800s); Doisteau; [sale, Drouot, 25 November 1909, lot 414]; William Randolph Hearst, New York and San Simeon, 1910–1943. Illus. M. R. Rogers and O. Goetz, *Handbook to the Lucy Maud Buckingham Collection* (Chicago, 1945), 63, no. 12, pls. XVII–XIX; Schädler 1983, 51, fig. 16; and Recht 1987, 344, no.1.09, pls. 32, 34.

Workshop of Tilman Riemenschneider, *Virgin and Child,* c. 1490–1493?, limewood, height 142 (56), The Detroit Institute of Arts, Gift of Mrs. Ralph Harman Booth in memory of her husband (43.2). Ex coll.: Rosenbaum, Frankfurt am Main; Mr. and Mrs. Ralph Harman Booth, Grosse Pointe, Michigan. Illus. *Sculptures of Tilman Riemenschneider* [exh. cat., North Carolina Museum of Art] (Raleigh, 1962), 38–39, no. VII.

Ulm, circle of Hans Multscher (active c. 1427–1467), *Saint Bartholomew,* c. 1450, limewood, height 117.5 (46¼), The Detroit Institute of Arts, Gift of Robert H. Tannahill (43.451). Ex coll.: Schnell, Ravensburg; [J. B. Neumann, New York]. Illus. Barnet 1989, 28–31, 33, figs. 1, 6.

Lower Bavaria, *Saint Barbara,* c. 1520, wood with polychromy, height 83.2 (32¾), Museum of Fine Arts, Boston, Gift of Mrs. Charles Gaston Smith's Group (1945.474). Ex coll.: Otto H. Kahn, New York and London. Illus. Gillerman 1989, 83, no. 60.

Tilman Riemenschneider, *Bishop Saint,* c. 1510–1520, limewood with traces of polychromy, height 82.3 (32 3/8), National Gallery of Art, Washington, Samuel H. Kress Collection (1961.1.1). Ex coll.: Wilhelm Sattler and his son Jens (d. 1901), Mainberg Castle (near Kitzingen), before 1826–1901; Benoit Oppenheim, Berlin, 1901–before 1927; [Munich art market, c. 1927–before 1934]; Henry Goldman, New York, 1934–before 1943; [New York art market, 1943]; [Duveen Brothers around this time]; Samuel H. Kress Foundation, 1944. (cat. 44)

Tilman Riemenschneider, *Saint Jerome with the Lion,* 1490–1495, alabaster, height 37.8 (14 7/8), The Cleveland Museum of Art, Purchase from the J. H. Wade Fund, 1946 (46.82). Ex coll.: Church of Saint Peter at Erfurt(?); cathedral provost Würschmidt in Erfurt by 1856; Dieburg near Darmstadt by 1860; [Frankfurt art dealers in 1896]; Mme. C. Lelong, Paris; [sale, Georges Petit, Paris, 1902, lot 147]; [Boibove, Paris]; Edouard Aynard, Lyon; [sale, Georges Petit, Paris, 1913, lot 278]; Harry Fuld, Frankfurt am Main, until after 1931; Mrs. Clementine Cramer, Fuld's sister, Northwood, England, before 1937 and until 1946; [Rosenberg and Stiebel, New York]. (cat. 11)

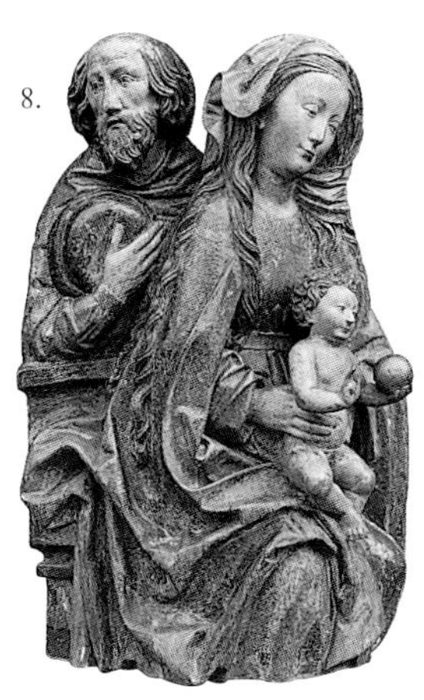

Alsace, influence of Niclaus Gerhaert von Leiden, *Saint Barbara,* c. 1490, limewood with traces of polychromy, height 81.2 (32), Museum of Fine Arts, Boston, Gift of Mrs. Charles Gaston Smith's Group (1947.1020). Ex coll.: [H. Schaeffer Gallery, New York]. Illus. Recht 1987, 337, no. XI.01, pl. 253; Gillerman 1989, 44–46, no. 26.

(**8.**) Niclaus Weckmann (Ulm, active 1481–1528), *Holy Family,* c. 1500, limewood? with polychromy, height 80 (31 1/2), The Metropolitan Museum of Art, Gift of Alastair B. Martin, 1948 (48.154.1). From the church at Guttenzell, district of Biberach, Upper Swabia. Ex coll.: Johannes Noll, Frankfurt am Main; [sale, Frankfurt am Main, 1912, no. 26, pl. 18]; Oskar Bondy, Vienna; [Leopold Blumka, Vienna and New York]; The Guennol Collection, New York (until 1948). Illus. Schädler 1992, 72, fig. 31.

Lower Saxony, winged altarpiece with the *Virgin in Glory,* dated 1524, limewood? and oak with polychromy, height 236.2 (93), Busch-Reisinger Museum, Cambridge, MA, Gift from an anonymous New York private collector (1949.306). Illus. Kuhn 1965, 75–76, no. 30., pl. XXX; and Osten 1965, 107, fig. 72.

Circle of Daniel Mauch (Ulm, 1477–Liège, 1540), *Bishop Saint* and *Saint Martin,* c. 1510–1515, limewood with polychromy and gilding, height 113.4; 114.4 (44 5/8; 45), The Metropolitan Museum of Art, Gift of Mrs. Russell C. Veit, 1950, in memory of her father, Maurice Bompard (50.233.1–2). Illus. Sophie Guillot de Suduiraut, *Sculptures allemandes de la fin du Moyen Age dans les collections publiques françaises 1400–1530* [exh. cat., Musée du Louvre], (Paris, 1991), 216, figs. a,b; and Agnes Cascio and Juliette Levy in *Sculptures médiévales allemandes, conservation et restauration, actes du colloque du Louvre…1991* (Paris, 1993), 325, 329 no. 2, figs. 1, 5.

Tilman Riemenschneider, *Virgin and Child,* c. 1500–1501, limewood, height 123 (48 3/8), Spencer Museum of Art, The University of Kansas, Museum purchase: Gift in memory of Professor Harry C. Thurnau through the Estate of Myrtle Elliott Thurnau (52.1). Ex coll.: Hans Schwarz, Vienna (collection auctioned in 1910 in Berlin); collection of the prince of Liechtenstein, Vaduz and Vienna; [Blumka Gallery, New York, acquired in May 1951]. The sculpture was purchased for the Spencer when John Maxon (d. 1977) was director (1948–1952); Maxon later became director of the Art Institute of Chicago. (cat. 22)

Swabia, *Three Kings* from an
Adoration group, before 1489,
poplar with polychromy,
height 101.6; 156.2; 164 (40;
61 ½; 64 ½), The Metropolitan
Museum of Art, The Cloisters
Collection, 1952 (52.83.1–3).
From the high altar of the
Cistercian abbey church at
Lichtenthal in Baden-Würt-
temberg, near Baden-Baden.
Ex coll.: private collection;
[sale, Sotheby's, London, 28
July 1939, lot 103]; [John Hunt,
Dublin]. Illus. *Spätgotik am
Oberrhein. Meisterwerke der
Plastik und des Kunsthandwerks
1450–1550* [exh. cat., Badisches
Landesmuseum] (Karlsruhe,
1970), 157, nos. 105–107, figs.
99, 101; William D. Wixom,
"Medieval Sculpture at The
Cloisters," *The Metropolitan
Museum of Art Bulletin* 46, no.
3 (Winter 1988), 18–19 (color
illus. showing the sculpture
after conservation).

(**9.**) Swabia, *Saints Vincent,
Urban, and Kilian(?),* c. 1510,
wood with later polychromy
and gilding, height 121.4; 141.5;
141 (47 ¾; 55 ¾; 55 ½), Wadsworth Atheneum, Hartford:
Gift of Mr. and Mrs. James
Lippincott Goodwin (1953.96);
and Purchase, Walter Keney
Fund (1953.97–98). Ex coll.:
[Blumka Gallery, New York].
The group was purchased
when Charles C. Cunningham
was director (1946–1966).
Illus. Gillerman 1989, 304–
305, no. 229.

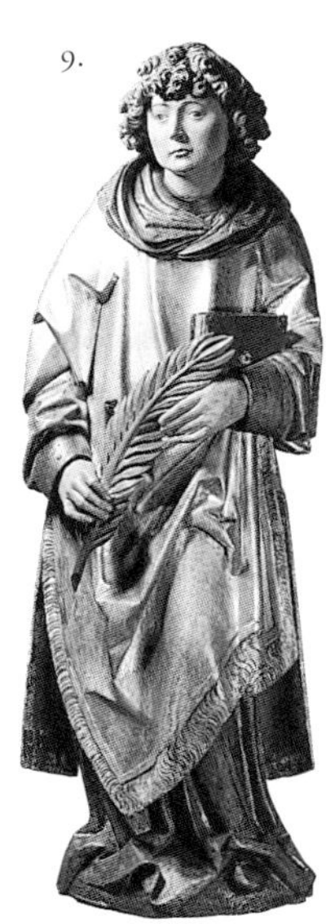
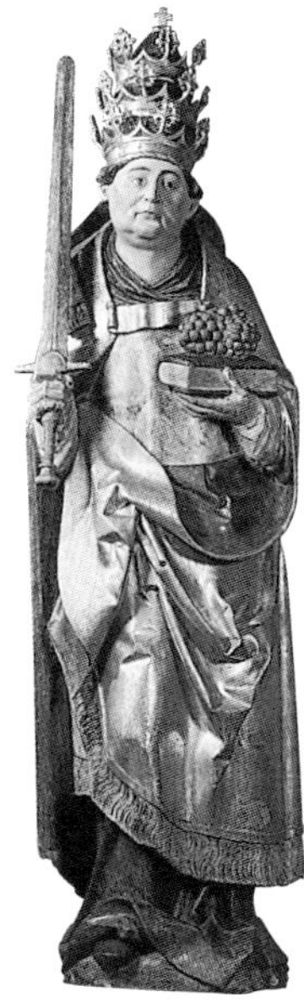
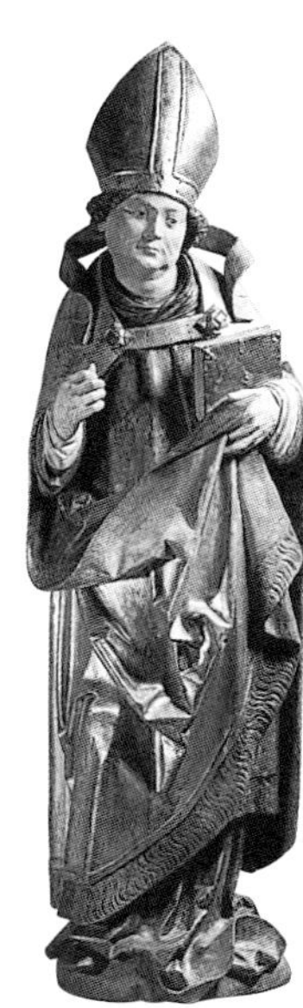

9.

Strasbourg, *Saint Barbara,*
c. 1500, limewood with poly-
chromy and gilding, height
127.2 (50 ⅛), The Metropolitan
Museum of Art, The Cloisters
Collection, 1955 (55.166).
Recently reattributed to the
young Conrad Meit by Alfred
Schädler. Ex coll.: Beinhaus,
Kippenheim; Henselmann,
Offenburg; [Henri Heilbron-
ner, Munich]. Color illus.
Wixom 1988, 27.

Upper Rhine, influence of
Niclaus Gerhaert von Leiden,
Virgin and Child, c. 1480,
wood with polychromy, height
99 (39), Jewett Art Center,
Wellesley College, Gift in
honor of Myrtilla Avery from
her students (1957.1). Ex coll.:
[Mathias Komor, New York].
Illus. Gillerman 1989, 256–257,
no. 200.

Bavaria, follower of Hans
Leinberger, *Saint John the
Baptist,* c. 1520, limewood with
polychromy, height 85.8 (33 ⅞),
Busch-Reisinger Museum,
Cambridge, MA, Museum
Association Fund (1957.124).
Ex coll.: R. Oertel, Munich;
[sale, R. Lepke, Berlin, 6–7
May 1913, 36, no. 120, pl. 74];
Oskar Bondy, Vienna; [Blumka
Gallery, New York]. Illus.
Kuhn 1965, 70–71, no. 26, pl.
XXVIII; Gillerman 1989, 211–
212, no. 171.

Workshop of Tilman Riemen-
schneider, *Saint Andrew,* c. 1505
limewood, height 103 (40 ½),
The High Museum of Art,
Atlanta, Samuel H. Kress Col-
lection (1958.57). Ex coll.:
Justus Bier, Widdersburg and
Louisville, KY; [Paul Drey
Gallery, New York]; Samuel H.
Kress Foundation, 1955–1958.
Illus. Justus Bier, *Tilmann
Riemenschneider: His Life and
Work* (Lexington, KY, 1982),
53–55, pl. 7a,b.

Tilman Riemenschneider, *Saint Stephen* and *Saint Lawrence,* limewood with polychromy and gilding, height 94.6; 92.7 (37¼; 36½), The Cleveland Museum of Art, Leonard C. Hanna Jr. Fund (59.42–43). Ex coll.: Reportedly from an altarpiece in the region of Rothenburg; von Gontard collection, Frankfurt am Main, until 1911; Richard von Passavant-Gontard, Frankfurt am Main, 1921–1929; Catalina von Pannwitz, De Hartekamp near Haarlem, The Netherlands, 1930–1956; [Rosenberg and Stiebel, New York, 1957–1959]. (cat. 32 A, D)

Attributed to Tilman Riemenschneider, *Pietà,* limewood, height 46 (18⅛), Rhode Island School of Design, Providence (1959.128). Ex coll.: Carl Streit, Bad Kissingen; Bayerisches Nationalmuseum, Munich. Illus. Raleigh 1962, 58–59, no. XVI.

Tilman Riemenschneider, *Saints Christopher, Eustace, and Erasmus (Three Helper Saints),* c. 1500–1504, limewood, height 53.8 (21⅛), The Metropolitan Museum of Art, The Cloisters Collection, 1961 (61.86). Ex coll.: Lord Delamere, United Kingdom; Dr. George Saint (d. 1957), Cheadle, Staffordshire, by 1951; Mary Saint, his wife, 1957–1960; [sale, Sotheby's, London, 14 October 1960, lot 52]; [Rosenberg and Stiebel, New York]. (cat. 23)

Upper Rhine, *Domestic Altarpiece with the Crucifixion,* 1490–1500, limewood, height 94 (37), The Metropolitan Museum of Art, The Cloisters Collection, 1961 (61.113). Ex coll.: Edouard Chappey, Paris; [Henry Daguerre, Paris]; Ambrose Monell, Tuxedo Park, New York; Oscar B. Cintas, New York; [Edward R. Lubin, New York]. Color illus. Wixom 1988, 17.

Swabia, attributed to Peter Köellin, *Virgin of Mercy,* c. 1470, limewood with polychromy and gilding, height 144.8 (57), North Carolina Museum of Art, Raleigh, Gift of R. J. Reynolds Tobacco Co. (61.13.1). Ex coll.: [Paul Drey Gallery, New York]. Color cover, Justus Bier, "The Statue in the North Carolina Museum of Art of a *Madonna with a Protective Cloak* by Peter Köellin of Esslingen," *North Carolina Museum of Art Bulletin* 9 (1970), 6–13, figs. 1–4.

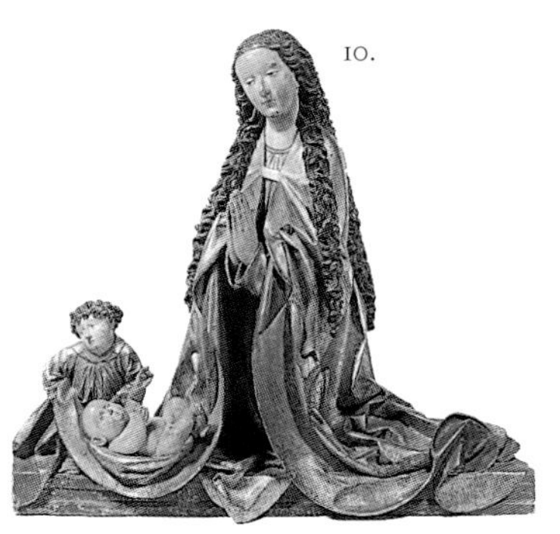

(**10.**) Upper Rhine, *Nativity,* c. 1490, limewood with polychromy and gilding, height 71.7 (28¼), Busch-Reisinger Museum, Cambridge, MA, Purchase, Antonia Paepcke DuBrul Fund (1963.1). Ex coll.: Richard von Passavant-Gontard, Frankfurt am Main; Dr. Walter von Pannwitz, Berlin. Illus. Kuhn 1965, 66–67, no. 22, pl. XIX; and Gillerman 1989, 196–197, no. 158.

Tyrol, workshop of Michael Pacher (active 1462–d. 1498), *Seated Virgin and Child,* c. 1470, stonepine with polychromy and gilding, height 74 (29), Museum of Fine Arts, Boston, Bequest of Dr. S. J. Thannhauser in memory of his wife, Franziska Reiner Thannhauser (1962.238). Ex coll.: Richard Oertel, Munich; Fischmann, Munich; Dr. and Mrs. Siegfried J. Thannhauser, Boston. Illus. Gillerman 1989, 89–90, no. 65.

Lower Swabia, circle of Hans Syfer, *Saint John the Evangelist,* c. 1490–1500, limewood, height without base 126.6 (49⅞), Busch-Reisinger Museum, Cambridge, MA, Gift of Mrs. Solomon R. Guggenheim (1964.5). Ex coll.: Mr. and Mrs. Solomon R. Guggenheim, New York. Illus. Kuhn 1965, 59–60, no. 16, pls. XIV, XV; and Gillerman 1989, 201, no. 162.

Tilman Riemenschneider, *Mourning Virgin* from a Crucifixion group, c. 1505–1510, limewood, height 59.1 (23¼), The Nelson-Atkins Museum of Art, Kansas City, Purchase: Nelson Trust (64.6). Ex coll.: Collegiate Church, Aschaffenburg, until early 1800s; Dr. Jacob von Hafner-Alteneck by 1851; Hans Schwarz; Dr. Walter von Pannwitz (d. 1920), Berlin; Catalina von Pannwitz, his wife, De Hartekamp near Haarlem, The Netherlands; [Rosenberg and Stiebel, New York]. (cat. 34)

Tilman Riemenschneider, *Female Saint,* c. 1490, limewood, height 96.5 (38), North Carolina Museum of Art, Raleigh, Purchased with funds from the North Carolina Art Society (Robert F. Phifer Bequest) and the State of North Carolina (68.33.1). Ex coll.: Wilhelm Gumprecht collection, Berlin, by the late 1890s, and auctioned in 1918; Dr. Franz Haniel, Munich. (cat. 10)

Follower of Tilman Riemenschneider, *Saint Anthony,* c. 1510, limewood, height 117.4 (46¼), Busch-Reisinger Museum, Cambridge, MA, Anonymous Special Gifts of Friends of Charles L. Kuhn (1969.214). Ex coll.: F. Hamel, Bavaria; unknown Belgian collection; [Rosenberg and Stiebel, New York]. Illus. Gillerman 1989, 204–205, no. 165.

• 1970s •

Tilman Riemenschneider, *Seated Bishop,* c. 1495–1500, limewood, height 91 (35⅞), The Metropolitan Museum of Art, The Cloisters Collection, 1970 (1970.137.1). Ex coll.: Count Hans Wilczeck, Vienna, in 1904; [Blumka Gallery, New York]. (cat. 17)

Tilman Riemenschneider, *Saint Sebastian,* c. 1510–1515, limewood, height 72 (28⅜), The Montreal Museum of Fine Arts Collection, Purchase, Gift of L.V. Randall and Horsley and Annie Townsend Bequest (1971.8). Ex coll.: Gedon collection, Munich (c. 1880); Pfälzische Landesgewerbeanstalt, Kaiserslautern (catalogues in 1885); William F. C. Ohly, Frankfurt am Main and London; acquired between 1933 and 1935 from Edmund Schilling by Lewis V. Randall, Bern and Montreal. (cat. 39 A)

Workshop of Tilman van der Burch (Lower Rhine, Cologne, active 1464–c. 1511), *Death of the Virgin,* late fifteenth century, oak, height 160.6 (63¼), The Metropolitan Museum of Art, The Cloisters Collection, 1973 (1973.348). Ex coll.: Augustin Lambert, Paris; Salavin, Paris. Color illus. Wixom 1988, 20–21.

Workshop of Tilman Riemenschneider, *Standing Bishop,* c. 1510, limewood with later polychromy and gilding, height 116.8 (46), The Metropolitan Museum of Art, The Cloisters Collection, 1975 (1975.25). Ex coll.: Kahle, Vienna; Julius Böhler Family Collection. Illus. Michele Marincola, Jack Soultanian, and Richard Newman, "Untersuchung eines nicht-polychromierten Holzbildwerkes in The Cloisters: Identifizierung einer ursprünglichen Oberfläche," *Zeitschrift für Kunsttechnologie und Konservierung* 11, no. 2 (1997), 238–248, figs. 1–14.

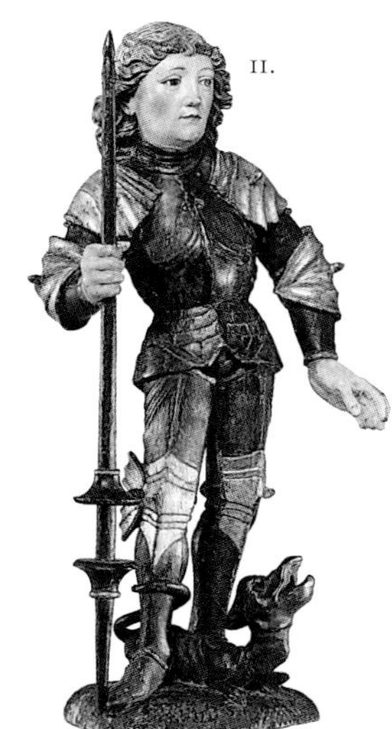

(**11.**) South Germany or Austria (possibly Vienna), *Saint George,* c. 1475, wood with polychromy, height 44.1 (17⅜), The Metropolitan Museum of Art, Bequest of Kurt John Winter, 1979 (1979.379). Ex coll.: August Carl, Lugano; Kurt John Winter, Scarsdale, NY. Illus. *Mirror of the Medieval World* [exh. cat., The Metropolitan Museum of Art] (New York, 1999), 193–194, no. 235.

Hans Leinberger (active 1510– c. 1540), *Saint Stephen,* c. 1525– 1530, limewood with traces of polychromy, height 83.8 (33), The Metropolitan Museum of Art, Bequest of Gula V. Hirschland, 1980 (1981.57.2). Ex coll.: Private collection (Baron Kornfeld?, Budapest); [Georg Schuster, Munich]; Gula V. Hirschland, Weston, CT. Illus. New York 1999, 226–227, no. 287.

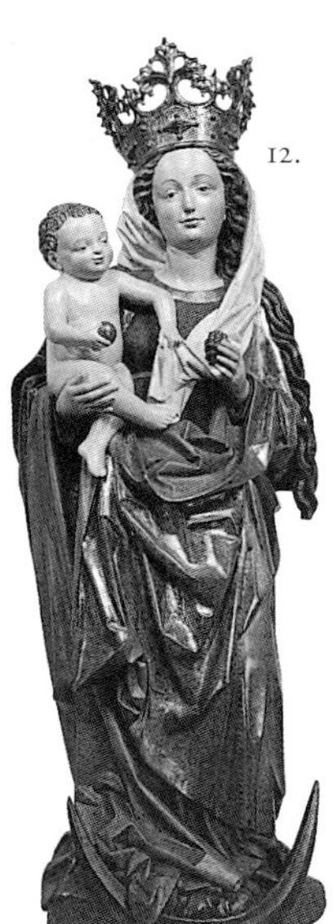

12.

(**12.**) Nuremberg, *Virgin and Child on the Crescent Moon,* c. 1470, limewood with poly- chromy and gilding, height 191.8 (75½), The Metropolitan Museum of Art, The Cloisters Collection, 1984 (1984.198). Ex coll.: Dr. Karl Krüger, until 1943; Tiroler Landesmuseum Ferdinandeum, Innsbruck; Dr. Peter Hierzenberger, Vienna; [sale, Sotheby Parke Bernet, London, 3 April 1984, lot 14, color illus.]. Illus. New York 1999, 185–186, no. 227.

Upper Bavaria, the Chiemgau, attributed to the Master of Rabenden, *Virgin and Child* from a Holy Kinship group, c. 1510–1515, limewood with traces of polychromy, height 60 (23⅝), The Metropolitan Museum of Art, The Cloisters Collection, 1987 (1987.15). Ex coll.: Bayerisches National- museum, Munich (1896–1965); [Galerie St. Raphael, Vienna]. Illus. New York 1999, 223–224, no. 284.

Attributed to Nicolas Hagen- ower (Strasbourg, c. 1445– d. before 1538), *Saint Anthony Abbot,* c. 1500, walnut, height 113.7 (44¾), The Metropoli- tan Museum of Art, The Clois- ters Collection, 1988 (1988.159). Ex coll.: [Julius Böhler, Munich]. Illus. New York 1999, 205, no. 248.

Workshop of Tilman Riemen- schneider, *Saint Sebastian,* c. 1515, limewood, height 95.6 (37⅝), New York, Private Collection. Purchased at Sotheby Parke Bernet, Lon- don, 10 March 1983, lot 31.

Swabia, *Private Devotional Shrine (Hausaltärchen),* about 1490, wood with polychromy, height 33.7 (13¼), The Metro- politan Museum of Art, The Cloisters Collection, 1991 (1991.10). Ex coll.: Wildendorf Castle, near Bubendorf, Can- ton Basel, Switzerland; [sale, Christies, Manson & Woods, London, 6 July 1990, lot 14]; [Albrecht Neuhaus, Würz- burg]. Illus. New York 1999, 191–192, no. 232.

Attributed to Niclaus Ger- haert von Leiden (active 1460– d. 1473), *Virgin and Child,* boxwood, height 33.7 (13¼), The Metropolitan Museum of Art, The Cloisters Collection and Lila Acheson Wallace Gift, 1996 (1996.14). Ex coll.: Anselm Salomon von Roth- schild, Vienna, before 1866– 1874; Nathaniel von Roth- schild, Vienna; Alphonse and Clarice de Rothschild; seized by the Nazis in 1939; recovered by Clarice de Rothschild by 1947; [Rosenberg and Stiebel, New York, 1948]; Julius Wilhelm Böhler (d. 1967), Munich; Julius Harry Böhler (d. 1979), Munich; Marion Böhler-Eitle (d. 1991), Munich; Florian Eitle, Starnberg, Germany. (cat. 6)

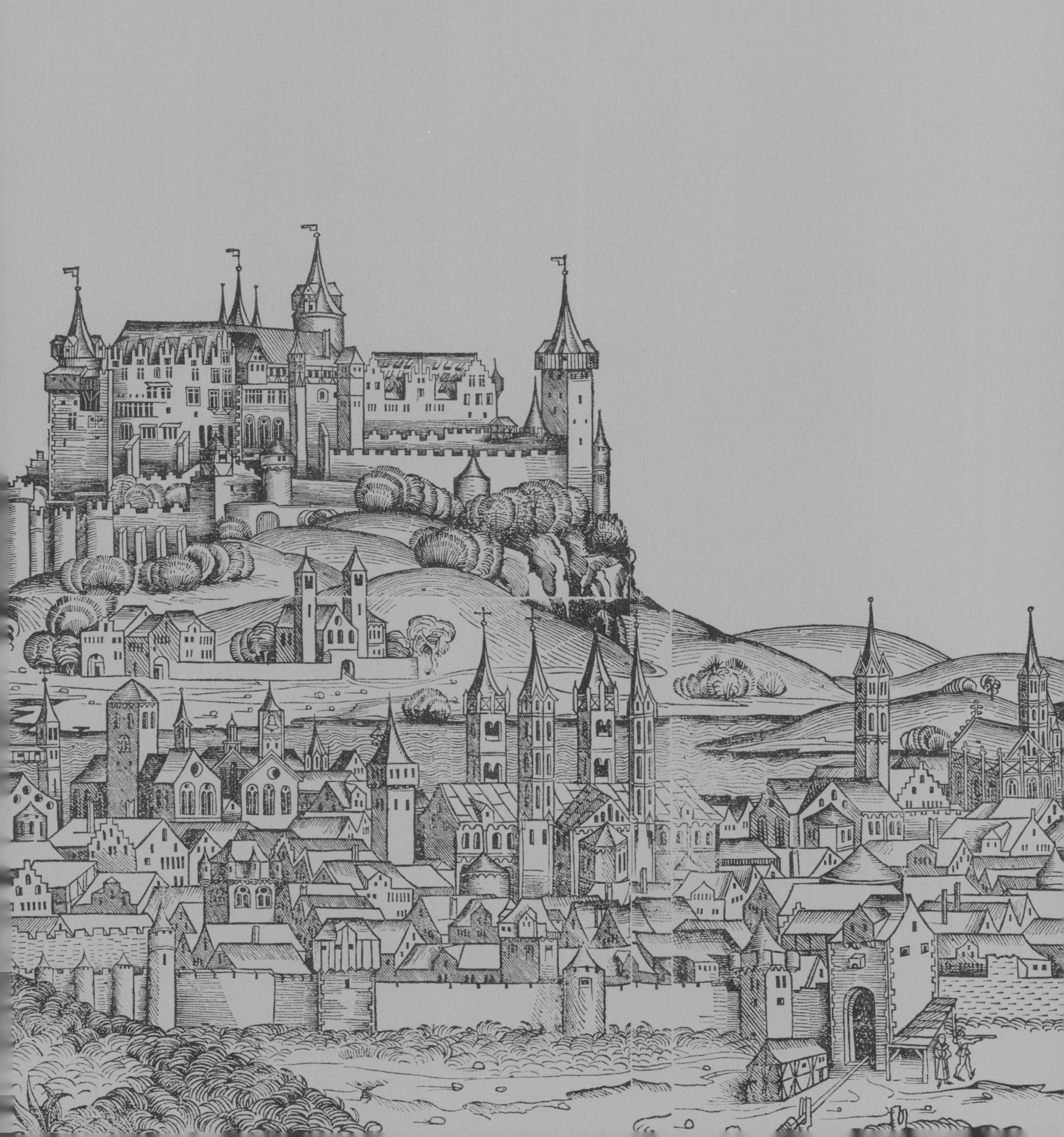

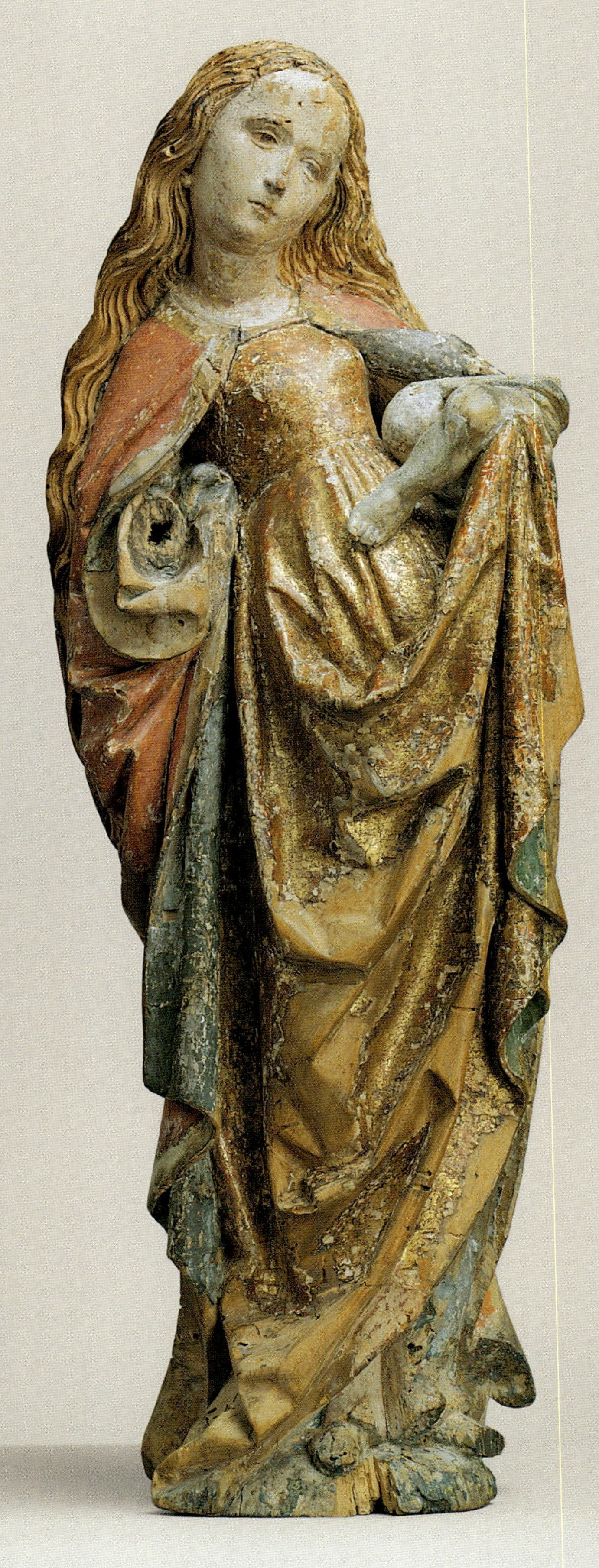

VIRGIN AND CHILD

c. 1480–1485, limewood with polychromy, 43.2 x 15.7 x 12 (17 x 6⅛ x 4¾), S. Mehringer, Munich

• *Technical Notes* •

In addition to the right hand of the Virgin and the upper portion of the child, the Virgin's left toe and sections of the base are missing, while the right heel of the child is cut out at a right angle. The legibility of the surface is somewhat confused by the patchy, successive layers of paint and gilding interspersed with areas of bare wood. Insect damage is relatively light; the open surface channels indicate activity after the figure was polychromed. In all probability the group was originally intended to be painted, but the degree to which this presumed polychrome is preserved has not been determined. The hair at the back appears to have been cut down, presumably later, perhaps for the attachment of an aureole.

• *Provenance* •

Acquired from the Munich trade in 1973.

• *Literature* •

Würzburg 1981, 224–225, 260, no. 41, figs. 147–149; Kalden 1990, 90 n. 348; Ruppert 1992, 99.

THE STANDING VIRGIN cradles the Christ child in her arm against her projecting hip; her tilted head and akimbo hip produce a distinctly S-curved stance. The child, whose torso and head are now missing, sits with his left leg crossed over his right. The supporting left hand of the Virgin is covered with the fabric of her gown, which she has drawn up, creating voluminous loops of deep drapery folds across her front and then rhythmic, tubular folds as the fabric falls from her hand to her feet. Her right forearm is missing. Her mantle, clasped at the chest with a cord, folds back over her upper left arm and, in counterpoint to the primary drapery passage, is drawn up under her right arm and secured by her elbow pressing against her side, thus creating a respondent com-plex of folds. In a visual echo, her hair flows over her shoulders and cascades down her back in a single, articulated mass. Standing on an island of textured ground, her feet peek out from beneath the drapery.

As nothing is known of Riemenschneider's activities prior to 1483, when he became a resident journeyman in Würzburg, and no surviving works by him are documented prior to the Münnerstadt altarpiece of 1490–1492, the attribution of works to his early career necessarily relies largely on stylistic considerations. In the present instance the affinities with his earliest alabaster carvings—the Amsterdam *Annunciation* of about 1485 and the *Saint Barbara* of about 1485–1490 (cats. 2 and 4)—have been pointed out.[1]

The exceptional dimensionality of Riemenschneider's early sculpture is manifest in this figure. Although essentially a high relief, as evidenced by the flattened and relatively unfinished back, the projecting volumes of the drapery give the illusion of a sculpture in the round. Viewable from a 180-degree vantage, one complex drapery passage counterpoises the next, each logically interrelated, bringing volumetric unity and coherence to the sculpture as a whole. Voids between drapery passages and undercut forms relieve the density of the volumes while structuring the figure's plastic complexity.

The mantle of this small polychromed Virgin rests on both shoulders, drops to the base on one side and then is partly hiked up under the arm on the other. With her left hand the Virgin lifts up the fulsome front of her gown, creating a series of descending pocket loops and a separate passage of zigzag folds as the drapery falls from the hand. The vacant spaces created between the latter drapery passage and the mantle falling from the upper arm and between the undercutting of the child and the surrounding drapery achieve a coherent dimensionality by rhythmically alternating voids and solids.

1. Schädler in Würzburg 1981, 225.

2. See Recht 1987, 244–245, 372, figs. 232–233. Unfortunately, nothing is known of the provenance.

3. Schädler in Würzburg 1981, 225. Ex coll.: Schneider-Hörig, Berlin. I am grateful to Dr. Nina Gockerell of the Bayerisches Nationalmuseum for making available a photograph of this sculpture.

4. Schädler in Würzburg 1981, 260. Jörg Rasmussen, "Tilman Riemenschneider–Frühe Werke," *Kunstchronik* 34, no. 11 (1981) 418, rejected Schädler's attribution; both Kalden 1990, 90 n. 348, and Ruppert 1992, 98–99, find it problematical, largely because neither accepts the Amsterdam *Annunciation,* to which Schädler stylistically relates the present polychromed Virgin, as an autograph work of Riemenschneider.

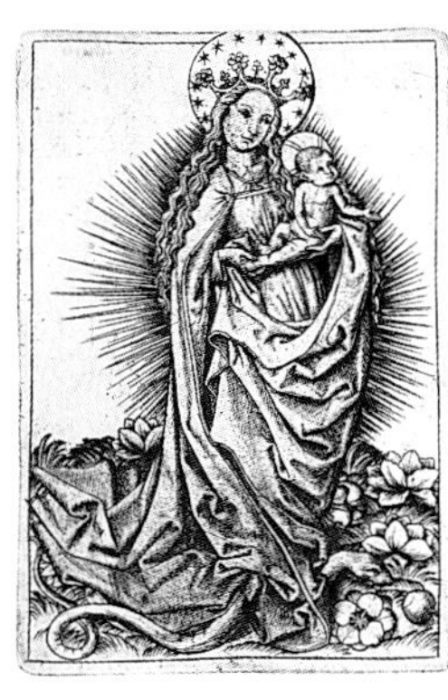

1.
Master E. S.,
*Virgin and Child Standing
on a Serpent,*
c. 1460–1470, engraving,
National Gallery
of Art, Washington,
Rosenwald Collection

Perhaps an early experiment with a fundamental sculptural concept, the simple expediency of lifting the front of the gown exists nowhere else in Riemenschneider's work and is only rarely encountered elsewhere. Closely related, however, is a limestone sculpture of a standing Virgin and child from Schüttern. Although more linear and erect, this refined sculpture, by a follower of Niclaus Gerhaert, employs the identical drapery concept, and both the treatment of the folds as well as the articulation of the hands are not unrelated, as Recht points out, to the sandstone *Anna Selbdritt* from Berlin, also by a follower of Gerhaert (cat. 8).[2] Further demonstrating the sources of influence, Schädler has correctly noted that a standing Virgin and child that probably originated in the Upper Rhineland about 1470–1480, but otherwise unrelated and now in a private collection, is compositionally so close to the present statuette that the two must have shared a common model or the same direct influence.[3]

Early in his career Riemenschneider adopted an alternative formula of drapery treatment, which he had evidently encountered during his early training in the region of the Upper Rhineland and subsequently employed to enhance the convincing volumes and dimensionality of his figures. Essentially, the mantle falls over the arm and down on one side, while it drops off the shoulder down to the hip level on the other side and is lifted back up and held against the torso. This creates a large looping fold that envelops the lower portion of the figure while affording a glimpse of the underlying and otherwise ambiguous corporeal form. As this drapery treatment appears almost simultaneously in the sculpture of Niclaus Gerhaert and his close circle as well as in the engravings of Master E. S. (fig. 1), its precise origin within the Upper Rhineland is difficult to establish. It recurs throughout Riemenschneider's early work: it is encountered in the two early alabaster works mentioned above; and likewise, in varying forms, in other sculpture dating up through the early 1490s, including the *Saint John the Baptist* and the *Saint Matthew* (cat. 13A) from the Münnerstadt altarpiece; both *Saint John the Baptist* (Chapuis essay, fig. 1) and the *Virgin and Child* from the parish church in Hassfurt; the *Saint John the Evangelist* from the parish church in Iphofen; and the Raleigh *Female Saint* (cat. 10).

In addition to the dimensionality of the figure and the skillful articulation of detail, the character and treatment of the face relate this statuette to Riemenschneider's early work. While sculpturally this piece has little to do with the Amsterdam Virgin (cat. 2), the faces of the two figures are extremely close.

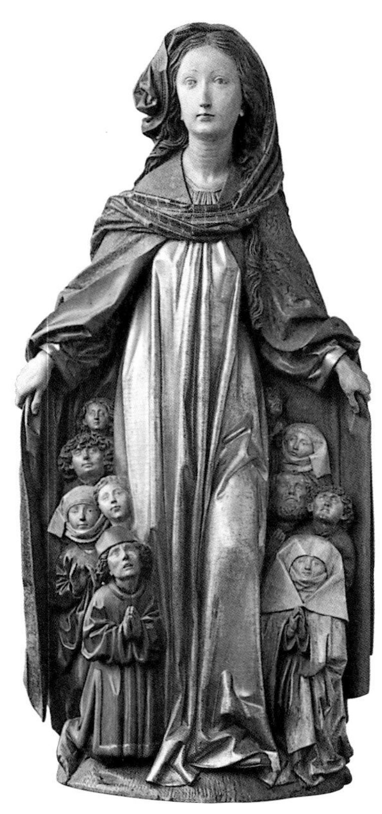

2.
Follower of Michel Erhart, *Virgin of Mercy,* c. 1480, limewood with original polychromy, Staatliche Museen zu Berlin, Skulpturensammlung

Bearing in mind that the features of the Amsterdam Virgin are slightly distorted, as the work was conceived to be viewed primarily in three-quarter profile —a sculptural ploy that is more highly developed in the apostles in the central shrine of the *Holy Blood* altarpiece (cat. 23, fig. 1)—both share the smooth, rounded forms of the face, the heavy-lidded oval eyes set under firm brows, the small, thin mouths, and nubby chins. This small polychromed Virgin, however, lacks the rather childlike aspect of Riemenschneider's Amsterdam Virgin and retains more of the calm but thoughtful countenance of Virgins by Michel Erhart and his followers, typified by the *Virgin of Mercy* of about 1480, from Ravensburg (fig. 2). The reliance on a sculptural type and the reference to a facial type both familiar from his early years suggests that the present Virgin may well date from the opening years of the 1480s, when Riemenschneider was already an accomplished sculptor, with an active career, and had not yet moved to Würzburg; thus the present polychromed statuette may well be, as Schädler was inclined to consider it,[4] the earliest of Riemenschneider's extant works. HUSBAND

ANNUNCIATION

c. 1485, alabaster, angel: 39.5 x 28.5 x 14 (15 ½ x 11 ¼ x 5 ½); Virgin: 41 x 34 x 14 (16 ⅛ x 13 ⅜ x 5 ½),
Rijksmuseum, Amsterdam

• *Technical Notes* •

The Virgin is missing the tips of the first three fingers of her left hand and two fingertips of her right hand; there are other losses in her hair, on the edge of the undercut section of her mantle, in the hem of her left sleeve, and in the edging of her mantle at her right wrist. There are substantial remains of gilding in her hair, on the lectern and edges of the pages of the book, and in the cusped border pattern of her sleeves and edging of her mantle, which is accented in black and red. Her irises are a grayish black, with black pupils accented with a fleck of white. The book cover retains traces of its original red pigment, as do her lips and nostrils. The ground is painted green. The top and left side of the book have a border described by double etched lines. The hair at the back of her head and over the right shoulder has been flattened. At the top of her head is a filled hole of about 1.5 cm in diameter and, behind that, a smaller filled hole of about 0.7 cm in diameter; on the underside are two rectangular slots, about 2 x 0.8 cm each, separated, in line, by about 6 cm.

The thumb and fingers of the angel's right hand are missing; the lower right arm appears to have been carved separately and then doweled to the figure. The lower section of the banderole is lost, and the toes are replaced. Substantial remains of gilding are found in the hair, the waist cord and the tassel of the hood, the lettering on the banderole, and the borders and hems (in the same pattern as on the garments of the Virgin). The ground is painted green, and the gilding in all areas except the hair was ornamented in red, green, and black. The gilded fringe of the cope is enhanced with alternating sections of red and green. In the absence of adequate analyses, it is not certain how much of the polychrome and gilding is original. A slot in the angel's right shoulder for the attachment of a wing has been filled. The back of the head has been flattened and reduced; it is also drilled with three holes of uncertain function, one filled, ranging from 0.5 to 0.7 cm in diameter. The hair has been drilled, leaving bore holes of about 0.5 to 0.8 cm in diameter. Holes at the top of the angel's head and in the base, like those in the Virgin, may have fixed the figure to a workbench clamp. The alabaster in both figures is heavily grained, with several dark flaws, some with minute occlusions. The backs of both figures have been sawn off in plane.

• *Provenance* •

By tradition, a monastery in Bamberg; [art dealer, Bamberg]; Max von Goldschmidt-Rothschild, Frankfurt; Fritz Mannheimer, Amsterdam, until his death in 1939; apparently acquired in 1941 by Hans Posse through Kajetan Mühlmann for the planned Führermuseum in Linz; after the capitulation of the Nazis, recovered from the Alt Aussee depot; sent by the Allies to the Central Collecting Point, Munich; received on loan by the State Office for Dispersed Art Works, The Hague, 1952; acquired by the Rijksmuseum, 1960.

• *Literature* •

Schmitt and Swarzenski 1921, 29, fig. 144; Bier 1925, 32 n. 4; Schrade 1927, 55–59 n. 145; Habicht 1931b, 5–6; Hannover 1931, 8, no. 8, fig. 3; Bier 1951, 228, 233, fig. 8; Bier 1957a, 10; Bier 1959b, 196, fig. 6; Raleigh 1962, 22–23, no. 2; Müller 1966, 224 n. 75; Schädler 1975, 102; Bier 1978, 155; Würzburg 1981, 257–260, 265, no. 55, figs. 184 and 185; Krohm 1982, 96–97, fig. 1; Sello 1983, 15, 54–55; Jopek 1988, 90–93, 156–157, no. 48, fig. 47; Ruppert 1992, 89, 95–99, fig. 59.

KNEELING AT AN ANGLE before a lectern, the Virgin gazes into undefined space, arrested in motion as she grasps a fold of her mantle with one hand and touches the cockled pages of the book with the

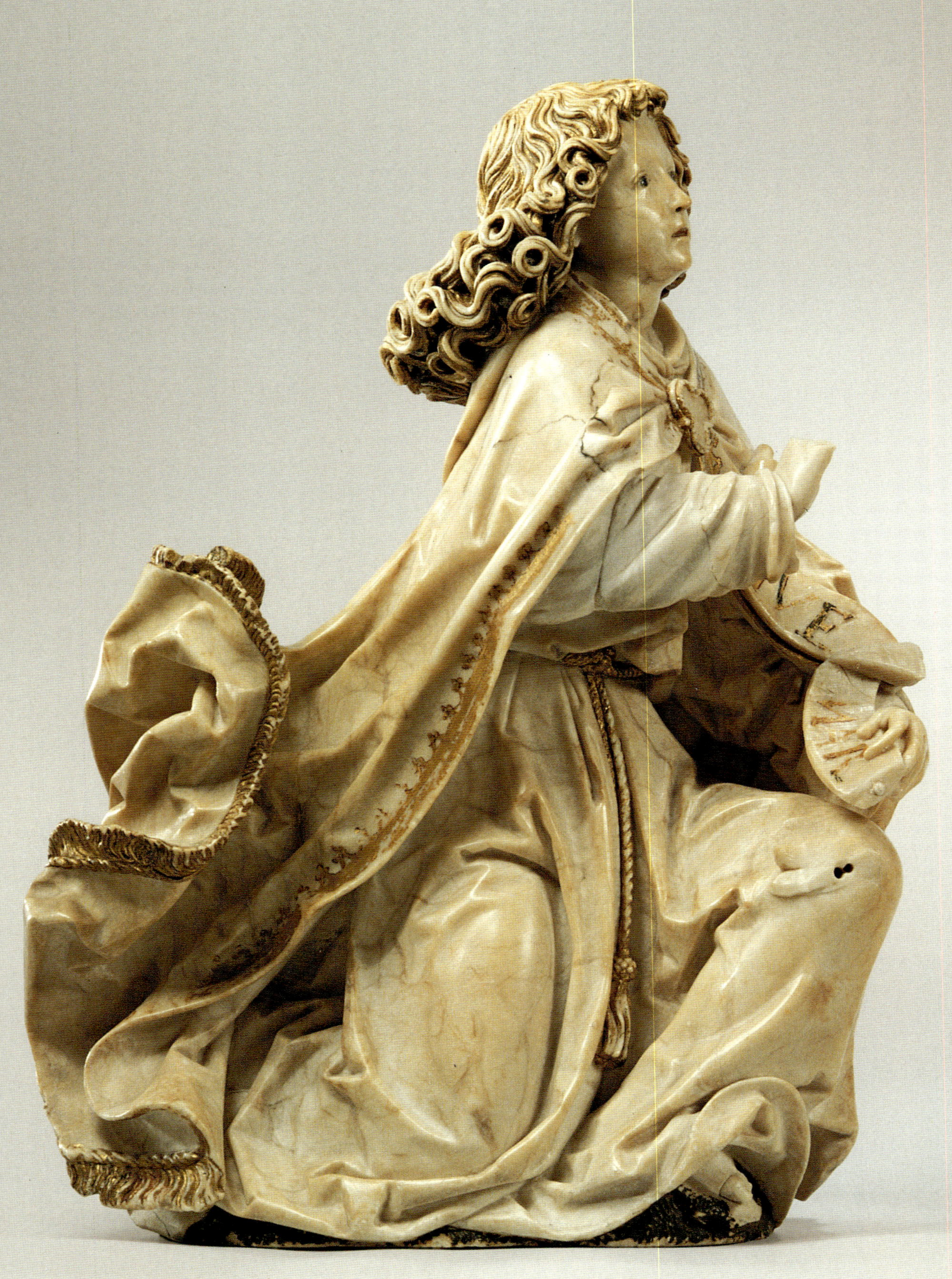

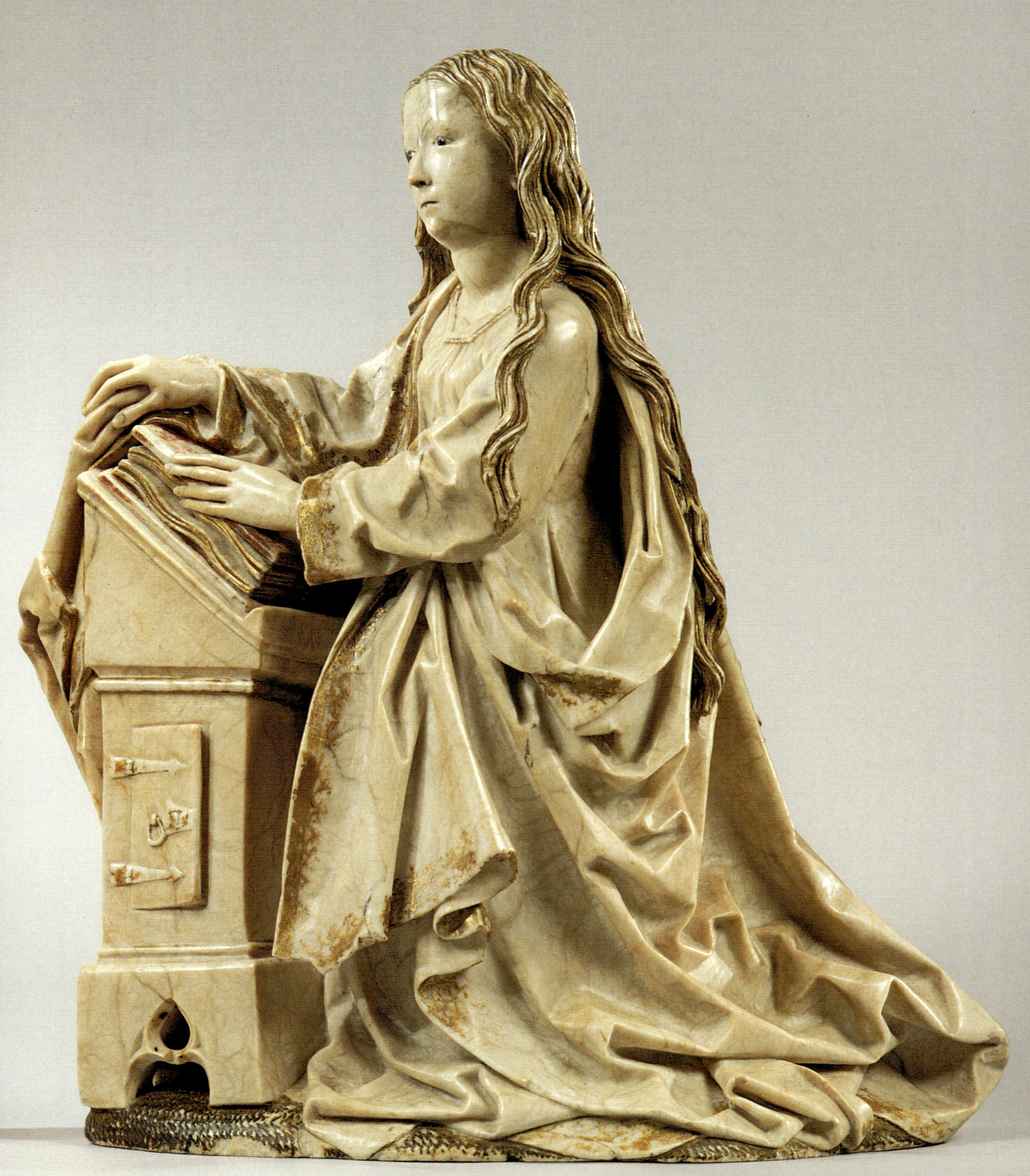

other. The mantle crosses over her shoulders and descends down her left side to be drawn up in a deep, generous loop, with the material held to her side by her elbow; the garment then falls in large, planar folds, with the rest of the fabric gathered in crumbled, angular folds at the edge of the textured ground that supports the figure. Her long, wavy hair falls down her back, with a separate strand, completely undercut at the shoulder, trailing down her left arm.

The youthful angel, on his right knee before the Virgin, raises his right hand in salutation while holding a banderole inscribed: AVE MAR(IA)....The angel's alb, tied at the waist by a tasseled cord, clings to his right thigh and drapes over his left knee, descending between in long tubular folds, then gathering along the edges of the textured ground on which the figure rests. The toes of the left foot emerge from beneath an upturned fold. The heavy, fringed cope, closed at his breast by a morse, falls over the angel's left arm and off his right shoulder, terminating in a dramatic upturned expanse of crumpled folds. The angel's luxurious curls have been drilled and deeply undercut.

Along with the small polychromed *Virgin and Child* (cat. 1) and the surviving high reliefs of a *Passion* altarpiece from Rothenburg (Chapuis essay, fig. 2), this engaging alabaster *Annunciation* must be numbered among Riemenschneider's earliest extant works, dating from around 1485, the year in which he became a master in Würzburg. The charm of this group is due in large part to the absorbed but insouciant aspect of the almost childlike figures. Yet to comprehend fully the significance of the momentous event in which they are participating, they express an abiding spiritual faith by their serene calm.

These figures are nonetheless dramatically charged. The Virgin is stopped in midaction: either she is in the process of opening the book, not yet aware of the angel's presence, or she is closing it, in dawning recognition of the impending event. Her unfocused gaze, like the ambiguity of the moment, interjects an element of tension. In contrast to the repose of the Virgin, the angel appears to have been captured in the last moment of entry: the agitated folds of his cope, airborne in forward motion, have not yet come to rest. His upraised right arm, the angled forward knee, and even the upturned fold revealing the foot, all further heighten the illusion of arrested momentum.

The composition of the group, with the Virgin facing the angel and the bookstand placed between the two—rather than the Virgin looking back over her shoulder toward the angel—is highly unusual. A

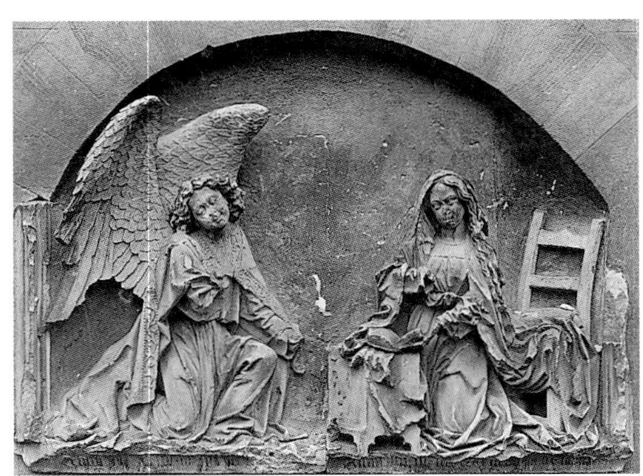

Circle of Niclaus Gerhaert von Leiden, *Annunciation from the Venningen Tomb*, c. 1459 or shortly after, sandstone, Speyer Cathedral

sculptural comparison is found in the earlier *Annunciation* from the tomb ensemble of Bishop Siegfried von Venningen (d. 1459) and his brother Canon Nicholaus von Venningen (d. 1483), which was originally erected in the cathedral cloister at Speyer (fig. 1). Müller considered this monument the most important work of the successors of Niclaus Gerhaert in the Middle Rhineland and suggested that Gerhaert's deeply undercut 1464 *Epitaph of a Canon* in Strasbourg Cathedral may have been the source of inspiration (see Krohm essay, fig. 1).[1] Other than the tilt of the angel's head, Riemenschneider's composition is essentially the same. The striking contrast of the Virgin's quietude with the agitated motion of the angel suggests that these two works must have shared, at the least, common inspiration.[2] In more general terms, the precise working of details that characterizes Upper Rhenish sculpture is evident in the virtuoso execution of the Amsterdam figures: the deep drilling of the angel's hair and the total undercutting of the Virgin's tresses invite comparison to the *Virgin and Child* from Dangolsheim (Krohm essay, fig. 2), which underscores the influence of Gerhaert and his immediate followers on Riemenschneider's early work.

In the Amsterdam Virgin, Riemenschneider has employed a sculptural formula often encountered in Upper Rhenish sculpture of the 1470s: a small-breasted figure in a tight-waisted dress, encompassed by a voluminous mantle that arcs around from behind and is drawn up and held against her side by her elbow; the enormous loop of drapery that results and the planar folds that descend from beneath her arm reveal the volume of the figure underneath. This motif appears in a number of works dating from Riemenschneider's early career and perhaps finds its most emphatic expression in the slightly later *Saint Barbara* (cat. 4).

1. Müller 1966, 106. The relationship was first pointed out in Schrade 1927, 58. Krohm considers this a work of Gerhaert himself.

2. In terms of the concept of the figures and the organization of drapery passages, Riemenschneider could well have been aware of the engraved *Annunciation* by Master E. S. (see cat. 21, fig. 1).

Schrade definitively placed the Amsterdam group early in Riemenschneider's career, and all authors thereafter—Bier repeatedly—have affirmed a date in the 1480s. Schädler argued for a date in the first half of the decade.[3] Jopek, who does not consider the work to be autograph, proposed a date about 1480.[4] Within Riemenschneider's oeuvre, the Virgin is closely related to the kneeling figure at the right of the mourning women in the predella from Riemenschneider's early *Passion* altarpiece (Krohm essay, fig. 8);[5] the characterization of the face and the treatment of the hair are so close as to be virtually interchangeable. The right figure of this group in turn shares a common model with the Virgin from an Adoration in the hospital church at Horb, a nearly contemporary work by the Michel Erhart workshop. The angel likewise may be compared, particularly in his face and hair, with the figure at the right of the other Lamentation figures in the predella from the *Passion* altarpiece (fig. 2). Riemenschneider's style defies linear interpretation, and as Schädler noted, an artist of this rank rises to a high level even at the outset of his career,[6] but the Amsterdam *Annunciation* is more independent of Upper Rhenish and Ulmish influence than is the small polychromed *Virgin and Child* (cat. 1) and most likely can be placed, along with the *Passion* altarpiece reliefs, about 1485 or shortly after.

The sawn backs of the Amsterdam figures establish the plane in which they were originally set; both figures, in fact, were angled slightly outward, increasing their dimensionality. Their original context is unknown, although the slight foreshortening indicates that they were placed in an elevated position. Certain details, such as the toes of the angel peeking out from under the alb and the drilling and undercutting of the hair of both figures, are visible only when viewed from well below the baseline; if the eye is any higher, one can see the unfinished part of the angel's hair. Moreover, for the toes on the angel's right foot to be visible, the figure, which has a maximum viewing incident of about 45 degrees off the back plane, also must have been separated from the left terminus of its housing by 5 or more centimeters.[7]

The Venningen angel may provide an indication of the Amsterdam angel's appearance with his nowlost wings. It is possible that the right wing was attached to the flattened area at the back of the head, employing the several dowel holes. The Venningen group might suggest a context for the Amsterdam

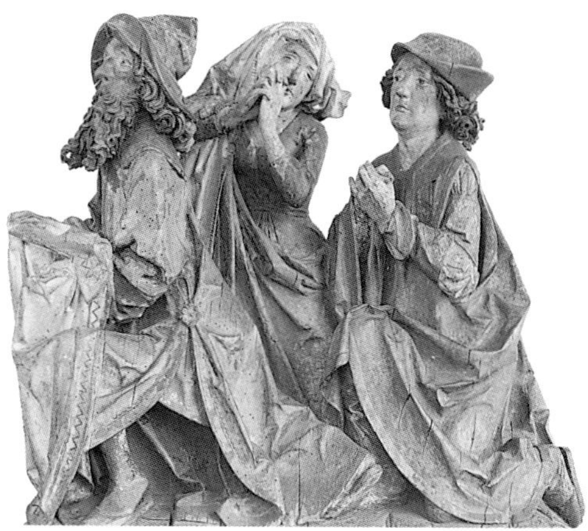

2.

Mourning Figures from the predella of a *Passion* altarpiece, c. 1485–1490, limewood with remains of original polychromy, Staatliche Museen zu Berlin, Skulpturensammlung

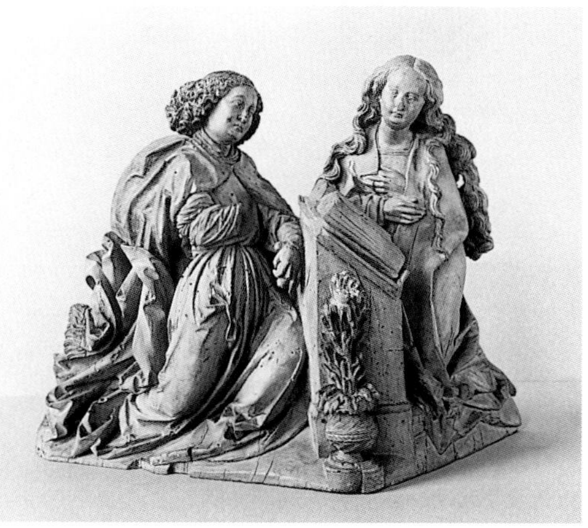

3.

Hans Wydyz, *Annunciation*, c. 1515, limewood, Staatliche Museen zu Berlin, Skulpturensammlung

Annunciation, considering the evident preference for alabaster over bronze in tomb and sepulchral monuments of this period. Another possibility is offered by a later *Annunciation* by Hans Wydyz (fig. 3), who was clearly aware of Riemenschneider's work: following the same, unusual iconographic type and angled out like the Amsterdam figures, this later limewood group is known to have belonged to a series of the Seven Joys of the Virgin, incorporated into a large rosary.[8] HUSBAND

3. Würzburg 1981, 260.

4. Jopek 1988, 91–92, 156. Ruppert 1992, 97, concurs.

5. The composition of the two *Passion* altarpiece figures appears again in a variant form in Riemenschneider's *Mourning Women* of about 1510 (cat. 37). It can also be seen in Nicolas Hagenower's 1501 *Deposition* in Collège Saint-Etienne, Strasbourg, supporting a widely circulated common model.

6. Würzburg 1981, 259.

7. Whether the composition incorporated other elements to indicate a domestic setting—as in the Venningen group—is uncertain; in any case, the textured ground on which each figure is placed should probably be considered a convention rather than a literal representation.

8. This *Annunciation*, somewhat smaller than that in Amsterdam, was executed about 1515 and is now in the Skulpturensammlung, Berlin. See Gross 1997, 23–25, no. II.8.

3

Franconian (Würzburg) / A N N U N C I A T I O N

1484, alabaster, Virgin: 49 x 36 x 16.5 (19 ¼ x 14 ⅛ x 6 ½); angel: 52.5 x 30 x 18 (20 ⅝ x 11 ¾ x 7 ⅛),
Bayerisches Nationalmuseum, Munich

• *Technical Notes* •

The right hand and the left index finger of the angel
are missing. The back of the Virgin's head is flattened
and drilled for attachment of perhaps a halo. The
angel's wings have extensive gilding. There are traces
of gilding in the hair and on the hems of both figures
as well as traces of red in the mantles and cloaks and
on the cloth of the Virgin's reading stand, often found
over the gold and presumably later. The tooled ground
on which each figure stands was largely polychromed
in green over blue. On the back of the angel, in period
numerals but with later strengthening in black paint,
is the date 1484. The inscription on the angel's banderole survives as pentimenti. The group was lightly
cleaned by Eugen Zepp in 1998–1999.

• *Provenance* •

From the private chapel of the cathedral canons' Rötelsee residence near Würzburg; acquired from the Martinengo collection, Würzburg, 1858.

• *Literature* •

Swarzenski 1921, 190–191, 195, no. 6, fig. 22; Zeissner
1950, 117–118; Müller 1966, 125, 217 n. 103, 224 n. 74;
Würzburg 1981, 261–263, no. 56; Krohm 1982, 32–
33, no. 3; Jopek 1988, 87–88, 90, 151–152, no. 45, fig.
41; Ruppert 1992, 101.

BOTH FIGURES ARE carved in high relief; the
backs have flat, unfinished surfaces with rough-hewn
projections at the bottom edges. The angel, with
attached gilded wings, rests on his left knee, with the
right one raised in a forward position; a banderole
curls from one hand to the other. His mantle, clasped
at the neck, drapes over his left shoulder and is drawn
up under his arm; on the other side it falls on the
shoulder then descends to his feet. The Virgin, kneeling at a bookstand, raises her right hand as she turns

to look back over her shoulder at the approaching
angel, which causes her right knee to lift off the ground.
Her left hand lies across the open book as she dis-
tractedly fingers a ribbonlike banderole (a bookmark?).
Over a loose-fitting gown she wears a mantle closed
by a chain above the breast. At her left the mantle
falls from her shoulder to the base; on her other side
it drops from her shoulder but is drawn up under her
arm in a large loop of drapery, which is secured against
her torso at the wrist. Both figures have long wavy
hair that falls in a single mass over their shoulders
and down their backs. Each rests on an island base
that is textured with a chisel; while the drapery of the
Virgin's robes conforms to the perimeter of her base,
that of the angel overlaps his.

The present figures have long been identified
with the alabaster *Annunciation* group cited as being
on the high altar of the chapel of the Rötelseehof,
Würzburg, in an inventory compiled by the Mainz
cleric Peter Trach and dated 29 March 1491.[1] According
to Zeissner, the chapel, intended for the veneration
of the Annunciation, was erected by cathedral provost
Kilian von Bibra (1426–1494) in 1484,[2] one year

1. Zeissner 1950, 118. The
document, no. 242/128, is in
the Staatsarchiv Würzburg.

2. Kilian's relative Lorenz von
Bibra was prince-bishop of
Würzburg from 1495 until his
death in 1519 and was a major
patron of Riemenschneider's.

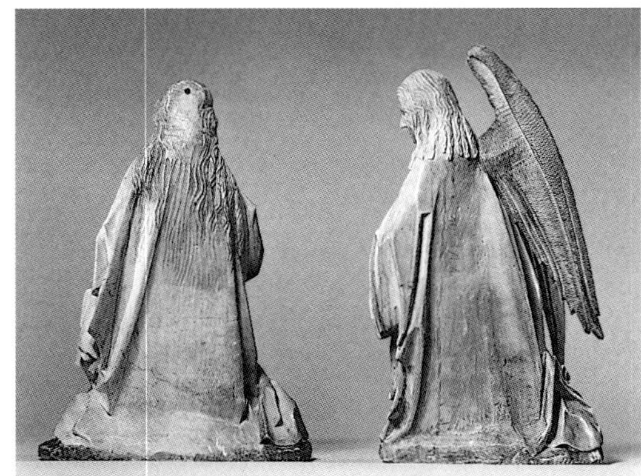

Back view of catalogue no. 3

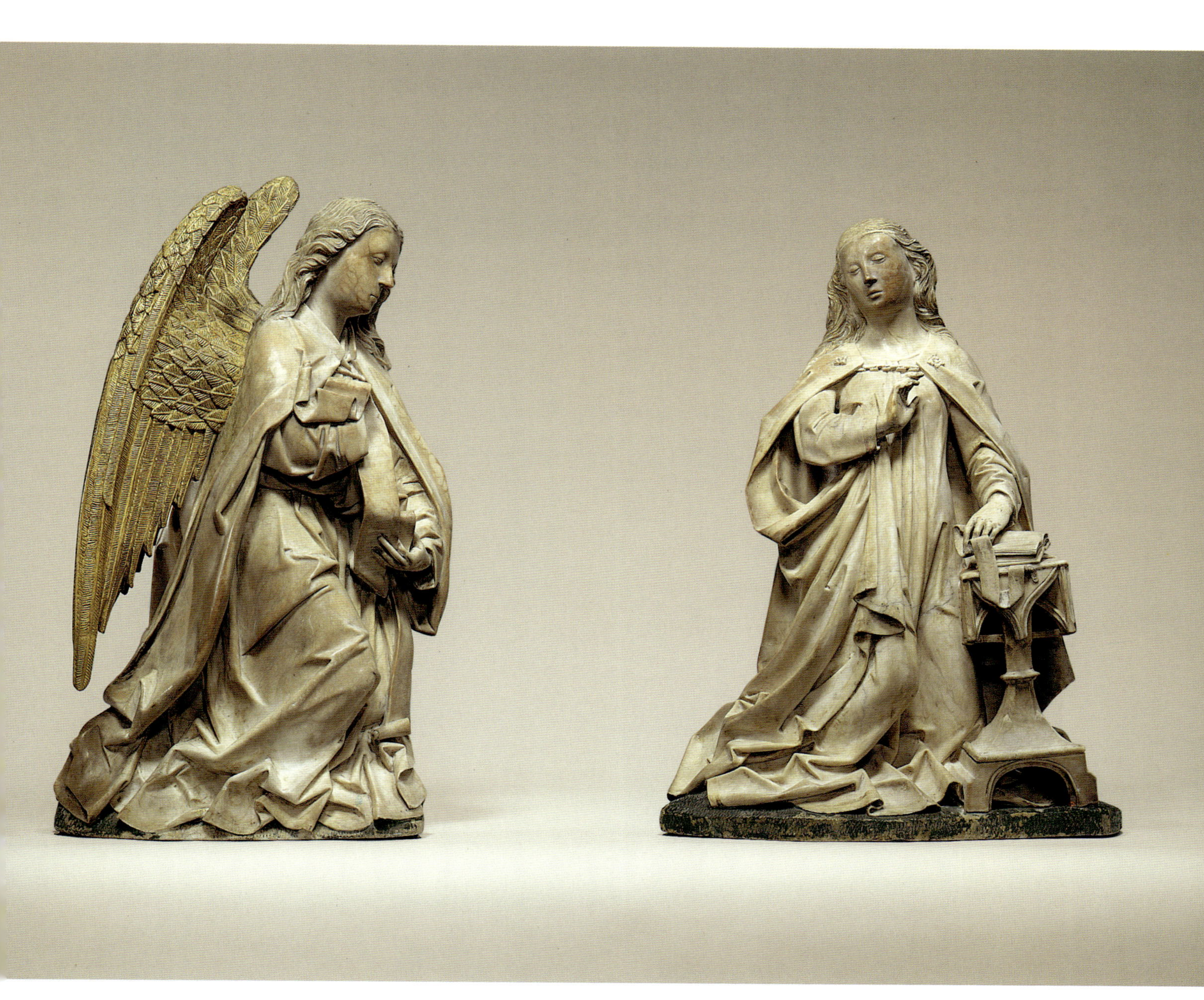

after Riemenschneider settled in Würzburg (the present angel is inscribed "1484" on the back). If, as generally assumed, the Munich *Annunciation* and that mentioned in the inventory are one and the same, this group may further be presumed to have been commissioned by Kilian von Bibra and probably executed in Würzburg. Another stone *Annunciation,* also dated 1484, was originally installed over the portal and is now in the Mainfränkisches Museum.[3]

Müller correctly asserted that the Munich group was not an import but an indigenous work echoing Netherlandish invention, and he compared it to two examples of regional alabaster carving: a *Virgin and Child* from the monastery of Saint Andrew in Halberstadt, now in the chapel of a Franciscan convent in Halberstadt; and the 1467 relief of Saint Michael in the Severikirche, Erfurt (fig. 1), both of which he suggested could even be by the same master.[4] To justify his attribution to Middle Franconia, Müller pointed to an alabaster *Virgin and Child* in the Liebieghaus, Frankfurt.[5] Noting the nearby alabaster quarries, Müller later wondered if the Munich *Annunciation* might have come from Erfurt.[6] Schädler believed the Munich work was the product of an earlier generation, stylistically indebted to Niclaus Gerhaert; he suggested less compellingly that a Würzburg origin is supported by the stylistic similarities with the Master with the Book tympanum

now in the Mainfränkisches Museum, Würzburg.[7] Jopek, noting that the 1484 *Annunciation* from the Rötelsee chapel portal is in a different realm stylistically, argued that the sculptor of the Munich group must have been exposed to stylistic influences well beyond Würzburg.[8]

Both figures of this accomplished *Annunciation* are carved with exceptional skill. One only need point to the deep undercutting, most obvious in the banderole of the angel or in the reading stand of the Virgin, and to the remarkable thinness of the drapery, most apparent in the passage of mantle drapery over the Virgin's left side, cut so finely that a hole has appeared. Essentially this work translates into sculpture an Annunciation type by Rogier van der Weyden, exemplified by the grisaille figures on the outer wings of the Beaune *Last Judgment* polyptych (fig. 2). In addition to the compositional arrangement, the angularity of the figures, draped in abstracted linear garments that fall in sweeping planes and gather at the base in crumpled folds, point to the Netherlandish influence of a previous generation. Yet Müller had good reason to invoke Niclaus Gerhaert; although this work is somewhat wooden in comparison, the voided loop of the Virgin's mantle, allowing a glimpse of the underlying form, constitutes a defining motif of the Strasbourg master's sculptural concept. Regional links are likewise in evidence: the idiosyncratic tex-

3. See Fritz Knapp, "Würzburg und seine Sammlungen," *Münchner Jahrbuch der bildenden Kunst* 10 (1916–1918), 118–119, fig. 17.

4. Müller 1959, 139–140. For the comparisons see Jopek 1988, 150–151, no. 44, fig. 39; and 146–147, no. 42, fig. 40, respectively.

5. Illus. Jopek 1988, 119–120, no. 15, fig. 26.

6. Müller 1966, 217 n. 103.

7. Muth 1982, 263.

8. Jopek 1988, 87.

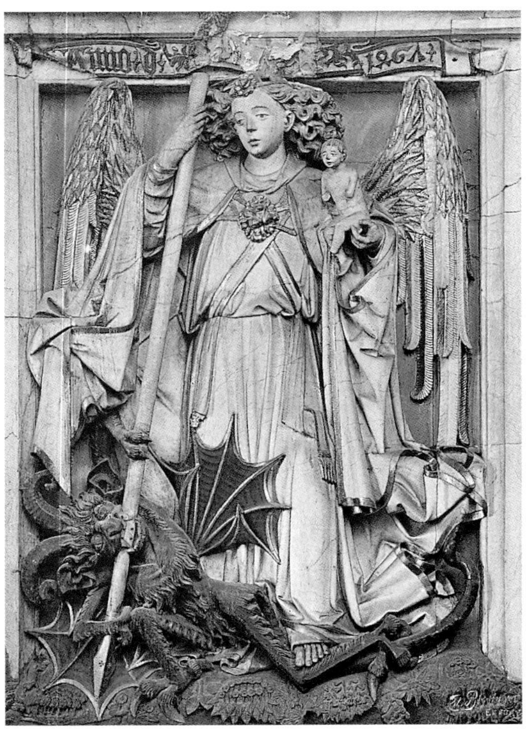

1.

Anonymous, *Saint Michael and the Dragon,* 1467, alabaster, Severikirche, Erfurt

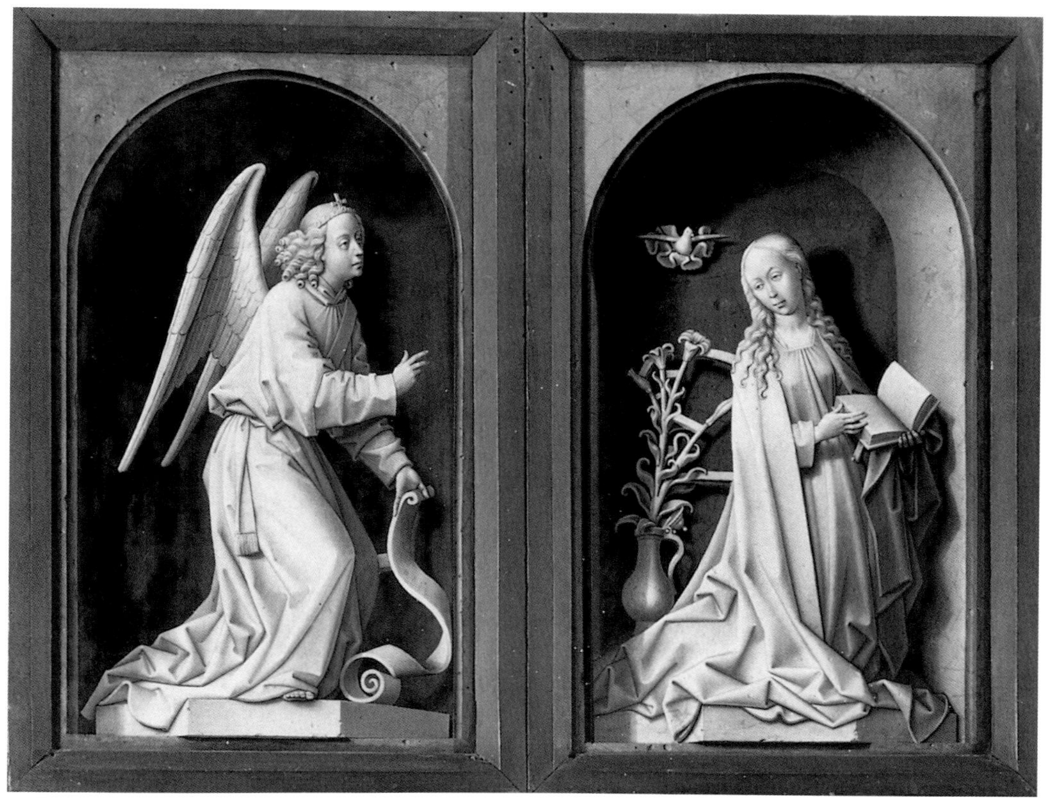

Rogier van der Weyden, Annunciation from the exterior wings of the *Last Judgment* polyptych, c. 1450,
oil on panel, Hôtel-Dieu, Beaune

turing of the angel's wings is virtually identical to that of Saint Michael's in the Erfurt relief (fig. 1). There is nothing that specifically points to a Würzburg workshop, but by the last decades of the fifteenth century the defining style of artistic centers had less to do with local tradition than with the training of individual masters and the workshops they established.

Judging by the nearly contemporaneous Amsterdam *Annunciation* (cat. 2), Riemenschneider was influenced very little by the Munich figures, if he knew them—or by Würzburg sculpture in general, if the Munich group may be viewed as representative. Both *Annunciation*s ultimately hark back to Netherlandish models, but this can be said about most high-quality alabaster carving. While both reflect the Upper Rhenish influence of Niclaus Gerhaert and his followers, the stiff, abstracted drapery of the Munich Virgin bears little resemblance to the fluid, extravagant treatment seen in the Amsterdam Virgin. Indeed, the carefree youthfulness of the Amsterdam figures, enveloped in exuberant, articulated folds and accented with aerial flutters, is in striking contrast to the somberness of the Munich figures. If Riemenschneider had seen the present group in the Rötelsee chapel when he arrived in Würzburg, he would surely have been impressed at least by the exacting artistic standards of the Würzburg Cathedral hierarchy, members of which were to become Riemenschneider's most powerful patrons.

The figures were conceived as a relatively freestanding group, intended to be set in the same plane, with a viewing incident of about 160 degrees, possibly recessed in a shallow niche. Because they appear to rely on the Rogerian formula, it is also possible that they were in separate niches or arcades. HUSBAND

4

c. 1485–1490, alabaster with traces of polychromy, 42 x 17 x 14 (16 ½ x 6 ⅝ x 5 ½), Private Collection

• *Technical Notes* •

The figure is carved in high relief, with the back, principally at the saint's right shoulder, and the top of her head left in a roughed out state. A conical hole about 1 cm in diameter in the top and two rectangular slots (about 1.5 x 0.5 x 0.8 cm) in the base appear to have been used to secure the figure to a workbench revolving clamp (see also cat. 2) rather than to its original housing. Four small drilled holes at the cardinal points just inside the roll of the turban may have been used (later) to attach a metalwork crown. Substantial remains of original gilding are found in the saint's hair, on the border of her mantle, and on the chalice. Her left arm has been broken through just below the shoulder and the back of her hand but reattached with adhesive and possibly iron dowels; there is discoloration at the breaks. The edges of the folds and mantle have suffered numerous chips and losses. The bowl of the chalice is lost, as is part of the mantle at the saint's left side (4 cm long) that shows traces of glue and restoration. Parts of the saint's right thumb and the fingers of her right hand are lost. The surface is rubbed in areas, and the incised zigzag pattern in the fur trim has lost much of its texture. There are considerable discoloring surface accretions.

• *Provenance* •

[Julius Böhler, Munich]; acquired by Ludwig Roselius, Bremen, 1929; by descent to the present owner.

• *Literature* •

Bier 1931, 451; Habicht 1931a, 109, 111 (fig.); Habicht 1931b, 5–6; Hannover 1931; Bier 1934, 334; Bier 1951, 228, 232–233, fig. 7; Bier 1957a, 9–12, esp. 10; Schmoll 1958, 101–102; Raleigh 1962, 20–21, no. 1; Müller 1966, 224–225 n. 75, pl. 173 B; Würzburg 1981, 10–11 (figs.), 225–236, 265; Bier 1982, 29 n. 12; Krohm 1982, 96–97 (ill.); Jopek 1988, 90–94, no. 46, fig. 44; Ruppert 1992, 89, 90–92, fig. 55; Kahsnitz 1997, 90–91, fig. 53; Söding 1998, 154–155, fig. 24.

THE STANDING SAINT holds the remains of a chalice in her right hand and steadies it with her left. A large rolled turban encircles her head, and from beneath her headdress long wavy hair falls down her back, reaching to below her hips. A single tress falls over her right shoulder and is gathered up under her right arm along with the trailing fabric of the turban; another long tress falls down her left side into the deep fold of her mantle. Her fitted, fur-trimmed dress with a low neckline is tightly drawn at the waist, below which the underlying form, obscured by broad drapery passages and accented with vertical folds, expands voluminously. Her mantle falls over her right shoulder; pulled up and tucked over her right arm, it descends in long, planar, slightly arcing folds, the foremost of which turns back against itself. On the saint's left side the expansive mantle falls off her shoulder to the ground and is gathered up and held against her torso by her wrist, resulting in a deep, looping fold that reveals the volume of the underlying torso and creates a series of arcing, tubular folds that converge at her left hand. The figure places her weight on her right leg, and the protruding knee of her left leg interrupts the descending drapery. The tip of her left shoe peeks out from beneath the hem of the mantle, among the softly crumpled gatherings of drapery at the ground.

The sculptural concept of this engaging statuette, more defined by the drapery than by the figure it envelops, derives from the juxtaposition of a youthful yet contemplative visage with an exuberant complex of drapery passages that obscure the figure's weighty but ambiguous corporeal presence while imbuing it with a rhythmic coherence. The saint seems to emerge from the enveloping folds of her mantle

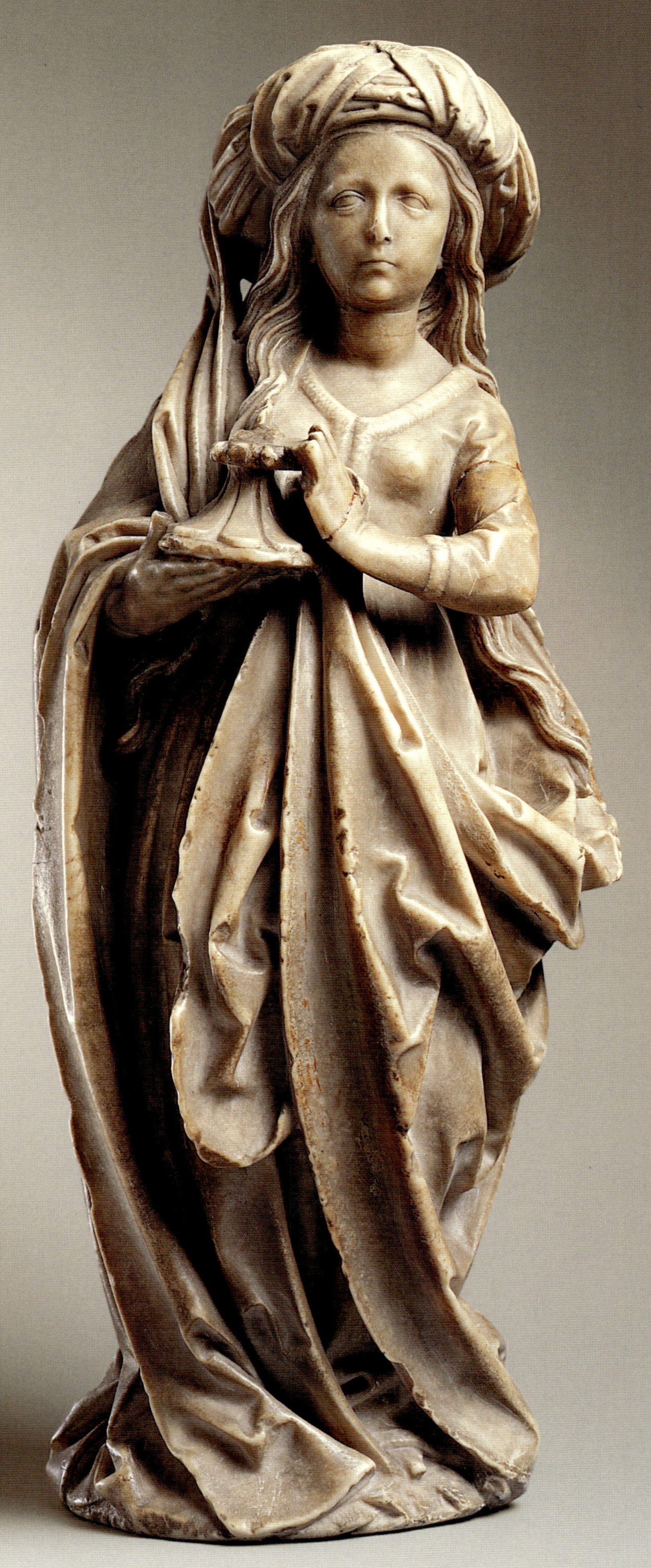

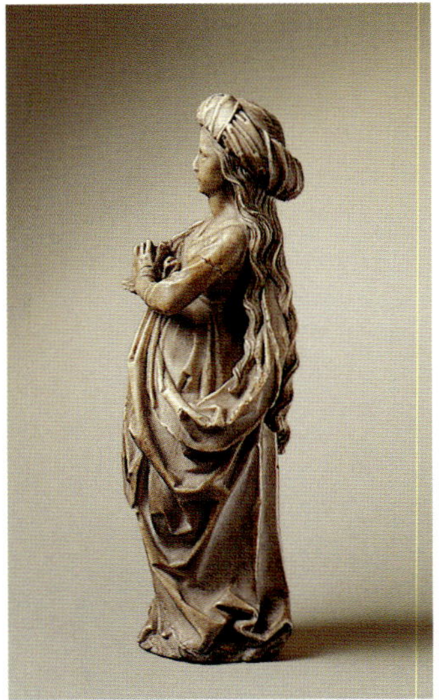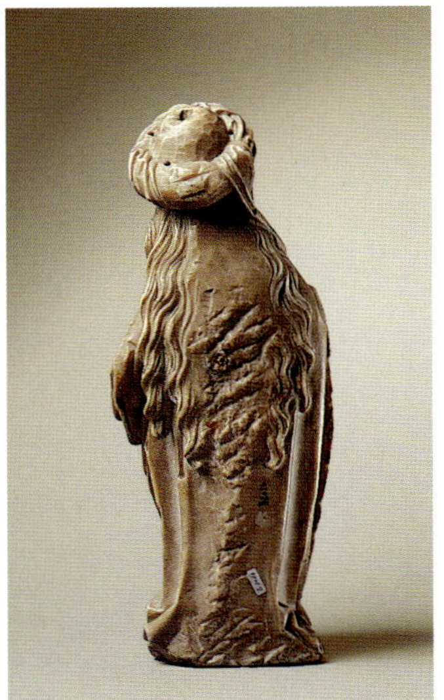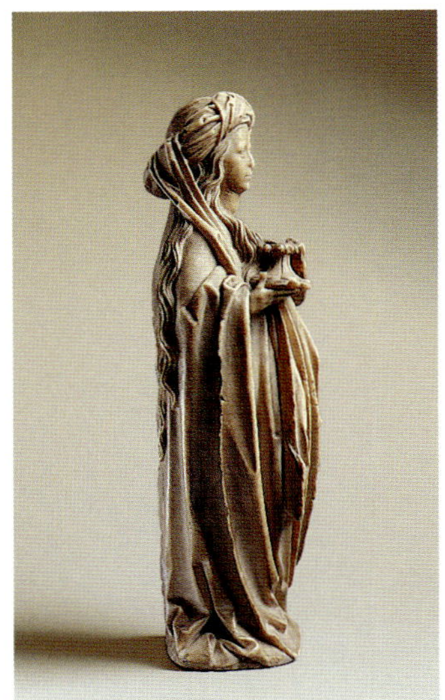

Left, back, and right views of catalogue no. 4

with numinous calm. The contrast of the gently rounded forms of the saint's face and décolleté with the agitated drapery passages that encompass the lower two-thirds of her body suggests a spiritual serenity rising from engulfing turbulence.

As in many works from Riemenschneider's early career, the *Saint Barbara* is notable for its plasticity and three-dimensionality. Although a high relief, the figure is fully legible from a 180-degree vantage, and every view provides a harmonious and integral aspect of the whole. The viewer is left with the impression of a sculpture in the round, an effect that relies largely on the drapery treatment and is enhanced by the slight spiraling of the figure as a result of the weight resting on one leg and by the exaggerated thrusting forward of the pelvis, particularly obvious in the left profile.

The drapery motif Riemenschneider uses here is encountered in the Amsterdam Virgin (cat. 2), but it is usually reserved for standing figures such as the Hassfurt *Saint John the Baptist* (Chapuis essay, fig. 1) or the Raleigh *Female Saint* (cat. 10). It can be seen in Upper Rhenish sculpture as early as the 1460s and more widely in the 1470s and 1480s. The motif emerges somewhat mutedly in a Virgin from an alabaster Crucifixion now in Strasbourg, generally dated between 1460 and 1470 (Krohm essay, fig. 6). A more expansive appearance is found in the *Mary Magdalen* from the parish church of Biengen, closely related to the Nördlingen altarpiece (cat. 5, fig. 2) and the circle of Niclaus Gerhaert. It is abundantly evident in the applewood *Virgin and Child* from Berlin (cat. 7), which Krohm attributes to a follower of Gerhaert and dates about 1470–1480. The motif finds its most

refined and dramatic expression in the Cloisters' boxwood *Virgin and Child,* here attributed to Niclaus Gerhaert and dated about 1470 (cat. 6).

The evident ubiquity of this drapery motif indicates that it was an established visual convention of the region, which Riemenschneider readily absorbed into his sculptural vocabulary in his formative years, which were assuredly spent in part in the Upper Rhineland. More immediately, however, Riemenschneider appears to have been influenced by the sculpture of Niclaus Gerhaert. The commanding formal conception of the *Saint Barbara,* the rhythmic balance of volumes, and the artistry with which the least details are executed place Riemenschneider, as Krohm rightly observes, squarely in the ranks of the followers of the Strasbourg master.[1]

Bier considered *Saint Barbara* the earliest of Riemenschneider's alabaster sculpture, dating it 1480–1490; he compared it to both *Mary Magdalen* and *Saint Elizabeth* from the 1490–1492 Münnerstadt altarpiece (cat. 13, figs. 1 and 2) and to the Hassfurt *Saint John,* at the same time noting the old-fashioned style of turban.[2] Krohm viewed the statuette as a touchstone among the earliest works and assigned it a date of about 1485, while Jopek and Kahsnitz have both placed it somewhat later, about 1490.[3] Söding, seeing the *Saint Barbara* as a foreshadow of the Münnerstadt *Mary Magdalen* and *Saint Elizabeth,* reverted to an earlier date of about 1485.[4] Comparison can also be profitably made with figural groups from the early Rothenburg *Passion* altarpiece, executed around 1485.[5] A pair of kneeling female mourners from the predella has the same childlike proportions, with large

1. Würzburg 1981, 12.

2. Raleigh 1962, 20.

3. Würzburg 1981, 12; Jopek 1988, 153; Kahsnitz 1997, 90–91.

4. Kahsnitz and Volk 1998, 154.

5. For a discussion of this altarpiece, particularly for issues of dating, see Würzburg 1981, 33–36, 50–56; Krohm 1982, 10–11; for a monographic treatment with specific reference to the Munich reliefs, see Kahsnitz 1997.

heads relative to body size (Krohm essay, fig. 8).[6] The left figure exhibits the same draped weightiness of the *Saint Barbara* and wears the same type of turban (the only other instance of this style of headdress in Riemenschneider's works). The right figure shares a strikingly similar facial type and nearly identical treatment of the hair. There are also correspondences with the large group of female mourners from the central shrine of the *Passion* altarpiece (Chapuis essay, fig. 2). The way the leftmost mourner holds her left hand and presses the folds of her mantle against her body is essentially the same in the *Saint Barbara*. One figure does not replicate the other; rather each seems to be an inventive variant of a common sculptural concept. Stylistic references to models presumably encountered during his years as a journeyman, less explicit

and abandoned in his later work, suggest that *Saint Barbara,* like the *Passion* altarpiece, must be numbered among Riemenschneider's early works, dating not much after 1485.

Like so much of Riemenschneider's sculpture, the *Saint Barbara* benefits from a high placement. While the original context is unknown, it seems likely that the figure was mounted on a wall or above a fireplace, much as is the *Trinity* depicted in the right wing of the Heinrich Werl altarpiece in the Prado (fig. 1). Placed against flat surface, the back must have projected sufficiently for the turban to clear; this projection may have been removed at a later date to accommodate an altered installation possibly accounting for the area that has been rather crudely chopped away. HUSBAND

6. Kahsnitz 1997, 90.

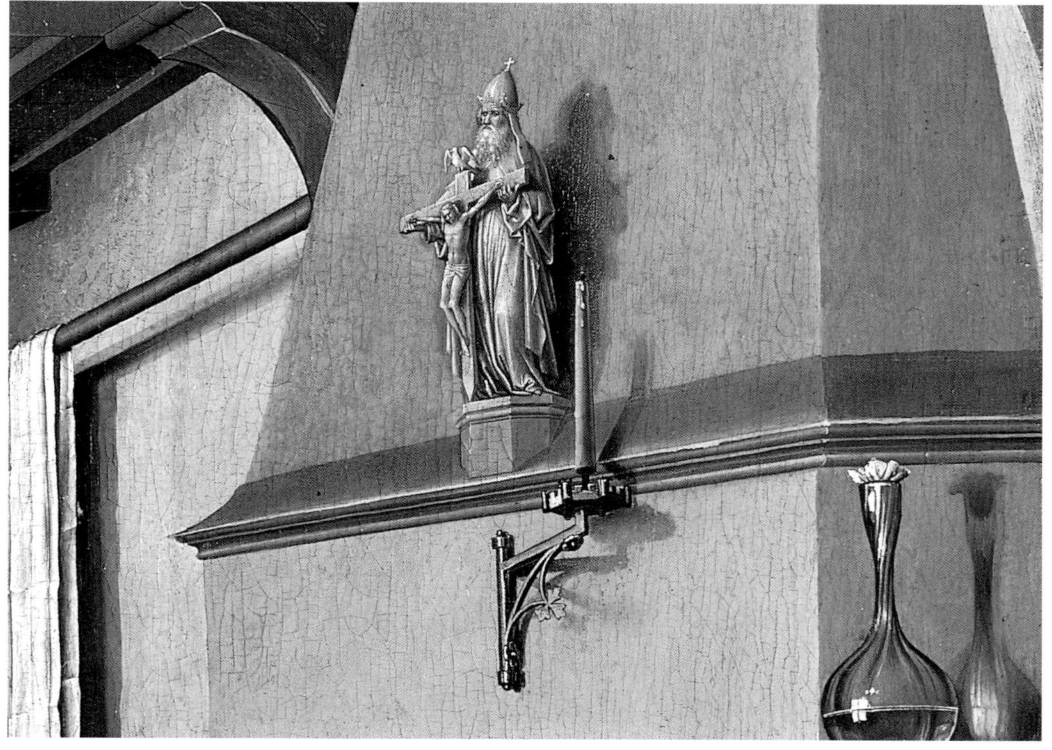

1.

Detail from the right wing of Robert Campin's or Rogier van der Weyden's triptych for Heinrich Werl,
1438, oil on panel, Museo del Prado, Madrid

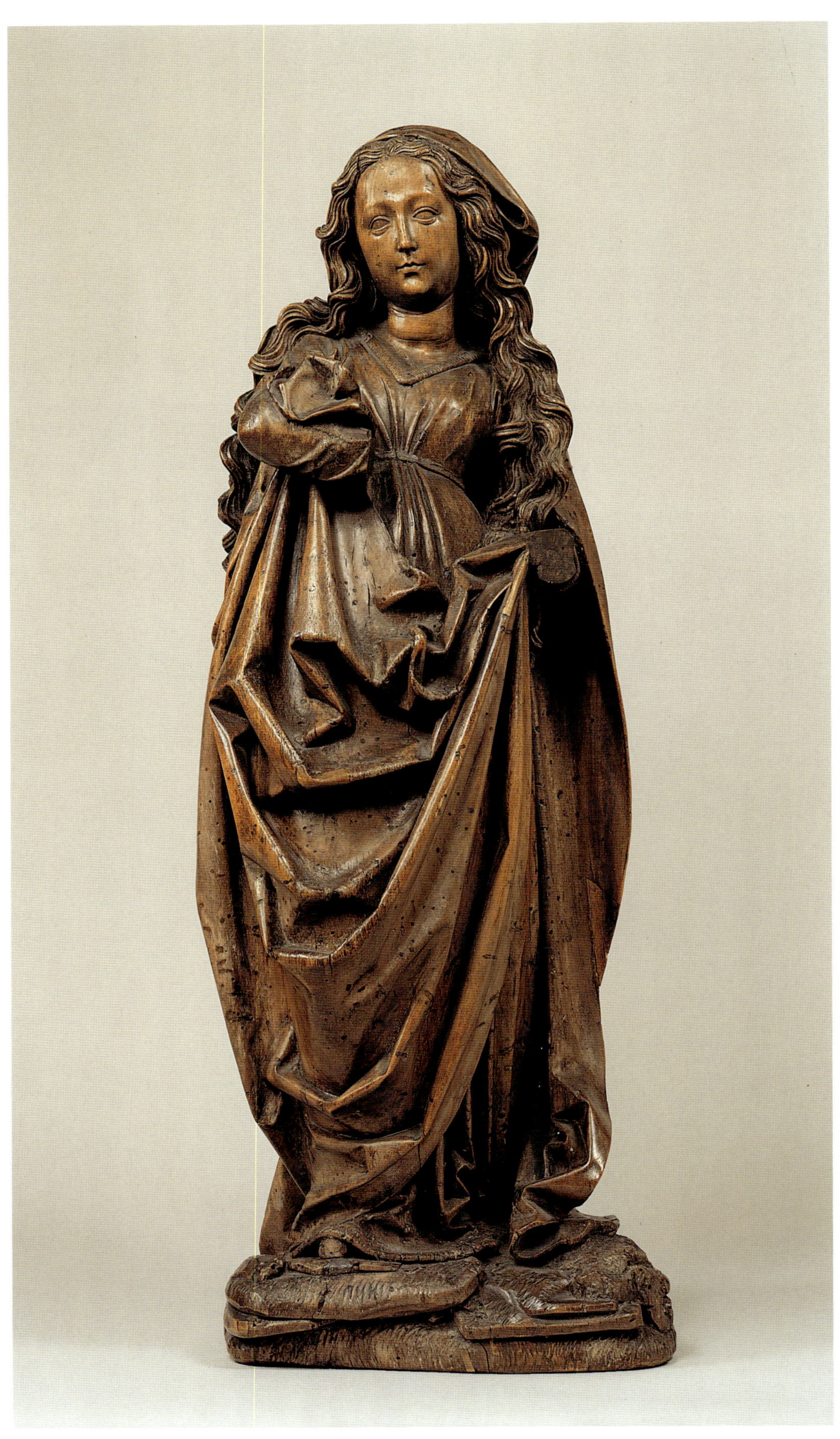

5

Attributed to Niclaus Gerhaert von Leiden / VIRGIN AND CHILD

c. 1465, limewood, 56.5 x 22.3 x 18.2 (22 ¼ x 8 ¾ x 7 ⅛); Staatliche Museen zu Berlin,
Skulpturensammlung

• Technical Notes •
The figure, which is cut from a single block of limewood with the grain running vertically, is carved fully
in the round, with deep folds and numerous areas of
undercutting. Remnants of a chalk ground and of
paint suggest that the sculpture was originally polychrome. The pupils and irises of the eyes are marked
with color applied directly to the wood. The hands,
which were originally carved separately and glued,
are missing, as is the object in the figure's right arm.
There are scattered small losses in the garment and
on the back of the base. A larger break in the border
of the cloak under the figure's left arm has been im-
properly restored, causing a distortion in the contour
of the figure. Insect channels are scattered over the
surface, some of which have been filled with beeswax.

• Provenance •
Private collection in Colmar, Alsace; acquired by the
museum in 1895.

• Literature •
Demmler 1925, 164–180, esp. 171–172; Pinder 1929,
388; Demmler 1930, 144–146; Fischel 1944, 109–123;
Berlin 1958, 38–39, no. 23; Deutsch 1964, 11–129, esp.
45–47; Beyer 1972, 151–156; Recht 1987, 223, 365 no.
VI.7; Krohm in Kahsnitz and Volk 1998, 109–128,
esp. 111–124.

THIS STATUETTE HAS traditionally been
called the "Small Dangolsheim Saint" because of its
stylistic proximity to the Virgin from Dangolsheim
in Alsace (Krohm essay, fig. 2). Originally polychromed, it has been stripped of its paint; the cloak
was most likely gilded. The Virgin is carved fully in
the round and stands on a grass-covered plinth of
earth and stone. A wide cloak rests on her shoulders
and wraps around in front of her body. The fabric is

gathered below her angled right arm and drawn across
to her left hip, where it is held in place by her other
arm. The large protective cloak thus arrayed before
the lower half of her body falls in a number of wide,
arcing folds, leaving open the area of her chest and
waist, which is accentuated by a belt. The visual anchors created by the cloth gathered at the left and
right are emphasized by the converging drapery folds,
which evidently have symbolic significance, pointing
to what the figure once held.

The loss of both hands and what they originally
held makes identification of the figure more difficult.
Older photographs reveal that at the time of its acquisition the sculpture held Barbara's attributes, a
book and a small crenelated tower; both the hands
and the attributes, however, were modern replacements. But the folds of the mantle and the figure's
raised right arm are articulated in such a way that the
viewer expects something more momentous. It is
probable that the figure represents a Virgin who holds
the Christ child across her breast. The child's head
seems to have been supported by the Virgin's right
arm and to have been cradled by the bunched-up
cloak in the bend of the arm. This interpretation is
supported by the emphasis on the figure's body, which
gave birth to Christ and which is revealed here by the
open cloak; by the maidenly face, which gracefully
tilts sideways, its beauty heightened by the mass of
magnificent curling hair; and finally by her somber
glance, which was probably somewhat auspiciously
cast over the child—apprehensive insofar as it seems
to contain a hint of budding knowledge about the
fate of her son.

The energy that unfolds in the cascade of curling hair emerging from below the Virgin's veil attests
to an almost unsurpassed virtuosity in carving. Her
tresses are contained in intertwined, swirling strands
and are particularly shown off in the back. Such a

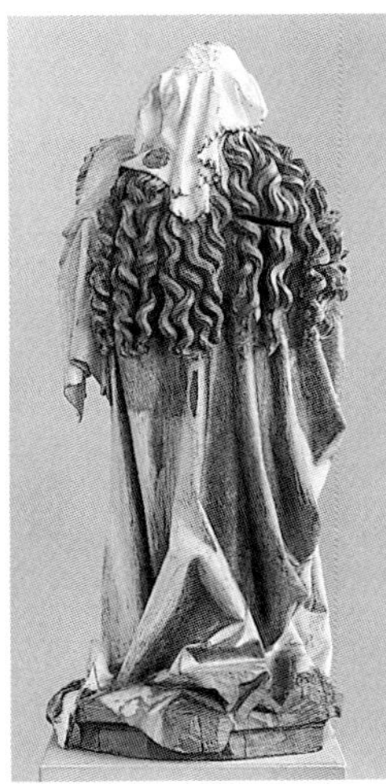

1.
Back view of Dangolsheim
Virgin and Child
(Krohm essay, fig. 2)

capriccio of innovative forms entails spontaneity in the creation and a superior realization of the conception. Very few sculptors of the late Gothic can be named who mastered their tools with similar skill. The dynamism in the wavy flow of the hair is directly reminiscent of that in the Dangolsheim Virgin (fig. 1). This was also the starting point for the curls on sculpture by Riemenschneider, which have an almost painterly effect (see cat. 45).

On the back of the present *Virgin and Child* one encounters a captivating arrangement of fabric, structured in long, continuous vertical columns that break into angled folds at the ground. Lateral and diagonal views of the figure direct the eye toward the front and the back. In its composition, which is decidedly not the sum of discrete points of view but is based on the concept that the sculpture is to be seen from all directions, the figure belongs among artistic innovations of its time.

The handling of the heavy mantle contrasts with that of the lightly sheathed body, probably even more than is true of the sandstone *Anna Selbdritt* in Berlin (cat. 8), which belongs in the same stylistic category. The "Small Dangolsheim Saint" thus shifts into the more immediate circle of wood sculpture linked to the Netherlandish sculptor Niclaus Gerhaert von Leiden, who worked in Strasbourg from 1460 to 1467, then in Vienna and Wiener Neustadt until his death in 1473. Among the works attributed to him are, above all, the Dangolsheim Virgin and the figures of 1462 from the shrine of the high altar of the Sankt Georgskirche in Nördlingen (fig. 2).[1] These attributions to Gerhaert, although not undisputed, are nowadays widely accepted. After the destruction during the Reformation of the high altar in the cathedral in Constance, for which Gerhaert had delivered the sculptural decoration in 1466, no other documented wooden sculpture by him is extant, only examples of stone sculpture. A figure such as the Dangolsheim Virgin is distinguished in its design by a conceptual intelligence found in Strasbourg at that time only in the stone sculpture of Niclaus Gerhaert.

Demmler had in 1925 already attributed the present statuette to the "Master of the Dangolsheim Virgin." Her kinship with this crucial work of the late Gothic lies mainly in her spatial conceptualization: she seems simultaneously to open to and withdraw from her surroundings. Another similarity to the Dangolsheim Virgin and the Nördlingen figures is the abstract rendering of the mantle and drapery motifs, which are not naturalistic but intended to heighten expressiveness. In the figural development seen here, the body is the core, perceived by the imagination even in those areas that are concealed and enveloped by the outer garment like a shell. The underlying principle of "core" and "shell," which determines the outer appearance of the figure, implies that what the eye cannot see is still present in the imagination. With regard to religious art, this means that the image of the saint now has a presence hitherto unknown. Gerhaert here continued a trend that had its origins in the cathedral sculpture of the thirteenth century and further development in the art of the French court around and after 1400 (especially the work of Netherlandish artist Claus Sluter at the Burgundian court in Dijon and of Jacques Morel, employed by the duke of Bourbon) and in Netherlandish art (in the work of the sculptor Jean Delemer from Tournai and in the painting of Jan van Eyck).

In the case of the Berlin statuette the question arises if it may not also be a work by Niclaus Gerhaert, although its material is limewood, not the more traditional Netherlandish medium of walnut, as was used for the Dangolsheim Virgin and the Nördlingen figures. In design and motif the present work is especially close to the Dangolsheim Virgin, but it does not approach her almost incomparable innovative power. This should not be interpreted as a lesser demand for quality but can possibly be explained as the result of a different, less prominent commission.

Yet the statuette does have unusual characteristics. Despite its small scale, the figure, especially in

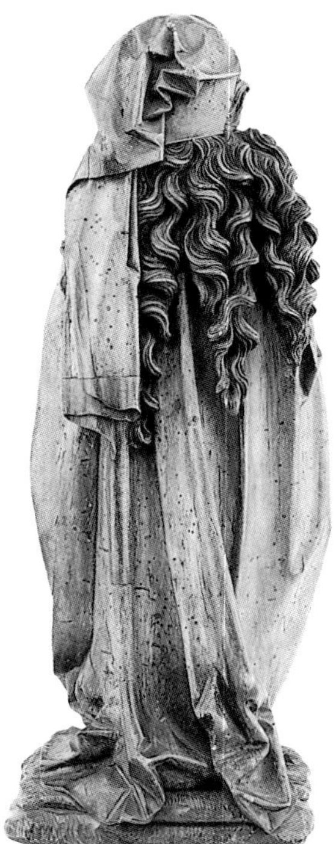

Back view of catalogue no. 5

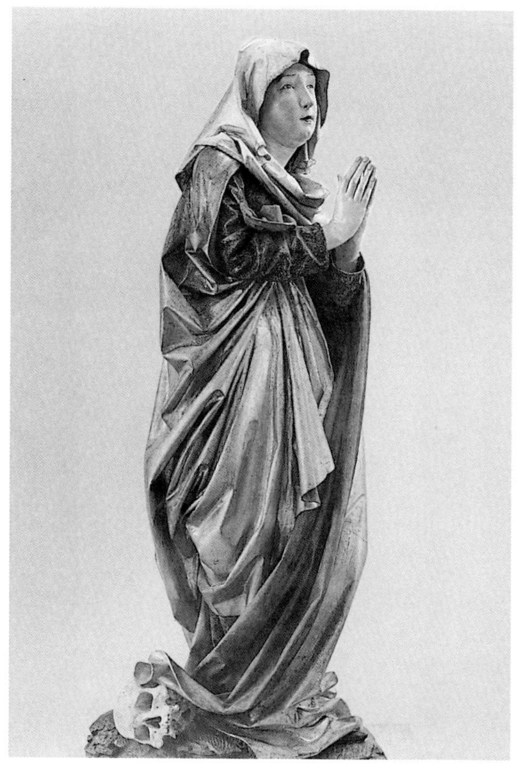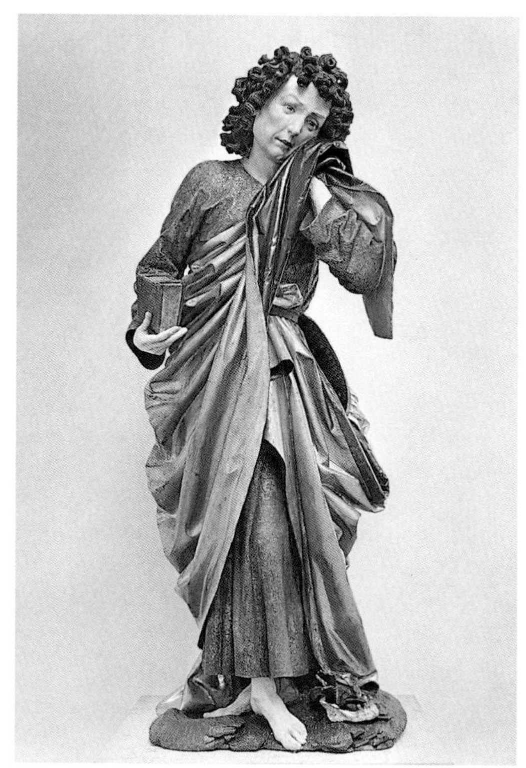

2.

Attributed to Niclaus Gerhaert von Leiden, *Mourning Virgin* and *John the Evangelist,* from the Crucifixion altarpiece,
1462, walnut with polychromy, Sankt Georgskirche, Nördlingen

the structure of the garment, gives the impression of a large format. Indeed, as the image seems to grow beyond its actual size, it belongs to a process according to which the Virgin, displayed in a private environment, was perceived like a vision.

The influence of Gerhaert's sculpture on Riemenschneider's stylistic development can be observed everywhere in the latter's early work. One may consider the alabaster figure of *Saint Barbara* (cat. 4) or the Münnerstadt angels (cat. 13, fig. 1), to mention just two examples here. Schrade recognized correctly in 1927 that the art of Riemenschneider had an immediate precursor in a work like the "Small Dangolsheim Saint," with its exquisite surface treatment and delicate modeling of the solemn yet gentle facial expression. He placed this statuette, as is commonly — yet erroneously — done today, close to the altarpiece in Lautenbach in the Renchtal, a late example of the Strasbourg tradition. Schrade showed this retable to derive from Gerhaert, distinguishing its authorship from that of the Blaubeuren altarpiece (Michel Erhart in Ulm). Schrade reached a remarkable conclusion: "For the first time our investigations... encounter a sculptor whose ability is the same as Riemenschneider's. One who, still influenced by the lasting impression of Gerhaert's factual sense, has the same discriminating perception for the aesthetic value of a painstakingly treated surface and who for that reason belongs in the same educational sphere as Riemenschneider. Someone who sculpts on a large scale and thinks in terms of concentrated masses, as does the man from Blaubeuren, cannot have been the teacher of a man who made the accuracy of his carved line an immutable characteristic of his art. Someone, however, who, just as the man from Lautenbach, feels the sensuality of the raw material so distinctly that he is able to fashion it into something alive in its own right, someone like that one would trust to have taught the young Riemenschneider." Schrade's observations, comparing the "Small Dangolsheim Saint" with the *Saint Barbara* in Munich, one of Riemenschneider's key works (Baxandall essay, fig. 2), emphatically stress the preeminent role of Gerhaert as a source of inspiration. KROHM

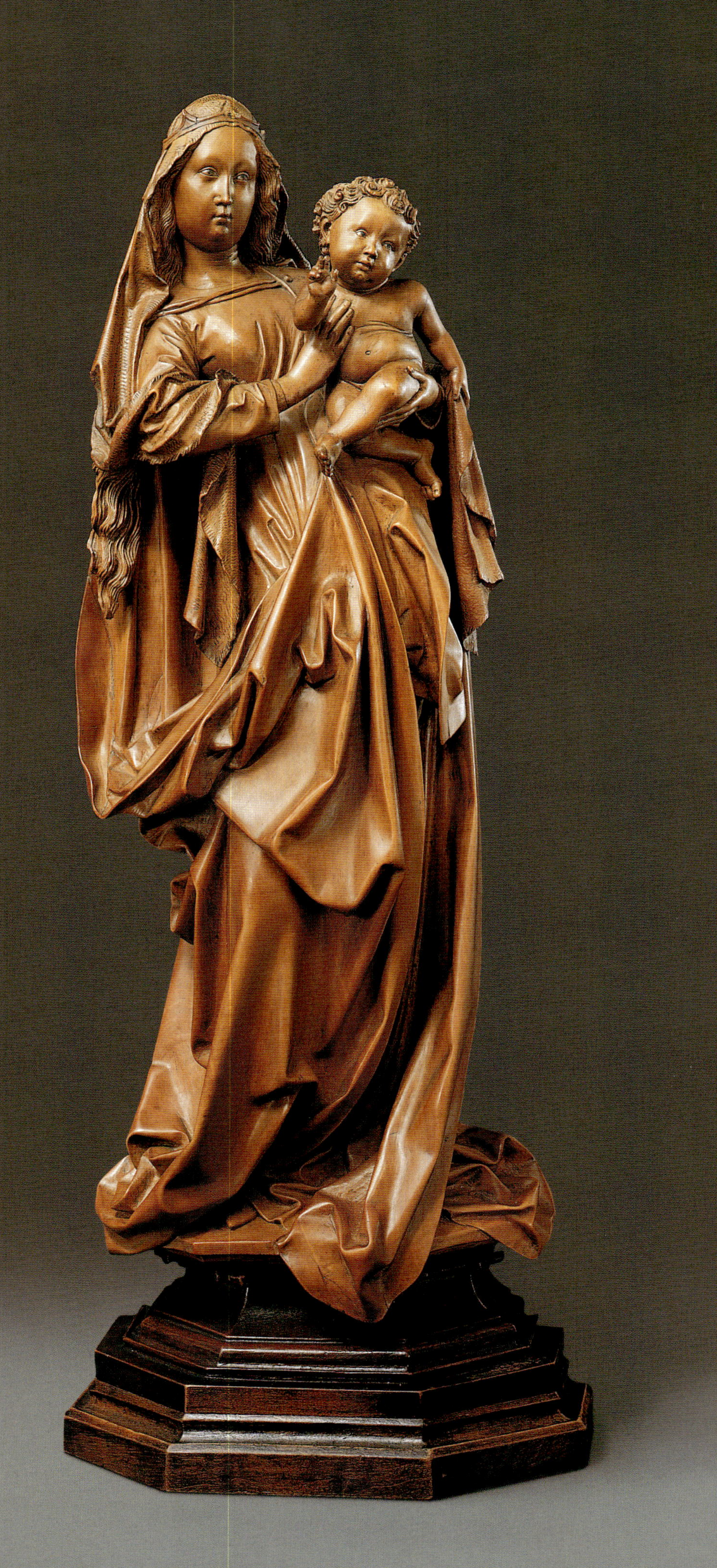

Attributed to Niclaus Gerhaert von Leiden / VIRGIN AND CHILD

c. 1470, boxwood, 33.7 x 14 x 7.6 (13¼ x 5¼ x 3), The Metropolitan Museum of Art, New York,
The Cloisters Collection and Lila Acheson Wallace Gift

• Technical Notes •

The sculpture is cut from a block of boxwood with the grain running vertically, to which a separate section was added at the time of carving to accommodate the drapery on the Virgin's right side. The figure is very well preserved, and the surfaces are intact. Intended as a monochrome, the work bears traces of color on the mouths and eyes that were strengthened at a later date. Replacements from before 1866 include both of the child's arms, curls at the back of his head, drapery held in his left hand, part of the Virgin's veil, and tips at the back and center front of her crown.[1] Also dating from before 1866 is the separately carved dark wooden base with its fictive Dürer monogram. Losses include points at the front of the Virgin's crown and the tips of the child's fingers raised in blessing. A portion of the Virgin's drapery below the child's right leg was broken away and reattached. Parallel notches below the Virgin's drapery at the back, created by the rocking motion of a chisel, are likely the sculptor's trial cuts before attempting the fine texture of the veil.[2]

• Provenance •

Anselm Salomon von Rothschild, Vienna, before 1866–1874; Nathaniel von Rothschild, Vienna; Alphonse and Clarice de Rothschild; seized by the Nazis in 1939; recovered by Clarice de Rothschild by 1947; [Rosenberg and Stiebel, New York, 1948]; Julius Wilhelm Böhler (d. 1967), Munich; Julius Harry Böhler (d. 1979), Munich; Marion Böhler-Eitle (d. 1991), Munich; Florian Eitle, Starnberg, Germany; acquired in 1996.

• Literature •

Schestag 1866, no. 31; Karlsruhe 1970, 97–98, figs. 26–27; Homolka 1972; Würzburg 1981, 172–173; Schädler 1983, 41–54, figs. 1–4, 7–8, 11, 13–14; Chamonikolasová 1995, 79–81, 83, fig. 8; Wixom 1996, 21 (ill.); New York 1999, 186–188, no. 228 (ill.).

NICLAUS GERHAERT WAS the finest and most influential sculptor working in the third quarter of the fifteenth century—a pivotal period in the development of late Gothic sculpture in northern Europe.[3] An artist of the generation preceding Tilman Riemenschneider, Gerhaert was either born or worked in Leiden, as suggested by his signature and his initials, which appear on three of his extant stone works: "nicola[us]. gerardi. de.leyd[en]," "n.v.l.," and "nic[o]laus.von.ley[d]en." In 1464 Gerhaert became a citizen of Strasbourg, where he was active in the years 1460–1467. His documented or signed works include the stone tomb of Jakob von Sierck (archbishop of Trier; d. 1456), dated 1462; the stone sculpture (now in fragments) for the portal of the new chancellery in Strasbourg dated 1463; the stone *Epitaph of a Canon* (Conrad von Busnang?), dated 1464 (Krohm essay, fig. 1); the destroyed wooden altarpiece of 1466 for the high altar in the cathedral in Constance; the red sandstone *Crucifix* dated 1467 in Baden-Baden (Krohm essay, fig. 13); and the red marble tomb of Emperor Friedrich III of around 1467–1472 in the Cathedral of Saint Stephen in Vienna. Except for the last, most of these commissions could have been seen by Riemenschneider. There are, in addition, eight undocumented works in wood and one in stone that have been seriously considered to be by Gerhaert.[4] All but one of these could also have been seen by Riemenschneider. The exception is the present statuette, a work for private devotion, which was probably carved when Gerhaert was in Vienna or Wiener Neustadt toward the end of his life.[5]

Extraordinary for its sense of elegant drama, its suggestion of monumentality, and its lyric homogeneity, this small sculpture is indeed an accomplished

1. Shestag 1866, no. 31 (ill.).

2. Taken from a conservation report by Jack Soultanian, objects conservator at the Metropolitan Museum of Art, dated 4 January 1996.

3. See Müller 1966, 79–82, 102, 106–108, 112–114, 122–123, 126–128, 134, 148, 168, 170, 176–177, 179, pls. 90–93, 95A; Baxandall 1980, 13, 15, 16, 19–21, 159–160, 248–251, pls. 6–10, 12.

4. See Schmoll 1958, 52–102; Alfred Schädler, "Studien zu Nicolaus Gerhaert," *Jahrbuch der Berliner Museen* 17 (1974), 46–62; Schädler 1983; Recht 1987, pt. 2, chap. 1, 115–185, nos. 1.01–.1.12, pls. 1, 3, 4, 6, 7, 9, 10, 12–17, 22, 25–36; *Skulpturengalerie der Staatlichen Museen zu Berlin Preussischer Kulturbesitz* (Berlin, 1989); Eva Zimmermann et al.,"Zuschreibungsprobleme. Beiträge des Berliner Colloquiums zur Dangolsheimer Muttergottes," *Jahrbuch Preussischer Kulturbesitz* 28 (1991) 223–267; Krohm in Kahsnitz and Volk 1998, 109–112; Wixom in New York 1999, 186–188, no. 228, color illus.

5. Schädler 1983; Wixom in New York 1999.

carving in fine-grained boxwood. The slim, high-waisted body of the Virgin serves as a pliant cylinder at the center of a lively envelope of drapery. While partly enclosing and obscuring the central volume, this drapery loops away spatially in places and takes on a life of its own in terms of curving, angular, fluted, and pocketlike folds. The squirming, cross-legged Christ child is another example of this spatial breaking away from the center. The rhythm and balance of the forms are counterpoised by the linear details and by such textural contrasts as that between the rich abundance of the waves of hair and the smooth, concave valleys of the drapery at the back, or between the overall hatching of the crenate veil and the smooth, polished planes of the Virgin's face and neck. Among the naturalistic details is the delicate manner in which the Virgin's fingertips press into the chubby flesh of the child, a detail carried over from central European and Rhenish sculpture of the late "Beautiful Style," dating from the first quarter of the fifteenth century.

The pros and cons of the attribution of this masterpiece to Niclaus Gerhaert (first proposed by Eva Zimmermann in 1970 and subscribed to by Hartmut Krohm in 1981) were carefully addressed in 1983 by Alfred Schädler, who was the first to conclude that this is a late work by the master, made about 1470 during the last period of his career, when he was working on the imperial tombs in Vienna and Wiener Neustadt. It must suffice here to cite a few of the characteristics of the present *Virgin and Child,* as well as the overall form of that work, which, in subtle combination with two of the master's signed and dated figures, the finest of the attributed works, and two of the workshop statues, support the attribution.[6] Among these details are the small but full oval face and the rounded brow of the Virgin; her small mouth, long pointed nose, and long and thick locks of wavy hair; her crenate veil and the thin ridges and narrow as well as wide valleys of the drapery folds, including the breaking folds and the concave pocket folds; and the formal concept of a narrow, elongated core partly enclosed by a surrounding and expansive envelope of drapery. The Christ child—naturalistic, chubby, and animated—with his enlarged head framed by tight, curly locks of hair, is also typical of the sculpture attributed to Gerhaert. The latter traits are also inherited from the earlier sculpture in the "Beautiful Style."

Kaliopi Chamonikolasová has recently provided a stunning confirmation of Schädler's attribution by firmly citing the Metropolitan's statuette as the most important link between the Viennese sculpture by Gerhaert or his workshop and those produced north of Vienna in Moravia. Primary among these Moravian monuments are two statues of the Virgin and child in the Moravian Gallery in Brno and a retable for the high altar of the Sankt Elisabethkirche in Košice, the latter dated by Chamonikolasová shortly after Gerhaert's death, or between about 1474 and 1477.[7] While each of these works displays a considerable correspondence in the proportions and the concept of folds of enveloping drapery, the Moravian style represents a further evolution toward late Gothic mannerism, in which the intricate configurations of the draperies begin to assume an even more independent status.

Datable around 1470, the present figure might also have been considered a possible source for the early works of Riemenschneider. Yet because it was probably carved after Gerhaert left the Rhineland and arrived in Vienna, it can only be cited generally as one example among several works, all of them earlier, by or attributed to Gerhaert that underscore Riemenschneider's debt (see also cat. 5).[8] Perhaps the closest stylistic analogies in the exhibition may be made with Riemenschneider's *Saint Barbara* of about 1485–1490, the *Virgin and Child* from about 1495–1500, and the *Saint Lawrence* of about 1502 (cats. 4, 19, 32 D). The

6. See Krohm essay, figs. 1, 2, 13, and cat. 5, fig. 2. See also Schädler 1983, figs. 18–19; and Schmoll 1958, figs. 16–20.

7. See Chamonikolasová 1995, figs. 1, 3, and 6.

8. See Schmoll 1958, 95–102, for a fuller discussion of the stylistic connections between Gerhaert's and Riemenschneider's work. See also Krohm's essay in this catalogue.

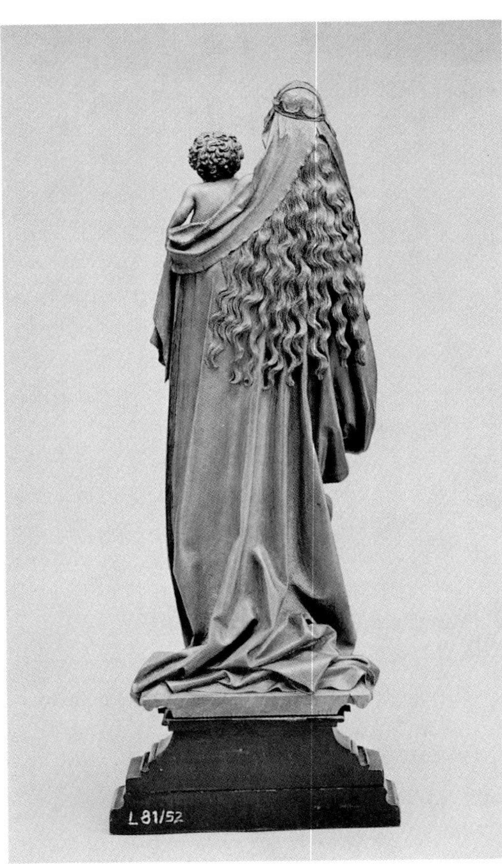

Back view of catalogue no. 6

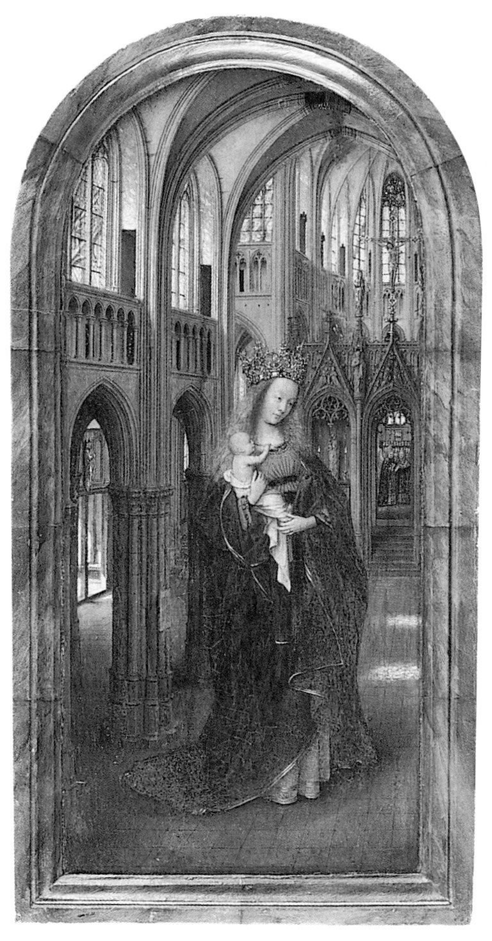

1.

Jan van Eyck, *The Virgin in a Church,* c. 1430, oil on panel,
Staatliche Museen zu Berlin, Gemäldegalerie

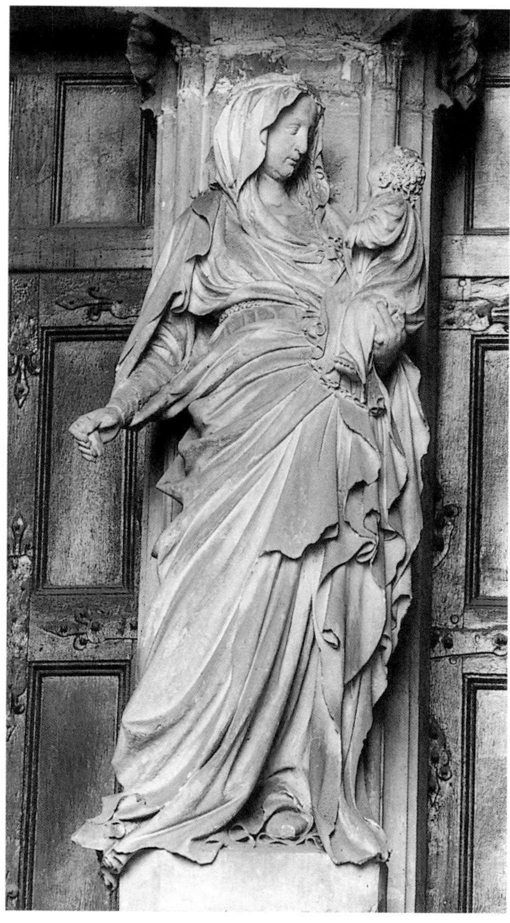

2.

Claus Sluter, *Virgin and Child,* c. 1390, limestone,
Chartreuse de Champmol, Dijon

contrapposto and spatial curve of each of these works, the slightness of the torsos, the expansive draperies that tend to obscure the lower part of the figures, the tendency to use small oval faces, and the interest in textural contrasts all seem to point to the achievement of Gerhaert. The proportions and animation of the Christ child in the present statuette also seem to be echoed in several of Riemenschneider's renderings of the Virgin and child (see cats. 9, 14, 19, 45).

More than this, Gerhaert may be seen as an essential link between Riemenschneider and still earlier styles: the elegant proportions and exquisite textures of Jan van Eyck (fig. 1) and the robust naturalism of Claus Sluter (fig. 2), who were Gerhaert's stylistic sources in the Burgundian territories. The authority of formal conception and eloquence of execution of the present *Virgin and Child* are evidence of a great artist. It is no wonder that, taken with the rest of Gerhaert's oeuvre, the artist had enormous influence in the Upper Rhineland, south Germany—including Franconia, where Riemenschneider worked—Vienna, and Moravia. WIXOM

7

c. 1470–1480, probably applewood, 24.8 x 10 x 7.8 (9 ¾ x 3 ⅞ x 3 ⅛), Staatliche Museen zu Berlin, Skulpturensammlung

• *Technical Notes* •

The figure, which is cut from a single piece of applewood, is carved fully in the round, with areas of deep undercutting. There are remnants of an ancient polychromy, which is not necessarily original. The accents of color in the irises, pupils, and lips, which lie directly on the wood, seem to have been retouched. The noses of the figures as well as strands of the Virgin's hair have been rubbed by repeated touching and presumably by kissing. There are minor losses in the veil, the mantle, and the base. The Virgin's left thumb and the first phalange of her left index finger are modern, unsatisfactory replacements.

• *Provenance* •

Acquired in 1917 as a gift; documented earlier in Landsberg am Lech.

• *Literature* •

Demmler 1925, 164–180, esp. 171–172; Pinder 1929, 385; Bange 1930, 3–4; Vöge 1950, 95; Metz 1966, 79, no. 397; Karlsruhe 1970, 149, no. 94; Deutsch 1977, 242–322, esp. 277–286; Mezenceva 1979, 57–60, esp. 59; Würzburg 1981, 231–233, no. 46; Krohm in Kahsnitz and Volk 1998, 109–128, esp. 125–126.

T H I S   E X Q U I S I T E   S T A T U E T T E   of the Virgin, whose figure and clothing are richly differentiated, exhibits highly accomplished carving skills. Despite traces of wear, the finely worked details are clearly evident. Yet the solemnity of the sculpture is not betrayed in artistic playfulness, for the Virgin's gaze and gesture express a serenity and calm reminiscent of works by Riemenschneider.

Although the small, graceful figure is seen to best effect from one direction, she is meant to be viewed from different vantages; the sides offer especially lovely impressions. The figure's plasticity, reflecting the artist's deliberate intention to achieve a comprehensive view, indicates the beginnings of a new approach to figurative art that reaches far beyond tradition. The Virgin steps forward with her right foot, which projects from beneath her robes and rests on a half moon on which a face is carved (identifying her as the woman from the Apocalypse described in Revelation 12:1). Synchronized with the movement created by this step, the Virgin assumes a gentle S-curved stance, with her upper body tilted to one side and her hip distinctly bent. This arcing is countered by the tilt of her head in the other direction, ending in line with the figure's center of gravity. The nude Christ child perches on his mother's left arm above her projecting hip, with his leg cupped by her hand. She braces the child against her chest with a tender, protective gesture. The child's right hand caresses her neck, while he touches her hand with the apple in his left hand, momentarily suspending his play. His face is turned to the viewer.

The counterpoint motion in the overall form is reinforced by the shape of the mantle. It has slipped from the Virgin's right shoulder and is draped in a wide loop over her projecting right leg toward her left hip. The parallel vertical folds of the mantle, which are strongly delineated and direct the viewer's attention to the child, accentuate the curves of the figure. Contrasts heighten the tension: one may observe the space between the mantle's volume and the body, the ridges and valleys defined by the draperies. The figure itself seems to unfold freely within the boundaries of its outer garment.

Although the drapery is purposefully laid out and arranged in proper sequences, it does not appear schematic. In contrast to the "Small Dangolsheim Saint" (cat. 5), which is perhaps by Niclaus Gerhaert, the drapery folds here give the impression of spontaneity. In keeping with the overall design, widely pro-

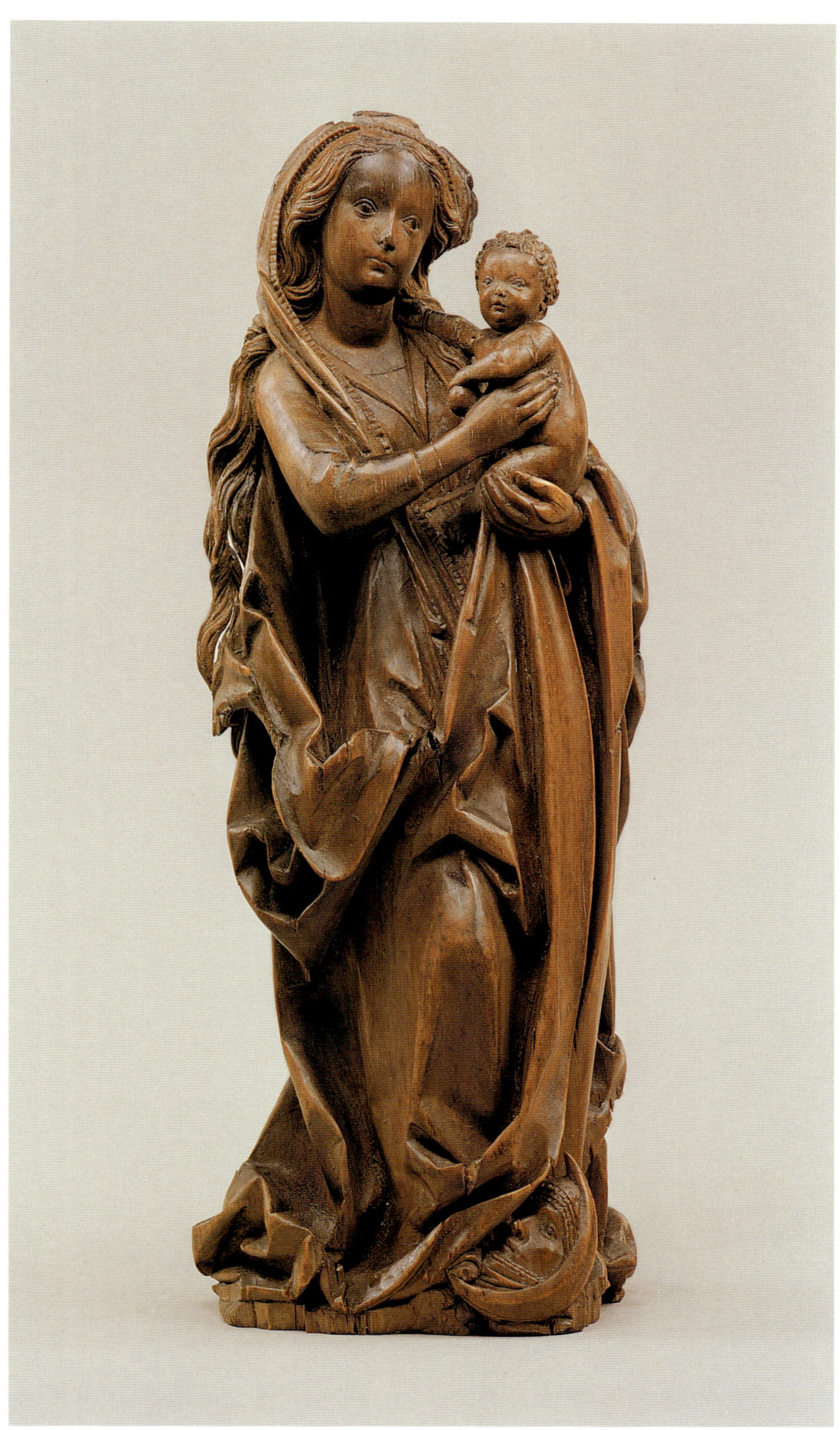

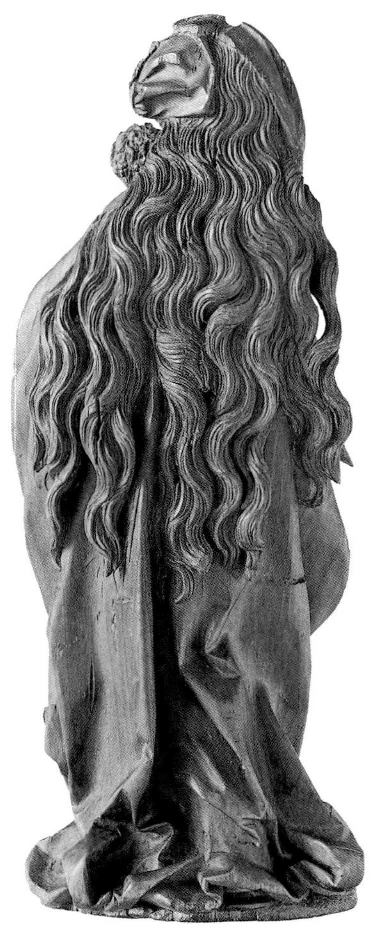

Back view of catalogue no. 7

jecting or billowing forms appear at the left, while tighter vertical ones are confined to the right. The execution of the back is no less captivating. Masses of curls cascade from the cowl-shaped veil and cover the Virgin's shoulders and back like a tapestry. At the bottom of the mantle the supporting leg is visible, its placement reinforced by stabilizing diagonal tubular folds.

The conceptualization of the statuette fully in the round, which broke with the prevailing style of the time, is based on innovations in the articulation of form by Netherlandish sculptor Niclaus Gerhaert. His work was crucial to the development of south German sculpture in the second half of the fifteenth century. The main characteristics of this composition are adopted from Gerhaert: the agile, swinging stance, developed through a forward step; and the copious, sometimes contrapuntal draping of the body. A similar design, even more closely based on Gerhaert, can be seen in the statuette of a Virgin newly acquired for the Cloisters (cat. 6). The same is true for its double, currently on the market. Schädler has attributed both figures to Gerhaert, but opinions are divided.

In general, the present statuette displays Gerhaert's formal language. Its type also suggests Gerhaert's circle, as does the stone Virgin commissioned by the canon Edmund von Malberg (d. 1478) from the cathedral cloister in Trier (fig. 1), a work probably of Strasbourg origins. Principal motifs are the child sitting on the lower left arm of the mother, and the Virgin protectively shielding his body with her extended right arm and open hand.[1] The more restrained representation, the reduction in dynamic tension, and the round, even face of the Berlin Virgin, with its serious large eyes, suggest that it was intended for contemplation.

A small engraving of a contemplative Virgin by Martin Schongauer from the 1470s (Krohm essay, fig. 4) seems to have been inspired by such a sculpture. Another work of the same type, and of especially high quality, is the sandstone Virgin in the outer frame of the tomb for Adalbert von Sachsen (d. 1484) in Mainz Cathedral. Another is the Virgin, dated c. 1480, from the Obstmarkt House no. 22 in Nuremberg.[2] Deutsch, who attributed the Berlin statuette to the

1. See Schmoll 1958, 52–102, esp. 59–68.

2. New York 1986, 162, no. 32.

Ulm sculptor Michel Erhart, suspected that it was a model made around 1474 for the high altar of the Ulm Minster, in recollection of Gerhaert's Virgin of 1466 for the high altar in the cathedral in Constance (destroyed, as was the one in Ulm, during the Reformation). Deutsch perceived reflections of the Ulm Virgin, about whose actual appearance nothing at all is known, in other Virgins of secondary quality, including the one in Ehrenstein near Ulm and one in the Detroit Institute of Arts.

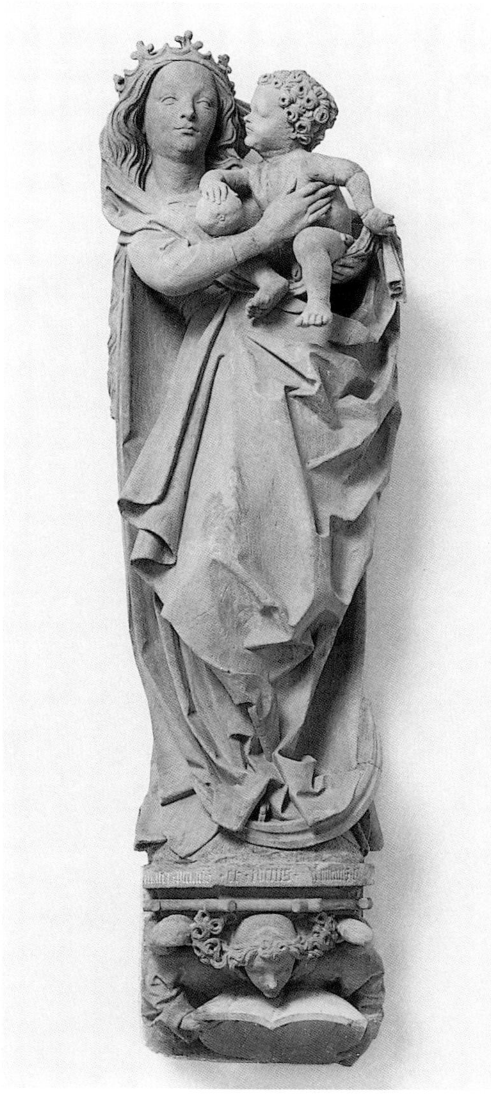

1.

Strasbourg, *Virgin and Child* with the coat
of arms of Edmund von Malberg, c. 1478, sandstone,
Dom- und Diözesanmusem, Trier

One can only guess the actual purpose of the statuette, since a thorough study is still lacking of the phenomenon of medieval miniature carvings in which site determines the sculptural means. But traces of wear on the face, nose, and forehead indicate that the figure was touched and kissed in veneration. It probably served as a private object of devotion but must have been appreciated as an accomplished work of art as well. Similar works from before 1500 have survived only in small numbers. The collecting of such sculpture began only in the later part of the sixteenth century, with the emergence of the *Kunstkabinett*.

While the figure may have served primarily as a goldsmith's model and secondarily as a devotional image, little is known about models for goldsmiths' work. A statue of a Virgin, still in private hands and attributed to Michel Erhart, is thought to have been the model for the silver figure from the Kaisheim cloister, today in the Berlin Skulpturensammlung.[3] Yet it is not even certain that models were created as patterns for large-scale figures, as Deutsch assumed. It is of course conceivable in a workshop such as Riemenschneider's, where standard models were used extensively, that drawings were not the only basis for final works, but that carved models or even clay examples also existed. It is also possible that workshop assistants recorded the most successful concepts for their own further use in the form of small models. This touches on the question of workshop praxis, for which current research cannot yet provide conclusive answers.

Its accomplished execution suggests that the Berlin Virgin belongs among the few statuettes of the time that may have served as models, although it was primarily a devotional image. Precursors from the thirteenth and fourteenth centuries are found in ivory, while many later examples in hardwood are suspected to be forgeries. It is no longer possible to determine the extent to which such small works circulated in the late fifteenth century. The relationship to a number of Virgins by Riemenschneider is unmistakable, however, not least in the opulent curls carved on the backs of these statues. His small Virgins, often in damaged condition, are usually not of the same remarkable quality as the applewood statuette. An exception is the Virgin formerly in the collection of Wilhelm Clemens, now in the Museum für Angewandte Kunst in Cologne (cat. 16), whose artistic caliber is outstanding. KROHM

3. Dietmar Lüdtke, *Die Statuetten der gotischen Goldschmiede. Studien zu den "autonomen" und vollrunden Bildwerken der Goldschmiedeplastik und den Statuettenreliquiaren in Europa zwischen 1230 und 1530.* Tuduv-Studien, vol. 4 (Munich, 1983), 318–319, no. 13.

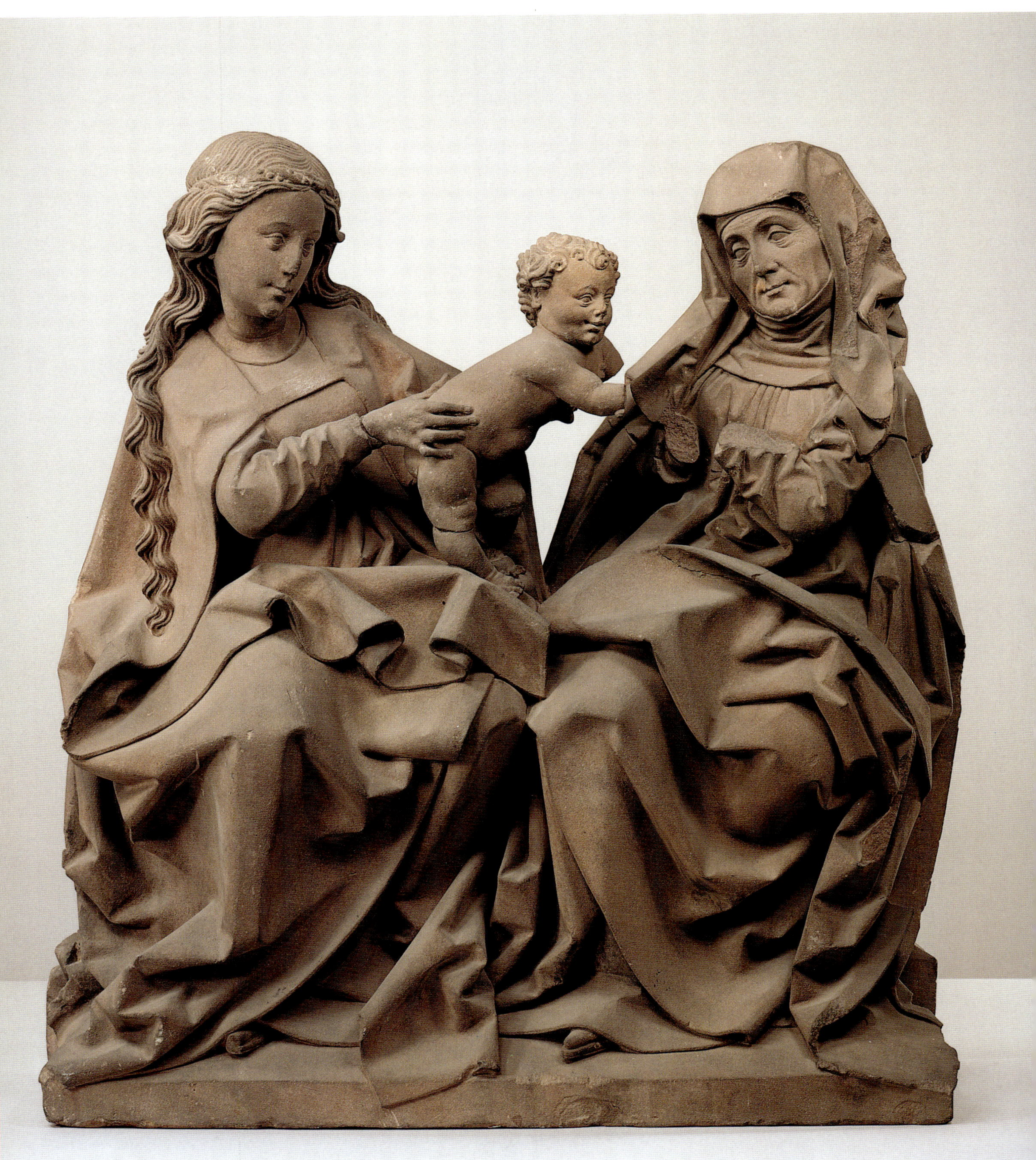

Strasbourg / SAINT ANNE WITH THE VIRGIN AND THE CHRIST CHILD
(ANNA SELBDRITT)

c. 1470/1480, sandstone, 65 x 60 x 25.8 (25⅝ x 23⅝ x 10⅛), Staatliche Museen zu Berlin,
Skulpturensammlung

• Technical Notes •

The group is cut from a large block of sandstone, the front of which has been finely carved, with no chisel marks; the entire visible surface has been evenly smoothed with polishing tools. Flesh and fabric have been treated similarly, with no differentiation in texture. On the back, the bottom half of the block is flat, while the contours of the figures at the top have been summarily rendered with flat and toothed chisels. The group was damaged in 1945 and had broken into three larger pieces and one smaller one. In addition to the loss of Saint Anne's hands and those of the child, Anne's head veil was chipped at that time. The separated parts of the sculpture were rejoined during a 1961 restoration (fig. 1). Earlier damage is evident on Mary's nose.

• Provenance •

From a niche above the door of the rectory in Trimbach near Wissembourg in Alsace, according to Wertheimer 1929; acquired by the museum in 1910 in Strasbourg.

• Literature •

Demmler 1921, 20–33, esp. 22–29; Sommer 1927, 112–114; Wertheimer 1929, 37–38; Pinder 1929, 356; Demmler 1930, 138; Frenz 1943, 51, 56, 67; Fischel 1944, 27–36; Schmoll 1958, 52–102, esp. 59–68; Paatz 1959, 68–94, esp. 86; Müller 1966, 102; Karlsruhe 1970, 100–102; Fründt 1972, 37–38, no. 26; Nuremberg 1983, 61–78, esp. 70–71; Recht 1987, 246–248, 373; Krohm 1989, 87–105; Wirtz 1994; Holger Quandt in Krohm 1996, 465–469; Paris 1996, 138–139; Gross 1997, 275.

THE YOUTHFUL MARY sits on a bench with Anne, who is depicted as an older matron. The women sit so close to one another that their knees almost touch, and because their garments are especially voluminous at the bottom, the bench is engulfed in drapery. The Virgin passes her child to Saint Anne with gentle prodding, sending him "on his way" to become acquainted with his grandmother. The principal motif is Mary's extended arms and hands, offering the boy support, as his unsteady pose and his straight right leg indicate a first attempt to walk (never before in medieval art has this been so astutely observed).

The relationship between the Virgin and Saint Anne is defined by movement and countermovement with respect to the child. While the seat is contiguous, creating a bridge in the area of the women's laps, their upper bodies lean outward, allowing them to direct their focus on the child in the center. This is reinforced by the inclination of their heads and by the orientation of their arms and hands. Their poses allow the child to be relatively unencumbered and prominent between them. The outward-leaning motion connotes a different meaning for each woman: in Mary

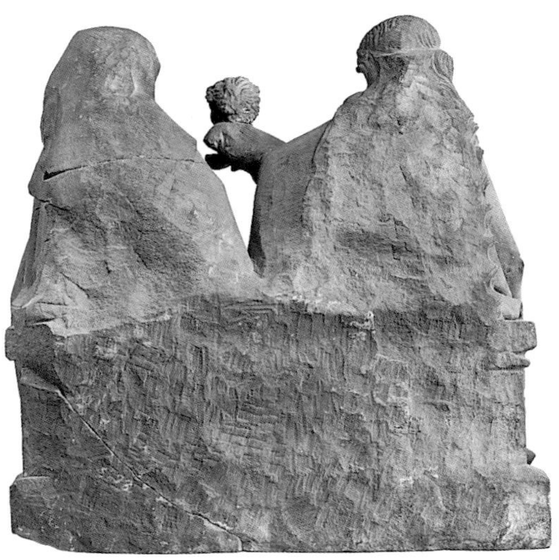

Back view of catalogue no. 8

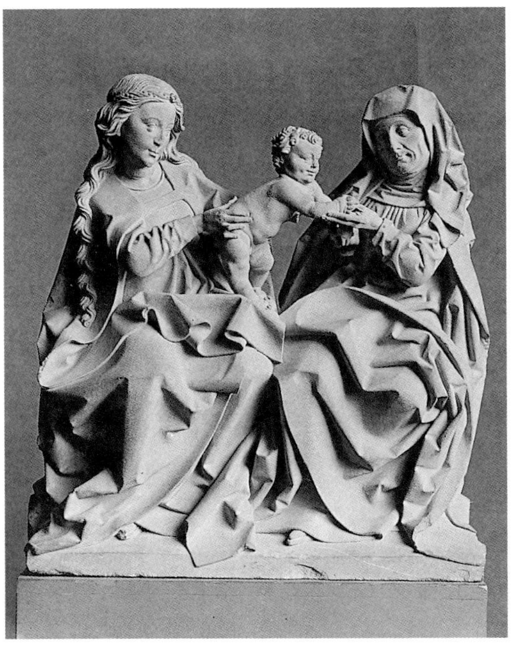

Plaster cast of *Anna Selbdritt* before it was damaged
in World War II

it signifies preparing the child to leave, an active role; in Saint Anne it characterizes a restrained and deferential, reserved reaction.

The group's spatial configuration can be compared with that of Niclaus Gerhaert's *Epitaph of a Canon* from 1464 in Strasbourg Cathedral (Krohm essay, fig. 1). In both works the representation alludes to an act of mercy, in this case the blessing of Saint Anne. As the mother of the Virgin Mary, she participates in the Redemption through Christ, which is the primary theme of the group.

The draperies, cast over the knees and varied in their design, establish not only junctures but also boundaries. A rhetoric is inherent in the folds, seldom as clearly pronounced as here, which supports the principal idea intimated in the child's urging forward and in the women's gestures: the wavy, directed expanse of the mantle running across the Virgin's lap ends in a point just at the child's feet; and the corresponding passage on Anne's lap is a smooth, arcing configuration that cascades over her left knee. In a work such as the *Noli me Tangere* relief from the Münnerstadt altarpiece (cat. 13 F), Riemenschneider combines a similar language of folds with Schongauer's use of the line as an expressive means.

Theodor Demmler in 1921 was the first to introduce the *Anna Selbdritt* group into literature as a work by Niclaus Gerhaert. This attribution, as Karl Hans Frenz convincingly demonstrated in 1939, cannot be sustained. Frenz was justified in relating the

piece to a work by an immediate follower of Gerhaert, the upward-looking figure from the tower in Strasbourg Cathedral (today in the Musée de l'Oeuvre Notre-Dame). Joseph A. Schmoll (also called Eisenwerth), who elaborated on this suggestion in 1958, also grouped in this context the canon and cathedral deacon Edmund von Malberg's stone Virgin from Trier, with its console and crest-bearing angel (cat. 7, fig. 1), as the work of a sculptor who must have been intimately familiar with Niclaus Gerhaert's art. Among the artists he considered were Hans Kamensetzer and in particular Bartolomäus Widitz, while Roland Recht added a further player from the Strasbourg tradition of that time, namely Lux Kotter. The Trier figure, also long thought to be a work by Gerhaert, was probably commissioned in Strasbourg, possibly by Edmund von Malberg himself just before his death in 1478.

With regard to the date of the *Anna Selbdritt,* Schmoll defined stylistic relationships between this group and the 1484/1485 sandstone figures on the pulpit in Strasbourg Cathedral, commissioned for the clergyman Geiler von Kaysersberg, which suggest a time toward the end of the 1470s or the beginning of the 1480s. Whether all of these works are by the same hand is of course open to discussion. They are probably by journeymen schooled in Gerhaert's style and active in the Strasbourg Cathedral workshop until Riemenschneider settled in Würzburg. This would account for Riemenschneider's apparently first-hand knowledge of these works. The *Anna Selbdritt* is clearly the creation of an outstanding artist.

Despite the heightened gesture and pose of the Dangolsheim Virgin or the Nördlingen figures (Krohm essay, fig. 2; and cat. 5, fig. 2), Gerhaert's motifs are developed with an informed understanding of organic contexts. The master gives exact indications of how one should visualize the body, posture, and movement, even in those areas hidden by the garment. By contrast, the sculptor of the *Anna Selbdritt* (as of the Trier Virgin and most of Gerhaert's followers), much as he may try to employ mass as a sculptural means, does not distinguish clearly between body and garment or the successive layers of a garment. On the one hand, body and garment become a less differentiated whole, while on the other hand, the configuration of folds that is so characteristic of Gerhaert in its directedness and interpretive role is paradoxically more poignant. Despite Gerhaert's more pronounced use of contrasts in the composition and the rhythm of movement, he ponders and subtly harmonizes posture and garment.

Considering the overall high quality of the sculpture, the reduction of formal means typical of Gerhaert is not to be seen as a flaw; rather the emphasis on figurative, symbolic points in the drapery bears witness to a conscious change in the mode of interpretation. A particular indication of the group's quality is the impeccable surface: subtly differentiated, it allows a delicate play of light and shadow. The body of the Christ child and the faces of both women give the impression of smooth skin in a way that will later be characteristic of Riemenschneider's stone sculpture (see Chapuis essay, fig. 3), while the garments achieve a high degree of abstraction. Comparing the Christ child of the *Anna Selbdritt* with that of the Strasbourg *Epitaph of a Canon* by Gerhaert, the naturalistic description of the latter stands out, despite both works' similarity to one another. In the works of Gerhaert's followers, as in those of Riemenschneider, mimesis gave way to an increasing idealization. Gerhaert shows Mary's fingertips pressing into the child's flesh as though moving a mass (one may also observe the callous hands of the canon); in the *Anna Selbdritt,* by contrast, the touch is rendered with restraint and achieves greater subtlety. Gerhaert

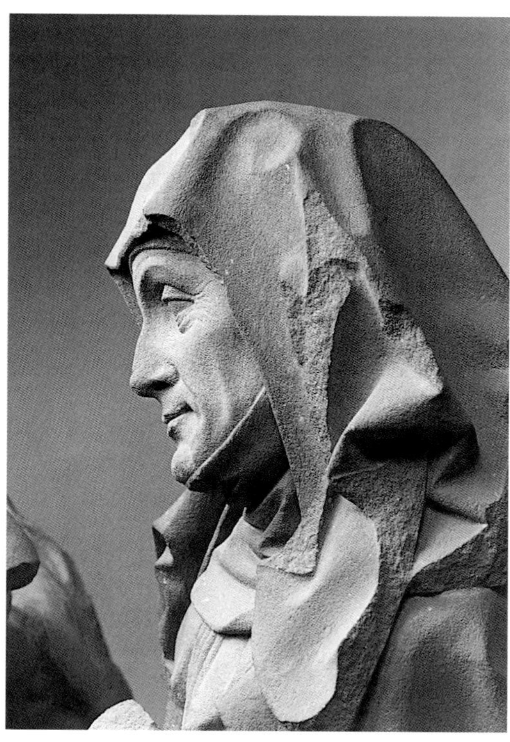

Detail of catalogue no. 8

relinquished an overly smooth appearance in favor of variety in his surfaces. Occasionally, following French custom, he further enhanced garment surfaces by texturing them with a toothed chisel. Instead of being highly polished, the face of the Strasbourg canon and of other figures conveys an impression of porous skin.

Particularly enchanting in the *Anna Selbdritt* is the contrast between young and old, sweetness and severity. The aging yet spiritually transformed visage of Anne seems especially original because of its lively execution; it is considered a facial type specific to Strasbourg sculpture. The sharp, precise cut in the border of the veil and wimple underscores her gaunt, almost bony features, framing the pensive and knowing eyes; at the same time these outlines are contrasted with feminine, soft lines in her face. Hubert Schrade and later Justus Bier correctly concluded that Riemenschneider adopted a vocabulary developed in Strasbourg for the face of his limewood *Saint Anne* of 1505–1506 in Munich (cat. 30).[1] Alfred Schädler pointed to comparable relationships in representations of Saint Peter, which are ultimately based on Gerhaert's circle.[2]

Most likely, the *Anna Selbdritt* was originally located not in Trimbach but in a more prominent location, perhaps even Strasbourg. The cultic context for such an innovative work remains to be determined. It cannot be completely excluded that the group is a copy of a work by Niclaus Gerhaert, but this hypothesis does not lead to any conclusion; in fact, it is contradicted by the uncharacteristic surface treatment. The sculptor of the *Anna Selbdritt* may himself have created the design for the work, inspired by Gerhaert's *Epitaph of a Canon.* The composition was known even to Albrecht Dürer (who stayed in the Upper Rhine in 1490–1494 during his journeyman's travels), as documented by a woodcut of 1511 (Bartsch 96) and a related drawing in the Vienna Albertina. Dürer's print, or even his sketch, may in turn have inspired the sculpture in the shrine of the *Saint Anne* altarpiece, with wings painted by Hans von Kulmbach, in the Lorenzkirche in Nuremberg.[3] Another important wood relief, today in the Vieux Saint-Pierre church in Strasbourg and attributed as a late work of Hans Wydyz, is probably based directly on the Berlin *Anna Selbdritt.* KROHM

1. Schrade 1927, 51–52 n. 419; Bier 1930, 46 n. 5.

2. Schädler 1983, 27–46, esp. 32-33.

3. Compare Ingo Trüper in Krohm and Oellermann 1992, 211–222.

9

FRAGMENT FROM AN ADORATION

1485–1490, limewood, 53.5 x 56.5 x 23 (21 x 22¼ x 9), Germanisches Nationalmuseum, Nuremberg

• Technical Notes •

The two larger figures are deeply hollowed out as separate elements up to the convergence of the king's hands with the child and the Virgin. This massing, while serving compositional purposes, gives strength to the connecting section of wood. It is possible that the group was carved out of the junction of two branches, the lower portions of the two main figures each corresponding to a radiating branch. By this reading, the insert that forms the drapery at the Virgin's lower right must be original. The right section of the Virgin, from the base up to her hand, is a separate piece of wood. The block is split at the base through the brim of the king's hat, and a further split runs through the child's right shoulder. A thinly carved area of drapery above the king's right calf has been broken through; it may originally have had a wood backing next to the one still in place. A similar breaking through is found between the Virgin's knees, an area that appears to have been strengthened by a mastic patch at the back. Nineteenth-century restorations can be discerned in several areas: part of the base in front of the king's knee, a section of the brim and crown of the hat, the edge of the Virgin's drapery just above the base at her lower left side, a portion of the drapery fold between her knees, the tips of the king's left thumb and the Virgin's left thumb, the right hand and the large right toe of the child. Throughout there are minute traces of both a chalk ground and polychromy: on the king, ground layers, red brown in the beard and hair, and vermilion in the mantle; on the Virgin, ground layers in the hair; on the casket, pale red in the tracery.[1]

• Provenance •

Acquired in 1861 from the collection of the Freiherren von Aufsess, founders of the Germanisches Nationalmuseum.

• Literature •

Bode 1885, 166; Tönnies 1900, 224; Kehrer 1904, 74, pl. 8; Haack 1906, 21–32; Grossmann 1909, 27; Kehrer 1909, 228; Wilm 1922, 41, 75; Schrade 1927, n. 225; Bier 1930, 50–53; Flesche and Beyer 1957, 12, pl. 50; Raleigh 1962, 42–43, no. 9; Würzburg 1981, 12, 199–201, no. 34; Ruppert 1992, 102, fig. 63.

THE SEATED VIRGIN, carved in high relief and only slightly flattened at the back, sits with the cross-legged child perched in her lap. She holds the king's offering, a casket with tracery relief, in her left hand and rests the other on the child's right knee. The child rests his left hand on the casket, while reaching toward the king with the other. The kneeling king gently grasps the child's extended right arm with both hands; his mouth partly open, he seems to look beyond the mother and child. The upper portion of the king is carved in the round, and on the ground in front of his right knee lies his hat. The cuff of his mantle has a punched decoration, while the collar is minutely dimpled in imitation of dense fabric or fur.

The composition of this group echoes that of Schongauer's 1482 *Adoration* engraving (fig. 1), both in the general arrangement of the figures and in such details as the placement of the king's hat.[2] The participants in the engraving seem to relate to one another, however, while Riemenschneider's figures appear psychologically distant. With no eye contact among the three, all seem lost in their own thoughts. Yet the complicated merging of hands and arms draws the eye to the center of the composition and gives focus to the physical presence of the child. And the prominence of the Virgin's knees under the heavy folds of her robes provides a strong visual support for the child as well. The unusual motif of the Virgin holding the magus' gift—which Riemenschneider also seems to have quoted from Schongauer—is given an endearing human touch by the child's possessive grasp.

1. See Würzburg 1981, 201.

2. While Riemenschneider used Schongauer's composition as a point of departure, his early collaborator, the painter Martin Schwarz, appropriated the composition wholesale in his *Blessed Virgin* altarpiece of about 1500, from Rothenburg, now in the Germanisches Nationalmuseum, Nuremberg.

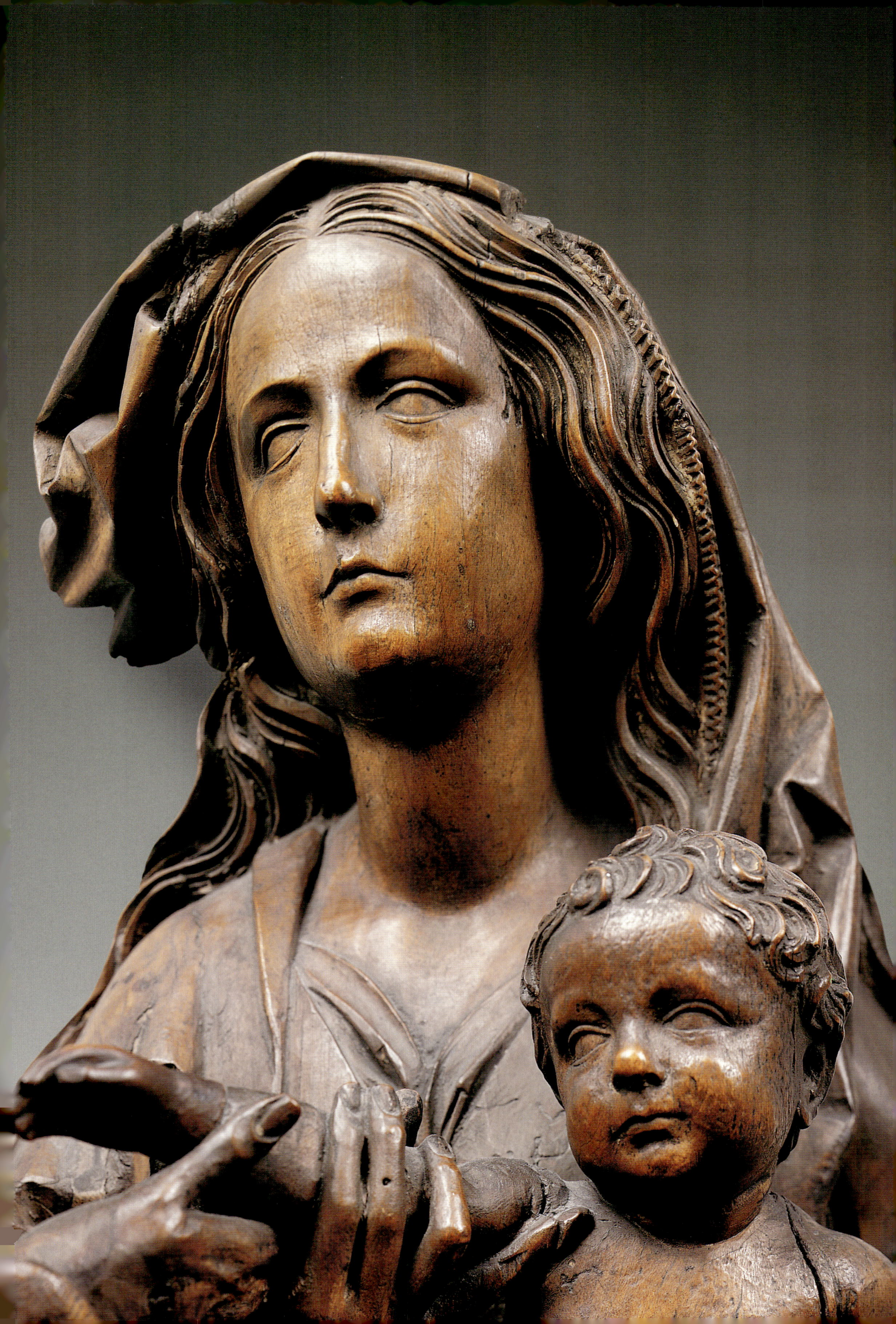

3. Anja Broschek, *Michel Erhart. Ein Beiträge zur schwäbischen Plastik der Spätgotik* (Berlin, 1973), 167–168, fig. 74.

4. Würzburg 1981, 199.

5. Kalden 1990, 109 n. 404. On the basis of this comparison, Kalden dates the Nuremberg group to 1490–1492.

6. Haack 1906, 242.

7. See Jopek 1988, 139–141, nos. 36–37, figs. 31–32.

Krohm has pointed to the similarity between the kneeling king and figures in the Berlin *Martyrdom of Saint Catherine* attributed to a follower of Michel Erhart, particularly in the generosity of form and in the plasticity of the fabric of the mantle prominently conforming to the king's thigh.[3] In the finely carved head of the magus Krohm noted a similarity to the busts in Heinrich Iselin's Weingarten choir stalls.[4] An even more compelling comparison with Erhart and his workshop is found in the head of Saint Onuphrius, now in the Kunstmuseum, Düsseldorf (fig. 2), which can be dated about 1480: the open mouth, the tilt of the head, the rich detailing of the beard and hair, and the very mien are remarkably close.

The face of the Virgin, on the other hand, is extremely close to that of the Hassfurt Virgin in its elongated structure and particularly in details such as the slanted, almond-shaped eyes with slightly swollen lower lids, the pursed mouth, and the dimpled chin. These distinguishing details, which hark back to the Ravensburg *Virgin of Mercy* of about 1480 by a follower of Erhart (cat. 1, fig. 2), anticipate the *Mary Magdalen* and *Saint Elizabeth* from the Münnerstadt altarpiece (cat. 13, figs. 1 and 2). The head type, drapery system, and general composition of the Nuremberg Virgin is virtually the same as that of the Mary Magdalen in the Münnerstadt *Noli me Tangere* relief (cat. 13 F),[5] which itself is dependent on Schongauer, suggesting that the present work was produced at a point of transition, when Riemenschneider had developed a new compositional formula for the Virgin and child but was stylistically still under the influence of Michel Erhart. By the time he used this composition again in the Münnerstadt altarpiece, Riemenschneider had achieved expressive independence.

In light of this, Krohm's arguments for ascribing an early date to the Nuremberg fragment—perhaps shortly after 1485, but certainly before the 1490–1492 altarpiece in Münnerstadt—become even more convincing. Underscoring the hazards of applying a linear framework to Riemenschneider's oeuvre, one can only remark that in comparison to the relatively static *Adoration* in the predella of the Creglingen altarpiece—a major work of Riemenschneider's mature period (Chapuis essay, fig. 7)—the emotionally charged Nuremberg *Adoration* is sculpturally more satisfying. This observation, in part, prompted Haack early in this century to pronounce its superiority.[6]

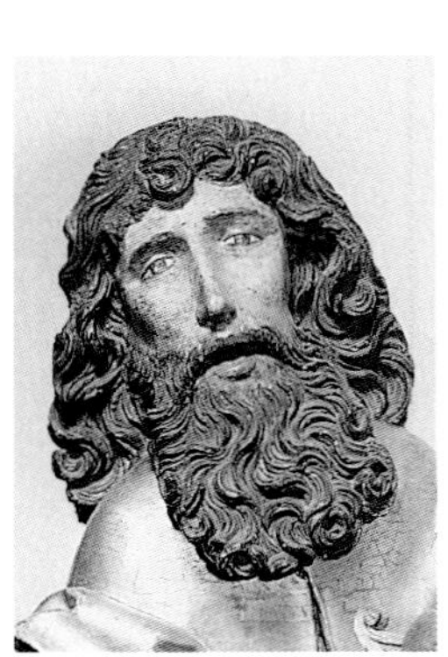

2.

Workshop or close follower of Michel Erhart, *Saint Onuphrius,* c. 1480, wood with ancient polychromy, Kunstmuseum, Düsseldorf

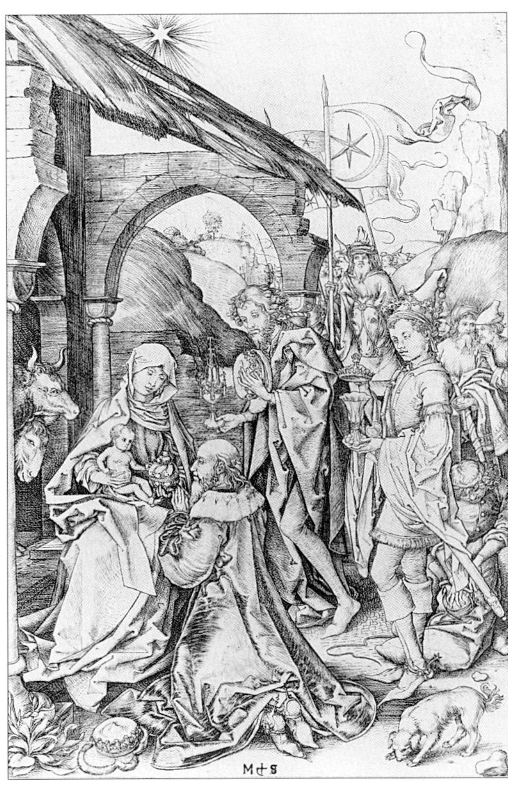

I.

Martin Schongauer, *Adoration of the Magi,* 1482, engraving, National Gallery of Art, Washington, Rosenwald Collection

While it is generally thought that these figures came from a predella, it is not possible to reconstruct the original appearance of the complete group. If Riemenschneider followed the formula common to central German alabaster relief carving of the 1470s,[7] the scene would have been organized horizontally, with the present figures flanked on either side by their narrative complements. If, on the other hand, the predella had multiple scenes, as does the predella in the Crelingen altarpiece, the composition, following Schongauer's model, would have been organized in a vertical format, with the other figures placed in receding planes. In either case, the deep undercutting and the partial carving in the round relieve the planar organization imposed by the limited depth of the shrine. The foreshortening of the king and the massing of drapery around the opened knees of the Virgin benefit from a low vantage, as one would have had before a high altarpiece. HUSBAND

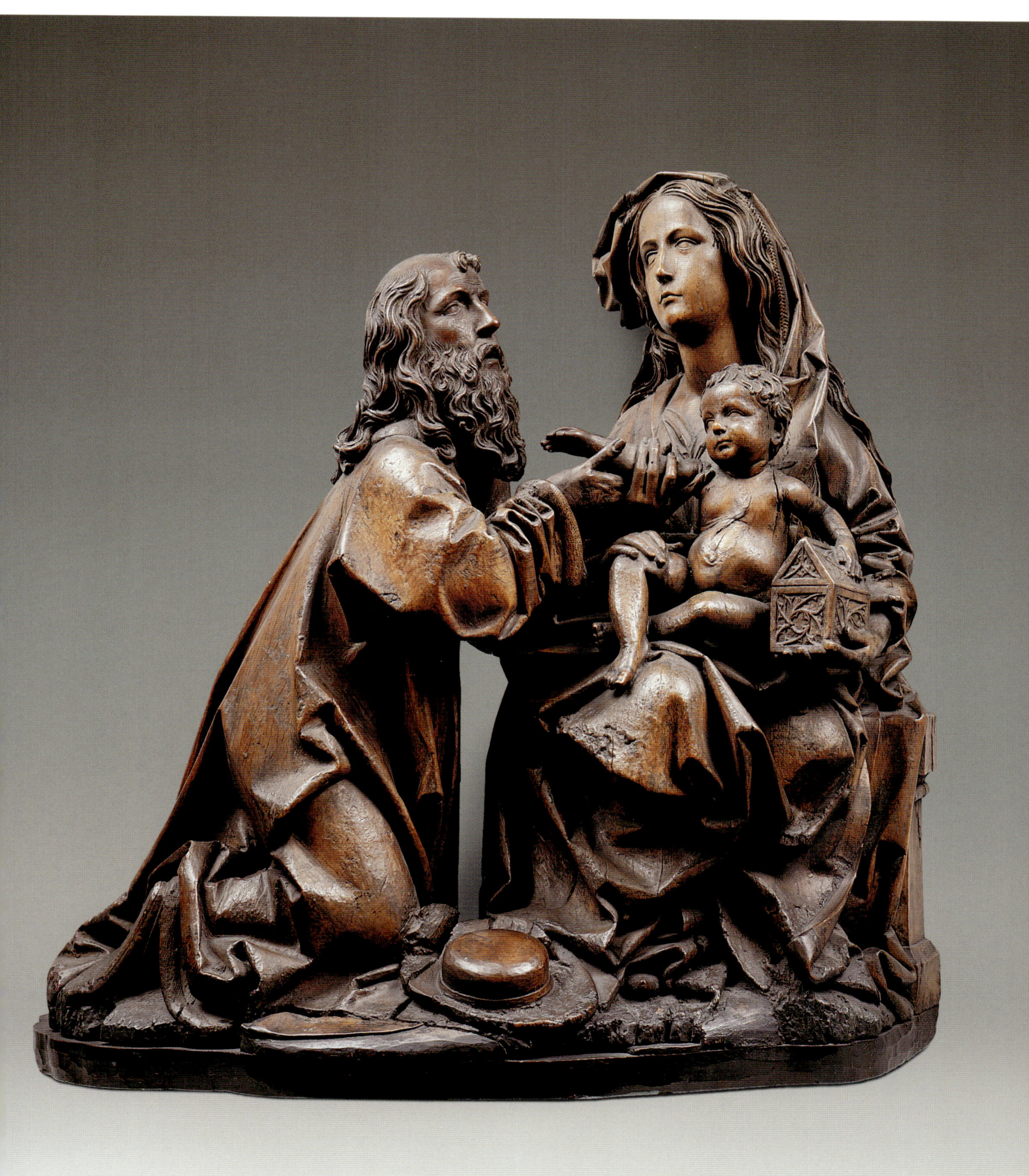

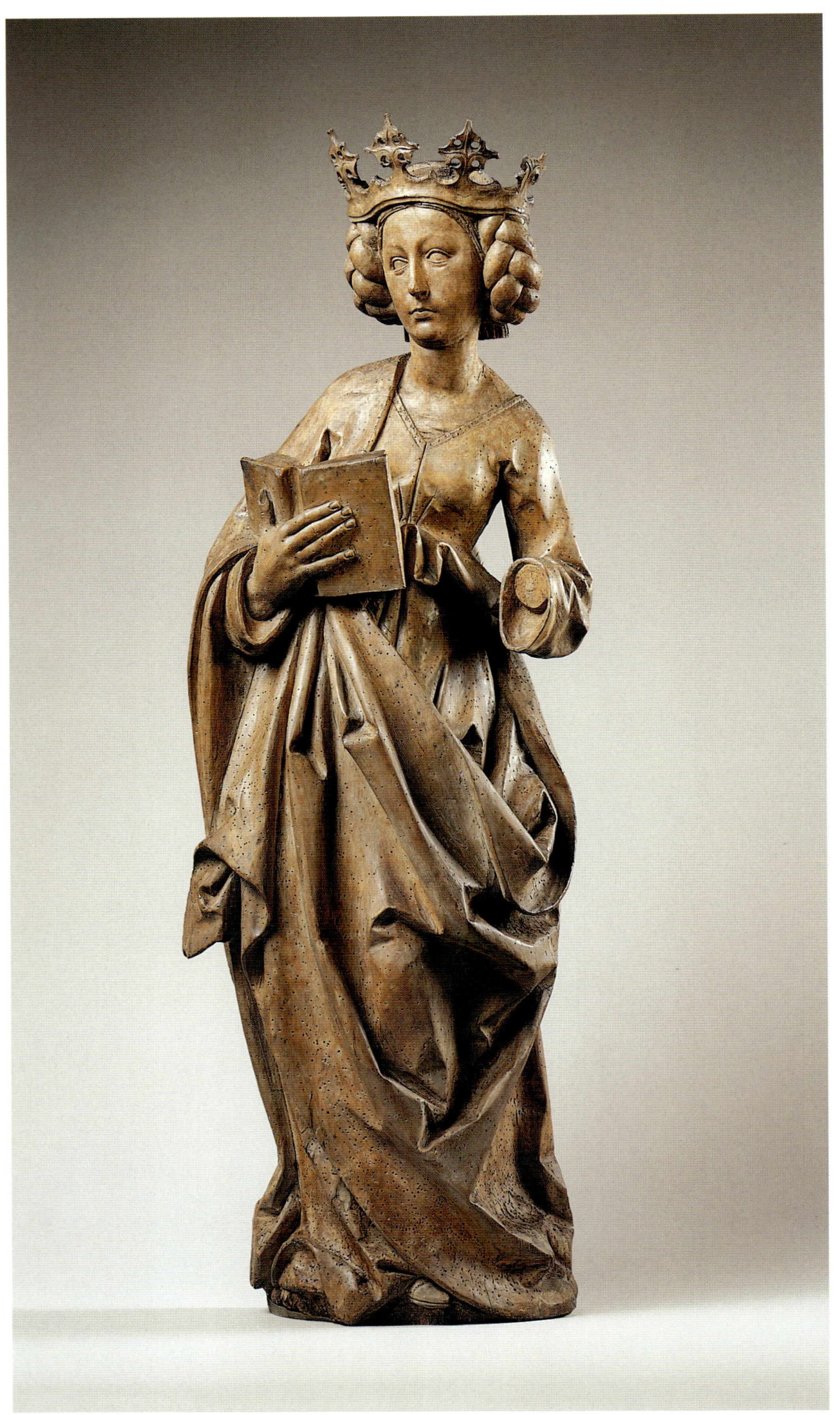

photographed during conservation

FEMALE SAINT

c. 1490, limewood, 96.5 x 31.7 x 18.4 (38 x 12 ½ x 7 ¼), North Carolina Museum of Art, Raleigh,
Purchased with funds from the North Carolina Art Society (Robert F. Phifer Bequest)
and the State of North Carolina

• *Technical Notes* •

The sculpture is carved in high relief from a single
block of limewood with the grain running vertically.
A small portion of the flattened back was hollowed
out, corresponding to the core of the tree trunk. A
substantial hole of uncertain age in the back presumably served to attach the figure to a background.
The five finials of the crown were carved separately
and inserted into the wood of the head. The work
has suffered seriously from insect damage, with holes
scattered over the entire surface but concentrated in
the head, neck, and along the figure's right side. It
was restored between 1904 and 1918, when most of
the insect holes were filled with a putty that discolored
over time, giving the surface a spotty appearance, and
a modern left hand grasping a chalice was replaced
by a hand holding a sword. The tip of the slipper is
also modern. In a conservation treatment carried out
in 1998–1999, Jack Soultanian cleaned the sculpture,
removing fills that covered large areas of the wood
beyond the holes and filling holes anew, especially in
the face, neck, and shoulders; he also toned certain
areas. In consultation with the staff of the North Carolina Museum of Art, it was decided that the modern left hand and sword should be removed. The sculpture was clearly intended to be polychrome, and it
bears remnants of paint of different natures and possibly different ages. These layers must have been removed before 1904, since a photograph published
that year shows the work without polychromy. The
surface bears the marks of a scraping tool.

• *Provenance* •

Wilhelm Gumprecht collection, Berlin, by the late
1890s and auctioned in 1918; acquired at that time or
shortly thereafter by Dr. Franz Haniel, Munich;
acquired from his estate by the museum in 1968.

• *Literature* •

Berlin 1904, 31; Bier 1978, 152; Bier 1980, 14–32; Bier
1982, 55–58.

THE BOOK AND THE CROWN, which dis-
tinguish this figure as an erudite princess, are the
attributes of both Saint Catherine and Saint Barbara.
The missing left hand originally held an attribute that
would have allowed definitive identification: a miniature tower or a chalice for Barbara, a sword or a spiked
wheel for Catherine. When the work was first published, in 1904, it was reproduced with a chalice in
the left hand—a modern restoration—and the saint
was identified as Barbara.[1] An auction catalogue of
1918 shows the figure, then called Catherine, holding
a sword in her left hand.[2] The thick, braided hair is
not specific to either saint and appears on Riemenschneider's depictions of other personages.[3]

In the present rendering the saint has interrupted
her reading and stares into the distance in front of
her. Her oval face, with a barely perceptible double
chin, is set on a curved, slightly swollen neck. The
figure is articulated along a generous curve that is
offset by her gently tilted head. Her right leg carries
the weight of her body, and her left knee pushes
against the front of her garment; the tip of her left
foot is visible at the juncture of her cloak and her
dress. Her dress has a V-shaped neckline, a tight-fitting
bodice, and loose sleeves. The fabric of this garment
is gathered at the belt in a series of short, radiating
folds. This motif is also found on one of the female
saints from Frankfurt, while the hair is combed in
straight vertical strands at the back of the head, as it
is on the other Frankfurt figure (cat. 32 C–D).

The cloak is essential in giving the work its
notable spatial presence. Covering the saint's right
shoulder, the mantle reappears at the left hip, engulfing
the front of the figure in a generous swath of drapery,

1. Berlin 1904, pl. 31.

2. Gumprecht auction catalogue
(Berlin, 1918), pl. 9/86.

3. See *Saint Dorothy*, c. 1500–
1505, limewood, formerly in the
Marienkapelle in Würzburg,
destroyed in World War II (Bier
1982, pl. 27); and Kunigunde
on the imperial tomb in Bamberg Cathedral (Chapuis essay,
fig. 4). The same hairstyle
appears on a female saint sold on
13 December 1984 at Sotheby's,
London, lot 76.

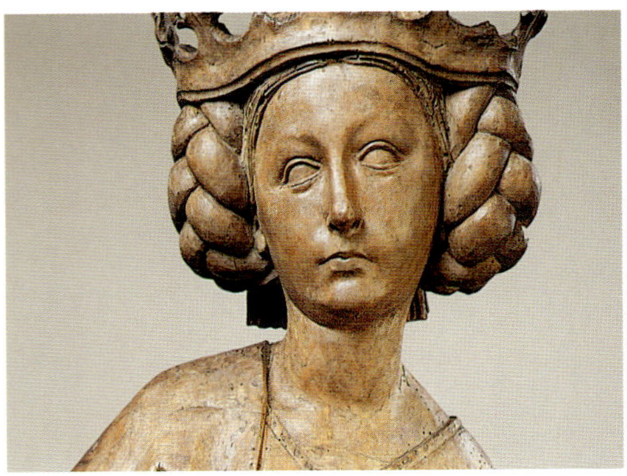 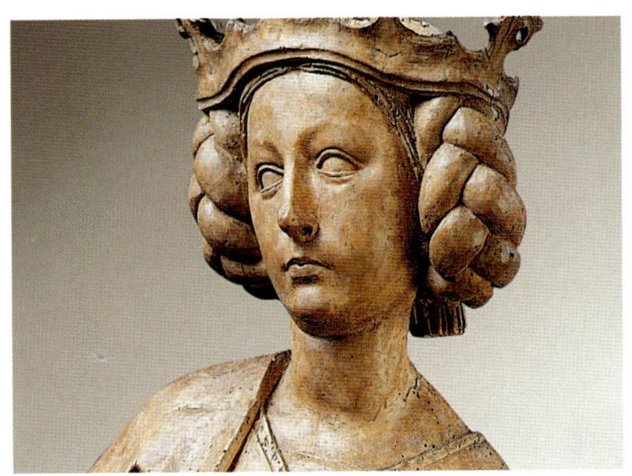

Details of catalogue no. 10 illustrating how the left eye is higher than the right (photographed during conservation)

4. See Bier 1982, 57. But the Raleigh figure only has the braided hair in common with Kunigunde, while the resemblance with the Creglingen Virgin is peripheral at best.

and is held against the body by the right wrist. This treatment is extremely close to that of the alabaster *Saint Barbara* (cat. 4): in both cases the mass of drapery surrounds the body in an oblique upward movement and converges in long tubular folds toward the right breast. The uncovered waist and left hip reveal how slender each figure actually is. The cloak gives a strong sense of volume to the attenuated body and functions like a shell around a core. Another early work, the Hassfurt *John the Baptist* (Chapuis essay, fig. 1), displays a similar motif of oblique, enveloping drapery.

This almost kinetic approach is characteristic of Niclaus Gerhaert, and it suggests the degree to which Riemenschneider's work, especially in his early career, was indebted to the older sculptor. A comparison with the Cloisters *Virgin and Child* ascribed to Gerhaert (cat. 6) reveals similarities. Like Riemenschneider's figures, the Cloisters figure—even more slender than they—is surrounded by the broad folds of a mantle that converge toward a point on her waist, an eloquent example of the "core and shell" treatment that gives spatial prominence to an otherwise frail body. The sculptor invites the viewer to follow the drapery folds, either mentally or literally, and to walk around the sculpture. This could not be done with the present *Female Saint* or with Riemenschneider's *Saint Barbara* or *Saint John the Baptist,* which were left flat at the back, but one imagines that the cloaks fall obliquely from the shoulder to the hip on the other side, and one reads the figures as continuous bodies in space. Like Gerhaert, Riemenschneider allowed drapery folds to fall over the edge of the base and to enter the space of the viewer.

Although dated to about 1505–1510 because of a perceived resemblance to images of Empress Kunigunde on the imperial tomb in Bamberg, dating to 1499–1513, and to the Virgin of the Creglingen altarpiece (Chapuis essay, figs. 4 and 5),[4] this female saint appears instead to have been sculpted in about 1490. The strong volumetric treatment of forms is characteristic of Riemenschneider's work at the time of the Münnerstadt altarpiece, as exemplified by its *Saint Elizabeth* (cat. 13, fig. 2). The dynamic effect of the drapery has its closest parallels in the *Saint Barbara* of about 1485–1490 and the Hassfurt *Saint John* of about 1490.

The Raleigh sculpture was clearly meant to be polychrome. While grand in conception, the piece does not exhibit the subtle treatment of surface that one expects from a work intended to remain uncolored, such as the Cloisters *Seated Bishop* (cat. 17). The treatment of individual folds is at times weak, suggesting that the sculptor expected to refine the final form in the chalk ground that would have been applied. He left disfiguring knife marks around the fingers on the book cover, a disturbing detail even from a distance, which polychromy would have concealed. Nowhere did the sculptor use punches to embellish the surface.

The composition of the work offers clues to its possible original installation. It is unlikely to have been made for a carved retable, for it is one of Riemenschneider's most volumetric creations and can be viewed from an arc of about 180 degrees; it is fully coherent when seen in full profile from either side. Much of this perspective would have been lost had the sculpture been installed in the shrine of an altarpiece, where its sides would be hidden. Rather, the Raleigh saint probably stood alone on a polygonal bracket under a baldachin on the wall of a chapel. The sculptural conception suggests that it was intended to be approached from the right—indeed, the drapery invites the viewer to walk from right to left, and the saint's left eye is higher than the right one, an optical correction that gives a stronger focus to the saint's gaze when seen from the right. CHAPUIS

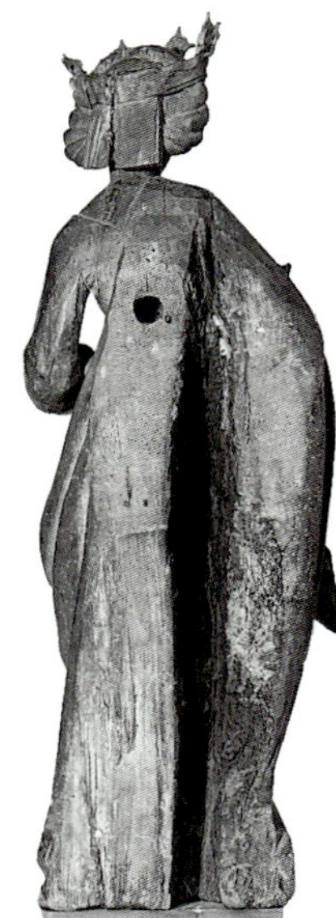

Back view of catalogue no. 10

II

1490–1495, alabaster; 37.8 x 28.1 x 15.9 (14 ⅞ x 11 x 6 ¼), The Cleveland Museum of Art, Purchase from the J. H. Wade Fund

• Technical Notes •

The back of the saint's head is flattened at an angle and drilled for a dowel, though the hole does not appear to have been used to attach the figure to a shrine. Different types of tooling texture the ground, the fur lining of the cowl, and the lion's fur. Two layers of gilding are discernible: a reddish orange layer, and a later one on a yellow ground. There are traces of gilding on the saint's left sleeve where it emerges from the mantle and on the hem of the mantle at the back of the figure. Traces of vermilion are found on the hat. A line of black appears under the left edge of the upper left eyelid, with further traces under the upper right eyelid. Traces of flesh color are seen in the saint's right ear and of gold in the lion's mane. The claws were black, while the paw appears to have been gilded. Extensive areas of the original green (azurite and yellow ocher) remain on the ground.[1] The drill holes in the hat are free of stains or wear marks, which would seem to preclude metalwork tassels.

Faults in the alabaster include one on the head that runs from below the saint's left eye across the bridge of his nose and the forehead to the lock of hair, then over the head through a fold in the cowl. Another is in the end of the drapery behind the lion, while another forms an ellipse on the lion's back. All have large black mineral occlusions. The underside of the sculpture is crosshatched for setting into a housing; there are no dowel holes. The notch in the base at the back may be for positioning the group, as it falls on the axis of the figure and is cut on a fault line or crack. Repaired sections of the sculpture include the right side of the cowl and the wrist and several fingers of the right hand.

• Provenance •

Traditionally said to have come from the Benedictine abbey church of Saint Peter at Erfurt; in the possession of cathedral provost Würschmidt in Erfurt by 1856 (see Förster 1856, 24) and a cleric (Würschmidt?) who had lived in Würzburg until he was pensioned and moved, by 1860, to Dieburg near Darmstadt (see Grossman 1909, 29–30, fig. 9); [Frankfurt art dealer(s) in 1896]; Madame C. Lelong in Paris until 1902; [sale catalogue, Georges Petit, Paris, 1902, no. 147]; [Boibove, Paris]; Edouard Aynard, Lyon; [sale catalogue, Georges Petit, Paris, 1913, no. 278]; Harry Fuld, Frankfurt, until after 1931; before 1937, to Fuld's sister, Mrs. Clementine Cramer, Northwood, England, until 1946, when it was acquired by the museum through Rosenberg and Stiebel, New York.

• Literature •

Förster 1856, 24; Grossmann 1909, 29–30; Swarzenski 1918, 85; Schmitt and Swarzenski 1921, 143; Swarzenski 1921, 169, 189, 191, fig. 20; Schrade 1927, n. 278; Hannover 1931, no. 10a; Bier 1931, 451–454; Habicht 1931b, 5–6; Bier 1934, 334; Schmitt 1937, 310, 322; Habicht 1937, 7, pl. 2, fig. 8; Bier 1937, 27, no. 54, pl. 54; Ring 1945, 192–193, fig. 5; Milliken 1946, 175–177; Davis 1949, 153; Bier 1956, 99–100, fig. 19; Raleigh 1962, 26–29, no. 3; Gerstenberg 1962, 206–207, 211–240 nn. 63–64; Müller 1966, 224–225 n. 75; Bier 1978, 156; Würzburg 1981, 10, 263–266, no. 57; Hubala 1982, 226–231; Krohm 1982, 96–97, fig. 6; Sello 1983, 15–16, pl. 52; Jopek 1988, 90–93, 154–156, no. 47, figs. 45–46; Kalden 1990, 107–108 n. 398; Krohm and Oellermann 1992, 102 nn. 17 and 18; Ruppert 1992, 89, 93–95, 101–102, 105, fig. 56.

DRESSED IN CARDINAL'S robes with a cowl draped over his head, Saint Jerome sits on a banquette, his hat in his lap. He tilts his head, looking down with a gentle but intent expression at the lion seated at his feet. Gazing away from its benefactor, the lion extends its left foreleg, which the saint grasps in

1. The pigments were identified by Michele Marincola using polarized light microscopy.

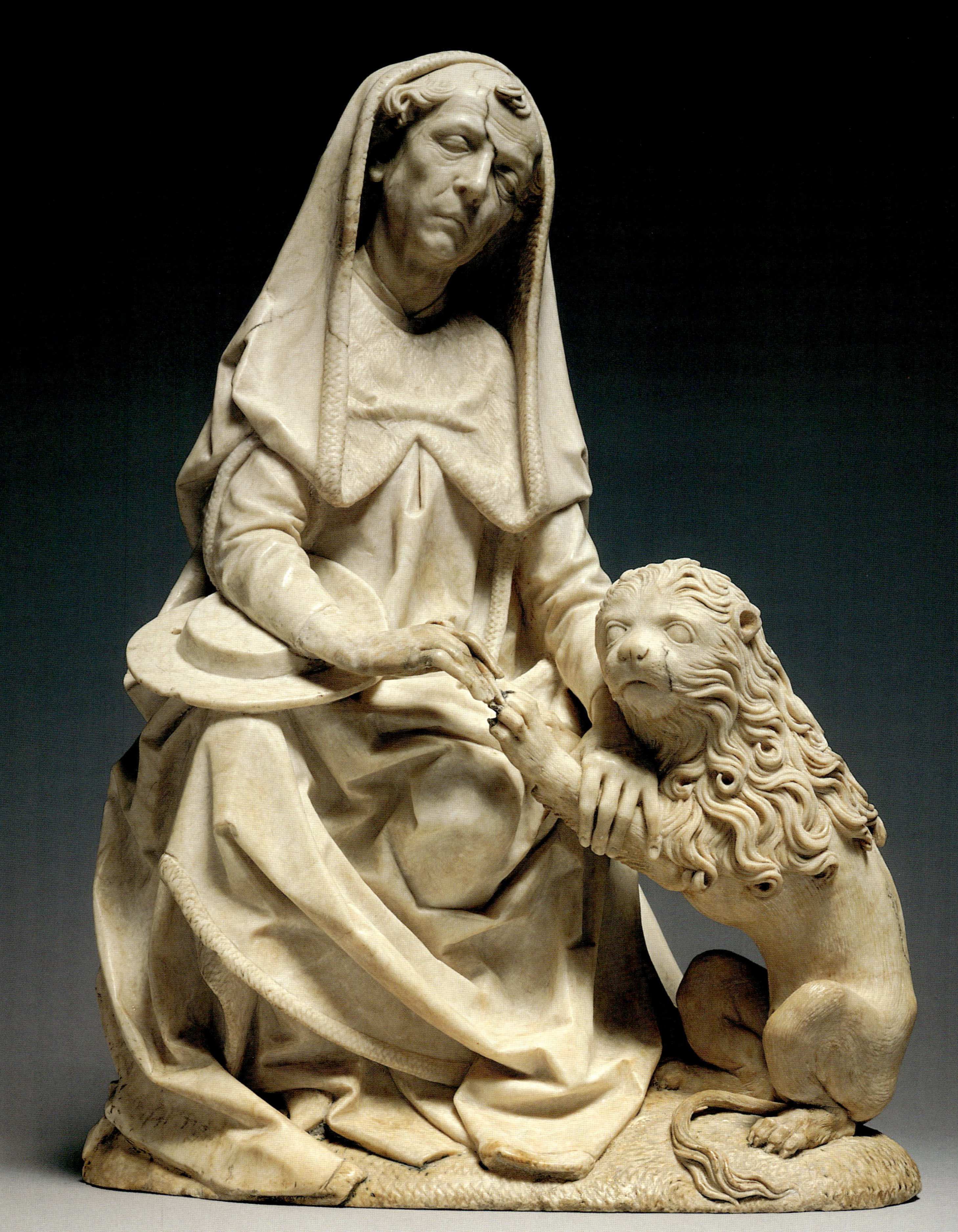

order to extract the thorn from the paw. The cowl descends in large, planar folds to the saint's shoulders, then falls past his waist in the back. Drapery conforms to the saint's projecting knees, which jut slightly to his right, then descends to the ground in arcing, tubular folds separated by deep recesses, ending in flat, reverse folds. At the back the robe meets one corner of the bench in an angular fold, then falls in broad planes to the ground, which is textured with short, parallel cuts. The lion, with its tail between its legs, has a richly textured mane and napped fur.

Perhaps the most accomplished of Riemenschneider's extant alabasters, the *Saint Jerome* presents subtly modeled and expressive features, a balanced composition, and an affecting relationship between the saint and his docile charge. Ring has pointed out the similarity between this group and a panel painting by a follower of Rogier van der Weyden (fig. 1).[2] The two depictions are so close that one assumes they both rely on a common source.[3]

Bier long maintained that the Cleveland sculpture was a mature, not an early work. Comparing Saint Jerome with the Saint Benedict in the relief "Delivering the Emperor of a Stone" on the Bamberg tomb of Heinrich and Kunigunde (fig. 2) and to the apostles of the Creglingen altarpiece, he argued for a date between 1505 and 1510.[4] Krohm viewed this relationship as merely a correspondence of motifs[5] and, observing the resemblance to the apostle Philip in the Creglingen altarpiece (Chapuis essay, fig. 7), suggested that the head type was already conventionalized by 1500 or soon after.[6] Noting the stylistic parallels with the Münnerstadt evangelists (cat. 13 A–D), Krohm followed Gerstenberg in finding a date around 1495 more acceptable. Jopek, pointing to the monument to Rudolf von Scherenberg (Kemperdick essay, fig. 1), argued for a slightly later date, between 1495 and 1500.[7] And Ruppert followed Krohm in assigning a date in the middle of the last decade.[8]

The contrapposto stance and canted head of the seated saint, the voluminous drapery passages, and the ambiguity of Jerome's underlying form are all characteristic of Ulm sculpture, particularly that of Michel Erhart and his immediate followers. The Berlin *Virgin and Child* attributed to Erhart (cat. 12) is remarkably close in sculptural conception. The heavy drapery in both, worked into constructions more plastic than any fabric could assume, was designed to bring volumetric definition to the sculpture. The handling is masterful in Jerome: his right knee is draped with a large fold that breaks into two arcing folds that echo the position of the arm, while the drapery clings to his left knee, creating a counterpoint between pro-

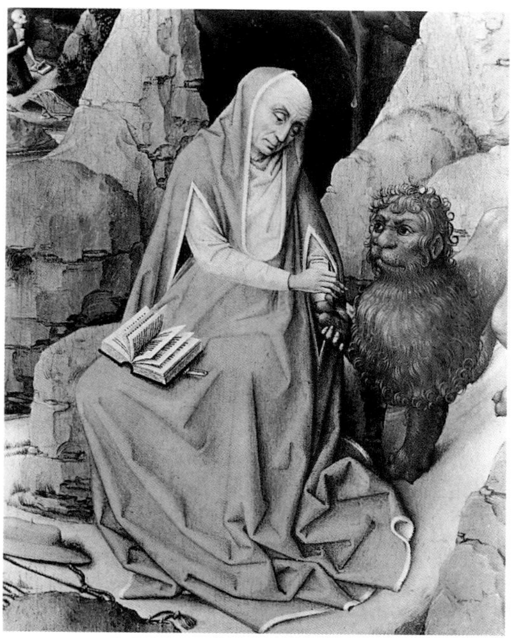

1.

Follower of Rogier van der Weyden,
Saint Jerome and the Lion, c. 1440–1450, oil on panel,
Detroit Institute of Arts

jecting and receding areas, between mass and void, between highlight and shadow. The handling of the drapery is also characteristic of Upper Rhenish and Swabian sculpture in the 1470s, and the conceptual proximity of *Saint Jerome* alone suggests an earlier rather than later dating. The same can be said of the Rogerian model.

Within Riemenschneider's oeuvre *Saint Jerome* is probably most closely related to the Münnerstadt evangelists Mark and Luke (cat. 13 B–C): these seated figures both exhibit a gentle contrapposto. Luke's head is set at an identical angle, and his right hand is similarly positioned. Mark's facial type is very like Jerome's, particularly in its soft fleshiness and its crescent-shaped eyes with heavy lids and double creases in the lower lids. The head of Mark's lion is close to its counterpart in the *Saint Jerome,* but also to that in the 1487 tomb of Eberhard von Grumbach in Rimpar (cat. 18, fig. 1) and that in the 1496–1499 monument to Rudolf von Scherenberg, suggesting that the type was conventionalized quite early and repeated for a decade or more.

The numerous occluded faults, the most prominent of which runs through Jerome's face, along with the extensive remnants of polychromy would seem to provide incontrovertible evidence that Riemenschneider intended the sculpture to be painted over most of its surface. Only the bench, Jerome's hair,

2. Ring 1945, 190.

3. Ring 1945, 190–191, cites two other panel paintings, both by followers of Hans Memling, that depict the scene in essentially the same formula: the left wing of the Sforza triptych, Musée d'art ancien, Brussels; and another, then in an English private collection.

4. Notably in his 1951 study of the alabasters, in the 1962 Raleigh exhibition catalogue, and in his 1982 monograph.

5. While Krohm's point is well taken, the Bamberg comparison is compelling. The facial type, which is found already in the *Saint Mark* from the Münnerstadt predella, is combined with a conventionalized treatment of a balding head, found also in the figures of Saint Peter in both the *Holy Blood* and the Creglingen altarpieces, and supports his reading of the similarity as a coincidence of motifs.

6. Würzburg 1981, 265.

7. Jopek 1988, 93, 154.

8. Ruppert 1992, 93.

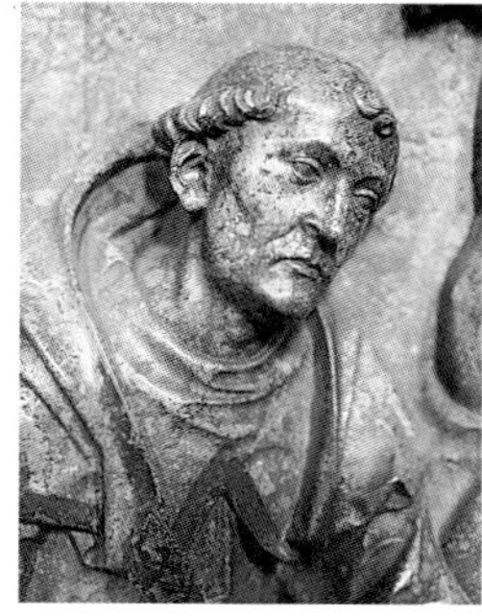

2.

Detail from the
"Delivering the Emperor
of a Stone" relief on
the tomb of Heinrich II
and Kunigunde,
1499–1513, Solnhofen
stone, Bamberg Cathedral

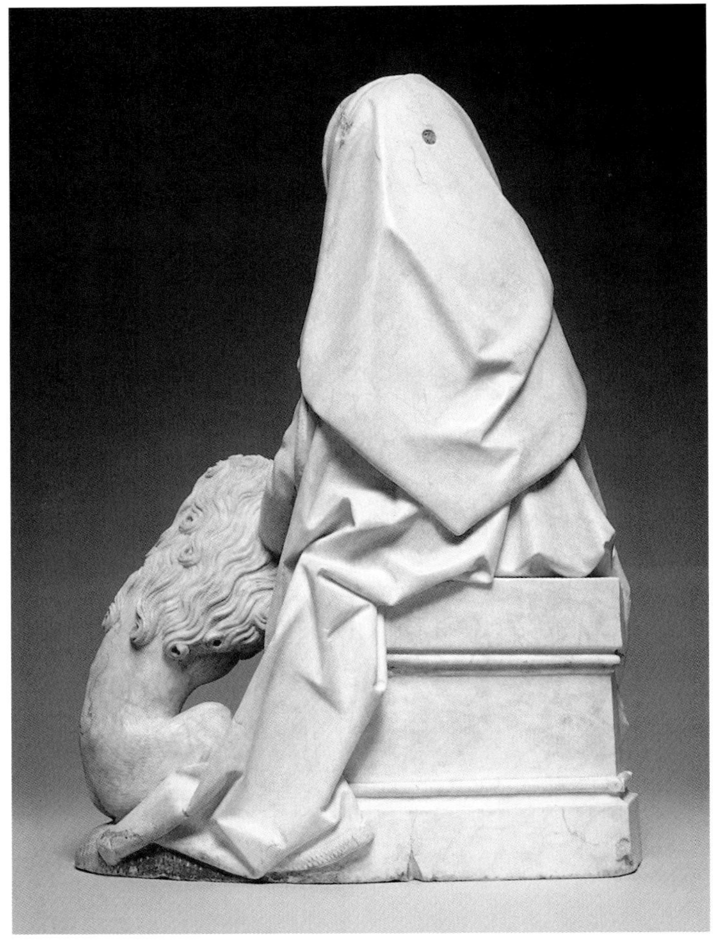

Back view of catalogue no. 11

and the lining of his mantle remained unpainted. And drill holes on the brim of the hat presumably allowed for the attachment of a red silk cord, no doubt with a cardinal's tassel. The overall effect was thus radically different than that presented by the now bare, polished surfaces. Evidently alabaster was valued more for its tractability than for its inherent aesthetic appeal. One wonders whether this was always the case, or whether, like limewood, there was a conflicted aesthetic regarding polychromed or monochromed surfaces.

Although the original context of the Cleveland *Saint Jerome* is unknown, Jopek has speculated that it may have been commissioned by someone connected with the University of Erfurt to adorn a study: this church father, who symbolized exacting theological scholarship, was viewed as the patron of the early humanists; furthermore, the sculpture is said to have come from Erfurt; and the work has an Erfurt provenance. Sculpturally, the group was conceived to be viewed from below eye level; only then do the foreshortening and the working of the saint's face become fully coherent and other details, such as the undercutting of the lion's tail, become visible. The back of the figure, while relatively planar, is fully, if economically, finished, but the sculpture was primarily intended to be viewed frontally, in a wide arc of about 70 degrees either side of center. The work would be well situated in a wall niche or on a bracket, on an open shelf, or atop a cupboard. From this point of view, the *Saint Jerome* and the Vienna *Adam* (cat. 20) may well be exceptional among Riemenschneider's surviving oeuvre: rather than objects of veneration, these figures seem to have been viewed as autonomous works of art to be contemplated and appreciated in a purely secular setting. HUSBAND

Attributed to Michel Erhart / SEATED VIRGIN AND CHILD

c. 1480, limewood, 39 x 36 x 19.5 (15⅜ x 14⅛ x 7⅝), Staatliche Museen zu Berlin, Skulpturensammlung

• *Technical Notes* •

The figure is hollowed out inside, and the opening is closed by an attached carved panel. The Virgin's right forearm and hand holding the nursing flask are thought to be additions, as are the right arm and left forearm of the child. The lower edge of the boulder base in the back has been reworked. No remnant of paint or chalk ground can be discerned with the naked eye, although one can assume that the sculpture was originally polychrome.

• *Provenance* •

Acquired in Munich by the museum in 1882.

• *Literature* •

Tönnies 1900, 234; Demmler 1925, 175; Otto 1927, 110–111; Wertheimer 1929, 91, 97 n. 14; Demmler 1930, 142; Hessig 1935, 102; Otto 1943, 67; Meier 1957, 291; Berlin 1958, 40–41; Deutsch 1969, 97–100d; Meurer 1993, 68–69, 77 nn. 28–29; Krohm in Kahsnitz and Volk 1998, 126–127.

THE VIRGIN IS seated on cushions placed on a rough masonry banquette, which is visible almost exclusively from the sides and back. She quiets the tiny Christ child in the broad expanse of her lap, nursing him from a flask. This uncommon motif, sometimes said to be a latter addition, could actually be original, given the unusually detailed character of the sculpture. Seen from the back, the flow of Mary's hair has a painterly quality akin to that of the applewood Virgin by a follower of Niclaus Gerhaert (cat. 7), while attesting to the influence of Gerhaert himself, seen, for instance, in the "Small Dangolsheim Saint" (see cat. 5). The accentuated tilt of the Virgin's head, which expresses her tender devotion to the child, is reminiscent of engravings by Master E. S. (see Lehrs 66), although in its meditative mood the sculpture

transcends this or any other printed source. The *Seated Virgin,* conceived to be seen from a number of vantage points, thus testifies to the use of formal precedents and to reflection on the nature of sculpture during an era that has been mistakenly thought to pay little attention to theoretical questions.

Earnest and reflective, the Virgin's countenance is especially captivating. An elegiac mood is expressed by the tilt of her head and her lowered gaze. Caring for her helpless child, she is bound in introspective anticipation. Resonances of the Passion are implicit in the theme of the Incarnation, and Mary's throne of stones could be understood as a reference to Golgotha. Certainly intended as an image for private devotion, the figure is highly unconventional, and it invites close and long scrutiny.

This figure of the Virgin is characteristic of work in Ulm, the second most important sculptural center in southern Germany after Strasbourg. It emphasizes

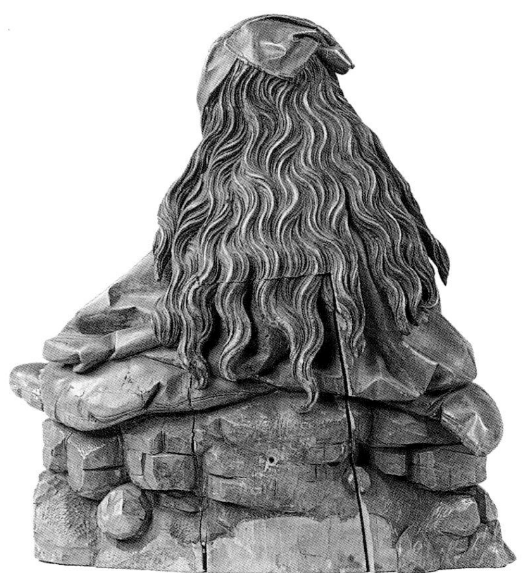

Back view of catalogue no. 12

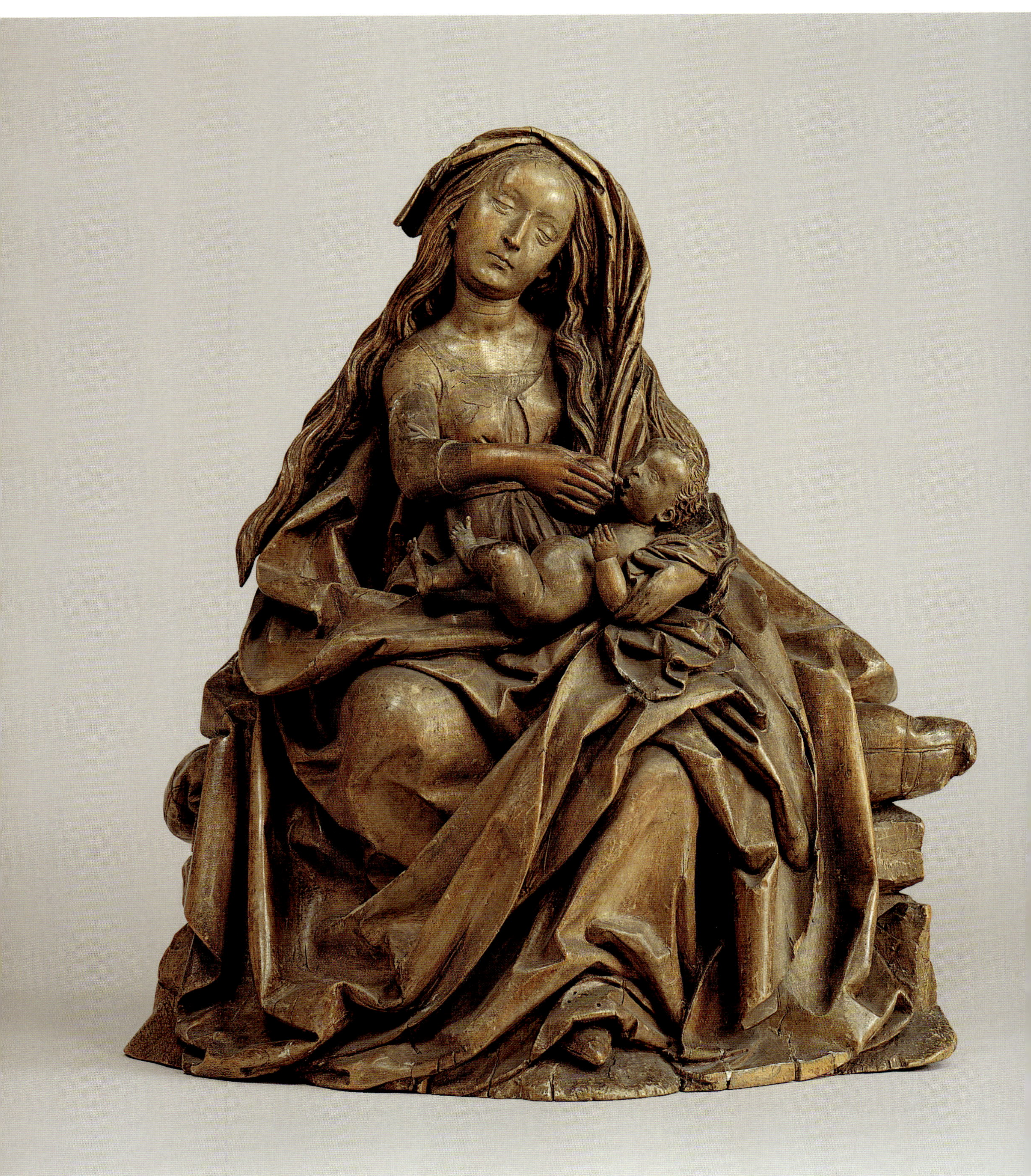

the contrast between the human figure and the wide, encompassing drapery. The facial type shows an unmistakable relationship with the female figure of the Vienna *Vanitas* group (Krohm essay, fig. 10), an allegory on the transitory nature of life. This work, until now attributed to Gregor Erhart, is more likely by the hand of his father, Michel, and should be dated around 1480.[1] The conception of the figure reveals the influence of early Netherlandish painting and the engravings of Master E.S. from the 1460s.

The Virgin from the Blaubeuren altarpiece, 1493/1494, is also a useful comparison (fig. 1). Despite differences in facial type and in scale, the multilayered, spatially rich drapery of this figure is reminiscent of the *Seated Virgin and Child.* The Blaubeuren Virgin is very different from the *Virgin of Mercy* in Berlin, which, dated around 1480 (cat. 1, fig. 2), has played a key role in the interpretation of Michel Erhart's oeuvre. The *Virgin of Mercy* exhibits a drastically simplified drapery treatment, which, surprisingly, most scholars have praised for its simple harmony of forms, naïveté, and original polychromy; it is seen as the ideal Gothic sculpture. Charm notwithstanding, she is less deserving of attribution to Michel Erhart than is the *Seated Virgin.*

The creator of the *Virgin of Mercy* from Ravensburg may have worked on the figural decoration of the choir stalls of Ulm Minster (fig. 2), at that time the most extensive sculptural program in south Germany. New research indicates Michel Erhart's marked participation in this project. The sculptor of the Ravensburg figure appears to have absorbed the formal advances of the Ulm choir stalls and to have taken them a step further in the creation of an engaging work of art. Examined independently of Erhart's oeuvre, however, the *Virgin of Mercy* suggests anew that there might be truth in an old tradition: an inscription originally belonging to the sculpture stated that it was carved by Friedrich Schramm of Ravensburg and polychromed by Christoph Keltenhofer.[2] Also from Ravensburg, and possibly from the same retable as the *Virgin of Mercy*, are reliefs of the *Mass of Saint Gregory* and the *Martyrdom of Saint Catherine,* both in Berlin, as well as one of the hermit Onuphrius, now in Düsseldorf (cat. 9, fig. 2).[3]

An attribution of the Berlin *Seated Virgin* to Michel Erhart, the most important sculptor in Ulm of the generation after Hans Multscher, could well lead to a fundamental redefinition of his oeuvre. Along with the Vienna *Vanitas,* two busts in the Victoria and Albert Museum, one of a young man and one of a woman (originally full figures), have been attributed to Gregor Erhart,[4] yet the young man bears

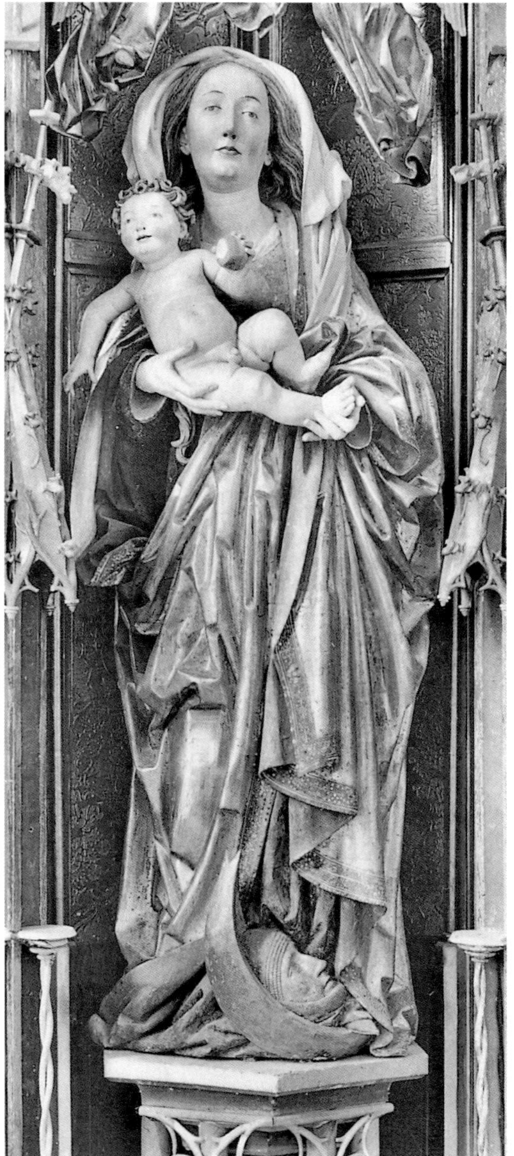

1.
Michel Erhart, detail from the
Blaubeuren altarpiece, 1493/1494, wood with original
polychromy, Klosterkirche, Blaubeuren

a resemblance to figures in the Blaubeuren altarpiece. The female figure in the *Vanitas* along with the youth in this group call to mind Riemenschneider's *Adam* and *Eve* from the Würzburg Marienkapelle (Chapuis essay, fig. 3) but can hardly be compared with the Mary Magdalen at the Louvre, a work influenced by Dürer and attributed to Gregor Erhart with some certainty.[5] There is additional evidence that another work should be attributed to Gregor Erhart, a Virgin and child from the Cistercian monastery of Kaisheim near Donauwörth, formerly in the Berlin Museum, and lost in World War II.[6]

1. For more discussion, see my essay in the present catalogue.

2. Peter Eikel, "Die Ravensburger Schutzmantelmaria. Beobachtungen zur Geschichte eines mittelalterlichen Kunstwerks," in Ernst Ziegler, ed., *Kunst und Kultur um den Bodensee. Zehn Jahre Museum Langenarge* (Sigmaringen, 1989), 111–120; Otto Rundel, "Johann Baptist von Hirscher (1728–1865) und seine Kunstsammlung," *Zeitschrift für Württembergische Landesgeschichte* 49 (1990), 295–319.

3. The figure was known as a king in the nineteenth century. See Jörg Rasmussen, "Ein wiedergefundenes Bildwerk von Michel Erhart," *Pantheon* 32 (1974), 351–354.

4. Baxandall 1974, 30–33, no. 4.

5. Alfred Schädler, "Gregor Erharts 'La Belle Allemande' im Louvre," *Aachener Kunstblätter* (1994), 365–376.

6. Demmler 1930, 212–213.

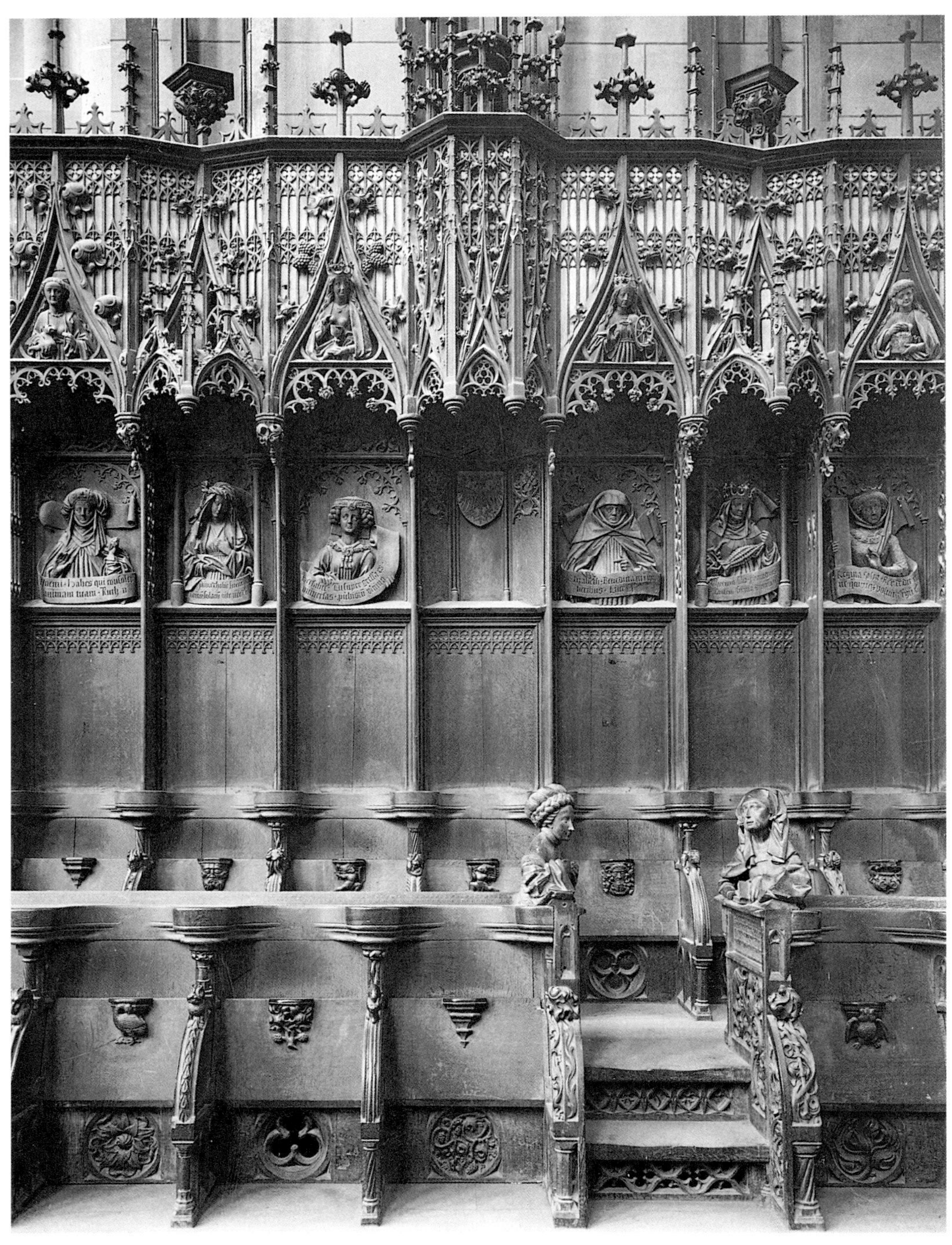

2.

Jörg Syrlin the Elder and Michel Erhart, choir stalls, 1469–1474, oak, Ulm Minster

If indeed the Berlin *Seated Virgin* is a work of Michel Erhart, it is undoubtedly the one sculpture besides the Vienna *Vanitas* that most clearly reveals the extent of Erhart's influence on Riemenschneider. A similarly introspective countenance is found on the *Magdalen* from the Münnerstadt altarpiece now in Munich (cat. 13, fig. 1) as well as on the contemporary bust of a Virgin in Sankt Burkard in Würzburg,

one of Riemenschneider's most important accomplishments (fig. 3).[7] Combining the melancholy and the elegiac, Riemenschneider's *Virgin and Child* from Burg Seebenstein of about 1495 (fig. 4) is extremely close to the *Seated Virgin*. The complex spatial effects achieved by the voluminous drapery of the *Seated Virgin* also reveal a profound knowledge of the art of Niclaus Gerhaert in Strasbourg; and are paralleled

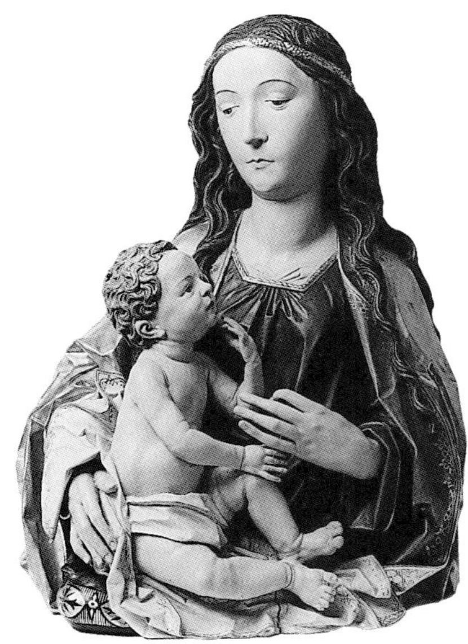

3.

Half-Length Virgin and Child, c. 1490, limewood with
modern polychromy, Sankt Burkardskirche, Würzburg

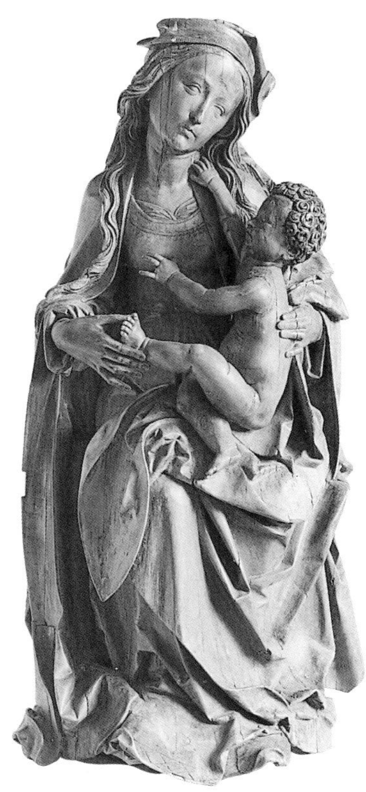

4.

Seated Virgin and Child, c. 1495, limewood, Private
Collection, Burg Seebenstein, Austria

in Riemenschneider's work of the early 1490s, above
all in the Münnerstadt altarpiece. This can be seen
specifically in *Saint Matthew* from the predella, the
angels surrounding the *Magdalen, Saint Elizabeth,*
and the *Trinity* (cat. 13A, figs. 1–3). Another example
from Riemenschneider's workshop worth mentioning here is the seated Saint Anthony from the church
of the Ursulines in Würzburg, which was burned in
World War II.[8]

It is apparently not true, as Justus Bier suggested,
that the sculptor, while still a journeyman, made an
altarpiece for the Benedictine Abbey of Wiblingen
near Ulm.[9] The assumption that an assistant would
be entrusted with the design of an entire altarpiece
is contradictory to the evidence presented by late
medieval sculptural practice as it is now understood.
The sculpture known in the scholarly literature as
parts of the "Wiblinger altarpiece," based on the
erroneous provenance of a relief fragment with male
mourners, now in Berlin (cat. 2, fig. 2), in fact come
from a *Passion* altarpiece made after 1485, when
Riemenschneider was already a master, for a church
in Rothenburg, probably that of the Franciscans.[10]

At the same time, both the Berlin *Seated Virgin*
and the *Vanitas* bear witness to Riemenschneider's

knowledge of artistic developments in Ulm. And
while it is impossible to tell how much he was influenced by the figural decoration of Michel Erhart's
sculpture on the high altar of Ulm Minster (1474–
1481) since this work was destroyed in 1531, we can
look for clues in the extant choir stalls (fig. 2). Wolfgang Deutsch and David Gropp have ascribed the
famous choir stall busts to Michel Erhart.[11] Questions
remain, however, concerning Jörg Syrlin's role in for-
mulating the figural style there,[12] and recent attributions of sculptural elements from the tabernacle and
the sedile to Syrlin need further consideration.[13] But
the influence of the Ulm school on Riemenschneider's style is especially evident in his work of the 1490s.
By then the sculptor had amassed a rich visual repertoire on which he could draw freely for inspiration,
depending on the specifics of individual commissions. KROHM

8. Würzburg 1981, 17.

9. Würzburg 1981, 24–69.

10. Examination by Peter Klein
of the cell structure of this work
and a group of female mourners
(Krohm essay, fig. 8) reveals that
they were cut from the same tree.

11. Wolfgang Deutsch, "Der
ehemalige Hochaltar und das
Chorgestühl, zur Syrlin- und zur
Bildhauerfrage," in *600 Jahre
Ulmer Münster,* ed. Hans Eugen
Specker and Reinhard Wort-
mann (Ulm, 1977), 242–322;
David Gropp, *Das Ulmer
Chorgestühl und Jörg Syrlin der
Ältere,* Neue Forschungen zur
deutschen Kunstgeschichte,
vol. 4 (Berlin, 1999).

12. Alfred Schädler, "Stetigkeit
und Wandel im Werk des
Veit Stoss," in Nuremberg 1983,
32–34.

13. Barbara Rommé, "Jörg Syrlin
der Jüngere und die Bildhauerfrage," *Zeitschrift für Württembergische Landesgeschichte* 50
(1991), 105–112; and Barbara
Rommé, "Überlegungen zu Jörg
Syrlin d. Ä. und zur Ausstattung
des Ulmer Münsterchores am
Ende des 15. Jahrhunderts,"
*Jahrbuch der Staatlichen Kunst-
sammlungen in Baden-Württemberg* 30 (1993), 7–23; Gerhard
Weilandt, "War der ältere
Sürlin Bildhauer?" *Jahrbuch der
Staatlichen Kunstsammlungen
in Baden-Württemberg* 28 (1991),
37–53. See also David Gropp,
"Der Prophetenzyklus am Sak-
ramentshaus des Ulmer Münsters," *Hans Multscher. Bildhauer
der Spätgotik in Ulm* (Ulm,
1997), 145–164.

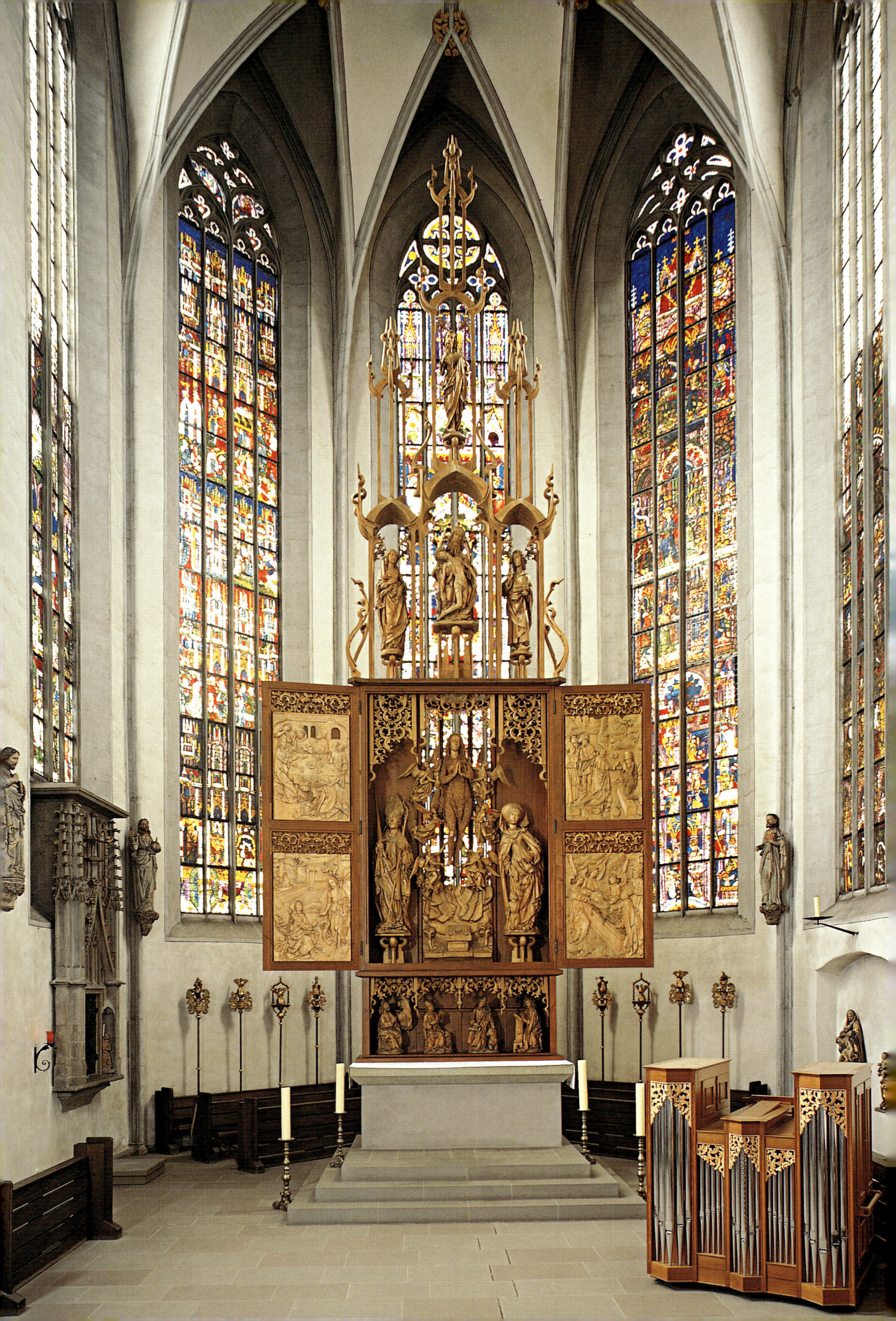

Six elements from the Münnerstadt altarpiece

13A   MATTHEW / from the predella

1490–1492, limewood, 72.5 x 35 x 32 (28½ x 13¾ x 12⅝), Staatliche Museen zu Berlin, Skulpturensammlung

13B   MARK / from the predella

1490–1492, limewood, 73.5 x 40 x 25 (29½ x 15¾ x 9⅞), Staatliche Museen zu Berlin, Skulpturensammlung

13C   LUKE / from the predella

1490–1492, limewood, 77.5 x 44 x 24 (29½ x 9½ x 9½), Staatliche Museen zu Berlin, Skulpturensammlung

13D   JOHN / from the predella

1490–1492, limewood, 73 x 45 x 25 (28¾ x 17¾ x 9⅞), Staatliche Museen zu Berlin, Skulpturensammlung

13E   CHRIST IN THE HOUSE OF SIMON / from the left wing

1490–1492, limewood, 143 x 102 x 4 (56¼ x 40⅛ x 1⅝), Bayerisches Nationalmuseum, Munich

13F   CHRIST APPEARING TO MARY MAGDALEN

("NOLI ME TANGERE") / from the left wing

1490–1492, limewood, 143.5 x 102 x 4 (56½ x 40⅛ x 1⅝), Staatliche Museen zu Berlin, Skulpturensammlung

Modern high altar with some of Riemenschneider's original elements, Church of Mary Magdalen, Münnerstadt

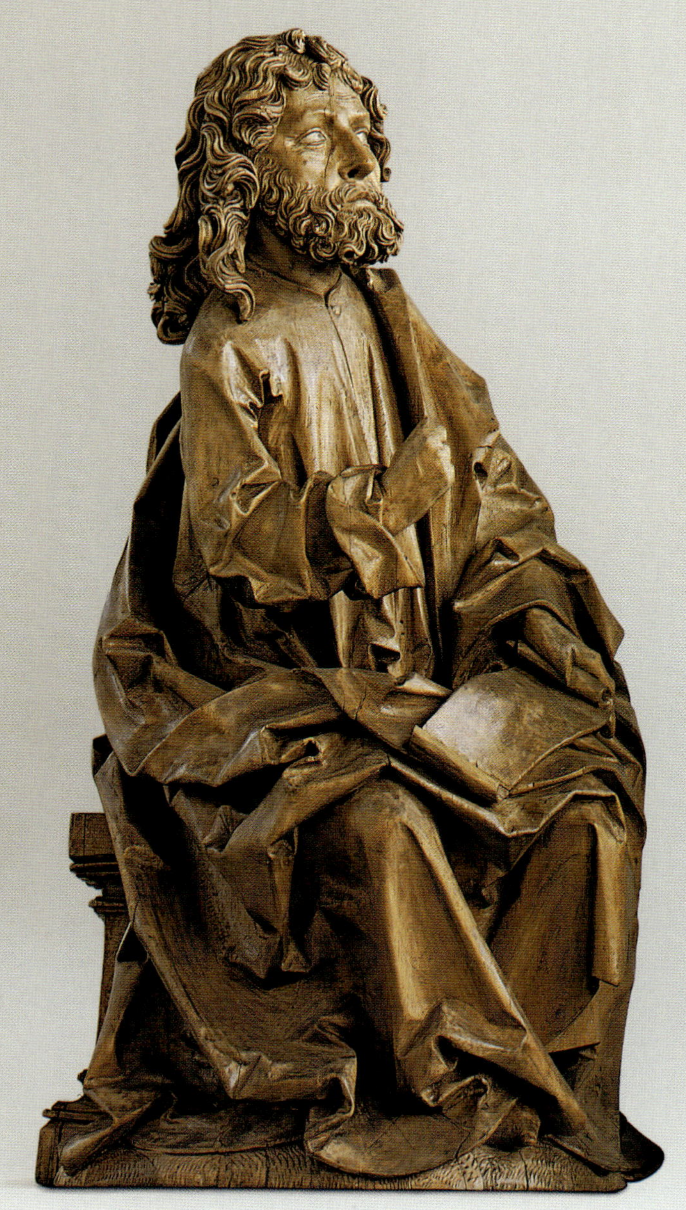

13 A

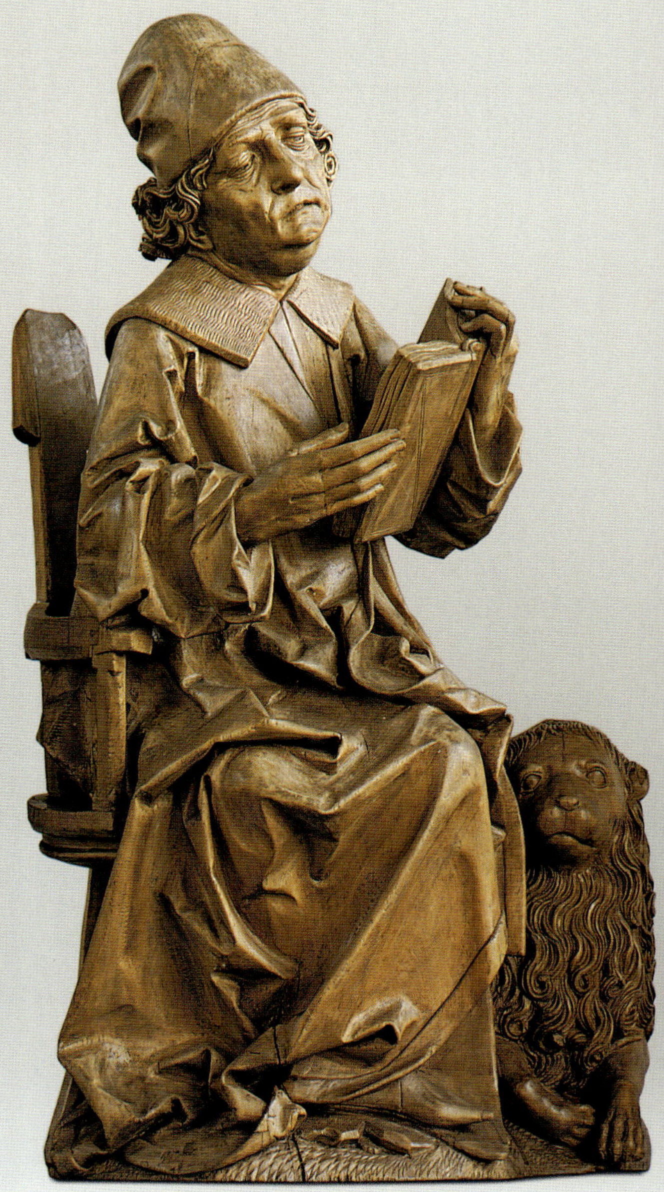

13 B

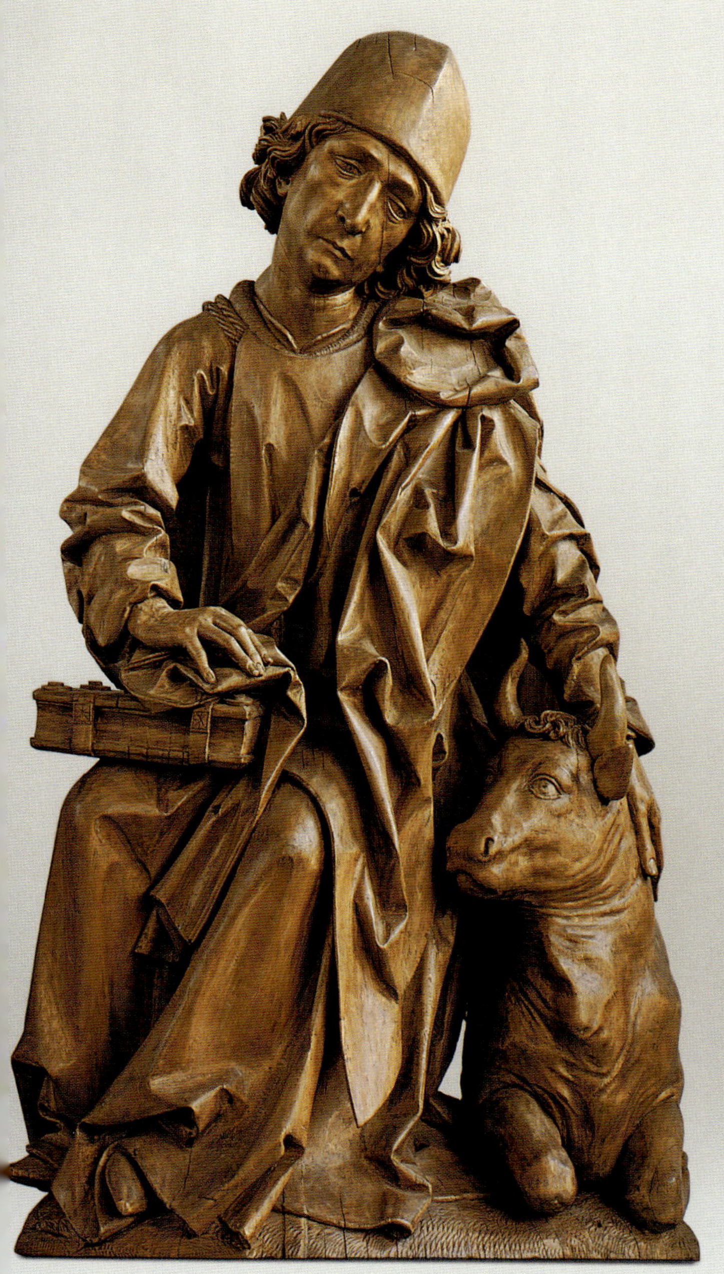

13 C

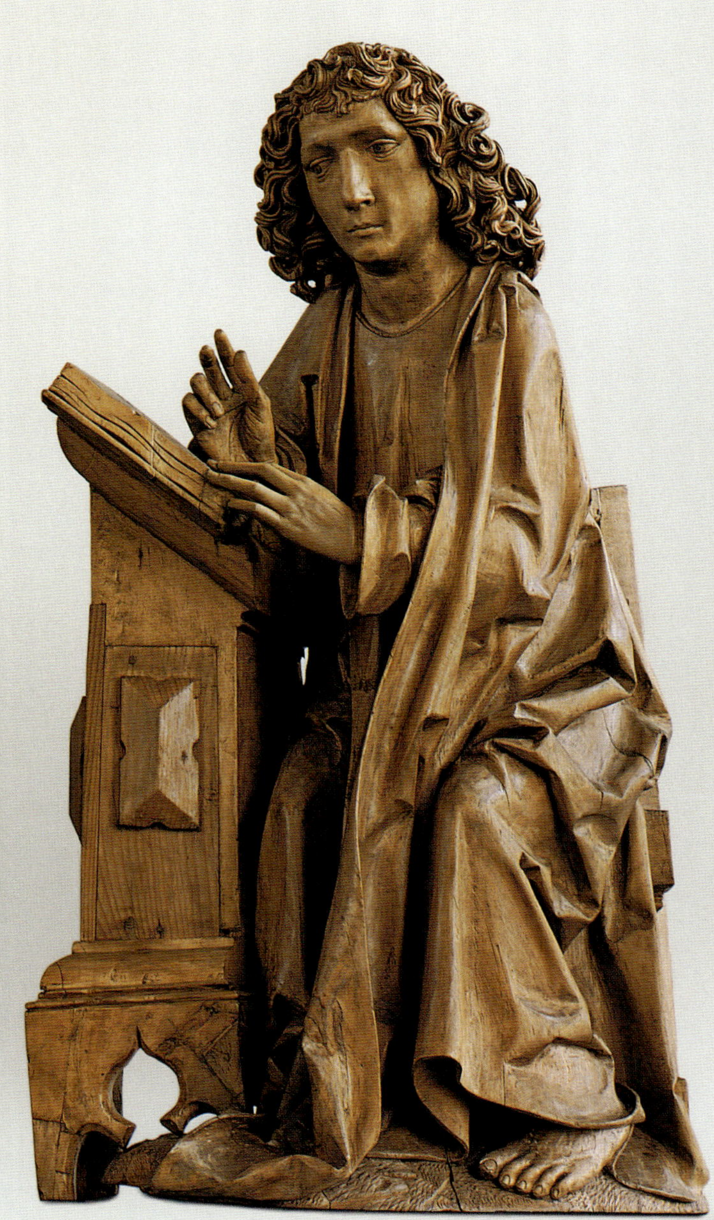

13 D

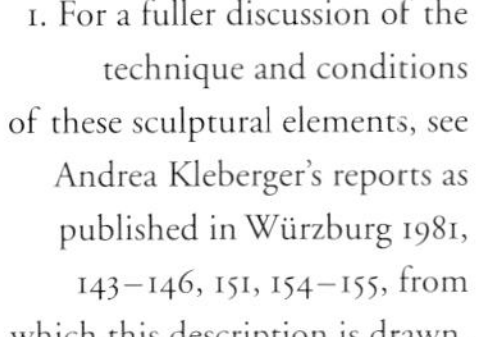

• Technical Notes •
Each evangelist is carved from a single block of limewood with the grain running vertically and the backs
hollowed out to prevent cracking. The two reliefs are
made of several boards of limewood joined vertically.
All sculptural elements contain original additions,
minor losses, and modern replacements. They have
suffered only moderately from insect damage. The
surfaces of the evangelists and the *Noli me Tangere*
relief are decorated with a carved zigzag pattern
(Tremolierung), while several areas of *Christ in the
House of Simon* are stippled to imitate fur or velvet.
Remnants of an original pigmented translucent layer
have been found on the evangelists and the *Noli me
Tangere* but not on *Christ in the House of Simon,*
whose surface is less well preserved. Analysis revealed
the layer to be protein (glue) containing small amounts
of oil mixed with black, calcium carbonate (chalk),
and yellow ocher. The eyes and eyebrows were originally painted black and the lips painted red.[1]

• Provenance •
The evangelists and both reliefs were removed from
the altarpiece during its 1649–1653 refurbishment.
The reliefs entered the collection of Wilhelm Sattler
at Mainberg Castle near Schweinfurt before 1826. The
Berlin museum acquired the evangelists at auction in
Vienna in 1887 and the *Noli me Tangere* relief at the
auction of the Sattler collection in Berlin in 1901. At
the same auction Benoit Oppenheim of Berlin purchased the relief of *Christ in the House of Simon,*
which was acquired in 1923 by Dr. Gerhart Bollert,
Berlin; in 1952 the Bollert family placed the relief
on long-term loan to the museum in Munich, which
acquired the work in 1979.

• Literature •
The extensive literature prior to 1980 is given in
Krohm and Oellermann 1980, 88–89; Würzburg 1981,
115–166; Boockmann 1994, 330–335; for later literature, see bibliographical references in Söding 1998.

THE RETABLE THAT Riemenschneider made
between 1490 and 1492 for the parish church of Mary
Magdalen in Münnerstadt is a key monument of his
art and a milestone in the development of late medieval sculpture. A dated work of the highest quality,
both in conception and execution, it serves as a touchstone for the reconstruction of Riemenschneider's
early oeuvre. Extensive archival documentation reveals
much about the commission and the production of
the work. Riemenschneider's largest altarpiece, it was
one of the earliest carved retables to be delivered

uncolored, a fact that apparently proved disturbing
for its commissioners and had to be remedied a few
years later. It is only because the retable was dismantled
in the seventeenth century that several of its elements
could be included in the exhibition.

• The Commission and the Iconographic Program •
In 1883 a chest in the church of Mary Magdalen was
found to contain a trove of archival material, including a contract with the sculptor, detailed directives on the iconographic program, and receipts for
payments, which thoroughly document the production of Riemenschneider's monumental altarpiece
and establish it as his earliest recorded commission
since he became a master in 1485.[2]

The town of Münnerstadt in Lower Franconia
had a population of between 2,000 and 2,500 inhabitants in the fifteenth century and drew its pros-
perity from its crafts *(Handwerk),* especially in cloth.
It fell equally under the authority of the prince-bishop
of Würzburg and the counts of Henneberg-Aschach.
The presence since 1220 of a branch of the Teutonic
Knights had a strong influence on the development
of the city. The knights' power was curtailed in 1335
when Münnerstadt assumed responsibility for its own
administration and justice, but they originally exerted
great power over the church of Mary Magdalen: they
appointed its parish priests, administered its income,
and supervised changes to its fabric. By the fifteenth
century the municipal council was in charge of the
church's income and ordered commissions, such as
Riemenschneider's for the high altar, but the Teutonic
Knights were directly involved in the process. In all
likelihood, the altarpiece was financed with donations
made by the burghers of the town as well as by religious confraternities.

On 26 June 1490 Riemenschneider reached a
contractual agreement with the burgomaster of Münnerstadt, members of the municipal council, and the
master builder of the church; witnesses included Nikolaus von Ebern, the commandant of the Teutonic
Knights, and Johan von Arnstein, the parish priest.
Riemenschneider agreed to deliver a large retable for
the high altar in the choir and to erect it himself by
Easter of 1492. The altarpiece would thus complete
the decoration of the choir, which had been built in
the early fifteenth century and elaborately glazed. The
sculptor was to receive the sum of 145 guilders, from
which, presumably, he would also pay the joiner who
was to provide the encasement for the altarpiece.
Riemenschneider was responsible for the execution
of the entire retable and contracted out a significant
part of the work. The carpentry of the retable was to

1. For a fuller discussion of the
technique and conditions
of these sculptural elements, see
Andrea Kleberger's reports as
published in Würzburg 1981,
143–146, 151, 154–155, from
which this description is drawn.

2. Unless otherwise specified,
the accounts given in this entry
are based on Krohm and
Oellermann 1980; and Krohm
in Würzburg 1981, 116–128.

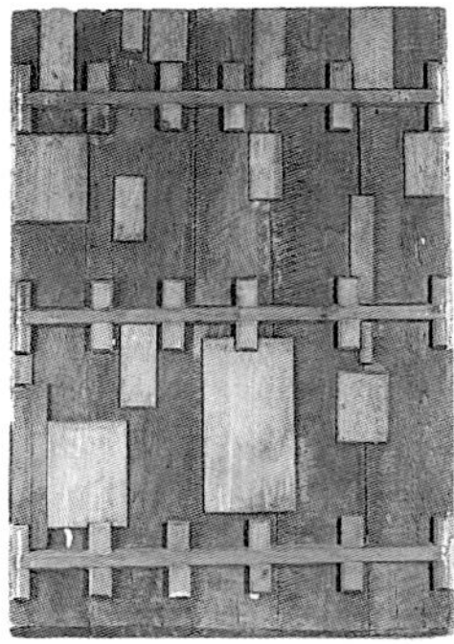

Back view of catalogue
no. 13 F

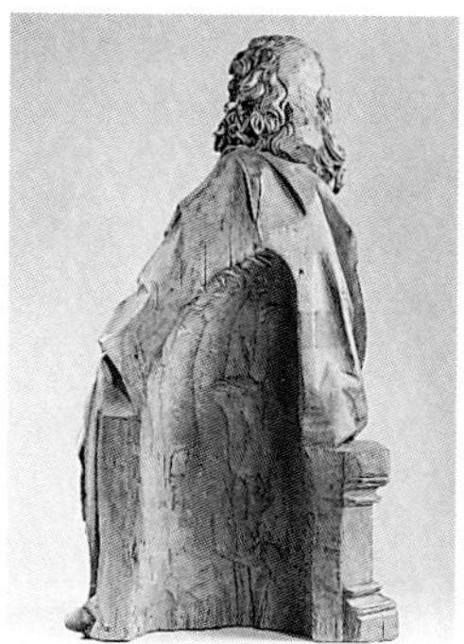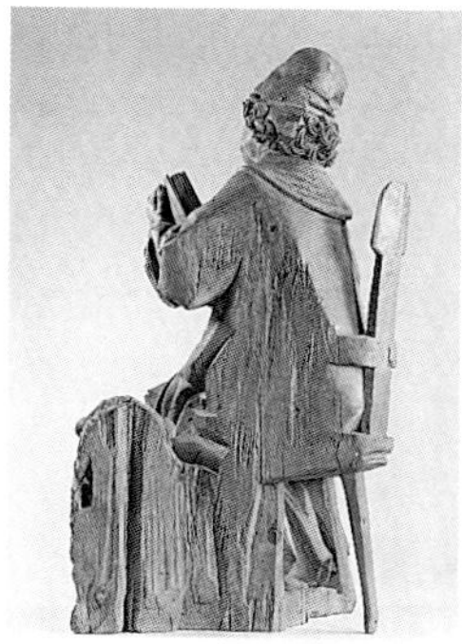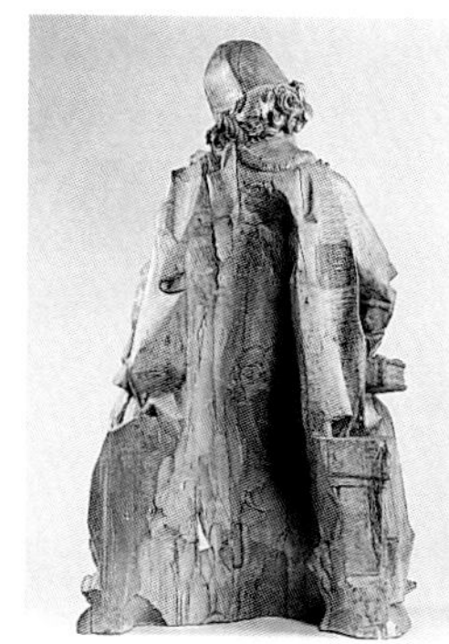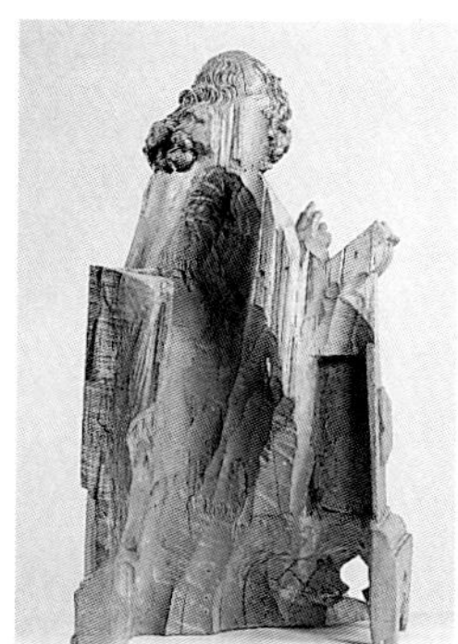

Back views of catalogue nos. 13A–D

follow his design. The price of 145 guilders is remarkably low, especially compared with the 220 guilders that Stoss received for the polychromy a few years later. Riemenschneider may have agreed to the low fee in order to secure the commission by ruling out competition and thereby to establish his reputation.[3] The Münnerstadt contract stipulates that Riemenschneider was to submit a presentation drawing *(Visierung),* which presumably defined the composition in general terms. No such drawing by the sculptor has survived.

In addition to the contract, a second document established in great detail the program of the altarpiece. The iconography was to center on Mary Magdalen, the patron saint of the church. Since the writings of Gregory the Great, medieval devotion—and therefore art—conflated three figures into Mary Magdalen: the woman with that name in the Gospels, whom Christ had delivered of seven demons and who attended his Passion and witnessed his resurrection; Mary of Bethany, the sister of Martha and Lazarus; and the repentant sinner who washed Christ's feet with her tears in the house of Simon. Popular piety grafted onto the Gospel accounts an eleventh-century French legend, according to which Mary Magdalen sailed with Martha, Lazarus, and the bishop Maximin to Provence, where she lived as a hermit for thirty years. Seven times a day, angels raised her to heaven, where she attended a celestial concert.[4] Viewed as a repentant harlot who had turned to Christ, she embodied the hope for redemption.

According to the specifications, the central shrine would contain three large figures: the patron saints of the city, the diocese, and the Teutonic Knights. In the middle Mary Magdalen, wearing a hair shirt, was to be shown being carried to heaven by six angels (fig. 1), a seventh one holding a crown above her head; under her feet would be a relief with an altar in a landscape.[5] To her right would stand Kilian, bishop and patron saint of the diocese of Würzburg, holding the sword of his martyrdom. To her left would appear Elizabeth of Hungary, patron of the Teutonic Knights, with a loaf of bread, a jug, and a cripple begging for alms at her feet (fig. 2). The superstructure would depict God the Father holding a crucifix with the dove of the Holy Spirit; the Trinity would be flanked by the Virgin (now lost) and John the Evangelist. At the top would stand a figure of John the Baptist. The predella would contain busts of the four evangelists with their symbols. The wings of the altarpiece would have four reliefs, not to exceed two or three fingers in thickness, with scenes from the life of Mary Magdalen: on the left wing, *Christ in the House of Simon* above the *Noli me Tangere;* and on the right, the Magdalen's last communion above her burial by angels. An elaborate diaphanous tracery surrounded the figures and grew into a tall superstructure, as seen in Creglingen.[6]

• *The Subsequent History of the Altarpiece* •
The altarpiece, completed half a year after the stipulated date of Easter 1492,[7] underwent radical change soon after its installation. Riemenschneider delivered the work uncolored. The contract makes no reference to polychromy; and given the price of gold leaf or natural ultramarine, such materials would have been mentioned separately had there been any intention of using them. It thus appears certain that the commissioners expected to receive an uncolored altarpiece. Yet on 7 October 1497 a report from nearby Hassfurt reveals that plans to paint the retable were under way: the burgomaster and council of Hassfurt recommended that their councilman Johann Moler be awarded the commission. The altarpiece was finally polychromed between February 1504 and June 1505 by the sculptor Veit Stoss (cats. 25 and 35), who had

3. Boockmann 1994, 331.

4. *Lexikon der christlichen Ikonographie,* ed. Wolfgang Braunfels (Rome, Freiburg, Basel, Vienna, 1974), 7:516–517; Louis Réau, *Iconographie de l'art chrétien* (Paris, 1958), 3.2: 846–859.

5. For the text of the commissioning document, see Krohm and Oellermann 1980, 91. The seventh angel holding a crown was either never carved or is lost, as is the landscape with a relief below the Magdalen.

6. Emericus Kratzer, parish priest in Geldersheim, described the Münnerstadt altarpiece in 1613 and noted that it had "an abundance of tracery, all carved and undercut" (Krohm and Oellermann 1980, 31, 97).

7. Riemenschneider received a final payment on 30 September 1492 (Würzburg 1981, 122).

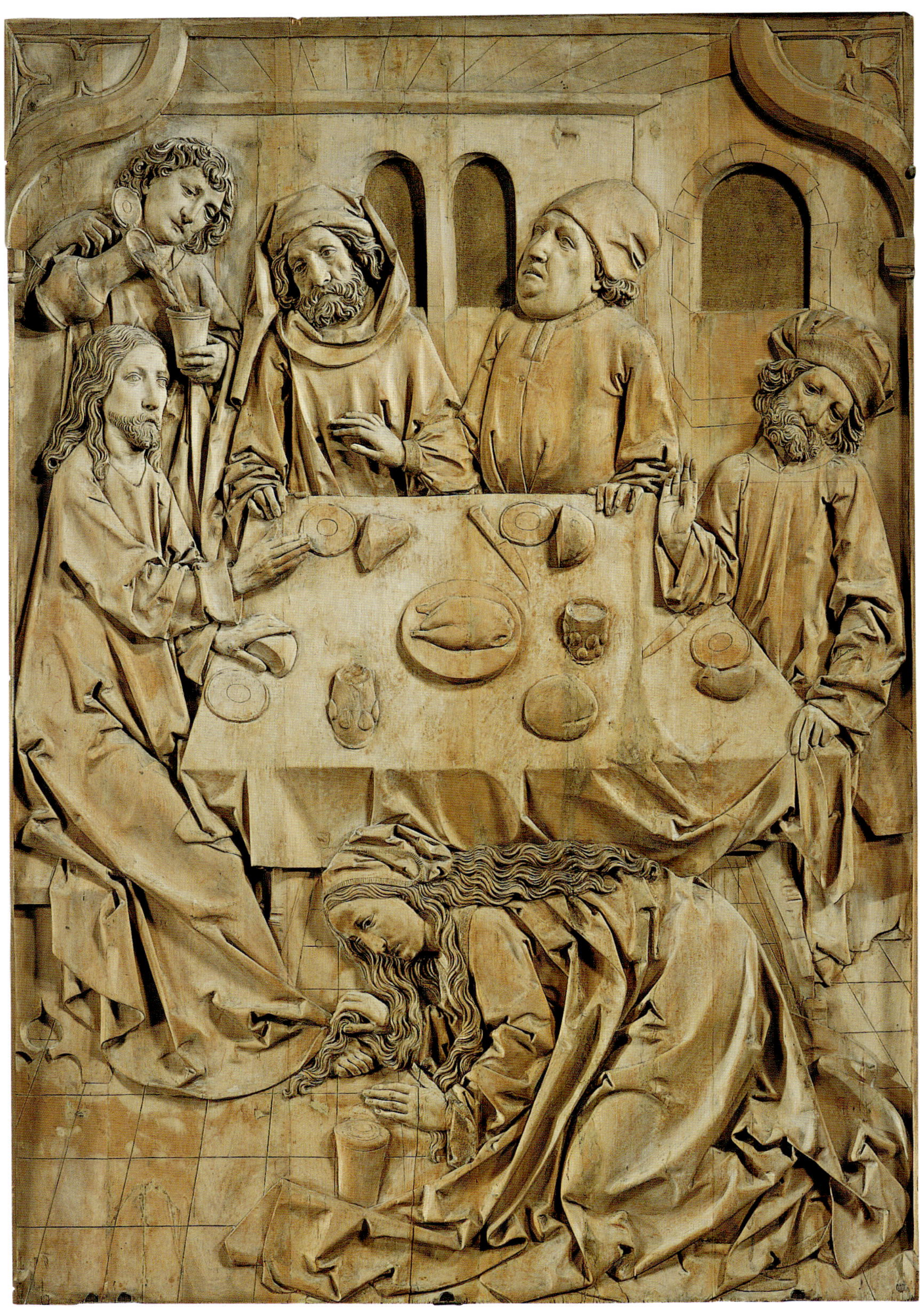

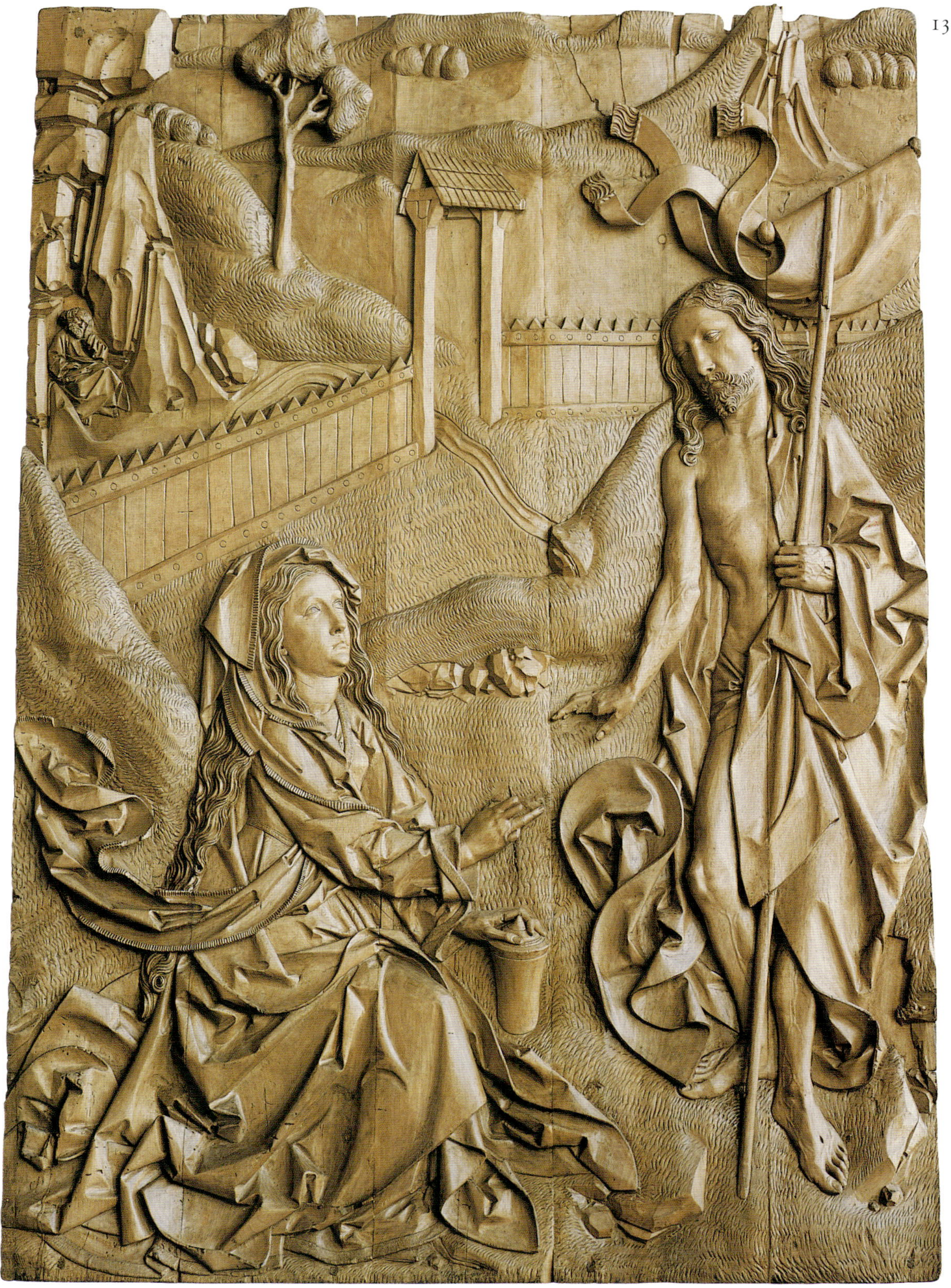

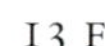

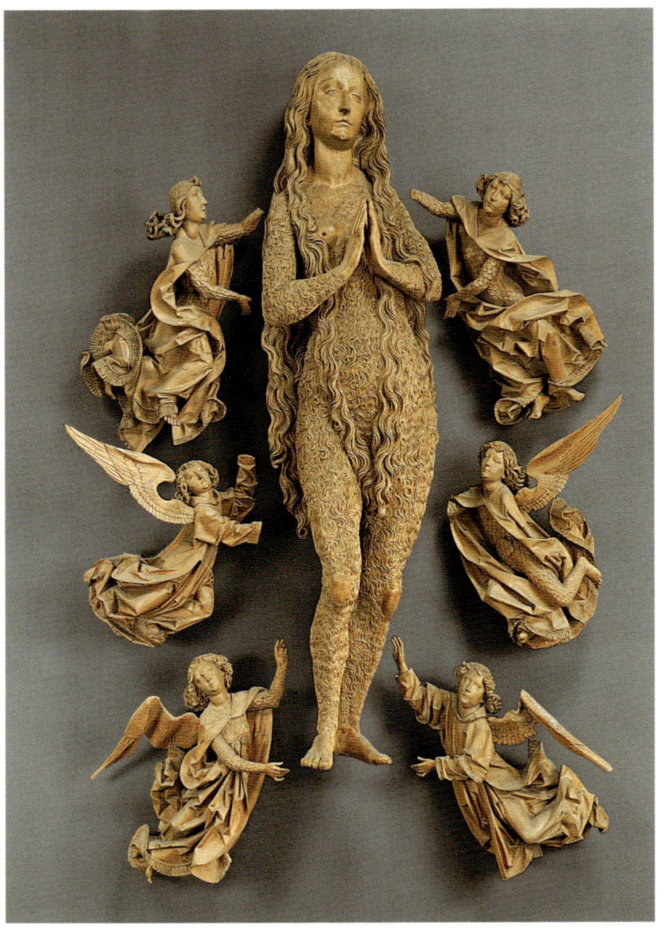

1.

The Assumption of Mary Magdalen, from the central shrine of the Münnerstadt altarpiece, 1490–1492,
limewood, Bayerisches Nationalmuseum, Munich

8. For a discussion of Stoss'
tribulations, see Krohm and
Oellermann 1980, 49.

9. Münnerstadt remained
Protestant until Bishop Julius
Echter established the Counter-
Reformation there in 1587
(Würzburg 1981, 117).

10. Würzburg 1981, 117.

come to Münnerstadt to flee Nuremberg, where he
was being sued for debts.[8] Stoss also painted four
scenes from the legend of Saint Kilian on the exterior
of the wings. Two painters from Würzburg came to
Münnerstadt to inspect the retable sometime before
June 1505 and determined that Stoss should be paid
220 guilders for his work—75 guilders more than
Riemenschneider had received for producing the whole
altarpiece. It is ironic that Stoss did the polychromy:
keenly aware that layers of ground and paint would
conceal the fineness of carving, he stated explicitly
some years later that the large altarpiece he had
made for the Carmelites in Nuremberg should not
be painted.

The retable survived the Peasants' Revolt of 1525
and Münnerstadt's temporary conversion to Protestantism[9] but not the baroque remodeling of the high
altar between 1649 and 1653. Riemenschneider's retable
was dismantled, and a monumental classicizing framework was erected in its stead that combined a painting of the *Noli me Tangere* with Riemenschneider's

Assumption of Mary Magdalen, Saint Kilian and *Saint
Elizabeth,* the *Trinity, John the Evangelist,* and *John
the Baptist.* At the same time, the Münnerstadt painter
Otto Sebastian Eigenbrodt was commissioned to
"clean the old paint off the sculpture from the high
altar," which probably meant the removal of Stoss'
polychromy.[10] In 1756 church authorities in Würzburg
ordered the removal of the *Assumption* group, no doubt
because the Magdalen's nudity was found offensive.

The altarpiece underwent a neo-Gothic refurbishment between 1833 and 1834, which incorporated
only the figures of Kilian, Elizabeth, John the Baptist, John the Evangelist, and the Trinity from the
original retable; these were stripped of their baroque
polychromy and painted anew. The neo-Gothic high
altar was destroyed in 1945, but fortunately the Riemenschneider figures had been evacuated. Following
extensive research by the Berlin museum in the 1970s,
a modern structure was erected in an attempt to present those works that have remained in Münnerstadt
at the proper height and in the proper light. This new

216

encasement must not be understood as a reconstruction but as an evocation of Riemenschneider's retable (see page 208). Later copies of the pieces that had found their way to Berlin and Munich were added to the presentation.[11] Despite the tribulations to which the altarpiece was subjected, it would appear that most figures survived, with the exception of the losses mentioned above.[12]

• *The Cohesion of the Retable and
the Sculptural Execution* •

Although the commissioners determined the iconography and the general placement of the figures, Riemenschneider was responsible for integrating all of the elements into a coherent design. The unifying theme of the altarpiece is the doctrine of redemption through Christ's death. On weekdays, as well as on Sundays throughout Lent and Advent, the central section was not visible, as the wings were shut. The evangelists in the predella provided the scriptural and visual foundation for the whole. Directly above,

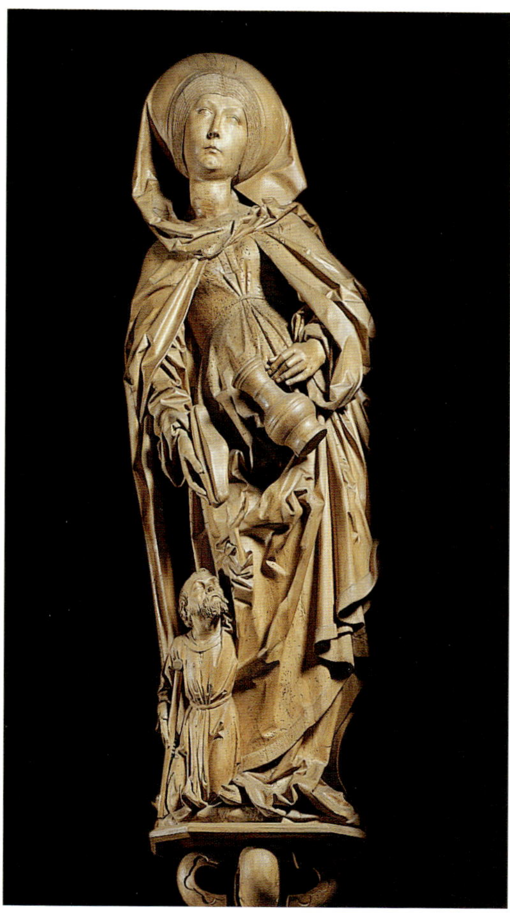

2.
Saint Elizabeth of Hungary, from the central shrine of
the Münnerstadt altarpiece, 1490–1492,
limewood, Church of Mary Magdalen, Münnerstadt

Christ's dead body in the Trinity was flanked by the Virgin and John the Evangelist, as it was at the Crucifixion. John the Baptist, at the top, pointed to the lamb as a reference to Christ as "the Lamb of God, who takes away the sin of the world" (John 1:29). When the wings were open, the concept of forgiveness was made all the more vivid by the scenes from the life of Mary Magdalen and her assumption into heaven. The corpus was innovative in that it was both a narrative tableau and a traditional altarpiece that juxtaposes standing figures *(Reihenaltar).*[13] The high placement of the over-life-size Magdalen, hovering above Kilian and Elizabeth, gave the retable a strong vertical pull. The abundant tracery that originally decorated the altarpiece further unified the various components of the ensemble.

Riemenschneider did not follow in detail all of the directives in the commissioning documents. The Trinity, for instance, does not represent Christ on the cross but supported by God's hands (fig. 3). This should not be interpreted solely as artistic license; the contract was drawn, after all, to bind the sculptor legally to the wishes of the patrons. It is possible, however, that Riemenschneider, as he proceeded with the execution of the figures, realized that certain changes in iconography would result in a more forceful rendering of a subject. The omission of the cross allowed him to fuse the two figures into a superb composition that, while powerful in its pathos, visually underscores the theological dogma that God the Father and God the Son are one. The lifeless body of Christ, held tenderly at the chest, breaks in an arc that is echoed by the line of the Father's drapery and is almost entirely encompassed in his silhouette. There was certainly communication between Riemenschneider and his patrons during the production of the retable, and the commissioners must have been aware of the modifications before delivery of the work.

• *The Four Evangelists* •

The evangelists in the predella represent another significant departure from the original specifications. The document states explicitly that they were to be represented as busts, which probably meant as half-length figures with arms and hands, as in the *Saint Kilian* formerly in the Neumünster in Würzburg (cat. 44, fig. 1). In addition, each was to be provided with his particular attribute and a bookstand. Instead, Riemenschneider depicted the evangelists full-length and gave only John the required bookstand.

Conceived to be viewed from the front, Riemenschneider's evangelists are at once unified and diverse. The arrangement of the figures from left to right

11. The new structure is based on inferred dimensions of the original altarpiece, an assumed proportional system, placement of the figures as described in documents, an analysis of the sculpture, and the findings of scientific examination (see Krohm and Oellermann 1980, 78–88; and Krohm 1985, 31–43). See also Kobler 1982, 199–206; Kalden 1990, 165–168; and Söding 1998.

12. Vetter 1980, 359.

13. Krohm and Oellermann 1980, 30.

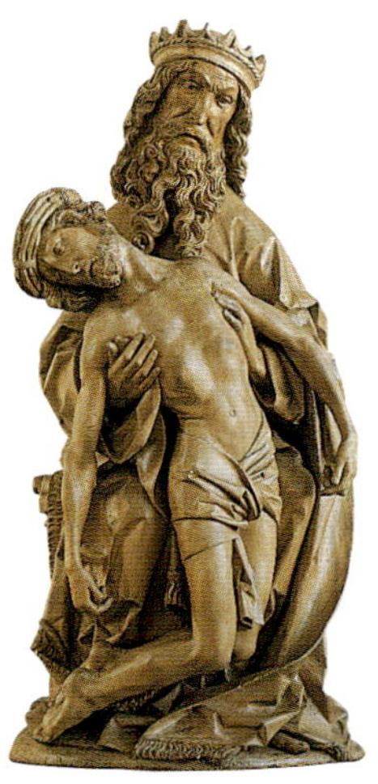

3.
Trinity, from the
superstructure of
the Münnerstadt altarpiece,
1490–1492, limewood,
Church of Mary Magdalen,
Münnerstadt

reflects the order in which their Gospels appear in the Bible. Their poses and the disposition of their draperies respond to one another and lead the eye toward the center of the group. They are highly differentiated in age, mood, and stance. Matthew and John, thought in the Middle Ages to be identical with their namesake apostles, are clothed in timeless draperies. Mark and Luke, by contrast, wear the cap and garb of the humanist. Riemenschneider here follows a tradition harking back to early Christian time, which recognized Matthew and John as eyewitnesses of Christ's ministry, whereas Mark and Luke, as supposed followers of Peter and Paul, are venerated as examples of pious learning.[14]

The bearded Matthew, turned three-quarters to the right, sits upright on a profiled rectangular bench, a scroll on his knee and a look of attentive expectation on his face. Originally looking up at his attribute, an angel, which was carved separately and attached to the back wall of the predella,[15] he appears to be listening to its words and preparing to write them down. The raising of his right hand, which once held a quill, has caused his mantle to fall off his right shoulder. The big sweep of drapery, familiar from other early works by Riemenschneider (see cats. 2, 4, 10), surrounds the figure and covers his lap. By giving emphasis to the right knee, this drapery underscores the oblique position of the figure and lends it great spatial presence.

Mark, with a docile lion at his feet, is also turned to the right, but less sharply than Matthew. Sitting on a wooden chair and leaning forward slightly, the aged, beardless author holds an open book. He has apparently completed his task: the absence of quills suggests that the text requires no correction. His knees project almost frontally, while his upper body is turned to the right, creating an unnatural torsion at the hips (note the relationship of the saint's left knee to his abdomen) and continuing the directional movement initiated by Matthew.

Luke too seems to have completed his task, holding the closed codex on his right knee. He does not touch the book directly but shields it with the cloth of his mantle in deference to its contents. With a melancholy expression emphasized by the tilt of his head, he affectionately caresses the neck of his ox, while the creature, its ears pricked up and eyes raised, seems aware of Luke's quiet sadness. The only evangelist to face the viewer, Luke turns his body toward Mark. The mantle gathered on his left shoulder covers the greater part of his torso and reinforces, through lucidly articulated folds, the grand oblique of the body.

John sits at a bookstand and amends his manuscript, apparently following the instructions of his attribute, the eagle, which must have been placed roughly above his book. Echoing the angle of Matthew's body, he is turned sharply to the left. Riemenschneider represented him as a lanky adolescent with abundant curly hair and bare feet, sitting on the edge of a chair. The saint's sense of purpose is almost tangible in his tense neck muscles and the angles of his body, though his drapery is quieter than that of the other figures. The mantle covers both shoulders and envelops the body, which remains legible through the fabric. The edge of the cloak falls in an uninterrupted oblique from the left shoulder to the front of the bookstand.

Early on, Riemenschneider developed most of the compositional and facial types that he and his workshop repeated, with variations, for the rest of his career.[16] Three of the evangelists from the Münnerstadt altarpiece are among his earliest formulations of these types. The faces of Matthew and Mark are reflected in the sandstone apostles for the Marienkapelle and in the figures for the *Holy Blood* and Creglingen altarpieces. Luke is the first of one of Riemenschneider's most ubiquitous types: the middle-aged man, with a strong narrow nose, half shut eyes set at an angle, thin narrow mouth, square jaws, and prominent cheekbones, conveying an expression both of melancholy and interiority. With variations in hair or beard, it reappears for years, on such figures as Saint Eustace in the Cloisters group (cat. 23) or in the effigy of Emperor Heinrich in Bamberg (Chapuis essay, fig. 4).

• *Christ in the House of Simon* •
The specifications accompanying the contract identify the subject of the upper relief of the left wing as "the scene in which Saint Mary Magdalen anoints Jesus' feet during the meal in Simon's house." The scriptural source, Luke 7:36–50, tells how Christ was having a meal in the house of a Pharisee named Simon, when a woman known in town as a sinner entered, bringing with her "an alabaster jar of ointment. She stood behind him at his feet, weeping, and began to bathe his feet with her tears and to dry them with her hair. Then she continued kissing his feet and anointing them with the ointment." In response to his host's evident disdain for the woman, Jesus said to him, "Simon, I have something to say to you:…her sins, which were many, have been forgiven; hence she has shown great love."

Riemenschneider draws elements from two graphic sources.[17] The first is a woodcut illustration

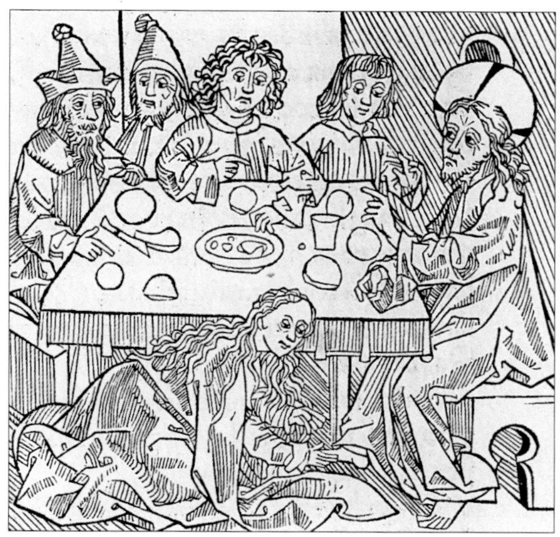

4.

Nuremberg, *Christ in the House of Simon*, woodcut,
from Anton Koberger's *Heiligenleben*, published in 1488,
The Metropolitan Museum of Art, New York

in Anton Koberger's *Heiligenleben,* published in
Nuremberg in 1488 (fig. 4), where the meal takes place
around a square table in a square room, with the back
wall parallel to the picture plane, the woman kneeling
in front of the table, and Christ sitting across from
Simon. The precise correspondence of Christ's hands
and of the arrangement of the Magdalen's drapery
confirms that Riemenschneider was familiar with the
woodcut. The attendant standing in the upper left
corner pouring wine derives from Israhel van Meckenem's engraving of the Last Supper from about 1480
(fig. 5).

While borrowing motifs from existing models,
Riemenschneider transcends them by creating a composition that is both formally more structured and
psychologically more charged. The addition of columns
to support the tracery in the upper corners suggests
that the viewer stands in front of the room and is
allowed to look in. Although the relief is extremely
shallow, the receding floor tile, ceiling, and table permit a coherent spatial reading. The figures seated
around the table glance at one another, establishing
interrelationships. The Magdalen, however, is isolated
from the other figures and from the viewer. Her head
is kept below the edge of the table, and the powerful curves of enveloping drapery form a barrier around
her while also giving prominence to the focus of the
composition. Prostrate, as though crushed by guilt,
the Magdalen seems oblivious to the reactions of on-
lookers. The scene is made all the more poignant by
Riemenschneider's decision to show her repenting
but not knowing her sins will be forgiven, because
Christ has not yet spoken.

Instead of anointing Christ's feet, as dictated by
the commission, the Magdalen here is drying them
off. Simon, sitting at the right,[18] lifts up the corner
of the tablecloth, not to have a better look at her but
to prevent his food from being soiled by contact with
a woman of ill repute.[19] His action and raised right
hand express his dismay at Christ for allowing her to
touch him. The bearded man behind the table follows attentively what is happening, while his fat,
beardless companion shows interest only in the wine
being poured.[20] The ointment jar, which the Magdalen will take to the tomb on Easter morning, is a
reminder of the Christian belief that forgiveness of
sins was achieved through Christ's death. Riemenschneider's ability to express in a lucid composition
emotions as diverse and contradictory as contrition,
love, hope, condemnation, compassion, and indiffer-
ence is no small measure of his talent as a narrator.

Noli me Tangere

The specifications accompanying the contract describe the subject of the relief to be installed in the
lower half of the left wing as "how Christ appeared
to her with a spade after the resurrection." Riemenschneider's relief is based on the account in John 20:
1–17. On the third day after the crucifixion, Mary
Magdalen went to the tomb where Jesus had been
laid, and seeing it open and empty, she alerted Peter
and John. After they left, she stood outside the tomb
weeping. Suddenly she saw Jesus standing next to her
but mistook him for the gardener and asked if he had
taken away Christ's body. When he addressed her by
name, she recognized him, but Jesus admonished
her, "do not hold on to me (*noli me tangere*), because
I have not yet ascended to the Father." Although the
commission dictated that Christ was to be depicted
with a spade, he holds instead the banner of the resurrection, which originally had a cross at the top.

The encounter portrayed by Riemenschneider
takes place in a hilly garden, which is enclosed by a
picket fence. The kneeling Magdalen reaches out to
Christ, who signals her not to touch him. Part of his
mantle has fallen off his right shoulder, revealing his
naked body underneath, and especially the wound in
his side, positive proof of the resurrection. In the left
background a diminutive bearded figure crouching
among rocks is the apostle Peter, whose anachron-
istic presence at the scene refers to a passage from the
Golden Legend by Jacobus of Voragine: after having
denied knowing Christ, Peter fled to a cave where he
wept for three days until Christ appeared to him.
Peter thus establishes a parallel with the Magdalen,
both in his repentance and in seeing the risen Christ.[21]

18. In my opinion Vetter 1980,
360, has convincingly argued
that only this figure can be
Simon; see also Krohm and
Oellermann 1980, 39.

19. Compare Schrade 1927, 40;
and Krohm and Oellermann
1980, 39.

20. For an eloquent and more
detailed discussion of the scene,
see Vetter 1980, 359–363.

21. Vetter 1980, 364; Krohm
in Würzburg 1981, 152; and *Le
Beau Martin. Actes du colloque
de Colmar 1991* (Colmar, 1991),
478.

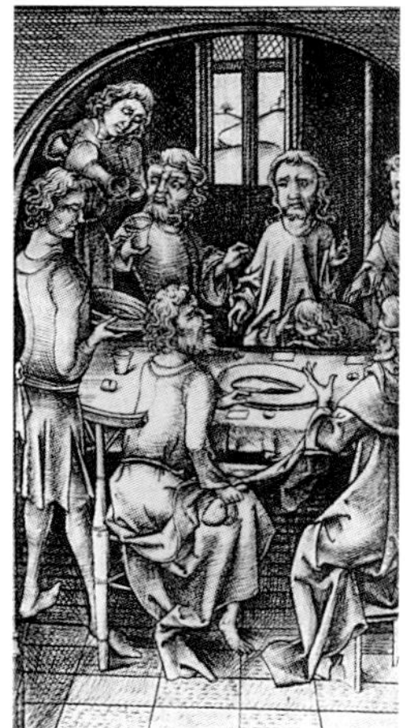

5.

Israhel van Meckenem,
detail of the
Last Supper, from *Christ
Washing the Feet of His
Apostles,* c. 1480, engraving,
National Gallery of Art,
Washington, Rosenwald
Collection

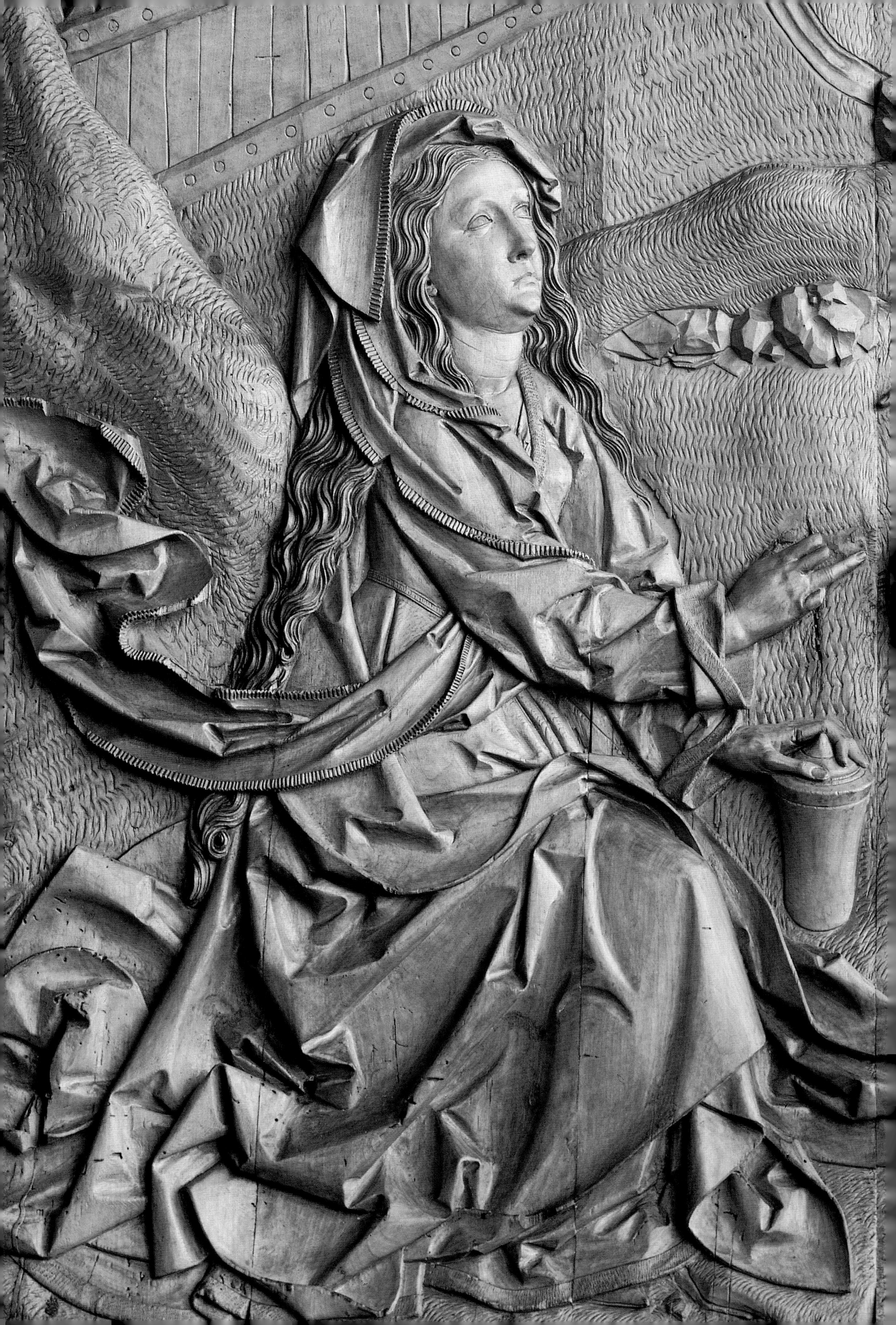

Like *Christ in the House of Simon,* the *Noli me Tangere* transforms an existing composition by another artist by giving different accents to the story.[22] The point of departure here is Martin Schongauer's engraving of the same subject of about 1475–1480 (fig. 6). Riemenschneider borrows the juxtaposition of the kneeling Magdalen on the left and the standing Christ on the right as well as specific details of landscape and costume. Everything else appears to have been reformulated into a new composition that not only is more emotionally charged but draws the viewer into the narrative.

The relationship between the two figures has changed, and so has the landscape that anchors it. The mood in the engraving is quieter: the figures are farther apart, the draperies are calmer, and the raised area on which Mary Magdalen kneels is separate from the ground on which Christ stands. The bare tree in the background emphasizes this separation, while the almost horizontal wattle fence, above which a wide landscape is perceived, establishes a stability in the composition.

In Riemenschneider's relief the encounter has a heightened sense of drama. The fluttering of the banner, of Christ's mantle, and of the Magdalen's veil reinforce the supernatural character of the scene. This motif, which is present in the Schongauer print, has been magnified in the relief, as though a powerful wind were blowing from the tomb (outside the scene depicted). The figures, which are closer to each other here and stand on the same terrain, also have quite different poses. Christ's slightly unstable stance has replaced the statuesque pose in the print. Likewise the Magdalen appears more unsteady here, where she has only one knee on the ground and seems about to stand up. Her veil no longer covers her hair but is falling. There is a greater sense of excitement and expectancy about her. Schongauer gives each figure a clear position in space, whereas Riemenschneider shows them drawn toward one another and yet unable to touch.

The landscape in the relief eloquently echoes this tension between movement and restraint. The horizon is not visible, which compresses the action into a shallower space. The hills also anchor the figures: one at the left creates a strong oblique that continues through the Magdalen to the drapery on the ground;

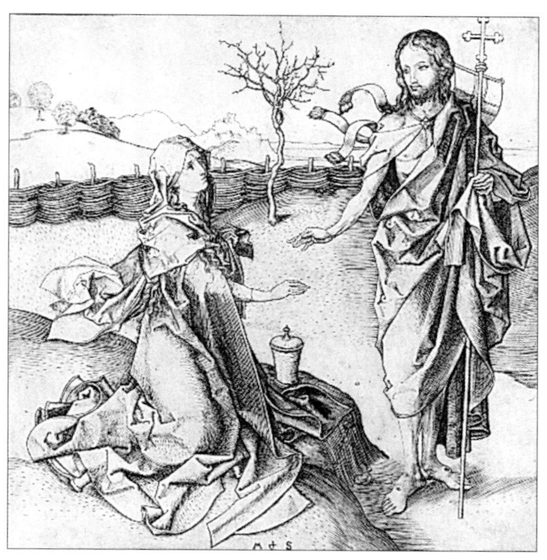

6.

Martin Schongauer, *Christ Appearing to Mary Magdalen ("Noli me Tangere"),* c. 1475–1480, engraving, National Gallery of Art, Washington, Rosenwald Collection

and one behind Christ follows the contour of his arm all the way to the Magdalen's uplifted face. The two segments of the fence meet at an angle at the gate and reflect in their orientation the gazes of the figures. Despite its extreme shallowness, the relief conveys the striking impression of depth, by means of the river flowing through the gate, the angled fence, and the juxtaposition of Christ's knee, drapery, and staff, which appear to be in different planes. The staff is in fact entirely undercut at the top (as is the stream of wine poured in the Munich relief), but covered by a portion of Christ's cloak at the bottom.

Krohm has rightly pointed to the "linear" quality of the relief. Paradoxically, Riemenschneider's figures seem to have less volume than Schongauer's: they are patterns in a plane. The landscape is extensively incised with zigzag patterns *(Tremolierung)* applied in different directions. The changes in the orientation of the pattern help distinguish one plane from another and are highly effective in creating depth in the landscape, corresponding to the hatch marks in the print; yet they also endow the landscape with a dramatic quality that is absent in Schongauer's serene composition. It is ironic that for a work intended to remain monochrome, their effect is almost coloristic. CHAPUIS

22. For an exhaustive analysis of the relationship of the relief to the print, see Krohm in Krohm and Oellermann 1992, on which many of these observations are based.

I4

c. 1490–1495, limewood, 116.8 x 34.9 x 26 (46 x 13¾ x 10¼), Museum of Fine Arts, Boston,
Gift in memory of Felix M. Warburg, by his wife, Frieda Schiff Warburg

• Technical Notes •

The entire sculpture is carved from a single block of wood, which has been deeply hollowed out (to a depth of 10.2 to 11.4 cm); the thinned wood, with an original inset, just below the Virgin's right hand has broken through. Losses include the third finger of the Virgin's right hand, and two fleurons are replacements of the nineteenth century or later. There are several splits where the wood is the thickest, notably at the base, vertically through the moon and the drapery that overlaps it; through the left side of the child; and through the Virgin's left wrist, which has been cut out and filled with a wedge. The edging of the veil has been textured with parallel cuts and the trim of her robe with zigzag cuts in imitation of fur. There is no punch work. A single circular hole in the Virgin's head, now plugged, and two small slots in the base appear to be left from the carver's vise. Black stain indicates the eyes of both figures; the whole work is coated in brown pigment, with brush marks evident on the underside of the child's left leg.

• Provenance •

Felix M. Warburg, Hamburg and New York; acquired by the museum in 1941.

• Literature •

Bier 1959a, 5–6; Raleigh 1962, 36–37, no. 6; Bier 1975, 45–47, 62 n. 23, fig. 5; Würzburg 1981, 20; Bier 1982, 35–37; Gillerman 1982, 147, no. 44; Kalden 1990, 109, 166.

THE BOSTON *Virgin and Child,* like many of Riemenschneider's earlier works, is conceptually rooted in the Upper Rhineland, particularly in the sculpture of Niclaus Gerhaert and his followers. The present figure—principally in the organization of the drapery, the upright position of the child, and the gesture of the Virgin holding the child's foot—may be compared to the Virgin from Wasserliesch, now in Trier (fig. 1). Certain details are remarkably similar to corresponding passages in the *Virgin and Child* from the cloister of the cathedral in Trier (cat. 7, fig. 1): the veil pulled over the Virgin's shoulder and diagonally across her torso; and the broad, planar treatment of the mantle, hiked up to reveal the garment underneath and drawn in at the ankles, with crumpled folds overlapping the prominent crescent moon. More generally, there is a correlation with the Master E. S. engraving of the *Virgin and Child on the Crescent Moon* (Lehrs 63) in the attenuation of the figure, the cant of the head, and the planar treatment of the drapery. The motif of the Christ child playing with his toe, on the other hand, seems to be a Netherlandish invention. It appears, for example, in Dirk Bouts' half-length *Virgin and Child* in Berlin. Riemenschneider, however, seems to have quoted this detail from the *Virgin and Child* of about 1440–1445, from the trumeau of the west portal of the Marienkapelle, Würzburg (fig. 2), which is the only other occurrence of the child crossing his left foot over his right and grasping it in his right hand.

Bier classified the known sculptural images of the Virgin and child into four compositional types reproduced by Riemenschneider and his workshop progressively throughout his career.[1] These findings were critically reevaluated by Holger Simon in his 1998 study of the Creglingen altarpiece.[2] The Boston *Virgin and Child,* along with a Virgin and child once in the Himmelstein collection, subsequently in the cathedral of Würzburg, then destroyed in 1945 (cat. 16, fig. 2), and the *Virgin and Child* in the Neumünster, Würzburg, which stands on a corbel dated 1493 (fig. 3), belong to the earliest of these four groups.[3] As the dated corbel is presumed to be original, the Neumünster Virgin is the earliest of only three figures

1. Bier 1975, 41–65; in a compressed form, he repeated his findings in the fourth volume of his monographic study, Bier 1978, 16–25.

2. Simon 1998, 167–179.

3. Bier 1975, 44–47, placed the Virgin from Werbach, lost in World War II (see cat. 19, fig. 1), in this early grouping, but it seems clear that this sculpture belongs in Simon's second group along with the *Virgin and Child* in Vienna and that in Karlsruhe (cat. 19, figs. 2 and 3).

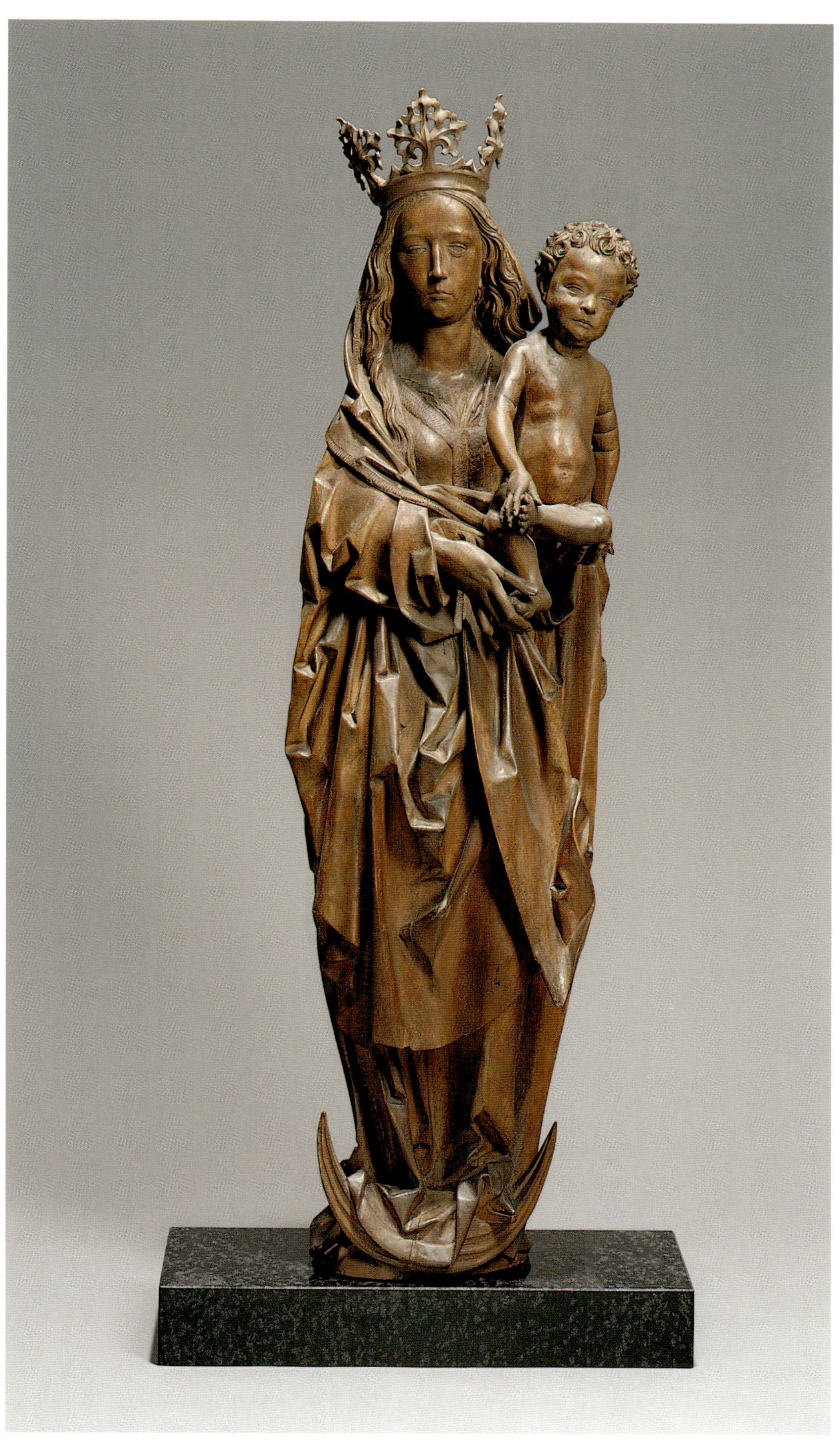

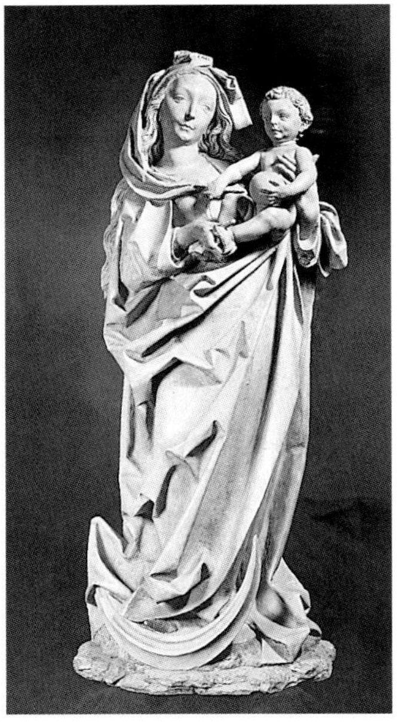

Circle of Niclaus Gerhaert von Leiden,
Virgin and Child on the Crescent Moon
from Wasserliesch, 1460–1470,
limestone, Bischöfliches Dom- und
Diözesanmuseum, Trier

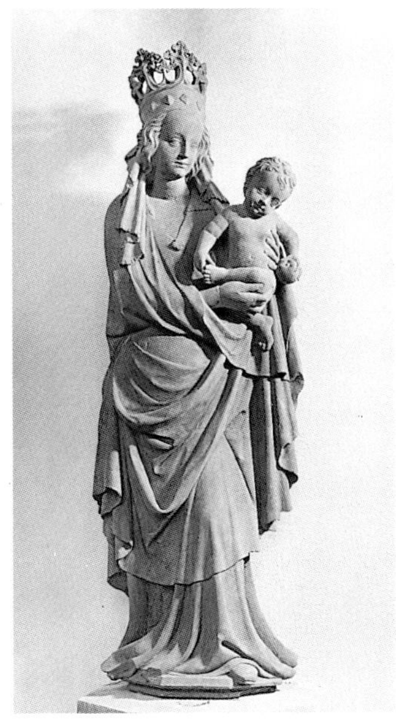

Würzburg, *Virgin and Child,* from the
trumeau of the west portal
of the Marienkapelle, c. 1440–1445,
sandstone, Mainfränkisches
Museum, Würzburg

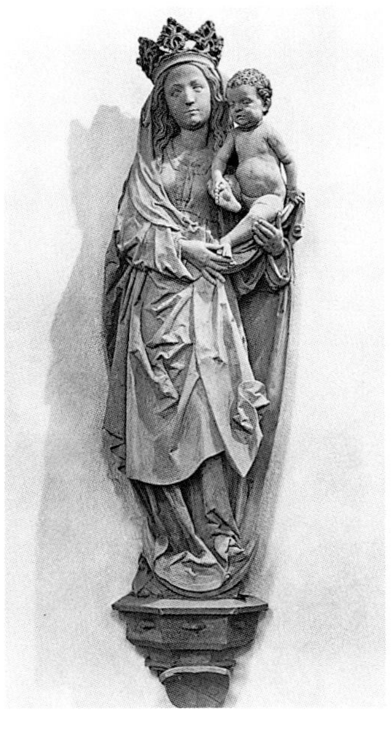

*Virgin and Child on the Crescent
Moon,* 1493, sandstone, Neumünster,
Würzburg

in the Riemenschneider oeuvre that have associated dates, making it pivotal in dating related works.

Bier correctly noted that Riemenschneider's earlier Virgin and child groups are markedly plastic, volumetric, and dimensional: their sculptural movement is defined not by an S-curve in a single plane, but by a spiral form rotated in space.[4] These images were intended to be viewed not only frontally but from any point in an arc of 180 degrees. While the Boston *Virgin and Child* is the most frontal of the three in this early group—the child is as upright and frontal as his mother—the diagonal direction of the veil across the Virgin's torso, paralleling her arm, leads the eye in a counterclockwise direction. The relatively simple organization of drapery on the Virgin's right side resolves in a massing of bold folds, projecting into space—one from the mantle drawn across her torso and the other from the mantle dropping off her right shoulder—with a void in between that cradles the upright Christ. The muted S-curve stance of the Virgin, the upright posture of the child, the crown, the narrowness of the drapery at the feet all reinforce the impression of exceptional height. On the other hand, the projecting points of the moon and jutting drapery folds, the Virgin's hand, and the child's limbs—all of which are completely undercut—relieve the verticality of the group.

The Himmelstein *Virgin and Child* generally employs the same drapery system, with individual folds corresponding closely, but the composition is less columnar. The Boston and Neumünster Virgins relate more closely. The patterns of drapery folds are the same in their essentials, although they are more effectively executed and rationally distributed in the Neumünster sculpture. Clarifying the concept of the drapery movement, different form is given to the folds of the mantle that wrap around the Virgin's arm than to those across her legs or those that descend from beneath her hand. And the mantle on the Virgin's right side is held up by the child, creating a curtain effect that visually gives support to the child and counterbalances the volume of the child with the void below. At the same time, this cloak partly reveals the underlying form of the Virgin, amplifying the gentle S-curve of her stance.

Bier, noting a strong resemblance between the faces of the Boston Virgin and the Münnerstadt *Mary Magdalen* (cat. 13, fig. 1), placed the present figure in the early 1490s, before the Neumünster group (which he gave an unsparing reading). He believed this work to have been executed under Riemenschneider's direction with the help of an assistant.[5] Kalden argued that the Boston sculpture was executed entirely by an assistant, and, pointing to the rigid stance of the Virgin, the stiff treatment of the drapery, the egg-shaped head, and the slight bend in the neck, posited that the same assistant was responsible for the figure of John the Evangelist in the superstructure of the Münnerstadt altarpiece.[6] Simon maintained that while it is possible to group figures within Riemenschneider's oeuvre according to formal or stylistic motifs, it is very difficult, in the absence of documentary evidence, to assign dates.[7] This is true in large part because Riemenschneider relied on numerous artistically voiceless assistants, who drew on workshop models to produce like images over extended periods of time. It certainly compounds the problem of distinguishing an "autograph" work.

The relationship of the Boston *Virgin and Child* to the Neumünster sandstone work is therefore difficult to parse. It is unlikely that the former is a model for the latter, for the sculptural concept as well as the refinements of detail are more clearly expressed in the Neumünster group than in its putative model (see cat. 45).[8] Indeed, it is not clear whether the Boston group preceded or followed the Neumünster version. It is probable that both relied on common models. While the formal treatment of the drapery is strikingly close, the facial types are altogether different, with the Boston Virgin's being elongated and melancholic and the Neumünster's being oval and contemplative. Likewise the characters of the two figures of the Christ child are very different. Both assume the beguiling pose of grasping one foot, but the expression of the Neumünster child seems distant and rueful, while that of the Boston child seems cheerful and carefree. In contrast to the more individualized head of the Christ child in the Neumünster group, the head of the Boston child is a stock type and can be seen in identical form, for example, in the *Anna Selbdritt* dated 1500.[9] The formal correspondences nonetheless suggest that the Boston sculpture was executed within a few years of 1493 by a sculptor who was not entirely able to convey the spatial relationships of the drapery patterns or the conceptual coherence of the sculpture. HUSBAND

6. Kalden 1990, 108–109.

7. Simon 1998, 170.

8. It is uncertain whether either the statuette in the Voralberger Landesmuseum, Bregenz (see Würzburg 1981, 225–227, figs. 150, 151), or the similar statuette in Euskirchen (Bier 1975, 48, fig. 8) was intended as a model for the Himmelstein Virgin, however close in formal terms they might be.

9. Inv. no. 14 067. See Muth 1982, 126-127, no. 27.

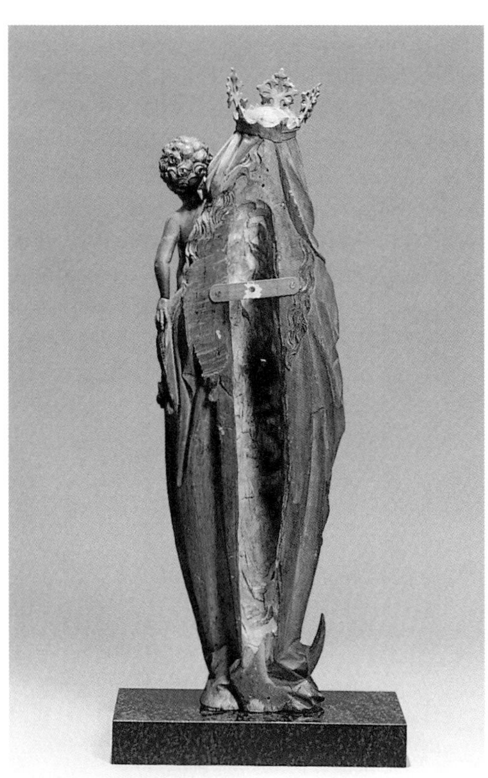

Back view of catalogue no. 14

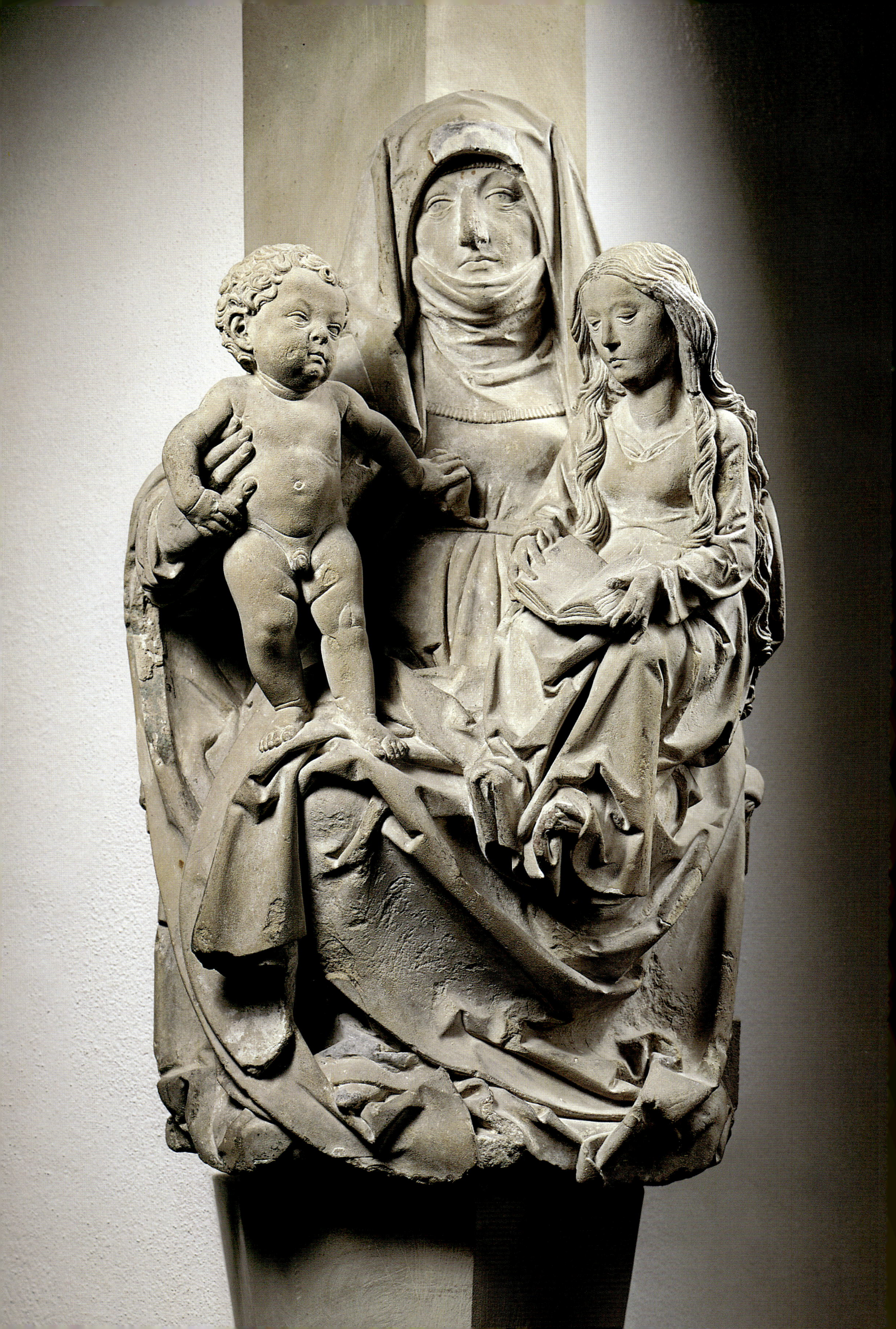

ENTHRONED SAINT ANNE WITH THE VIRGIN AND THE CHRIST CHILD
(ANNA SELBDRITT)

c. 1490–1495, sandstone, 78 x 48 x 30 cm (30¾ x 18⅞ x 11¾), Mainfränkisches Museum, Würzburg, Freunde Mainfränkischer Kunst und Geschichte

• *Technical Notes* •

The group is carved from a single block of greenish gray, fine-grained sandstone. Two areas—the front of Saint Anne's veil and the locks at the Virgin's left temple—are additions but appear to be original.[1] Compared with other sandstone sculpture by Riemenschneider, which has been largely reworked by restorers, the *Anna Selbdritt* is in remarkably good condition, and its surface is largely original.[2] Missing chips are scattered over the surface, especially along drapery folds and in the Virgin's hair and fingers. Modern replacements include Saint Anne's nose, the tip of her right foot, and the child's penis.[3] According to Bodo Buczynski and Artur Kratz, most of Riemenschneider's sandstone sculpture was intended to remain uncolored, with the Neumünster Virgin (cat. 14, fig. 3) being a notable exception.[4] Traces of pigment of undetermined age suggest that the *Anna Selbdritt* was painted at some point, however, and the eyes of the figures were painted directly on the stone.[5] The back of the figure is carved at an angle of about 140 degrees, according to Mainfränkisches Museum conservator Stephanie Kleidt, presumably to allow its placement against an octagonal column.

• *Provenance* •

Said to come from the convent of the Benedictine nuns in Kitzingen near Würzburg; [Seligsberger in Würzburg]; acquired in 1905 by the Fränkischer Kunst- und Altertumsverein Würzburg, whose collections form the Mainfränkisches Museum.

• *Literature* •

Weber 1911, 20, 98–99; Schrade 1927, 171–174 n. 416; Bier 1930, 46, 196; Diehl 1936, 21; Bier 1944–1945, 23, 24, 27 n. 53; Freeden 1954, 157–160; Gerstenberg 1962, 216 n. 68; Freeden 1981, 40, 50; Würzburg 1981, 253–255; Muth 1982, 82–87; Kalden 1990, 137 n. 507.

SITTING ON A rectangular cushioned throne and wearing the headdress and wimple typical of older women, Saint Anne holds the Virgin Mary and the Christ child on her knees. Mary, whose youthful face and uncovered head and neck contrast with the rendering of her mother, is engrossed in her reading. The pudgy Christ child engages in a balancing act on Anne's knee, reaching for her breast for support. His precarious stance contrasts with the mass and static pose of his grandmother, and it introduces a keen sense of life into the group. This impression is also conveyed by the gentleness of Anne's grasp, Christ's reaching for her little finger, and the almost playful expression on his face. This representation, traditionally known by its German name, *Anna Selbdritt,* emphasizes Anne's role as Christ's ancestor, and thereby as a link in the doctrine of redemption; the pear in the child's left hand is a reference to the original sin and thus to his Atonement, or Passion. The many representations of the subject reflect the popularity of the cult of Saint Anne in Germany. While sometimes shown in the same scale as her mother (see cat. 8), the Virgin is more often depicted smaller, as here, to give Anne greater prominence.

As is the case with other examples of Riemenschneider's best work (see cat. 11), the sculptural conception of this group reflects its intended placement. The ensemble was apparently installed against an octagonal column.[6] One of Riemenschneider's most plastic works, the *Anna Selbdritt* is carved three-quarters in the round, and it invites approaches from multiple viewpoints. Seen in full profile from either side, the sculpture is entirely coherent. Saint Anne's arms, embracing the smaller figures, lead the eye from the sides toward the center of the group, encouraging the viewer to walk around it. This movement is echoed on either side by the broader folds of the mantle that run obliquely from Saint Anne's elbows

1. Muth 1982, 86.

2. See Würzburg 1981, 249, for diagrams documenting the surface of the *Adam* and *Eve* from the Marienkapelle.

3. Muth 1982, 86.

4. Würzburg 1981, 335–336.

5. Würzburg 1981, 253–255.

6. Freeden 1981, 40; see also Würzburg 1981. In addition, the underside of the sculpture shows evidence of having been originally mounted on an octagonal console.

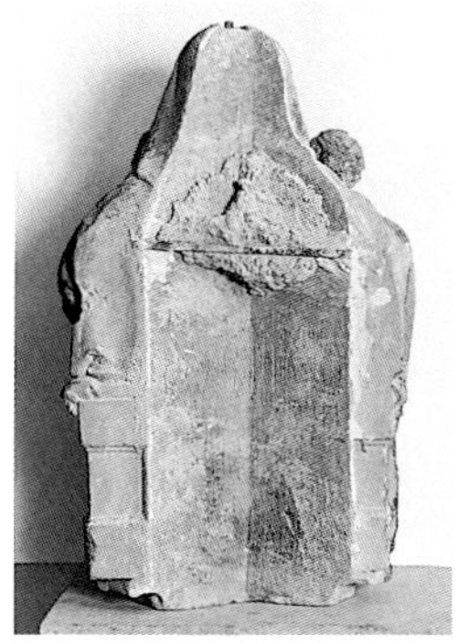

Back view of
catalogue no. 15

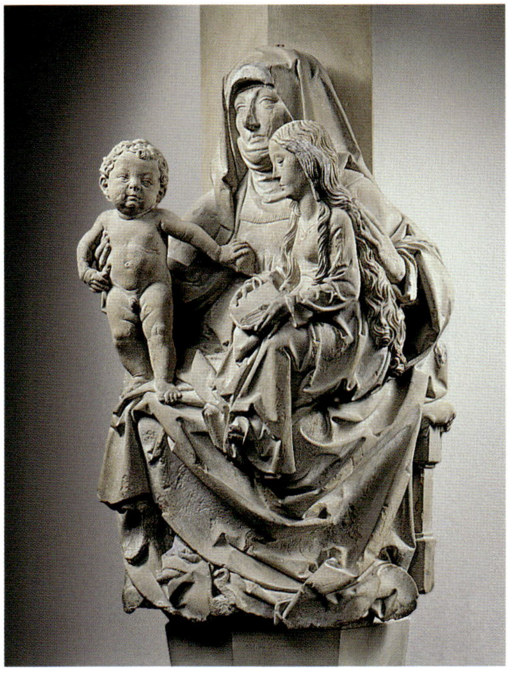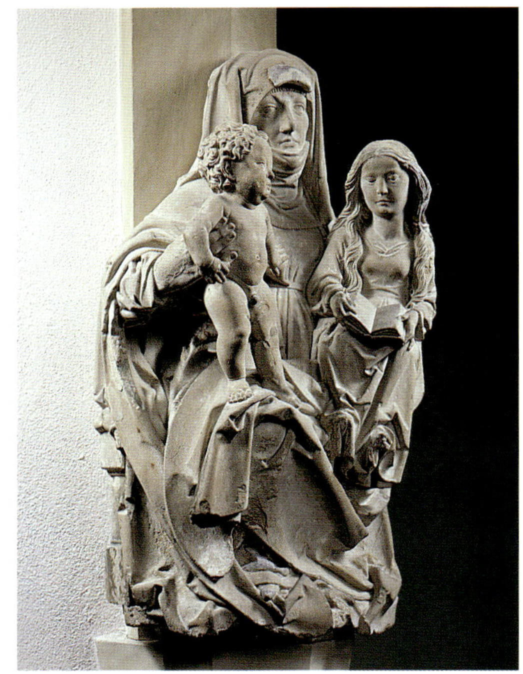

Alternate views of catalogue no. 15

7. Würzburg 1981, 336.

8. I am grateful to Michele Marincola for clarifying the physical qualities of stone as a sculptor's medium.

9. For a review of the different opinions expressed on the date of the group see Alfred Schädler in Würzburg 1981, 253; Schädler dates the sculpture early, as does Muth 1982, 82—to 1490–1495 and to c. 1495, respectively.

10. Muth 1982, 82.

to the front of the sculpture. The monolithic impression is strengthened by the absence of major verticals in the cloak, most of the folds in the front being oblique. The drapery at the bottom rests on a polygonal base, which itself was certainly supported by a console. The sculpture was presumably surmounted by a canopy.

While Riemenschneider is now best known for his carved altarpieces and other works in wood, his fame in the early decades of his rediscovery was based on his sandstone sculpture. Often these monumental works are anchored in an architectural framework and are simply too large and heavy to transport safely. The *Anna Selbdritt* from Würzburg is an eloquent illustration of Riemenschneider's mastery of sculpture in stone. The material presents different qualities than wood does. Sandstone is brittle because of its crystalline structure, while wood is tougher because of its cellular structure. Although stone breaks easily if dropped or struck, it offers greater resistance to precision cutting with a chisel than wood does. The sculptor must therefore combine physical strength with self-control, removing layer after layer of material toward the intended form.[7] The present sculpture is distinguished by the attention lavished on details, such as the intricately rendered hair of the smaller figures. Saint Anne's hands, in which veins and sinews are apparent, achieve the same sophistication in surface treatment as Riemenschneider's best works in

wood (see cat. 24). His virtuosity as a stone carver resides in his ability, despite the fragility and intractability of his material, to achieve several areas of deep undercutting: the stone is pierced and penetrated so that the Christ child is entirely freestanding.[8]

Several features of the Würzburg *Anna Selbdritt* allow it to be dated to the early years of the sculptor's career.[9] The work is related to sculpture from Strasbourg, which is probably one of the places Riemenschneider was trained. Comparison to a sandstone group of the same subject made in Strasbourg (cat. 8) reveals a strong resemblance not only in the facial type of the Virgin but also in the placement of broad areas of drapery across the knees. In addition, portions of Saint Anne's drapery project over the polygonal base, a motif favored by Niclaus Gerhaert, who was active in Strasbourg (cat. 6). The spatial presence of the sculpture, due in part to its intended installation against a column, also places this work in Riemenschneider's early oeuvre. The volumetric treatment of form and a certain naive charm in the depiction of the Christ child connect this work with the Cologne *Virgin and Child* (cat. 16). As Muth pointed out, the sensitive surface treatment of the sandstone here recalls works in that material from about 1490, such as the tombstone of Eberhard von Grumbach in Rimpar (cat. 18, fig. 1) and the *Adam* and *Eve* from the Marienkapelle (Chapuis essay, fig. 3), although the latter do not achieve the same degree of spatial presence.[10] CHAPUIS

VIRGIN AND CHILD ON THE CRESCENT MOON

c. 1495, limewood, 76.5 x 27 x 19 (34⅛ x 10⅝ x 7½), Museum für Angewandte Kunst, Cologne,
Sammlung Wilhelm Clemens

• Technical Notes•

The sculpture is carved from a single block of limewood with the grain running vertically; the back was
neatly hollowed out to minimize cracking. In 1960 a
private conservator removed a layer of nineteenth-
century polychromy, under which lay remnants of
older paint and bole. Although these were mostly
removed,[1] some traces are still visible. It is unclear
whether the wood originally had a monochrome layer
or layers of paint and gilding. At present, only the
pupils of the figures' eyes are painted, which gives
direction to their gaze. Despite minor breaks—such
as finials of the Virgin's crown, a portion of her veil,
parts of the drapery, the child's toes, the small fingers
of the child's hands and of the Virgin's left hand—
the sculpture is in good condition overall. There are
small additions in the Virgin's left hand, the drapery
under her right hand, the child's abdomen and shoulders, and the right side of the base. The wood has suffered little from insect damage except in the lower
frontal portion of the dress; losses, especially near the
base, and insect tunnels have been filled with beeswax
and are unobtrusive, as are the few cracks, now filled
with wedge-shaped repairs.[2] An elongated burn runs
through the V-shaped folds of the Virgin's cloak, to
one side of her protruding knee.[3]

• Provenance •

The sculpture was acquired in 1909 on the Munich
art market by the painter Wilhelm Clemens, who bequeathed it with his collection to the Cologne Kunstgewerbemuseum (Museum für Angewandte Kunst)
in 1921. It is probably the same Virgin and child that
belonged to administrative counsel Martinengo in
the nineteenth century, and later to Canon Wicken-
mayer, both in Würzburg, then entered the collection of Ferdinand Broili in Paris, from whom it was
acquired, before 1884, by the Munich collector Brauer.

• Literature •

Straus-Ernst 1921, 15; Creutz 1922, 419; Schäfer 1923,
22; Haedecke 1961; Klesse and Haedecke 1963, no. 67;
Volk 1971; Bier 1975; Würzburg 1981, 230–231; Bier
1982, 89–90; Kalden 1990, 91; Söding 1998, 154–155.

LIKE OTHER IMAGES of the Virgin and child
by Riemenschneider (see cats. 14, 45), this sculpture
refers to the woman described in the Apocalypse—
"a woman clothed with the sun, with the moon under her feet, and on her head a crown of twelve stars"
(Revelation 12:1)—the hem of her garment falling
over a crescent moon and her crown bearing twelve
finials. Images of the Virgin as the woman of the
Apocalypse became extremely popular in the late
1400s and were produced in large numbers after Six-
tus IV granted an indulgence of 11,000 years for each
specific prayer said in front of one of them.[4] Mary
was often called the second Eve, who, by giving birth
to Christ, brought redemption to mankind. The pear
held by the Christ child is clearly an allusion to the
original sin and, by extension, to his future Passion.

The Cologne group is among Riemenschneider's most appealing and sculpturally complex images
of the Virgin and child. Although Mary's slender body
is articulated in a broad S-curve, the figure makes a
solid, monolithic impression. She holds her elbows
not against her body but at a slight distance, causing
the contour of her cloak to form a bracket on either
side of her body. The effect of the encompassing com-
plexes of drapery engenders the overall volume of the
figure, relative to her seemingly slight stature.[5] The
sense of mass is heightened by several horizontal
accents, such as the position of the Christ child or
the portion of the Virgin's cloak draped around the
front of her body, the hem curving below her knees
like an apron. The weightiness of the figure finds a
psychological echo in Mary's broad, pensive face. Her

1. Bier 1975, 43; Würzburg
1981, 230.

2. For a more detailed published
discussion of the sculpture's
condition, see Bier 1975, 61.

3. Bier 1975, 61. I am grateful to
Hans-Werner Nett, conservator
at the Museum für Angewandte
Kunst, for kindly providing
me with a detailed condition
report on the sculpture.

4. Sixten Ringbom, "*Maria in
Sole* and the Virgin of the
Rosary," *Journal of the Warburg
and Courtauld Institutes* 2
(1962), 326.

5. Krohm 1998, 116, describing
this phenomenon in the sculpture of Niclaus Gerhaert von
Leiden, used the metaphor of
the core and the shell (see also
cat. 5).

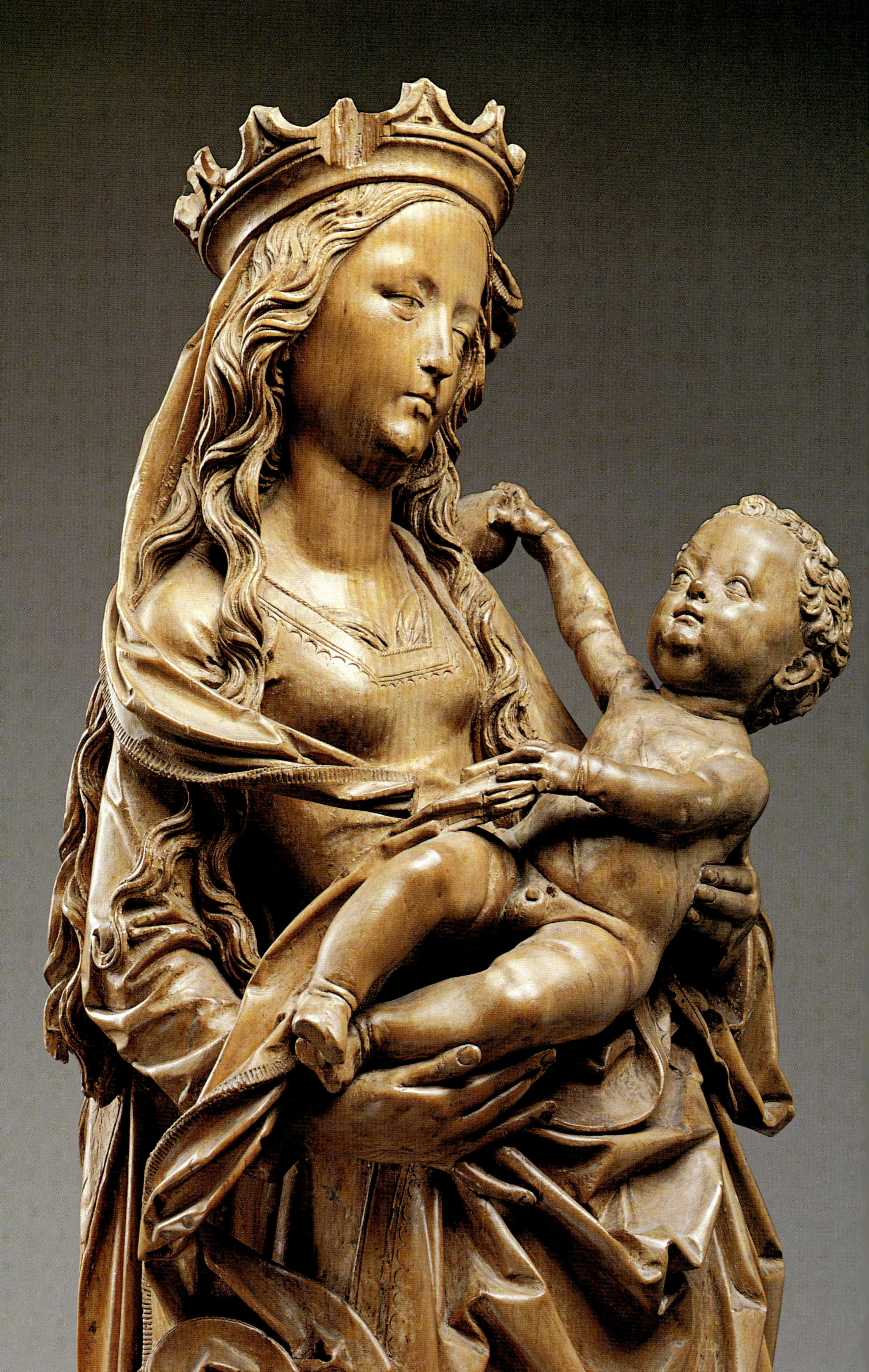

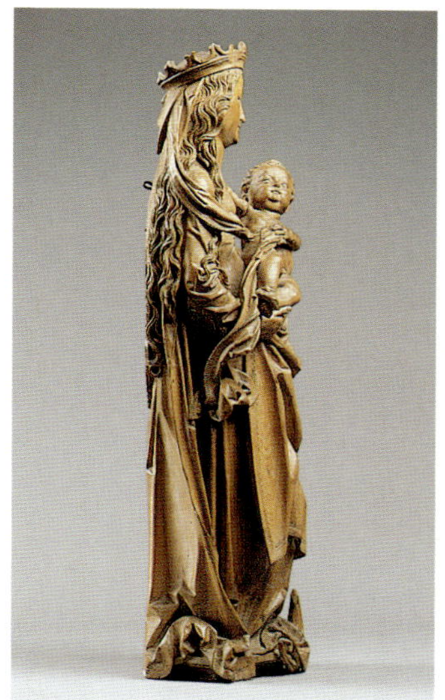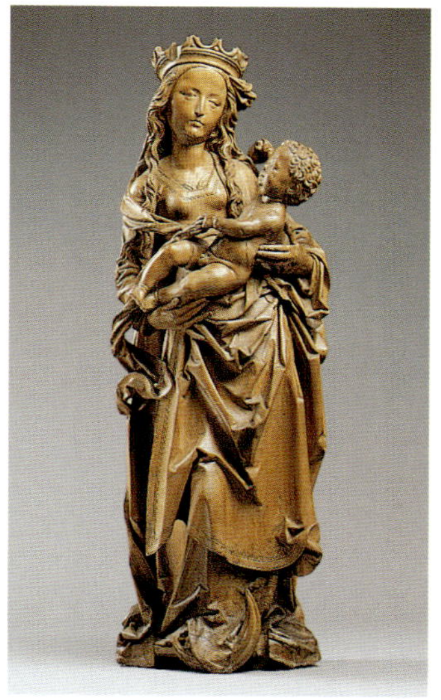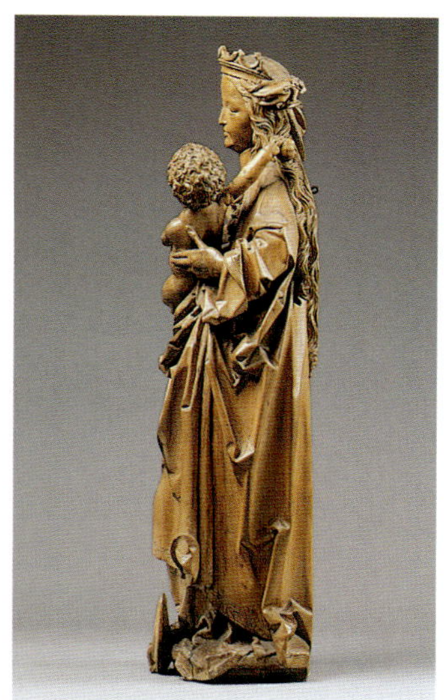

Alternate views of catalogue no. 16

painted eyes are directed at her child, whose playfulness contrasts with her serious expression and static pose. With one hand the child pulls her veil, creating a calligraphic swirl of fabric arrested in midair. His legs seeming to wiggle like those of an infant, he balances a pear on her shoulder while looking at her attentively.

This work stands out in Riemenschneider's oeuvre by its depth. The figure allows the viewer to move around it in an arc of 180 degrees. As profile views reveal, the sides are carved with as much attention to detail as the front—the strands of hair falling behind the Virgin's right shoulder, for instance, are as exquisitely rendered as the ones in front of it. More important, the sculpture is not an assemblage of different views, but a continuous figure in space. Spatial elements lead the eye around the figure and thereby encourage movement. The head veil, pulled by the child, forms a visual arrow that draws one from the left side to the front of the sculpture. The oblique positioning of the infant leads the eye across the figure to the right, and his right arm, paralleling the Virgin's left, points to the profile view. The intelligence of the spatial conception is evident in the detail of the head veil, caught under the crown on the Virgin's left side and reappearing over the opposite shoulder. Although the viewer cannot walk around the sculpture—the back is flat, and the piece was made to stand in front of a wall—one can mentally follow the veil behind her neck and think of the sculpture as a continuum in space. This conception of a sculpture as a spiral, or a volume winding about a center, is one

of Riemenschneider's most fundamental borrowings from Niclaus Gerhaert (see cat. 7).

The sculpture offers a few clues as to its possible original function and context. The superb execution, apparent in the sensitive treatment of surfaces, the carefully cut decoration of the costume, and the meticulous attention to detail, suggests that it was intended for relatively close viewing. It is unlikely that the group was part of a retable, because its placement in a shrine would have concealed its sides. Rather, it was probably intended as a cult figure, made to stand on a console against a wall or a pillar, possibly over a small altar, where it could be seen from a half circle. The latter is supported by presence of an elongated burn mark, probably caused by a candle, on one of the large triangular folds on the front of the figure. Since the sculpture invites the beholder to move from left to right, it is attractive to hypothesize that this was how it was originally approached, by entering its site, perhaps a lateral chapel, from the left. Some of Riemenschneider's finest works clearly take into account the intended position of the viewer—for instance, the Cleveland *Saint Jerome* (cat. 11)—or refer to the space for which they were intended, such as the *Holy Blood* altarpiece in Rothenburg. The Cologne *Virgin and Child,* it seems, is no exception.

In the absence of documentary evidence, it is solely through stylistic analysis that one can reach a date for the Cologne Virgin. Bier, the first to address this issue fully, correctly pointed out the resemblance of the Cologne sculpture to the much larger sandstone Virgin in Würzburg (fig. 1). Indeed, the two

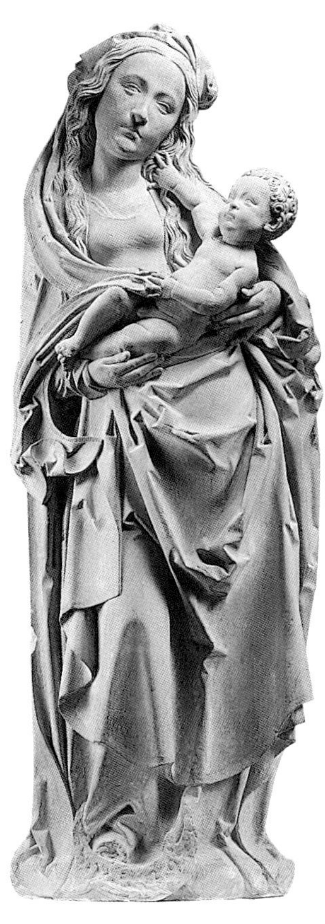

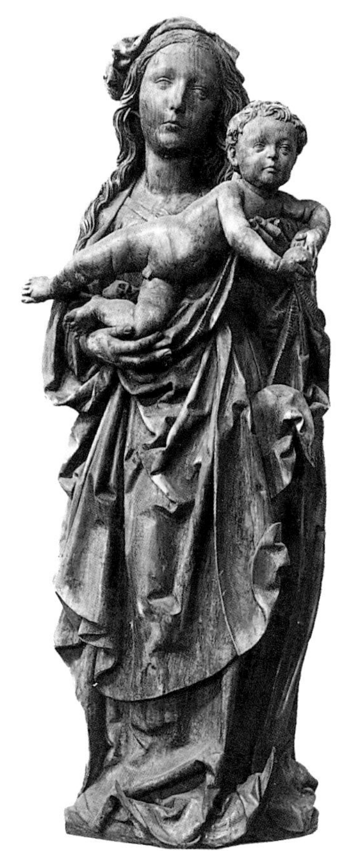

1.

Virgin and Child, c. 1518–1520, sandstone, Mainfränkisches
Museum, Würzburg

2.

Virgin and Child from the Himmelstein Collection,
c. 1493, limewood, formerly Würzburg Cathedral
(destroyed in World War II)

6. Bier 1975, 54–56.

7. Freeden 1956, 28; Schädler
1975, 103–104; Muth 1982,
100, with references to earlier
literature; Maek-Gérard
1985, 238.

8. Schädler 1975, 104; Würzburg 1981, 230–231. Although
both authors consider the
Cologne sculpture to be close to
the Neumünster Virgin, dated
1493, Timothy Husband has
observed that the Himmelstein
Virgin, in its sculptural mass
alone, offers in fact a closer
resemblance.

works share the arrangement of the figure along a
broad S-pattern, the inclination of the Virgin's head,
the positioning of the Christ child across her body,
and the head veil pulled by the child over the Virgin's
right shoulder (see also cat. 22). Bier less convincingly
suggested that Riemenschneider carved the Cologne
sculpture as a model for the one in Würzburg, and
he dated both to about 1505, between the Rothenburg and Creglingen altarpieces.[6] While some similarities in composition are evident, the two Virgins
represent radically different spatial conceptions, which
point to separate moments in Riemenschneider's development as sculptor. Conceived as a high relief for
frontal viewing, the Würzburg figure presents the
planar arrangement of forms that typifies Riemenschneider's late works, such as the Dumbarton Oaks
Virgin and Child (cat. 45) or the Maidbronn *Lamentation* of 1519–1523 (Chapuis essay, fig. 9). This has
led several authors to assign a date of 1518–1520 to

the Würzburg Virgin and to the very similar sandstone *Virgin and Child,* now in the Liebieghaus in
Frankfurt (cat. 28, fig. 3).[7] By contrast, the Cologne
sculpture is a voluminous figure that invites the viewer
to move around it and examine it from different angles.
The continuity of form in space, which is clearly a
major feature of the Cologne group, plays no role in
the Würzburg sculpture and therefore precludes the
possibility of one having been created as a preliminary stage of the other. Both Alfred Schädler and
Peter Bloch placed the Cologne Virgin in Riemenschneider's early work.[8] In its spatial presence, its use
of horizontal accents, the liveliness and type of its
Christ child, and its arrangement of the draperies in
short crumpled folds, the sculpture is very close to
the Himmelstein *Virgin and Child* of about 1493 (fig.
2). In view of these similarities, it would appear to
have been carved at about the same time. CHAPUIS

232

17

c. 1495–1500, limewood, 91 x 36 x 18.5 (35 ⅞ x 14 ⅛ x 7 ¼), The Metropolitan Museum of Art, New York, The Cloisters Collection

• *Technical Notes* •

The sculpture is cut from a large block of relatively unblemished limewood with the grain running vertically, to which several pieces of the same wood have been attached. The surface treatment is consistent throughout, suggesting that the additions are original and that they were doweled and glued to the larger block before carving. The additions serve two purposes: some increase the width of the principal block (one long piece running from the saint's right shoulder to the chair, and one making up the triangular fold of drapery over his left knee); others appear to be repairs where the artist may have carved too deeply or where knots may have jeopardized the stability of the sculpture (two rectangular pieces of wood, glued from the back, under the saint's left arm). The back was hollowed out with broad curved chisels held perpendicular to the direction of the grain. The wood is extremely thin in portions of the drapery, while other areas, such as the head, are fully in the round.

Several technical features support the contention that the sculpture was not originally polychromed. Even in the deepest folds, there are no traces of medieval paint or a chalk ground, which usually survive even a thorough cleaning. Furthermore, the surface shows no clear signs of having been scraped to remove a prior polychromy. More important, many of the subtlest details of the carving, such as the wrinkles in the face, would have been obscured by even a thin layer of chalk ground. Although the surface is not elaborated with the contrasting textures seen on the later monochromes, such as the privately owned *Female Saint* and the Munich *Saint Barbara* (cat. 43A, and cat. 43, fig. 1), the level of decorative carving is comparable to that of the Münnerstadt figures (cat. 13).

The figure has lost its hands, which were carved individually and doweled to the body. Traces of glue indicate that the miter and cope were originally decorated with wooden appliqué elements, some of which remain. The piece has suffered from insect damage, especially in its lower half. After an extensive technical examination, Rudolf Meyer removed the nineteenth-century polychromy in 1972. The insect channels have been left apparent, except in the face, where they were found distracting and were filled with beeswax. In 1998 Michele Marincola retouched these fills, which had discolored, and carried out a technical examination. Cross-section analysis of the surface of the *Seated Bishop* was completed in 1998, but no trace of a pigmented coating was found. The remains of an original finish may have been removed inadvertently during a prior restoration.

• *Provenance* •

In the collection of Count Hans Wilczek, Burg Kreuzenstein (near Vienna), in 1904; acquired from the Blumka Gallery in 1970.

• *Literature* •

Leisching 1908, fig. 55, no. 116; Nostitz 1975; Würzburg 1981, 210–213; *Metropolitan Museum of Art Guide* (New York, 1983), 374–375; Wixom 1988, 28–29.

WEARING A MITER and a fringed cope over a belted tunic, the aged bishop is depicted full-length. He sits erect, with his feet tucked under his chair. The figure is turned to his left so that his legs and head are viewed obliquely, while his upper body is depicted slightly more frontally; his gaze is focused on a point to his left. In the original state of the sculpture, the saint's hands would have emphasized the broad S-curve of the drapery, his left hand being higher than the right. The loss of the hands, and therefore of distinguishing attributes, precludes a precise identification, although either Burchard or Kilian, both patron saints of Würzburg, are possible candidates.

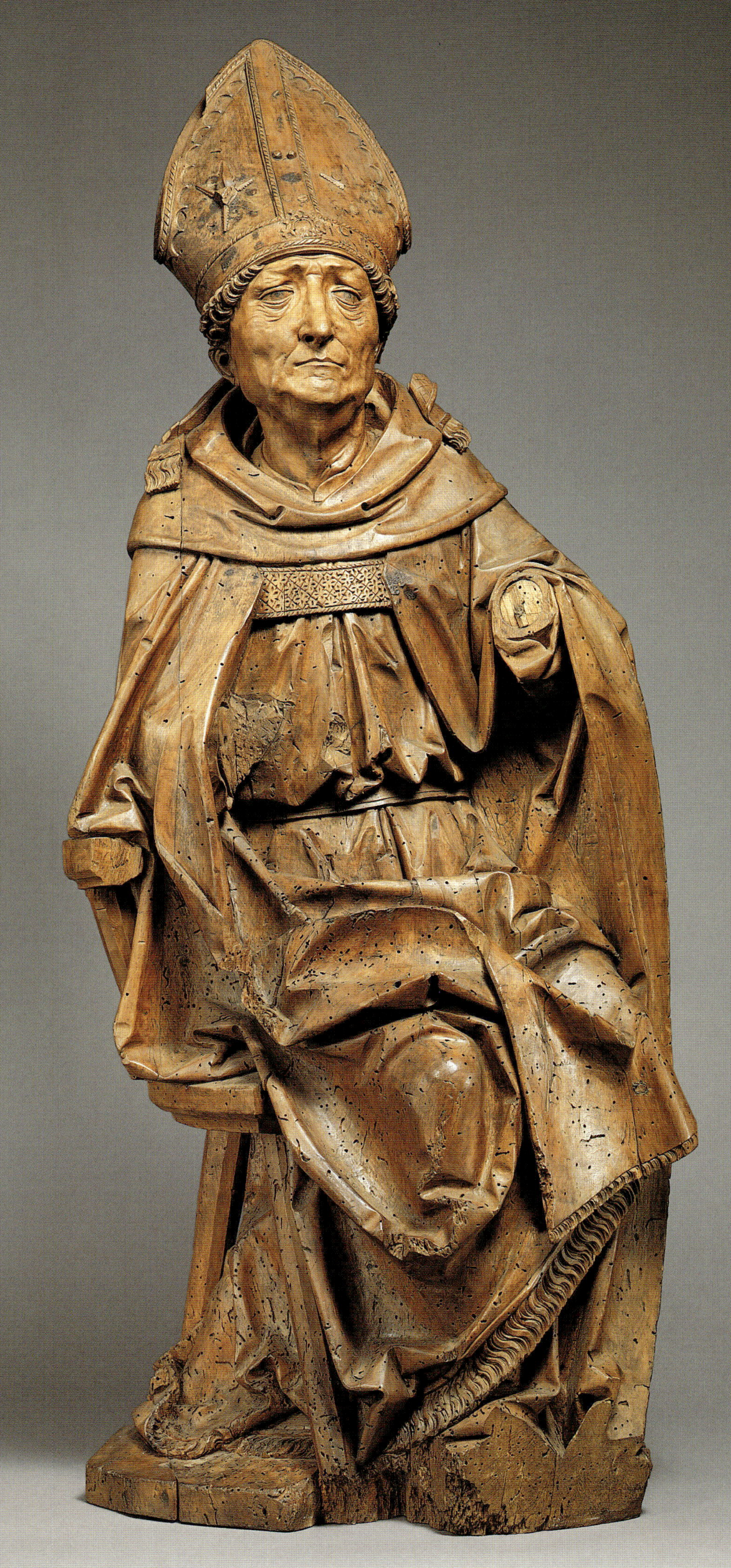

The pose of the figure suggests that it might instead be a church father—Saint Augustine, bishop of Hippo, or Saint Ambrose, bishop of Milan—and might have been part of a *Church Fathers* altarpiece.[1] The work is too large to have served as an object for private devotion, and, unlike the Munich *Saint James* and the Washington *Bishop Saint* (cats. 31 and 44), it does not face the viewer and thus would not have been an independent cult figure. Late Gothic retables that incorporate individual statues side by side, as opposed to those with a unified composition (see Chapuis essay, fig. 5), usually show the figures standing. By contrast, the church fathers, whose iconography derives from classical authors' portraits, were often depicted sitting at a desk or lectern, surrounded by scholars' attributes, and reading or writing in a book. A contemporary example is Michael Pacher's *Church Fathers* altarpiece, made for the church of Neustift near Brixen (fig. 1). The torsion in the body of the Cloisters bishop and the position of his hands would have accommodated a lectern, while his gaze suggests that he would originally have been placed at the left side of an altarpiece. Given his size, it is improbable that he would have been installed in a predella, as were the more diminutive Münnerstadt evangelists. In all likelihood he sat in the central shrine of a smaller altarpiece, as one of the four church fathers: Ambrose, Augustine, Gregory, or Jerome.

Although actually a high relief, this sculpture conveys a striking sense of volume and depth through a rich play of interconnecting curves. The general pattern of the drapery follows a broad, three-dimensional S-shape. The folds fall from the saint's right shoulder onto the chair, then across his lap to his left knee. The middle section of the body is an area of great spatial complexity, with its twisting motion and the deep undercutting of fabric, which adds to the sense of volume. The vertical folds of the cope function as brackets around this area, and the bishop's right knee, pressing against the garment, is the center of a vortex of deep folds.

The sculpture has its closest parallels, both in conception and in quality, in the evangelists from the Münnerstadt altarpiece of 1492–1494. The pose and the orchestration of the drapery are comparable to those of the *Saint Matthew,* with its oblique positioning of the legs and more frontal view of the upper body. The bishop's right arm is covered by his cope, while his elbow, distinguishable through the

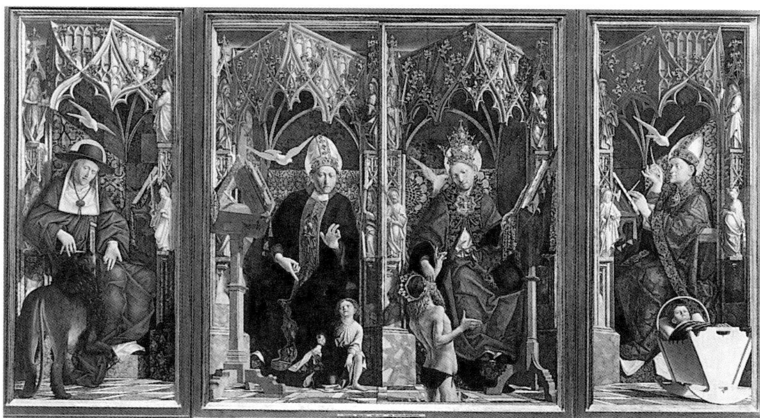

1.

Michael Pacher, *Church Fathers* altarpiece, interior of the wings, c. 1480, oil and tempera on fir, Bayerische Staatsgemäldesammlungen, Munich, Alte Pinakothek

fabric, pushes the garment away from his body. The same effect is achieved with the left arm of the Münnerstadt *Saint John.* Krohm has pointed out that the Cloisters bishop shows a more systematized organization of drapery patterns, especially in the lower portion of the figure, suggesting a slightly later date than the Münnerstadt evangelists.[2]

The date of about 1495–1500 is supported by the extremely sensitive treatment of the face, which achieves a certain psychological depth. Through delicate carving, Riemenschneider describes the structure of the skull and the jowly flesh of the bishop. Several authors have commented on the resemblance of this face to that of Rudolf von Scherenberg, bishop of Würzburg, whose effigy Riemenschneider carved between 1496 and 1499 (see Kemperdick essay, fig. 1).[3] Indeed, both heads show sunken cheeks, a finely drawn mouth with thin lips, a square chin, and curved grooves under the eyes. Although each visage is a striking physiognomy, neither is properly speaking a portrait. Scherenberg died three years before Riemenschneider received the commission for the monument from his successor, Lorenz von Bibra. It would appear that both bishops follow a type—that of an old man—which Riemenschneider probably developed while beginning to work on the Scherenberg monument. The connections with both the Scherenberg effigy and the Münnerstadt evangelists support a date for the Cloisters bishop of around 1495–1500, making it one of the few surviving major works in wood from the middle of the decade.
CHAPUIS

1. This hypothesis was first put forward by Krohm in Würzburg 1981, 211.

2. Würzburg 1981, 211.

3. Nostitz 1975, 55; Krohm in Würzburg 1981, 211; Wixom 1988, 29.

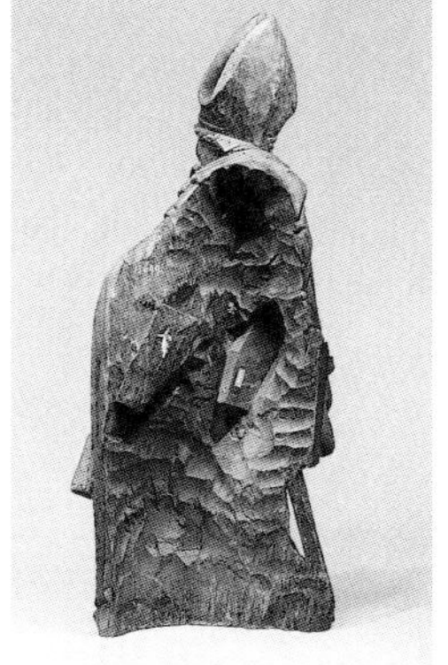

Back view of catalogue no. 17

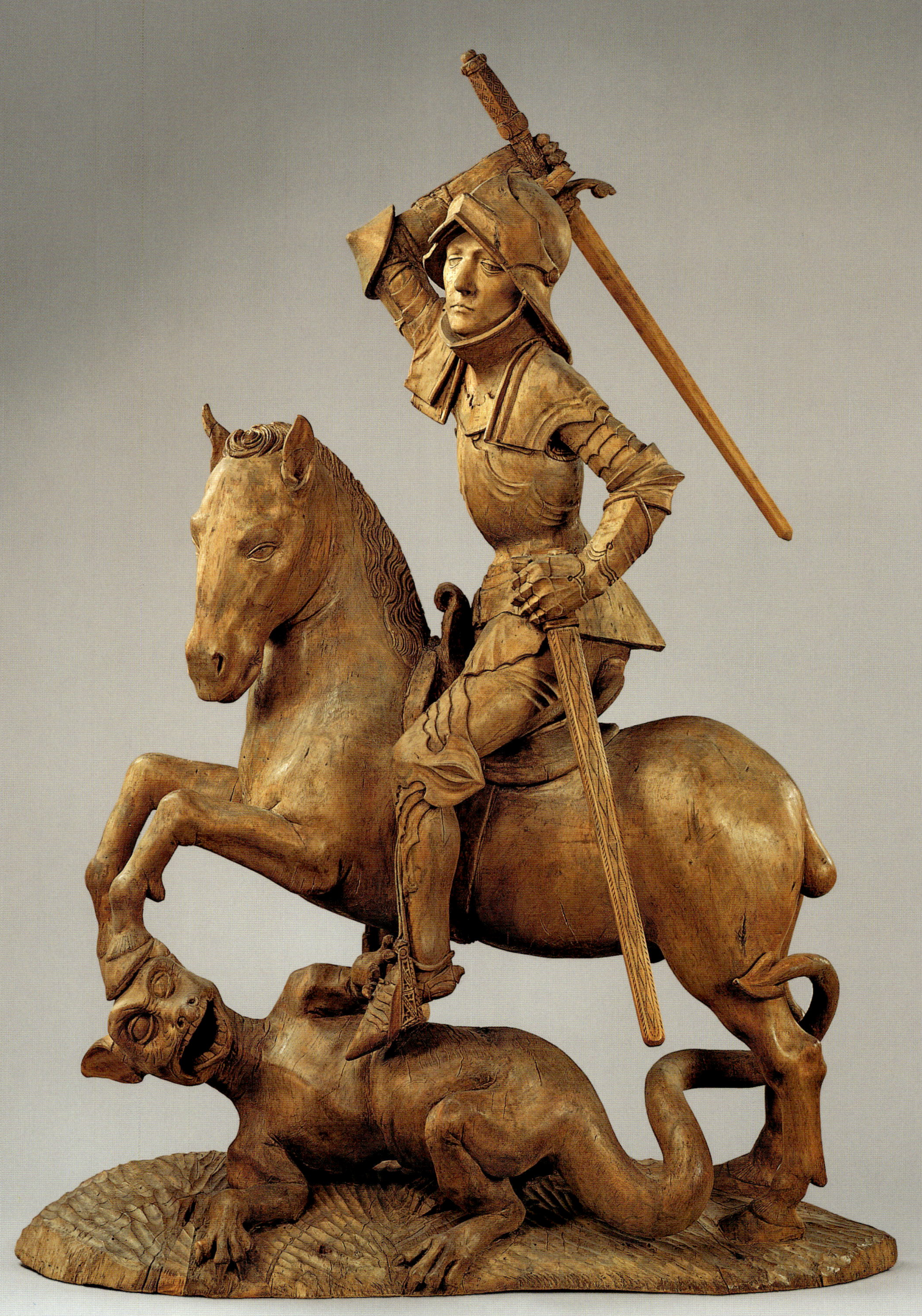

SAINT GEORGE AND THE DRAGON

1485–1490, limewood, 78.5 x 56.5 x 23.5 (30⅞ x 22¼ x 9¼), Staatliche Museen zu Berlin,
Skulpturensammlung

• Technical Notes •

This composition was apparently carved from a section of wood taken from directly above the inverted crotch of two branches; the section was split vertically, and half was used for this group. The wood at the back of the figures was closest to the bark, a piece of which can be seen around the saddle. Inset pieces of wood on the back of the horse—one (5 x 13 cm) on the flank and another (8 x 7.5 cm) on the shoulder—must have filled in compromised areas of the wood. Additional inserts are found on the back, including a wedge (10 x 3 cm) on the dragon's hip, a section (8.5 x 3 cm) in the base, and a section (6 x 43.5 x 5 cm) along the edge of the base. Replacements include the sword and sheath, the horse's left ear (the tip of the right being reattached), the dragon's right ear (the left being reattached), the tip of the dragon's tail, and the claws of both first toes. The sculpture was originally polychromed, but the minute traces of paint on the dragon's head are insufficient to determine its character. After removal of the paint, probably in the nineteenth century, a brown stain was applied. A black stain defines the pupils. In 1900 the bridle had a leather attachment, for which tiny wooden pegs survive. Insect damage had been filled with wax. The figure was conserved in 1986 by Monika List.

• Provenance •

Acquired in Würzburg by the museum, 1887.

• Literature •

Tönnies 1900, 258; Vöge 1910, 102, pl. 209; Demmler 1923, 8; Bier 1982, 121.

IN THE FULL ARMOR of a medieval knight, Saint George straddles his horse as it rears on its hind legs over the dragon. With his right hand raised over his head, he brandishes his freshly drawn sword, as his left hand steadies the sheath. Lying underneath the horse, the defeated dragon, with its pointed tail entwined in the horse's hind legs, futilely attempts to defend itself by tripping up the steed. The group stands on an island of ground textured with cuts of a rounded chisel.

Only recently, after a long period of neglect, was this appealing composition again recognized as an early work by Riemenschneider.[1] The youthful Saint George, with a wistful, even melancholy expression, focuses not on the dragon, but on an indeterminate point in space. He is not in fact represented as a heroic warrior engaged in mortal combat with a fierce dragon. Rather, the way he raises his sword should be understood as a gesture of triumph over evil, symbolized by the less-than-fearsome creature below. The horse, rearing on its hind legs like a heroic bronze, reinforces the triumphal context and further indicates that this independent group was conceived as an iconic, rather than a narrative image.

Sculpturally, the work is more complex than the forthright imagery would suggest. Its general form is determined by the annular section of the tree from which it was carved; the front of the group was closest to the heart wood, and the back closest to the bark. Thus Saint George's head, paralleling that of the horse, turns toward the viewer in three-quarter profile, conforming to the arcing of the wood. Capitalizing on necessity, Riemenschneider organized his composition in four distinct zones—the ground, the dragon, the horse, and George himself—rising within a triangular configuration. And he weighted the group toward the viewer. In their turning motions, both Saint George and his mount place their weight on the side facing the viewer, so that the left front hoof of the horse connects with the dragon, but not the right, and likewise the left foot of George, but not his right. The effect is further amplified by the care-

1. I am grateful to Hartmut Krohm for providing me with the text of his unpublished 1988 catalogue entry on this sculpture.

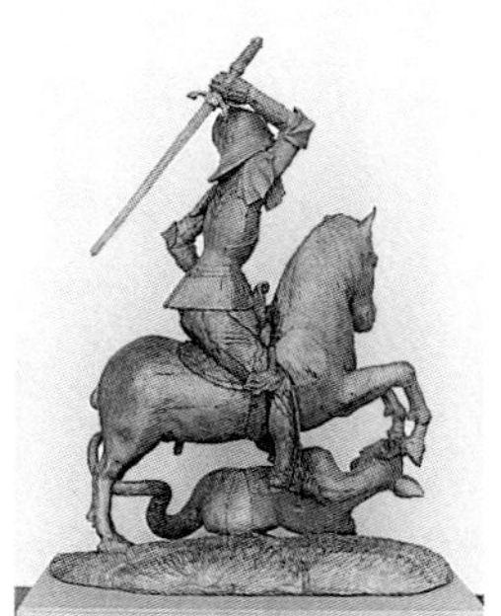

Back view of
catalogue no. 18

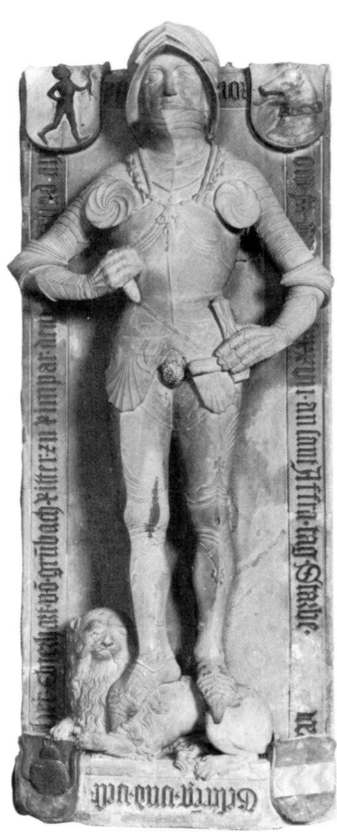

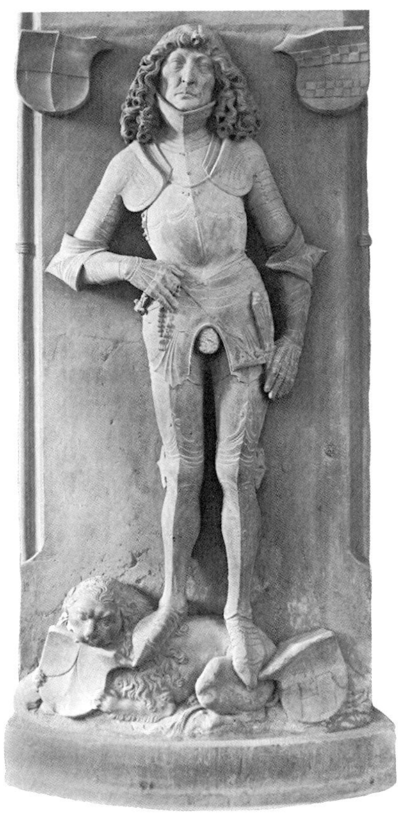

1.

Monument to Eberhard von Grumbach, c. 1487,
sandstone, Pfarrkirche, Rimpar

2.

Monument to Konrad von Schaumberg, c. 1499,
sandstone, Marienkapelle, Würzburg

fully calculated spaces that separate the component elements of the composition, creating an interplay of alternating solids and voids.

While carved entirely in the round, the *Saint George* was intended to be viewed from the front, within a vantage of about 80 degrees off either side of center. All detail and action are concentrated within this arc. The back, summarily finished and of minimal descriptive value, was not meant to be seen. In this sense the group was conceived much as the Cleveland *Saint Jerome* was (cat. 11); though possibly freestanding, it was probably set in a shallow niche or shrine or in the baldachin tracery of an altarpiece. The patching of the imperfect wood assuredly indicates that the work was originally polychromed.

According to Krohm, who rediscovered *Saint George and the Dragon* and recognized it as an autograph work of Riemenschneider,[2] this group can be numbered among the sculptor's earliest works, dating from the same period as the funerary slab of Eberhard von Grumbach (d. 1487), which may have been completed during the lifetime of the knight (fig. 1). The armor is nearly identical in structure and detail. Likewise, the treatment of the faces and the taut flesh

is very similar. Krohm also points to the funerary monument in the Marienkapelle, Würzburg, to Konrad von Schaumberg (fig. 2), who died on a trip to the Holy Land in 1499. Like Saint George, the tomb figures wear their armor weightlessly, their movement seemingly unencumbered by the heavy plate. Typical of Riemenschneider's facial types of the 1490s are the slightly slanted eyes, the long bridge of the nose, the narrow mouth, and the high cheekbones. A comparison of the *Saint George*'s features can also be made to the *Saint Sebastian* of about 1490 in Munich (cat. 20, fig. 1), to *John the Evangelist* from the 1490–1492 Münnerstadt altarpiece (cat. 13 D), and to the *Adam* of 1491–1493 from the south portal of the Marienkapelle (Chapuis essay, fig. 3).

The renewed popularity of Saint George as a symbol of the Christian chivalric order was given considerable impetus by propaganda campaigns aimed at the political aggrandizement of both Friedrich III (who brought chivalric identity to the Hapsburgs with the founding of the order of Saint George in 1469) and Maximilian I. HUSBAND

2. Bier 1978, 151, listed the group under works attributed to Riemenschneider on a stylistic basis and dated it about 1500; it goes unmentioned in his text. The same applies to Bier 1982, 121.

VIRGIN AND CHILD

c. 1495–1500, limewood, 30 x 11 x 8.5 cm (11 ¾ x 4 ⅜ x 3 ⅜), Mainfränkisches Museum, Würzburg, Stadt Würzburg

• Technical Notes •

The sculpture is cut from a single block of limewood with the grain running vertically. The wood has several knots—one on the Child's hip and another in the drapery in front of the Virgin's left shin—some of which have been removed and the resulting holes plugged, presumably later, with a different wood. The sculpture, carved fully in the round, has suffered several losses: the child's right arm, right leg, and left foot; and the Virgin's left little finger and part of her right thumb. There are portions missing from the base, at the front and at the left, and there is damage to the Virgin's nose and right cheek. These damages are ancient, and the sculpture has clearly endured considerable handling, because the breaks in these areas are not clean, but rubbed. The sculpture exhibits only minor insect damage. There are traces of red and blue paint on the wood, and the figure has clearly been freed of a polychromy of uncertain age.

• Provenance •

Acquired in 1969 from a private collection in Seligenstadt am Main with funds given by Deutsche Bank on the seventieth birthday of Dr. G. Henle.

• Literature •

Freeden 1973, 283; Bier 1975, 49–50; Bier 1978, 150; Würzburg 1981, 15, 228–229; Muth 1982, 118–121; Zimmermann 1985, 336; Kalden 1990, 90–91; Simon 1998, 177–178.

AMONG THE HANDFUL of small works ascribed to Riemenschneider, this statuette of a Virgin and child stands out, both for the intelligence of its sculptural conception and for its delicate execution. The Virgin holds the Christ child across her body in an almost reclining position. With her left leg carrying her weight, her body is articulated in a broad S-shape. Her head is inclined toward the child, the true focus of the composition. Emphasizing this focus and unifying the different planes of the sculpture, a veil wraps around her head, across her right shoulder and breast, and behind the child, who dangles it from his left hand, where it flutters toward the back of the figure. The Virgin's right knee causes wide, oblique folds in her garment to converge on the child.

Despite its diminutive scale, the statuette is characterized by a forceful sense of volume: areas of deep carving, such as the gathering of the mantle under the child's feet or the space under the Virgin's left hand, contrast with areas of high relief and create a rich play of light and dark. The quality of the execution is apparent in such details as the Virgin's coherently articulated right leg, whose volumes are legible through the fabric of the dress. Long, wavy strands of hair fall down the Virgin's back, joining wide folds of drapery to form another broad curve.

The Würzburg statuette occupies a particular place in the development of Riemenschneider's Virgins. It combines features from two compositions formulated in the early 1490s, and it appears to have functioned in turn as a prototype for larger sculpture until just before 1520. The general articulation of the figure and the lines of the drapery seem to derive from the *Virgin and Child* from Werbach in the Tauber Valley (fig. 1), which displayed the same volumetric treatment of form and the same conception of the figure as a spiral in space seen in the large figures from the Münnerstadt altarpiece, especially the *Mary Magdalen* and the *Saint Elizabeth* (cat. 13, figs. 1, 2). It has thus rightly been considered contemporary and dated to about 1490–1492.[1] The Würzburg Virgin also bears notable formal resemblance to a statuette of similar dimensions in Bregenz, Austria. Both are carved in the round and share the disposition of the body along a broad S-shape, the expansion of the figure in width,

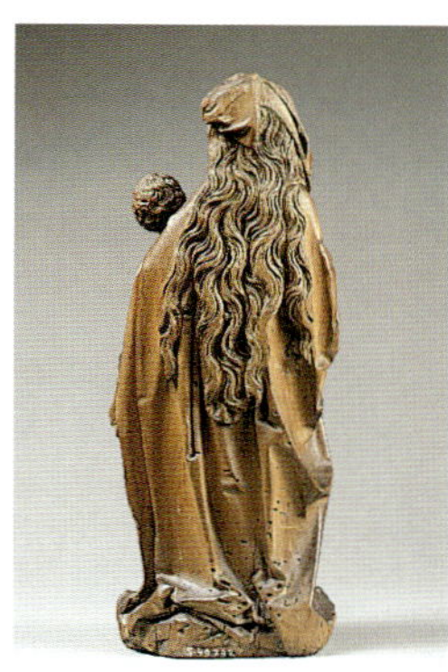

Back view of catalogue no. 19

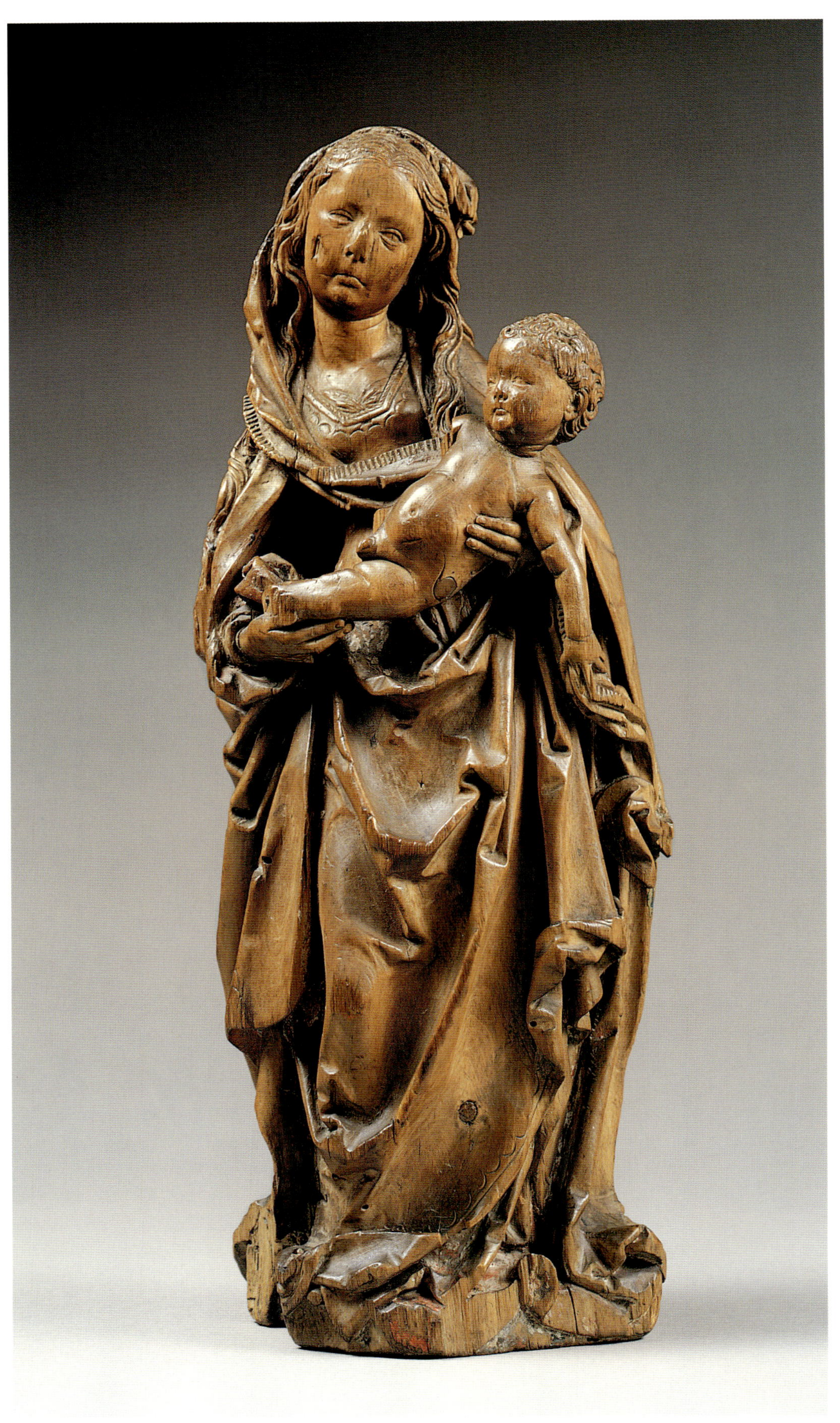

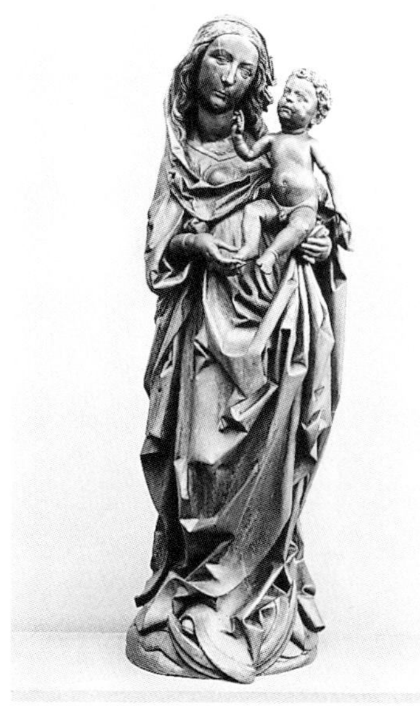

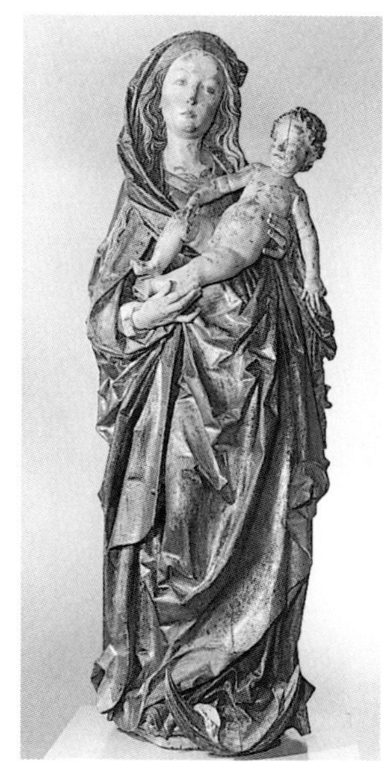

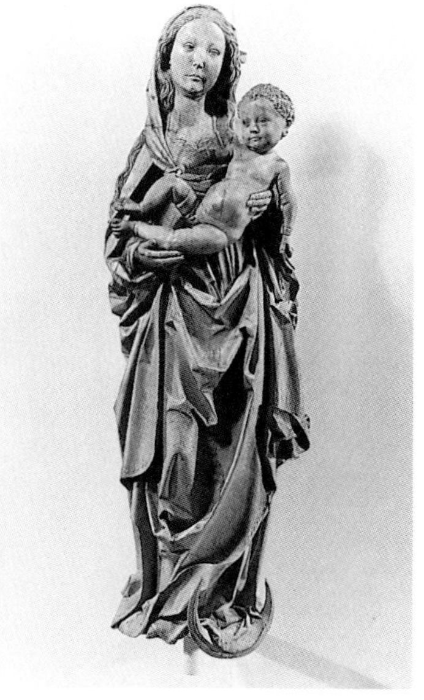

1.

Virgin and Child from Werbach,
c. 1490–1492, limewood, formerly Staatliche
Museen, Berlin (lost in World War II)

2.

Virgin and Child, c. 1500,
limewood with ancient
polychromy, Kunsthistorisches
Museum, Vienna

3.

Virgin and Child, c. 1510–1520,
limewood, Badisches Landesmuseum,
Karlsruhe

and the almost horizontal position of the Christ child. The Bregenz *Virgin and Child,* possibly a model for the so-called Himmelstein Virgin of the mid-1490s (cat. 16, fig. 2), appears to have been created about 1490–1495.[2]

There is an even more direct correspondence between the Würzburg statuette and another sculpture, a monumental *Virgin and Child* in Vienna (fig. 2). The differences between the two works are minor. The Vienna Christ child, who appears to be a toddler rather than an infant, projects beyond the Virgin's left shoulder to a greater degree. The relationship between mother and child is less intimate, with the Virgin presenting the child to the viewer, instead of leaning toward him. The larger sculpture otherwise duplicates the composition of the Würzburg statuette so precisely that one can assume it reflects the original position of such missing elements as the child's right arm and leg. The Vienna sculpture, which like the Würzburg statuette is intended for frontal viewing, is generally dated to about 1500.[3]

Although the precise nature of models in late medieval sculptors' workshops is a matter of debate, their existence and use are attested by the repetition of figural compositions over an extended period of time.[4] Several elements suggest that the Würzburg statuette may have functioned as the model on which the Vienna sculpture was based. Like two other works in this exhibition that may have served as models, the Montreal *Saint Sebastian* and the Dumbarton Oaks

Virgin and Child (cats. 39 A and 45), the Würzburg statuette exhibits a sensitive and detailed treatment of surface. Furthermore, although the Vienna sculpture is hollowed out in the back, the Würzburg figure, like the Dumbarton Oaks Virgin, is carved fully in the round, which allowed the composition to be modified for a variety of purposes. It could be enlarged and the back flattened to create a figure to be set in a retable or as a cult image above an altar. If the work would also be visible from the back—as a hanging sculpture or a figure carried in procession—the model provided indications for the treatment of the back. Finally, as in the Dumbarton Oaks Virgin, the wood used for the Würzburg statuette is of poor quality. It has several prominent knots, which would be disturbing on a small object used for private daily devotions.

That the Würzburg, not the Vienna, sculpture remained in the shop for several years is attested by a *Virgin and Child* in Karlsruhe, datable after 1510 (fig. 3).[5] The Karlsruhe sculpture follows the Würzburg composition in two points where it differs from that in Vienna: the child's head is upright, not tilted back, and is more closely aligned with the Virgin's head; and the Virgin's left fingers are positioned on the child's body as they are in Würzburg. The existence of the Karlsruhe figure illustrates that once a compositional scheme had been found satisfactory, it retained currency in Riemenschneider's shop, sometimes for decades.[6] CHAPUIS

1. Bier 1975, 44–47; Krohm in Würzburg 1981, 15–17.

2. See Bloch in Würzburg 1981, 225–228, with illustration.

3. Bier 1975, 49–50; Krohm in Würzburg 1981, 15; Muth 1982; Trnek 1988, 144.

4. Krohm, for instance, sees this work not as a model but as a high-quality sculpture made specifically for private devotion. It certainly served this function, but not necessarily from the start, as it has been rubbed by touch and presumably kissing, after several elements broke off.

5. For the dating of the Karlsruhe piece, see Zimmermann 1985, 333–337.

6. The composition of the Würzburg statuette was also repeated in a sculpture in the Zichy-Thyssen collection in Buenos Aires (reproduced as fig. 54 in Simon 1998).

241 • *catalogue no. 19*

2O

1495–1505, pearwood, 24 (9½) high (without base), Kunsthistorisches Museum, Vienna, Kunstkammer

• *Technical Notes* •
The left arm appears to have been carved separately and is attached at the shoulder. There is a knot in the wood in the left pectoral. The brownish patination is of a later date.

• *Provenance* •
Acquired in 1866 from the Böhm collection; Ambras Castle until 1875, then transferred to the museum in Vienna.

• *Literature* •
Weber 1911, 273; Bier 1925, 68 n. 2; Schrade 1927, 27–33; Schädler 1975, 105 n. 15; Muth 1981, 5, fig. 4; Würzburg 1981, 233–238, no. 47; Vetter 1982, 66–67; Schädler 1991, 48–51, figs. 12–13; Vetter 1991, 80, fig. 12.

WITH HIS WEIGHT resting on his left foot and his right leg flexed at the knee, the naked Adam gently tilts his head to his left, counterbalancing the long torso that, as a response to his projecting left hip, cants in the opposite direction. He presses a leafy branch of modesty against his body with his left hand, while holding the forbidden apple in the other; both arms, flexed at the elbow, pull away from the torso. His face, with raised brows, pronounced cheekbones, strong nose, and diminutive mouth, is framed by abundant curls of hair; his contemplative gaze is directed downward at an undefined point before him. Slender and lithe, Adam is graced with a youthful and athletic physique, the musculature of which is carefully observed, notwithstanding the slightly overscaled head, hands, and feet. The figure is all the more comely for the balanced pose, emphasized by the right foot that barely contacts the ground.

Carved fully in the round, this exquisite statuette can be viewed to great advantage from every aspect. The S-curve pose of the figure, which in reality would be strained and mannered, reads here as naturalistic and thoroughly convincing. The illusion is sustained in part by a stabilizing vertical axis that runs from the supporting foot to the center of the head and by a counterclockwise spiraling movement, led by the left arm, and followed by the head, right knee, then the trailing right arm. The seeming naturalism of the figure is enhanced by the sensitive rendering of the anatomy, notably in such details as the protrusion of ribs and the veined hands and forearms.

Clearly this is a youthful figure, endowed with a firm and lissome body, yet his face projects a spiritual burden beyond his years, through the lowered corners of the mouth, the furrowed eyebrows over downcast eyes, and the double-lined lower lids. The fact that Adam holds the leaf of modesty and the apple of temptation at the same level—rather than the more usual reaching up for the apple or bringing it toward his mouth—suggests that the consequences of his actions have already dawned on him. Riemenschneider's ability to create an image of such psychological penetration through artifice and manipulation of reality that nonetheless strikes the eye as the embodiment of poignant naturalism is no mean measure of his sculptural genius.

This diminutive figure has not easily found a place in Riemenschneider's oeuvre. Schlosser, who first published the piece in 1910, ascribed it to "the hand of a Würzburg master."[1] Weber, in the following year, was the first to consider it a study for the sandstone *Adam* from the south portal of the Würzburg Marienkapelle (Chapuis essay, fig. 3).[2] Bier implied an attribution to Riemenschneider by indicating that a comparison to the sandstone *Adam* was justified only in that the statuette "pointed already to the loose, fluid style of the Creglingen altar."[3] Schrade placed the Vienna statuette after the Würzburg *Adam* on the basis of its "more formal consciousness" and

1. Julius Schlosser, *Werke der Kleinplastik in der Skulpturensammlung des A. H. Kaiserhauses,* vol. 2 (Vienna, 1910), 1–2.

2. Weber 1911, 273.

3. Bier 1925, 68 n. 2.

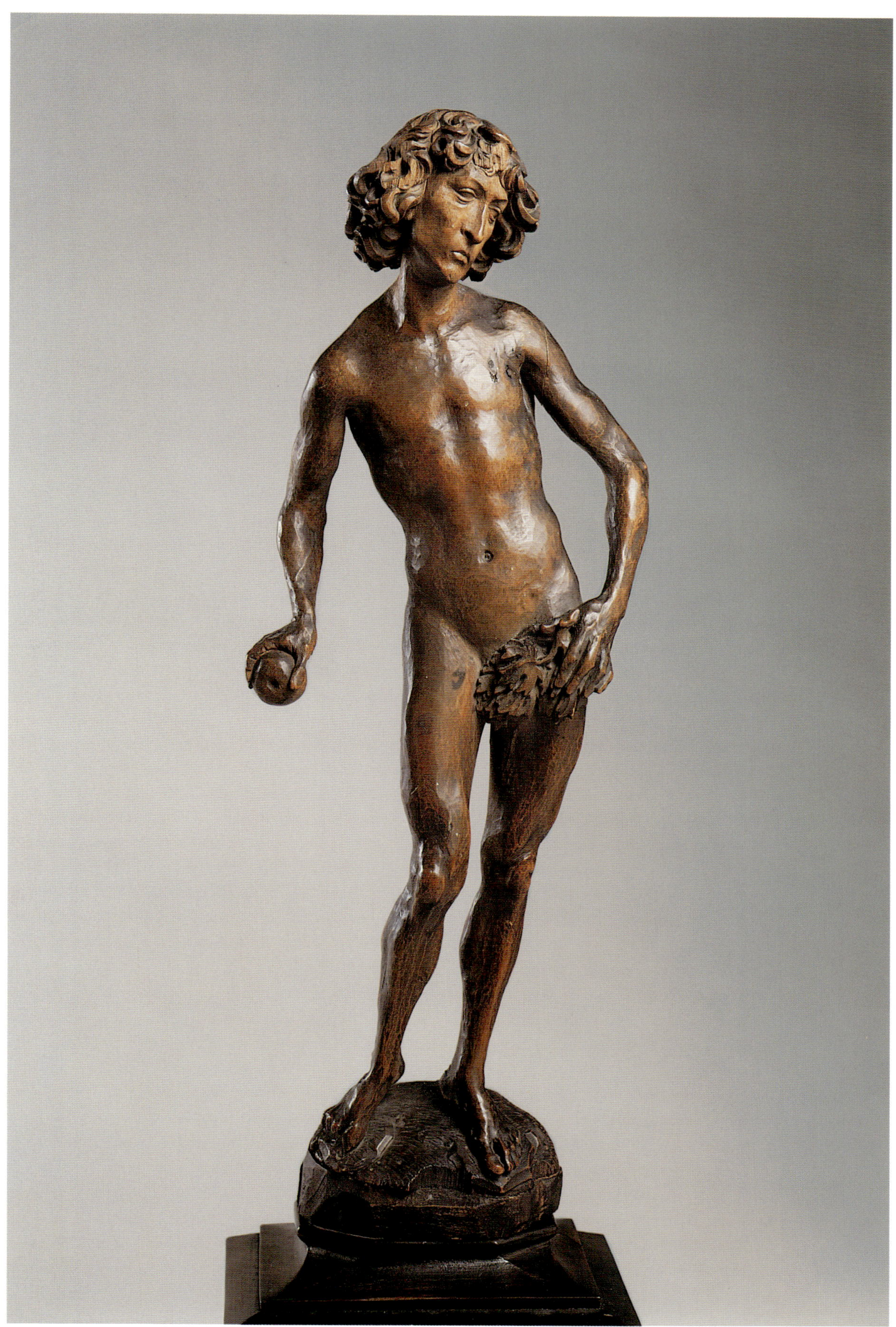

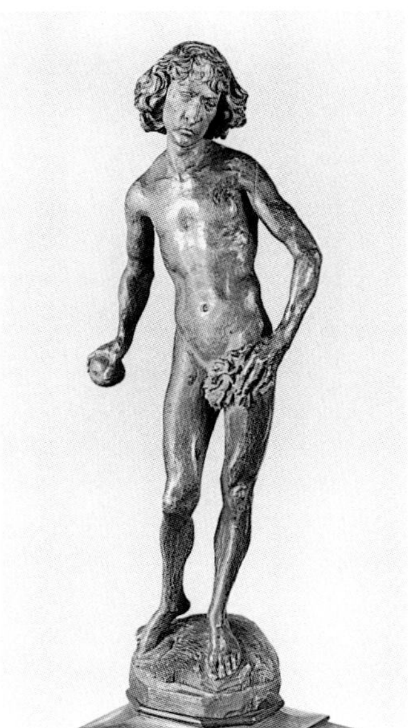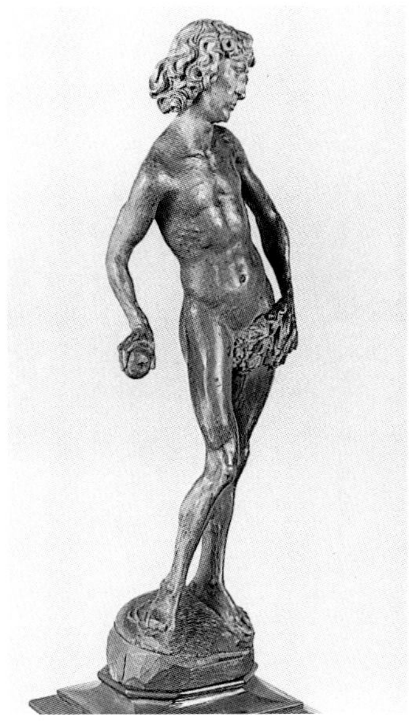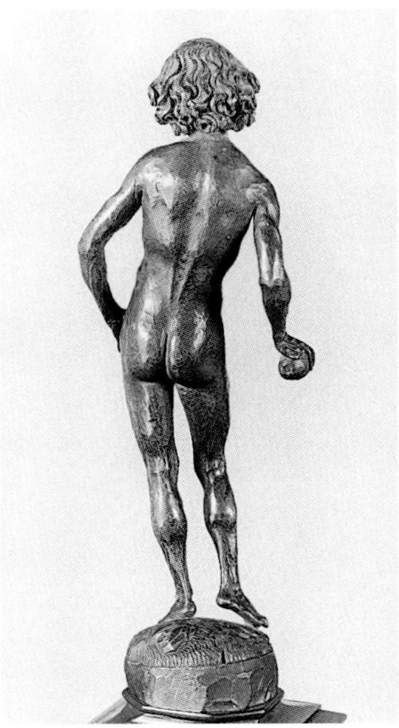

Front, side, and back views of catalogue no. 20

4. Schrade 1927, 27.

5. Kunsthistorisches Museum, *Gefälschte Kunstwerke* (Vienna, 1937), 7, no. 21.

6. Schädler 1975, n. 105, considered the statuette an unfinished collector's cabinet object.

7. Würzburg 1981, 235.

8. Jörg Rasmussen, "Tilman Riemenschneider–Frühe Werke," *Kunstchronik* 34, no. 11 (1981), 418.

9. Kalden 1990, 92 n. 356.

10. Muth 1981, 5; Würzburg 1981, 233.

11. See Karlsruhe 1970, 151–152, no. 98, fig. 92.

12. Vetter 1991, 80, figs. 13 and 1, respectively.

13. Compare the Würzburg *Virgin and Child* (cat. 19) and the fragmentary corpus (Würzburg 1981, 238–239, no. 50).

viewed it as being more in the orbit of Renaissance *Kleinkunst*.[4] Planiscig and Kris quite to the contrary included the figure in their 1937 Vienna exhibition, having deemed it a revivalism of the Romantic period from the first half of the nineteenth century.[5] The scholarly discussion was thereby brought to a halt until Schädler reevaluated the piece in 1975,[6] redeeming it from its vilified status and instigating its return to exhibition. Schädler subsequently declared that, although its date remains problematic, the statuette is an autograph work, comparable to the Würzburg *Adam* and to the *Saint Sebastian* in Munich (fig. 1).[7] The similarities to the former were so convincing to Schädler that he was inclined to place the Vienna *Adam* in the 1490s, before 1500. The rehabilitated status of the figure was accepted by Rasmussen, who compared it to the Darmstadt *Crucifixion* (cat. 33),[8] while Kalden found the "balletic movement" and the face—particularly the narrow bridge of the nose and the flaring nostrils—sufficiently unusual in Riemenschneider's work to question both the attribution and the early dating.[9]

The residual carving marks on the surface of body and the summary rendering of the hair, interpreted as evidence of the statuette's unfinished state,[10] have been compared to that of the corpus from the Amerbach-Kabinett, now in the Historisches Museum, Basel.[11] The rough cutting of the latter, however, is not comparable to the finely faceted surface of the Vienna *Adam*. And the expressiveness of the face and the anatomical particulars of the present work, including the veined arms or the protruding ribs, are hardly characteristic of an unfinished sculpture. Indeed, any additional smoothing of the surface would have erased many of these delicate details. The planar surfaces of the face suggest the underlying bone structure and bring a pathos and monumentality to this diminutive sculpture in a way that highly polished surfaces cannot (compare cat. 2). With nothing wanting in the physical definition or the emotive value of this sculpture, one can reasonably conclude that the Vienna *Adam* was, for all of Riemenschneider's intents and purposes, finished.

The function of the Vienna *Adam* does elude definitive answer. It may have been intended as a model for large-scale sculpture, and the close correspondences with the Marienkapelle *Adam* have frequently been pointed out. Vetter's reconstruction of the sandstone *Adam,* based on the Regnier 1848 pre-restoration engraving, even allows Adam to hold an apple in the same unusual manner as the Vienna statuette.[12] Yet while extant figures that appear to have served as models were generally somewhat smaller than the works based on them, the Vienna *Adam* is significantly smaller.[13] Moreover, the Würzburg *Adam* seems to have been conceived for entirely different circumstances, thus the similarities are superficial. It was designed to stand on an elevated corbel against a pilaster under an architectural canopy; the figure is essentially erect, with little contrapposto, and the broad, planar features of the body and uplifted head are calculated for viewing from a distant and limited vantage. The figure is iconic and hieratic. The Vienna *Adam,* to the contrary, was conceived as a figure in the round: the contrapposto stance, bodily torsion, and modeled forms must be scrutinized from every aspect to comprehend the subtlety of the harmonious compositional balance. The tension of forms counterpoised in space and the psychological intensity of the downcast face combine in an emotionally charged figure that is both animated and intimate.

Schädler suggests compellingly that the Vienna *Adam* was part of a freestanding Temptation group, such as that by Hans Wydyz, executed in nearly the same scale around 1505 (fig. 2).[14] It is conceivable that Riemenschneider later reinterpreted the Würzburg *Adam*—essentially a disengaged relief—in a fully three-dimensional form. A later date for the Vienna *Adam,* between 1495 and 1505, is also supported by the pathos it expresses, foreshadowing the stoical and internalized emotional intensity that characterizes the sculptor's later work, such as the *Salvator Mundi* from

Biebelried, securely dated between 1508 and 1510. By comparison, the 1491–1493 Würzburg *Adam* is relatively static and limited in expression.

The *Adam* statuette has something of a Renaissance aura to it—an observation that earlier brought it opprobrium—almost suggesting a wood sculptor's response to a fifteenth-century north Italian bronze. In a period of increasing Italianate influences in the North, Adam with a pendant Eve, in a freestanding group, was not infrequently invoked as an expedient for the study of nude forms while preserving the respectability of the subject. Without the attributes this figure could be readily mistaken for a Northern interpretation of a Renaissance bronze—or a model for one, as the surface is remarkably similar to that of a wax worked up with a tooling knife—and thus may be evidence of Riemenschneider in a rare expression of Renaissance interest. HUSBAND

14. For a discussion of the Wydyz group, see Gross 1997, 298–300, no II.2.

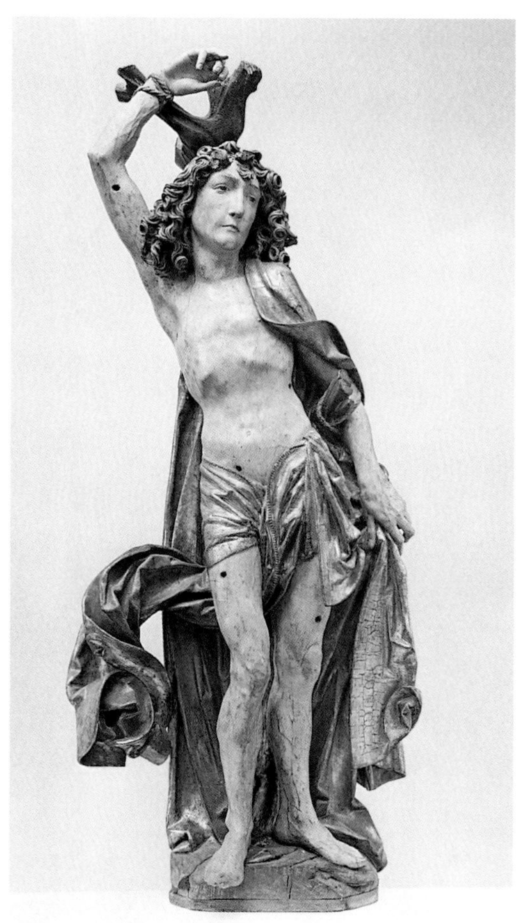

1.

Saint Sebastian, c. 1490, limewood with mostly original polychromy, Bayerisches Nationalmuseum, Munich

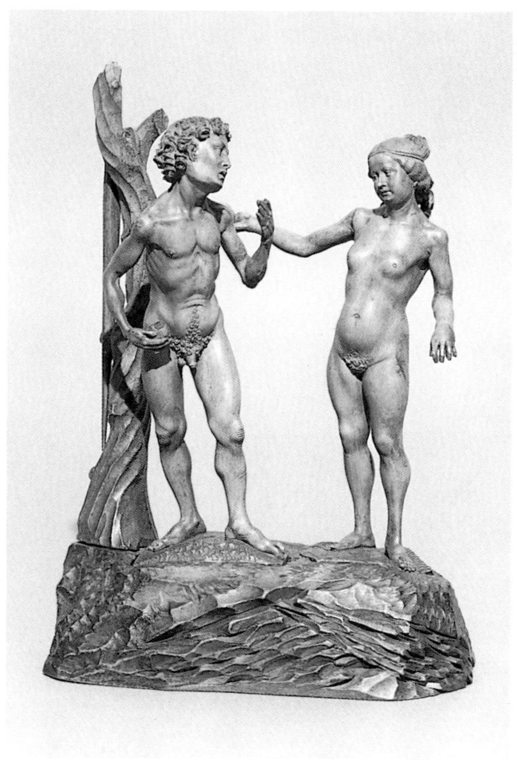

2.

Hans Wydyz, *The Fall of Man,* c. 1505, boxwood, Historisches Museum, Basel

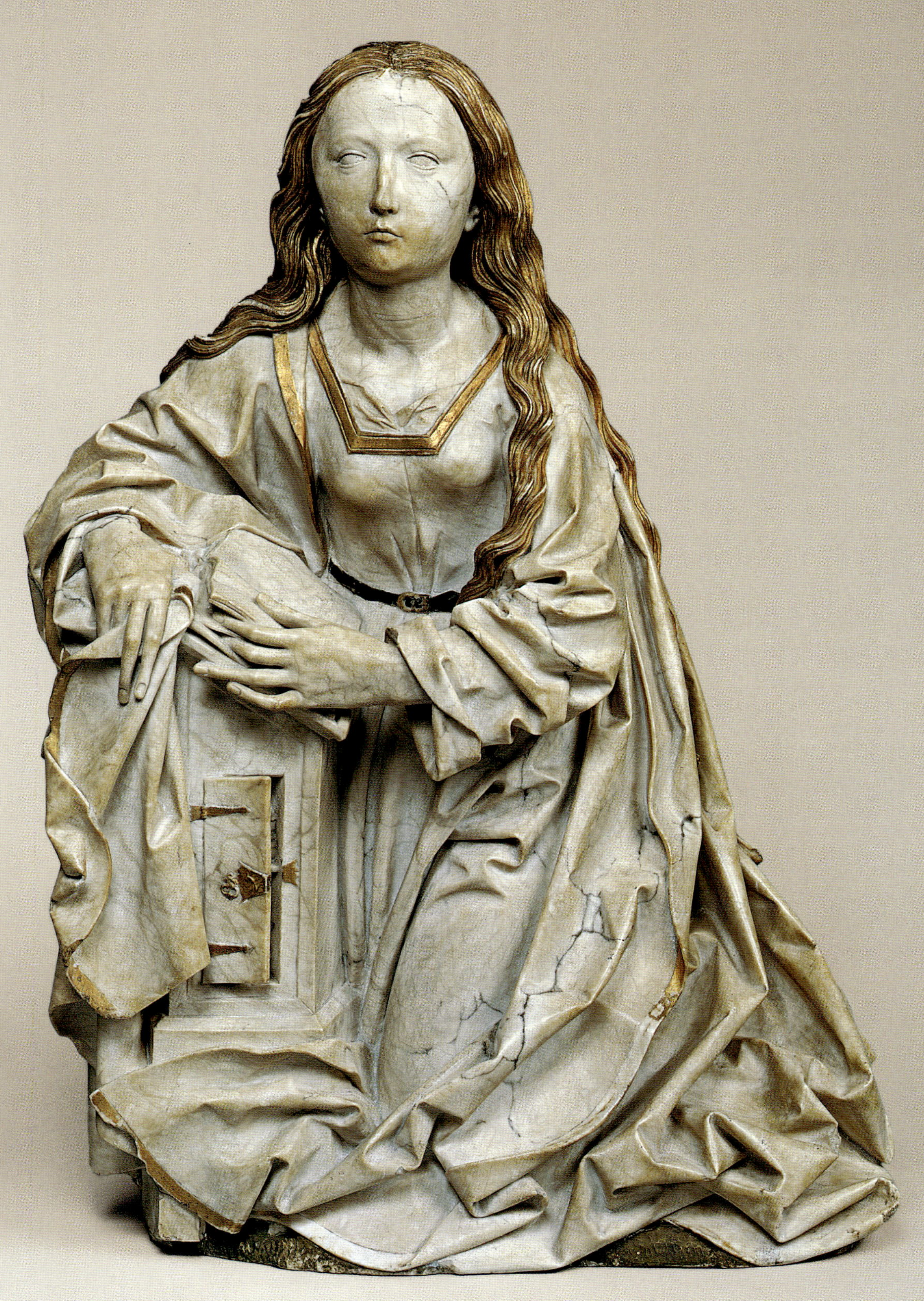

VIRGIN ANNUNCIATE

c. 1500, alabaster, 54 x 36.5 x 17 (21¼ x 14⅜ x 6⅝), Musée du Louvre, Paris

• *Technical Notes* •

Considerable remains of gilding are found in the Virgin's hair, on the border and interior of her mantle, the neckline of her dress, the buckle of her girdle, and the hardware on the door of the easel. The girdle is painted black, the patches of ground, green. The alabaster is marked with an overall network of veining, including several long, discolored faults, notable in the main fold of the mantle paralleling the Virgin's left leg. A fill has been inset at the base of the easel, and damage at the back of her head has been repaired. The flat back of the sculpture has the rough parallel marks of the cutting chisel. There are chips and minor losses to the edge of the mantle and to the cuff.

• *Provenance* •

Traditionally said to have come from the Benedictine abbey church of Saint Peter at Erfurt; in the possession of cathedral provost Würschmidt in Erfurt by 1856 (see Förster 1856, 23–24) and a cleric (Würschmidt?) who had lived in Würzburg until he was pensioned and moved, by 1860, to Dieburg near Darmstadt (see Grossman 1909, 30, fig. 10), along with the Cleveland *Saint Jerome* (cat. 11); [Frankfurt art dealer(s) in 1896]; Leopold Goldschmidt, Frankfurt; acquired by the Louvre in 1904.

• *Literature* •

Förster 1856, 23–24; Vitry 1908, 217; Grossmann 1909, 30; Swarzenski 1921, 195; Schmitt and Swarzenski 1921, 169; Louvre 1922, 67, no. 555; Schrade 1927, 59 n. 5, 156–157; Bier 1931, 451; Habicht 1931b, 5–6; Hannover 1931, no. 6; Milliken 1946, 176–177; Bier 1951, 228–229, 231, 233–234, figs. 9, 10; Gerstenberg 1962, 80; Raleigh 1962, 30–31, no. 4; Müller 1966, 178, 224–225, nos. 74, 75; Bier 1978, 156; Würzburg 1981, 266–268, no. 58; Krohm 1982, 96–97, fig. 2; Sello 1983, 15–16, fig. 39; Jopek 1988, 90–94; Kalden 1990, 116,

fig. 64; Paris 1991, 184–186, no. 48; Ruppert 1992, 100–102; Ruppert 1993, 255; Gaborit 1994, 96.

KNEELING BEFORE a reading stand, with her head and torso turned to the front, the Virgin fingers the pages of a book with her left hand, while her right arm rests on the lectern; drapery partly covers the book and engulfs the back of the stand. A fold of her mantle held under her first two fingers descends in a planar passage, partly covering the side of the bookstand. From her left shoulder the mantle falls in a long arc, the edge turning over on itself until it crosses her left knee and meets the lectern, where, in a gravity-defying flourish, it turns the corner and covers the front base of the structure. Separated by a long tress of hair, another long fold behind the first likewise arcs down, its tubular form angled here and there. This motif is repeated yet again, and the drapery terminates in a gathering of deeply crevassed, angular folds. The door on the front of the reading stand is ajar, revealing two books on the top shelf and a vase below. Patches of the textured ground on which the figure is placed are just visible.

This commanding figure — by far the largest of Riemenschneider's extant alabasters — invites comparison with the Amsterdam *Annunciation* (cat. 2). Other than subject and authorship, however, the two have surprisingly little in common. The Paris figure, unlike the Amsterdam group, is conceived as a high relief, with the Virgin set frontally and carved in plane with a rough-sawn back. While the intended angle of viewing is about the same as for both works — that is, not more than about 45 degrees from either side of center — the present figure projects forward, and both sides have to be seen for one to comprehend the sculptural concept fully. The extraordinary passage on the Virgin's left side, with arcing mantle folds alternating with tresses of hair, can be seen only at the extreme

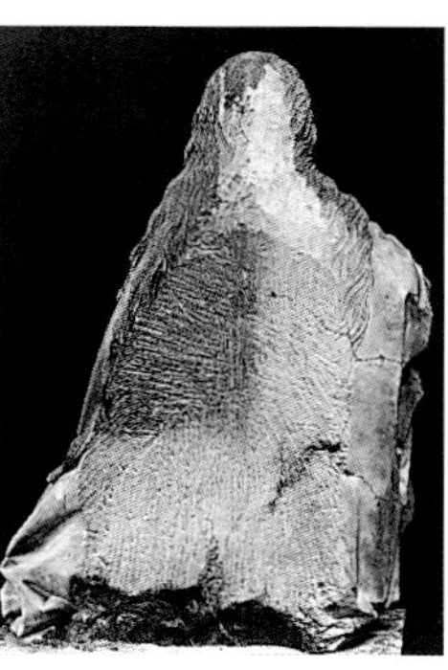

Back view of
catalogue no. 21

of the viewing angle. The same is true of the complex of drapery folds across the back of the lectern, a passage that is essentially at a right angle to the front of the Virgin. The figures in the Amsterdam *Annunciation,* on the other hand, are angled off their back plane into a three-quarter view, making the front and side viewable from one point. In other words, the Amsterdam group was conceived to be viewed from a fixed point (perhaps on one's knees), while the Louvre figure requires the viewer to move.

Movement is at the core of the sculptural conception: the Virgin kneels not in front of the bookstand, but at a slight angle to it; her head and torso are turned frontally at a right angle to the lectern. Thus a counterclockwise motion is established, and the entire drapery system responds. As the Virgin draws up the mantle in her right hand, the resulting folds move counterclockwise. As she turns to her left, she pulls three long, arcing folds from a crumbled mass of fabric at the floor that spiral upward from front to back, each separated by a long tress of hair, and converge at the Virgin's shoulders in an eloquent drapery passage at her left side. The line of one tress of hair hanging straight down over her left shoulder and another pulled over her right shoulder further emphasizes the counterclockwise movement. Even the partly open door of the pulpit, with its intriguing contents—an idea that appears to be borrowed from Master E. S. (fig. 1)—

draws the viewer to the right in order to peek into the interior.

The sculptural concept of this figure required Riemenschneider to provide clearer definition of the underlying anatomy. Below the tiny waist of the Amsterdam Virgin, anatomical definition is lost in the considerable envelope of drapery. While comparably substantial below the waist, the mantle of the Louvre Virgin falls off her shoulder and down her side to reveal the robed figure beneath. The clinging drapery clearly defines her left thigh, which also clarifies the turning motion of the figure and the different planes described by the legs and hips as opposed to the head and torso. The counterclockwise turn indicates that the lost annunciate angel approached from the Virgin's left, not her right, as in the Amsterdam group.[1]

The verticality at the left side of the sculpture, which would have conformed to the wall of an enclosing shrine, supports this reading and indicates that the composition, with the annunciate angel approaching the Virgin from behind, depended on an iconographic model that can ultimately be traced back to a Netherlandish source, as in the Petrus Christus *Annunciation* from the left wing of a triptych dated 1452 (fig. 2).[2] Aware of the angel's presence, the Virgin diverts her attention from the pages of the book and begins to turn away from her lectern in acknowledgment.

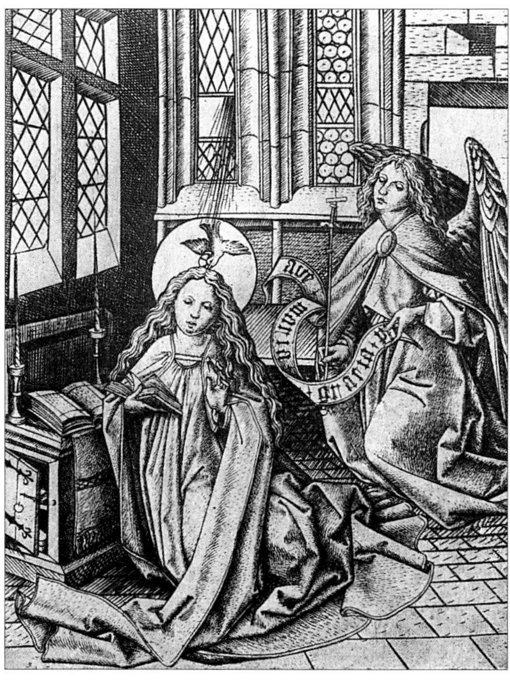

1.

Master E. S., *Annunciation,* c. 1465, engraving, The Metropolitan Museum of Art, New York

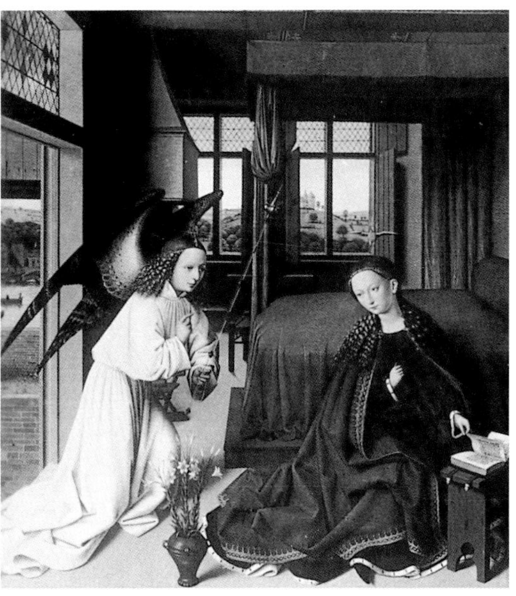

2.

Petrus Christus, *Annunciation,* 1452, oil on panel, Staatliche Museen zu Berlin, Gemäldegalerie

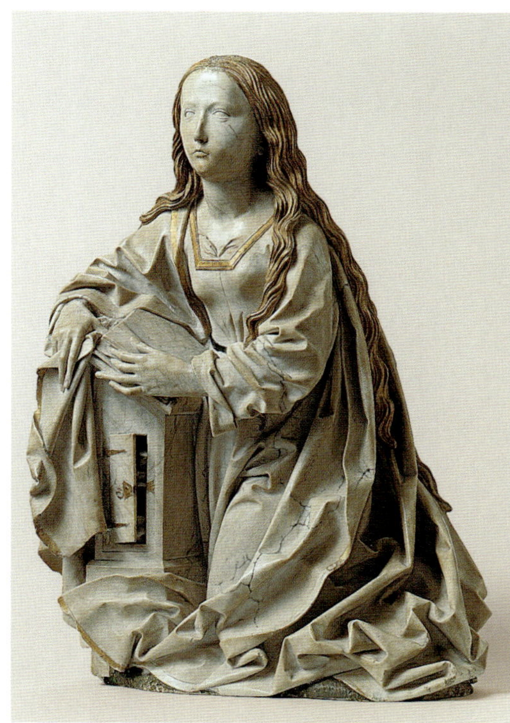

Alternate view of catalogue no. 21

The Louvre and Amsterdam Virgins are of very different character, made all the more apparent by their identical costumes. The Louvre figure, although certainly a young woman, has nothing of the child-like mien of the Amsterdam Virgin. Her broad, fleshy face, with its small mouth and delicate nose, reveals the serenity and dignified composure of a more mature and experienced woman. This aspect is also found in the well-preserved face of *Eve* from the south portal of the Marienkapelle, Würzburg (Chapuis essay, fig. 3); Eve's face is more elongated, and while the features are treated identically, the Virgin's are relatively more generous. A closer comparison, however, is found in the head of Kunigunde from the "Miracle of the Crystal Bowl" relief on the imperial tomb in Bamberg (fig. 3), commissioned in 1499 but completed only in 1513. The treatment of Kunigunde's face is so close to that of the Louvre Virgin, that one face would seem interchangeable with the other. Bier believed that the Miracle relief was one of the last to be completed and dated it to about 1510.[3]

Scholars have consistently dated the Louvre Virgin to the 1490s. Bier, who included the sculpture in his 1962 exhibition but not in his final monographic study of 1982, dated it about 1490—earlier than the

Saint Jerome (cat. 11) and the same year as the Münnerstadt *Mary Magdalen* (cat. 13, fig. 1).[4] Krohm also saw a close relationship with the Mary Magdalen in the *Last Communion* relief from the Münnerstadt altarpiece and therefore dated the Louvre Virgin about 1493–1495.[5] Jopek felt that the figure corresponded to other Riemenschneider Virgins in the modeling of the face but lacked plastic tension and could not be reconciled stylistically with the *Saint Jerome*; he concluded that the Paris sculpture, which he dated about 1490, was not an autograph work.[6] Ruppert similarly did not accept the attribution to Riemenschneider.[7] Guillot de Suduiraut, on the other hand, accepted Krohm's arguments and dated the Virgin to 1495 or somewhat before.[8] Kalden, also seeing stylistic similarities with the head of Kunigunde in the Miracle relief in Bamberg but finding the drapery characteristic of earlier work, proposed a date of 1495–1496.[9] The close correspondence of facial types would, however, seem to support a somewhat later dating, perhaps toward the end of the decade.

The attribution of both the Amsterdam *Annunciation* and the Louvre *Annunciate Virgin* to Riemenschneider has come under question in the more recent literature, while that of the *Saint Barbara* and the *Saint Jerome* (cats. 4 and 11) has generally enjoyed acceptance. Even though these alabasters may have been executed over a longer period of time than has heretofore been argued—from the early 1480s to around 1500—the problem has arisen largely from the difficulty of comfortably placing these stylistically divergent works in a linear chronology. In the case of Riemenschneider, this is probably a misguided expectation, for he was fully capable of adopting or developing different solutions to suit his intentions, as his several and often-repeated compositional formulas for the standing Virgin and child eloquently establish.[10] Moreover, given the nature of late medieval workshops in general and Riemenschneider's large and productive workshop in particular, it is futile to try to identify different hands, for in the end the master's style becomes the workshop style. As scholars have generally found these four alabasters to be quintessentially Riemenschneider, each in its own way, all must be accorded a place in the Riemenschneider canon, even as our understanding of that is evolving.
HUSBAND

3. Bier 1947, 114.

4. Raleigh 1962, 30.

5. Würzburg 1981, 268.

6. Jopek 1988, 92, 158.

7. Ruppert 1992, 100; reiterated in Ruppert 1993, 254.

8. Paris 1991, 184.

9. Kalden 1990, 116 n. 425.

10. For an extended discussion of the development of different formulas, see Bier 1975, 41–64; a reprise is found in Simon 1998, 167–176.

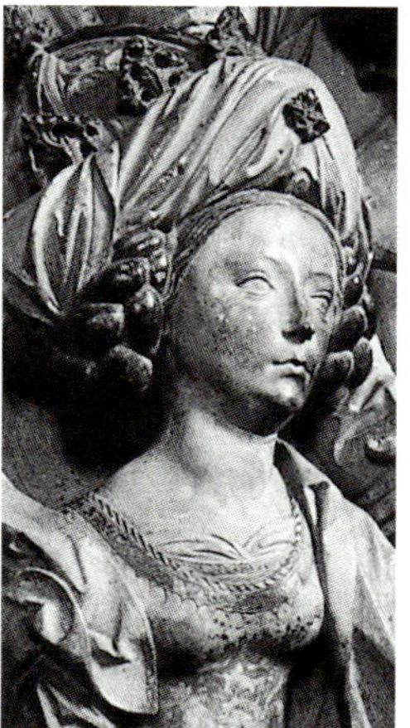

3.
Detail from the "Miracle of the Crystal Bowl" relief on the tomb of Heinrich II and Kunigunde, 1499–1513, Solnhofen stone, Bamberg Cathedral

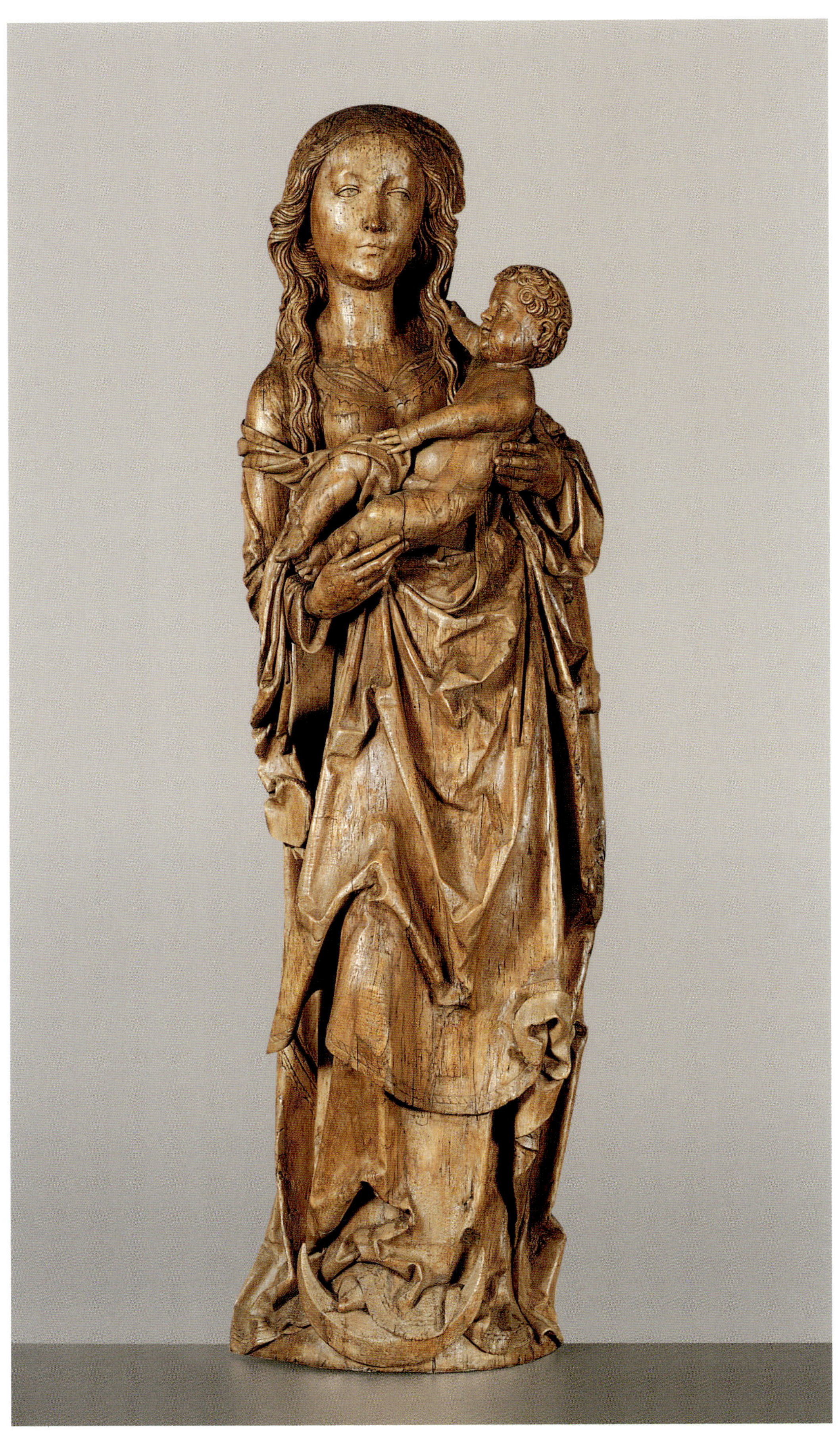

VIRGIN AND CHILD ON THE CRESCENT MOON

c. 1500–1501, limewood, 123 x 36.8 x 21 (48⅜ x 14½ x 8¼), Spencer Museum of Art,
The University of Kansas, Museum purchase: Gift in memory of Professor Harry C. Thurnau
through the Estate of Myrtle Elliot Thurnau

• Technical Notes •
The sculpture is cut from a single piece of limewood
with the grain running vertically. The back is partly
hollowed out, and workbench holes are visible in the
head and in the base. Replacements include the tips
of the crescent moon and several areas of drapery.
An inscription on the back, "Ronovirt von Lorz/
Worudle [or Wandle?]," records an earlier restoration.
The broad treatment of surfaces, absence of punched
ornament, and roughness of the cut decoration could
suggest that the sculpture was originally intended to
be polychrome. When it entered the museum's collection in 1952, it had a dark brown stain,[1] some of
which was removed in a conservation treatment
carried out in 1978 by Forrest R. Bailey, conservator
of paintings at the William Rockhill Nelson Gallery
of Art, Kansas City.[2] The work was treated a second
time in 1984 by Mayda Goodberry, art object conservator in Blair, Nebraska, who evened out the surface and repositioned the child's apparently original
but misplaced right arm.[3] In its present position, however, the arm appears to be too low; it was probably
resting on an apple, which was balanced on the Virgin's shoulder, as in the Cologne *Virgin and Child*
(cat. 16). There are several vertical cracks, including
one that runs across the child's legs above the knees
and another (17.2 cm long) that runs up from the
bottom in the lower left portion of the base.

• Provenance •
Hans Schwarz, Vienna (collection auctioned in Berlin,
1910); collection of the prince of Liechtenstein, Vaduz
and Vienna; [Blumka Gallery, New York, May 1951];
acquired by the museum in 1952.

• Literature •
Bier 1952, 1–6; Bier 1959a, 2–15; Raleigh 1962, 34–
35; Bier 1978, 150; Bier 1982, 41–43; Kalden 1990, 115.

WITH HER FOOT on the crescent moon, identifying her as the woman of the Apocalypse (Revelation 12:1), the Virgin looks out into the distance while
holding the Christ child across her body in a reclining position. Her calm, erect pose contrasts with the
liveliness of the child. The composition appears to
derive from the *Virgin and Child* in Cologne, either
directly or through a work that recorded the placement and gestures of the child as well as the general
organization of the drapery and details of the costume. Although the Spencer Virgin lacks a crown, her
veil rests on the left side of her head, falls down her
back, is pulled around her right arm by the child,
then flutters down her right side. She wears a cloak
that has fallen off her right shoulder but rests on her
left shoulder and wraps around the front of her body
like an apron. The similar pose, with the weight borne
by the left leg and the right knee pushing against the
fabric, causes the garment to drape in a similar pattern. Other details also correspond, such as the strands
of hair falling both in front and behind the right
shoulder and the scalloped decoration along the edge
of the cloak and the neckline.

There are also radical differences between the
two works, the most notable being the greater sculptural mass of the Cologne figure, despite its smaller
dimensions. While the Spencer Virgin repeats the
motifs of the figure in Cologne, it is more elongated.
The concentric, rounded drapery folds have become
V-shaped; the Virgin's arms are held close to the body
and her head is held upright; the Spencer figure also
lacks the cloak at the right, which adds breadth to
the Cologne Virgin and functions almost as a background against which to read the figure. The narrower
proportions of the Spencer Virgin appear to be due
in part to the block of wood from which it was carved.
The sculptor seems to have used half of a tree trunk,
which necessarily imposes limitations. The side views

1. Personal communication of
Marilyn Stokstad, professor
of art history, The University of
Kansas.

2. Conservation report on file
at the museum.

3. Conservation report on file
at the museum.

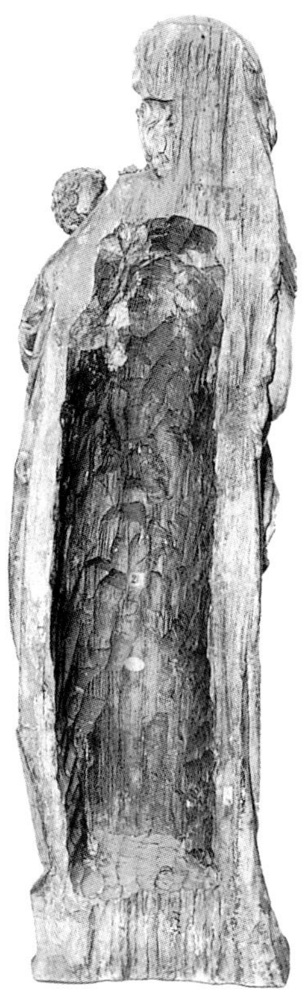

Back view of catalogue no. 22

make this point quite clearly: the child is held closer
to the Virgin's body, and her cloak does not project
as far forward. The Spencer figure also has a more restricted arc of address. The back is entirely flat, its
profile view is not inviting, and the cloak does not
wrap around the figure in such a way as to allow a
smooth transition from side to front.

Iris Kalden noted a resemblance between the
Spencer Virgin and the effigy of Kunigunde on the
imperial tomb in Bamberg (Chapuis essay, fig. 4).[4]
Both share the same facial type, with squarish jaws,
high forehead, and slightly arched eyebrows. Both
have elongated proportions and exhibit drapery folds
that are shallower and less angular than those on the
Cologne Virgin. It thus seems reasonable to suggest
that the Spencer figure was carved at roughly the same
time, about 1500–1501. CHAPUIS

4. Kalden 1990, 115 n. 422.

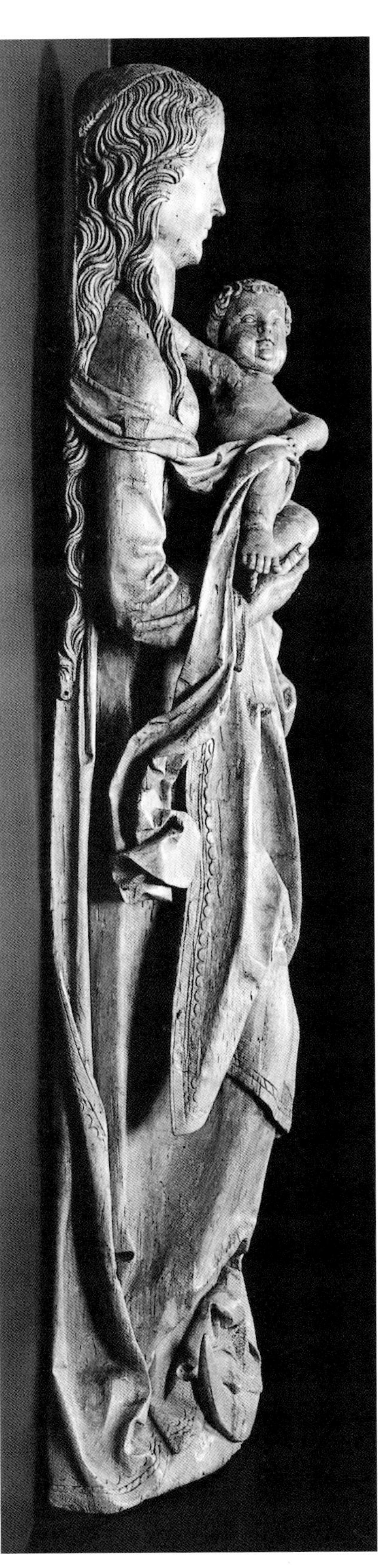

Side view of catalogue no. 22

SAINTS CHRISTOPHER, EUSTACE, AND ERASMUS (THREE HELPER SAINTS)

c. 1500–1504, limewood, 53.8 x 34.5 x 13.5 (21⅛ x 13⅝ x 5¼), The Metropolitan Museum of Art,
New York, The Cloisters Collection

• Technical Notes •

The sculpture is cut from a large block of limewood
with vertical grain, to which a smaller piece of the
same material was appended; the join runs vertically
at Christopher's right shoulder. As the carving is consistent throughout, the addition is clearly contemporary and was glued on after the smoothing of the
back. This procedure, possibly necessary because of
a defect in the wood, was common in Riemenschneider's shop (see also cat. 17). The sculptor did
not hollow out the back but finished it flat, presumably because the shallow depth and small size of the
relief would not have presented any serious risk of
cracking. An original repair runs vertically through
Erasmus' upper body, neck, and chin. There is only
minor insect damage, concentrated at the left. Missing elements include the head and right arm of the
Christ child on Christopher's back (the head carved
separately and attached with a dowel), the crook and
lower portion of Erasmus' crozier as well as the greater
part of his spindle, and a triangular section of the
ground to the right of Christopher's left foot. Traces
of a chalk ground in the deep folds and insect channels reveal that the sculpture was painted at some
point. Restoration treatments in 1956 and 1961 removed
most traces of paint and obscured the material record
by adding a tinted varnish, making it impossible on
the basis of technical analysis to determine an original layer. The high level of detailed carving suggests,
however, that the group was initially monochrome.
A modern dark brown layer and nineteenth-century
additions, including the head and right arm of the
Christ child, were removed in 1956 when the sculpture was on loan to the Victoria and Albert Museum.
The work received a light cleaning and surface coating by Mojmir Frinta in 1961 after its acquisition
for the Cloisters.

• Provenance •

Lord Delamere, United Kingdom; Dr. George Saint
(d. 1957), Cheadle, Staffordshire, by 1951; Mary Saint,
his wife, 1957–1960 (on loan to the Victoria and
Albert Museum, 1951–1952 and 1956–1957); [Sotheby's,
London, 14 October 1960, no. 52]; [Rosenberg and
Stiebel, New York]; acquired for the Cloisters in 1961.

• Literature •

Bier 1963, 44–47; Bier 1975, 45; Nostitz 1975; Würzburg 1981, 214–216; *Metropolitan Museum of Art Guide*
(New York, 1987), 150–151; Wixom 1988, 29; Young
1988, 132–133; Kalden 1990, 97, 110.

THE FIGURES IN this relief represent three of
the Fourteen Helper Saints, who had been venerated
as a group since the early 1300s. They consisted of
three bishops: Denis, Erasmus, and Blaise; three virgins: Barbara, Margaret, and Catherine; three knights:
George, Acacius, and Eustace; the physician Panta-
leon, the monk Gilles, the deacon Cyriacus, the boy
Vitus, and the giant Christopher. Their cult became
particularly strong in southern Germany after 1446,
when they appeared in a vision to a shepherd from
the Cistercian monastery of Langheim in Upper Franconia. Two years later a chapel was erected on the site,
which became a major center of pilgrimage.[1] Each
saint was thought to protect against distinct ailments
or to help in specific situations, and their popularity
was enhanced by their perceived cumulative powers.

According to the *Golden Legend,* Christopher
was a giant Canaanite, whose ambition it was to serve
the most powerful man on earth. First he served a
king, but after discovering that the king was afraid of
the devil, he went on to serve the devil, only to realize that the devil was afraid of Christ. Wanting to
serve Christ, he followed the instructions of a hermit and went to live on the bank of a river, carrying

1. *Lexikon der christlichen
Ikonographie,* ed. Wolfgang
Braunfels (Rome, Freiburg,
Basel, Vienna, 1974),
8:546–548.

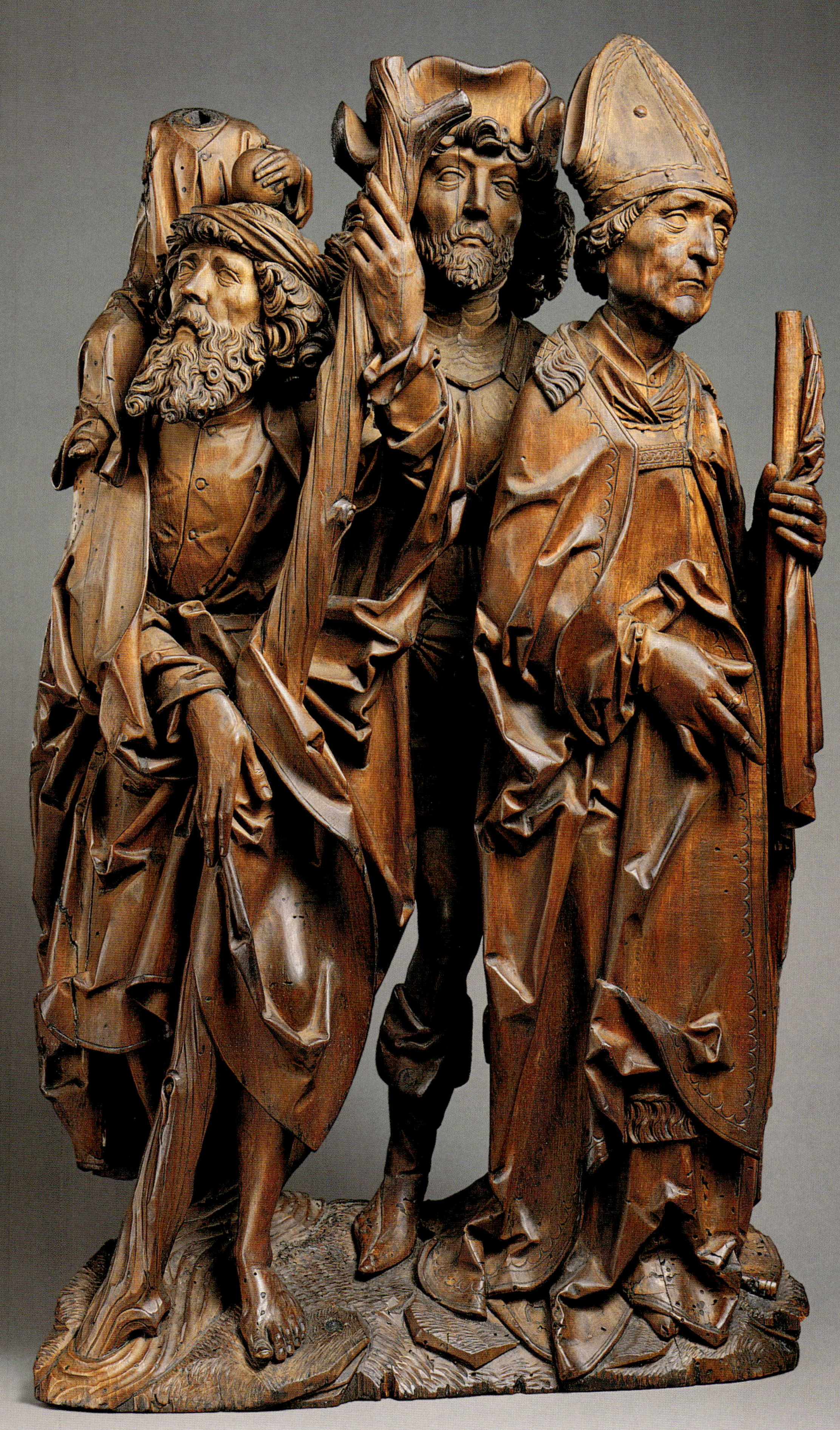

travelers to the other side. One night he carried a little child, who, growing heavier and heavier, told him that he was bearing the weight of the world on his shoulders, thereby revealing himself to be Christ. Riemenschneider depicted the saint as he ended his crossing, with one foot still in the river and the other on the shore. His left hand grasps a staff for support, and his back arches under his load. Looking up at the child, he furrows his brow as if listening with attention.

The middle figure is Eustace, a general in Trajan's army who was converted to Christianity while hunting when he saw a crucifix in the antlers of a stag. He is distinguishable by his armor, but in addition to a gauntlet and breastplate, he wears, rather oddly, a fur-lined tunic, boots of soft leather, and a hat with a wide, undulating brim. Erasmus, on the right, was a Syrian bishop who was miraculously transported to Campania and put to a particularly gruesome death by disembowelment, his tormentors making an incision in his abdomen and cranking out his intestines.[2] He stands here in full episcopal regalia, his left hand resting on his crozier, of which the crook and lower portion are missing, and his right hand holding a section of a spindle, the instrument of his martyrdom.

The fourteen saints from which this group was taken originally stood friezelike in two staggered rows, which allowed the composition to remain compact and several of the figures to be rendered in abbreviated fashion, as is Eustace. Separate sections of three or four figures would have been assembled in front of a flat background. The ends of the plinth, scored to give better purchase for the glue, are cut at sharp angles so that the base has a keystone shape and adjacent segments could be joined without an obvious seam; presumably adjoining bases would have been cut in a keystone shape with the longer edge at the back rather than the front. The line of figures was also to appear seamless: the left edge of Christopher's drapery would probably have been hidden by the figure to his right, while Erasmus would have stood partly in front of the figure to his left. This arrangement was surely dictated by the specifications of the commission and the site of installation. The main challenge was fusing the group into an organic whole, which the sculptor accomplished by introducing elements that lead the eye from the sides toward what would have been the center of the frieze. Although Christopher looks to the left, his walking stick and the torsion in his body direct attention strongly to the right; Eustace faces the viewer, while Erasmus is turned to the right. The general reading movement of the relief is thus left to right, suggesting that it originally stood in the left half of the ensemble.[3]

With an estimated original width of about 1.6 meters, the complete group could have formed either the predella of a small altarpiece or, more likely, an independent relief in a niche or a shrine. Riemenschneider's predella figures are usually quite broadly treated (see cat. 13 A – D). The Cloisters relief, by contrast, exhibits a meticulous rendering of detail, including the twisted border on Erasmus' miter and the simulation of moving water around Christopher's foot and walking stick. Christopher's beard and hair are chiseled as finely as if they were of metal, the buttons of his doublet cause the fabric to crease, and his hands display an intricate tracery of veins and sinews. All of this suggests that the ensemble was to be the sole focus of the viewer. It also implies that the group was intended to remain uncolored, beyond the usual indication of pupils and lips. The finest details, such as the stippled imitation of fur on the hem of Eustace's tunic, would have been obscured under even a thin layer of ground.

The relief was entirely unknown until it surfaced in an English collection in the 1950s, but Justus Bier's opinion, published soon after the sculpture's acquisition for the Cloisters in 1961, has carried great weight.[4] It is known that in 1494 Johann von Allendorf, chancellor to Prince-Bishop Rudolf von Scherenberg, commissioned a group of Fourteen Helper Saints from Riemenschneider for the church of the Hofspital in Würzburg, which was dedicated to them and which he had endowed. Bier considered the Cloisters relief to be the sole surviving fragment of this group. Nothing is known about the specifics of Allendorf's commission, however, and given the popularity of the theme in southern Germany, the connection is circumstantial at best. Furthermore, the style of the Cloisters relief does not bear out Bier's dating. Compared with the Cloisters *Seated Bishop* (cat. 17), created around the mid-1490s,[5] its somewhat rigid and disciplined treatment of draperies is difficult to reconcile with the fairly homogeneous style of the early works. A closer comparison can be seen in the *Holy Blood* altarpiece of 1501–1504 (fig. 1), with its linear conception of draperies.[6] Despite the shallower depth of carving, the Cloisters piece exhibits elegant passages that have parallels in Rothenburg. Christopher's cloak, curving around his left shoulder and elbow, then wrapping around the stick and covering his left knee, allows a coherent spatial reading of elements in different planes. Similarly, in the Rothenburg composition Judas' right hand reaches from the background to lift up the front of his garment, pulling the fabric from the foreground into the middle ground. There are also repetitions of gesture, such as

2. Louis Réau, *Iconographie de l'art chrétien* (Paris, 1958), 3.1: 437–438.

3. The Mainfränkisches Museum, Würzburg, owns a complete relief of the Fourteen Helper Saints carved by a follower of Riemenschneider in the 1520s. The saints stand in three staggered rows, and various compositional elements point toward the center of the group (see Muth 1982, 210–211 [ill.]).

4. Raleigh 1962, 44–47; Bier 1963; see also Bier 1982, 37–41.

5. As far as I know, Justus Bier never expressed an opinion in print on the Cloisters *Seated Bishop,* not even in his 1982 monograph. He was aware of the sculpture, however, since Charles von Nostitz had contacted him when he prepared his 1975 article on these two works at the Cloisters.

6. See Würzburg 1981, 214. Bier 1982, 40, pointed out the similarity in draperies.

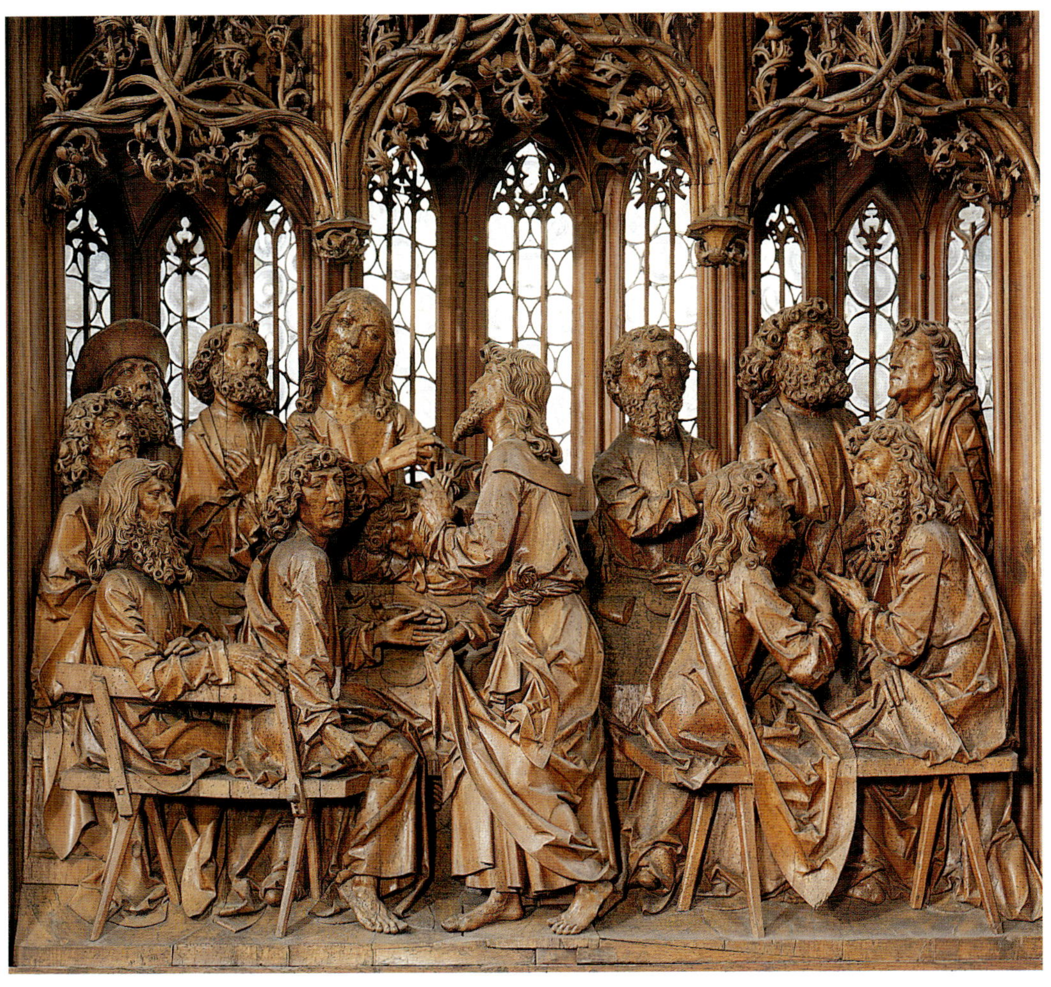

Holy Blood altarpiece, detail of the central shrine, 1501–1504, Jakobskirche, Rothenburg

7. Kalden 1990, 97, fig. 314.

Christopher's eloquent right hand, bent at the wrist with the little finger separated from the rest, which almost duplicates that of the bearded apostle in the left foreground of the Rothenburg altarpiece.

The presence of certain facial types also supports a dating of about 1500–1504. Erasmus seems a slightly younger version of Rudolf von Scherenberg, whose funerary monument Riemenschneider carved between 1496 and 1499 (Kemperdick essay, fig. 1). Christopher's face appears to follow that of the second apostle from the right in the background of the Rothenburg altarpiece. The slightly melancholy expression of Eustace follows one of Riemenschneider's most widespread types, first formulated in the *Saint Luke* of the Münnerstadt altarpiece (cat. 13 c) but also in the later Stuttgart *Saint James* (cat. 31, fig. 1).[7] CHAPUIS

SAINT MATTHIAS

c. 1500–1505, limewood, 104.5 x 32 x 19 (41⅛ x 12⅝ x 7½), Staatliche Museen zu Berlin,
Skulpturensammlung

• *Technical Notes* •

The sculpture is cut from a relatively unblemished piece of limewood with the grain running vertically. The back was not hollowed out, as it was in the great majority of figures of this size, but was carved flat (see also cat. 42). Despite some insect damage, confined largely to the lower area, the work is in good condition. The surface is quite dark, especially at the bottom, perhaps owing to the accumulation of dirt and wax or to the application of a stain. The saint's left hand is modern; other replacements include the lower corner of the drapery in front, the edges of the cloak on the right side of the plinth, and the vertical edge of the cloak at the left. The border of the cloak bears a carved inscription, with appliqué wooden gems between the words and a series of half-moon shapes cut with the chisel. A filled dowel hole in the front of the figure, roughly in front of his left knee, may have served for the attachment of the saint's attribute, an axe.

The fine surface decoration — especially the coloristic stippling on the border of the cloak that allows the inscription to stand out, or the imitation of fur on the collar — suggests that the sculpture was originally intended to remain uncolored. There is indication, however, that the figure was painted at a later point. Some insect channels run parallel to the surface, indicating that the surface was scraped with a tool to remove polychromy. This is supported by the presence of traces of a white ground layer in some of the deepest drapery folds.

• *Provenance* •

Acquired by the museum in 1905 in Frankfurt am Main.

• *Literature* •

Bier 1930, 27 n. 1; Bier 1931, 22; Demmler 1936, 172; Bier 1978, 151; Muth 1982, 68; Kalden 1990, 93, 133.

AN INSCRIPTION ON the border of the cloak identifies this figure as Matthias, who succeeded Judas as the twelfth apostle. It reads: "O ERBARME / O MARIA DV MVDER ALLE / MARIA GRACIA / O MARIA HILE VNS AVS ALLER NOT DENS PIT / ON HEILEIGER SANT MATIAS PIT G" (Oh, have mercy, Mary, mother of all men. Thanks be given to you, Mary. Oh, Mary, protect us from every danger, we pray you. Saint Matthias, pray to God).[1] The saint's left hand probably once held his attribute, the axe with which he was beheaded. Depicted as a mature man, with a full face and a mass of curly hair, Matthias stands erect on a patch of rocks and grass. His head is turned to his right, his gaze focused on a point over our heads. His bare feet contrast with the richness of his garments, which include a cloak with a bejeweled border worn over a long robe with loose sleeves and an ermine collar.

The Berlin *Matthias* is a work of exceptional quality, which sets standards for the attribution of other works to Riemenschneider. The intelligence of the sculptural conception is apparent in the subtle dialogue of quiet and active passages. At first glance, one reads the sculpture as a static form, because of the rooted stance and the long tubular folds of his robe. But the body is conceived as a series of elements arranged obliquely along a vertical axis: the saint's left foot defines the first oblique accent, with the shoulders countered in the opposing direction, and the head turned toward the right shoulder.[2]

The cloak functions as a shell, surrounding the figure and giving it great spatial presence, a concept particularly favored by Niclaus Gerhaert (see cat. 5), whose influence marked most of Riemenschneider's career. The garment, which has fallen from the saint's right shoulder, descends along his right side to the ground, where it covers part of his right foot. His right arm echoes this line, reaching around to grasp

1. The translation given here is based on research by Matthias Fritz, as yet unpublished.

2. See the Montreal *Saint Sebastian* (cat. 39A), where complex torsion in the body is more apparent because the figure is nude.

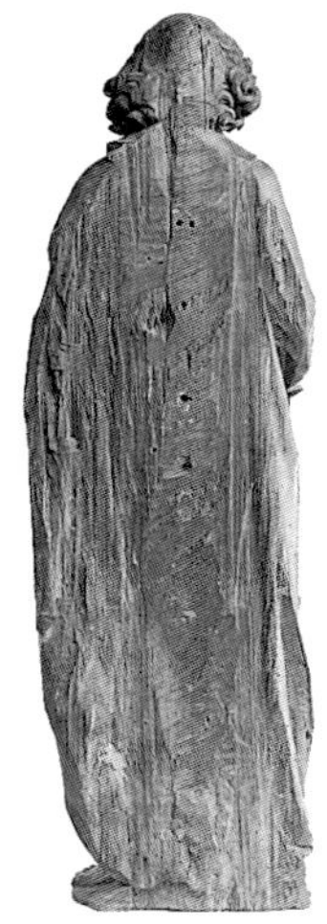

Back view of
catalogue no. 24

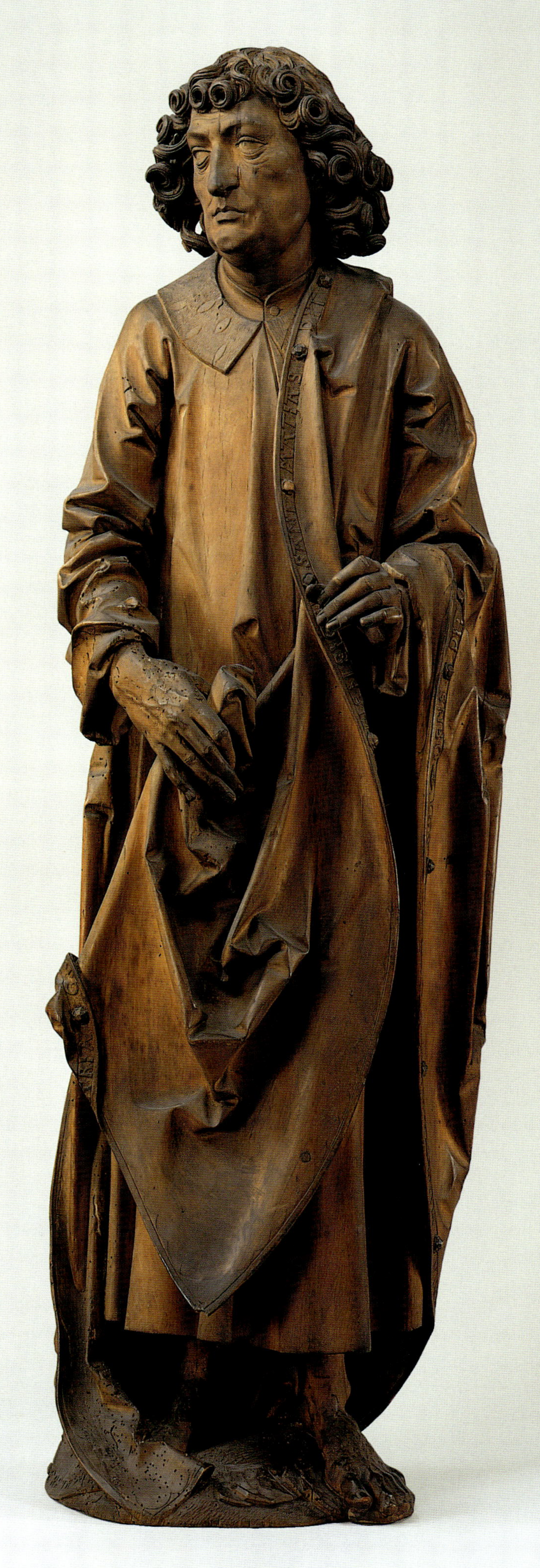

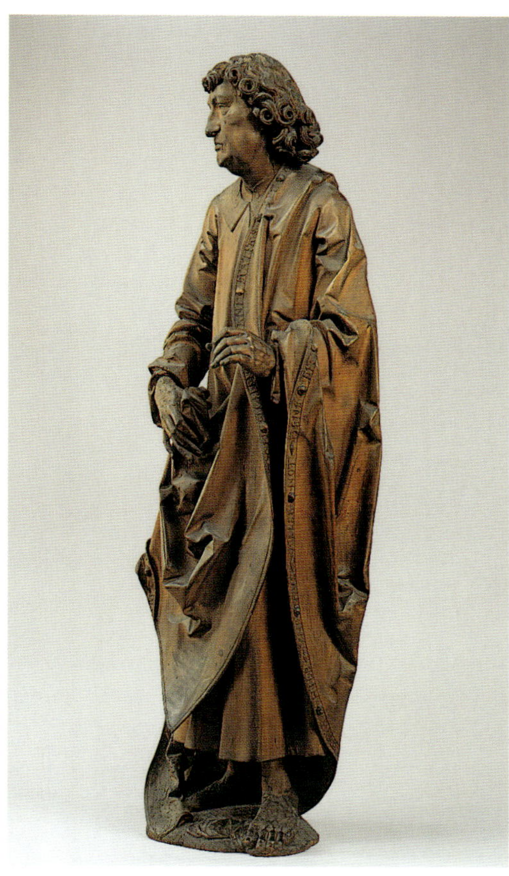

Alternate view of catalogue no. 24

a portion of drapery in front. Although the sculpture is not fully in the round, one reads the cloak as continuing across the saint's back to his left shoulder, where it falls on either side of his left arm. Turned inside out at the front, the cloak forms a generous drapery swirl, actually separated from the figure by deep undercutting and offering a rich play of light and dark. This handling calls to mind the sculpture of Veit Stoss, whose *Archangel Raphael and the Young Tobias* (cat. 25) reveals a similar bravura for more theatrical effects. Riemenschneider's use of the motif creates a grand calligraphic form, especially noticeable in the series of short angular folds surrounded by large, flat areas.

The quality of the carving is extremely high. The curls in the hair, for instance, are bored out and stand away from the head. This depth of undercutting is typical of Riemenschneider's best work, such as the reliefs from his *Passion* altarpiece and the figures in his *Holy Blood* altarpiece (Chapuis essay, figs. 2 and 6). The saint's right hand is among the most expressive in Riemenschneider's oeuvre. Coherently articulated, with a vital delineation of sinews and veins, its ele-

gance is quite remarkable. The expressive face, too, conveys seriousness and a sense of purpose.

The composition of the Berlin sculpture is extremely close to that of the sandstone *Matthias* in the Mainfränkisches Museum (fig. 1), one of the fourteen figures produced in Riemenschneider's shop for the decoration of the Marienkapelle in Würzburg between 1500 and 1506. The stance, costume, and draperies are repeated with minor variations. The one major difference is the head: a youthful dreamy countenance in the sandstone has replaced the gravity of the older apostle's face, and the head is tilted back slightly. Unlike the *Adam* and *Eve* of 1491–1493, which stood on either side of the south portal of the Marienkapelle, at the level of the tympanum where they could be seen well from the ground (Krohm essay, fig. 5), the figures of Christ, the twelve apostles, and John the Baptist were made to be placed high on the buttresses. Their execution is far less accomplished, and it is generally agreed that Riemenschneider was responsible only for their conception, leaving the actual carving to assistants. This conclusion is borne out by the fee paid for the two commissions: Riemenschneider received 120 guilders for the *Adam* and *Eve,* as opposed to 10 guilders for each of the fourteen later figures.[3]

The limewood and the sandstone versions of Matthias are clearly related and probably contemporary, but not much can be surmised about the original context of the Berlin *Saint Matthias* in the absence of documents. It probably stood in an altarpiece with other carved figures, as it is best viewed within an angle of only about 100 degrees, which is typical for figures in a shrine (see cat. 32A–D). If the other figures in this altarpiece were of equal quality, this must have been one of Riemenschneider's most accomplished works.

The Berlin sculpture is important in another regard, throwing light on Riemenschneider's origins. While civil registers in Würzburg list the sculptor as coming from Osterode am Harz, archival research by Walter Prochaska has revealed that Riemenschneider's father, Tilman the Elder, was in Heiligenstadt im Eichsfeld until December 1465, when he moved to Osterode. Riemenschneider's uncle Nikolaus is mentioned in Heiligenstadt since 1423.[4] Prochaska's conclusion that Riemenschneider must have been born in Heiligenstadt—about 1460—has been confirmed by philological analysis of the inscription on the cloak of the Berlin sculpture done by Matthias Fritz, revealing it to be in the dialect of northwestern Thuringia typical of the Heiligenstadt region.[5] CHAPUIS

3. See Muth 1982, 29, 52.

4. See Prochaska's essay, with references to his earlier publications, in Würzburg 1981, 385–388.

5. I am grateful to Dr. Fritz for making his research available before its publication, and to Hartmut Krohm for drawing it to my attention.

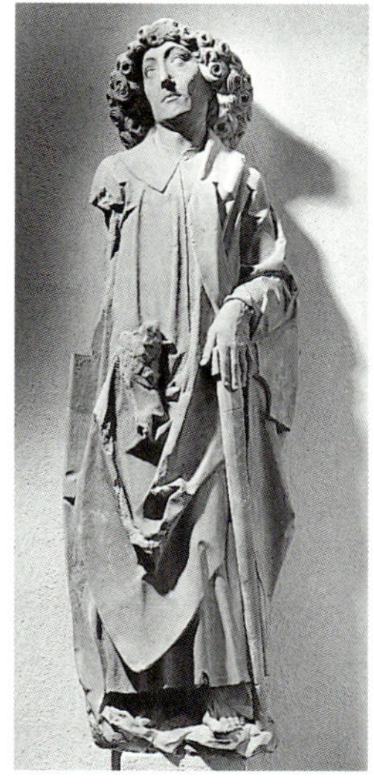

1.

Saint Matthias from the Marienkapelle, 1500–1506, sandstone, Mainfränkisches Museum, Würzburg

25

Raphael, 1516, limewood, 94.5 x 48 x 38 (37¼ x 18⅞ x 15), Germanisches Nationalmuseum, Nuremberg, on loan from the Governing Body of the Lutheran Church of Saint James

Tobias, 1516, limewood, 85 x 34.5 x 31 (33½ x 13⅝ x 12¼), Germanisches Nationalmuseum, Nuremberg, on loan from the City of Nuremberg

• *Technical Notes* •

Each figure is cut from a single block of limewood with the grain running vertically and no additions except for modern restorations. The figures have been hollowed out deeply in the back: the angel entirely, and Tobias up to the waist. The hair on the back of the heads is not finished but only roughed out. The sculpture was originally monochrome, with a light brown translucent layer and touches of color in the eyes and the lips, now lost. The curls of hair on the right side of Raphael's head have suffered severely from insect damage, as has the back of Tobias below the belt. There is less serious insect damage over the entire surface of the group. Raphael has suffered the following losses: his right fingers after the first joint, his right thumb and right big toe—which are replacements—a box in his right hand, and his left small finger. Tobias has no right hand; apparently it was never carved because it would not have been visible in the original installation. His left hand once held a fish, carved separately and hanging from a string.[1]

• *Provenance* •

Dominican church in Nuremberg (demolished in the nineteenth century). Raphael: Jakobskirche, Nuremberg (nineteenth century); Tobias: municipal art collections (nineteenth century).

• *Literature* •

Johann Jakob Schwarz, 1737, 18, 20 (Stadtbibliothek Nürnberg, Hs. Will II, 1395 fol.); Lösch 1825, 42; Bode 1885, 125; Schäfer 1896, pl. 28; Daun 1903, 149–150, fig. 78; Daun 1906, 91, fig. 100; Josephi 1910, no. 305 (ill.); Lossnitzer 1912, 130–131, 200 nn. 408–410, pl. 46; Daun 1916, 210–212, pl. 59.2; Bock 1924, 201–202; Nuremberg 1933, nos. 23, 24; Lutze 1937, 186–188 (ill.); Dettloff 1961, 1:132–133, 301, 2: pl. 189; Pilz 1964, 66–67; Lutze 1968, 49–50, figs. 62–63; Weskott 1975, 18, 136 n. 59; Baxandall 1980, 272–273, pl. 47; Kepinski 1981, 79–80, pls. 141–146; Liebmann 1982, 357, 364–365, fig. 197; Nuremberg 1983, 142–149, figs. 94–97; Vetter and Oellermann 1984, 311–320, figs. 2, 5–10; Kahsnitz 1984, 42–44 (ill.); Rasmussen 1985, 121–122, fig. 70; New York 1986, 249–251, no. 93, pl. 251.

VEIT STOSS WAS Riemenschneider's most important contemporary and is often seen as his polar opposite. The early style of Stoss, who was born in Horb am Neckar in Swabia around 1447, suggests that he was trained in the Upper Rhine region. His oeuvre, like Riemenschneider's, testifies to his awareness of Niclaus Gerhaert, of Ulm sculpture—especially that of Jörg Syrlin—and of prints by Master E. S. and Martin Schongauer. Like Riemenschneider, Stoss demonstrated his virtuosity in carving materials as diverse as limewood, sandstone, and marble. He settled in Nuremberg before 1476 but the following year moved to Krakow, where his first documented work, the monumental *Death of the Virgin* altarpiece in the church of Saint Mary, dates from 1477–1489. During his stay in Krakow he created a stone *Crucifix* for Heinrich Slacker, also in the church of Saint Mary, as well as the red marble tomb of King Kasimir IV Jagiello in Wawel Cathedral, which is signed and dated 1492. In 1496 Stoss returned to Nuremberg, where he stayed, with a long interruption, until his death in 1533. His first documented work in Nuremberg is the so-called Volckamer Donation of 1499 in the Sankt

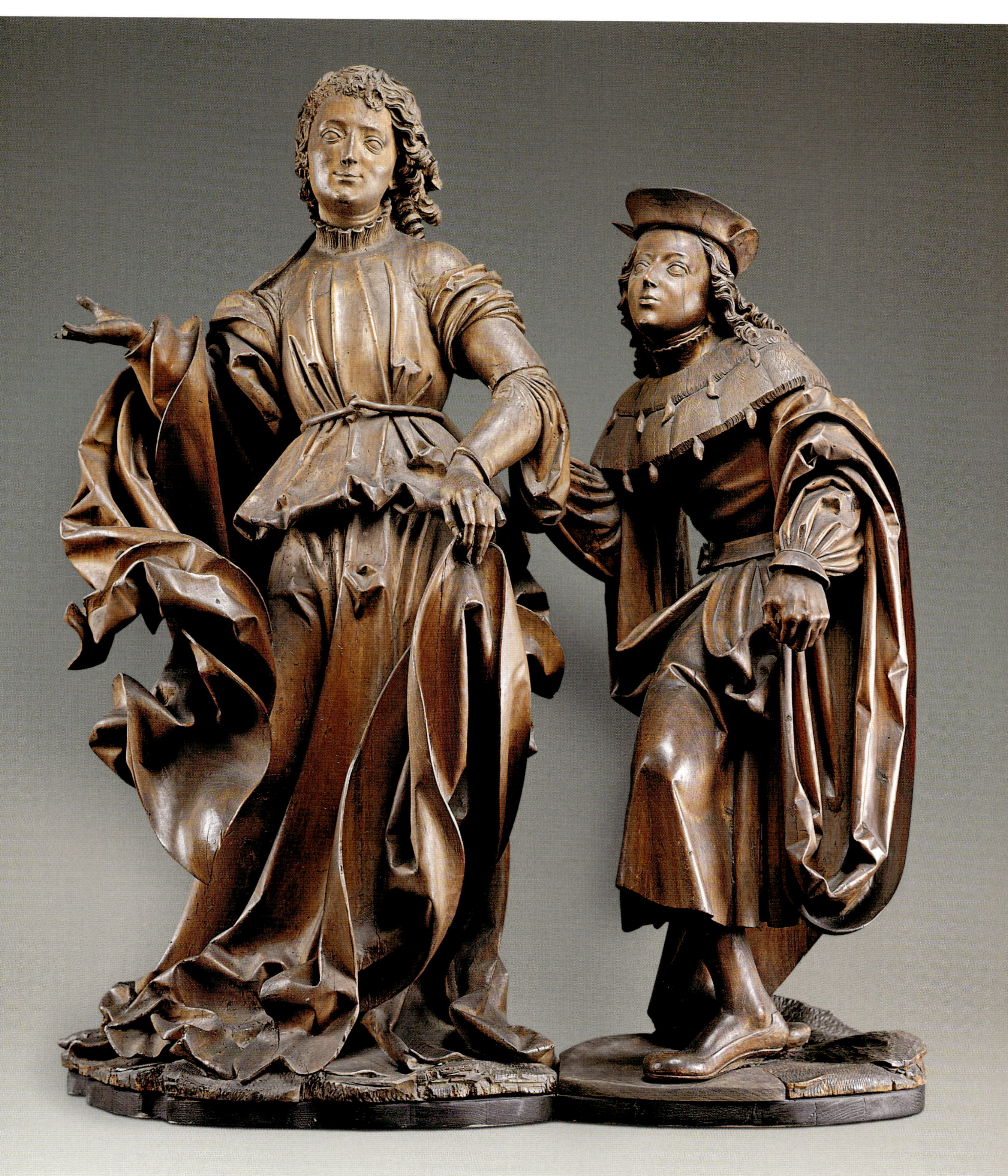

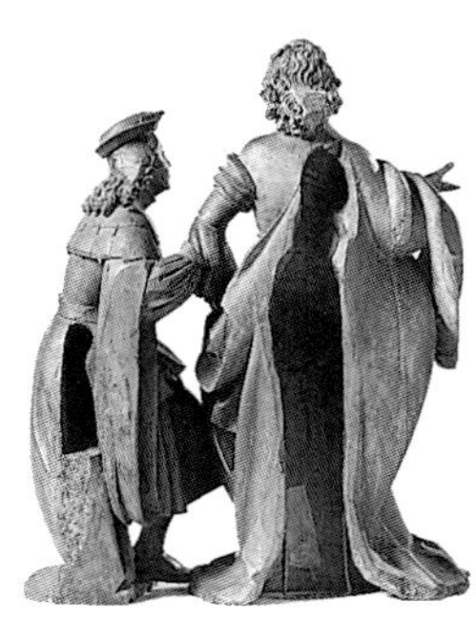

Back view of
catalogue no. 25

Sebalduskirche, an ambitious ensemble in limewood and sandstone.

Stoss' repeated involvement in risky financial ventures led to his imprisonment in 1503, but through the personal intervention of Lorenz von Bibra, prince-bishop of Würzburg, he escaped blinding or execution. In 1504 he fled to Münnerstadt, where he polychromed Riemenschneider's *Mary Magdalen* altarpiece (see cat. 13) and painted scenes from the life of Saint Kilian on its wings. In 1507 he was received in audience in Ulm by Emperor Maximilian, who may have helped his rehabilitation in Nuremberg. The works he created after his return include a dramatic over-life-size *Crucifix* of 1505–1510 for the Heiliggeist-Spital (Germanisches Nationalmuseum) and a monumental *Saint Andrew* of 1510–1520 in the Sebalduskirche (Baxandall essay, fig. 8). In addition to the *Archangel Raphael and the Young Tobias*, dated 1516, and his *Nativity* altarpiece, commissioned in 1520 by his son Dr. Andreas Stoss, prior of the Carmelite convent in Nuremberg (now in Bamberg Cathedral), the most sublime work of this late period is his *Annunciation* of 1517–1518 in the Lorenzkirche (Marincola essay, fig. 1).[2] Hallmarks of Stoss' highly personal style include the expressive use of drapery patterns and keen attention to details.

This unusually dramatic group of Tobias and the angel Raphael was described by Johann Jakob

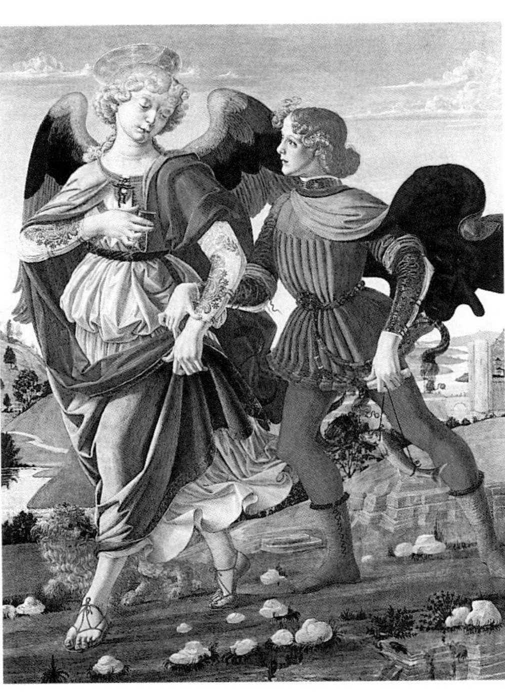

1.
Follower of Andrea del Verrocchio, *Tobias and the Angel,*
c. 1470–1475, egg tempera on poplar, the Trustees of the
National Gallery, London

Schwartz in 1737 as being located on the south side of the nave of the Dominican church in Nuremberg. It was placed against the column closest to the choir and inscribed with the date 1516, the initials R. T., and a shield with the arms of Raffaello Torrigiani (c. 1480–1531), a wealthy Florentine silk and jewel merchant, who sojourned in Nuremberg between 1516 and 1518.[3] The subject, almost nonexistent in German art, had particular resonance for the donor: it represented his patron saint, the archangel Raphael, who was also revered as the protector of travelers. The subject was popular in Torrigiani's native Tuscany, and Stoss' group bears resemblance to Florentine models, such as the *Tobias and the Angel* of about 1470–1475 by a follower of Andrea del Verrocchio (fig. 1), especially in the positioning of the figures, in the double-belted costume of the angel, and in Tobias' holding gently onto Raphael's left wrist. There are relationships to other Florentine depictions of the theme, which suggests that Torrigiani either specified the details of the iconography or provided Stoss with a model, such as a print or a drawing.

The subject is derived from the Old Testament book of Tobit, which tells of a God-fearing Jew living in exile in Assyria. Tobit loses his eyesight and descends into poverty as a result of good deeds that bring him into the king's disfavor. His devoted son Tobias restores his fortunes with the assistance of the archangel Raphael, who is disguised as a kinsman. Raphael travels with Tobias to reclaim money Tobit had left in trust with a relative. Along the way the angel instructs the young man to cut open a large fish from the Tigris River and to save the fish gall, heart, and liver to use as medicine. The gall becomes the agent for the miraculous restoration of Tobit's sight.

Veit Stoss included all the details required to tell the story, though the fish once held by Tobias and the box of fish gall in the angel's right hand are now missing (both elements are present in the painting by the follower of Verrocchio). Even though he chose to depict the angel without wings, Stoss established a clear contrast between the two figures that identifies Raphael as a celestial being while emphasizing Tobias' earthbound nature. Raphael appears to glide over the ground without actually touching it. Only his right foot, which is bare, is visible, while the actual placement of his left leg is entirely ambiguous. His left hand holds a portion of his garment, while his mantle drapes around his raised right arm and swirls in a florid drapery passage of extreme finesse that is almost entirely freestanding. The grand flourishes of Raphael's garments convey an almost supernatural animation. Tobias, by contrast, is clearly a terrestrial creature. Un-

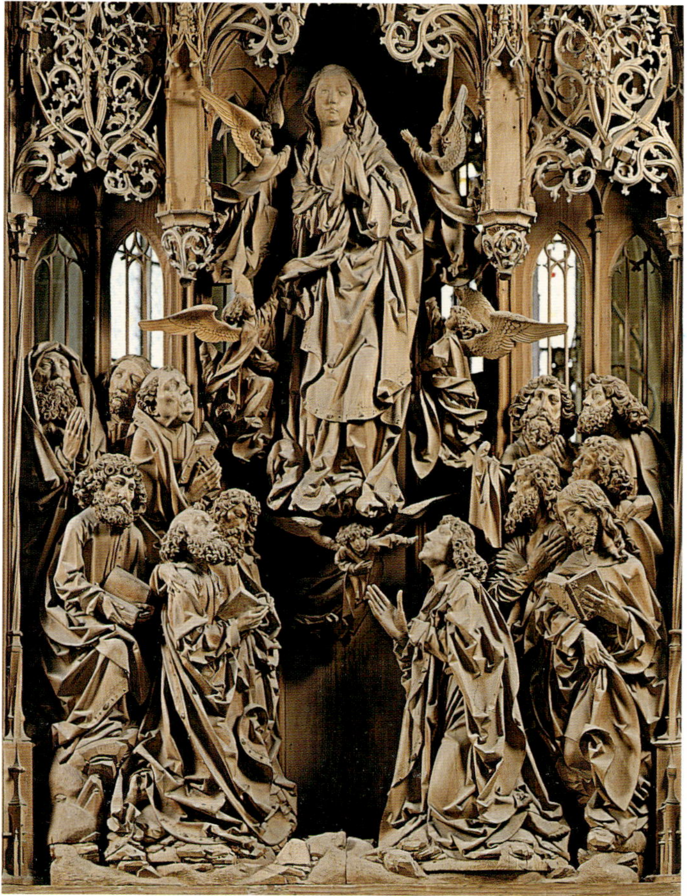

Assumption of the Virgin altarpiece, detail of the central shrine, c. 1505–1510, Herrgottskirche, Creglingen

like the "timelessness" of Raphael's drapery, Tobias' costume, which responds to the pull of gravity, is contemporary and expensive. He wears a short robe with puffed sleeves, a belted cloak with a double ermine collar, shoes, and a beret with a high brim. The awkward twisting of his feet suggests that he was originally walking toward the right, and that Gabriel, leading him, rectified his course.[4]

The intelligence of the sculptural conception and the virtuosity of the carving establish this group as one of Stoss' most accomplished masterpieces. The spatial animation of the almost free-hanging yet enveloping drapery defies belief. The sense of arrested movement and the psychological relationship between the two figures are extremely subtle. Originally made to be seen against a column, the sculpture is conceived to accommodate a variety of vantage points, from which the spatial complexity of the whole becomes apparent. A work that makes a subject of its very virtuosity, it develops the great sculptural and spatial naturalism and the interest in contrasting textures

shown by Niclaus Gerhaert (cats. 5 and 6) into a kind of Gothic baroque style.

The contrast between this group and the roughly contemporary works by Riemenschneider could not be more dramatic (see cat. 24). Riemenschneider's emphasis is more subdued in the rendering of figures and more planar in the treatment of draperies, increasingly so as his style evolved in such works as the Dumbarton Oaks *Virgin and Child* (cat. 45). The closest analogy can be found in Riemenschneider's central shrine for the Creglingen altarpiece of about 1505–1510, with its *Assumption of the Virgin* (fig. 2), showing the apostles below and the angels above clustered around the rising Virgin in an intricate spatial, chiaroscuro, and psychological involvement. The great spirituality of this masterpiece suggests that Riemenschneider's underlying aims were quite different from those of Veit Stoss. The figures of Raphael and Tobias, while more worldly in their costumed elegance, are also perhaps more humanist in their response to the Florentine Renaissance. WIXOM

4. Nuremberg 1983, 142–143.

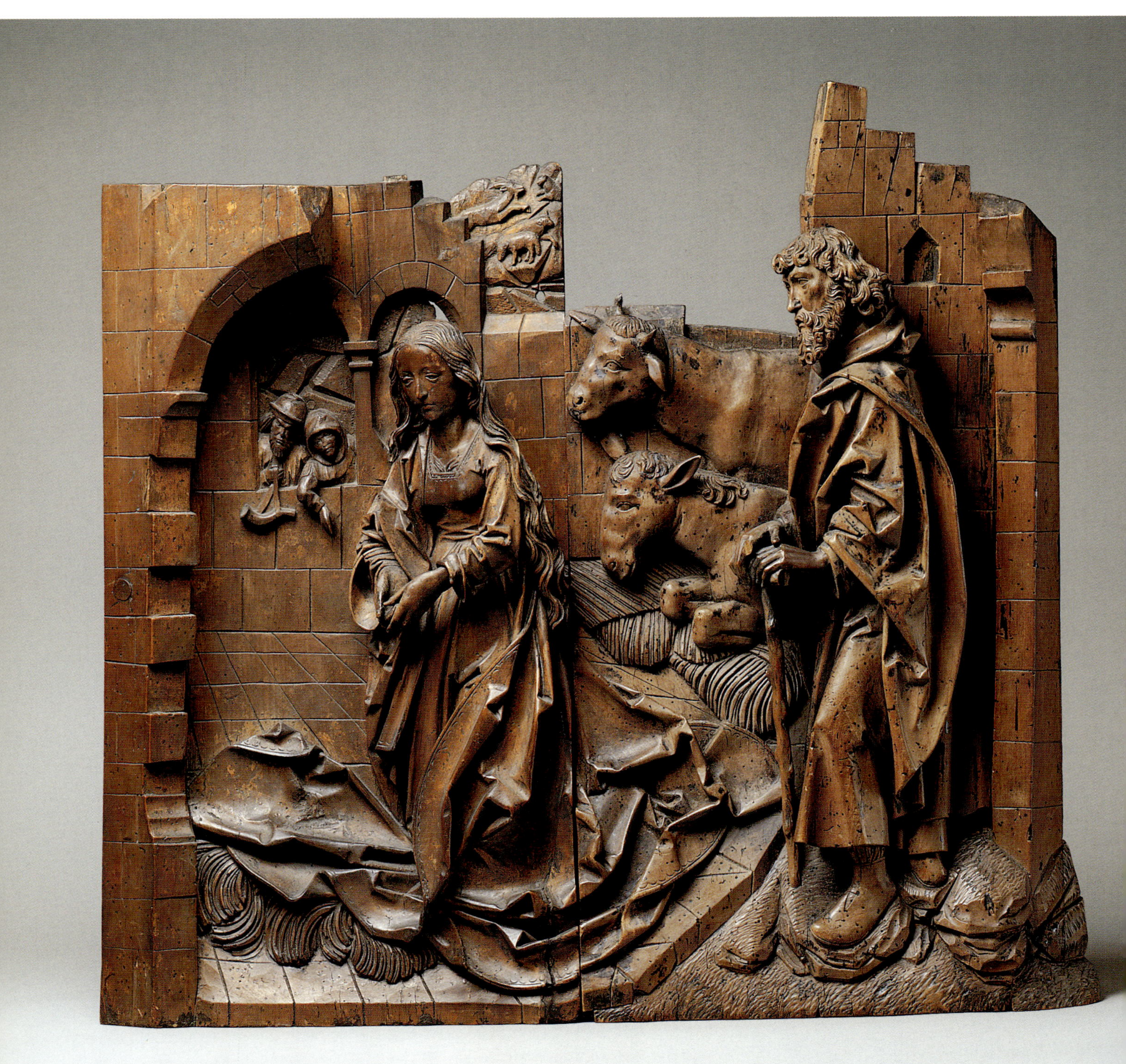

NATIVITY

c. 1502–1505, limewood, 61 x 66 x 10 (24 x 26 x 3⅞), Staatliche Museen zu Berlin,
Skulpturensammlung (left half); Stiftsmuseum der Stadt Aschaffenburg (right half)

• *Technical Notes* •
The relief, carved of limewood, consists of two main vertical sections. Originally joined together, they broke apart prior to 1845 (when the left half entered the collection in Berlin). The background landscape was carved separately and attached to the back of the relief. Portions of the landscape are missing, especially in the right half. The original Christ child, now missing, was also individually carved, and it must have been glued in place since there is no sign of nails or dowels. The niche behind Joseph originally contained a candlestick. A dark surface layer covers the left half of the relief, and traces of dark brown define the pupils of the Virgin's eyes. The right half shows remnants of a dark brown surface layer, but there appears to be no trace of paint in Joseph's eyes. Minor modern replacements include a lock of Joseph's hair, the back of his right hand, and several inserts in the drapery of both figures.[1]

• *Provenance* •
The right half of the relief appeared on the art market in Berlin [Ferdinand Knapp]; acquired by Dr. Aloys Lautenschläger, Berlin, who bequeathed it to the museum in Aschaffenburg in 1943. The left half was acquired from the royal collections by the museum in Berlin in 1845; it remained in East Berlin after World War II; was placed on long-term loan to the Aschaffenburg museum in 1994, where both halves have been reassembled.

• *Literature* •
Bode 1885, 166; Tönnies 1900, 222; Weber 1911, 240; Adelmann 1910, 60; Vöge 1910, 106; Cornell 1924; Demmler 1930, 461; Aschaffenburg 1949, no. 191; Bier 1955b, 168–172 nn. 26, 28; Bier 1957b, 207–209; Aschaffenburg 1957, no. 211; Aachen 1958, no. 104; Raleigh 1962, 52–53; Schneider 1964, 22–23; Augs-

burg 1965, nos. 7–10, 72; Treutwein 1981, 263–265; Kalden 1990, 119 n. 435; Aschaffenburg 1994, 84–85.

THIS RELIEF OF the Nativity no doubt originally formed part of the wing or predella of a lost altarpiece by Riemenschneider, which presumably included other depictions of Christ's infancy or the life of the Virgin. The setting is defined by an imposing stone structure reminiscent of Romanesque architecture. At the left the Virgin kneels on a tiled floor that establishes recession in space. Over a tight-waisted dress she wears a mantle that descends in a grand spiral from her right shoulder, wrapping behind her back to the front, where it is spread out over bundles of straw. She folds her hands in a prayerful gesture and bends forward slightly toward the empty space where the Christ child originally lay.[2] At the right, isolated on the rocky ledge of a grassy patch of earth, Joseph stands facing the scene, with one foot forward and both hands on his walking stick. He seems to have just entered, an impression enhanced by the dynamic folds of his mantle, thrown over his left shoulder, and by the open archway behind him. A donkey and an ox resting on straw placed over the tile floor belong to the same space as the Virgin and child. Through a window in the rear wall two shepherds witness the Nativity. Farther in the distance some sheep and a leaping goat are visible; this detail is probably a fragment of an Annunciation to the Shepherds.

Riemenschneider's image, a fine example of his narrative carvings, refers to the account of the Nativity in Luke 2:1–17. By including the ox and ass, the relief also seems to depend on apocryphal gospels or hagiographical writings such as Jacobus de Voragine's *Golden Legend*. Together with the shepherds, these animals were featured in performances of the Nativity staged in churches during Advent. In theological thought the ox and ass were considered sym-

1. Bier 1955b, 168–169 n. 26.

2. Bier 1955b, 169 n. 28.

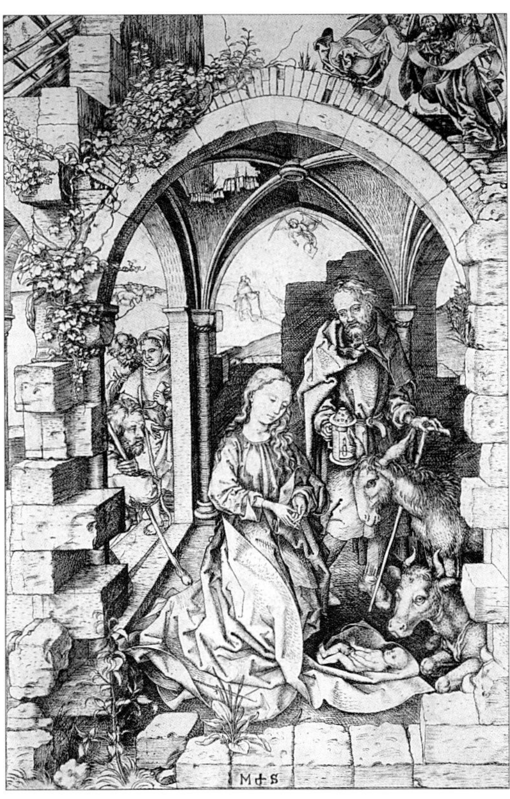

1.

Martin Schongauer, *Nativity,* c. 1475, engraving, National
Gallery of Art, Washington, Gift of W. G. Russell Allen

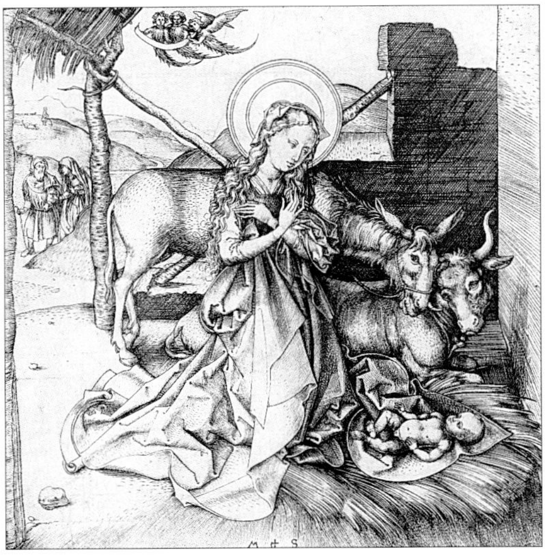

2.

Martin Schongauer, *Nativity,* c. 1480/1490, engraving,
National Gallery of Art, Washington, Rosenwald Collection

3. Karl Young, "Officium
Pastorum: A Study of the
Dramatic Developments within
the Liturgy of Christmas,"
*Transactions of the Wisconsin
Academy of Sciences, Arts, and
Letters* 17 (1914), 1:299–396;
Cornell 1924; Treutwein 1981,
263–265.

4. Bier 1955b, 169–171; Bier
1957b, 207–209.

5. Bier 1955b, 170–171; Alfred
Stange and Norbert Lieb, *Hans
Holbein der Ältere* (Munich
and Berlin, 1960), no. 4; Augsburg 1965, nos. 7–10.

6. Stange and Lieb 1960, nos.
17, 75; Augsburg 1965, no. 72.

7. Bier 1955b, 171–172; Raleigh
1962, 52–53.

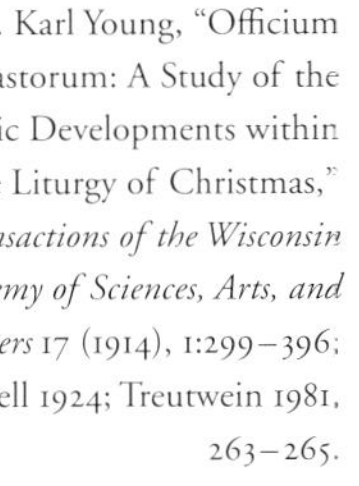

bolic of the Old and the New Law.[3] Other details
also have symbolic connotations. The Romanesque
style of the architecture refers to the Synagogue of
the Old Law, which served as the foundation for the
Ecclesia of the New Law. It is difficult to determine
if these associations were commonly and consciously
observed in Riemenschneider's time, or if these
motifs were simply integral to the pictorial tradition.

Justus Bier pointed out that the Aschaffenburg
Nativity was based on two engravings of the *Nativity* by Martin Schongauer (figs. 1 and 2), which the
sculptor transformed into an original composition.[4]
He selected discrete details from both prints, such as
the abstract representation of bundles of straw or the
shepherd's horn, and quoted more directly the Virgin and her drapery, though in reverse. Another model
for Riemenschneider's composition, especially for the
figure of Joseph, was an engraving by Israhel van
Meckenem (fig. 3) that freely copied the *Nativity* from
Hans Holbein the Elder's Weingarten altarpiece. Dated
1493, this altarpiece was a collaboration between Holbein and Michel Erhart of Ulm, who influenced
Riemenschneider (see cats. 9, 11, 12). Although Riemenschneider had already established himself in
Würzburg by this time, his direct knowledge of this

work cannot be excluded, but it is more likely that
he knew it through Van Meckenem's print.[5]

Newly discovered evidence supports Riemenschneider's personal knowledge of another *Nativity*
by Holbein, dated 1500–1501, which belonged to a
destroyed altarpiece for the Dominican church in
Frankfurt am Main. The painting is known only by
a contemporary drawing after it in Berlin's Kupferstichkabinett, sometimes believed to be by Holbein.[6]
While the principal arrangement of the composition
differs from that in the Aschaffenburg *Nativity,* certain correspondences go beyond pure accident. Most
striking are the floor tiles, which are conspicuously
absent in the prints mentioned above. Moreover, the
fragment of an Annunciation to the Shepherds in the
background of the relief seems, judging from the
drawn copy, to reveal a stunning similarity to the gen-
relike depiction of the goat and sheep in Holbein's
panel. Although Riemenschneider could have known
Holbein's composition from a drawn copy, such as
the one in Berlin, he may easily have seen the actual
altarpiece, given the relatively short distance between
Würzburg and Frankfurt, comfortably connected by
the river Main.

Within the surviving oeuvre of Riemenschneider and his workshop the *Nativity* in Aschaffenburg
is one of four representations of this subject, including a relief on the right wing of the Creglingen altarpiece from about 1505–1510 (fig. 4). The Aschaffenburg relief exhibits the highest quality carving and
the most inventive composition. Bier argued convincingly that it was largely an autograph work by
Riemenschneider.[7] The hand of collaborators may

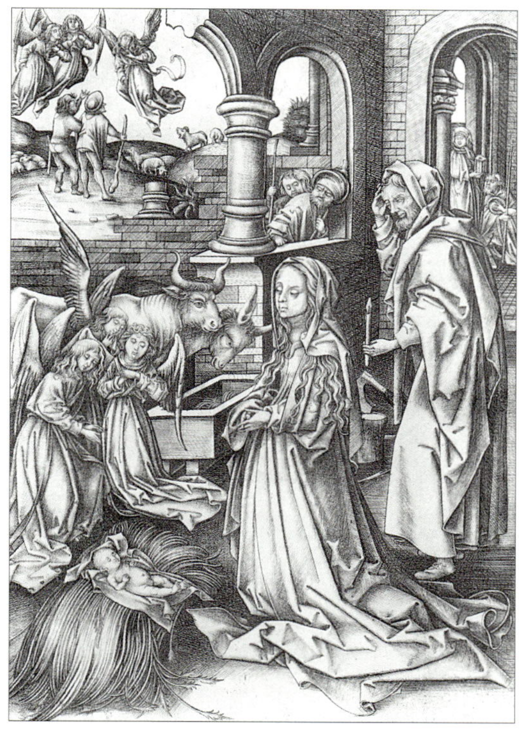

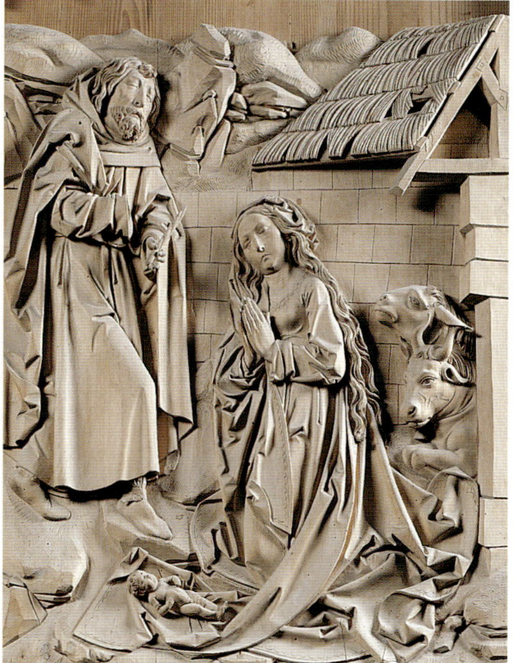

3.

Israhel van Meckenem, *Nativity,* engraving,
after 1493, National Gallery of Art, Washington,
Rosenwald Collection

4.

Nativity in the right wing of the
Creglingen altarpiece, c. 1505-1510, limewood,
Herrgottskirche, Creglingen

be detected in the shepherds, but the Virgin and Joseph seem to be the work of the master. The conceptual strength of the Aschaffenburg relief, most notable in the integration of various pictorial sources into a harmonious original composition and its mastery of complicated spatial structures and their narrative implications, supports Bier's attribution to Riemenschneider himself. By contrast, the artist (or his workshop) based the Creglingen *Nativity* scene solely on Schongauer's prints. Stylistic comparisions with the effigy of Heinrich II on the imperial tomb in Bamberg and the *Holy Blood* altarpiece in Rothenburg (Chapuis essay, figs. 4 and 5) support a date for the Aschaffenburg *Nativity* of about 1502–1505. BORCHERT

Pupil of Veit Stoss / B A P T I S M   O F   C H R I S T

c. 1480–1490, limewood with polychromy, 121.9 x 101.6 x 7.6 (48 x 40 x 3), The Metropolitan
Museum of Art, New York, Rogers Fund

• *Technical Notes* •

The relief is made of three main pieces of wood,
probably limewood, joined with the grain running
vertically. They measure, from right to left, 5 cm, 48
cm, and 48 cm wide at the bottom. A fourth board
was cut to follow roughly the contour of John's back,
and it does not extend to the bottom. A strip of limewood, 2–2.5 cm thick, runs horizontally across the
bottom and appears to be original since the join is
covered with matted plant fiber, as was the join between Christ and John. The lateral edges of the panel
are beveled to fit into the frame of an altarpiece wing.
The knot of Christ's loincloth was carved separately
and fastened to the panel with a nail.

Although the colors have altered over time, the
relief has retained much of its original polychromy.
The flesh tones are fairly well preserved, and reflections are painted in the eyes. The background rocks,
by contrast, show significant paint loss, as does John's
camel's hair garment. The reds are achieved in two
layers: a crimson red lake over a bright underlayer.
The blue lining of Christ's drapery consists of pigment over a layer of black. Silver leaf covered with a
translucent greenish glaze, of which only fragments
remain, suggested the shine of the water in the river.
Most remarkable is the differentiation in Christ's garment held by the angel, which was executed in matte
gilding (as were the angel's wings), while its border is
burnished and was decorated by two different punches.
This matte surface contrasts with the highly burnished
water gilding of the angel's robe.

• *Provenance* •

Acquired by the Metropolitan Museum from Lipp-
mann in 1912.

• *Literature* •

Kahsnitz in New York 1986, 236–237.

T H E   F O U R   G O S P E L S all tell of John the Baptist, who announced the coming of Christ, urged
people to turn to God for forgiveness, and baptized
them in the river Jordan. Jesus, too, came to be baptized by John, despite John's protest of his own un-
worthiness. In this relief John stands on the bank of
the river, wearing the camel's hair specified in the
scriptures, his right hand raised over Christ in blessing. Although not mentioned in the Gospel accounts,
one or more angels holding Christ's garments are
often included in renderings of the scene. One important element is missing from the relief. After the
baptism Christ saw "the heavens torn apart and the
Spirit descending like a dove on him. And a voice
came from heaven, 'You are my Son, the Beloved;
with you I am well pleased'" (Mark 1:10–11). When
complete, the relief probably showed the blessing
figure of God the Father and the dove of the Holy
Spirit, possibly in the upper left background.

The relief, from the interior of a wing from a
lost or uncompleted altarpiece, follows an engraving
by Martin Schongauer of about 1480, nearly contemporary (fig. 1). Schongauer's composition became the
prototype for numerous renderings of the scene in
German art, and it was repeated thirty years later by
Riemenschneider's shop on the left wing of the Gerolzhofen altarpiece from around 1513 (Chapuis essay,
fig. 11). The present relief compresses the main elements of Schongauer's horizontal composition into
a vertical format, no doubt dictated by the dimensions of the altarpiece shutter the relief was to decorate. While the angel in the engraving stands isolated
on the right, as a visual counterpoint for the figure
of John and the rocks on the left, he stands close to
Christ in this relief. Schongauer achieves a much
greater integration of the two main figures, whose
contours echo one another. John is clearly kneeling
as a sign of deference, and his body forms a visual

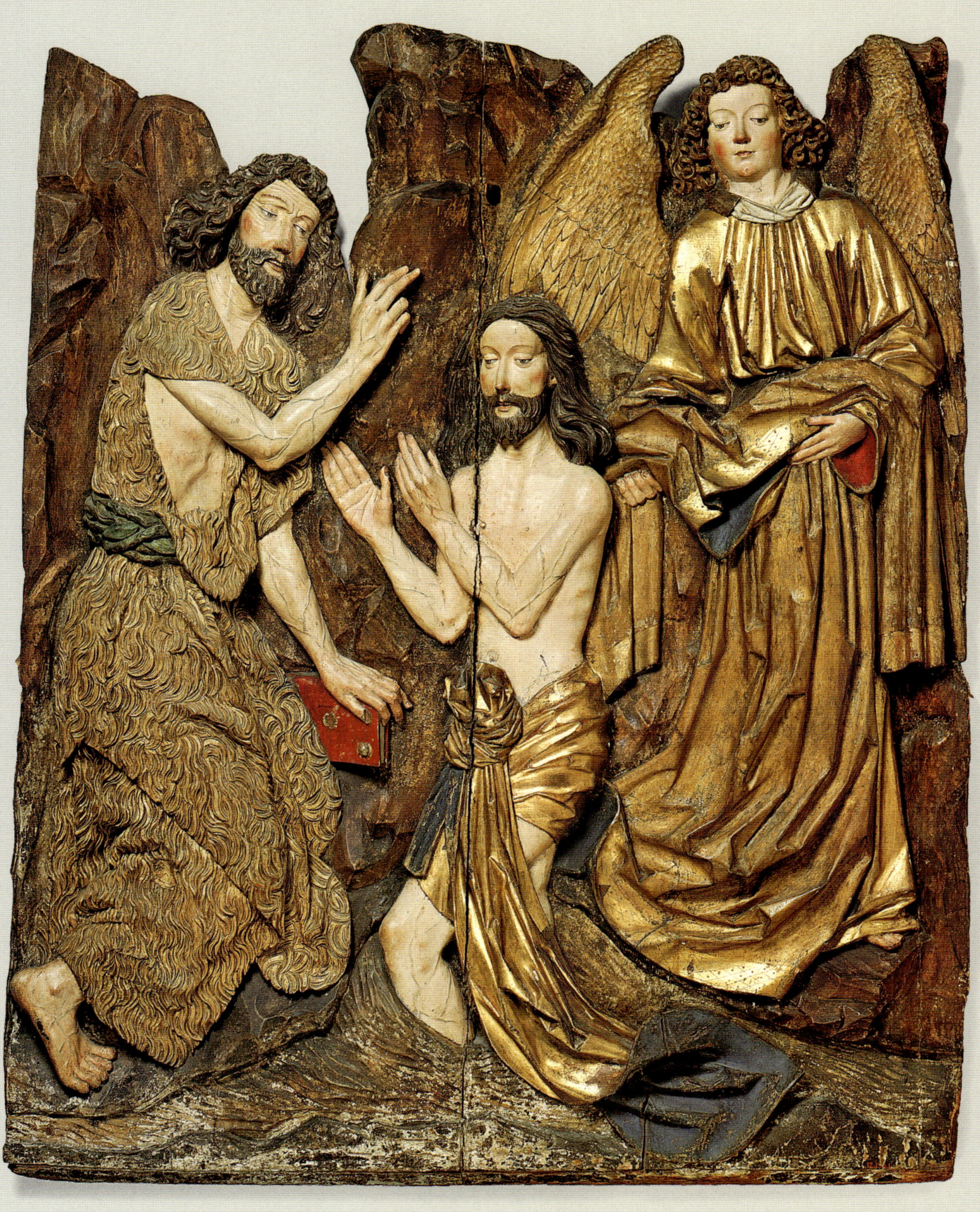

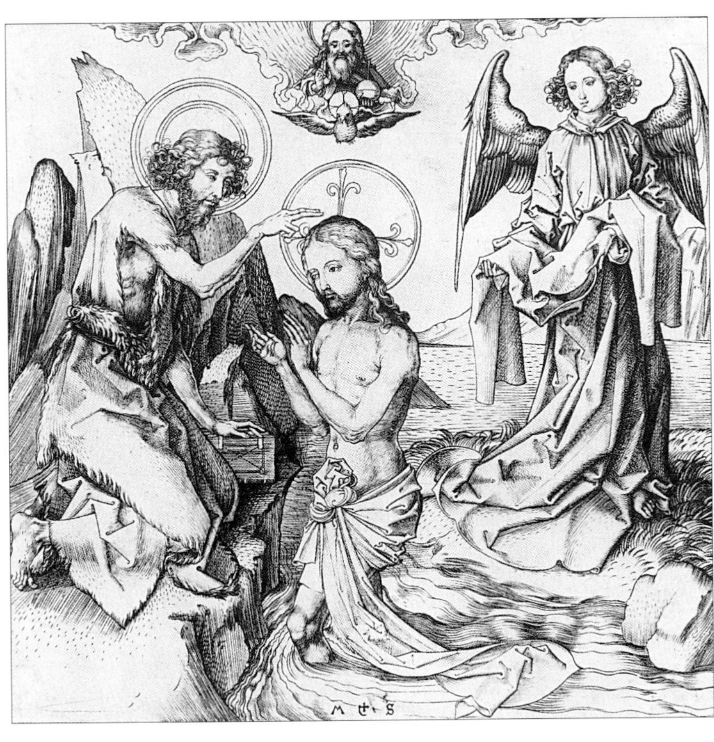

1.

Martin Schongauer, *Baptism of Christ,* c. 1480, engraving, National Gallery of Art, Washington, Rosenwald Collection

1. The Metropolitan Museum catalogue of medieval art records the suggestion of Dr. Andrew Ciechanowiscki, dated 15 January 1959, that if the relief actually came from Krakow it would have been "part of the now incomplete altarpiece by Veit Stoss in Saint Florian church there" and the relief might have been carved by a son of the master.

2. Kepinski 1981, pls. 31–32, 35–36; Piotr Skubiszewski, "Der Osterzyklus im Marienaltar des Veit Stoss," in *Veit Stoss. Die Vorträge des Nürnberger Symposions* (Munich, 1985), 123–128, figs. 73–74.

3. Kahsnitz 1997, 36–37, figs. 15–16.

bracket for Christ's upper body. This relationship is diluted in the relief, where the two figures, now turned toward the viewer, are more erect. The sculptor has thoroughly changed the background, replacing Schongauer's vast expanse of water with a wall of rock, thus reducing the sense of spatial recession, as appropriate to the relief's intended function and context.

This polychrome low relief appears to be by a pupil of Veit Stoss working in Krakow, where the sculptor sojourned from 1477 to 1496 (see cats. 25 and 35). This assumption is based on the work's resemblance to several of the reliefs carved by assistants for Stoss' monumental *Death of the Virgin* altarpiece of 1477–1489, made for the high altar of the church of Saint Mary.[1] The shared elements include the awkward poses and gestures, the elongated physiognomies of the bearded figures, the narrowed eyes, and the bland facial expressions. For these reasons it is inconceivable that the New York relief (or the *Harrowing of Hell* and *Noli me Tangere* of the Krakow altarpiece[2])

could have been designed and carved by the master himself. Yet it is difficult to identify which assistant was responsible; there is a possibility that one of Stoss' two sons participated.

The New York *Baptism of Christ* is valuable as an example of polychrome low-relief carving designed for the moveable wings of late Gothic altarpieces. It is almost contemporaneous with Riemenschneider's early *Passion* altarpiece of 1485–1490 from Rothenburg (see Chapuis essay, fig. 2), portions of which are now dispersed. The wings, principally by Riemenschneider's workshop and now in the Schlossmuseum in Berchtesgaden, are similar in their dependence on Schongauer and in their representation of steeply angled spaces punctuated by awkwardly placed figures and obvious gestures.[3] The qualitative advance in expressiveness and eloquent carving seen in Riemenschneider's subsequent Münnerstadt wing reliefs (cat. 13 E–F) demonstrates how a tradition can be imbued with new life. WIXOM

VIRGIN AND CHILD ON THE CRESCENT MOON

c. 1503–1505, limewood, 139 x 47 x 26 cm (54¾ x 18½ x 10¼), Museum für Kunst und Gewerbe,
Hamburg

• Technical Notes •

The figure is cut from a single block of limewood
with the grain running vertically and the entire length
of the back hollowed out. The sculptor Georg Schuster of Munich restored the work in or before 1921,
making several additions: both of the child's arms
and the parts of the veil he holds, his toes and genitals,
large portions of the base (including the crescent
moon), and the edge of the drapery on the Virgin's
right side.[1] He also reworked the back of the Virgin's
head and recarved the veil along the right side of her
neck. There is a complete lack of decorative carving
as often seen on Riemenschneider's monochromes,
but the work seems to have been polychromed only
significantly after its completion, for the ground and
paint layers cover cracks. The polychromy was removed (possibly in the nineteenth century), and the
surface exhibits scraping marks in many areas, such as
the Virgin's left knee. Traces of the ground still remain,
which may be why a dark varnish has been applied.

• Provenance •

From a chapel around St. Leon near Wiesloch; Gustav Seitz, Külsheim, by 1885; his son, the sculptor
Seitz, Freiburg im Breisgau, by 1911; [sold after 1911
to the dealer Lösl in Leutkirch]; Weiller collection,
Frankfurt, by 1921; Carl von Weinberg, Frankfurt, by
1931; acquired with the entire Von Weinberg collection by the city of Frankfurt and exhibited at the
Städtische Galerie (Liebieghaus); after the capitulation of the Nazi regime, it was sent by the Allies to
the Central Collecting Point in Wiesbaden and, in
accordance with Restitution Laws, returned to Carl
von Weinberg's heirs; [Heinrich, Frankfurt]; from
whom it was acquired by the museum in Hamburg
in 1950.

• Literature •

Weber 1911, 223; Schmitt and Swarzenski 1921, no.
142; Anonymous 1928, 72–73; Demmler 1928, 1–2;
Hannover 1931, 3, no. 12; Raleigh 1962, 40–41; Bier
1975, 52–53; Bier 1978, 16, 23–25, 152; Würzburg 1981,
229; Kalden 1990, 120, 122, 135; Simon 1998, 173, 176.

LIKE MANY OF Riemenschneider's images of the
Virgin and child (see cats. 14, 16, 45), this imposing
group presents Mary as the woman of the Apocalypse
(Revelation 12:1), with her left foot on a crescent
moon. The chubby Christ child, held gently under
his right arm and under his feet, is in a half-sitting,
half-reclining position and grabs his mother's veil with
both hands. The mood is one of solemn melancholy
mixed with tenderness. The Virgin, presenting the
child to the beholder, seems to gaze straight ahead,
her head slightly bent, while the child looks off to
the right.

The drapery responds to the poses of the figures. The child's body forms a distinct curve, which
is echoed and expanded in the series of concentric
U-shaped folds below him. Converging folds at the
Virgin's left hip lead the eye to her left hand, emphasizing her support for the child's legs through the fabric of her veil. This detail is particularly noticeable
from slightly to the right of center, which seems to be
the intended direction of approach, as suggested by the
child's gaze. Figural distortions, such as the Virgin's
extremely long thighs, suggest that the sculpture was
intended to be installed quite high, where a fore-
shortened viewpoint would make the proportions
appear natural. Ironically, this vantage was achieved
during the sculpture's execution, when the figure was
placed horizontally on a workbench. The work can
be fully appreciated within an angle of about 120
degrees, inviting the viewer to walk around it.

1. Bier 1978, 24.

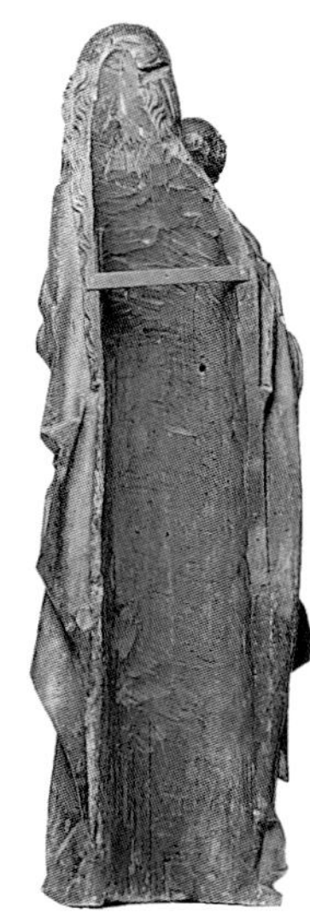

Back view of
catalogue no. 28

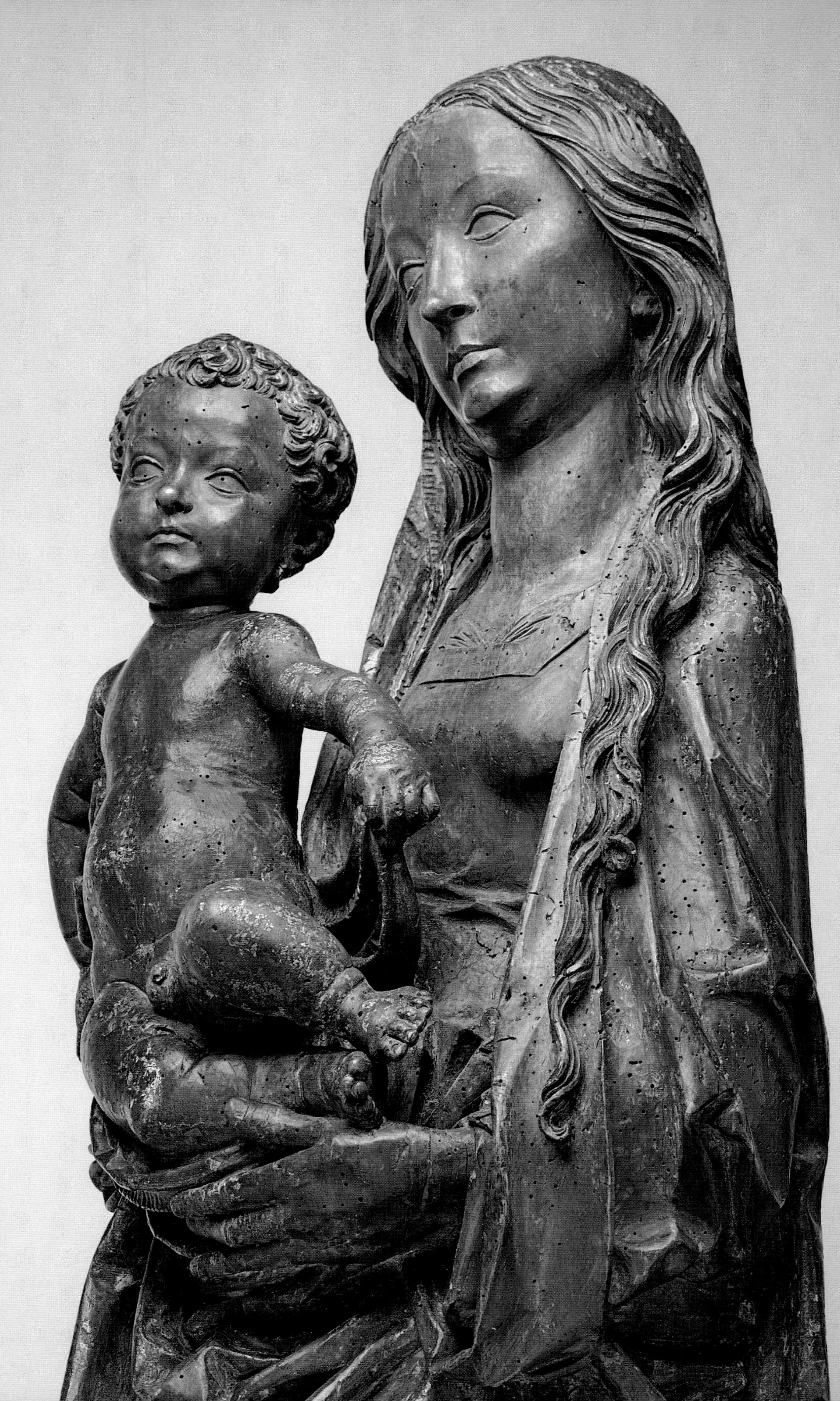

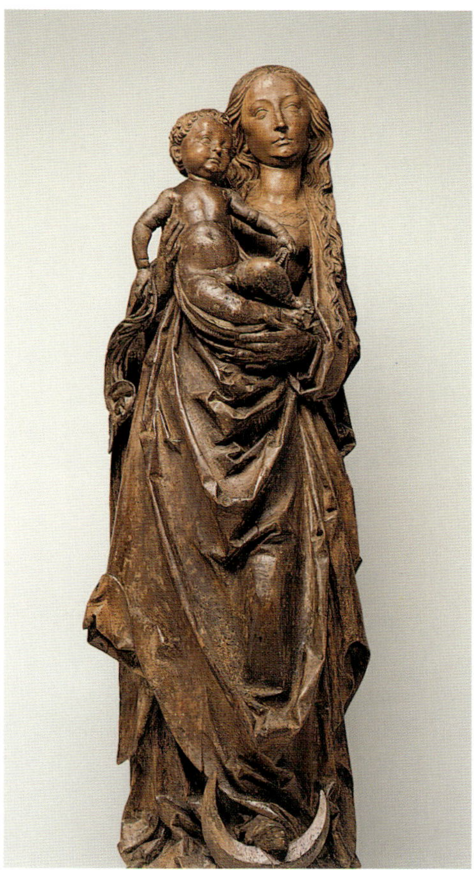

Front view of catalogue no. 28

The Hamburg sculpture belongs to a group of eight images of the Virgin and child that follow the same composition: those in Munich, Hannover, Frankfurt, and Zurich (figs. 1–4), as well as three in Würzburg, including one view of the *Double-Sided Virgin and Child* (cat. 29), a group in the Martin-von-Wagner Museum, and a recently discovered Virgin and child just acquired by the Mainfränkisches Museum. Allowing for minor variations, the drapery patterns and the articulation of Mary's body are virtually identical. Over a dress, which is almost entirely hidden, she wears a wide, presumably rectangular cloak that she seems to have pulled to her left side: it rests on both shoulders, surrounds her left arm, is held there against her hip, then covers the entire front of her body before falling over her right wrist. In all versions of this type, the weight of the body rests on the Virgin's right leg, which establishes the disposition of the figure along an inverted S-curve and prompts her left knee to push forward against the fabric of her cloak. The most distinctive pattern in the drapery is the repetition of concentric U- or V-shaped folds, which extend from the child's leg to below the Virgin's knee and converge at her hips.

Created over a period of about twenty years, these images reveal the prevalence of compositional types in Riemenschneider's oeuvre. While some are difficult to date precisely, circumstantial evidence suggests the place of others in the production of Riemenschneider's shop. The Hamburg sculpture appears to be among the earliest and to have been created in about 1503–1505. Its drapery breaks in crisp folds, with narrow crests. And in the area where the folds converge toward the left wrist, it is defined with the same rhythmic accents as the funerary monument of Dorothea von Wertheim (cat. 41, fig. 1), probably commissioned shortly after her death on 24 March 1503.[2] The *Virgin and Child* from the Gerolzhofen retable in Munich (fig. 1) can be dated to after 1513, since two reliefs on the wings are based on prints by Albrecht Dürer of 1511 and by Lucas von Leiden of 1512–1513.[3] The Gerolzhofen Virgin evidences a more rigid organization of draperies and is conceived for more restricted frontal viewing than the Hamburg sculpture. The Virgin from Gramschatz in Hannover (fig. 2), although definitely of a higher quality than the Gerolzhofen figure, exhibits the same treatment of drapery and the same spatial conception and must

2. Bier 1978, 24–25. Kalden 1990, 120, dates the sculpture slightly earlier, to 1501–1503.

3. Kalden 1990, 81, 134–135.

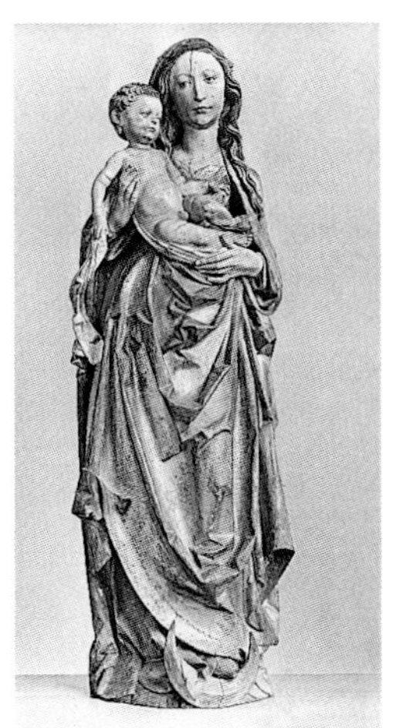

1.

Virgin and Child from the
Gerolzhofen altarpiece,
c. 1513–1515, limewood
with ancient polychromy,
Bayerisches
Nationalmuseum, Munich

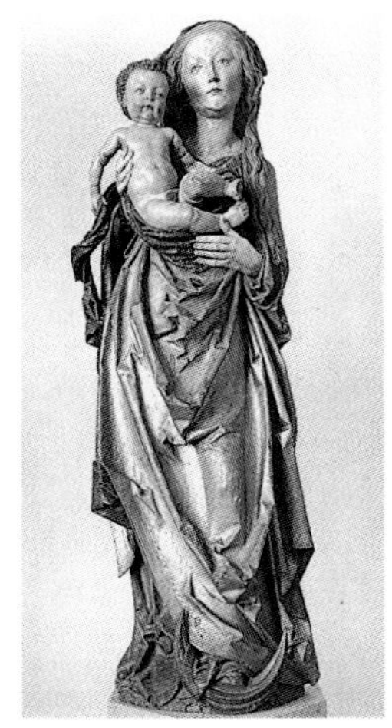

2.

Virgin and Child from
Gramschatz, c. 1515,
limewood with ancient
polychromy, Nieder-
sächsisches Landesmuseum,
Hannover

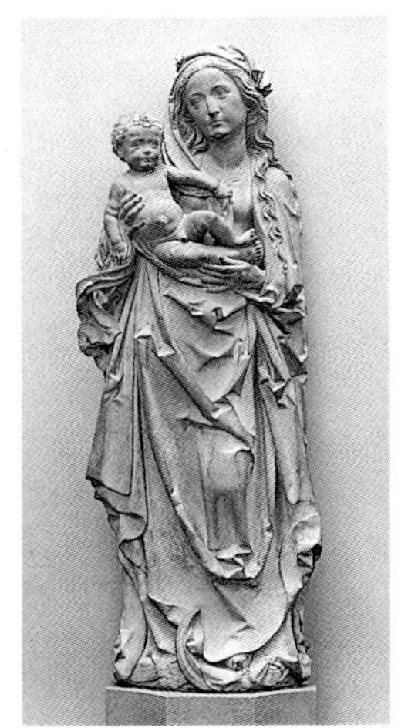

3.

Virgin and Child,
c. 1520, sandstone,
Liebieghaus-Museum
alter Plastik,
Frankfurt am Main

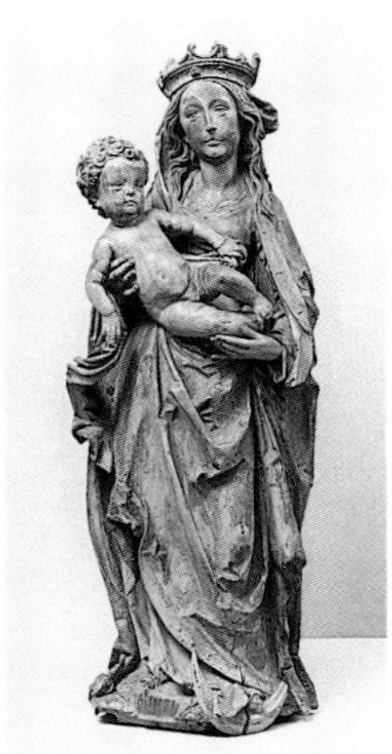

4.

Virgin and Child,
c. 1500, limewood,
Anda-Bührle Collection,
Zurich

4. Bier 1978, 22; and Maek-Gérard 1985, 237–239.

5. Riemenschneider's images of the Virgin and child fall into four compositional types (see also cats. 14, 16, and 19), suggesting that as many models existed in the workshop (Simon 1998, 173–179).

6. Würzburg 1981, 229–230; both Kalden 1990, 90–91, and Simon 1998, 177–178, consider the Zurich statuette as the model for the group.

7. I am grateful to James Draper, curator of European sculpture and decorative arts at the Metropolitan Museum, for his explanation of the pointing method.

therefore be roughly contemporary. A variation from the end of Riemenschneider's career is the grand sandstone relief in the Liebieghaus in Frankfurt (fig. 3). Made for strict frontal viewing, the figure is much broader than any other work in the group. It is close in style to the funerary monument of Lorenz von Bibra of 1515–1522 and the Maidbronn *Lamentation* of about 1519–1523, two works with which it must be contemporary (Kemperdick essay, fig. 2; Chapuis essay, fig. 9).[4]

These repetitions of form seem to imply the existence of a model that would have established the composition and preserved it over a period of twenty years.[5] Only one work could qualify as the model for the Hamburg sculpture: the statuette in the Anda-Bührle collection in Zurich (fig. 4).[6] Datable to about 1500 by virtue of its resemblance in facial type to the Cologne Virgin (cat. 16), this figure would thus be the earliest in the group. It is carved fully in the round (see also cat. 19) and is the smallest figure in the group (see cats. 39 A and 45). Equally important, it is distinguished by a highly detailed treatment of surface.

Ironically, the Hamburg sculpture itself served as a model, although not in the Middle Ages. Hand-drawn crosses and lines on the faces of the Virgin and child mark salient points such as the eyebrows, cheeks, chin, bridge of the nose, along the nose, and across the lips. This pointing method, using calipers, allows the precise duplication of a sculpture as well as its enlargement or reduction. Employed by the Greeks and Romans, this method of making copies was not revived in Europe until the baroque era; it was especially popular in the nineteenth century, when exact copies were much in demand.[7] In the late medieval era models seem to have been replicated more freely.

CHAPUIS

DOUBLE-SIDED VIRGIN AND CHILD ON THE CRESCENT MOON

1500–1520, limewood, Virgin with child on her left arm: 90.5 x 29 x 13 (35 ⅝ x 11 ⅜ x 5 ⅛);
Virgin with child on her right arm: 90.5 x 30 x 13.5 (35 ⅝ x 11 ¾ x 5 ¼), Mainfränkisches Museum,
Würzburg, Freunde Mainfränkischer Kunst und Geschichte

• Technical Notes •

The two sides were each cut from a separate piece of limewood with the grain running vertically and the backs hollowed out. Prior to 1893 they were sawn apart during a restoration.[1] The wood, relatively free of knots, appears to have been still fresh when carved, for many cracks had to be filled with wooden wedges. The top of the head of each Virgin is cut to accommodate a crown, now lost. Other losses include the tip of the right middle finger of the Virgin with the child on her left as well as the right toes and left lower arm of the child. The Virgin with the child on her right is missing the toes of the child's left foot. There are traces of at least three polychromy campaigns. Scraping marks abound, probably a result of paint removal, and the figures seem to have been resurfaced. The forged-iron band that surrounds the work replaced a more elaborate modern one in 1958. Christina Hoffart lightly cleaned the sculpture in 1997.

• Provenance •

Originally in the church of Saint Barbara (destroyed in 1824); Philipp Rottenhäuser, Würzburg; acquired in 1893 by the Fränkischer Kunst- und Altertumsverein, Würzburg, whose collection is now in the Mainfränkisches Museum.

• Literature •

Tönnies 1900, 227, 229; Adelmann 1910, 84; Schrade 1927, 102 n. 223; Schädler 1975, 102; Bier 1975, 63 n. 46; Freeden 1981, 39, 51; Muth 1982, 154–161; Kalden 1990, 141–142; Simon 1998, 176.

WHILE PRESENT-DAY museum visitors are accustomed to seeing sculpture on pedestals at eye level, much medieval sculpture was originally installed quite high—on façades, on the columns of ecclesiastical and secular buildings, or hanging from the vault of a church, as was this *Double-Sided Virgin and Child.* Consisting of two half-round figures conceived to fit back to back, the sculpture was originally suspended above an elaborate chandelier in the church of Saint Barbara in Würzburg, which was part of a Carmelite convent. Sculpted shafts of light radiated from the group, defining the subject as the Virgin of the Apocalypse (Revelation 12:1), a woman standing on the crescent moon and clothed in the sun. The stylized bands of clouds at the figures' feet heighten the impression that they are hovering above the ground. The modern iron band around the composition is intended to suggest the mandorla effect of the rays and to allow the sculpture to be hung today in a way that conveys a sense of its original installation.

Devotion to the Virgin of the Apocalypse and to the Virgin of the Rosary gained momentum in the late fifteenth century, and the two themes were often conflated into one representation, as prayers to these images brought with them the promise of considerable indulgences (see also cat. 45, fig. 1).[2] The metal chandelier below the *Double-Sided Virgin* probably bore fifty-five candles, standing for the fifty Ave Marias and the five Paternosters of a full rosary cycle.[3] Such an object would have hung freely in space and would have been visible from a variety of viewpoints.

Although the compositions are not strictly speaking mirror images, the silhouettes are contiguous enough so that when viewed frontally only one figure is visible. The differences between the two sides include the pose of the Christ child and the organization of the drapery. The child on the Virgin's left arm leans forward and reaches with his right hand toward his mother's breast for support while he gestures toward the viewer with his left arm. The Virgin's pose responds to the movement of the child, with her left leg carrying the weight of her body and her upper body leaning back. The pattern of her drapery fol-

1. Muth 1982, 160.

2. Sixten Ringbom, *"Maria in Sole* and the Virgin of the Rosary," *Journal of the Warburg and Courtauld Institutes* 2 (1962), 326–330.

3. Muth 1982, 154.

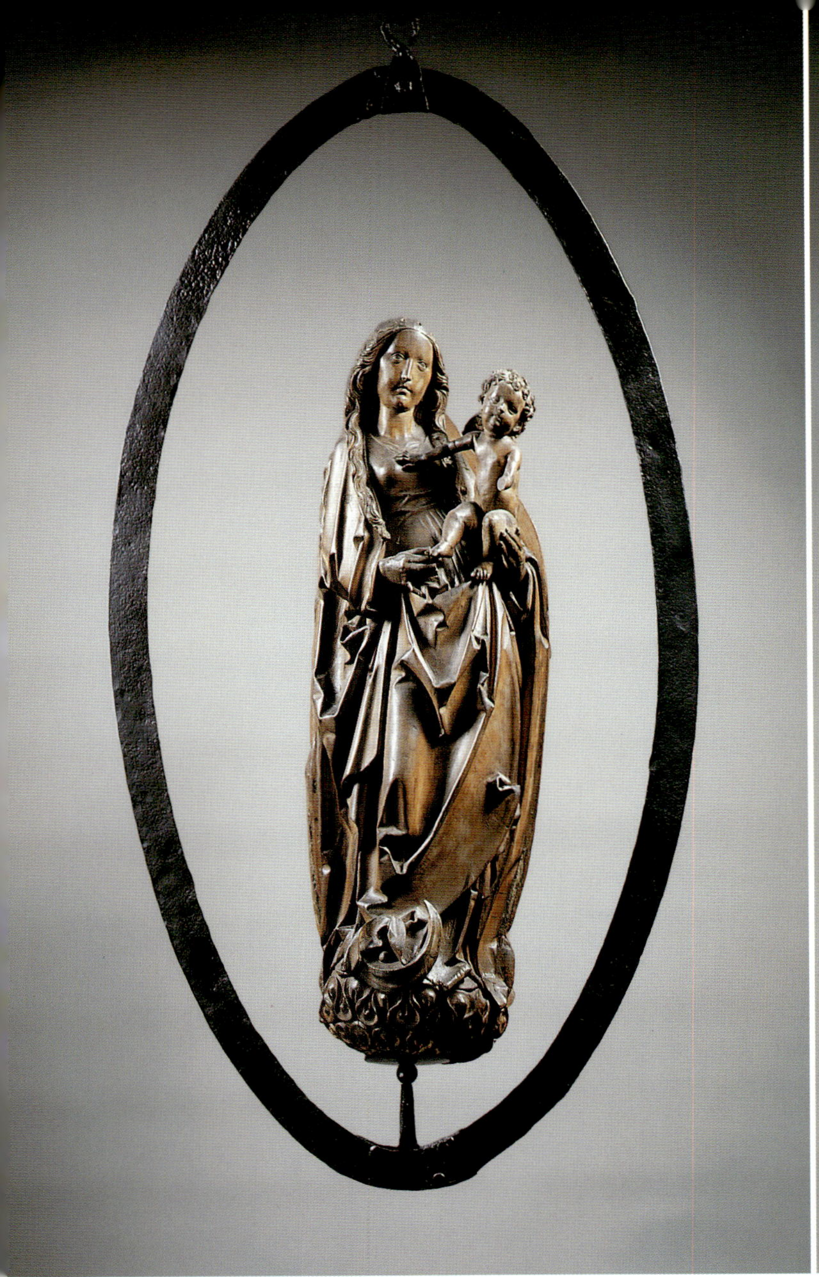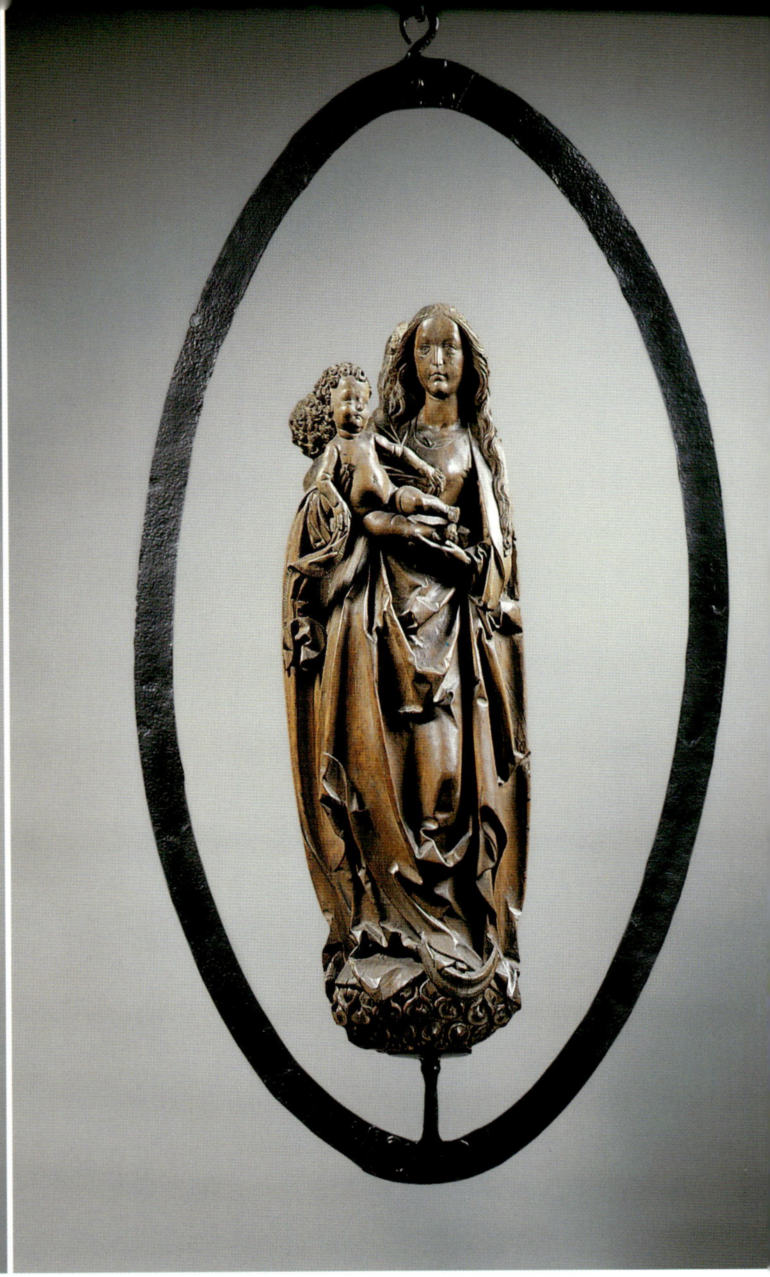

4. Muth 1982, 156.

5. See also Muth 1982, 158; Kalden 1990, 142; and Simon 1998, 176.

6. Adelmann 1910, 84.

7. Kalden 1990, 142, where an attempt is made to distinguish between different collaborators in Riemenschneider's shop, considered this the work of an assistant whose style is not recognizable in other works.

lows the articulation of her body.[4] The other Virgin follows a compositional type that Riemenschneider first conceived in about 1500 and produced with minor variations until almost 1520 (see cat. 28).[5] The child, held under his right arm and right calf, is half reclining and grabs the Virgin's veil with both hands. The Virgin's weight is shifted to her right leg, with her left knee projecting forward against her cloak, which creases in concentric U-shaped folds.

Riemenschneider and his assistants often took into consideration the intended installation when embarking on a new sculpture, and the apparent weaknesses in the *Double-Sided Virgin* would have been minimized in its suspension above a chandelier. The figures are characterized by a broad treatment of surfaces, in the draperies as well as in the faces, and the articulation of the fabric does not achieve the crispness of the examples in Hamburg, Munich, and Hannover (see cat. 28, figs. 1, 2). The hands are rendered

summarily, with little indication of joints or veins. Compared with the Hamburg Virgin, the faces of these two appear flat, with strikingly small eyes. The absence of any surface decoration, either cut or punched, suggests that the sculpture was conceived to be polychrome. Some degree of modeling would have been achieved in the application of ground and paint layers, and from a distance the sculpture would have gained volume and differentiation once it stood above a ring of fifty-five flickering candles. Nevertheless, Adelmann concluded that the carving had probably been done without the actual participation of Riemenschneider.[6] The sculpture appears to be the work of an assistant, who followed a model in the workshop for one side, while modifying it for the other. In view of the apparent absence of other works by this assistant,[7] it is difficult to situate this sculpture more precisely in the production of Riemenschneider's shop. CHAPUIS

SAINT ANNE

c. 1505–1506, limewood, 75 x 51 x 22.5 (29 ½ x 20 ⅛ x 8 ⅞), Bayerisches Nationalmuseum, Munich

• *Technical Notes* •

The figure and the background are carved from a single block of limewood with the grain running vertically; the wood is hollowed out only in the area of the figure. While the sculpture is largely a relief, the head is carved fully in the round. The sculpture is a fragment of a larger whole, and the overall state of preservation is poor. The piece has suffered severely from insect damage, scattered over the entire surface, with many holes filled with a brown material. The surface appears very dirty and dull, as if covered with wax, and damaged underneath. The saint's right hand is missing, as is the edge of the curved drapery fold below the spine of the book. The left thumb, the tip of the shoe, and a wedge in the left end of the base are modern replacements. A section of the veil is missing above the left eye. The work was conceived as a polychrome: the tooled decoration, consisting of large crescents along the edge of the garment, or the crude fringe on the veil and on the wall covering would all have remained visible through layers of paint. Moreover, the artist attempted to repair a long crack, running vertically across the breast: he made scratches into the surface, to which a piece of fabric would have been attached. This would then have been covered by layers of ground and paint.

• *Provenance* •

Probably from the Marienkapelle in Rothenburg (destroyed in 1810); collection of the sculptor Behrens in the region of Rothenburg; acquired in Würzburg by the Munich museum in 1892.

• *Literature* •

Tönnies 1900, 133–135; Weber 1911, 174–175, 198–202; Demmler 1921, 26–29; Bier 1930, 44–55; Bier 1937, 21; Bier 1944–1945, 21–37; Müller 1959, 142; Schädler 1975, 100; Freeden 1981, 36; Würzburg 1981,

217; Bier 1982, 95; Kalden 1990, 98, 119 n. 435; Kahsnitz 1997, 18 n. 18.

WITH HER HEAD and chin covered, as was customary for older women, Saint Anne sits on a narrow bench, balancing an open book on her right knee. Having interrupted her reading, she looks up, turns slightly to her left, and raises her right arm. A curtain serves as a backdrop. The sculpture is a fragment of a larger composition, most likely a representation of the "Anna Selbdritt" theme: Saint Anne with her daughter the Virgin Mary and the Christ child. Instead of the massive arrangement of Riemenschneider's sandstone group from Würzburg (cat. 15), in which Anne holds the child and the diminutive Virgin on her lap, the Munich ensemble was conceived as a horizontal composition, with the Virgin as an adult woman, seated next to her mother, as in the sandstone group made in Strasbourg in about 1480 (cat. 8). The Christ child was probably reaching from the Virgin's lap over to his grandmother or standing on the bench between the two women. Anne's raised right arm is clearly meant to support the child. Although the bench must have been continuous across the width of the composition, the slanted foreground stage was not: Mary's feet were probably resting, like Anne's, on a polygonal base. The curtain is cut irregularly at the top, and it is unclear how much higher it originally extended.

The present figure is traditionally regarded as a fragment of a *Saint Anne* altarpiece that Riemenschneider delivered for the Marienkapelle in Rothenburg in April 1506.[1] The altarpiece had been commissioned in January 1505, and the sculptor was to be paid 50 guilders for the entire work, both shrine and sculpture. Bier concluded that the *Saint Anne* altarpiece must have been about half as large as the *Holy Blood* altarpiece in Rothenburg (Chapuis essay,

1. First proposed in Tönnies 1900, 133–135; and developed in Bier 1930, 46–55. Only Weber 1911, 174, 198–199, disagreed.

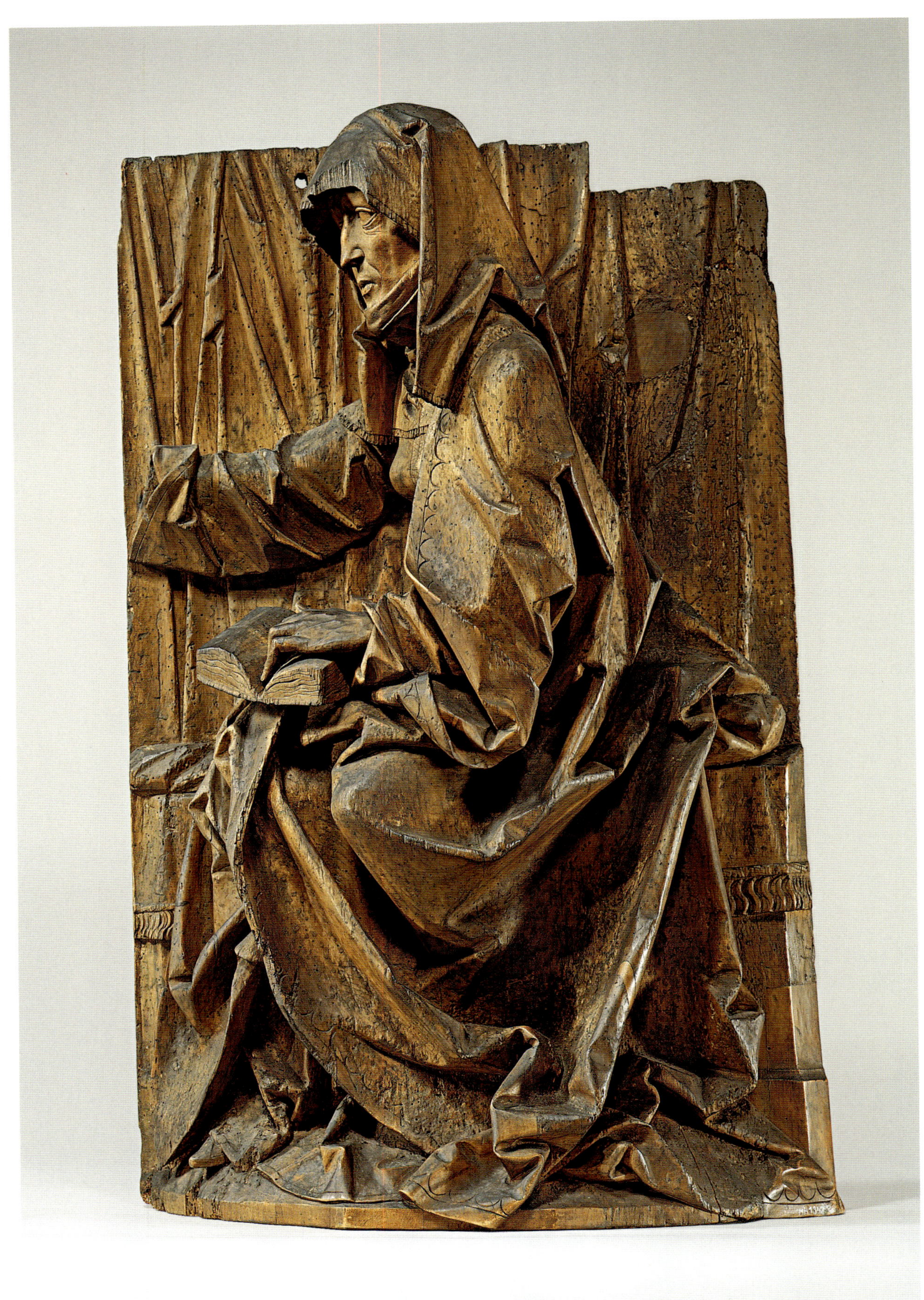

278

fig. 5), for which Riemenschneider received the same sum for only the figures.[2] This suggestion is congruent with the dimensions of the Munich relief. The Marienkapelle, destroyed in 1810, had three altars: a high altar dedicated to the Virgin; and two lateral altars, one dedicated to Saint Nicholas and the other to the Magi. Riemenschneider's retable seems to have been destined for the last of these: the first document related to the commission speaks of a tableau *(tafel)* for "Rudolff's altar"; and a priest named Heinrich Rudolff had said Mass at the altar of the Three Magi between 1483 and 1505. Subsequent documents, which clearly refer to the same commission, describe the work as both the "tableau on the altar of Saint Anne" and as the "Saint Anne tableau."[3] But it was fairly common for a retable to have a different dedication from the altar for which it was intended.[4]

The documents for this commission do not describe its iconography in any detail, but Saint Anne is necessarily depicted with the Virgin and child: they allow her to be identified and, as such, function as her attributes. This type of representation, known as *Anna Selbdritt* (roughly, "Anne, Three-in-One"), was extremely popular in Germany and expressed Christ's descent from Anne. It could easily be expanded into the theme of the Holy Kinship by including any number of Christ's relatives. A reduced version might show Joseph (Mary's husband) and Joachim (Anne's husband) standing behind the bench. The background in this relief would not accommodate such figures (compare cat. 36A–B), thus the subject of the central shrine was most likely an *Anna Selbdritt*.[5] The wings probably contained scenes from the life of Saint Anne, such as the meeting of Anne and Joachim at the Golden Gate—after both had been told that the aged Anne would bear a child—and the birth of the Virgin.

The formal treatment of the Munich figure is congruent with Riemenschneider's works from the early 1500s, which is consistent with its having been part of an altarpiece delivered in 1506 for the Rothenburg Marienkapelle. A comparison with another seated figure of similar size, the Cloisters bishop of about 1495–1500 (cat. 17), brings to the fore the characteristics of the Munich *Saint Anne*. The Cloisters bishop, although actually shallower, has a greater spatial presence than the Munich relief. This is the result of its more convoluted drapery, which accentuates elements of the anatomy (such as his right knee), and the more detailed treatment of surfaces that evokes different materials. By contrast, the drapery of the *Saint Anne*,

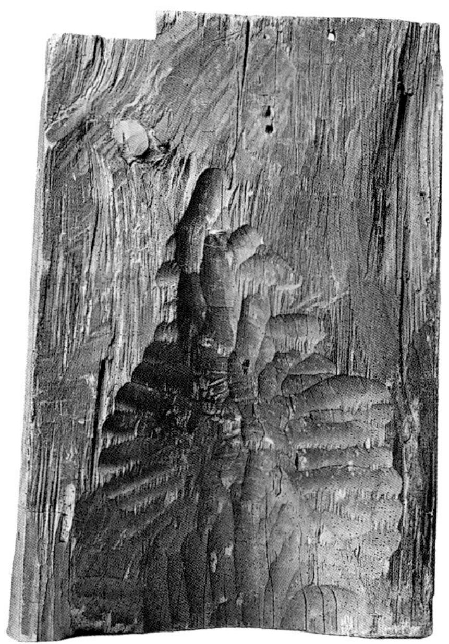

Back view of catalogue no. 30

which is treated more uniformly, is independent of the human figure beneath it and has been systematized into a more cohesive arrangement of forms. Anne's left knee, for instance, is surrounded by concentric arrangements of long, angular folds that have little to do with the body beneath. Anatomical correctness is of marginal relevance (the right arm is too long, the thighs too short). Rather, the lucid, linear treatment of drapery is paramount. The *Saint Anne* has parallels in the figures from the *Holy Blood* altarpiece of 1501–1504 in Rothenburg, especially the apostles sitting in front of the table (cat. 23, fig. 1).[6] Narrow tubular folds, articulated around nervous accents, interrupt large passages of flat or slightly crumpled fabric. The cloth has achieved autonomy and creates a grand calligraphy of form. This treatment is also apparent in the contemporary fragments from a *Holy Kinship* altarpiece (cat. 36A–B).

The Munich *Saint Anne* represents a new facial type for the older women with veil.[7] Compared with the Würzburg Saint Anne (cat. 15), the Munich figure's face is leaner, with a more defined bone structure, hollow cheeks, and deeply grooved wrinkles around her eyes and mouth. This type is strongly indebted to the Saint Anne from Strasbourg (cat. 8), long ascribed to Niclaus Gerhaert. Both visages are conceived as series of planes meeting at sharp angles rather than as continuous volumes in space. Gerhaert remained a potent source of inspiration until the end of Riemenschneider's career. CHAPUIS

2. Timothy Husband points out that this could also mean that less of Riemenschneider's personal participation was expected.

3. Documents of 2 January 1505, 19 April 1506, and 21 June 1506, transcribed in Bier 1930a, 175–176.

4. See Bier 1930, 53–55, although there are problems with his hypothesis. On the lack of consistency between the subject of an altarpiece and the dedication of the altar, see Bier 1960, 225 n. 16b.

5. Bier 1930, 48–49.

6. See Kalden 1990, 119 n. 435; and Krohm in Würzburg 1981, 217.

7. Kalden 1990, 98.

31

c. 1505, limewood, 148 x 52 x 23 (58¼ x 20½ x 9), Bayerisches Nationalmuseum, Munich

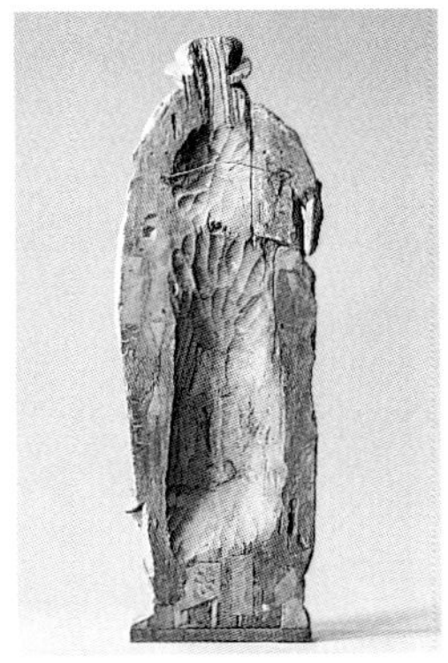

Back view of
catalogue no. 31

1. This observation was made
by Michele Marincola.

2. Louis Réau, *Iconographie
de l'art chrétien* (Paris, 1958), 3.2:
190–193.

3. Gerstenberg 1955, 206.

4. Müller 1959, 146, reported
that a shell adorned the hat. A
hole in the brim where the shell
was probably attached appears
in the center; the shell may have
been carved separately.

5. See Gerstenberg 1955, 206,
which considers the Stuttgart
version to be the earlier of
the two.

• *Technical Notes* •

The sculpture is carved from a piece of limewood
with the grain running vertically. The back of the
sculpture is hollowed out in two areas: a narrow chan-
nel from the head to the shoulders and a wider con-
cavity from the waist to the ankles. Blocks of wood
glued into the hollowed-out back indicate where
Riemenschneider accidentally cut through the thin
walls of the sculpture during its carving (see also cat.
17). Some additions may be original, including the
saint's right cheek, right shoulder, and the back of his
left hand. The condition is problematic. The wood
has suffered severely from biological attack, which has
required several replacements, including the entire
base below the bottom of the cloak, the saint's right
hand, and portions of the drapery and hat. The cloak
and tunic were originally decorated with attachments,
perhaps wooden pearls, secured by small wooden
dowels that are now flush with the surface, positioned
along the hem at intervals of about 1.5 cm.[1] The hat
was once adorned with a shell, James' attribute. Traces
of paint are visible in some areas, but the application
of a tinted oil-resin varnish to the surface complicates
the determination of its original finish. Mr. Kovacs,
conservator at the Bayerisches Nationalmuseum,
examined and treated the sculpture in 1979–1980.

• *Provenance* •

Acquired in 1890 from the Carl Streit collection in
Kissingen.

• *Literature* •

Bode 1885, 172; Streit 1888, 18; Tönnies 1900, 255;
Weber 1911, 207; Schrade 1927, 105–107; Bier 1930,
139–140; Knapp 1935, 22; Demmler 1936, 70–73;
Müller 1959, 146; Muth 1982, 62; Kalden 1990, 118–
119 n. 432; Kahsnitz 1997, 20.

JAMES THE GREATER was one of the three
disciples, including his brother John the Evangelist
and Peter, who were present at the Transfiguration
and at the Agony in the Garden. Although James had
no historical ties with Spain, legend had it that he
had preached in that country and that his relics had
been brought to Galicia. From the tenth century on,
thousands of pilgrims journeyed each year to Compostella, which became the primary pilgrimage des-
tination in Europe after Jerusalem and Rome.[2] By the
late Middle Ages images of Saint James were installed
all over the Continent in stations on the roads to
Compostella.[3]

Following tradition, Riemenschneider depicted
the apostle as the patron of pilgrims, with a broad-
rimmed hat[4] and a food bag hanging from a strap
across his chest. A water gourd was probably attached
to his walking stick, now missing its upper and lower
portions. Riemenschneider's apostle appears to have
been on the road for several days. His emaciated face,
with hollow cheeks, deeply grooved forehead, arched
eyebrows, and haggard expression, conveys exhaustion. His mouth is open, revealing the upper teeth,
as though he were about to halt his march and catch
his breath.

The Munich sculpture seems to be an elaboration on an earlier version of the subject (fig. 1).[5] Beyond the obvious resemblance in costume dictated
by the iconography, the figures have similar stances.
Each saint's left leg supports his body weight, while
the right knee pushes forward against the drapery;
the head is turned slightly to the figure's left; and his
right arm is bent and held close to the body. In both
cases the cloak is turned inside out over the saint's
right shoulder and appears to wrap around the back
of the body to the left shoulder, where it is held by
one hand.

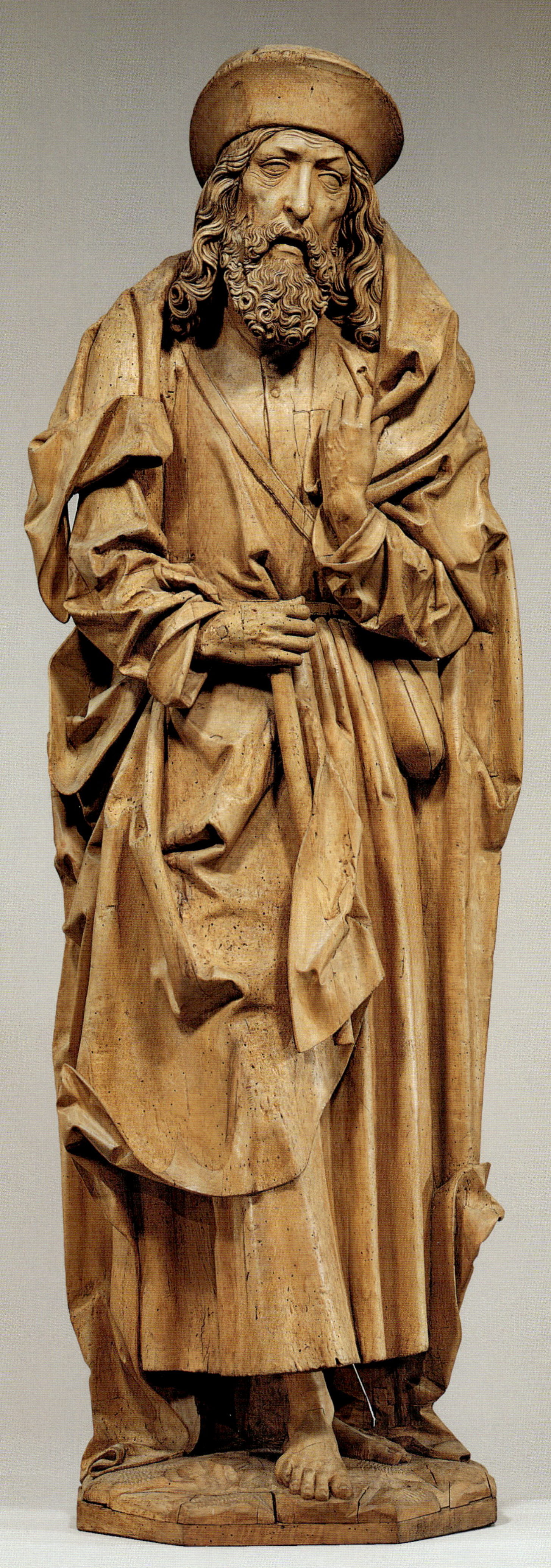

6. Bier 1930, 140.

7. For instance, Kalden 1990, 118.

8. Knapp 1935, 22.

The formal treatment of the Munich sculpture suits the subject better and makes it a more effective object of devotion. The Stuttgart figure depicts a younger man, who lacks the gravity and meditative presence of the Munich saint. His face is idealized and shows no sign of age or suffering. The slim, erect body of this figure is coherently articulated and legible through the drapery. The Munich saint, by comparison, is conceived as a *Gewandfigur* in which the general form is defined more by the drapery than by the anatomy (the latter is clearly wanting, as apparent in the too short arms). The wrinkles on the forehead and under the eyes of the Munich figure are chiseled with as much care as the curls of his beard, and they leave no doubt that he has a full life behind him. More important, though, the saint appears to be walking. When viewed frontally, his right leg is positioned at the center of figure, and his left knee is directly behind. This gives the figure a feeling of imbalance and forward movement, an impression reinforced by the hunched posture.

Because of its strong iconic presence, it is appealing to hypothesize that the Munich *Saint James* was originally conceived to stand on its own rather than as one of several statues in a carved retable. Indeed, the impressive figure does not respond to its surroundings but is entirely self-contained. The arch of drapery over the shoulders, the bent arms, and the left hand holding the cloak all lead the eye to the ascetic, visionary face. The figure encourages the mobility of the viewer within an arc of about 120 degrees, but it is not conceived to be seen strictly from the side, which suggests that it was originally installed in a shallow niche or shrine. Certain technical details, including the lack of carved or punched decoration and the broad treatment of surfaces, suggest that the sculpture was conceived to be polychrome.

Like the Berlin *Matthias* (cat. 24), the *Saint James* bears a strong resemblance to one of the sandstone apostles produced by Riemenschneider and his shop between 1500 and 1506 for the buttresses of the Marienkapelle in Würzburg. The saint in question is not James the Greater, but his namesake, James the Less (fig. 2). The configuration of the drapery is very similar; in each case the cloak covers the figure's left shoulder, where it is grasped by the left hand, while it is held like an apron against the body on the other side by the right hand. The positions of the arms and legs are also similar. The head of *James the Less* is turned sharply to the figure's right, and in its original installation on the Marienkapelle it would have been looking at *John the Greater* on the adjacent buttress.[6] The Munich sculpture is often thought to be con-

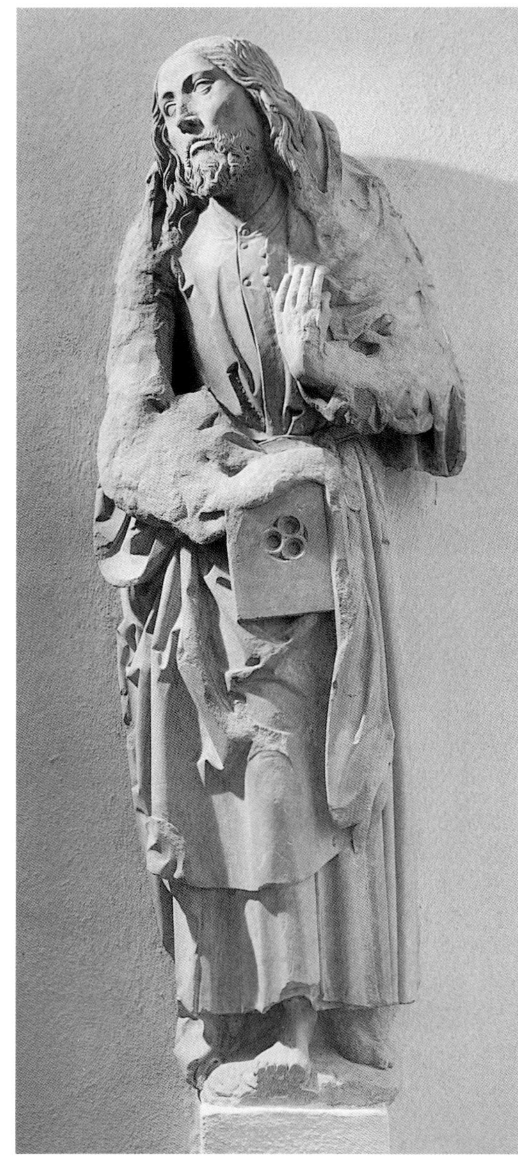

2.

Saint James the Less from the Marienkapelle, 1500–1506, sandstone, Mainfränkisches Museum, Würzburg

temporary with the series of apostles for the Marienkapelle,[7] and on occasion it has been considered the model for *James the Less*.[8] This is unlikely, since the sandstone figure has a very different focus, specifically in its response to its intended surroundings. The Munich saint seems to be the earlier of the two, however. Indeed, the position of the legs, which suggests walking and which is present in both works, is appropriate for James the Greater, the patron of pilgrims, but not necessary for James the Less. This observation and the broad arc of address suggest that the Munich figure was carved in about 1505. CHAPUIS

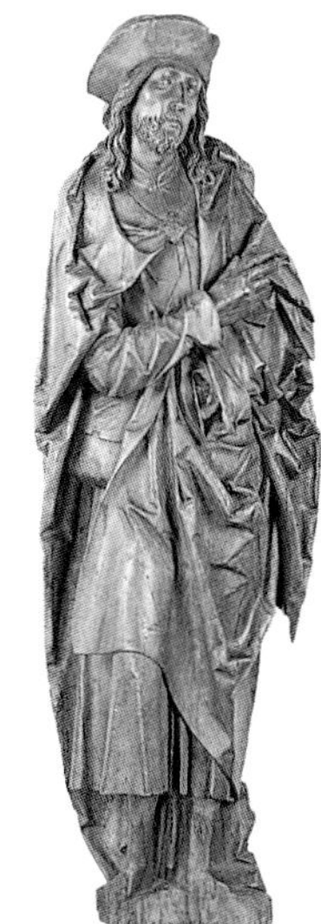

1.

Saint James the Greater,
c. 1500–1505, limewood,
Württembergisches
Landesmuseum, Stuttgart

Four saints from an altarpiece

32A   SAINT STEPHEN

c. 1508, limewood with polychromy, 92.7 x 34 x 17 (36½ x 13⅜ x 6⅝), The Cleveland Museum
of Art, Leonard C. Hanna Jr. Fund

32B   FEMALE SAINT (WITH BOOK)

c. 1500–1510, limewood with polychromy, 98 x 29 x 23 (38⅝ x 11⅜ x 9), Historisches Museum,
Frankfurt am Main

32C   FEMALE SAINT (WITHOUT BOOK)

c. 1500–1510, limewood with polychromy, 101 x 28 x 22 (39¾ x 11 x 8⅝), Historisches Museum,
Frankfurt am Main

32D   SAINT LAWRENCE

c. 1502, limewood with polychromy, 94.6 x 39.5 x 20 (37¼ x 15½ x 7⅞), The Cleveland Museum
of Art, Leonard C. Hanna Jr. Fund

• *Technical Notes* •

Each of the Cleveland figures is carved from a single
block of limewood with the grain running vertically
and the back neatly hollowed to prevent cracking.
Lawrence's left hand, which is original, was carved
separately and attached to the arm with a dowel. The
gridiron is a modern replacement except for the
handle, appearing on photographs as early as 1921.
The same photographs show Stephen holding a mar-
tyr's palm in his left hand. It is unclear whether this
palm was original; it was still in place by 1929 but had
been removed by the time the Cleveland museum
acquired the works.[1]

The Cleveland saints have retained much of their
original polychromy. The paint on Lawrence's face
and hands, although somewhat abraded, is largely
original, as it is on his cuffs, hair, and alb. The gilding of his dalmatic, however, is heavily restored. Most
of the paint and gilding visible on Stephen is from a
nineteenth-century restoration that closely follows
the original, although traces of original pigments are
preserved in the lower layers. When the saints were
acquired in 1959, the albs of both were decorated with
applied dots stamped out of gilded paper. Thought
at the time to be baroque additions, they were removed; but this type of decoration has subsequently
been observed on other late medieval sculpture. In
fact, the dots on Stephen's alb were nineteenth-century restorations, closely following the originals on
Lawrence's garment (see Marincola's essay in the present catalogue).

The female saints from Frankfurt were each cut
from a single member of relatively unblemished limewood with the grain running vertically and the back
hollowed out. The left hand of the better-preserved
figure (32B), which appears to be original, was carved
separately and attached with a dowel. Her neckline
is decorated with a pattern of diamonds and crosses
that is very close to that on the morse of the Cloisters bishop (cat. 17). While the azurite blue of her
dress has been repainted, both the gold of her cloak
and the paint on her face appear to be largely original.

1. For the 1921 photographs,
see Schmitt and Swarzenski 1921,
figs. 138–139. The state of the
figures in 1929 is illustrated
in Schilling 1929. See Wixom
1959, 196, for the state of the
figures in 1959.

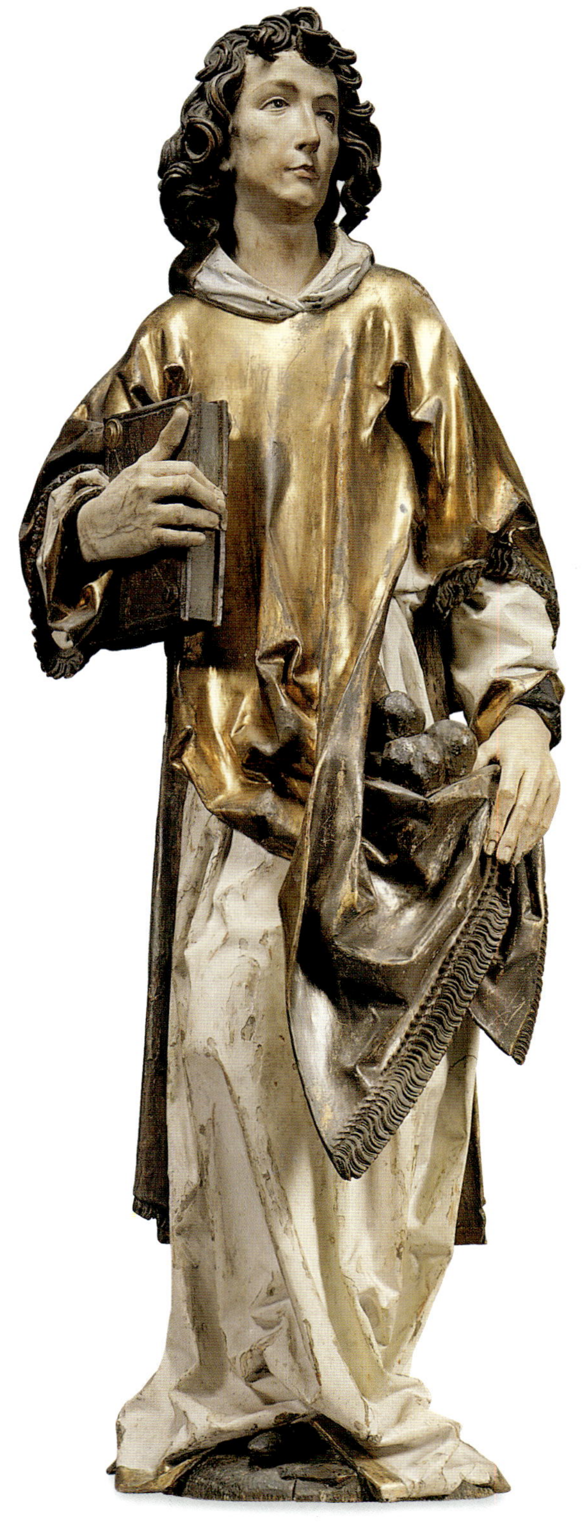

32 A

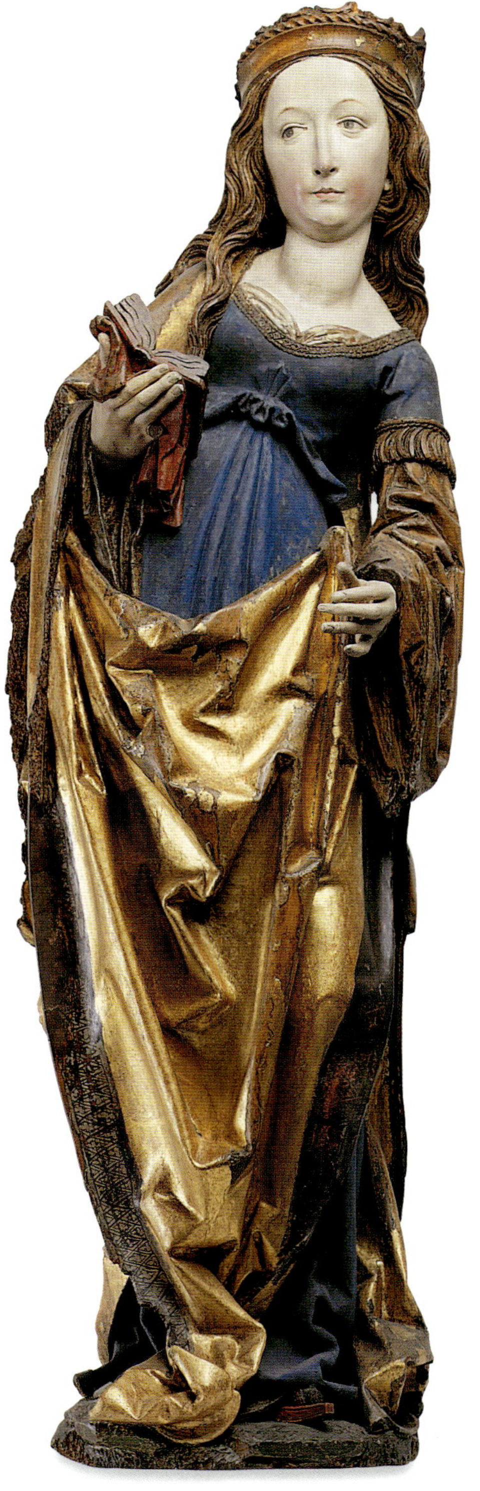

32 B

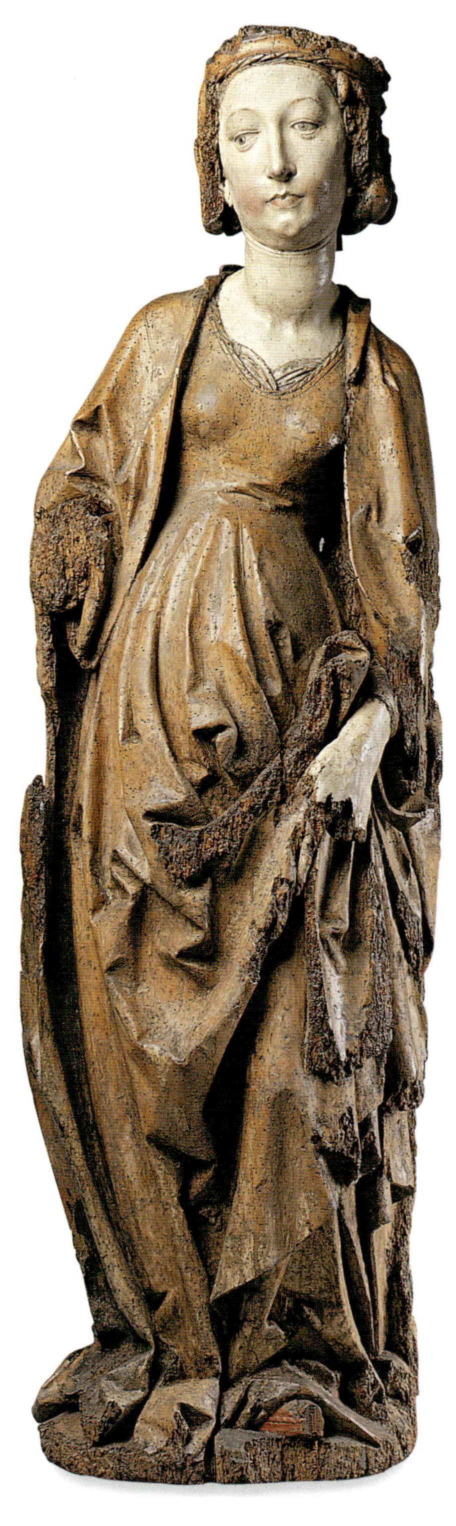

32 C

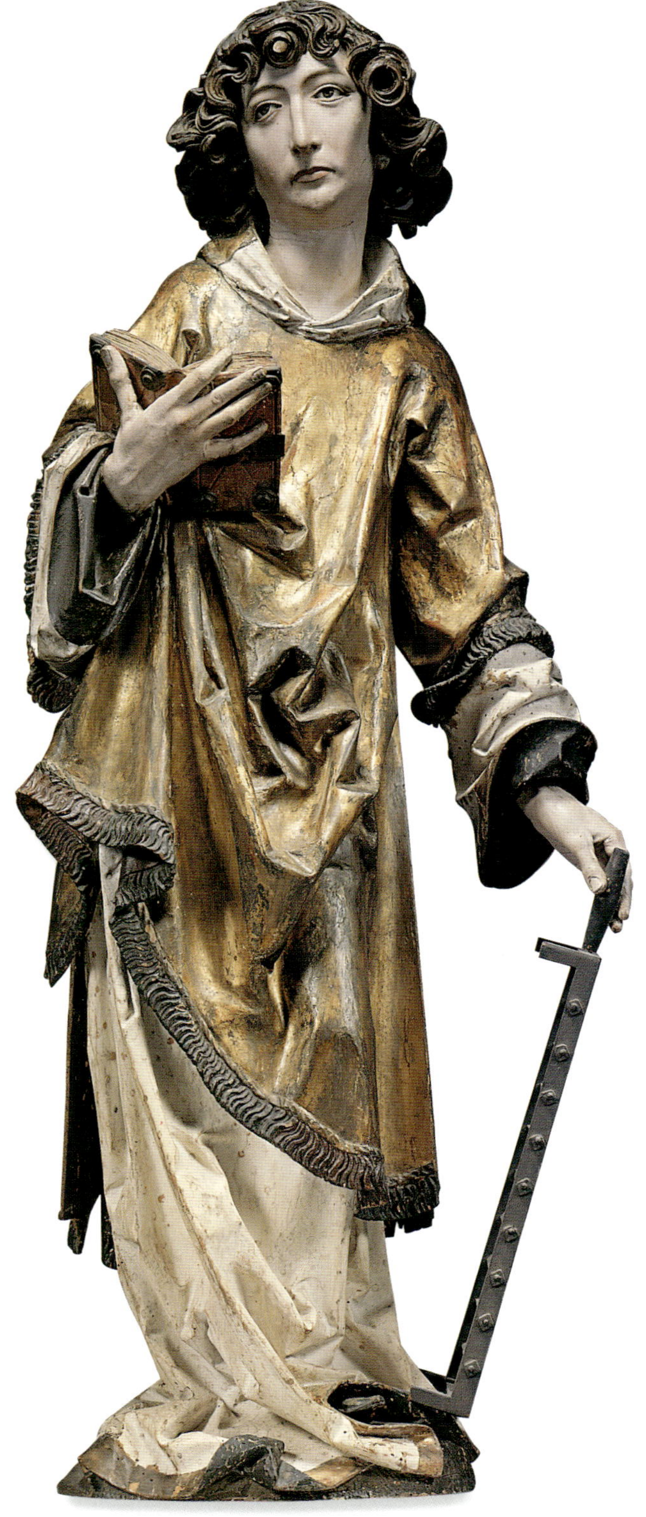

32 D

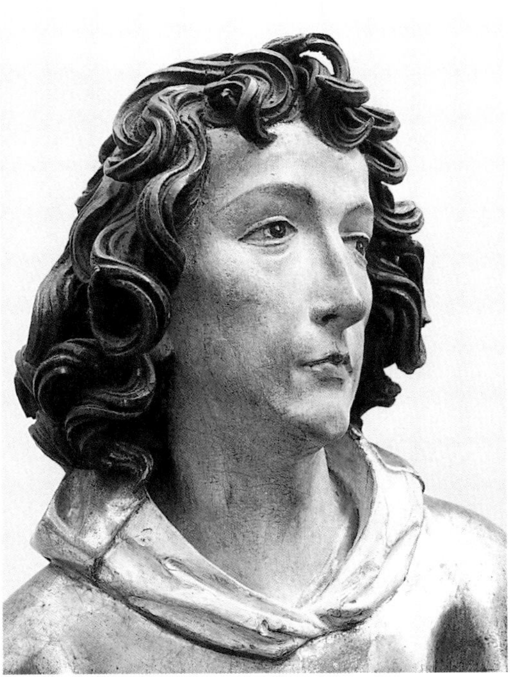

Detail of catalogue no. 32 A

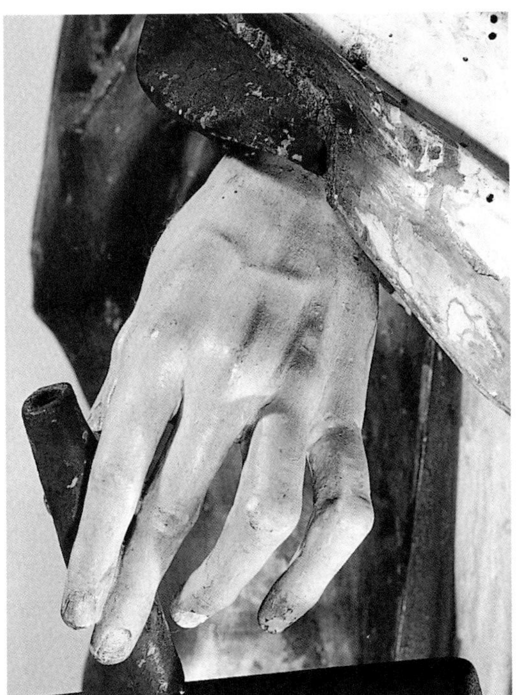

Detail of catalogue no. 32 D

The decoration combines gold and silver leaf; a yellow lacquer was applied on the silver leaf, while a layer containing glue appears to have been applied on the gold to reduce its shine. The saint's right side has suffered from insect damage and fluctuations in humidity. The damage in her companion (32 C) is much more severe, resulting in the loss of her entire right arm below the elbow, much of her left hand, her crown, and large areas of her drapery. In addition, the polychromy has been removed, except for the flesh tones, which are very similar to those of the other figure. A. Kratz restored both figures in 1956. Andrea Kleberger examined them in 1977.[2] Both were cleaned after 1977 by Bernhard Decker under the supervision of Andrea Kleberger.

2. This description is based on Kleberger's examination report, on file at the Historisches Museum, Frankfurt am Main.

• *Provenance* •

All four reportedly from an altarpiece from the region of Rothenburg. Both Cleveland saints in the von Gontard collection, Frankfurt, until 1911 (Lawrence reportedly acquired in 1855; Stephen in 1881); Richard von Passavant-Gontard, Frankfurt, 1921–1929; Baroness Catalina von Pannwitz, De Hartekamp near Haarlem, The Netherlands, 1930–1956; [Rosenberg and Stiebel, New York, 1957–1959]; acquired by the Cleveland museum in 1959. Both female saints purchased by the Frankfurt museum: the better-preserved one (32 B) on 13 December 1878, and the other (32 C) on 10 November 1881.

• *Literature* •

Bode 1885, 165; Streit 1888, 23; Tönnies 1900, 261, nos. 2–3; Weber 1911, 192; Schmitt and Swarzenski 1921, 28, nos. 138–139; Schilling 1929, 187; Frankfurt 1929, 22, nos. 92–93; Bier 1930a, 10; Bier 1934, 333–334; Wixom 1959; Bier 1960; Würzburg 1981, 30, 32 n. 5; Kalden 1990, 108, 110; Krohm in Krohm and Oellermann 1992, 92–95; Nicolaisen 1991, 272–273.

SINCE THE publication of Wilhelm von Bode's *Geschichte der deutschen Plastik* in 1885, students of German sculpture have been aware that the two deacons in Cleveland and the two female saints in Frankfurt were originally part of the same altarpiece. This exhibition reunites them for the first time in almost two hundred years. Despite differences that suggest separate moments in Riemenschneider's development and the participation of more than one sculptor, there can be little doubt that the four figures once belonged together. There are indisputable similarities in size, sculptural mass, and technical details such as polychromy, being carved three-quarters in the round, and the way they were hollowed out.

Although the historical saints Stephen and Lawrence lived in different centuries—the first and the third, respectively—they are often represented together as deacons, officers in the Church who ministered to the poor. As depicted here, their vestments are typical of that office: over white long-sleeved albs, they wear fringed dalmatics with the characteristic wide sleeves and slits up the sides. Their books symbolize their role as preachers and guardians of the Gospel. They are identified by the instruments of their martyrdoms: the rocks in Stephen's dalmatic refer to his having been stoned for alleged blasphemy, while Lawrence's miniature gridiron alludes to his having been burned alive by the Romans for failing to hand over the Church's treasures, which he had distributed to the poor.

In the absence of distinctive attributes except for their crowns, the two female saints are more difficult to identify. One (32 B) was probably Saint Catherine: the book is among her attributes, and the angle of her left elbow and position of her fingers suggest that she could originally have been holding a sword, with which she was executed. The other figure (32 C) could be Barbara or Kunigunde, both of royal lineage and commonly venerated in central Germany.[3] Since the three other saints in this group hold books, it is attractive to consider that she might be Barbara, whose possible attributes include a book, a chalice, and a miniature tower.

William D. Wixom has pointed out that the deacon saints were inspired by engravings by Martin Schongauer (figs. 1 and 2). Similarities include the general poses of the figures and the arrangement of the draperies. In both the print and the sculpture Stephen lifts the front of his dalmatic to display the stones of his martyrdom, creating a large inverted triangle of drapery. Likewise, Lawrence's right arm holds a portion of his dalmatic against his body, causing the fringed edge of the garment to form a Z pattern, ending in a sweeping curve across the figure's legs.

While Riemenschneider and his collaborators often referred to engravings by Master E. S., Schongauer, Dürer, Lucas van Leiden, and Israhel van Meckenem with varying degrees of dependency,[4] the Cleveland saints reveal a remarkable creativity. Because an engraving necessarily gives a single view of a subject, the sculptor must literally round out the two-dimensional image. Riemenschneider endowed his figures with a sense of movement that is wholly absent from Schongauer's engravings. Schongauer's deacons stand erect, their contemplative faces on the same axis as their bodies; this gives them a columnar quality that would, ironically, befit sculpture better than prints. Riemenschneider, by contrast, articulates his bodies along a subtle play of contrasting lines that opens the figures to the surrounding space. Like Schongauer, he shows the stones in Stephen's vestment, but he turns the dalmatic inside out in a dynamic forward sweep of drapery. The saint's head is turned sharply to the right,

with an acute expression of alertness and expectancy. The broad sweeping curve in Lawrence's alb, running from his left foot to his right hand, is echoed by the fringed border and two folds in the dalmatic; these curves are countered by the vertical line of the vestment on the right and mirrored by the oblique of the saint's left arm, which continues in the tilt of his head. Although some of Schongauer's engravings show female figures lifting a portion of their garment, either upward or across their body, none exhibits such a compositional closeness to the Frankfurt female saints as to be considered their source.[5]

There are distinctions both in the sculptural conception and in the quality of execution of the individual figures. Although the Cleveland saints are equally accomplished in their carving, their formal treatments differ, which led Wixom and Bier to conclude that they were probably produced in different years. The very high quality of both figures is evident in such details as the deeply undercut locks of hair—carved in the same technique as on reliefs from the early *Passion* altarpiece or on the *Holy Blood* altarpiece (Chapuis essay, figs. 2 and 6)—or the hands in which tendons and veins suggest a sense of life and tension, also seen in the Berlin *Matthias* (cat. 24). Stephen's slender proportions, the broad treatment of his drapery, and his facial type call to mind figures from the Creglingen altarpiece of around 1505–1510 (cat. 25, fig. 2). The swirling twist in his dalmatic, which reveals the underside of his garment, is found in the figure at the right foreground of the central shrine, and the treatment of freestanding locks of hair recalls that of the two apostles in the right background. Stephen's facial type—with its thin, straight nose, pointed chin, and prominent cheekbones—resembles that of Saint John in the Creglingen altarpiece as well as that of the *Saint Kolonat* (destroyed in World War II) Riemenschneider produced between 1508 and 1510 for the high altar of Würzburg Cathedral (fig. 3). By contrast, Lawrence resembles works created shortly after 1500. His stance and the organization of his drapery, for instance, mirror those of Empress Kunigunde on the lid of the Bamberg imperial tomb, carved in about 1501 (Chapuis essay, fig. 4). The contour of the body forms an arc on one side and a straight line on the other, the knee pushes against the fabric of the garment, one shoulder is higher than the other, and the head is tilted in that direction. The front center of the drapery in both is crumpled in short angular folds surrounded by broader, U-shaped folds. In view of these similarities, it would appear that Saint Lawrence was carved in about 1502, and Saint Stephen in about 1508.

3. Kunigunde, wife of Heinrich II, was depicted on the imperial tomb in Bamberg with a similar hairstyle. Her attributes include the imperial insignia, a model of Bamberg Cathedral, and a ploughshare (falsely accused of adultery, she proved her innocence by walking on red-hot ploughshares; Louis Réau, *Iconographie de l'art chrétien* [Paris, 1958], 3.1: 354).

4. See in particular Bier 1957b and Krohm in Krohm and Oellermann 1992.

5. See in particular Saint Agnes, the First Wise Virgin, the Fifth Wise Virgin (Lehrs 67, 76, 80).

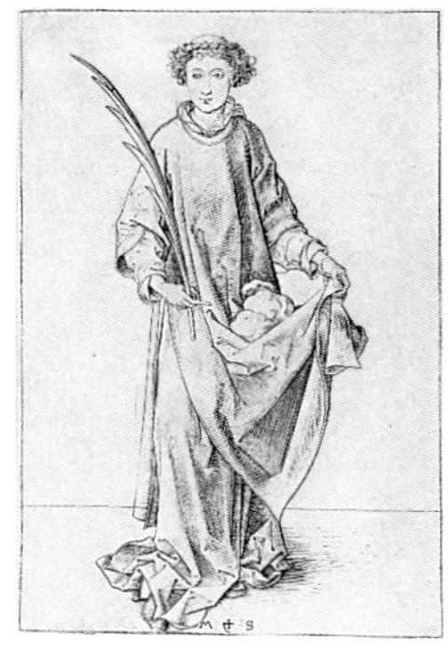

1.

Martin Schongauer, *Saint Stephen*, c. 1480, engraving, National Gallery of Art, Washington, Rosenwald Collection

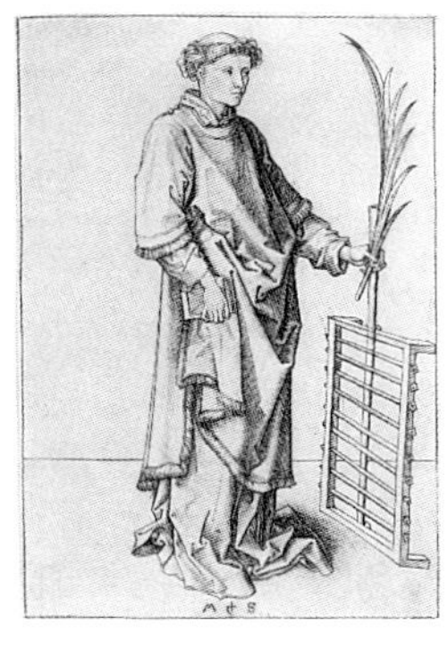

2.

Martin Schongauer, *Saint Lawrence*, c. 1480, engraving, National Gallery of Art, Washington, Rosenwald Collection

6. See Würzburg 1981, 30, 32 n. 5; and Marincola's essay in the present catalogue. Krohm points out that most of Riemenschneider's sculpture retaining the original polychromy seems to come from Rothenburg.

7. Bier 1930, 9–10; Bier 1960, 216.

The female saints are more difficult to locate precisely in the production of Riemenschneider and his shop, because they combine motifs found in sculpture created at different times. The figure that could be Catherine (32 B) is related to Lawrence in the way the center of her cloak breaks into a series of short, angular folds that achieve a rich contrast of light and dark. Like him, she supports her weight on her right leg, with her left knee pushing against the fabric of her robes. Also like him, her shoulders are on an oblique line, and her head is tilted the other direction. One strand of her hair falls in front of her right shoulder, while the hair on the other side is behind her shoulder, which conveys the illusion that the saint is slowly turning her head; a female saint of about 1515–1520 in a private collection (cat. 43 A) exhibits a similar feature. The figure that could be Barbara or Kunigunde (32 C) seems to echo the figure of Stephen. Her left hand, like his, hangs down to lift a portion of her drapery, while her right arm is bent at the elbow. One shoulder is higher than the other, and her head is turned toward the raised shoulder. Her hair arrangement, consisting of two rolled-up braids and a comb

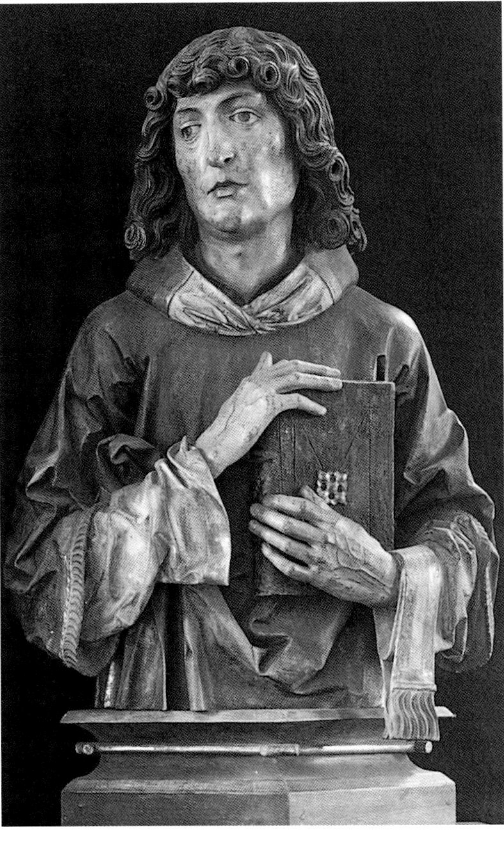

3.

Saint Kolonat, 1508–1510, limewood with ancient polychromy, formerly Neumünster, Würzburg (destroyed in World War II)

pattern at the back, is similar to that of the Raleigh female saint (cat. 10); the effigy of Kunigunde in Bamberg has the same heavy braids. The motif of the dress pulled up on the right side, creating an oblique movement contrary to the main fall of drapery, first appears in Riemenschneider's oeuvre on the Münnerstadt *Saint Elizabeth* of 1490–1492 (cat. 13, fig. 2). Both Frankfurt figures also have in common with the Raleigh female saint the broad oval face and the slightly swollen neck.

The Frankfurt saints do not display the same quality of sculptural execution as the Cleveland deacons, implying the participation of another sculptor. The lesser quality is apparent in the right hand of the female saint holding the book, which, compared with Lawrence's right hand, lacks its vital delineation and organic coherence. Likewise, the mantle of the other female saint does not exhibit the logical, crisp treatment of drapery of the Cleveland figures.

The Cleveland and Frankfurt figures, whose polychromy is consistent, are crucial reminders of the degree to which color often shaped the perception of Riemenschneider's sculpture. The blush on the cheeks, the red lips, pensive eyes, even the painted locks of hair on Lawrence's forehead, all add dramatically to the sense of life. The use of gold and silver leaf clarifies the distinction between the interior and the exterior of the dalmatics, and it marks the border of one female saint's mantle. The albs of the deacon saints are rendered in a matte white, very close to that found on the *Passion* reliefs, to suggest the quality of the cloth. While Riemenschneider is usually celebrated as one of the earliest sculptors to relinquish polychromy, a study of his works reveals that many were in fact originally colored. As discussed by Stephan Kemperdick elsewhere in this catalogue, guild regulations in Würzburg stipulated that the polychromy of sculpture could not be carried out in the sculptor's workshop but had to be executed by a specialized painter. Studying the groups in Frankfurt and Cleveland, Andrea Kleberger and Michele Marincola independently came to the conclusion that the four figures had probably been painted by Martin Schwarz, the Franciscan monk in Rothenburg who polychromed Riemenschneider's early *Passion* altarpiece.[6]

Elaborating on Bode's remark that the four figures came from a retable in the region of Rothenburg, Justus Bier proposed that this could have been an All Saints altarpiece for the church of the Dominican nuns in Rothenburg for which Riemenschneider received payments between 1507 and 1510.[7] The church, destroyed in 1813, was described in 1729 by the chronicler Johann Ludwig Schäffer as containing

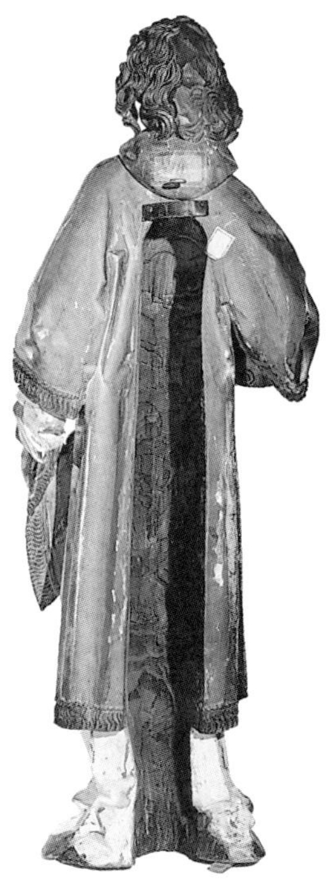

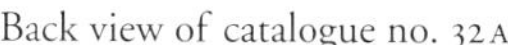

Back view of catalogue no. 32 A

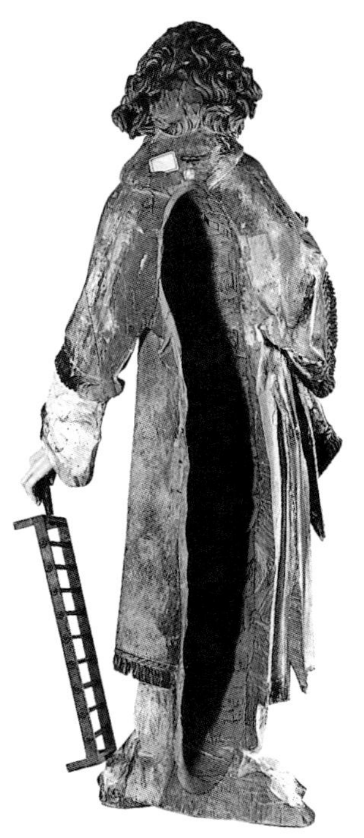

Back view of catalogue no. 32 D

"very beautifully carved and painted retables."[8] There were four of them, dedicated to Saint Catherine, All Saints, Our Lady, and Corpus Christi.[9] Bier suggested that the All Saints iconography could have been reduced to four figures, two males and two females. But the documents reveal that the joiner responsible for the encasement of the altarpiece received 50 guilders—which is as much as Erhart Harschner received for the framework of the *Holy Blood* altarpiece—suggesting a considerable structure. Although payment records do not specify how many figures the corpus contained, they do mention two angels and indicate that Riemenschneider carved a crucifix, presumably for the superstructure.[10]

There is circumstantial evidence to support Bier's hypothesis, which has generally been well received in the literature[11] and which rests on the absence of other existing fragments that could be identified as coming from this *All Saints* altarpiece. First, Martin Schwarz did several works for the church of the Dominican nuns in Rothenburg: he painted the wings of the *Our Lady* altarpiece (Germanisches Nationalmuseum, Nuremberg) and is documented as having polychromed carved processional staffs for the nuns in 1496 or 1497.[12] Second, the incomplete payment records for the *All Saints* altarpiece cover a period of at least four years, which is in keeping with the conclusion that the execution of the Cleveland saints was completed over several years. Third, the altar table

was found in 1812 to contain relics of Margaret, Kunigunde, and Lawrence.[13] While Lawrence is one of the Cleveland saints, the more damaged of two Frankfurt figures could conceivably be Kunigunde.

Whether or not the Frankfurt and Cleveland figures were once part of the Rothenburg *All Saints* altarpiece, they certainly stood in the corpus of a retable on either side of a central figure. In accordance with the All Saints iconography, which derives from the adoration of the Lamb by all nations (Revelation 6:9–12), the central figure could have been a Virgin and child, a personification of the Church (Ecclesia), a Trinity, or an Agnus Dei.[14] The articulation of the figures suggests their possible placement in the shrine. Stephen would definitely have stood to the left of the central figure, probably directly beside the left wall of the shrine, as suggested by the sharp turn of his head toward the right. Lawrence probably stood against the right side of the shrine, since his head is slightly inclined toward the left. Although the relative placement of the female figures is more difficult to determine, it is attractive to hypothesize that the figure with the book stood at the left, between Stephen and the central figure, while her companion stood in the corresponding spot on the right. Indeed, since the articulation of the latter echoes that of Stephen, her placement between the central element and Lawrence would have given diversity to the rhythm of the figures.
CHAPUIS

8. Würzburg 1981, 30.

9. Bier 1930, 9.

10. The use of "uff" *(auf)* for the crucifix suggests that it was intended to be positioned higher than the figures and the angels, which were to stand in the retable (Bier 1930, 169).

11. A notable exception being Kahsnitz 1997, 108 n. 36.

12. Würzburg 1981, 30; see also Oellermann in Würzburg 1981, 285–302; and Kahsnitz 1997, 25–27.

13. Würzburg 1981, 32 n. 5.

14. See *Lexikon der christlichen Ikonographie,* ed. Wolfgang Braunfels (Rome, Freiburg, Basel, Vienna, 1974), 1:101–104.

33

c. 1500–1510, limewood, Christ: 50.5 (19 ⅞) high; Virgin: 44.8 (17 ⅝) high; John: 46 (18 ⅛) high,
Hessisches Landesmuseum, Darmstadt

1. Weber 1884, 31; Würzburg 1981, 241.

2. Bier 1930, 2–3 n. 3; Bier 1978, 78–79 n. 62, Peter Bloch in Würzburg 1981, 241. Kalden 1990, 92 n. 359, believes the Darmstadt *Crucifixion* to be the work of a collaborator.

• Technical Notes •

The three figures are each made from a single piece of limewood with the grain running vertically. They are carved fully in the round, though the backs are less plastic. As was common in medieval sculpture, the arms of Christ were carved separately and attached to the corpus by wooden dowels or nails. A hole was drilled into the lower back to attach the figure to the modern cross. The backs of Saint John and the Virgin show similar holes, probably used to stabilize the figures against the background of a shrine in the nineteenth century. Both the Virgin and the Evangelist are attached to the base with two wooden dowels. A wooden strip about 1 cm wide has been added to the base of Saint John, probably to bring the two attending figures to the same height. Only a few traces of an old gilding, probably from the eighteenth or early nineteenth century, are discernible.[1] The extremely refined execution alone suggests that the group was conceived as a monochrome.

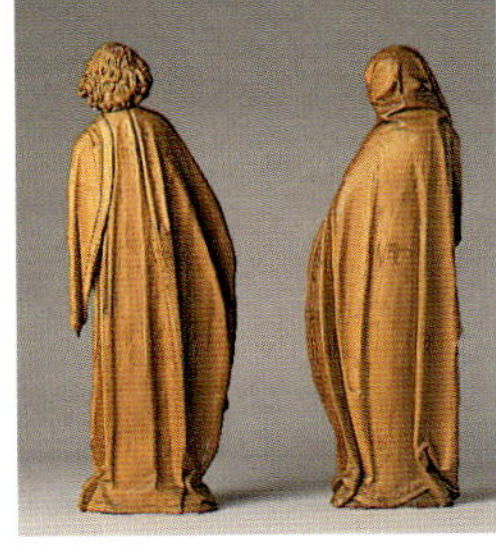

Back view of Saint John
and the Virgin
from catalogue no. 33

• Provenance •

Formerly in the possession of the Holzhausen family in Frankfurt am Main; acquired by the museum in Darmstadt at some point in the nineteenth century.

• Literature •

Weber 1884, 31; Bode 1885, 173; Streit 1888, 15; Weber 1888, 55; Tönnies 1900, 174; Adelmann 1910, 76; Weber 1911, 167, 232–233; Schrade 1927, nn. 298–299; Bier 1930, 2–3 n. 3; Knapp 1931, 21; Knapp 1935, 27; Demmler 1939, 72–73; Hotz 1961, 88; Bier 1978, 78–79; Würzburg 1981, 240–241; Kalden 1990, 92 n. 359.

CHRIST HANGS from the cross, a nail in each hand and another in his feet. His head drops deeply toward his right shoulder, on which locks of his hair fall from beneath the crown of thorns. His body is slender and exquisitely modeled, even in the back, with a clear understanding of anatomy. It breaks in an almost imperceptible arc to the right, then markedly at the neck. The loincloth wraps around his body and extends at either side in artificial flourishes, typical of late Gothic carvings of the Crucifixion. Above Christ's head the original banderole, with the inscription "INRI," has been attached to a cross made in the late nineteenth century, which replaces the lost or destroyed original. The modern cross is inserted into the ground, a sculpted mound of earth that alludes to the hill of Golgotha (Matthew 27:33).

On the ground to the left of the cross stands the Virgin, and to the right, John the Evangelist. Both turn toward the cross, their poses almost symmetrical: the figure of Mary is articulated in the characteristic S-shape, while John's is the reverse. The Virgin wears a fitted dress with a long mantle that is draped around her in graceful, calligraphic folds that emphasize her curved stance and give a compelling impression of depth and volume. In an expression of grief, she has covered her head with a long veil that is pulled low over her forehead and extends over her shoulders to her hands, crossed in front. The corresponding figure of Saint John, whose wide cape similarly underscores his dynamically curved stance, provides compositional and emotional balance to the Virgin's mourning figure. His cloak, with its conspicuous ornamentation, is worn loosely over a short tunic that leaves his bare feet visible. With his arms crossed above his waist, he holds his Gospel in his right hand and gathers his robe in the other.

The figure of Christ, by virtue of its superb quality, has been convincingly attributed to Riemenschneider himself. Those of the Virgin and Saint John are usually considered to be the work of a gifted collaborator who carefully followed the master's model.[2] The Darmstadt *Crucifixion* is one of the most beau-

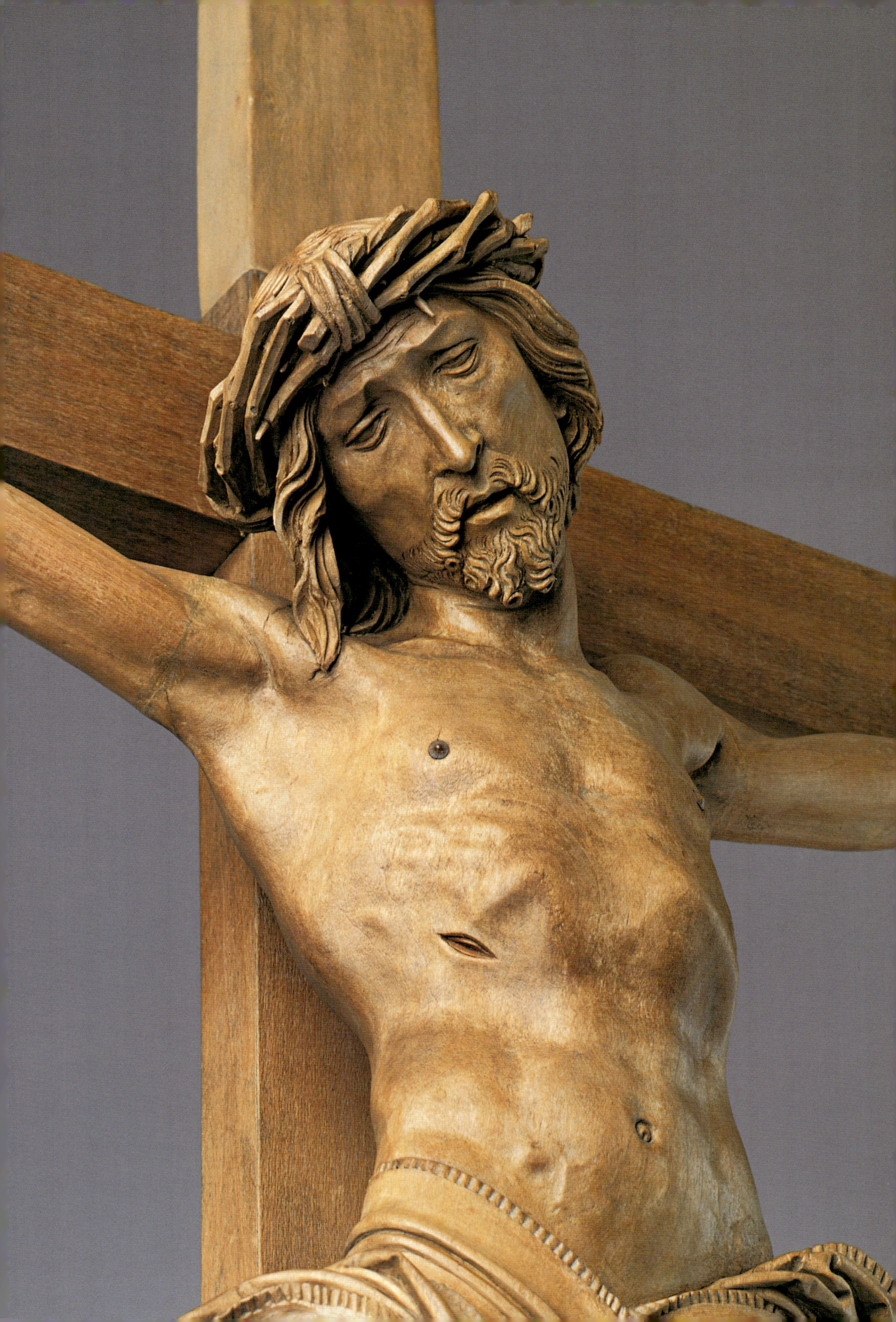

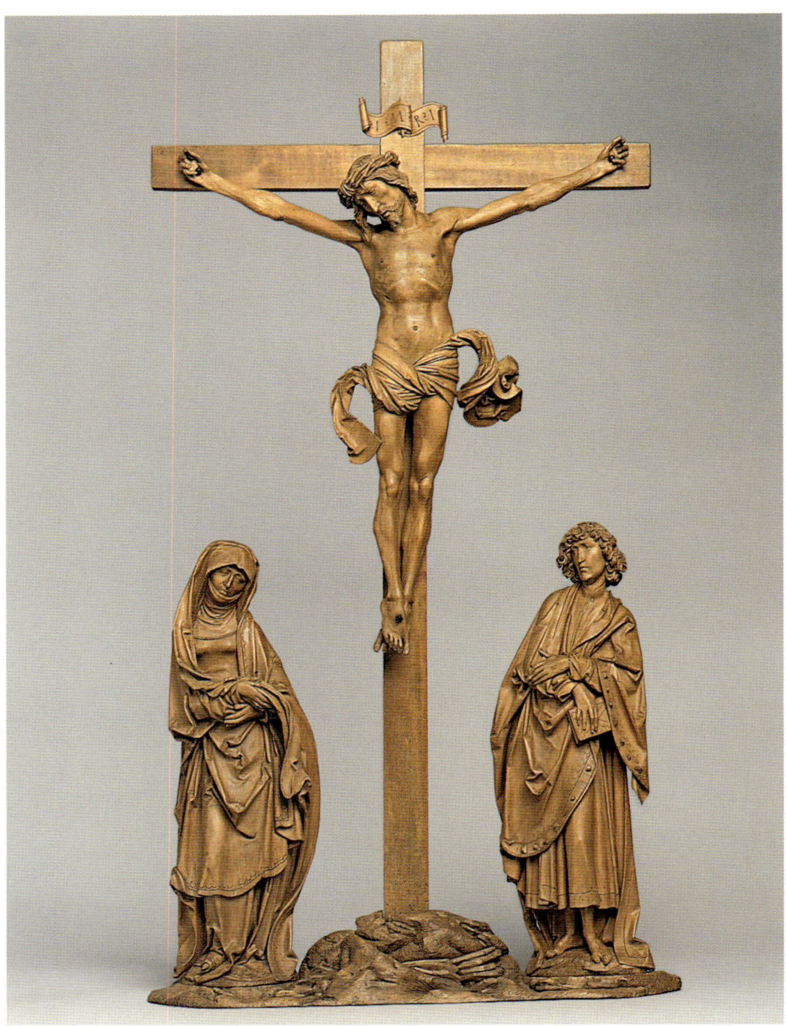

Catalogue no. 33

tifully carved pieces among Riemenschneider's surviving oeuvre.

The original context and function are unknown.
Knapp suggested it was a workshop model.[3] Given
its relatively small size and refined execution, it seems
much more likely that the group was made as an object of private devotion. Since the figures are carved in
the round, they would surely not have been displayed
within a wooden enclosure, as they were in the nineteenth century. Instead, the work must have been
placed on a house altar, allowing the beholder to ad-
mire it closely from at least three sides. The quality
of the work, which is enhanced by its outstanding
condition and by the almost painterly modeling of
the elegant body of Christ, would certainly have
satisfied even the most discerning patron. Surprisingly, the material of the Darmstadt *Crucifixion*, which
has long been mistaken for pearwood, is actually the
less costly limewood.[4]

There are indications that Riemenschneider must
indeed have had a remarkable artistic reputation for
his crucifixes, since he was involved in several prestigious commissions. The elector Friedrich the Wise
ordered a crucifix for the castle chapel in Wittenberg
in 1505–1506 from a Würzburg sculptor generally
identified as Riemenschneider. Riemenschneider probably also made a Crucifixion in the first decade of the
sixteenth century for the important collegiate church
in Aschaffenburg (cat. 34).[5] His reputation was presumably established by the dramatic early *Passion*
altarpiece for Rothenburg of which the Heroldsberg
Crucifix (Krohm essay, fig. 12) may have been the focal
point. It would have been further enhanced by a
crucifix he produced in about 1495 for Würzburg
Cathedral, destroyed in World War II.

The Darmstadt *Crucifixion* belongs to some
twenty crucifixes that have been associated with Riemenschneider or his workshop or followers. Only few

are considered to be autograph works by the master.[6] The supposedly early crucifixes in Heroldsberg and Insingen, the destroyed crucifix from Würzburg Cathedral, and even the Steinach *Crucifix* of 1516 (Chapuis essay, fig. 10) seem in general to derive from a type introduced by Niclaus Gerhaert in his wooden *Crucifixion* of 1462 from the Nördlingen altarpiece and his stone *Crucifix* of 1467 in Baden-Baden (Krohm essay, fig. 13). The Darmstadt *Crucifixion,* in contrast to Riemenschneider's considerably larger figures of Christ, has a decidedly different appearance, foreshadowing the Renaissance, in its small size and the elegant, almost sensual, modeling of Christ's body.

Several characteristics of the Darmstadt *Crucifixion* may also be seen in a *Crucifixion* from the parish church in Aub (fig. 1), for which Bier proposed a date of around 1500.[7] While there are crucial variations between the two works, similarities include the elongated and delicately modeled body of Christ, the S-shaped pose of the Virgin, and to a lesser degree the responding curve of Saint John. In Aub, Christ's head is more upright, his ribs are more pronounced, and the arc of his body is less graceful. The pose and type of the Evangelist are very different, although the curved contour of the figure gives a similar effect.

The drapery patterns in the garment worn by the Virgin, despite slight differences in the two figures' postures, are closely related in their principal movements. Both may have followed a common workshop model, possibly also reflected in the *Mourning Virgin* from Kansas City (cat. 34), which originally formed part of Riemenschneider's *Crucifixion* for the collegiate church in Aschaffenburg.[8]

For the purpose of establishing a date for the Darmstadt *Crucifixion,* the figure of Christ provides numerous clues. Related to several works by Riemenschneider's atelier, the Darmstadt corpus most closely resembles that on the Detwang altarpiece (fig. 2), which is of a similar high quality of sculptural execution. Both works share the refined and subtle modeling of Christ's body and the lively calligraphy of the loincloth flourishes, while the Darmstadt figure is still more elongated and more noticeably curved. The attenuation of the body is replaced in Detwang by a more rigid anatomy. Within a gradual stylistic development, the Darmstadt *Crucifixion* could be placed between the Aub and Detwang *Crucifixion*s, therefore roughly between 1500, which is the supposed dating of the sculpture in Aub, and 1510, the circumstantial date of the Detwang altarpiece.

BORCHERT

6. See Krohm's survey of the development of Riemenschneider's crucifixes in Würzburg 1981, 58–62. See also Krohm's essay in the present catalogue.

7. Bier 1925, 106; Bier 1982, 75; a later dating of after 1510 is proposed in Schrade 1927, 141.

8. The reconstruction in Schneider 1990, 58, fig. 56, is incorrect. Comparison to both Riemenschneider's Aub and Darmstadt *Crucifixion*s strongly suggests that the Virgin was originally positioned to the left of the cross, while Saint John was positioned to the right.

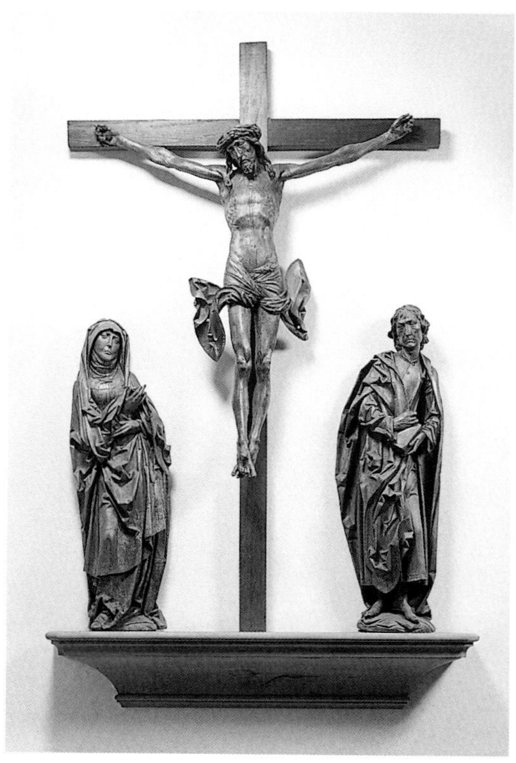

1.

Crucifixion, c. 1500, limewood, Pfarrkirche, Aub

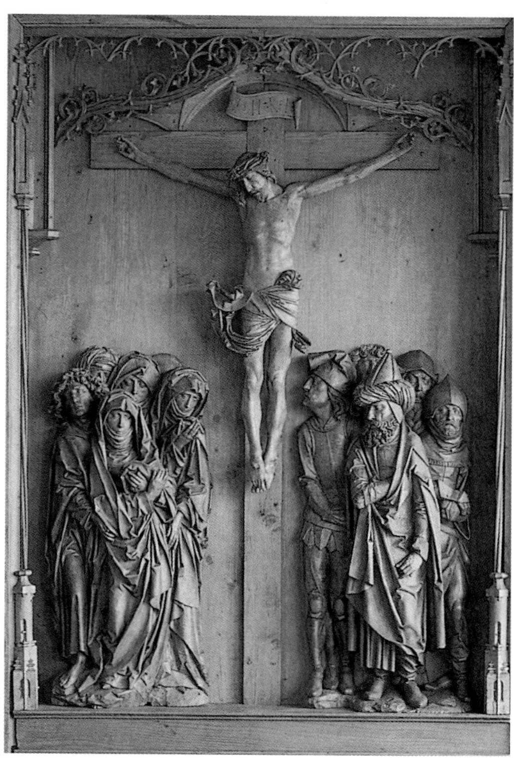

2.

Crucifixion, c. 1510, limewood, Pfarrkirche, Detwang

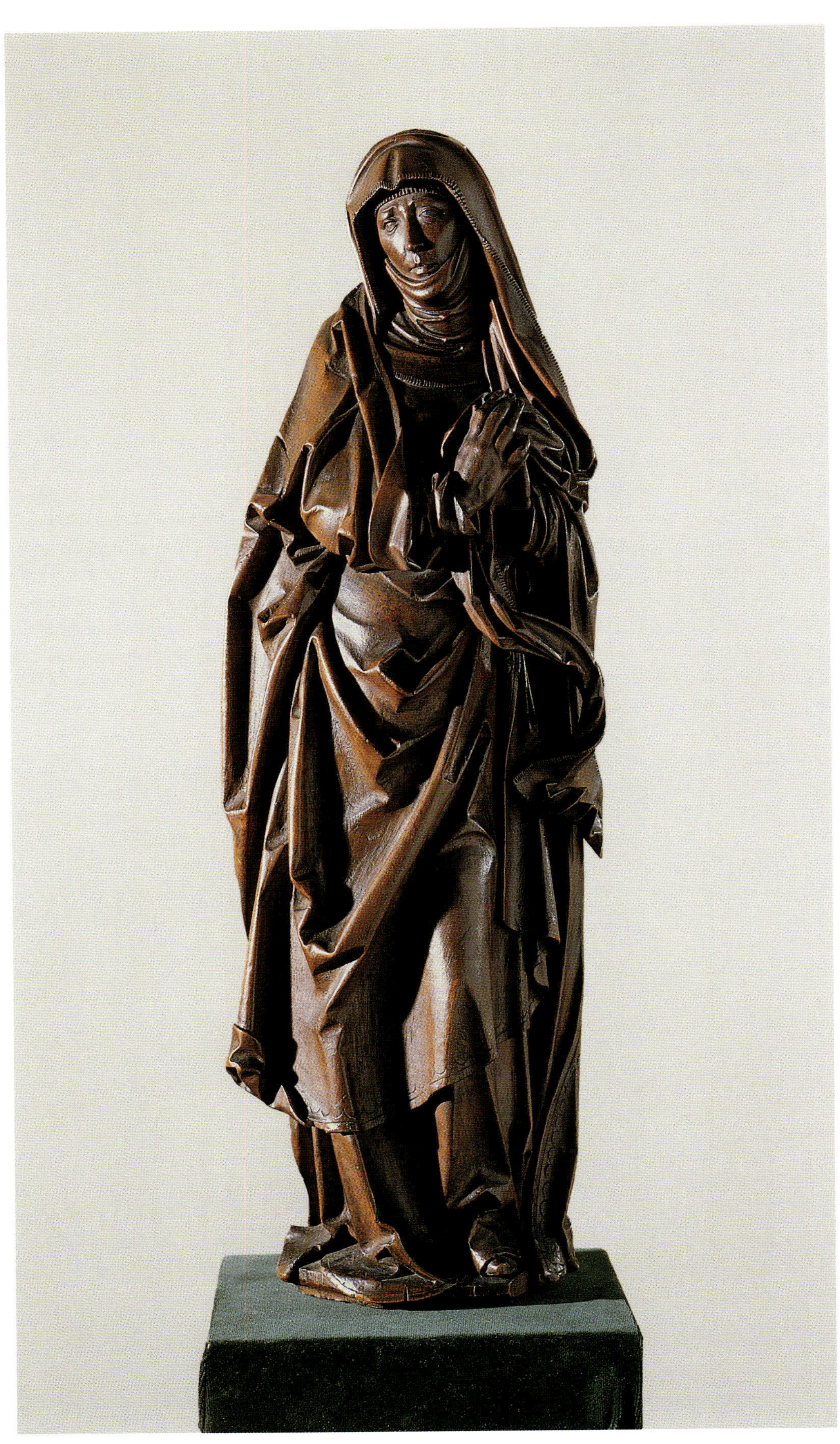

MOURNING VIRGIN

c. 1505–1510, limewood, 59.1 x 22.9 x 13.3 (23 ¼ x 9 x 5 ¼), The Nelson-Atkins Museum of Art,
Kansas City, Purchase: Nelson Trust

• *Technical Notes* •

The sculpture is cut from a single member of limewood with the grain running vertically. It is carved
fully in the round, although the back is rather flat,
with long vertical folds. Two holes have been drilled
in the back for attachment to a mount. Except for
the dark brown stain applied to the wood to make it
resemble oak, the work is in remarkably good condition. There is no significant insect damage, and only
a few small losses, including the tip of the Virgin's
right little finger and a minute triangular segment of
the polygonal base. The figure was painted at some
point, and paint particles are discernible on the wood
under the brown stain.

• *Provenance* •

In the Collegiate Church, Aschaffenburg, until the
early nineteenth century; Dr. Jacob von Hafner-
Alteneck by 1851; Hans Schwarz; Dr. Walter von Pannwitz (d. 1920); Catalina von Pannwitz, his wife, De
Hartekamp near Haarlem, The Netherlands; [Ros-
enberg and Stiebel, New York]; acquired by the
museum in Kansas City in 1964.

• *Literature* •

Bode 1885, 173; Hefner-Alteneck 1886, 471; Friedländer and Falke 1925, 12; Hannover 1931, 16, no. 32; Taggart and McKenna 1973, 71; Bier 1978, 149; Bier 1982,
70–73; Oklahoma City 1985, 139, no. 38; Ward and
Fidler 1993, 143.

THIS EXPRESSIVE sculpture of the Virgin originally stood to the left of the cross in a Crucifixion
group, with John the Evangelist on the other side.
These two personages are traditionally singled out,
excluding other witnesses to the Crucifixion, based
on the account in John's Gospel: "When Jesus saw
his mother, and the disciple whom he loved standing near, he said to his mother, 'Woman, behold your
son!' Then he said to the disciple, 'Behold your mother!'
And from that hour the disciple took her to his own
home" (John 19:26–27). This reduction of the narrative allows both the sculptor and the viewer to
focus on the emotions of the figures.

In medieval devotional texts, such as *Meditations
on the Life of Christ* or the writings of Ludolph of
Saxony, there is marked shift in emphasis from the
subject matter to the reaction expected of the readers. Readers are encouraged to ponder the suffering
of Christ and the Virgin and to enter into their experience. In its expression of extreme grief, the Kansas
City Virgin is a visual equivalent to such writings: it
offers a dramatic rendering of suffering, which the
viewer is invited to share. The *Crucifixion* remained
in the Collegiate Church at Aschaffenburg until the
early nineteenth century, when it was replaced by a
neo-Gothic altarpiece; the *Crucifix* is now in Berlin,
while the *Saint John* is lost.[1]

With her head and chin covered, as customary
for older women and women in mourning, the Virgin looks away from her dying son. Her furrowed
brow, the deep grooves under her eyes, and her barely
parted lips express unspeakable sorrow. The body is
articulated along oblique lines, with her hips and legs
facing to her right, her upper torso and clasped hands
twisting to her left, and her head turned back to her
right. The agitated drapery patterns reflect this con-
torted pose and suggest enervation and exhaustion,
an impression also conveyed by the fluttering veil,
which adds to the overall sense of despair.

The Kansas City statuette achieves a compelling
spatial presence by its sculptural handling and by its
arc of address. It has considerable mass, with areas of
deep undercutting between the face and the head covering, under the Virgin's hands, and around the almost
free-hanging end of the swirling veil. The viewer reads

1. Bier 1982, 72–73.

2. See also Bier 1982, 72.

3. A literal copy of the Kansas City figure, of almost identical height, was sold as lot 24 on 2 March 1984, at Sotheby's, New York. The sculpture is described in the catalogue as being made of pinewood, a species not found in any work ascribed to Riemenschneider or his shop.

the form as existing in three dimensions, which gives depth to the figure as a whole. Furthermore, the composition is made to be seen from several viewpoints within an angle of about 120 degrees. Indeed, the particularly complex area of the Virgin's hands and fluttering head veil gains coherence when seen from the right: only then does her left forearm properly recede in space and the veil unfold into its wide, fanlike structure. The averted face of the Virgin draws the viewer around to the left to meet its gaze.

The Kansas City figure combines elements from several compositions, most from around 1500–1510. The expressive gesture of the head inclined toward a shoulder is found, for instance, in one of the women in Stuttgart from about 1510 (cat. 37); this woman's head veil is also similar, with a vertical crease in the

center of the forehead. The same motif appears in the mourning Virgin in Darmstadt and that in Aub of about 1500 (cat. 33, fig. 1). The Kansas City sculpture is related in general terms to these two Virgins. Like them, her stance forms a generous curve on one side, which is offset by the tilt of her head; she holds a portion of her veil, a detail present in Stuttgart as well, which seems to have been a standard expressive gesture used by Riemenschneider and his shop. The Kansas City Virgin differs from the one in Darmstadt in the more angular treatment of the drapery and in the more schematic facial type. The closest parallel for the face is seen in the Virgin in *Christ among the Doctors* in the predella of the Creglingen altarpiece (fig. 1).[2] All these elements suggest that the Kansas City figure was created between 1505 and 1510.[3] CHAPUIS

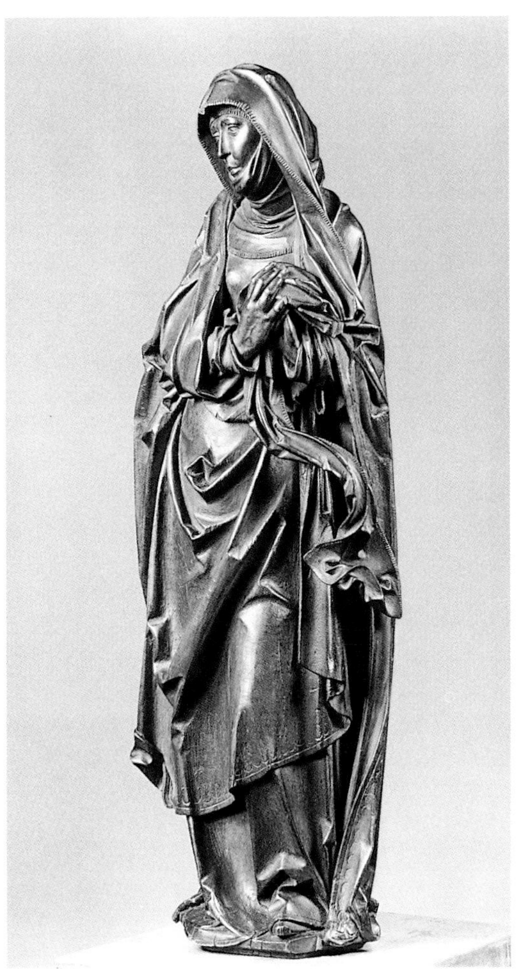

Alternate view of catalogue no. 34

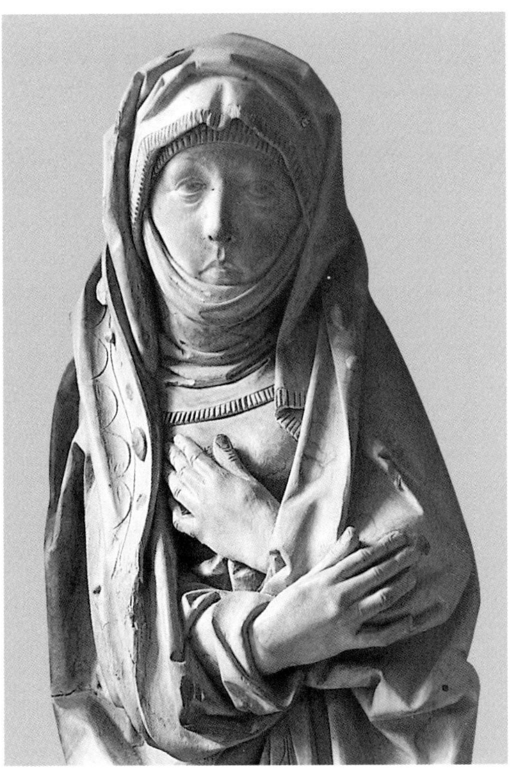

1.

Detail of the Virgin in *Christ among the Doctors,* in the predella of the Creglingen altarpiece, c. 1505–1510, limewood, Herrgottskirche, Creglingen

Veit Stoss / MOURNING VIRGIN

c. 1500–1510, pearwood, 31.4 x 9.8 x 8.5 (12 ⅜ x 3 ⅞ x 3 ⅜), The Cleveland Museum of Art,
Purchase from the J. H. Wade Fund

• *Technical Notes* •

This statuette, which was carved fully in the round, was cut from a single piece of pearwood with the grain running vertically. There are several losses, notably the figure's arms and hands, the front edge of her veil, the edge of the mantle at her left (which has been re-carved), and large portions of the base. The mantle has been pierced in six places, presumably during the removal of a layer of later polychromy, remnants of which are discernible on both the interior and exterior of the cloak. Two small holes on the figure's chest, probably not original, may have served to attach a later metal brooch or pendant, now lost.[1]

• *Provenance* •

Andreas Colli, Innsbruck, in 1933; acquired by the Cleveland museum in 1939.

• *Literature* •

Nuremberg 1933, no. 12; Dettloff 1961, 1:113–114, 302, 2: figs. 237–238; Lutze 1968, 51, fig. 65; Rasmussen 1976, 108–110, fig. 3; Baxandall 1980, 271; Beck in Frankfurt 1981, 200–201, fig. 53; Kahsnitz in New York 1986, 243–245, no. 91.

THIS ELOQUENT YET fragmentary figure does not appear to have been a model, for no full-scale mourning Virgin from a Crucifixion group by Veit Stoss is clearly based on it.[2] The Cleveland statuette in its original condition and polish was undoubtedly intended to serve as part of a household Crucifixion group, like Riemenschneider's Darmstadt *Crucifixion* (cat. 33). Its conception seems entirely appropriate for private devotions in a family chapel or, "even more likely, the study of a connoisseur, who was probably also a cleric."[3] The Virgin was to be viewed by a worshipper from a position somewhat below, as suggested by the elongated proportions of the figure.

The grievous losses, sensitively and correctly observed by Rainer Kahsnitz,[4] require a careful reading of the composition, inferring the sculptor's intentions. In general terms the figure would have been much more mysterious and mournful than it now appears: the edges of the mantle and veil enclosed the slight figure and tearful head more fully, like the closing valves of a shell. The sense of pathos would have been far more acute, as the Virgin seemed to be enfolded in shadows. Stoss had already perfected his ability to convey deep emotional states in the figures of the central shrine of his *Death of the Virgin* altarpiece of 1477–1489 in Krakow.[5] In its original condition this virtuoso carving would have been an even more successful miniature than the more famous, mannered, and possible slightly earlier boxwood statuette in the Victoria and Albert Museum.[6] These two figures are the only surviving examples of Stoss' mastery of small-scale sculpture.

A stylistic debt to Niclaus Gerhaert von Leiden is clearly evident in the Cleveland Virgin (see cats. 5 and 6). The extremely elongated proportions and high waistline, for example, recall especially those of the New York boxwood statuette, attributed to Gerhaert (cat. 6), which may represent the nature of the source for the deep enclosing envelope of the mantle, the long parabolic curves at the sides and back, and the exploitation of spatially conceived shallow hollows and deeply recessed folds. One might even wonder whether Veit Stoss could have seen the New York statuette in Vienna en route to and from Krakow. Stoss' engraving of the *Virgin with a Pomegranate* (Lehrs 5) and his drawing of *Saint Martha* with an aspergillum and holy water bucket seem to support this possibility.[7]

The sculptural contrast with Tilman Riemenschneider's figures of the same subject could not be greater. Riemenschneider's *Mourning Virgin* of around

1. See the extensive description of the condition provided by Kahsnitz in New York 1986, 243.

2. A comparison with the *Mourning Virgin* of the Crucifixion group of around 1506, Sebalduskirche in Nuremberg, is still instructive.

3. New York 1986, 244.

4. New York 1986, 243–244.

5. See, for example, the central grieving apostle with upraised arms, in Piotr Skubiszewski, "Der Stil des Veit Stoss," *Zeitschrift für Kunstgeschichte* 41 (1978), 109, 112, fig. 13. Some of the emotional motifs may have been based on the inventions of Rogier van der Weyden.

6. New York 1986, 241–243, no. 90 (fig.), 244.

7. Fritz Koreny, "Die Kupferstiche des Veit Stoss," in *Veit Stoss. Die Vorträge des Nürnberger Symposions* (Munich, 1985), 156–160, figs. 103, 107.

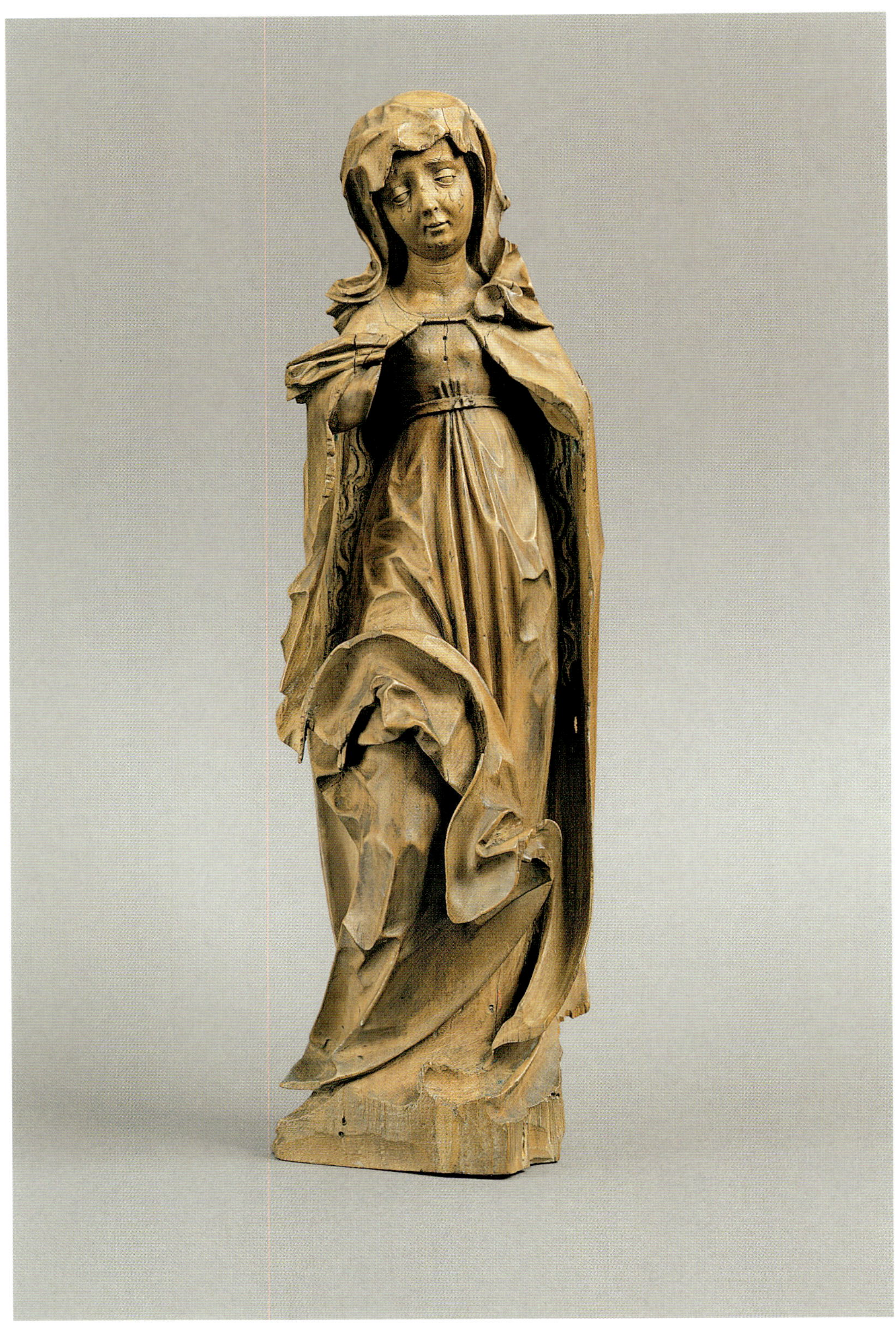

1500 in the parish church at Aub (cat. 33, fig. 1) and his *Mourning Virgin* of about 1510 from Kansas City (cat. 34) are each eloquent in an entirely different way from Stoss' aesthetic and his concern for three-dimensionality. Riemenschneider instead emphasizes a more planar, relieflike effect. Yet in these works, both sculptors were accomplished masters in empathetic expression intended to engage the devout observer in a deeply felt emotion of mourning. WIXOM

Two elements from a Holy Kinship altarpiece

36A   MARY CLEOPHAS AND ALPHAUS

c. 1505–1510, limewood, 117 x 50 x 24 (46⅛ x 19⅝ x 9⅜); Württembergisches Landesmuseum,
Stuttgart

36B   MARY SALOME AND ZEBEDEE

c. 1505–1510, limewood, 119.4 x 49.5 x 29 (47 x 19½ x 11⅜), Victoria and Albert Museum, London

• Technical Notes •

Each group was carved from a single block of limewood with the grain running vertically and the backs hollowed out (the one in London considerably less deeply). Ornament was applied using punches or by incising the wood, which suggests that the works were conceived as monochromes.

In the Stuttgart sculpture the missing hand of Mary Cleophas had been attached to the arm with a nail. The tip of her nose appears to be a modern repair in a different wood. A portion of Alphaus' beard to the left of his mouth is missing; the corresponding curl on the right seems to be a later replacement. Two cushion tassels are lost, and minor parts of the drapery are missing. Serious insect damage at the lower right has caused considerable loss of the original wood. Wormholes have not been filled. The work has been aggressively cleaned. There are no traces of polychromy, but small remnants of glue have been found. Traces of wax are found on the surface, along with numerous whitish stains of unclear origin. The pupils of the eyes have been indicated in dark paint, but the red color once recorded on the lips seems to have been removed during this century.[1]

In the London group the lower part of Zebedee's left hand was carved separately and inserted. The tip of Mary Salome's nose is a later repair. The lower section of the bench at the left is a pine replacement, attached with a nail. A piece of wood has been irregularly fitted under the left edge of the sculpture. The cushion tassels are missing. Although the pupils of the eyes are defined in black paint, there is no trace of polychromy, as the work has been covered with a dark glaze. Wormholes have been filled. An inscription on the back records an 1817 restoration.

• Provenance •

London: [Léon Gauchez, Paris]; bought by the Victoria and Albert Museum in 1878 as being by Jörg Syrlin the Elder.

Stuttgart: Princes of Oettingen-Wallerstein, Maihingen (until 1947–1948), then Harburg Castle; acquired by the Württembergisches Landesmuseum in 1994.

• Literature •

Bode 1885, 166; Weber 1888, 67; Streit 1888, 18; Tönnies 1900, 237–238; Adelmann 1910, 60–61; Weber 1911, 270–271; Schrade 1927, 173–174 n. 421; Bier 1930, 47–48 n. 1; Maskell 1931, 110, 112, 115–117; Demmler 1932, 209–210; Bier 1944–1945, 22–23; Winzinger 1951, 129–137; Freeden 1951, 347; Manchester 1961, 25, no. 67; Paatz 1963, 92–93 n. 301; Baxandall 1974, 48; Bier 1978, 116; Muth 1982, 276–278; Esser 1986, 86, 164, 241; Kalden 1990, 119 n. 435; Meurer 1995, 185.

THE THEME OF the Holy Kinship, which enjoyed great popularity in Germany, is based on the so-called Trinubium legend, which maintained that Saint Anne, the mother of the Virgin Mary, was married three times. With Joachim, she conceived the Virgin Mary, who later gave birth to Christ. With Cleophas, she had another daughter, Mary Cleophas,

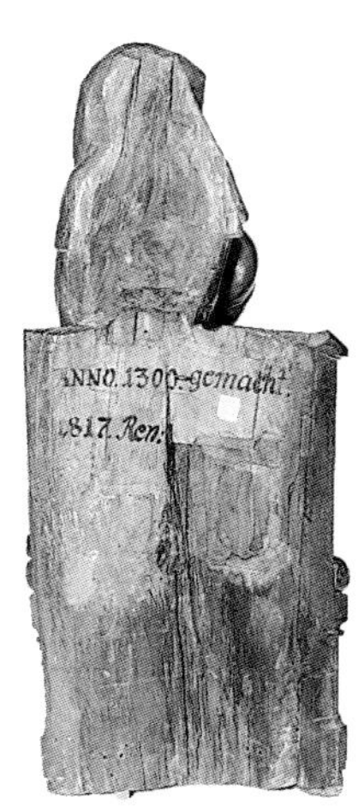

Back view of
catalogue no. 36 B

1. Winzinger 1951, 130, still noted the red color of Mary Cleophas' lips. I am grateful to Heribert Meurer and Hans Westhoff for allowing me to see the conservation report on file in the Württembergisches Landesmuseum.

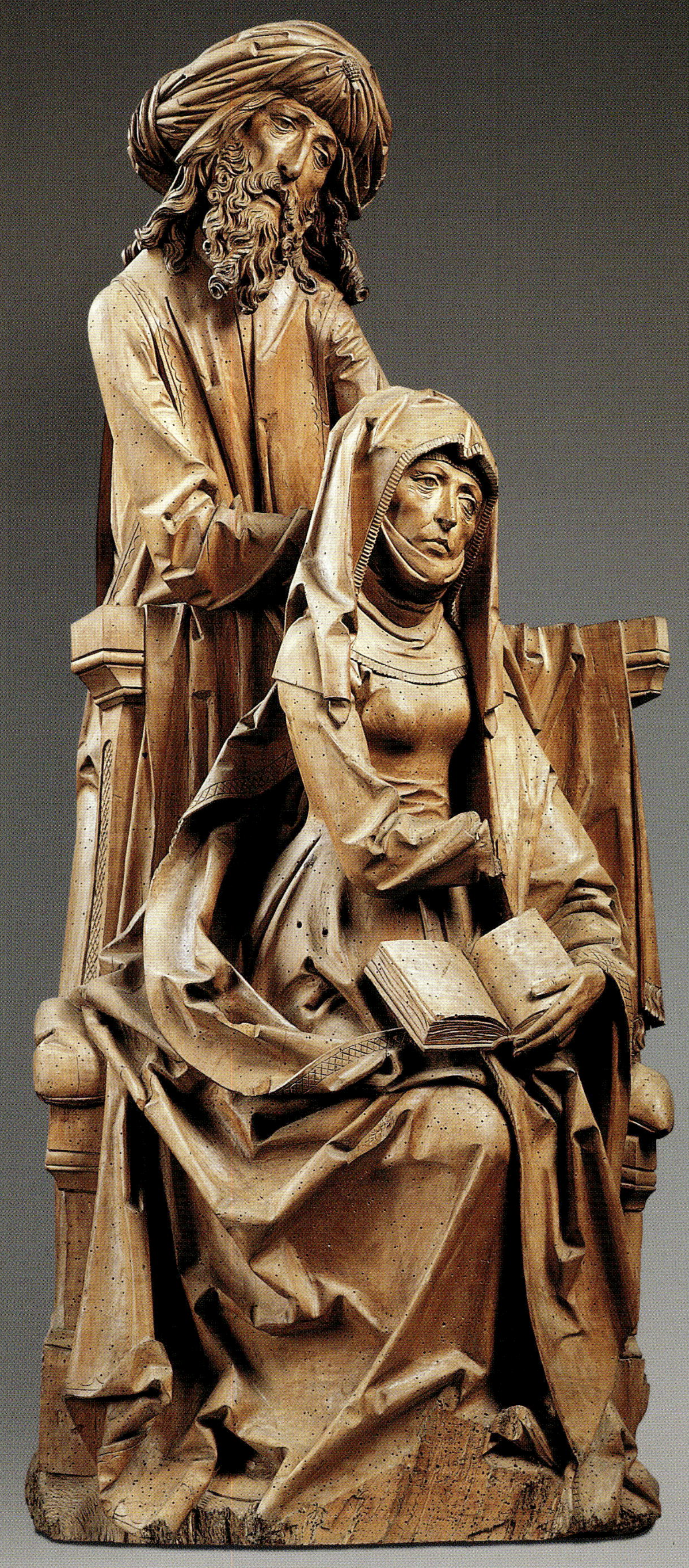

36 A

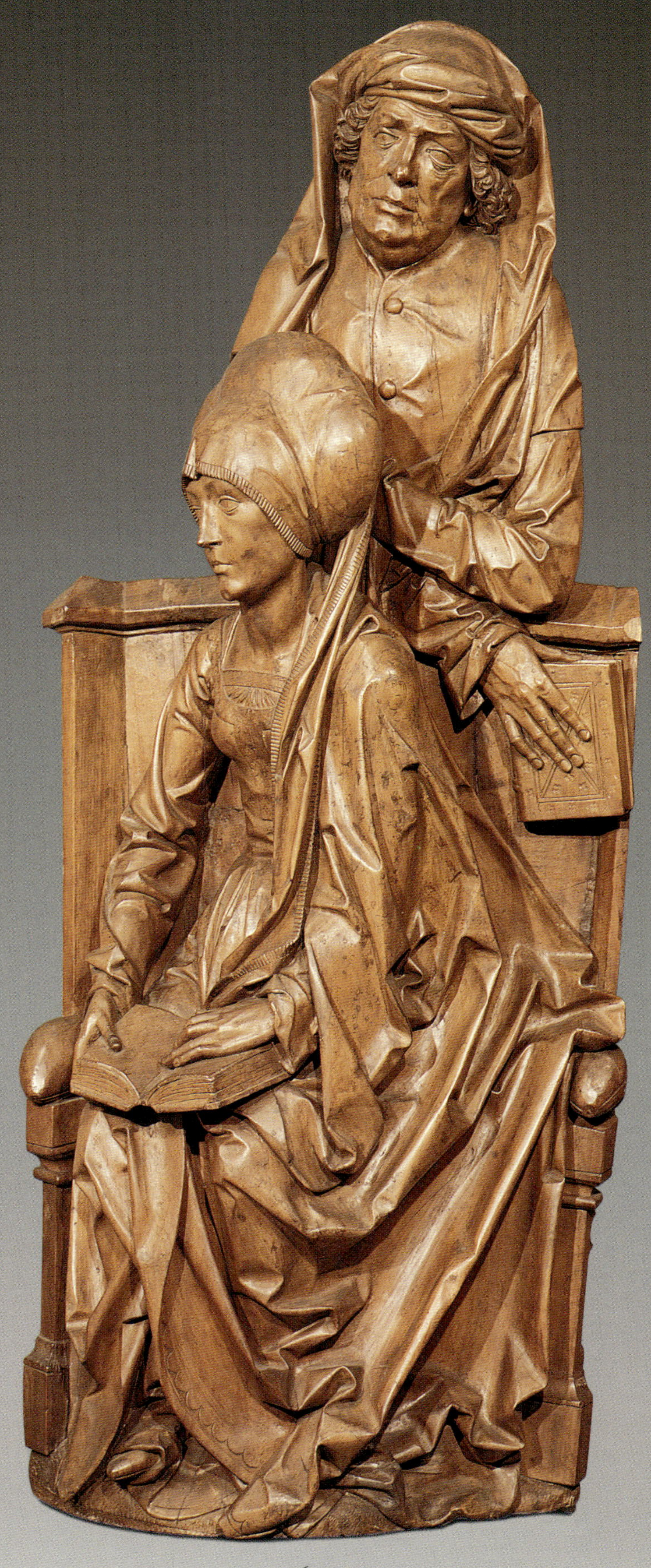

36 B

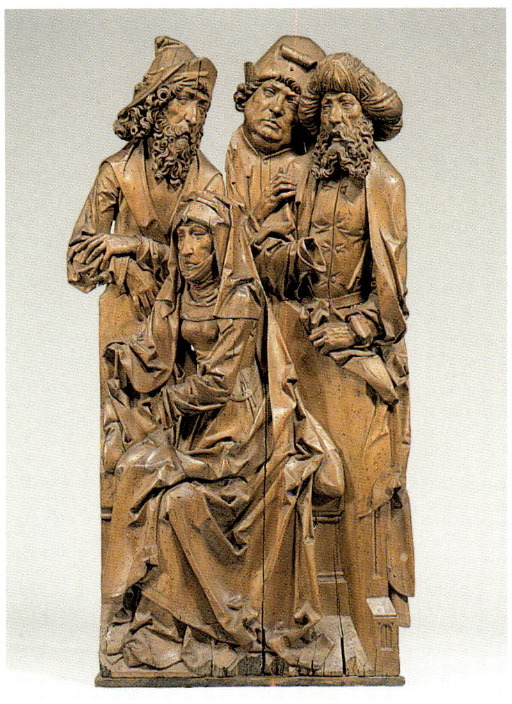

1.

Saint Anne and Her Three Husbands from a *Holy Kinship* altarpiece, c. 1505–1510, limewood, Private Collection, on loan to the Bayerisches Nationalmuseum, Munich

The representation of Mary Salome and Zebedee in London appears to be almost the mirror opposite. Mary Salome is also seated on a large cushioned throne with an open book on her lap, but she turns to her right. She wears a fashionable costume with an ornamented border and a mantle draped over her left shoulder that falls in an elegant curve over her arm and throne to the ground. Her bulbous coif and long veil were typical for married women in Germany at about 1500. Behind her, Zebedee leans with both elbows on the back of the throne, holding a closed book with a stamped cover in his right hand. Dressed in a buttoned coat, he wears a chaperon on his head that falls over his shoulders. Unlike Alphaus in the Stuttgart group, Zebedee faces the viewer frontally. His highly individual physiognomy is that of an aged man, with flaccid muscles and projecting cheekbones.

The groups in Stuttgart and London are extremely close in their refined execution and their ornamentation. In addition, when placed side by side, the two benches form an angle that causes both female figures to face toward each other.[3] This unusual detail supports the traditional assumption that the groups must originally have belonged at either side of a large altarpiece. The differences are minor. While the group in Stuttgart seems to be based on figural and facial types that were commonly employed by Riemenschneider and his workshop, the London group is related to some of the more individualized sepulchral portraits by Riemenschneider, such as the funerary monument of Dorothea von Wertheim in Grünsfeld (cat. 41, fig. 1). The face of Alphaus is like those of several disciples in the *Holy Blood* altarpiece (cat. 23, fig. 1) and the presumed figure of Nicodemus in the *Lamentation* from Grossostheim (cat. 38). The image of Mary Cleophas resembles a type that Riemenschneider used in representations of the mourning Virgin — such as those in the Maidbronn *Lamentation* and the Detwang *Crucifixion* (Chapuis essay, fig. 9; and cat. 33, fig. 2) — or of Saint Anne, such as that in Munich (cat. 30).

Any attempt to reconstruct the original context of the groups in Stuttgart and London faces the question of whether a third fragment in Munich, representing Saint Anne and her three husbands (fig. 1), originally belonged to the same altarpiece. Although compatible in subject matter and in height and width, the Munich relief is significantly shallower. Demmler, Bier, and Muth concluded that the three segments came from different retables, although they acknowledged the similarities.[4] Winzinger, by contrast, proposed a reconstruction of an altarpiece with the Munich relief at the center paired with a now-lost

2. See Esser 1986; see also Ewald Maria Vetter and Alfred Walz, "Die Rolle des Monogrammisten A.G. im Werk Riemenschneiders," *Anzeiger des Germanischen Nationalmuseums* (1980), 68–69.

3. My thanks to Heribert Meurer, Norbert Jopek, and Timothy Husband for pointing out this detail.

4. Demmler 1932; Bier 1930, 47–48 n. 3; Bier 1973, 150 n. 21; Muth 1982, 176–178.

who married Alphaus and had three sons: Christ's disciples Simon the Zealot, Judas Thaddeus, and James the Less. And with Salomas, Anne bore a third daughter, Mary Salome, who married Zebedee and had two sons, James the Greater and John the Evangelist, who were also to become disciples of Christ.

Despite regional variations, the Holy Kinship iconography followed two basic types.[2] The condensed version consisted only of Saint Anne with her three husbands and the Holy Family. The more extended, and apparently more popular treatment of the subject also included Mary Cleophas, Mary Salome, and their husbands and children. The two groups in Stuttgart and London, which are among the finest works by Riemenschneider, clearly belonged to such an ensemble.

Mary Cleophas is seated on a cushioned throne with a high back. Turning to her left, she holds an open book on her lap with her left hand, while she reaches forward with her other hand, now lost. She wears a simple dress, while the mantle over her left shoulder wraps around her right side in a broad loop of drapery to cover her knees. A wimple covers her head and chin, its striated border framing a pensive face. Her husband Alphaus stands behind her, resting his right elbow on the back of the seat. Wearing a turban on his head and a sleeveless tunic over a simple shirt, the old man also turns to his left.

Holy Family on the left, and the Stuttgart and London groups on the wings.[5] Baxandall also thought that the three fragments originally belonged together, but he believed that the groups in Stuttgart and London were too deep to have been installed on the wings.[6]

That one of the essential iconographic components of the Holy Kinship theme had been omitted in earlier discussions was realized only when Esser introduced the question of the original positioning of the six children of Mary Cleophas and Mary Salome within the composition.[7] The shallower carving of the Munich fragment could have allowed small figures of children to be placed in front of the group, while the somewhat smaller rendering of Saint Anne and her husbands would have given the impression of their being set back in space. The central panels were probably mounted on an elevated pedestal so that the heads of the figures would have been at the same height as those on each side or perhaps higher to accentuate the hierarchy of the Holy Kinship, with Saint Anne, the Virgin Mary, and the Christ child at the top. The groups in London and Stuttgart would thus have functioned as spatial brackets for the children in the central shrine of the retable.

Such a composition can be seen in the *Holy Kinship* altarpiece in Lübeck (fig. 2). Attributed to the Master of the Prenzlau Altarpiece, who was active in Lübeck after 1510 and trained with Riemenschneider around 1505, this retable is dated around 1510–1515.[8] Hasse considered the composition to be based on a Riemenschneider original,[9] and although it is certainly not a literal copy, it may nevertheless provide a sense of how the lost altarpiece looked. Taking into account the composition in Lübeck and the scale of the groups in London and Stuttgart, a reconstructed *Holy Kinship* altarpiece by Riemenschneider would likely have measured about 3–4 meters across. With wings, this altarpiece would have been among the artist's larger works. It seems to have influenced a number of works executed by Riemenschneider's workshop or followers. In addition to the Lübeck altarpiece, there are two fragments from a *Holy Kinship* altarpiece supposedly from Creglingen and another two fragments of the same subject in the Mainfränkisches Museum in Würzburg. It has been noted that the drapery patterns of the Virgin's garment in the latter correspond strikingly with those on Mary Cleophas' mantle in Stuttgart.[10] The *Holy Kinship* altarpiece by a weak follower of Riemenschneider in the Hessisches Landesmuseum, Darmstadt, often believed to be related to the lost work of the Würzburg sculptor, seems to be much further from Riemenschneider's original.[11] BORCHERT

5. Winzinger 1951, 129–137.

6. Baxandall 1974, 48.

7. Esser 1986, 241.

8. This altarpiece was once discussed as an early work by the Lübeck sculptor Benedikt Dreyer. This attribution was corrected by Max Hasse, who renamed the artist "Master of the Burgkloster Holy Kinship," whom he still distinguished from the Master of the Prenzlau Altarpiece ("Benedict Dreyer," *Niederdeutsche Beiträge zur Kunstgeschichte* 21 [1982], 9–58, esp. 38–42, and 56 n. 65). The present attribution has been suggested by Hartmut Krohm.

9. Hasse 1964, 42, 147; Hasse 1982, 41–44, 57 n. 70.

10. Bier 1930, 47–48 n. 3; Muth 1982, 176–178.

11. See Bier 1930, 47–48 n. 3.

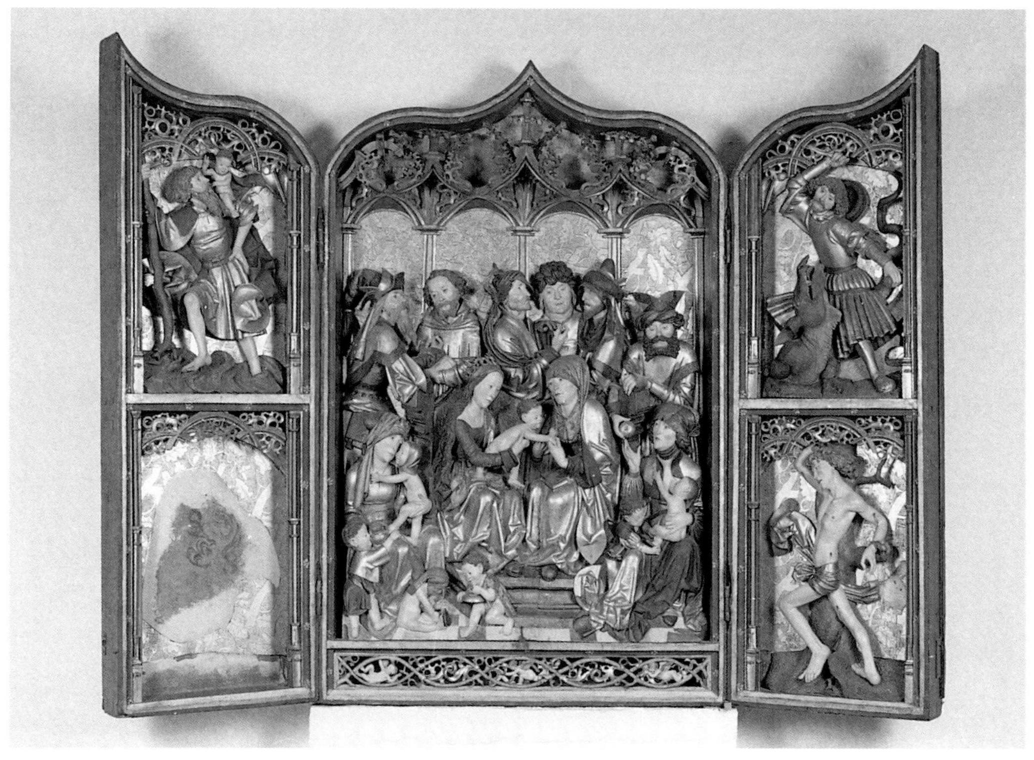

2.

Master of the Prenzlau Altarpiece, *Holy Kinship* altarpiece, c. 1510–1515, oak with polychromy,
Museum für Kunst- und Kulturgeschichte der Hansestadt Lübeck

37

c. 1510, limewood, woman at left: 55 x 43 x 24.5 (21 ⅝ x 16 ⅞ x 9 ⅝); woman at right:
62 x 43 x 24.5 (24 ⅜ x 16 ⅞ x 9 ⅝), Württembergisches Landesmuseum, Stuttgart

• Technical Notes •

The two figures were carved out of a single block of unblemished limewood with the grain running vertically and diagonally; the backs were hollowed out to a thickness of about 4–5 cm.[1] The modeling of the surfaces is especially refined within an arc of about 120 degrees. The missing hands of the woman at the right were carved separately and attached by wooden dowels (dowel holes 1.2 cm in diameter are still apparent). The hands broke off prior to 1886, when Weber saw the work in restoration at the workshop of Ulm sculptor Federlein.[2] Other damage to this figure includes the loss of a 2.5 cm length from her veil, replacement of a 2 cm section of drapery, considerable deterioration of the wood in her right arm, and slight abrasion of her nose. The woman at the left is generally in better condition, although parts of a finger have broken off. In 1886 the group was mounted on two boards of soft wood about 2 cm thick. Indications of grass, produced with the sculptor's chisel, are visible near the right end. This undamaged edge is bevelled, probably to create a smooth joint with an adjacent section of the composition. A rectangular opening (13 x 5 x 2 cm) in the back between the figures, which shows remnants of glue with some blue coloring, suggests that the work was once attached to a carved background. The group has traces of several campaigns of polychromy, the oldest one containing pigments used in the sixteenth century, as well as the remains of a translucent pigmented layer, suggesting that if the sculpture left Riemenschneider's workshop as a monochrome, it was polychromed shortly afterward.[3]

• Provenance •

In the possession of prelate Schwarz in Ellwangen; purchased by the museum in 1885 from Mrs. E. Schwarz in Stuttgart.

• Literature •

Weber 1888, 66–67; Grossmann 1909, 28; Josephi 1910, 192–193; Vöge 1910, 102; Weber 1911, 269–270; Baum 1917, 283–284; Schrade 1927, 149–150 n. 329; Bier 1930, 102; Muth and Schneiders 1982, 140; Würzburg 1981, 50; Kalden 1990, 161, 168–169.

T H E   M O U R N I N G   W O M A N at the right dominates this composition: not only is she closer to the viewer but her body and draperies define a strong triangular form. Turning toward her left, she rests most of her weight on her right knee. She wears a close-fitted dress and a mantle that covers her left shoulder and descends to the ground behind her but leaves her right shoulder and arm open. The cascade of drapery unfolds in an almost linear triangular shape that echoes the overall form of the figure. This drapery pattern is joined by a loop of fabric that descends from the woman's head veil, which she gathers up under her right arm. The veil leaves her forehead uncovered, and long strands of hair run down her back and in front of her right shoulder. With her eyes half-closed and the sides of her mouth drawn down, her expression is one of wordless grief. Yet her gaze is directed ahead, and her hands, now lost, would have reached out in front of her.

The mourner on the left, in contrast to the more open stance of her companion, is engulfed in a heavy mantle that conceals her body from head to toe. Crouched behind the other figure, she seems to turn in a spiraling motion that reinforces the sense of her withdrawal and despair. With her left knee on the ground, she twists to her left, bowing her head toward the other woman. Both hands are drawn up in front of her face, clasping her garment to cover her mouth. Her gesture of grief and anguish follows a centuries-old tradition, known both from religious imagery and funerary sculpture.[4]

1. This description is based on an exhaustive condition report by Hans Westhoff, on file in the conservation department of the Württembergisches Landesmuseum, Stuttgart. I would like to thank Hans Westhoff and Heribert Meurer for allowing me to see this material and discussing its content with me.

2. Weber 1911, 269–270.

3. Johannes Taubert, "Zur Oberflächengestalt der sogenannten ungefassten spätgotischen Holzplastik," *Städel-Jahrbuch* 1 (1967), 119–139.

4. Schrade 1927, 150, pointed to the similarity between this figure and one of the mourning women from the Detwang altarpiece.

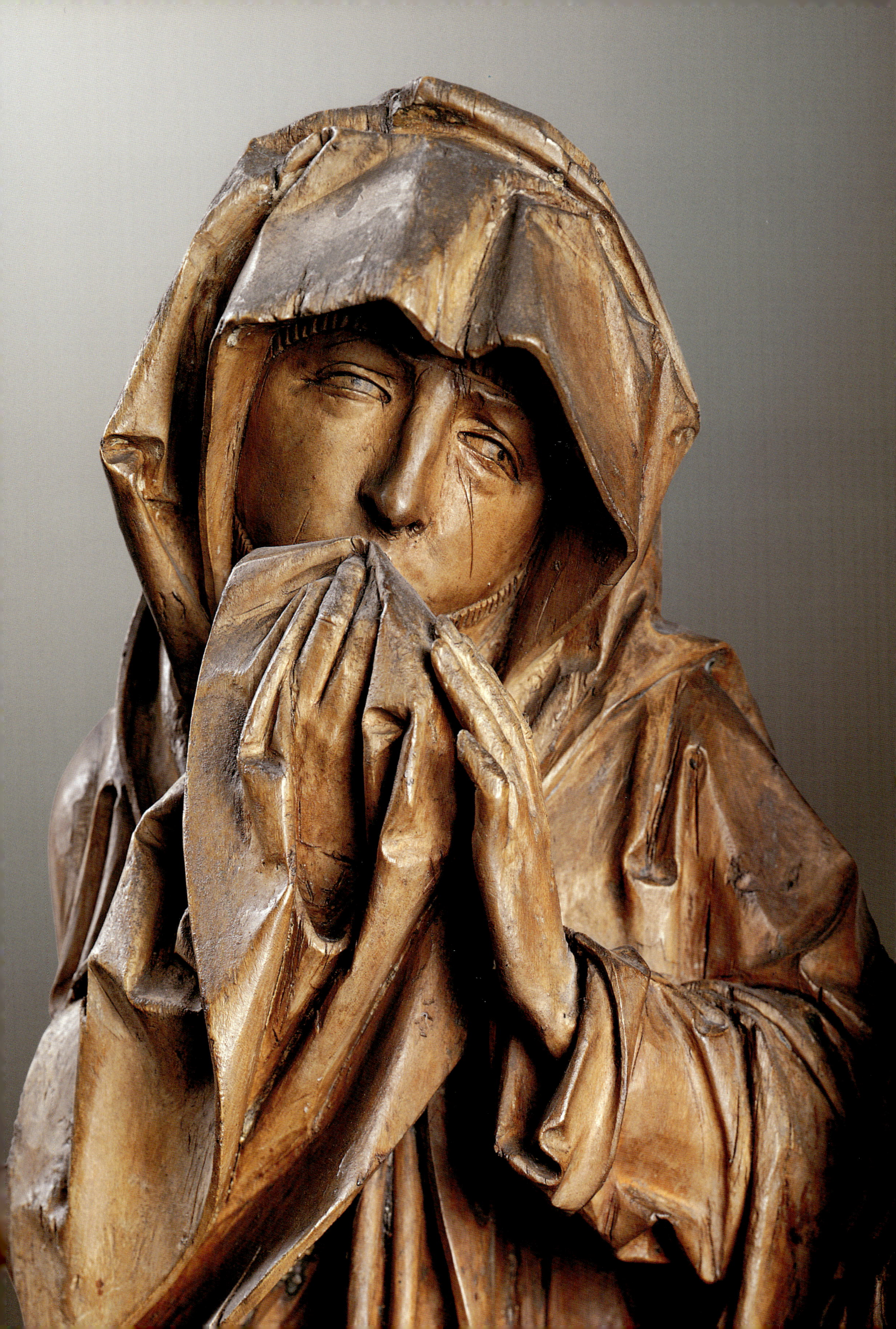

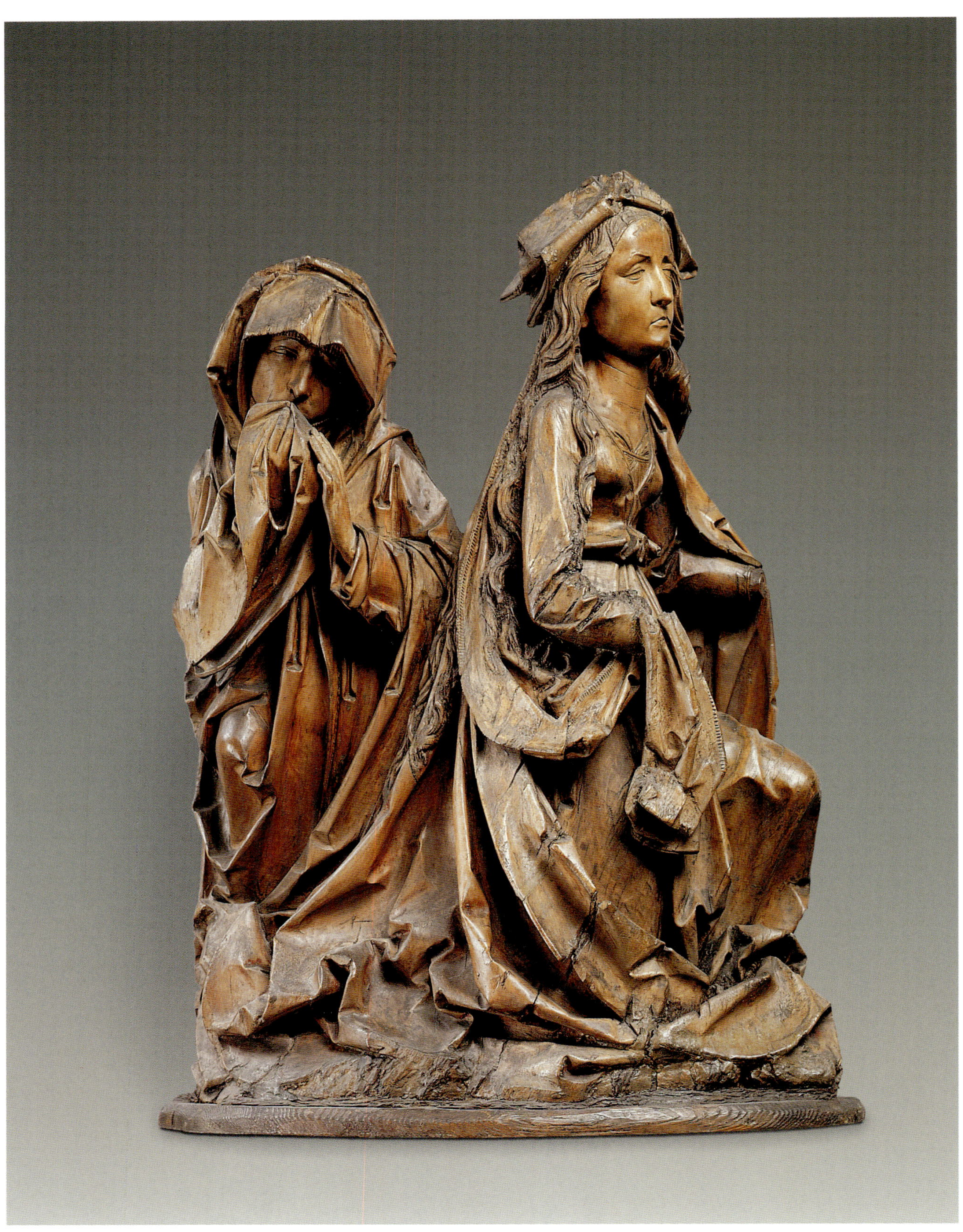

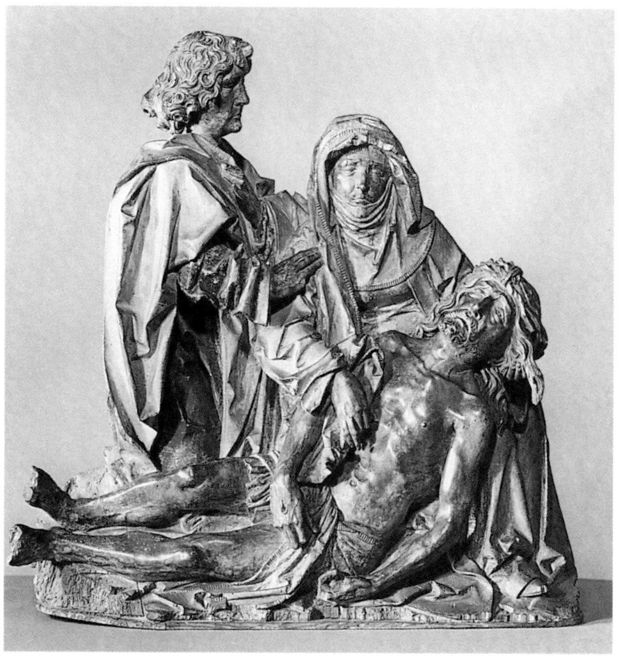

Lamentation, c. 1500–1510, limewood, Germanisches Nationalmuseum, Nuremberg

The Stuttgart *Mourning Women* originally formed part of a composition that depicted either a Descent from the Cross or a Lamentation, and it was most likely installed in the predella of a larger altarpiece.[5] Because a Crucifixion probably provided the focus for the altarpiece, it has been argued that the Stuttgart group and a Lamentation in Nuremberg (fig. 1) — of considerably lower quality and smaller scale — belonged to a lost predella for Riemenschneider's *Crucifixion* altarpiece in Detwang (cat. 33, fig. 2).[6] Recent technical research on the Detwang altarpiece, however, has shown that the retable could not have had a sculpted predella.[7]

In the general placement and articulation of the figures the *Mourning Women* in Stuttgart seem to be very close to another group of female mourners of higher quality in the Skulpturensammlung in Berlin (Krohm essay, fig. 8), originally part of the predella of an early *Passion* altarpiece from Rothenburg.[8] Yet there are notable differences. The mourning gesture of the woman on the left in the Berlin group, which derives from Netherlandish models, as Vöge pointed out,[9] has been completely transformed in the Stuttgart fragment. The hands are no longer held directly in front of the face, but over the mouth in a gesture that articulates the tension between being drawn to the object of one's sorrow and holding back strong emotion; she assumes a closed, introspective posture, with her veil extending forward to cast her face in deep shadow. Instead of facing outward, the whole body of this figure is inclined toward the presumed center of the lost Lamentation, reinforcing the position of the other woman in the group. This would indicate a principal shift toward a more unified composition.

Nicolas Hagenower's *Lamentation* of 1501, in the Collège Saint-Etienne, Strasbourg (Krohm essay, fig. 9), is believed to follow the same composition as the predella of the *Passion* altarpiece from Rothenburg.[10] Comparing the Stuttgart women with the corresponding figures in Hagenower's *Lamentation* suggests how different this lost work by Riemenschneider must have been. Its composition seems to have concentrated attention, by means of pose and gesture, on the central figure of the dead Christ. The Stuttgart fragment also seems to take into account the possibility of different points of view. Not only do the positions of the two women and the patterns of their draperies evoke movement, but the Stuttgart fragment deliberately seems to reward the viewer's curiosity by offering different vistas from which the group unfolds, step by step, its entire three-dimensionality. This conscious approach toward the possibilities that are unique to the medium of sculpture is indicative of the artistic development of Riemenschneider and his workshop and points specifically to the artist's mature works, as exemplified by his monumental limewood altarpieces of about 1505–1510 in Creglingen and Detwang. BORCHERT

5. Schrade 1927, 149.

6. Kalden 1990, 161, 168–169. Bier 1933, 25–28, attributed the group in Nuremberg to Peter Breuer.

7. Eike Oellermann and Karin Oellermann, "Das Detwanger Retabel und sein Detail," in *Der Detwanger Altar von Tilman Riemenschneider* (Wiesbaden, 1966), 31.

8. For a discussion of this retable, see Würzburg 1981, 24– 72, esp. 24–28; Kahsnitz 1997, 21–34, esp. 32–36, and 108 n. 39. See also Krohm's essay in the present catalogue.

9. Vöge 1910, 102; Krohm in Würzburg 1981, 50.

10. Würzburg 1981, 50; see also Schrade 1927, 150 n. 330, which mentioned the connection of the Berlin fragment and Hagenower's *Lamentation.*

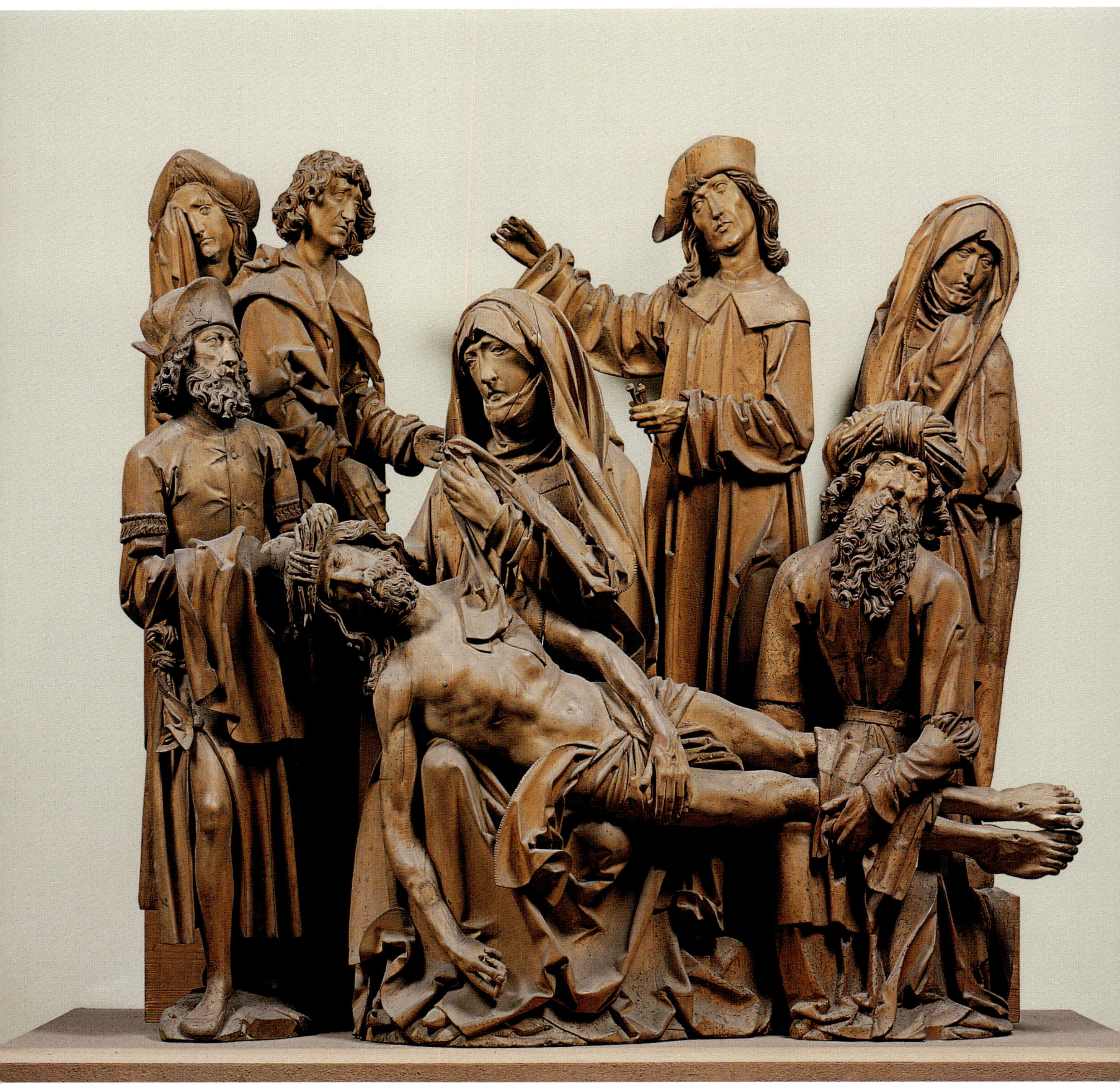

LAMENTATION

c. 1510, limewood, 172 x 151 x 39 (67 ¾ x 59 ½ x 15 ⅜), Parish of Saints Peter and Paul, Grossostheim

• *Technical Notes* •

Two of the foreground figures were carved from single blocks of limewood, with the grain running vertically, to which elements were added; but the Virgin and Christ were carved from separate blocks of limewood joined by dowels. Christ's feet, for instance, are attached to his legs where they are supported under a cloth, and the cloth itself is made from two pieces of wood joined by dowels. Other smaller segments of wood have been inserted into or attached to the larger blocks—to form Christ's shoulder, for example. The Virgin, Christ, and the male figure at the right are carved fully in the round. The man standing to the left on a round pedestal carved from the same block of limewood is less detailed in back than on the front and sides; his left arm, which is hidden, has been scraped down, presumably to allow the figures in the background to be closely integrated with those in the foreground.[1]

The background figures were carved in high relief with their backs hollowed out, except for the man behind the Virgin, who would have been standing below the cross, now lost. The two at the left were carved from a single piece, and a flattened area of the woman's drapery corresponds exactly with the scraped-down arm and shoulder of the man in front, allowing a precise positioning of the figures; the hands of the man, altered perhaps in the nineteenth century, were joined to the figure by dowels. The carving of the woman at the right was apparently too shallow, and two strips of wood were doweled to the back— 6 cm thick on the right, and 4 cm on the left.[2] This may have been the least expensive and most pragmatic way to solve the problem.

It is unclear if the work was originally polychromed. During restoration carried out in 1955 by Ludwig Gramberger from Würzburg, the nineteenth-century polychromy was removed, along with rem-

nants of an older polychromy, perhaps dating to the seventeenth or eighteenth century.[4]

• *Provenance* •

Donated to the church of Saints Peter and Paul, Grossostheim, in 1849.

• *Literature* •

Grossmann 1909, 23; Feulner 1927, 20, 156; Tiemann 1930, 14; Bier 1936; Hotz 1956, 217–226; Freeden 1965, 39; Bier 1973, 149–151; Würzburg 1981, 187–188, 320–332; Schneider 1990, 71–73; Kalden 1990, 130–132; Desel 1993, 27.

THE SEATED VIRGIN, wearing a heavy mantle and a head veil pulled low over her forehead, holds the dead Christ on her lap. Her sorrowful face, encircled by the bands of her wimple, is turned toward her son's head, which she supports with her right arm and presents to the beholder. Her gaze is unfocused, and with her left hand she grasps the end of her veil to dry her tears. Just released from the cross, Christ's body falls loosely toward the ground, his arms in gentle arcs and his legs supported by a kneeling male figure usually identified as Nicodemus.[3] Represented as an old man with a long beard, he wears a turban and a coat with segmented sleeves. He looks up and slightly to the side, almost facing the viewer. His posture, with its conspicuously lowered shoulders, seems a physical expression of the burden of sorrow that he and his companions bear.

In contrast to the Virgin and Nicodemus, Joseph of Arimathea stands calmly beside Christ's head holding a shroud. He wears a cap with a high brim and a coat with fringed sleeves. His tranquil pose—evident in the noble disposition of his bare right leg—provides a counterpoint to the emotive gestures of the other foreground figures attending Christ's body.

1. Andrea Kleberger notes that the projections on the background figures mesh with concavities in the back of the foreground figures.

2. Würzburg 1981, 325–327.

3. Hotz 1956, 218, and Freeden 1965, 39, refer to this figure as Simon of Cyrene. While the man is in the position traditionally reserved for Nicodemus, it is true that Nicodemus is usually depicted without a beard.

4. Bier 1978, 149 n. 18.

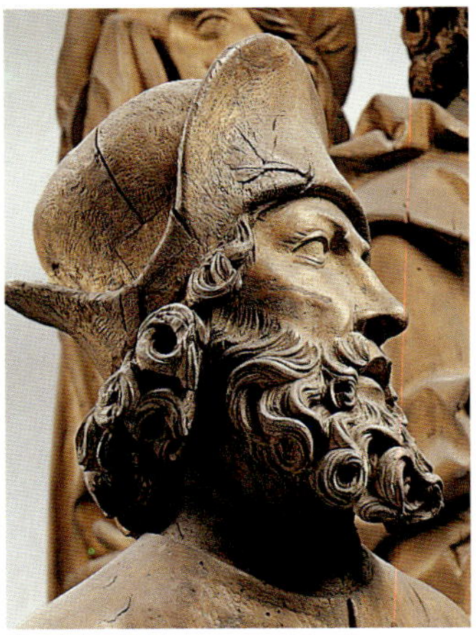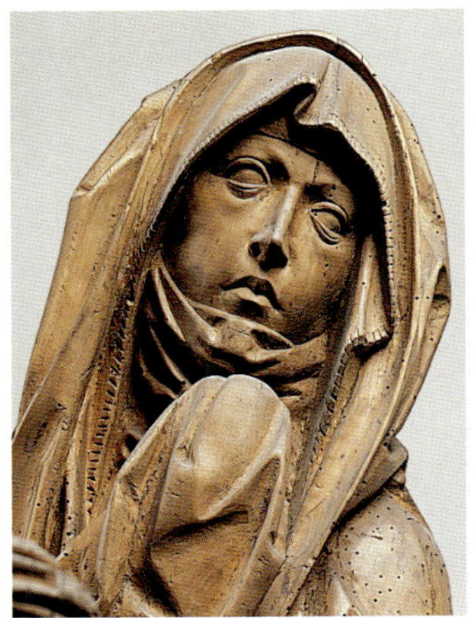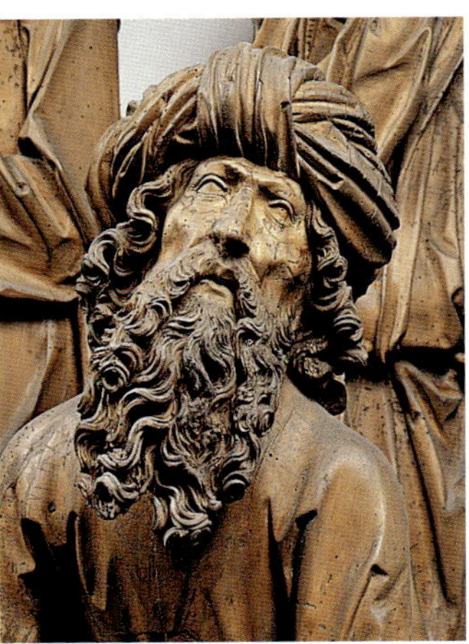

Details of Joseph of Arimathea, Mary Cleophas, and Nicodemus from catalogue no. 38

5. Würzburg 1981, 325–326.

6. Bier 1978, 149 n. 18.

A second row of figures, now elevated on a re-constructed pedestal,[5] includes Mary Magdalen and John the Evangelist at the left and a beardless man and Mary Cleophas at the right. The Magdalen, identified by her fashionable dress, stands behind the Evangelist and Joseph of Arimathea. She lifts part of her robe to dry her tears, hiding half of her face. Saint John turns toward the Virgin and originally reached out to touch her shoulder. Facing him, a man with long hair, wearing a simple hat and a coat with a wide collar, holds the nails of the Crucifixion in one hand while pointing up with the other hand to where the cross would have been. This figure is usually identified as the centurion who oversaw the Crucifixion, although his dress is decidedly civilian and he does not wear weapons. With his gesture of presentation, he plays a prominent role in the composition. At the right another mourning woman, thought to be Mary Cleophas, stands draped in a mantle that covers her completely and accentuates her S-shaped stance. She and Mary Magdalen bracket the scene in a manner that is typical for Riemenschneider—with both outside figures bending away from the center of the group.

The sculpture convincingly integrates the body of Christ into the overall composition. The parallel lines of Christ's and the Virgin's arms mark a strong oblique that ties the group together. This accent is re-inforced below by the corresponding line of Christ's right arm and repeated above by the pointing gesture of the man in the background. At the right an opposing oblique is established by the tilted heads of Mary Cleophas and Nicodemus, echoed by the angle of Nicodemus' left forearm and the loose end of Christ's loincloth.

The Grossostheim *Lamentation* combines several pictorial types. The Virgin with the dead Christ clearly derives from popular devotional images of the Pietà, common in German sculpture by the fourteenth century. And Joseph of Arimathea, Nicodemus, the mourning women, and Saint John are all traditional participants in Passion iconography. Neither the Pietà nor the Lamentation are mentioned in the Gospels but found their sources in hymns, prayers, and devotional literature. The writings of Thomas à Kempis, for example, connected both themes, encouraging the devout to ponder their meaning. The Virgin's compassion was thus promoted as the pious layman's model for his own commiseration; perhaps as a consequence, images of the Pietà began to flourish in private rather than public spaces. Occasionally supplemented by John the Evangelist and one or two mourning women, the Pietà was easily transformed into an image of the Lamentation, to which Joseph of Arimathea and Nicodemus were sometimes added.

Eschewing anecdotal detail in favor of a solemn configuration, the Grossostheim *Lamentation* achieves a strong iconic presence that invites contemplation. Through variations in the individual posture, gesture, and facial appearance of the Virgin, the two Marys, Nicodemus, and Joseph of Arimathea, Riemenschneider gave visual expression to different levels of grief and compassion, encouraging the viewer to empathize with the figures and to replicate their emotions. The affecting quality of the composition is especially compelling in its representation of Christ, turned toward the beholder: his face, body, and stigmata are presented frontally, encouraging a direct confrontation with the object of the devout compassion.

In view of the sculpture's unknown whereabouts before 1849, when it was given to the church at Grossostheim, its original function is a matter of debate.[6] Hotz, Bier, and Kalden thought it had been the cen-

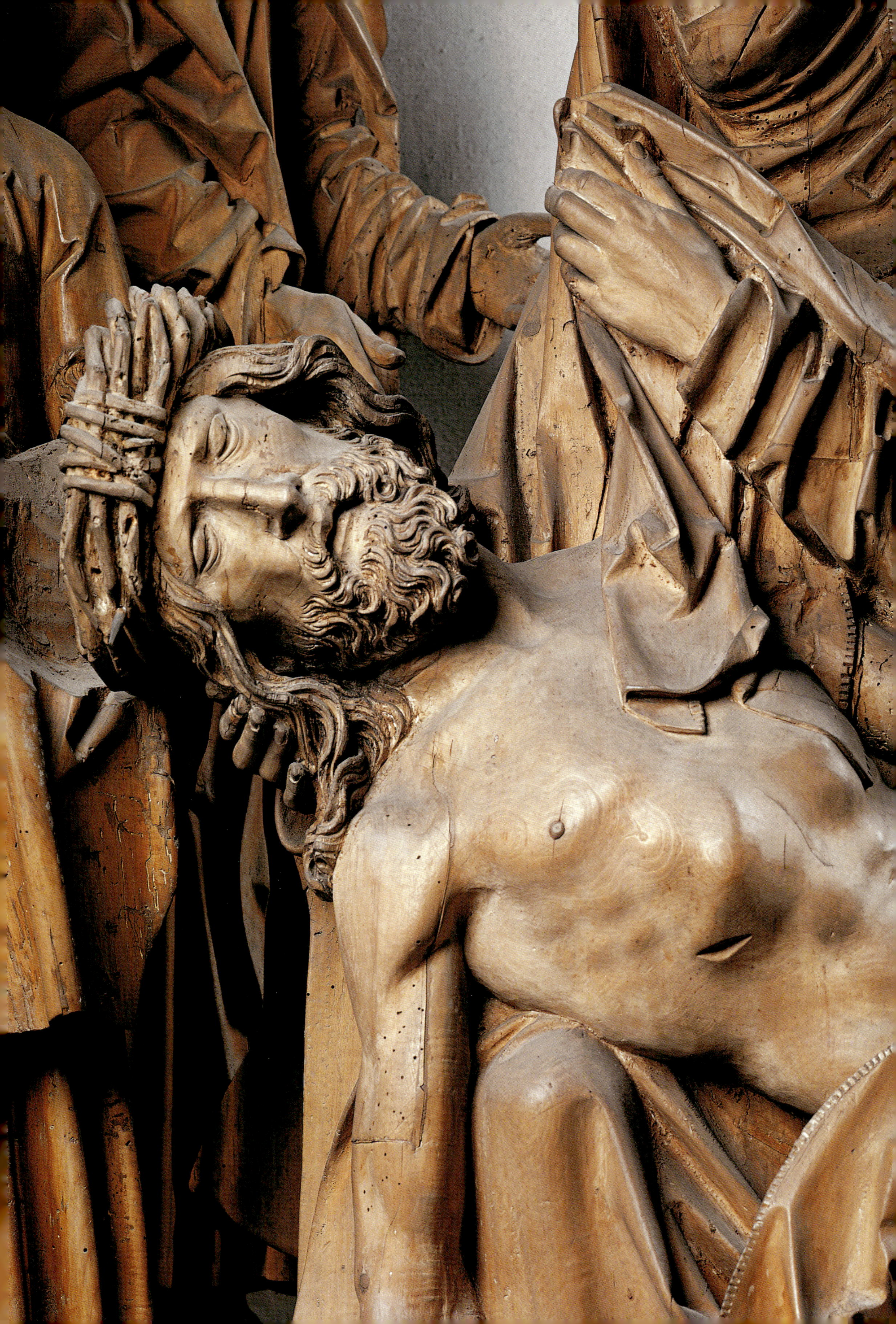

7. Würzburg 1981, 325–327;
see technical notes.

8. Würzburg 1981, 188.

9. Bier 1978, 150–151.

10. Bier 1936, 1:57–59; Hotz
1956, 217–226; Bier 1978,
149–151.

11. Würzburg 1981, 188.

12. Kalden 1990, 130–131.

ter of an altarpiece. When Andrea Kleberger convincingly reconstructed the figural arrangement of the *Lamentation* on the basis of technical examination, she proposed that the sculpture was originally framed by a shrine.[7] Hartmut Krohm has pointed out that large sculptural ensembles, which were not uncommon in Germany, were installed both inside and outside churches.[8] Some subjects, such as the Crucifixion or the Agony in the Garden, were rendered in stone and clearly intended for placement out of doors. Other popular images, like Entombments, were often made in wood and displayed within the church or its chapels. The latter probably could have been the case with the Grossostheim *Lamentation* in light of its material and its meditative character.

The participation of several sculptors is evident in the execution of individual figures; but the relationship of the Grossostheim *Lamentation* to Riemenschneider and his workshop has been controversial. Bier considered the Virgin, Christ, and Nicodemus to be largely autograph, although the remaining figures, which are rendered in a significantly smaller size and are of considerably lesser quality, would appear to be by assistants.[9] Pointing out the group's similarities to fragments of a *Holy Kinship* altarpiece in Stuttgart and London (cat. 36), he argued that both were based on artistic achievements that Riemenschneider reached only in his Detwang altarpiece of about 1510 (cat. 33, fig. 2).[10] Because of the composite quality of the group and its "bulky" appearance, Krohm doubted that this work could have been made by Riemenschneider or his workshop.[11] More recently, Kalden has linked the Grossostheim *Lamentation* to the Windsheim altarpiece of around 1508 (cat. 40, fig. 1) and attributed the principal figures to a collaborator of Riemenschneider's.[12] But a comparison with Riemenschneider's late Maidbronn *Lamentation* (Chapuis essay, fig. 9) clearly reveals that the ensemble in Grossostheim is markedly less subtle, both in terms of refinement of execution and of conceptual power of composition, than the master's last autograph work.

BORCHERT

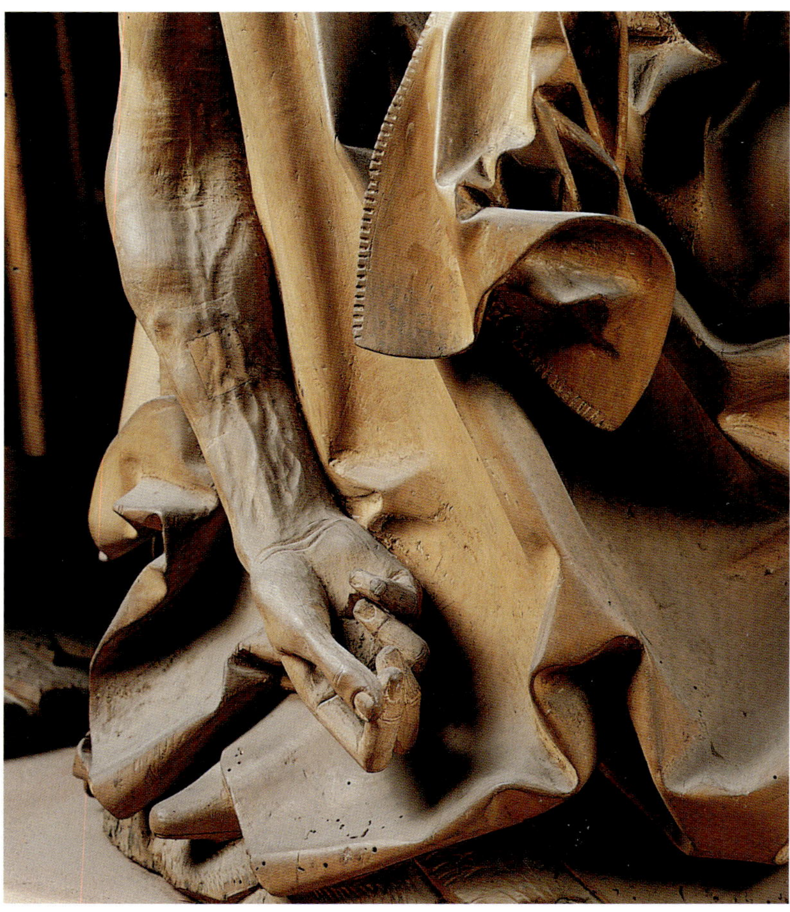

Detail of catalogue no. 38

39A SAINT SEBASTIAN

c. 1510–1515, limewood, 72 x 24 x 9.5 (28 ⅜ x 9 ½ x 3 ¾), The Montreal Museum of Fine Arts
Collection, Purchase, Gift of L. V. Randall and Horsley and Annie Townsend Bequest

39B SAINT SEBASTIAN

after 1510, limewood, 101 x 30 x 14 (39 ⅞ x 11 ¾ x 5 ½), Private Collection

• *Technical Notes* •

The sculpture from Montreal, carved from a single
piece of limewood with the grain running vertically,
has survived as a fragment. The most significant loss
is the saint's left arm from below the elbow; there are
other losses to the hair, feet, tree trunk, base, and several areas of drapery. Cracks in the wood and large
insect channels are scattered over the entire surface.
This damage had occurred by 1936.[1] Fears concerning the stability of the sculpture led to its conservation treatment in 1974, when it was impregnated with
Acryloid B72, some splits were filled with Multiwax
and pigment, and the surface was polished.[2] The fills
had discolored and the surface had become glossy, as
seen in the reproduction on page 314, taken before
conservation treatment in 1998 / 1999. Traces of a
whitish ground and of a bluish layer in deeper folds
reveal that the work was painted at some point.

The figure from a private collection is cut from
a single piece of limewood with the grain running
vertically and its back hollowed to prevent cracking.
A few vertical splits have been filled with shims of
wood, but the sculpture shows little sign of insect
damage. The surface is shiny, as if the work had been
impregnated with wax. Although the hem of the cloak
displays the incised scalloped pattern familiar from
other works ascribed to Riemenschneider, the cutting is quite coarse, suggesting that the sculpture was
intended to be polychrome, although no traces of
pigment remain.

• *Provenance* •

Montreal: Gedon collection, Munich, about 1880;
catalogued in 1885 as being in the collection of the
Pfälzische Landesgewerbeanstalt, Kaiserslautern;

William F. C. Ohly, Frankfurt am Main and London;
acquired between 1933 and 1935 from Edmund
Schilling by Lewis V. Randall of Bern and Montreal;
acquired by the museum in 1971.

Private Collection: Acquired in 1928 from Johannes
Hinrichsen, Berlin, by Ludwig Roselius, Bremen; by
descent to the present owner.

• *Literature* •

Montreal: Bier 1936; Bier 1937, 27; Bier 1954, 107–
109 n. 15; Bier 1959–1960, 6 n. 31; Raleigh 1962, 60–
63; New York 1968, no. 68; Carter 1971, 17–23; Carter
1972, 164; Bergmann 1972, 18; Bier 1982, 65–68;
Kalden 1990, 91–92.

Private Collection: Falke 1928, II:566; Habicht 1931a,
106; Hannover 1931, 16, no. 33; Bier 1936, 151; Raleigh
1962, 61–63.

SEBASTIAN WAS one of the most venerated saints
of the later Middle Ages. A third-century Roman
officer, he was shot with arrows as punishment for
his public support of the Christian faith. As Apollo's
arrows were thought in antiquity to cause disease, so
in the Middle Ages an arrow was seen to symbolize
the plague, a divine retribution for the sins of mankind. Sebastian was thus believed to protect against
the plague and other epidemics that regularly deci-
mated the population of Europe. His cult was particularly widespread in Germany, where he was sometimes included among the Fourteen Helper Saints
(see cat. 23). His popularity was also great as the
patron of archers and their guilds.[3]

Riemenschneider depicted Sebastian as a half-
naked youth, his right hand tied to a tree trunk behind

1. Photographs published in
Bier 1936.

2. Condition report, dated
28 January 1975, by R. Hardy,
assistant conservator at the
Montreal Museum of Fine
Arts (on file at the museum).

3. Louis Réau, *Iconographie
de l'art chrétien* (Paris, 1958),
3.3: 1190–1191.

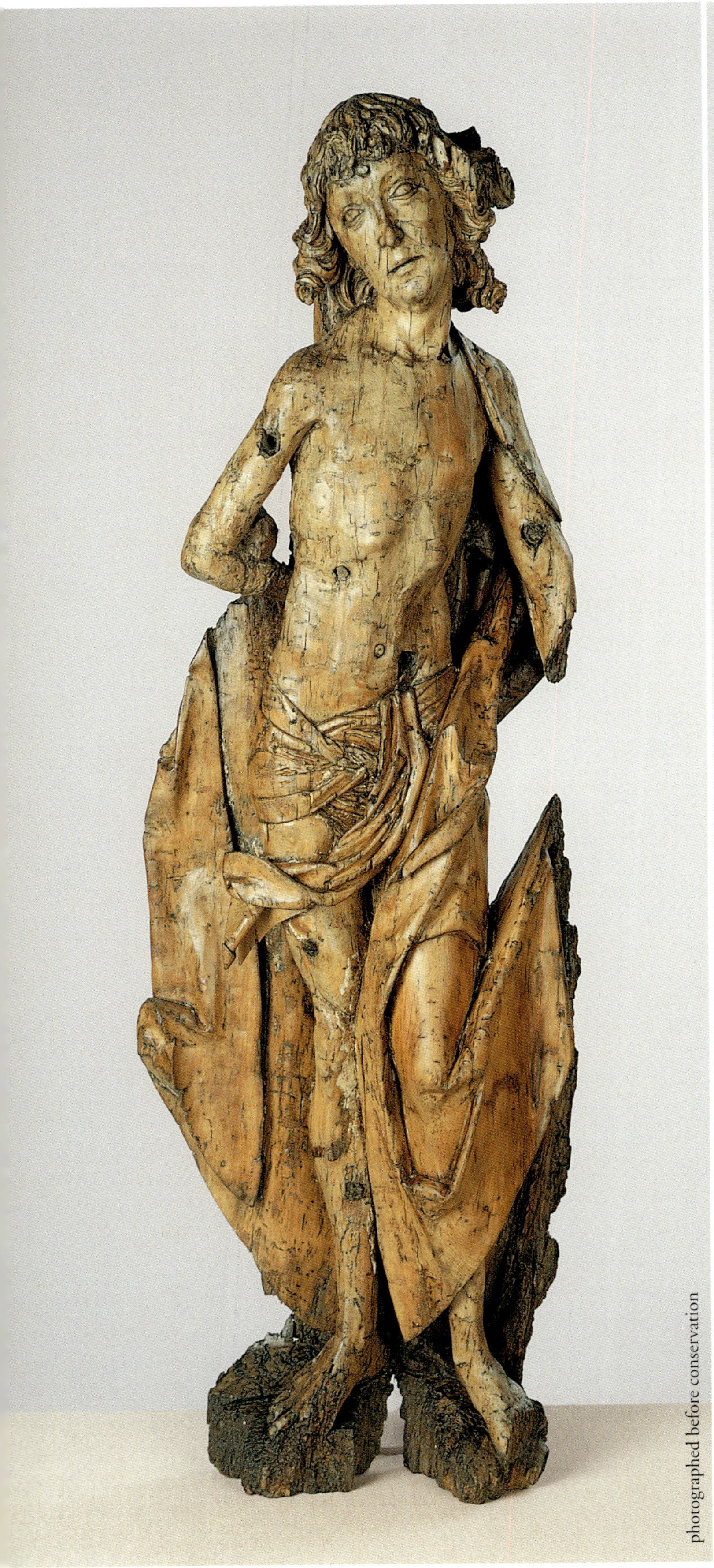

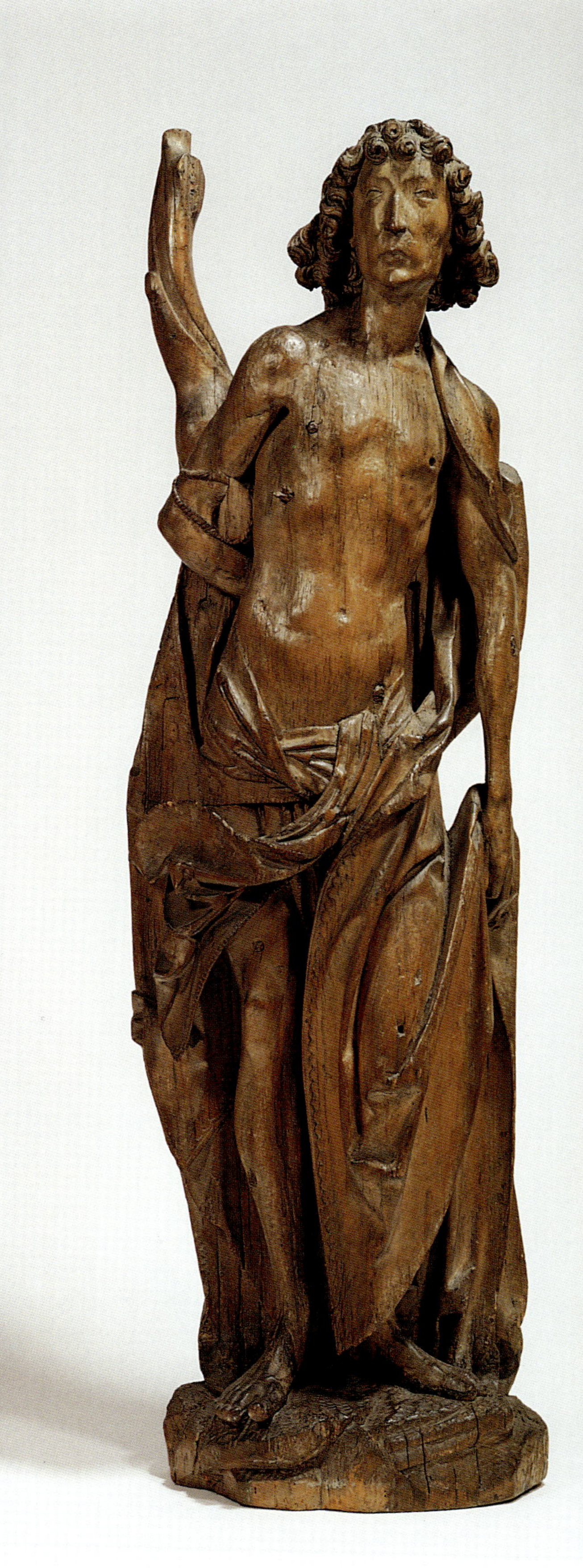

39 A

39 B

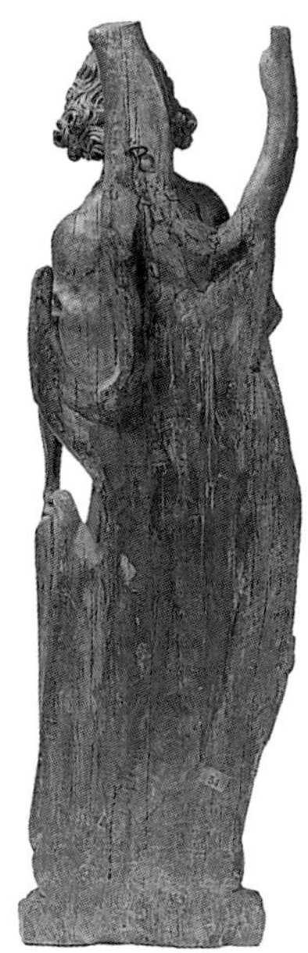

Back view of catalogue no. 39 B

his back. Originally arrows were wedged into the holes drilled in several areas of the figure. The intelligence of the sculptural conception is apparent in the subtle articulation of the figure, which conveys a keen sense of movement and spatial presence, although it is only a high relief. The loincloth and hips are depicted frontally, while all other components of the body turn at angles to one another. The placement of the saint's right hand behind his back causes his right shoulder to be thrust forward and his upper body to twist to his left. The left knee, coming forward, counterbalances the right shoulder, as does the tilted head, which turns to his right. The cloak emphasizes the organization of volumes and contributes to the spatial reading of the figure. The fabric has fallen from the saint's projecting right shoulder but covers his receding left shoulder. Where it is juxtaposed with the legs, it establishes an impression of depth, reading as one of three elements in different planes (see also cat. 42). It unites background and foreground, functioning both as a foil against which one reads the body along the saint's right side and as a shell, held out by the missing left hand, that wraps around the figure and covers the leg (see also cat. 43 A). The drapery comments almost musically on the movement and volume of the figure, and it creates a mandorla around the silhouette.[4]

The damages to the surface do not obscure the high quality of the carving, which is particularly evident in the sensitive treatment of the torso. The coherence of the anatomy, which is not inferior to that of the Vienna *Adam* (cat. 20), is illustrated in details such as the rib cage or the carefully observed junction of the neck and shoulders, with its tendons, collar-

bones, and Adam's apple. The play of light brings into relief the refined definition of the figure. The hair, by contrast, is treated in a more summary fashion.

Comparison with the securely dated *Adam* of 1491–1493 from the Marienkapelle in Würzburg (Chapuis essay, fig. 3) reveals a more planar arrangement of forms. While the *Adam* invites the viewer to move around him so as to take in the full profile views, the Montreal sculpture is conceived essentially for frontal viewing within an arc of roughly 90 degrees; if one moves much farther to the right, one loses the visual bracket of drapery on the left, for instance. As is the case with most of Riemenschneider's sculpture, the intended vantage point is low: the elongated proportions of the figure fall into place and the slanted base allows the feet to remain coherent when viewed from below.

The Montreal *Saint Sebastian* seems to be a rare example of a model by Riemenschneider (see also cats. 19 and 45), a high-quality sculpture, presumably autograph, of a popular subject made to remain in the workshop as a visual reference for assistants, perhaps working without the actual participation of the master. This is borne out by the existence of at least ten variants of the Montreal composition, each apparently by a different sculptor.[5] What would distinguish the Montreal figure as the model is its smaller size and its superior quality, both in its articulation and execution. Each copy varies, some reproducing the presumed model more closely than others. One version in a private collection (cat. 39 B) is instructive because it reproduces the prototype faithfully and thus conveys an idea of the missing elements in the Montreal figure. The mandorla effect of the composition would have been stronger when the drapery on the right was intact and formed a broader curve. The left arm would have hung down, with the hand lifting up the lower portion of the cloak. The loose end of the loincloth was longer, and the larger area of fluttering drapery would have added to the sense of movement. Branches may have extended over the figure from the tree trunk, and the right elbow was probably positioned around a stump coming from the tree. The privately owned figure differs from the one in Montreal in its more upright head and its feet being more firmly planted on the ground. Two variants, including one in the Bayerisches Nationalmuseum in Munich that is now installed in the central shrine of the Gerolzhofen altarpiece (fig. 1), reproduce the composition in reverse.

The planar arrangement of forms and the limited arc of address of the Montreal figure suggest that it was created in about 1510–1515. CHAPUIS

4. Bier 1936, 22; Kalden 1990, 91–92.

5. Listed and reproduced in Raleigh 1962, 60–63.

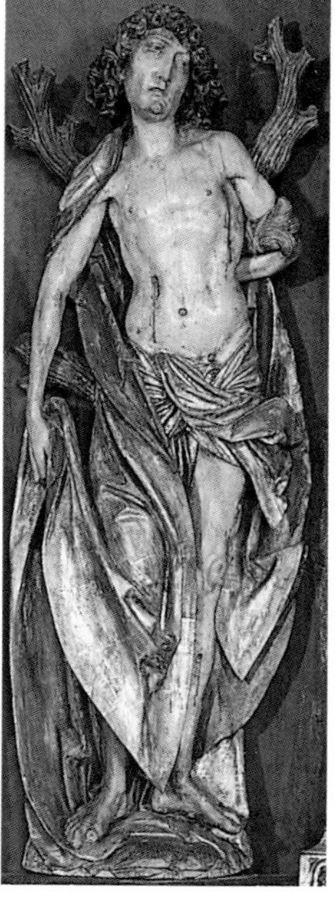

1.
Saint Sebastian in the Gerolzhofen altarpiece, c. 1510–1520, limewood with ancient polychromy, Bayerisches Nationalmuseum, Munich

4O A–C

Three Saints

40A SAINT JAMES THE GREATER

c. 1510–1515, limewood, 153 x 42 x 20 (60 ¼ x 16 ½ x 7 ⅞), Parish of Saint James, Grosslangheim

40B SAINT ANTHONY ABBOT

c. 1510–1515, limewood, 145 x 38 x 23 (57 ⅛ x 15 x 9), Parish of Saint James, Grosslangheim

40C SAINT LAWRENCE

c. 1510–1515, limewood, 133 x 36 x 22 (52 ⅜ x 14 ⅛ x 8 ⅝), Parish of Saint James, Grosslangheim

• *Technical Notes* •

Each figure was carved from a single piece of lime-wood with the grain running vertically. The sculpture of James seems to be intact, but the attributes of Anthony and Lawrence, which must have been carved separately and attached, are now lost. Although there is insect damage scattered over the surface of all three figures, the works appear to have suffered few major losses, except for the tip of Lawrence's drapery, at the height of his right knee. The pupils of each saint are painted with dark color. The works were restored in 1966 by Theo Spiegel of Würzburg.

• *Provenance* •

Probably made or acquired for the chapel of Saint Anthony or the parish church of Saint James in Grosslangheim during the sixteenth century.

• *Literature* •

Lill and Weysser 1911; Weber 1911, 116–117; Muth and Schneiders 1982; Freeden 1981, 48; Müller 1997, 48–50.

SAINT JAMES THE GREATER, the patron saint of pilgrims, wears a buttoned garment reaching almost to his ankles and a mantle that is draped over his shoulders and held together by a morse at his chest. His cape descends around him in lavishly carved folds, especially at his left side, where it is held up by the left arm and covers the front of his body like an apron. The longer strand of wavy hair on his left shoulder echoes the more abundant flow of drapery on this side. The borders of his garment and cape are decorated with rows of incised scalloped motifs. The saint wears a high-brimmed hat, which originally bore a shell, and carries a pilgrim's bag under his right arm (see also cat. 31). His hands cross in front, with his left hand touching his bag and his right pointing in the other direction. Standing in a slightly S-shaped pose, the saint rests most of his weight on his left leg, with his right knee projecting forward and his head turned a little toward his left.

Saint Anthony Abbot, often considered the founder of monasticism, wears a long cape over a simple belted robe. His wrinkled, expressive face is that of an old man, with the characteristic, double-pointed beard. His head is covered by a monk's cowl. In his left hand he holds an open book to his chest, its stamped cover facing the viewer. In his right he might originally have held a T-shaped staff with a bell, his attribute, which is now lost. Since Antonine monks bred pigs in the Middle Ages, this animal is the saint's other attribute, and one may have originally stood at his feet. Anthony's pose follows the typical S-shape, known from many sculptors of the late Gothic period. The figure achieves a three-dimensional presence through a subtle orchestration of drapery. The cape, which rests on both shoulders, falls on either side of the saint's left arm, contributing to the overall sculptural mass, while on the other side it is held away by his arm, adding width to the slender figure.

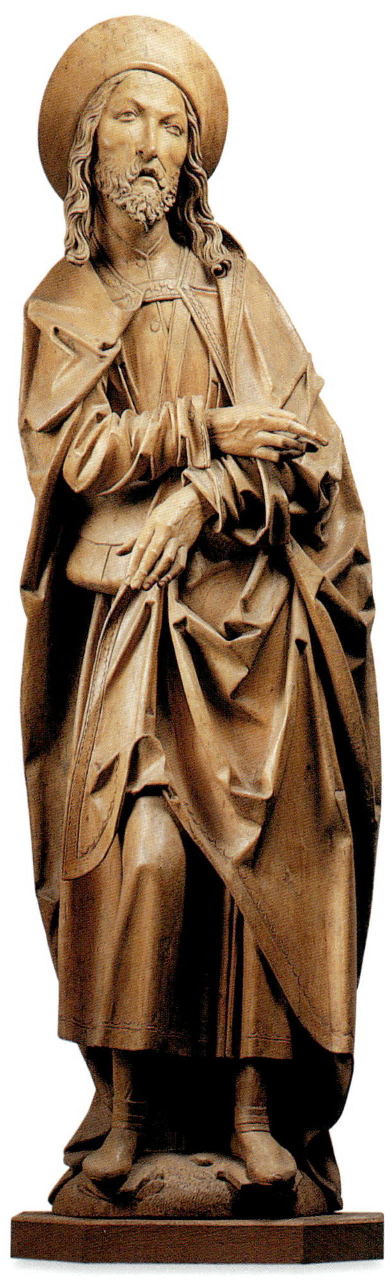

40 A

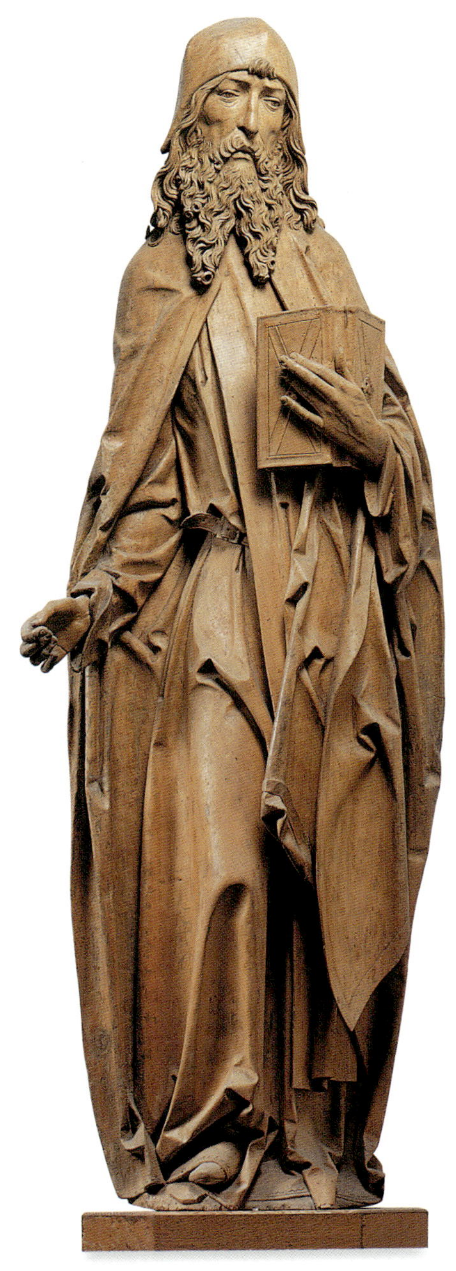

40 B

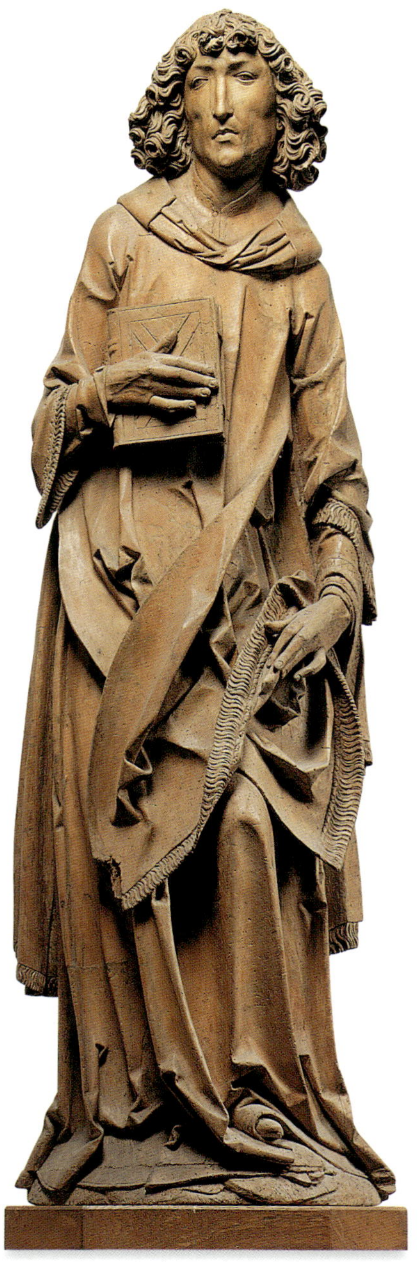

40 C

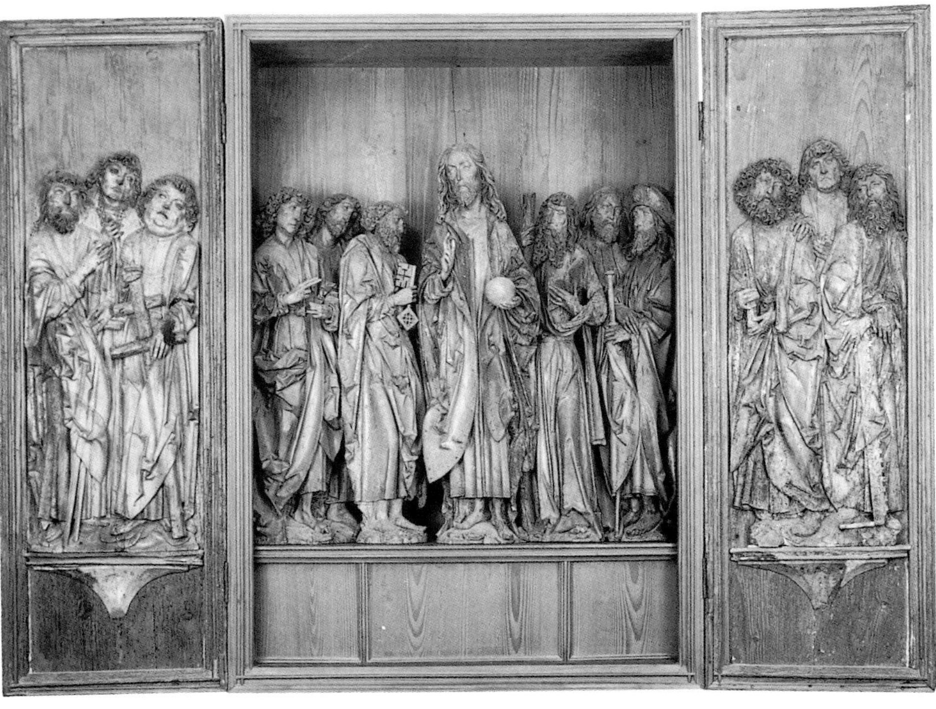

Christ and the Apostles altarpiece from Windsheim, before 1509, limewood, Kurpfälzisches Museum der Stadt Heidelberg

1. Weber 1911, 116–117.

2. Muth and Schneiders 1982, 92.

3. Müller 1997, 48.

Saint Lawrence's stance is the mirror reverse, with his weight borne on his right leg and his left knee projecting forward. His bare head is turned slightly to his right, and his gaze focuses in the same direction but without establishing eye contact with the viewer. He wears a long alb under a fringed dalmatic, a costume indicative of his office of deacon. His right hand holds a closed book against his chest, while his left must have once held a gridiron as a sign of his martyrdom. The position of the saint's left hand is reminiscent of that of the Cleveland *Saint Stephen* (cat. 32 A). It holds the fringed edge of the dalmatic, so that its interior side is revealed, creating a broad, pointed sweep of drapery across the front of the figure. Encircled by a mass of curly hair, his face is that of a young man and is obviously based on a type commonly associated with Saint John the Evangelist.

In each of these last two figures the lower part of the body is disproportionately long, giving a somewhat awkward impression. This may be one reason the saints in Grosslangheim have received so little critical attention until recently. The first scholar to mention them was Anton Weber, who in 1911 attributed them to Anthonius Reuss of Iphofen, a follower of Riemenschneider.[1] Weber did not describe the Saint James, which may not have been on display in Grosslangheim at the time. The saints were not discussed again in the Riemenschneider literature until Muth reintroduced them in 1982, recognizing that they were

of much higher quality than the average production of followers of Riemenschneider or his school.[2]

The personal relationship between the rulers of Würzburg and Grosslangheim in the early sixteenth century offers a plausible explanation as to how sculpture by Riemenschneider could have come to the small village. Bishop Lorenz von Bibra, one of the sculptor's most eminent patrons, had close contacts with Count Heinz Truchsen of Langheim, whose possessions included the little market town of Grosslangheim. Thus it is possible that the nobleman followed the recommendation of the prince-bishop in commissioning sculpture for his private chapel — where the figures are displayed today — or for the village's parish church.[3] Yet Riemenschneider's reputation was well established throughout Franconia by then, and he would have been an obvious choice for the project.

Although the three saints are approximately the same depth, the figure of James appears more naturalistic and much more voluminous, in part because the folds in his drapery are more deeply carved, and in part because the elongated proportions of Saints Anthony and Lawrence make them appear flatter. This casts doubt on whether the three saints belonged to the same altarpiece. The slight difference in height seems to argue against this possibility. Saint James the Greater, as the patron saint of Grosslangheim's parish church, was more likely intended for the church, either as a cult figure or as part of a retable. Anthony and Lawrence could easily have served as pendants, and they would have been thematically suited for an altarpiece in the private chapel, which was dedicated to Saint Anthony. Both were venerated among the Fourteen Helper Saints (see cat. 23) and may have stood in the shrine of a retable on either side of a Virgin and child. If wings were added to this ensemble, as is likely, it may have resembled the altarpiece from the Saint John the Baptist chapel in Gerolzhofen, now in the Bayerisches Nationalmuseum in Munich and generally dated between 1513 and 1515 (Chapuis essay, fig. 11). The elongated proportions of Saints Anthony and Lawrence would seem to indicate that they were installed quite high above the eye of the viewer, since they consciously take into account the optical distortions of a low perspective.

It is not clear whether the three figures were produced at the same time. Their similar depth seems to be their most telling common feature, and exactly this feature ties the saints to two other retables, usually attributed to Riemenschneider and his workshop between 1510 and 1515: the above-mentioned altarpiece from Gerolzhofen and that from Windsheim (fig. 1). The figures of Anthony and Lawrence also relate to these two altarpieces stylistically. The Saint Lawrence shares the same facial type as John the Evangelist at the left of the central shrine in the Windsheim retable. Saint Anthony's face, with its finely carved beard, resembles that of the Windsheim Saint Andrew, standing to the right of Christ. The figure of the Grosslangheim Saint James the Greater seems to be of generally higher quality, especially in its persuasive illusion of volume and space, but also in the detailed characterization of the physiognomy. Riemenschneider's own part in the production of this sculpture, it seems, was greater than in the other two works from Grosslangheim. BORCHERT

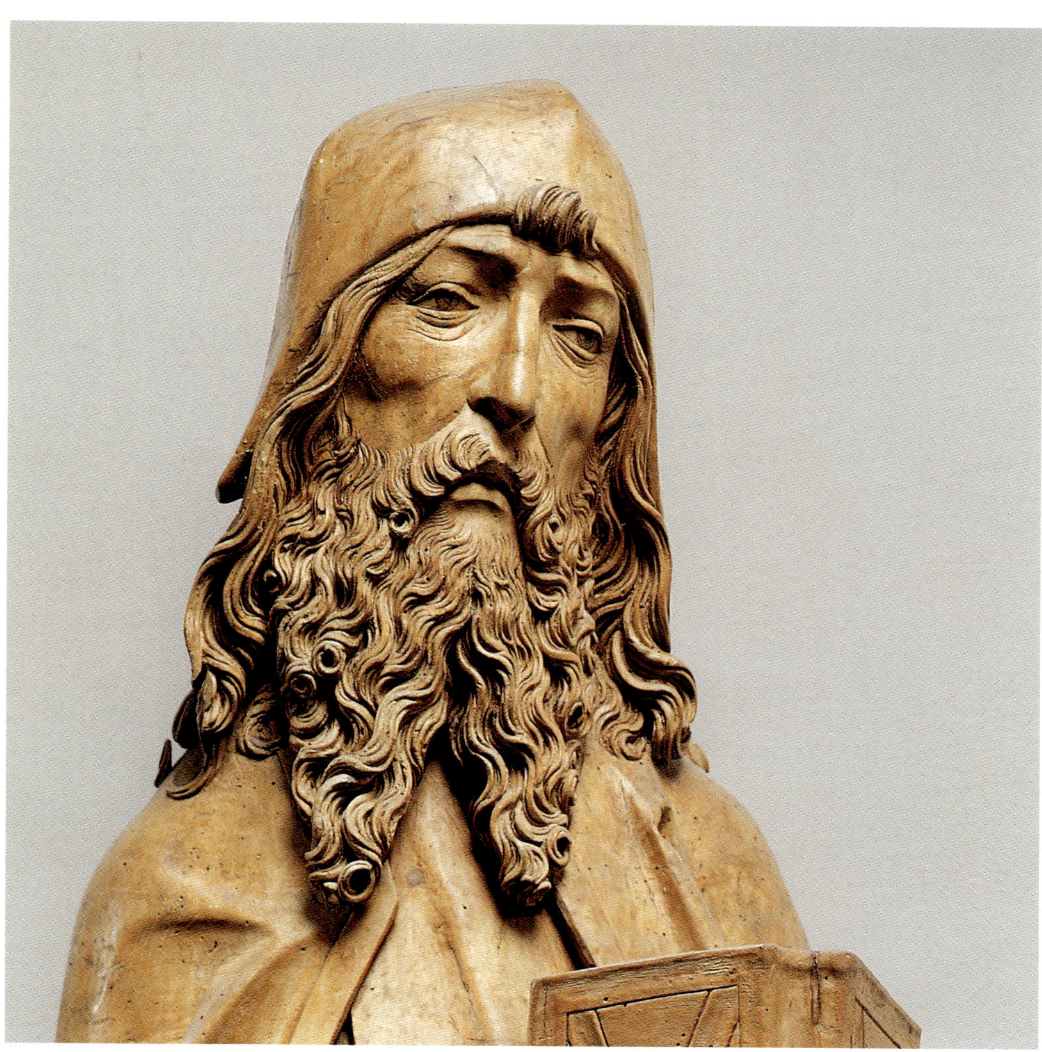

Detail of catalogue no. 40 B

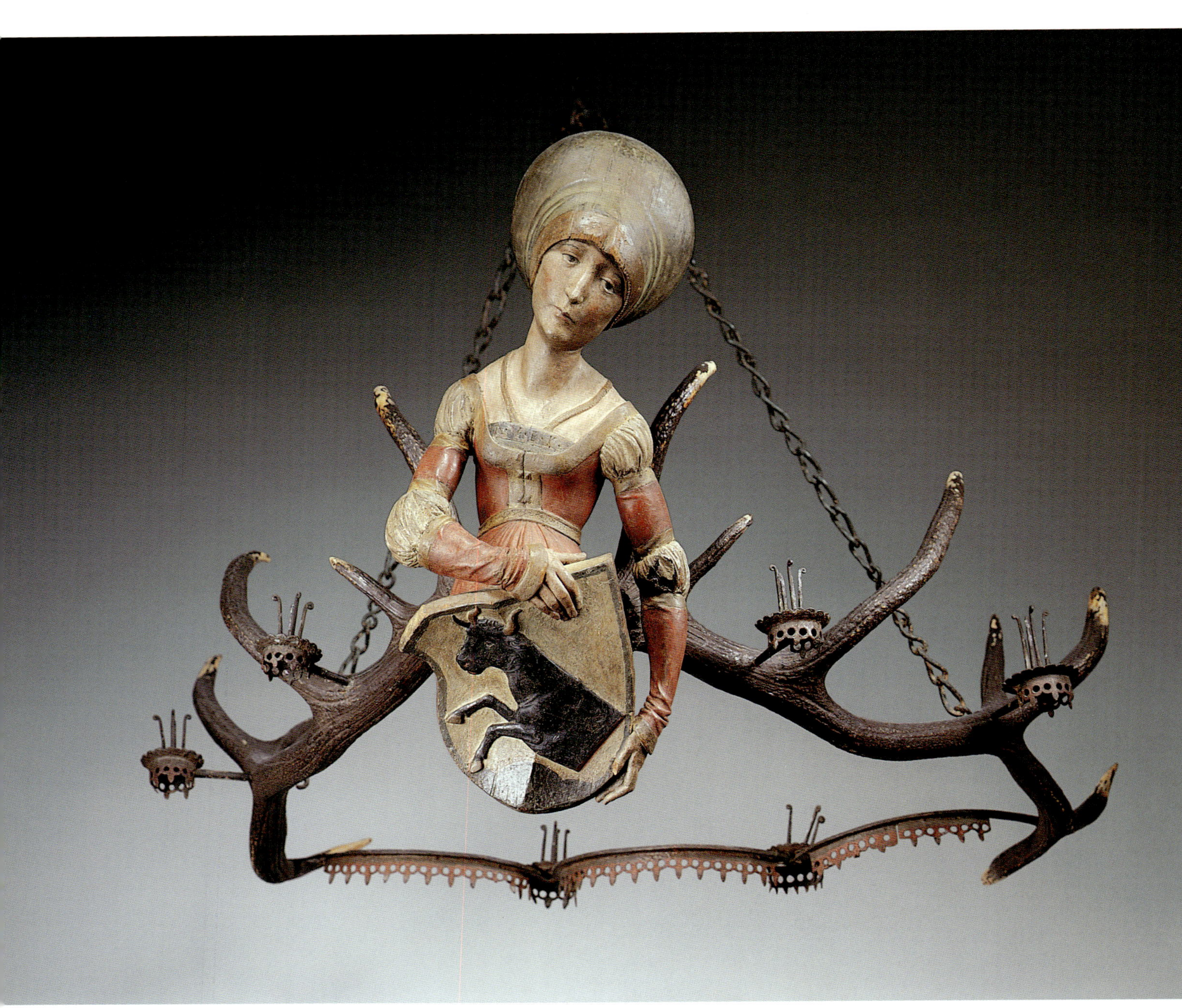

LÜSTERWEIBCHEN

c. 1510–1515, limewood with modern polychromy, antlers, and iron, 57 x 27 x 16 (22⅜ x 10⅝ x 6¼) (measurements without antlers), Private Collection

• *Technical Notes* •

The figure is cut from one block of limewood with two large attachments: the right arm between the elbow and the waist; and the rear half of the clouds carved in the back with part of the dress. The antlers, screwed directly into the back of the figure, are not original.[1] They were taken from a nineteenth-century *Lüsterweibchen* and added to the present work after 1925.[2] The figure, described as "colorless" in 1901,[3] has been painted since. The segments of the sleeves were once connected by cords attached to small dowels, one of which, on the figure's right shoulder, still has a fragment of a Z-spun, two-ply silk or linen cord, probably originally black, attached to it. The sculpture was examined and treated in 1998 by Annette Kollmann, a private conservator in Leonberg.

• *Provenance* •

From the town hall in Ochsenfurt am Main; reportedly sold by the haberdasher Herbig, burgomaster of Ochsenfurt from 1865 to 1877, to the Munich jeweler Franz Greb, who was himself from Ochsenfurt; auctioned in 1908 with the Greb collection at Helbing's, Munich; Goldschmidt-Rothschild collection, Frankfurt, by 1911 until at least 1923; possibly Brown collection, Baden near Zurich; acquired by Julius Böhler, Munich, in 1925; by descent to the present owner (long-term loan to the Mainfränkisches Museum, Würzburg, since 1981).

• *Literature* •

Friedländer 1901a, 326; Weber 1911, 248; Wilm 1923, 151; Bier 1931, 451; Hannover 1931, 8, no. 9; Demmler 1936, 82–83; Bier 1937, 28; Gerstenberg 1962, 216–218; Bier 1978, 103, 154; Freeden 1981, 36; Muth 1982, 260–261; Kalden 1990, 112.

WHILE RIEMENSCHNEIDER, like other sculptors of his time, must have produced numerous objects with a secular function, only a handful has survived. This *Lüsterweibchen*—normally referred to by the German name, which means "little chandelier woman"—is certainly the most appealing of them. Such chandeliers characteristically consist of a female bust or upper torso, often holding an armorial shield, to which a pair of antlers, set horizontally, is then attached like a double tail. In the present example a curved iron band links the ends of the horns, and seven forged-iron candleholders are attached to the antlers and the band; three iron chains allow the suspension of the chandelier from a ceiling beam. Clouds are carved at the back of the figure where the antlers meet the body. This floating, composite creature exemplifies the late medieval fascination with the fantastic.[4]

As has been pointed out, Riemenschneider's figure is anything but grotesque.[5] Her regular features express a dignified poise that would befit any of his female saints; the visage is indeed very close to that of *Saint Elizabeth* in Nuremberg (cat. 43B).[6] With her right elbow bent and her right hand resting at the top of the coat of arms, she stretches her whole upper body, even leaning her head, to reach the lower contour of the shield with her left hand. Her long arms are echoed by the curves of the antlers, and the line continues in her graceful hands, with slightly bent fingers, that seem to be barely touching the shield, adding to an impression of weightlessness. The imposing headdress, which is also worn by Mary Salome in the London fragment of a *Holy Kinship* altarpiece (cat. 36B) and by Dorothea von Wertheim on her funerary monument in Grünsfeld (fig. 1), offers a visual counterweight to the shield.[7]

1. Reproduced without antlers in Wilm 1923, 151, fig. 41.

2. Personal communication of Mr. Florian Eitle, of the Kunsthandlung Julius Böhler, Munich.

3. Friedländer 1901a, 326.

4. Gerstenberg 1962, 216–218.

5. Muth 1982, 260.

6. Gerstenberg 1962, 216.

7. Gerstenberg 1962, 218; Muth 1982, 260.

8. Discovered by Annette Kollmann; I am grateful to Michele Marincola for her description of this detail.

9. Bier 1978, 99.

10. Muth 1982. 260.

11. Bier 1982, 105, fig. 39.

The elegant costume is particularly rich. The slender body is encased in a low-cut dress with a tight-fitting bodice. Covering the breast, an undergarment bears the inscription "AV • E • K," which defies interpretation. A heavy necklace rests on the shoulders and falls into the corset. The narrow sleeves, which cover the greater part of the hands, consist of two separate segments, with puffs of gathered linen at the shoulders and the elbows. Comparison with the similarly coiffed Nuremberg *Saint Elizabeth* makes the point that such revealing attire would have been indecorous on a Virgin or a female saint (except perhaps Mary Magdalen before her conversion). But a secular figure could be dressed at the height of contemporary fashion. Riemenschneider's other *Lüsterweibchen* (fig. 2) likewise wears a tight dress with décolletage and slit sleeves, while a beret rests stylishly on her head.

The *Lüsterweibchen* from Ochsenfurt is a rare example of a work by Riemenschneider that combined different media: two others are the *Saint Jerome* in Cleveland, which had a silk cord dangling from the cardinal's hat, and the *Saint George* in Berlin, which seems to have had a leather bridle and reins (cats. 11 and 18). In addition to antlers and ironwork, this little chandelier woman originally had textile cords attached to the sleeves.[8] The dress with segmented sleeves is not an imagined, but a faithful rendering of a contemporary style of clothing that appears in paintings of around this time (fig. 3). Crisscrossed laces tied the sections of the sleeves together, at both shoulders and elbows. On the *Lüsterweibchen* remains of tiny, protruding dowels on both sleeves clearly allowed the attachment of an actual cord that would have run, possibly in zigzag, over the shirt.

The arms on the shield, showing the front half of an ox, are those of the Franconian town of Ochsenfurt am Main, and the provenance of the object can be traced to the local town hall *(Rathaus)*. Riemenschneider had received another commission from Ochsenfurt: for a canopy over a baptismal font in the parish church, which he delivered in 1514.[9] Construction on the town hall began before 1497 and must have been completed by 1513, the date engraved above the entrance to the council chamber. In all likelihood, the *Lüsterweibchen* was commissioned for this space, and the completion of the room provides a point of reference to date the sculpture.[10] The figure's resemblance to the Nuremberg *Saint Elizabeth* supports a date of about 1510–1515.

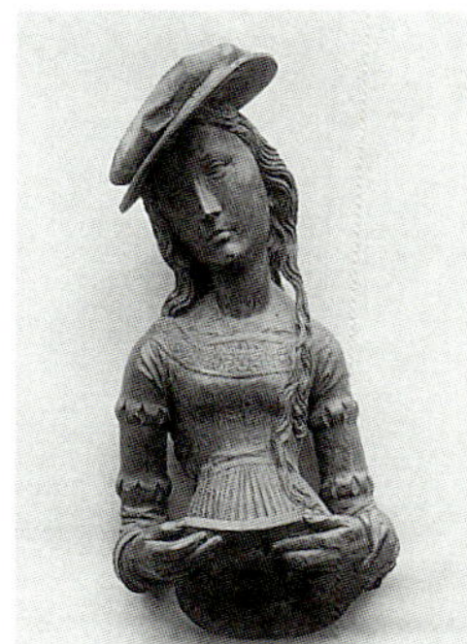

2.

Lüsterweibchen,
c. 1505–1510, limewood,
Private Collection

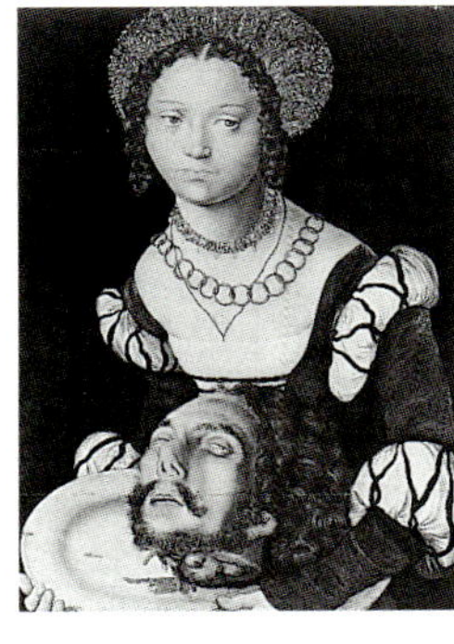

3.

Lucas Cranach the Elder,
Salome, c. 1510–1512, oil
on panel, Bayerisches
Nationalmuseum, Munich

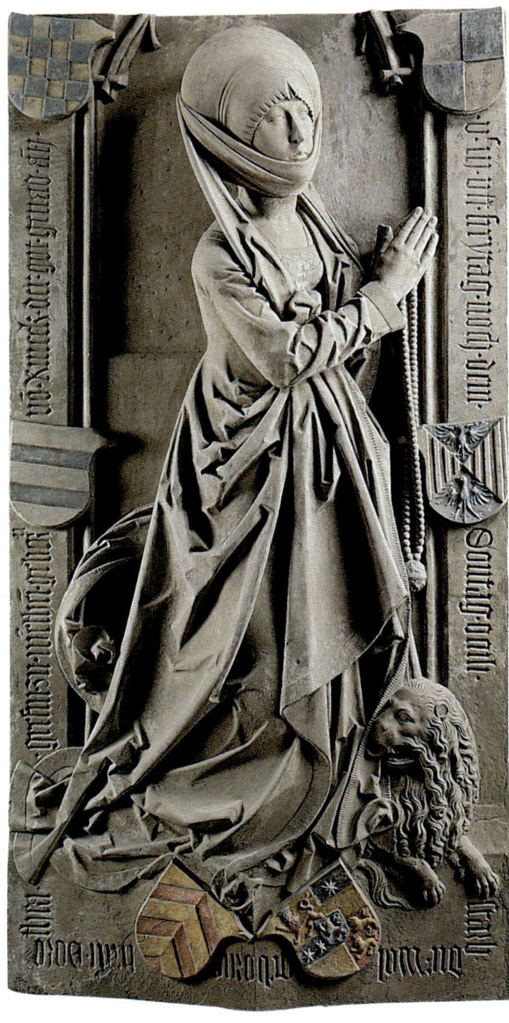

1.

Monument to Dorothea von Wertheim, after 1503,
sandstone, Pfarrkirche, Grünsfeld

It is not clear whether the *Lüsterweibchen* was originally intended to be polychromed. Traces of earlier paint under the modern polychromy do not give a clear indication of the original appearance. Justus Bier argued that Riemenschneider's other *Lüsterweibchen* was intended as a monochrome work, because the finely cut diaper pattern on her garment would have been obscured by a layer of ground, however fine.[11] The presence of colored cord on the Ochsenfurt *Lüsterweibchen* suggests that the work was in fact polychrome. If nothing else, it is certain that the shield was painted, for heraldry cannot be identified without tinctures. CHAPUIS

LAMENTATION

c. 1515, limewood, 102 x 97 x 22 (40 ⅛ x 38 ⅛ x 8 ⅝), Kunstsammlungen Böttcherstrasse, Bremen

• *Technical Notes* •

The figures are carved from a block consisting of four pieces of limewood joined vertically. There are numerous additions, especially in the lower portion of the work; many are original, such as the long curved fold of John's cloak and part of the edge of the Virgin's veil extending from her shoulder to John's forearm. The back is flat, not hollowed out (see also cats. 24 and 39A). The sculpture has suffered severely from insect damage; most channels run along the surface, which indicates that the work was painted. Indeed, it bears traces of three layers of paint. Several details suggest that the group was originally intended to be polychrome. The wood is of poor quality, with disfiguring knots left unrepaired, even in an important area like Christ's chest. In addition, several splits in the wood were filled with shims, through which insect tunnels run, suggesting that repairs were original. Finally, the surface is left rough in several areas, and there is little surface decoration. The sculpture was treated in 1993/1994 by conservator Dietmar Wohl of Münster, who removed an ancient discolored wax layer, consolidated loose areas, and removed or integrated discolored fills.[1]

• *Provenance* •

Collection of Dr. Franz von Defregger, Munich, by 1911; whereabouts unknown between 1911 and 1929; collection of Dr. Wilhelm Krumm, Munich, by 1929; acquired in 1930 by Ludwig Roselius (1874–1943), Bremen; sold by his son, Dr. Ludwig Roselius, in 1979, to General Foods (with Böttcherstrasse and Kaffee Hag Company); repurchased by Dr. Roselius in 1981; acquired in 1988 by the city of Bremen.

• *Literature* •

Bier 1973, 138, 154; Bier 1978, 154; Bier 1982, 104; Kalden 1990, 130 n. 477.

THE LAMENTATION over Christ's dead body, occurring between the Descent from the Cross and the Entombment, marks a contemplative break in the narrative of the Passion. The subject, which is not described in the Gospels, was first depicted in Byzantine art and entered Western Europe through Italian art in the fourteenth century. Its popularity in the West was greatly enhanced by the *Revelations* of Bridget of Sweden,[2] a fourteenth-century mystic whose writings belong to a body of devotional literature that encourages the reader to ponder events in the life of the Virgin and of Christ and to replicate their feelings. As a meditative rather than narrative theme, the Lamentation allows both artists and viewers to focus on the emotions of the participants.

Riemenschneider's imposing Bremen group combines three figures in a pyramidal composition. The dead Christ, thematically the most important, lies in the foreground, and his legs rest horizontally on the Virgin's garment, while his upper body leans upright against her right knee. His lifeless head, with half-shut eyes and parted lips, is supported by Mary's right hand. The Virgin is half-sitting, half-kneeling behind him, and her general form, with its broad sweep of drapery, echoes that of Christ. This similarity of form expresses the Virgin's compassion for the suffering of her son, a notion that was first articulated by Bernard of Clairvaux in the twelfth century and that had become doctrine by the fifteenth.[3] Facing the viewer, the disciple John stands behind the Virgin at the apex of the pyramid. The oblique alignment of the three heads — each turned in a different direction — dominates the composition. Following Christ's admonition at the Crucifixion to take care of Mary as of his own mother (John 19:26–27), John shows his solicitude by supporting her and gently reaching around to touch her wrist. His concern for her exemplifies admonitions to the reader in devotional literature to

1. Report dated 15 March 1994, on file at the museum.

2. Louis Réau, *Iconographie de l'art chrétien* (Paris, 1958), 2.2: 519.

3. Otto von Simson, "Compassio and Co-redemptio in Roger van der Weyden's Descent from the Cross," *Art Bulletin* 35 (1953), 9–16, esp. 11.

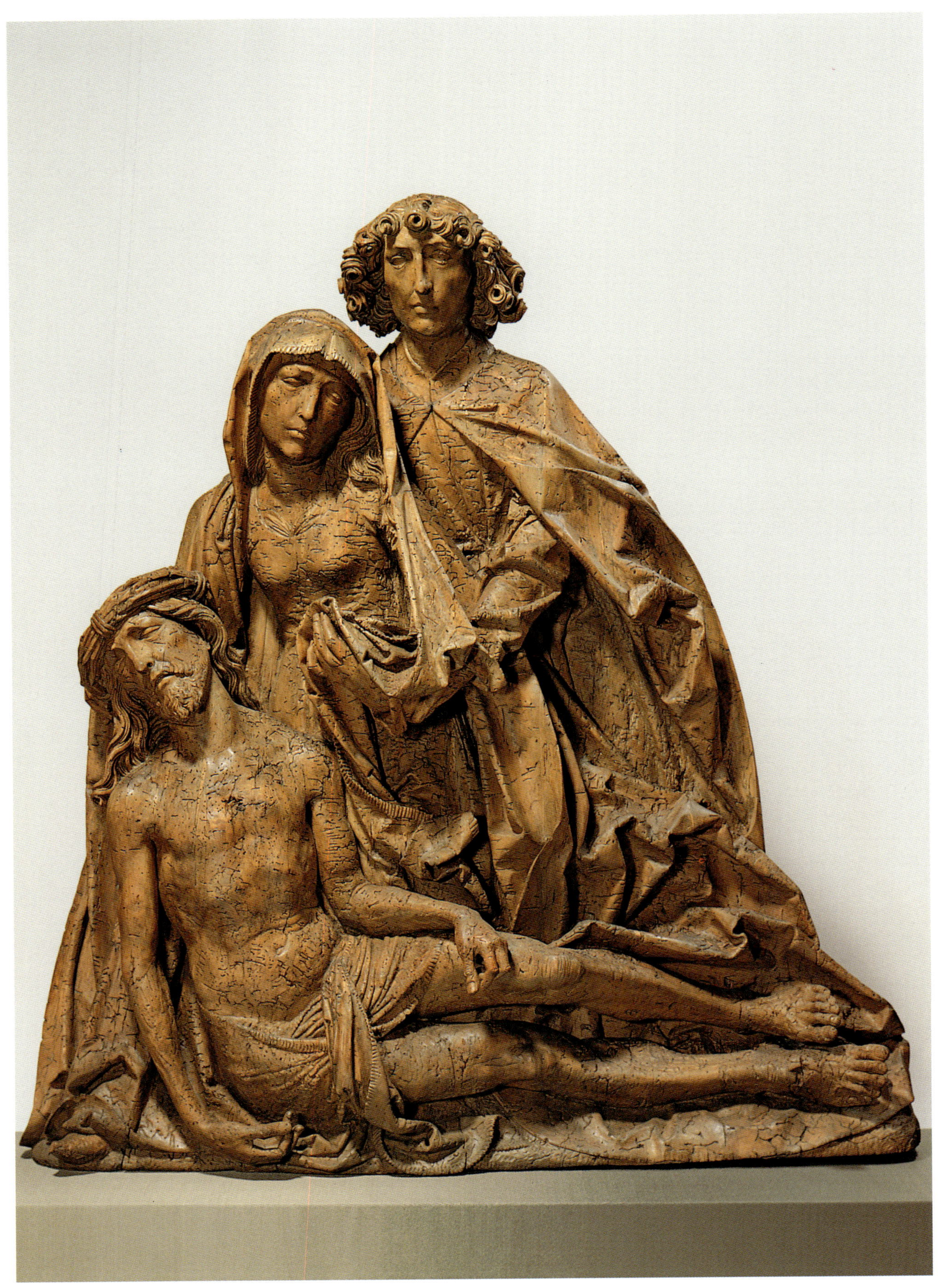

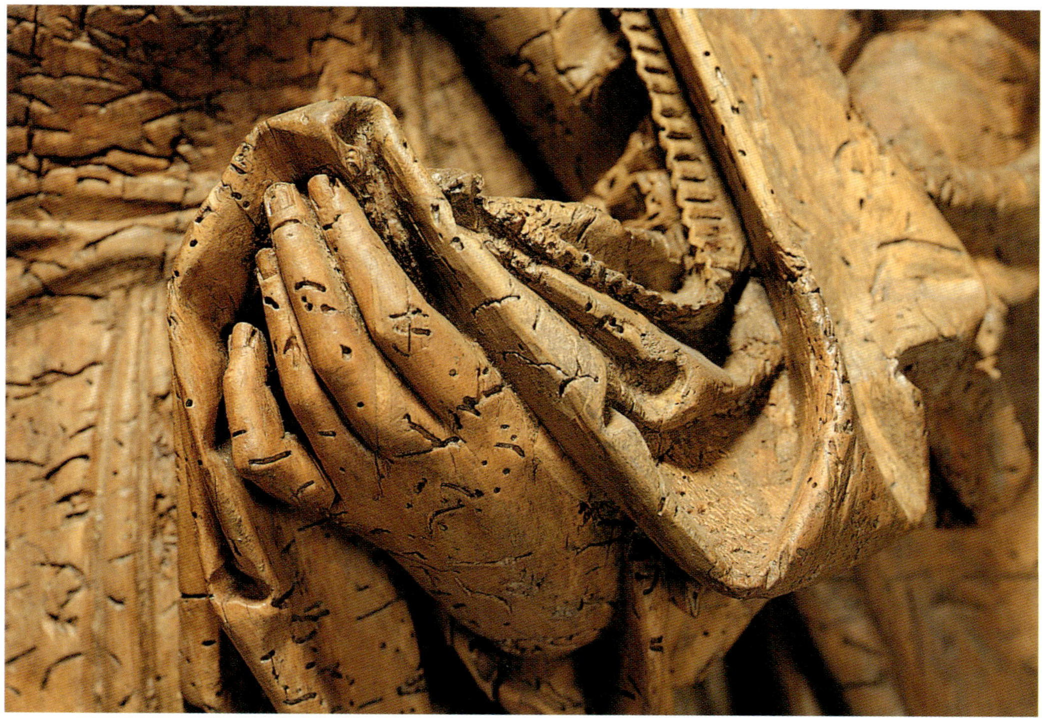

Detail of catalogue no. 42

share the suffering of the holy persons in the Scriptures. John's expression of muted, accepting grief contrasts with the desolation on the Virgin's face.

The focal point of the composition, as Bier pointed out, is the Virgin's left hand,[4] delicately holding the end of her veil, as if she were about to dry her tears. The hand expresses her sorrow, and in its action and articulation, it contrasts with Christ's limp, lifeless hands. In addition, as John touches Mary's hand, this detail serves to unite the two figures, both emotionally and spatially. The Bremen sculpture conveys a sense of muted pathos on a monumental scale that seems to anticipate the grand sandstone relief in Maidbronn of a few years later, a sculpture of the same subject also arranged in a triangular composition (Chapuis essay, fig. 9). The emotional appeal was even greater originally, when the sculpture was polychromed: it is likely that the eyes of Mary and John were red, tears rolling down their cheeks, and that their complexions contrasted with Christ's deadly pallor, his wounds colored red.

A remarkable quality of the Bremen group is that, despite its physical shallowness, it achieves a striking spatial presence and three-dimensionality. The volume of the group increases as one steps away from it and views it in its entirety from a distance.

One sees each figure in relation to the others and mentally places them in different planes. This sculptural device of juxtaposing several elements, which creates the illusion of depth when the forms are read together, is characteristic of Riemenschneider's works in the second decade of the sixteenth century (see also cats. 39 A and 43 A). Other details support this dating. The drapery patterns are simplified and reduced in number when compared, for instance, to the *Holy Blood* altarpiece of 1501–1504 in Rothenburg (cat. 23, fig. 1). The limited arc of address and the planar treatment of forms are also hallmarks of Riemenschneider's later years (see cat. 45).

In the absence of documents, the sculpture itself must provide the clues to its original installation. Because of the inherent horizontality of the subject, the Lamentation often appeared in the predella of a retable, as in Riemenschneider's now dismantled early *Passion* altarpiece (cat. 2, fig. 2). But the height of the Bremen group would seem to preclude its installation in a predella, as does its pyramidal composition. Since the sculpture is intended strictly for frontal viewing, it appears likelier that it was made to stand in a niche, either in a wall or in front of one. The niche might have been squarish, with an ogival upper contour and tracery in the upper corners. CHAPUIS

4. Bier 1973, 154.

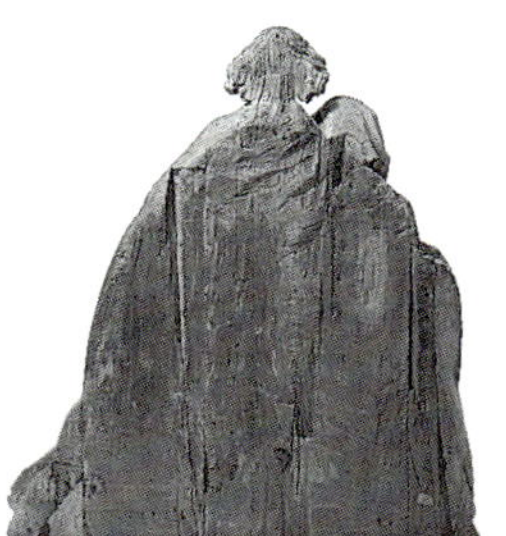

Back view of
catalogue no. 42

43 A–C

Three Saints

43A **FEMALE SAINT**
c. 1515–1520, limewood, 106.7 x 33 x 16.8 (42 x 13 x 6⅝), Private Collection

43B **SAINT ELIZABETH OF HUNGARY**
c. 1510–1515, limewood with ancient polychromy, 109 x 33.5 x 17.5 (42⅞ x 13⅛ x 6⅞),
Germanisches Nationalmuseum, Nuremberg

43C **SAINT CATHERINE**
c. 1505, limewood, 104.7 x 31.8 x 19 (41¼ x 12½ x 7½), Private Collection

• *Technical Notes* •

Each of the three figures is carved from a single piece of limewood with the grain running vertically and the backs hollowed. Each has a vertical slot about 5.7 cm long in the back at the shoulders by which it was attached to a retable. Insect damage is minor, and it does not affect the aesthetic appeal of the works.

The most obvious damages in the unidentified saint are the loss of her right hand and attribute and the presence of two wide cracks, one in her turban and the other down her left side. The *Elizabeth* has two areas of repair in the back, the upper one closing a hole near her left arm. There is a rectangular repair at the front, probably modern, in the saint's right shoulder. The most conspicuous damage is the loss of her left hand and attribute and of a significant part of the base. Fragments of the veil are missing as well as the pointed edge of the headdress at the figure's right side. The *Catherine,* identified by the inscription "KATHERI" on her undergarment, is missing her right hand, which originally held an attribute, probably a wheel. Other losses include a long vertical portion of the cloak that falls from her left arm, the tip of her nose, the tip of her left index finger, and a portion of the drapery on the left side of the base. A vertical crack runs down her left temple.

The elaborate ornamentation of the surfaces strongly suggests that these works were meant to remain uncolored. Indeed, the stippled imitation of velvet on the border of the bodices is visible on the unnamed female saint and *Catherine* but hidden by a layer of ground on the *Elizabeth*—which retains substantial areas of old polychromy, perhaps from the seventeenth or eighteenth century—except where the paint has flaked off. The female saint and *Catherine* also preserve nine distinct tool marks, including three different punches, whereas the incised pattern of scallops and dots along the edges of *Elizabeth*'s cloak is filled with paint and discernible only under raking light. A combination of abstract engraved designs (lines, vines, and diamonds) with punch marks is seen on both the female saint and *Catherine.* The bottom edge of *Elizabeth*'s cloak is decorated with wooden appliqué pearls and oblong gems.

The figures were painted at some later point. Traces of gilding with a red glaze are seen in many areas on the female saint and *Catherine.* These layers were overpainted twice, probably in the nineteenth century.[1] The paint on the two privately owned figures was removed in the late nineteenth or early twentieth century by treating the surfaces with a caustic material, which caused bleaching and dessication of the wood. The *Saint Catherine* was then stained dark brown, either to conceal damage to the surface or simply to imitate another wood. The female saint was spared this treatment.

1. Using polarized light microscopy, Michele Marincola identified one of the components of the upper layer as artificial ultramarine, not commercially available in Germany until 1830.

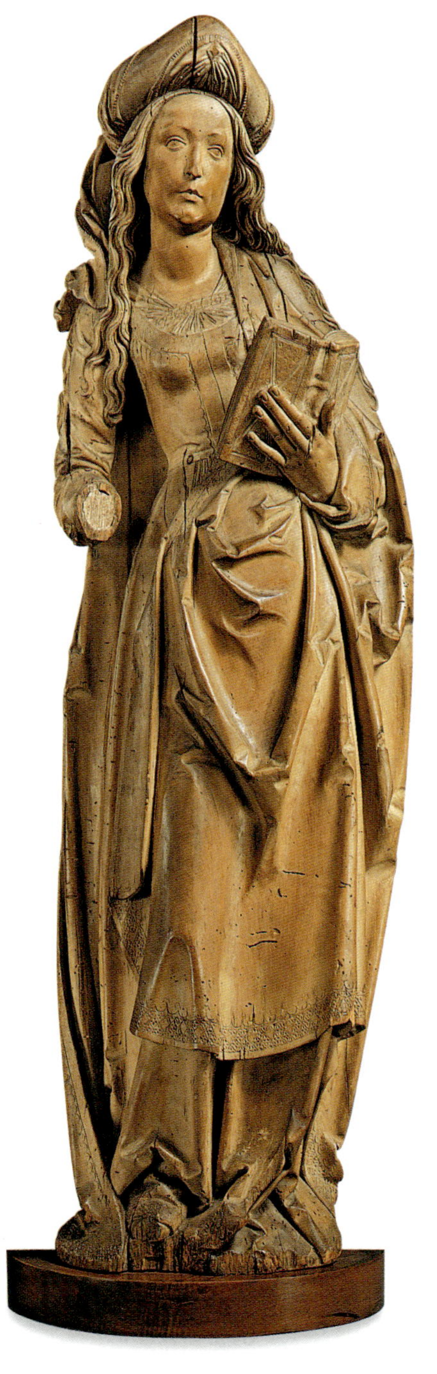

43 A

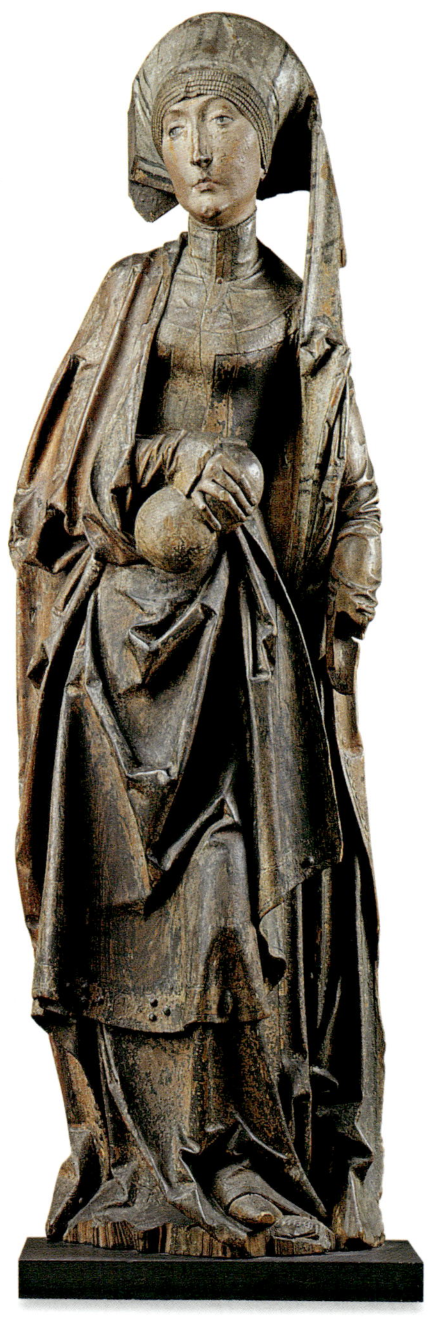

43 B

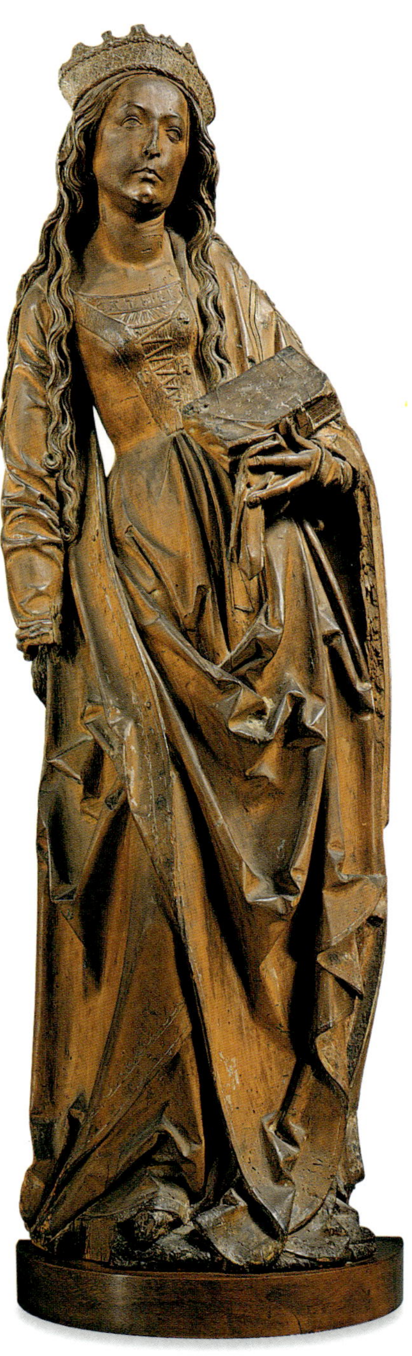

43 C

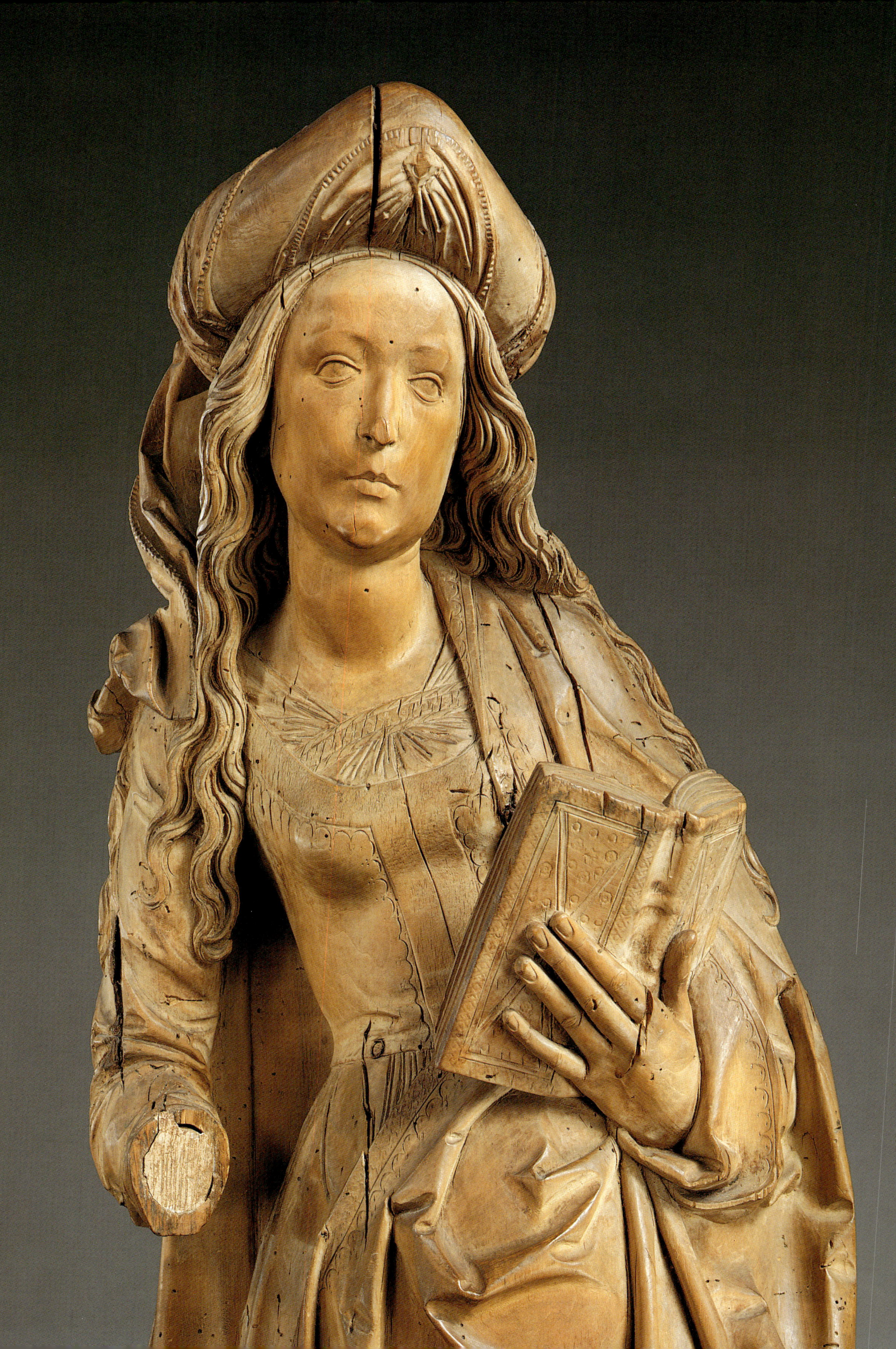

• Provenance •
The female saint and Catherine: Acquired in 1927 from Georg Schuster in Munich by the father of the present owners.

Elizabeth: Acquired by the Germanisches National-museum in September 1922 from Lehrer Lieb in Heuchelheim near Schlüsselfeld/Ofr.

• Literature •
Female saint: Hannover 1931, 12, no. 16.

Elizabeth: Hampe 1922–1923; Anonymous 1923, 428; Wilm 1923, 112–113, pl. 170; Bier 1925, 7; Gerstenberg 1962, 216, pl. 215; Schrade 1927, 171 n. 409; Germanisches Nationalmuseum 1977, 63; Germanisches Nationalmuseum 1997, 66.

Catherine: Hannover 1931, 12, no. 17; Bier 1978, 31; Finn 1997, 22–25.

WHILE THE ELIZABETH from Nuremberg has been discussed in the Riemenschneider literature for decades, the two other figures are among the great discoveries of this exhibition. Accessible to the general public only once in this century, during the exhibition in Hannover in 1931, they are known to only a handful of scholars. Although their surfaces have received very different treatments over time, there is little doubt that these three figures originally belonged to the same retable: all are high reliefs, of essentially equal size, with a rectangular slot in the back—a very specific means of attachment to the encasement of an altarpiece, which appears in none of Riemenschneider's other extant figures.[2] Yet they exhibit different sculptural conceptions that can be linked with distinct moments in Riemenschneider's development as a sculptor. Because the privately owned figures are virtually unknown and unpublished, they warrant more extensive discussion.

Catherine has the attributes of a learned princess: carrying a book and wearing a crown. Her right hand, now missing, probably displayed an instrument of her martyrdom, most likely the spiked wheel (she would have had to bend her elbow to hold a sword, whereas having her arm hanging down would allow the hand to rest on a wheel). Elizabeth, daughter of the king of Hungary and widow of the landgrave of Thuringia, achieved sanctity through her works of charity. The loaf of bread she carries here refers to her feeding the poor, as does her other attribute, a pewter jug or flagon, which she probably held in her left hand, now lost (see cat. 13, fig. 2). Her modest, matronly attire, with her neck and head covered,

reflects her widowhood. The loss of the other female saint's right hand, and therefore of a specific attribute, prevents her precise identification. She could be Barbara, who, like Catherine, carries a book, a reference to her study of the Scriptures when she was confined in a tower. Her turban, although worn by the *Saint Barbara* in Munich (fig. 1), is not specific to that saint; it is also found on images of Dorothy and Elizabeth attributable to Riemenschneider and his shop.[3] If this figure were indeed Barbara, it would probably have carried either a chalice or a miniature tower.

The *Saint Catherine* shows a volumetric treatment of form and angular drapery patterns, creating a rich play of light and shadow in a manner typical of Riemenschneider's work of around 1505. When viewed frontally, the left contour of the figure follows a vertical, while the right contour defines a sweeping curve, gently offset by the tilted head. Seen slightly from the left, however, the figure is conceived as an S in space, with the head leaning forward over the torso, while her drapery sweeps forward in a generous mass over her lower body. From the same angle, the grand *Virgin and Child* of about 1500 in Vienna (cat. 19, fig. 2) achieves a similar effect. The *Saint Catherine*'s profile and drapery patterns also recall those in the *Virgin and Child* of about 1505 in Hamburg (cat. 28). And like the drapery in the *Saint Matthias* of

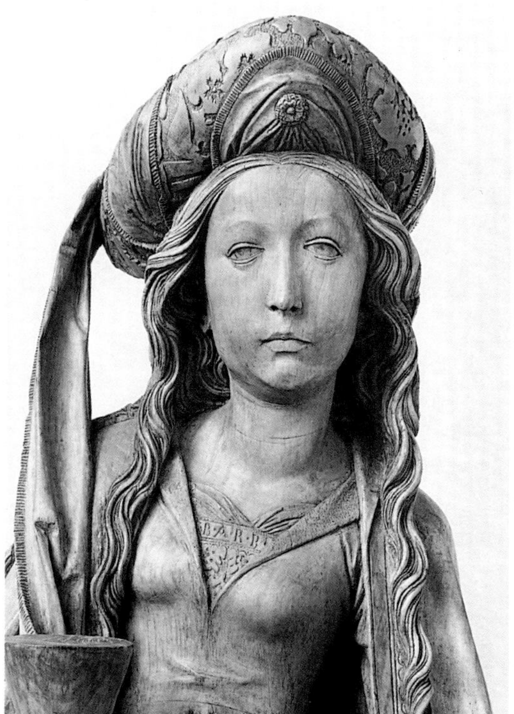

1.
Saint Barbara, c. 1510, limewood, Bayerisches Nationalmuseum, Munich

2. It is Michele Marincola who first recognized that the Nuremberg figure belonged to the same ensemble as the two privately owned pieces. I am grateful for her willingness to discuss the results of her examination of these works, which she will publish fully elsewhere.

3. See Dorothy, formerly in Würzburg Cathedral (destroyed in World War II) in Bier 1982, fig. 27; and Elizabeth, by a follower of Riemenschneider (Germanisches Nationalmuseum, Nuremberg) in Hannover 1931, 10, fig. 4.

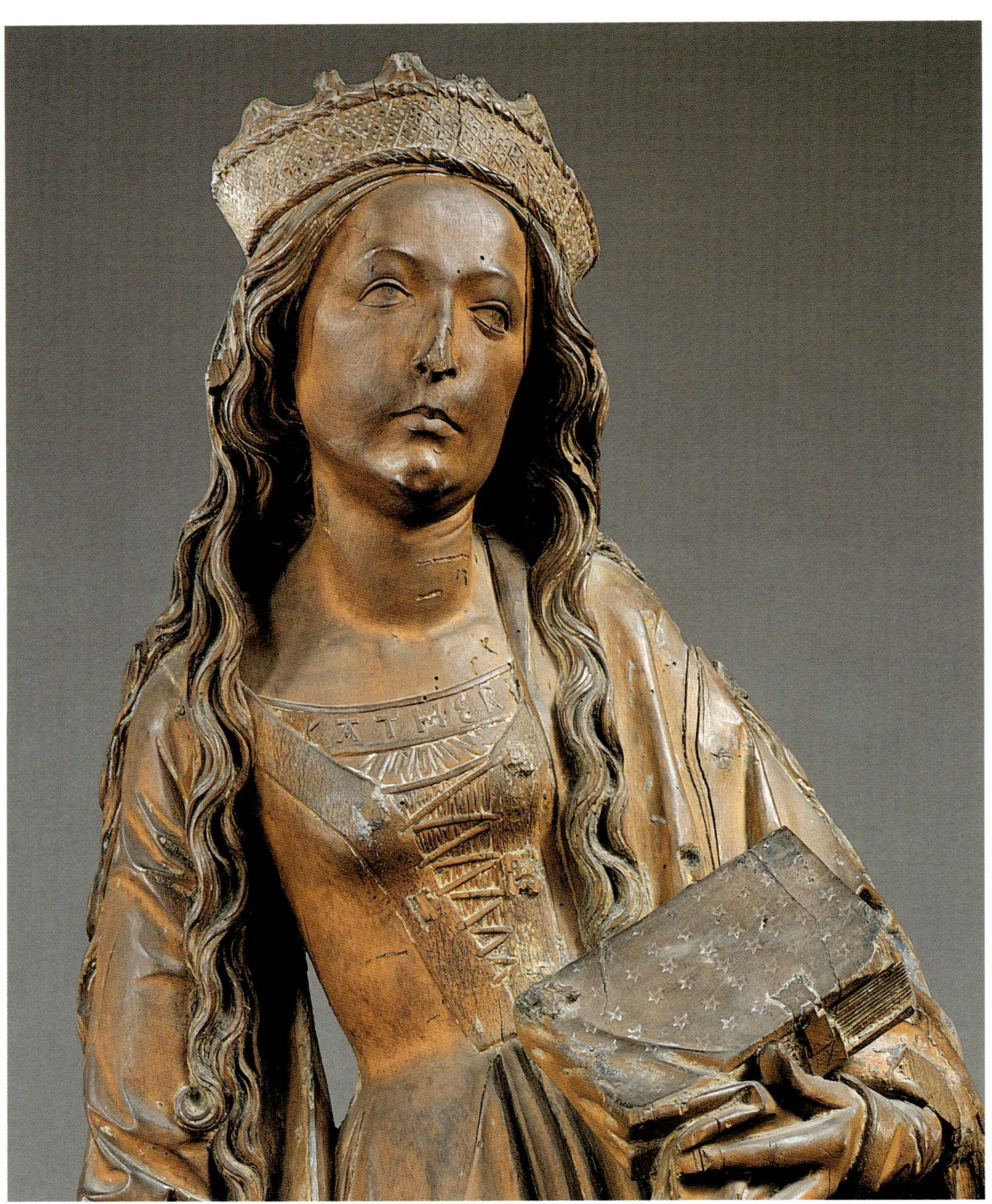

Detail of catalogue no. 43C

about 1500–1505 in Berlin (cat. 24), her cloak is reversed so that the interior covers the front of the figure in a broad inverted triangle; the center of this area is enlivened by a calligraphy of short angular folds. The resemblances would have been even greater when the *Saint Catherine* was in its original state and the left edge of her cloak was intact.

The slender figure of the *Saint Elizabeth* is articulated along an inverted S-curve, with the arcing of her body offset by the tilt of her head. Her mantle rests on her right shoulder and is drawn up under her arm and held against the body at the wrist, covering the front of the figure with V-shaped folds of drapery. The cloak functions as both a backdrop and a shell and gives the body spatial presence, as it does in the Munich *Saint Barbara* of about 1510. Her veil falls in front of her left shoulder where the mantle has fallen away, while the other side of the headdress is positioned behind the right shoulder; this conveys the illusion that the figure is turning her head. Her silhouette forms a vertical on one side and a curve on the other, just as do those of the other two saints. Her hanging arm, encased in a narrow sleeve that breaks in rounded folds at the elbow, is identical to that of

330

Saint Catherine. The treatment of her drapery, with
its slightly rounder folds, is reminiscent of the garments of Peter and John on the Windsheim altarpiece
completed in 1509, now in Heidelberg (cat. 40, fig. 1).

The third female saint is distinguished by her
commanding presence, the lucid arrangement of
forms, and the more planar treatment of volumes, all
achieved with sculptural virtuosity, establishing this
figure as a major work of Riemenschneider's late style.
Although essentially a high relief, this figure conveys
a striking sense of movement and volume. Despite
its shallowness, it is read as a body in space, the cloak
serving both as a shell on the right and as a backdrop
on the left. An impression of movement is communicated by the general articulation of the figure along
an elegant S-curve, with the saint's left leg supporting the weight of her body. In addition, the hair that
falls down her back on the right and in front of her
shoulder on the left suggests that the saint is turning
her head. The facial type and headdress bear a striking resemblance to the Munich *Saint Barbara.* Each
has an elongated face with almond-shaped eyes, a
straight nose, narrow mouth, dimpled chin, and a
thin, supple neck marked with horizontal creases.
Although both figures have the same erect pose and
slender proportions, *Barbara* displays a more volumetric treatment of forms and a crisper, more angular drapery pattern, which represent an earlier moment
in Riemenschneider's evolution. The sculptural conception of the unnamed female saint is very close to
that of the sandstone *Virgin and Child* in Würzburg,
datable to about 1518–1520 (cat. 16, fig. 1), and of the
superb *Virgin and Child* at Dumbarton Oaks from
around 1521 (cat. 45). These figures share the same
S-curve stance and compression of volumes into one
plane—emphasized by the apronlike drapery in the
front of each figure—an arrangement that invites
frontal viewing. The fabric depicted in these three
works has lost some of the crispness of earlier drapery, bending in fewer, rounder folds. In view of
the similarities with the Munich *Saint Barbara* on the
one hand and the later images of the Virgin on the
other, it seems reasonable to assume that Riemenschneider carved this unidentified female saint between about 1515 and 1520.

The *Saint Catherine, Saint Elizabeth,* and the
third female saint were certainly made for the central
shrine of a carved retable, and their individual sculptural conception suggests their original placement.
The shrine probably contained four figures, standing
in two groups on either side of a central figure, such
as the Virgin and child, as in Michel Erhart's Blaubeuren altarpiece (fig. 2). *Catherine* probably stood

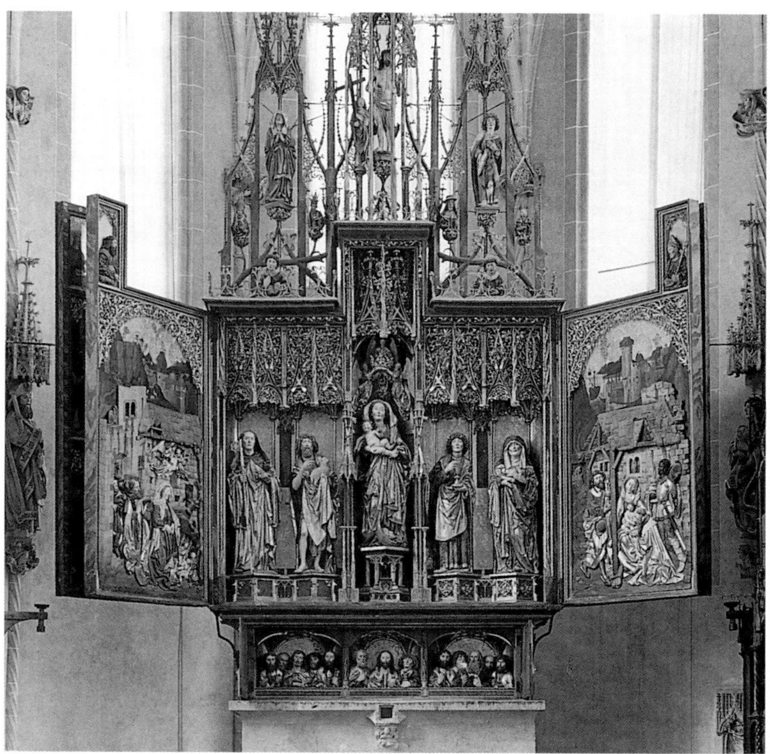

2.

Michel Erhart, Blaubeuren altarpiece, 1493/1494, Klosterkirche, Blaubeuren

directly to the right of the central figure, for her drapery is most coherent when seen from slightly to the
left. *Elizabeth* seems to have stood directly to the left
of the central figure, where the space under the cloak
covering her right wrist would have been seen most
clearly, giving the figure depth and volume. The third
female saint is conceived to be viewed more sharply
from the right, so she would probably have stood to
the left of *Elizabeth.* From this angle, her book would
have hidden a knot in the wood at her waist and her
veil would have been most effective as a space-creating
device. This reconstruction, which presupposes an
ideal vantage point facing the central figure of the
shrine, allows both *Saint Elizabeth* and the female
saint to be read as S-shapes in a plane, while *Catherine* becomes a broad S-form in space. To date, no
other surviving sculpture ascribed to Riemenschneider seems to have belonged to this altarpiece.

The span of years in which these figures seem
to have been produced suggests that Riemenschneider worked on the retable, with interruptions, for at
least ten years, if not longer. This would be in keeping with documentary evidence that the sculptor
sometimes worked on a commission for many years.
Judging from the extremely fine surface treatment
and rich tooling, it is clear that this retable was intended to remain uncolored. CHAPUIS

44

c. 1515–1520, limewood, 82.3 x 47.2 x 30.2 (32⅜ x 18½ x 11⅞), National Gallery of Art, Washington, Samuel H. Kress Collection

• *Technical Notes* •

The sculpture is made of two blocks of limewood with the grain running vertically. The larger block comprises the majority of the figure, with the saint's left shoulder made separately. Two cracks run vertically through the face and the miter. A long vertical repair in the back required a wood insert from the base through the saint's right shoulder. The crook of the crozier, carved separately and attached with a dowel, is lost. Modern replacements include the tip of the index and middle fingers of the right hand, the tip of the drapery fold held in the left hand, and part of the lappet of the miter at the saint's right side.

In all likelihood, the sculpture was originally a full-length figure that was cut down and converted into a reliquary. A narrow opening in the back, through which the sculptor hollowed out the figure to prevent cracking, was enlarged and made square so that it could be closed with a door or panel. A coarse diamond shape was carved into the saint's chest to allow for the installation of a large jewel, recorded in a photograph published in 1888;[1] this area is now painted red. The miter was decorated with appliqué on either side of the vertical band (see also cat. 17); the 1888 photograph shows that these were jewels, which have been replaced by wooden plugs.

It is not clear whether the sculpture was originally intended to be polychromed. The face is carved with sensitivity, and finely rendered details such as the hair, the fringe on the infulae, or the relief imitation of embroidery on the miter, would have been obscured, though still perceptible, under a layer of ground. The irises and pupils are painted in black directly on the wood, which could indicate monochromy, but this feature was also used on figures meant to be colored as a means to give the eyes focus during carving. The work was painted at least twice, perhaps three times: an azurite-colored mineral blue pigment is found on the lining of the pluvial, under a layer of paint; gilding on a pale orange bole appears on the outside of the pluvial; a red stainlike material directly on the wood of the mouth is overlaid with two layers of red.[2] The polychromy was removed between 1901 and 1904, when the bust was published variously as polychrome and uncolored.[3] A knifelike tool left scrape marks over the entire surface of the sculpture.

• *Provenance* •

Wilhelm Sattler and his son Jens (d. 1901), Mainberg Castle near Kitzingen, before 1826 until 1901; Benoit Oppenheim, Berlin, 1901 until before 1927; [Munich art market, c. 1927 to before 1934]; Henry Goldman, New York, by 1934 until before 1943; [New York art market, 1943]; [Duveen Brothers at some point]; Samuel H. Kress Collection, New York, 1944; acquired by the museum in 1961.[4]

• *Literature* •

Streit 1888, 18, pl. 47; Tönnies 1900, 256–257; Friedländer 1901b, 468; Weber 1911, 223–233; Bier 1943; Bier 1946, 128, 137; Frankfurter 1946, 26–29; Bier 1955a, 112; Bier 1959a, 14 n. 9; National Gallery of Art 1959; National Gallery of Art 1965, 166; Middeldorf 1976, 124–125; Pope-Hennessy 1976, 72; Walker 1976, 620, 635, fig. 986; Muth and Schneiders 1978, 108, no. 113; Freeden 1981, 38, pl. 79; Bier 1982, 75–77; Muth 1982, 20; Kalden 1990, 108 n. 398; *National Gallery of Art, Washington*, 1992, 292.

WITH HIS HEAD slightly inclined and a pensive expression on his youthful face, the bishop raises his right hand in blessing. His left hand holds his crozier staff and what appears to be a portion of the sudarium; the crook of the crozier is lost. The figure is traditionally identified as Saint Burchard, the first bishop of Würzburg, who helped convert the Germans to

1. Streit 1888, pl. 47.

2. These observations were made by Michele Marincola, who studied the sculpture with a binocular microscope on 16 December 1997, with kind permission of Alison Luchs, curator of sculpture, and Shelley Sturman, head of objects conservation, at the National Gallery of Art.

3. As reported by Luchs in the draft of an entry on the *Bishop Saint* to be published in the National Gallery's systematic catalogue of the collection.

4. As reported by Luchs.

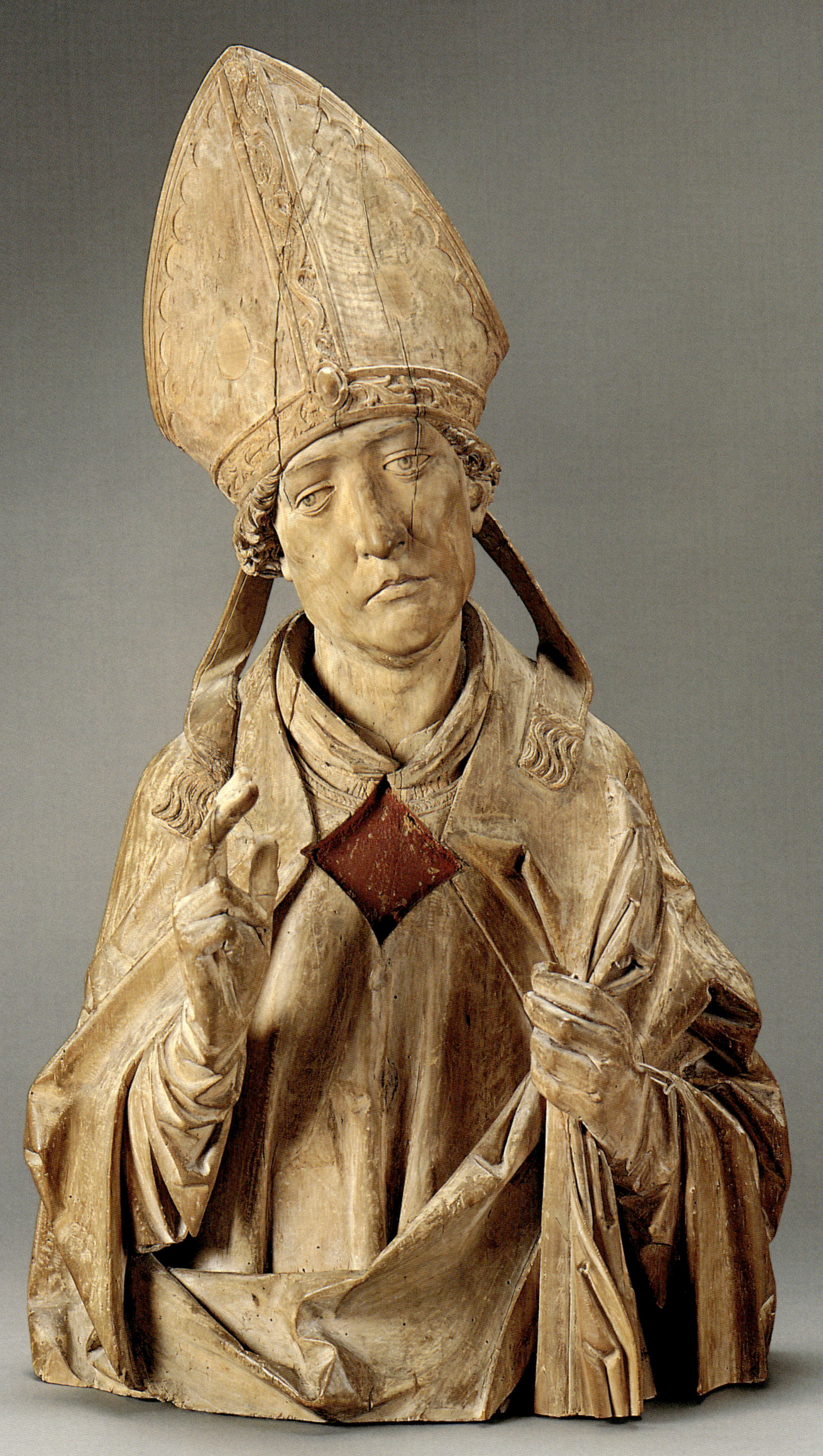

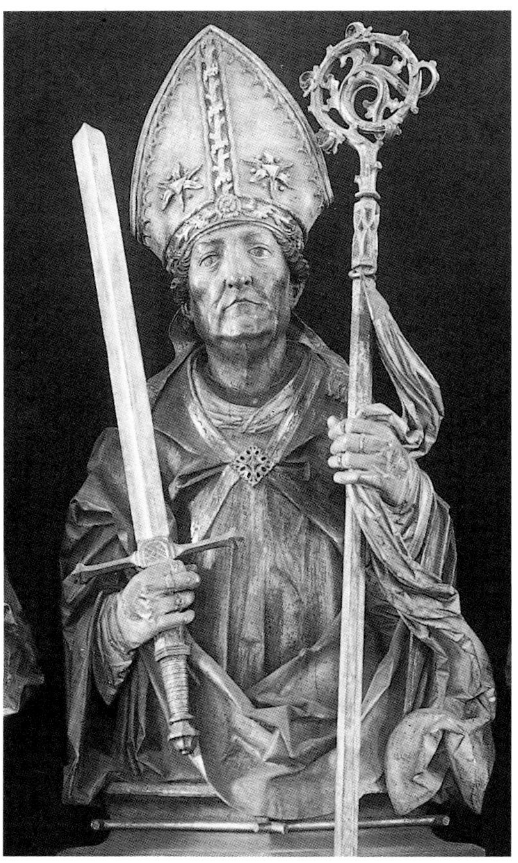

I.

Saint Kilian, 1508–1510, limewood with ancient polychromy, formerly Neumünster, Würzburg (destroyed in World War II)

favored by Niclaus Gerhaert (cats. 5 and 6) and used by Claus Sluter, which remained a constant in Riemenschneider's oeuvre (see cats. 16 and 45). Kilian's staff, which did not rest on the base but literally entered the space of the viewer, was another means to blur the aesthetic boundary of the base and unite the work of art with the world in which it functioned.

The conclusion is inescapable that the "Saint Burchard" has been severely altered. Nothing softens the abrupt horizontal of its lower edge. The verticals of the drapery on the right run perpendicular to the cut, as does the staff, which is held close to the body, suggesting strongly that the figure was originally full length. Furthermore, while Kilian looks up, with his chin raised, "Burchard" inclines his head forward, so that the face would be legible from below. The positioning of both hands is consistent with Riemenschneider's full-length depictions of bishops, such as the funerary monuments of Rudolf von Scherenberg and Lorenz von Bibra (Kemperdick essay, figs. 1 and 2). A blessing hand is raised, by definition, and a crozier is necessarily held with the hand positioned in front of the body, at a height between the shoulder and the elbow. The curved drapery fold across the front of the saint is seen on most of these works. Finally, Riemenschneider's busts were modeled fully in the round, whereas the back of the "Saint Burchard" is carved in low relief.[7]

In view of its composition, it is fair to assume that the "Saint Burchard" was conceived as an independent cult figure, made to stand above an altar or on a column in a church. Indeed, the saint is focused entirely on what is in front of him and does not react to anything on either side, as one would expect if he had been one of several figures in a shrine. The life-size figure must originally have been installed quite high, with the feet at the viewer's eye level. This is confirmed by the optical correction in the rendering of the left hand, which is distorted and too small when seen frontally, but anatomically coherent when viewed in strong foreshortening.[8]

The sculpture bears the hallmarks of Riemenschneider's late style. Its volumes have been compressed into a planar arrangement of forms. Like the Dumbarton Oaks *Virgin and Child* (cat. 45), it is intended essentially for frontal viewing and does not invite the mobility of the viewer. The face, carved with sensitivity, has been reduced to the essential features, in what Bier calls a "clarity of form and restraint of expression."[9] Its closeness, both in facial type and sculptural treatment to Riemenschneider's *Lamentation* of 1519–1523 in Maidbronn (Chapuis essay, fig. 9) supports a dating about 1520. CHAPUIS

5. Louis Réau, *Iconographie de l'art chrétien* (Paris, 1958), 3.1: 253; Bier 1982, 76.

6. Compare Bier 1943, 159–160; Bier 1955a, 112; Bier 1959a, 14 n. 9; and Bier 1982, 76.

7. Bier 1982, 76.

8. An observation first made by Catherine Metzger, paintings conservator at the National Gallery of Art.

9. Bier 1982, 77.

Christianity in the eighth century and whose attributes are a bishop's robe, a crozier, and sometimes the model of a church.[5] But it could theoretically be any other bishop saint, such as Louis of Toulouse, Blaise, or Martin of Tours. The figure is not Kilian, another patron saint of Würzburg, who is normally depicted with the sword of his martyrdom, as in the bust that Riemenschneider carved between 1508 and 1510 for the high altar of Würzburg Cathedral (fig. 1); this sculpture, which was moved in the eighteenth century to the adjacent Neumünster, burned in 1945.

Comparison with the *Saint Kilian* is instructive because it sheds light on the original form of the Washington sculpture. Indeed, there has been some debate on whether the "Saint Burchard" was created as a bust or cut down from a full-length figure.[6] The Neumünster saint was clearly conceived as a bust resting on a polygonal base, and the sculptor lavished attention on the junction between the figure and the base. He concealed the transition between vertical folds and the horizontal base with a broad sweep of drapery extending from one wrist to the other. Several folds of fabric fell in front of the base, a detail

334

VIRGIN AND CHILD ON THE CRESCENT MOON

1521–1522, limewood, 95.2 x 35 x 21 (37 ½ x 13 ¾ x 8 ¼), Dumbarton Oaks, Washington, DC,
House Collection

• Technical Notes •

The sculpture is made of four large pieces of limewood assembled with wooden dowels and iron nails,[1]
which allowed the sculptor to carve out the core without leaving a hole in the back of the figure.[2] This
method has its drawbacks, and a wide crack runs along
a join in the Virgin's left side. The artist used poor-
quality wood and did not remove several knots, which
caused further splits: the most notable knot is in the
Virgin's right arm; another is in the drapery in front
near the hem of the cloak. There are numerous smaller
additions. For example, the Virgin's right hand and
both of the child's arms were carved separately and
pegged to the body; the hand and the child's right
arm are replacements. The child's left cheek has an
old repair, possibly contemporary with the execution
of the sculpture, which may have been caused by a
knot. Losses include the fingers and thumb of his left
hand, and the left tip of the crescent moon. At the
top of the large block making up the back of the
figure, a piece has been lost, interrupting the flow of
hair. An area in the center of the back was flattened,
cutting through the carved hair; it was probably
at the same time that two holes were drilled in the
area, presumably for the attachment of the figure to
a support.

It is almost certain that the sculpture was not
originally intended to be polychrome, despite the
poor quality of the wood. Not only were the irises of
both figures painted black but, more important, the
incised zigzags along the edge of the cloak include
the faint impressions of two different punches (a six-
lobed floret surrounded by three small circles[3]), which
would have been obliterated by polychromy. At some
point, however, the sculpture did receive a layer of
paint, traces of which are visible in the hair and in
the deep drapery folds. The paint was removed in a
rather aggressive fashion, presumably in the nine-

teenth century, using an alkali solution that raised the
wood grain. The sculpture was conserved in 1999 by
Michele Marincola in preparation for this exhibition.

• Provenance •

[Reportedly acquired in Vienna around 1910 by Wilhelm Böhler, Munich (according to Bier 1982, 80)];
[Siegfried Lämmle, Munich, before 1935]; [offered in
the trade by Julius Böhler, H. Heilbronner, and Siegfried Lämmle, Munich, in 1935]; [Richard H. Zinser,
Stuttgart and Forest Hills, New York, 1935]; [Jacob
Hirsch, New York]; purchased on 13 February 1937
by Mr. and Mrs. Robert Wood Bliss, Washington,
DC; Dumbarton Oaks, Washington, DC, House Collection, since 1940.

• Literature •

Bier 1937, 30; Gerstenberg 1941, 192; Muth 1954, 164;
Kuhn 1974, 244–247; Bier 1975, 60; Bier 1978, 95–
97; Bier 1982, 78–80; Kalden 1990, 93–94, 141–142;
Vikan 1995, 133–135; Simon 1998, 177.

HER RIGHT FOOT on the crescent moon, the
Virgin holds the Christ child on her left hip and looks
ahead with a melancholy air at a point above the
viewer's head. The child, with a full face and happy
expression, is among Riemenschneider's most engaging: he gestures playfully and leans forward, turning
to look at his mother. His shirt is open in the front,
and part of it is swept back off his left leg, as if by a
draft of air, adding to the sense of liveliness and immediacy. The Virgin, wearing a dress with a tight-
fitting bodice, is swathed in a cloak that covers both
shoulders and is held by each wrist across the front
of her body like an apron. With her weight resting
on her left leg, her right knee pushing forward against
her drapery, her hips and shoulders slanted on
opposing lines, and her head inclined toward the

1. The largest block comprises
the front of the figure; the
second largest the back, with
most of the hair; and the third
largest the left side of the Virgin's
drapery. A fourth block makes
up the fold of the drapery at the
Virgin's left knee.

2. The edges of the different
pieces do not match on the
interior.

3. I am grateful to Michele
Marincola for pointing out that
the floret is identical to that
found on the female saint in a
private collection (cat. 43A).

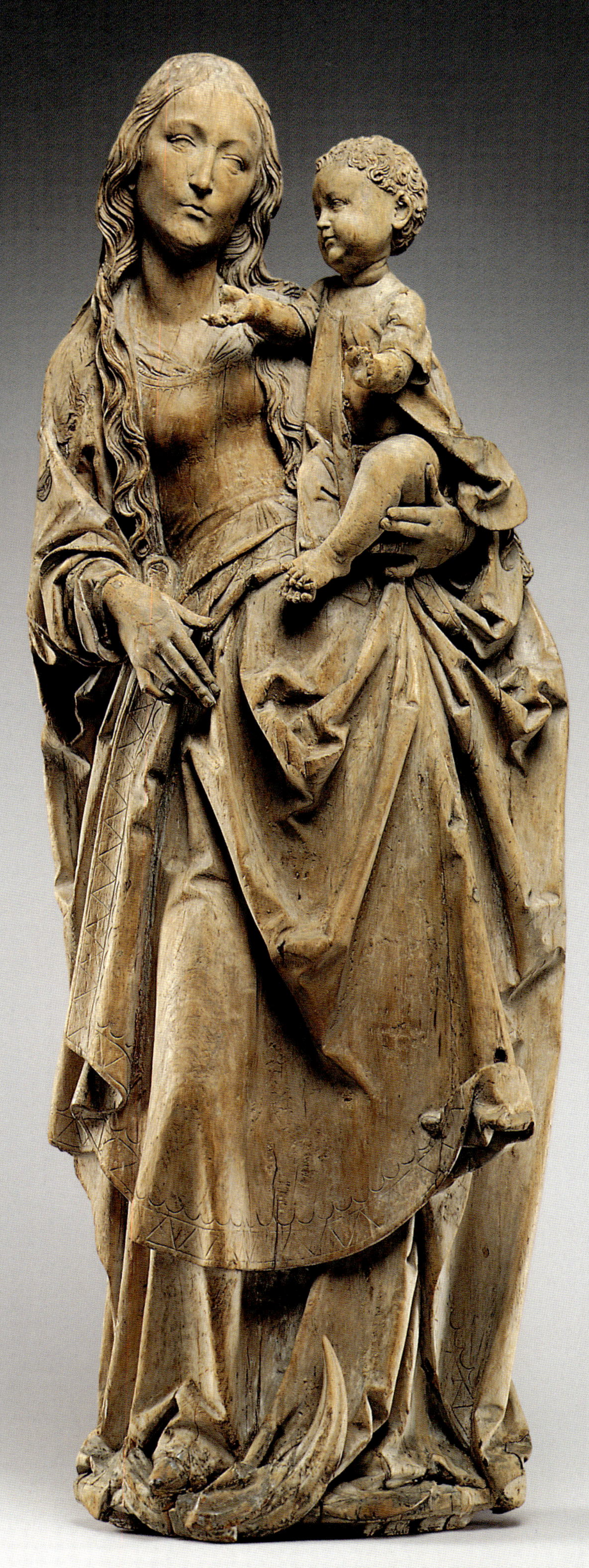

child, this grand figure is articulated along a generous S-curve. Her long, wavy hair falls down her back. The superb quality of the sculptural execution is evident in such details as the meticulous rendering of the child's mouth (in which two teeth are visible), in his coherent anatomy, and in the Virgin's elegant left hand.

This serene image of the Virgin and child is crucial for an understanding of Riemenschneider's art. Since its publication by Justus Bier in 1937,[4] the figure has been considered the model for the much larger *Virgin of the Rosary* in the pilgrimage church of Volkach (fig. 1), a sculpture documented to have been commissioned in 1521 and installed in the church in the following year.[5] The compositions of the two works are indeed extremely close, although the carving of the Dumbarton Oaks figure is of much higher quality than that of the Volkach Virgin; the implication is that an entirely autograph work was enlarged by assistants without the actual participation of the master. Furthermore, while most of Riemenschneider's figures are hollowed out in the back, those at Dumbarton Oaks and in Volkach are carved fully in the round. Each sculpture was made with essentially two viewpoints in mind—from the front and from the back—which would seem to reflect the intended placement of the Volkach sculpture, suspended from the arch at the entrance of the church choir.

A comparison of the two figures brings out their differences as well. The calmer Volkach Child is naked, and his arms are not raised but reach downward. The long strand of hair that falls in front of the right shoulder of the Dumbarton Oaks Virgin has been replaced in the Volkach Virgin by a veil that covers her head and flutters at her side. The Volkach Virgin also has a broader, flatter face.

These differences suggest that sculptors in Riemenschneider's shop enjoyed a certain freedom. Like the Montreal *Saint Sebastian* (cat. 39 A), whose function as a model is intimated by the existence of at least ten figures that seem to derive from it, the Dumbarton Oaks Virgin is characterized by a sensitive and detailed execution, which would have been particularly helpful for sculptors following the master's prototype.[6] The obvious discrepancy between the superb execution and the poor quality of the wood strongly suggests that the sculpture was not intended to leave the shop as an independent work and shows how thrifty Riemenschneider was with material.

While most likely carved in conjunction with the commission of the Volkach *Virgin of the Rosary,* the Dumbarton Oaks Virgin could have been replicated on other occasions. The Volkach Virgin stands on clouds, and her back is entirely covered with styl-

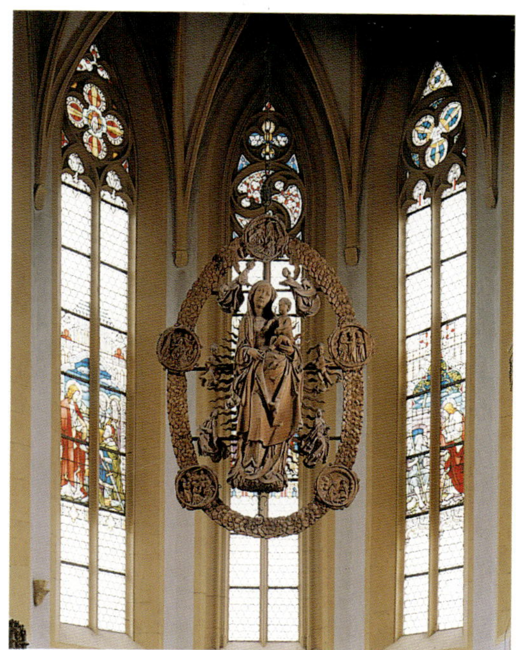

1.

Virgin of the Rosary, 1521–1522, limewood, Sankt Maria im Weingarten, Volkach

ized clouds (fig. 2), in keeping with her iconography as a heavenly vision and her function as a hanging image of the Virgin. The Dumbarton Oaks figure, by contrast, stands on a polygonal base, which emphasizes her "earthly" character, and her back is carved with hair, not clouds. The details specific to the theme of the *Virgin of the Rosary* were thus included only in the commissioned image.

Because it is circumstantially dated, the Dumbarton Oaks figure stands as a testament to the vitality of Riemenschneider's creative powers in his later years. Comparison with an earlier work of equal quality, the *Virgin and Child* in Cologne (cat. 16), brings the hallmarks of Riemenschneider's late style to the fore. While the Cologne figure is characterized by a volumetric treatment that encourages the viewer to move around it in an arc of about 180 degrees, the volumes of the Washington Virgin are compressed into a series of planes, and the work is essentially intended for frontal viewing. This flattening of form is also apparent in the Virgin's face, which has been reduced to the essential features. Equally important, the angular drapery pattern has been simplified, with fewer, rounder folds. This "classic simplicity and grandeur"[7] is typical of the best works of Riemenschneider's last years (see also Chapuis essay, fig. 9).

Comparison with the boxwood *Virgin and Child* at the Cloisters (cat. 6) reveals just how pervasive Niclaus Gerhaert's influence was on Riemenschnei-

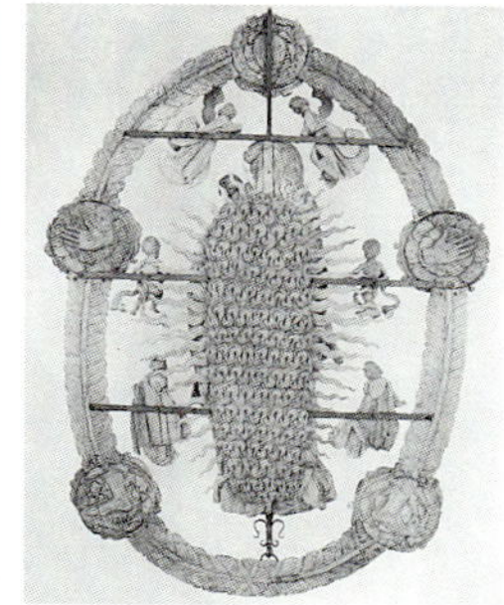

2.

Back view of

Virgin of the Rosary

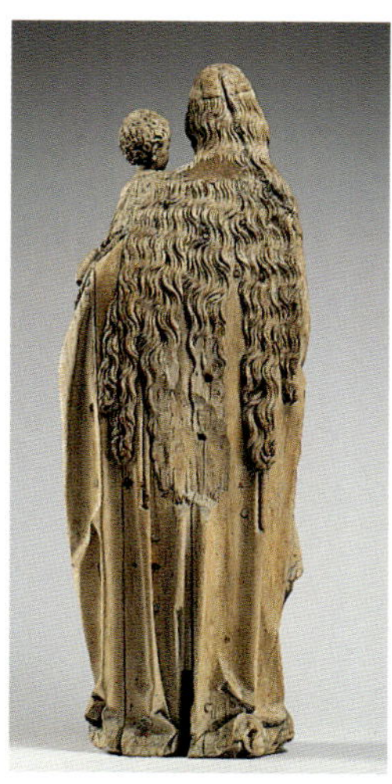

Back view of

catalogue no. 45

4. Bier 1937, 30.

5. Kalden 1990, 93–94, argues that although immediately preceding the Volkach Virgin the Dumbarton Oaks figure was not created necessarily as a model for it, but as a general model for the workshop; see also Muth 1954, 164.

6. Kalden 1990, 90.

7. Bier 1982, 79.

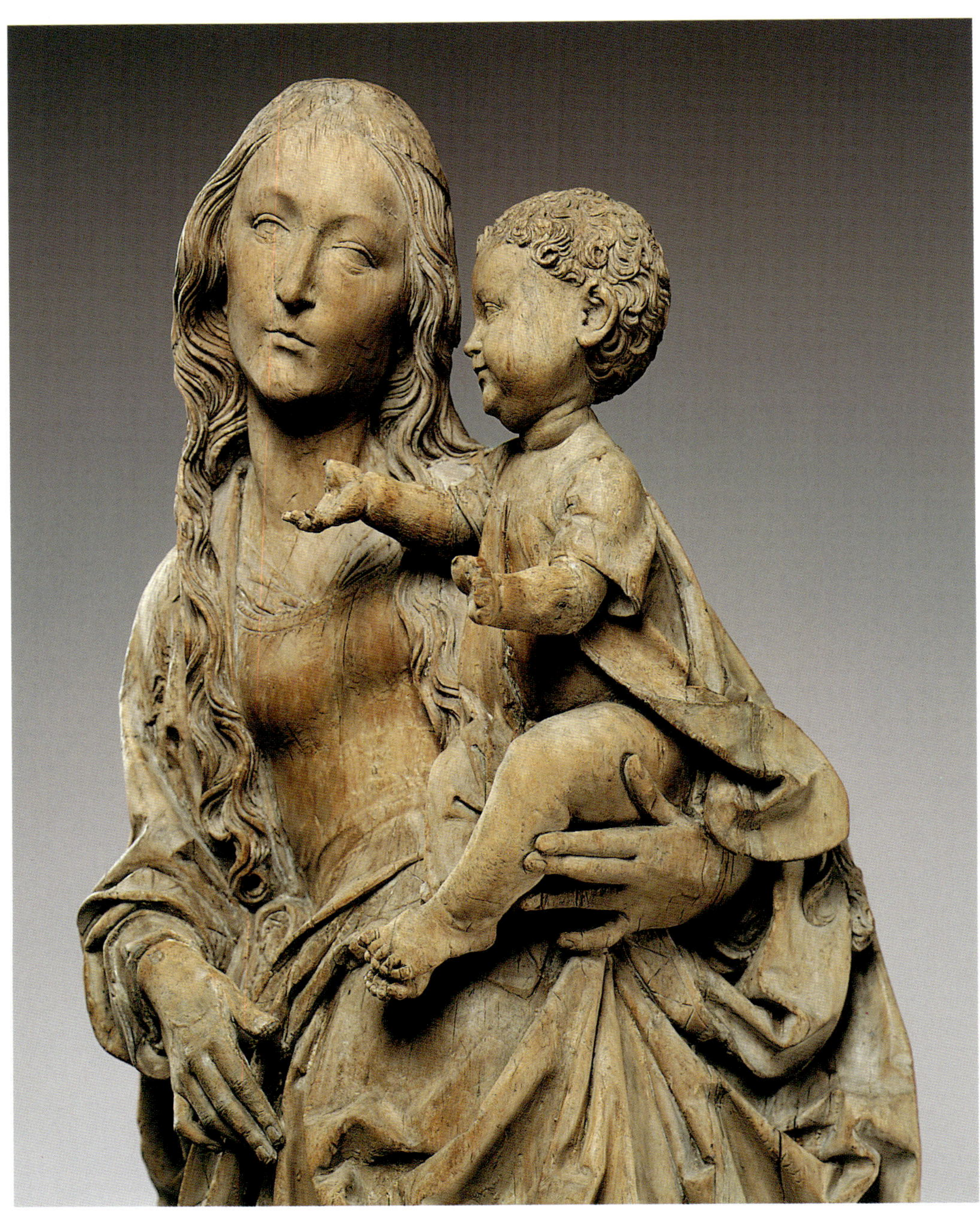

Detail of catalogue no. 45 (photographed during conservation)

der's art, even at the very end of his career. While highly stylized, Riemenschneider's masterworks retain a selective attention to naturalistic details. This is expressed here in the Virgin's exquisite left hand, with the thumb pushing into the flesh of the child's thigh, a motif present both on the Cloisters Virgin and on the Dangolsheim Virgin in Berlin (Krohm essay, fig. 2). As in these two works and in the earlier Cologne Virgin, the Dumbarton Oaks figure also stands on a polygonal base over which parts of her drapery fall. This detail is significant, because it reveals a similar reflection on the nature of sculpture. Sculpture is separated from the world in which it functions by its base, as a painting is set apart by its frame. By allowing the Virgin's garment to fall over the edge of the base, the artist blurs this boundary. The sculpture can then be perceived as a living woman, standing on a pedestal, appearing to be a sculpture appearing to be the Virgin. This conceit dramatically enhances the immediacy of the sculpture as an object of veneration, because it connects the world of the image with that of the viewer. CHAPUIS

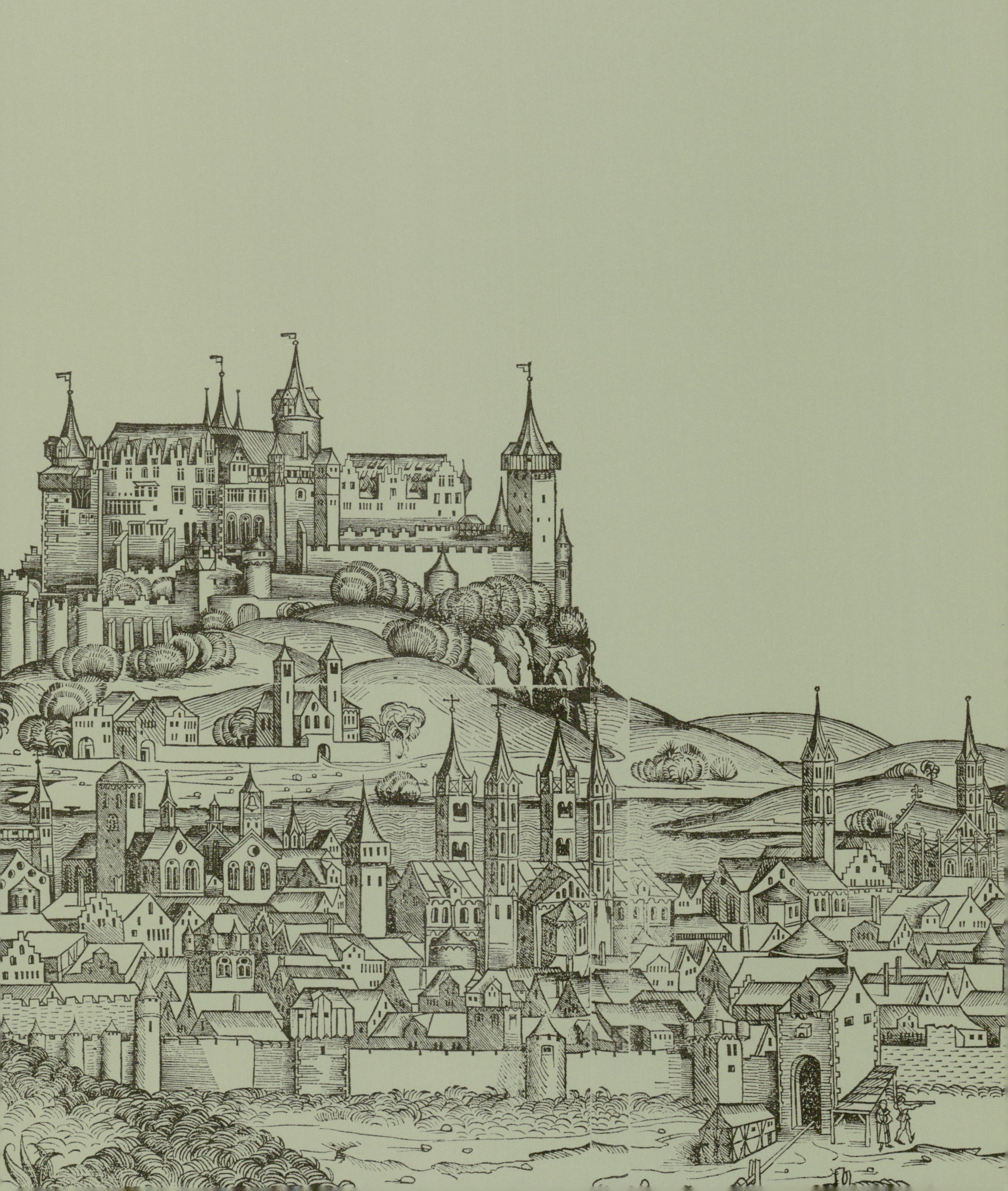

• References Cited •

An exhaustive bibliography is given in Eberlein, Johann Konrad. "Bibliographie zu Leben und Werk Tilman Rimenschneiders." *Beiträge zur fränkischen Kunstgeschichte* 3 (1998), 171–220.

Claudia Lichte's guide to the Riemenschneider collection in the Mainfränkisches Museum, Würzburg, was published in Munich, London, and New York in 1999, as the present catalogue was going to press.

EXHIBITION CATALOGUES

Albrecht Dürer. Oeuvre gravé. Musée du Petit Palais. Paris, 1996.

Aus 1000 Jahren Stift und Stadt Aschaffenburg. Stiftsmuseum der Stadt Aschaffenburg, 1957.

Bier, Justus. *Sculptures of Tilmann Riemenschneider.* North Carolina Museum of Art. Raleigh, 1962.

Dürers Verwandlung in der Skulptur zwischen Renaissance und Barock. Liebieghaus-Museum alter Plastik. Frankfurt am Main, 1981.

Friedländer, Max. J. *Deutsche und Niederländische Holzbildwerke im Berliner Privatbesitz.* Kunstgeschichtliche Gesellschaft. Berlin, 1904.

German Art 1400–1800 from Collections in Great Britain. City Art Gallery. Manchester, 1961.

Gothic and Renaissance Art in Nuremberg 1300–1550. The Metropolitan Museum of Art. New York, 1986.

Guillot de Suduiraut, Sophie. *Sculptures allemandes de la fin du Moyen Age.* Musée du Louvre. Paris, 1991.

Hans Holbein der Ältere und die Kunst der Spätgotik. Maximilianmuseum. Augsburg, 1965.

Kahsnitz, Rainer, ed. *Veit Stoss in Nürnberg.* Germanisches Nationalmuseum, Nuremberg. Munich, 1983.

Maedebach, Heino, ed. *Deutsche Bildwerke aus sieben Jahrhunderten.* Staatliche Museen. Berlin, 1958.

Medieval Art from Private Collections. The Metropolitan Museum of Art, The Cloisters. New York, 1968.

Mickenberg, David. *Songs of Glory: Medieval Art from 900–1500.* Oklahoma Museum of Art. Oklahoma City, 1985.

Mirror of the Medieval World. The Metropolitan Museum of Art. New York, 1999.

Riemenschneider Gedächtnis-Ausstellung 1931 des Museums für Kunst und Landesgeschichte. Provinzial-Museum. Hannover, 1931.

Sammlung R. von Passavant-Gontard. Städelsches Kunstinstitut. 3d ed. Frankfurt am Main, 1929.

Tilman Riemenschneider. Frühe Werke. Mainfränkisches Museum Würzburg. Regensburg, 1981.

Unsere Liebe Frau. Suermondt-Ludwig-Museum. Aachen, 1958.

Veit Stoss. Germanisches Nationalmuseum. Nuremberg, 1933.

Zimmermann, Eva. *Spätgotik am Oberrhein: Meisterwerke der Plastik und des Kunsthandwerks 1450–1550.* Badisches Landesmuseum. Karlsruhe, 1970.

MONOGRAPHS, ARTICLES, COLLECTION CATALOGUES

Adelmann, Karl. "Tilman Riemenschneider." *Walhalla* 6 (1910), 1–113.

Anonymous. "Ausstellung Gotischer Kunst im Künstlerhaus, Berlin." *Der Cicerone* 20 (1928), 72–73.

Anonymous. "Die wichtigsten Neuerwerbungen des Germanischen Museums in Nürnberg." *Der Cicerone* 15 (1923), 428.

Museen der Stadt Aschaffenburg. Stiftsmuseum der Stadt Aschaffenburg, 1949.

Stiftsmuseum der Stadt Aschaffenburg. Texts by Ingrid Jenderko-Sichelschmidt, Markus Marquart, and Gerhard Ermischer. Munich, 1994.

Bange, Ernst Friedrich, ed. *Die Bildwerke des Deutschen Museums.* Vol. 4. *Die Bildwerke in Holz, Stein und Ton. Kleinplastik.* Berlin, 1930.

Baum, Julius. *Katalog der Kgl. Altertümersammlung in Stuttgart.* Vol. 3. *Deutsche Bildwerke des 10. bis 18. Jahrhunderts.* Stuttgart and Berlin, 1917.

Baxandall, Michael. *South German Sculpture 1480–1530.* Victoria and Albert Museum. London, 1974.

———. *The Limewood Sculptors of Renaissance Germany.* New Haven and London, 1980.

Bergmann, Rosemarie. "Montreal. Neuerwerbung des Museums of Fine Arts." *Weltkunst* 42, no. 1 (1972), 18.

Beyer, Victor. "Autour du retable de Lautenbach (Bade). L'énigme d'une sainte Madeleine inconnue." *Cahiers alsaciens d'archéologie, d'art, et d'histoire* 16 (1972), 151–156.

Bier, Justus. *Tilmann Riemenschneider. Die frühen Werke.* Würzburg, 1925.

———. *Tilmann Riemenschneider. Die reifen Werke.* Augsburg, 1930.

———. "Riemenschneider-Ausstellungen im Gedächtnisjahr 1931." *Pantheon* 8 (1931), 451–454.

———. "Riemenschneider oder Peter Breuer?" *Pantheon* 11 (1933), 25–28.

———. "Tilman Riemenschneider." In Ulrich Thieme and Felix Becker, eds. *Allgemeines Lexikon der bildenden Künstler von der Antike bis zur Gegenwart.* 28:331–336. Leipzig, 1934.

———. "Ein unbekannter Sebastian von Tilmann Riemenschneider." *Pantheon* 17 (1936), 151–153.

———. *Tilmann Riemenschneider. Ein Gedenkbuch zur 400 jährigen Wiederkehr seines Todestages.* 2nd ed. Vienna, 1937.

———. "The Bust of a Bishop by Tilmann Riemenschneider." *Art Quarterly* 6 (1943), 158–166.

———. "An Anna Selbdritt by Riemenschneider." *Journal of the Walters Art Gallery* 7–8 (1944–1945), 10–37.

———. "A Bust of St. Urban by Tilmann Riemenschneider." *Art Quarterly* 9 (1946), 128–139.

———. "Riemenschneider's St. Jerome and His Other Works in Alabaster." *Art Bulletin* 33 (1951), 226–234.

———. "A Virgin with the Christ Child by Tilmann Riemenschneider." *Register of the Museum of Art of the University of Kansas* 2, no. 3 (1952), 1–6.

———. "Ein Sebastiansfragment von Tilmann Riemenschneider. Ein Beitrag zur Typologie der Riemenschneiderschen Sebastiandarstellungen." *Münchner Jahrbuch der bildenden Kunst* 5 (1954), 102–110.

———. "Riemenschneider as a Goldsmith's Model Maker." *Art Bulletin* 37 (1955), 102–112. [Bier 1955a]

———. "Riemenschneiders Weihnachtsdarstellungen und das neuentdeckte Fragment im Aschaffenburger Museum." *Aschaffenburger Jahrbuch* 2 (1955), 163–172. [Bier 1955b]

———. "Riemenschneider und die Schaumünzen des Lorenz von Bibra. Ein Beitrag zur Frage der frühesten deutschen Gussmedaille." *Münchner Jahrbuch der bildenden Kunst* 7 (1956), 95–110.

———. "Die Anfänge Tilmann Riemenschneiders." *Kunstgeschichtliche Gesellschaft zu Berlin, Nr. 5, Sitzungsberichte* (1957), 9–12. [Bier 1957a]

———. "Riemenschneider's Use of Graphic Sources." *Gazette des Beaux-Arts* 99, no. 50 (1957), 203–222. [Bier 1957b]

———. "A Virgin with the Christ Child by Tilmann Riemenschneider." *Register of the Museum of Art of the University of Kansas* 2, no. 2 (1959), 2–15. [Bier 1959a]

———. "Ein Werk Riemenschneiders aus seiner Strassburger Zeit." *Jahrbuch der Berliner Museen* 1 (1959), 190–197. [Bier 1959b]

———. "A Pietà by Tilmann Riemenschneider." *Bulletin of the Rhode Island School of Design* 46, no. 3 (1959–1960), 1–4.

———. "Two Statues: St. Stephen and St. Lawrence by Riemenschneider in the Cleveland Museum of Art." *Art Quarterly* 23 (1960), 215–227.

———. "Riemenschneider's Helpers in Need." *The Metropolitan Museum of Art Bulletin* 21 (1963), 317–326.

———. *Tilmann Riemenschneider. Die späten Werke in Stein.* Vienna, 1973.

———. "Riemenschneiders Marienstatuen und die Clemens-Madonna im Kölner Kunstgewerbemuseum." *Wallraf-Richartz-Jahrbuch* 37 (1975), 41–64.

———. *Tilmann Riemenschneider. Die späten Werke in Holz.* Vienna, 1978.

———. "Riemenschneider's St. Catherine in the North Carolina Museum of Art." *North Carolina Museum of Art Bulletin* 14 (1980), 15–32.

———. *Tilmann Riemenschneider. His Life and Work.* Lexington, KY, 1982.

Bock, Friedrich. "Das Nürnberger Predigerkloster, Beiträge zu seiner Geschichte." *Mitteilungen des Vereins für Geschichte der Stadt Nürnberg* 25 (1924), 145–213.

Bode, Wilhelm von. *Geschichte der Deutschen Plastik.* Vol. 2. *Geschichte der Deutschen Kunst.* Berlin, 1885.

Boockmann, Hartmut. "Bemerkungen zu den nichtpolychromierten Holzbildwerken des ausgehenden Mittelalters." *Zeitschrift für Kunstgeschichte* 57 (1994), 330–335.

Carter, David Giles. "Riemenschneider's St. Sebastian: Haunting Beauty and Nobility of Form." *M3*, no. 3 (1971), 17–23.

———. "Montreal Museum of Fine Arts Acquisition." *Pantheon* 30 (1972), 164.

Chamonikolasová, Kaliopi. "Nicolaus Gerhaert of Leyden in the Moravian Context." *Wiener Jahrbuch* 47 (1995), 79–83.

Cornell, Henrik. *The Iconography of the Nativity of Christ.* Uppsala, 1924.

Creutz, Max. "Die Sammlung Clemens in Köln. I. Plastik und Kunstgewerbe." *Der Cicerone* 14 (1922), 413–420.

Daun, Berthold. *Veit Stoss und seine Schule in Deutschland, Polen und Ungarn.* Leipzig, 1903.

———. *Veit Stoss.* Bielefeld and Leipzig, 1906.

———. *Veit Stoss und seine Schule in Deutschland, Polen, Ungarn und Siebenbürgen.* Leipzig, 1916.

Davis, R. S. *Masterpieces of Sculpture. Supplement to the Bulletin of the Minneapolis Institute of Arts* 38 (1949).

Demmler, Theodor. "Beiträge zur Kenntnis des Bildhauers Nicolaus Gerhaert von Leiden." *Jahrbuch der Preussischen Kunstsammlungen* 42 (1921), 20–33.

———. *Tilman Riemenschneider.* Berlin, 1923.

———. "Der Meister der Dangolsheimer Madonna." *Jahrbuch der Preussischen Kunstsammlungen* 46 (1925), 164–180.

———. "Gotikausstellung in Berlin." *Kunstchronik und Kunstliteratur. Beilage zur Zeitschrift für bildende Kunst* 62 (1928).

———, ed. *Die Bildwerke des Deutschen Museums.* Vol. 3. *Die Bildwerke in Holz, Stein und Ton. Grossplastik.* Berlin, 1930.

———. "Ein unbekannter Riemenschneider." *Pantheon* 10 (1932), 209–211.

———. *Die Meisterwerke Tilman Riemenschneiders.* Berlin, 1936; 2nd ed. 1939.

Desel, Jutta Barbara. *"Vom Leiden Christi oder von dem schmerzlichen Mitleiden Marias." Die vielfigurige Beweinung Christi im Kontext thüringischer Schnitzretabel der Spätgotik.* Alfter, 1994.

Dettloff, Felix. *Wit Stosz.* Breslau, 1961.

Deutsch, Wolfgang. "Die Konstanzer Bildschnitzer der Spätgotik und ihr Verhältnis zu Niklaus Gerhaert." *Schriften des Vereins für Geschichte des Bodensees und seiner Umgebung* 82 (1964), 11–129.

———. "Michel Erhart und sein Verhältnis zu Gregor Erhart und Syrlin dem Älteren." Unpublished typescript, 1969.

———. "Der ehemalige Hochaltar und das Chorgestühl, zur Syrlin- und zur Bildhauerfrage." In *600 Jahre Ulmer Münster.* Edited by Hans Eugen Specker and Reinhard Wortmann, 242–322. Ulm, 1977.

Diehl, August. *Tilman Riemenschneider, der grosse deutsche Bildhauer und Bildschnitzer.* Würzburg, 1936.

Esser, Werner. *Die Heilige Sippe. Studien zu einem spätmittelalterlichen Bildthema in Deutschland und den Niederlanden.* Bonn, 1986.

Falke, Otto von. "Ein Neuentdeckter Tilmann Riemenschneider." *Pantheon* 1 (1928), 566.

Feulner, Adolf. *Die deutsche Plastik des 16. Jahrhunderts.* Munich, 1927.

Finn, David. "A Sculpture by Tilmann Riemenschneider." *Sculpture Review* 46 (1997), 22–25.

Fischel, Lilli. *Nicolaus Gerhaert und die Bildhauer der deutschen Spätgotik.* Munich, 1944.

Flesche, Hermann, Günther Beyer, and Klaus Beyer. *Tilman Riemenschneider.* Dresden, 1957.

Förster, Ernst. *Denkmale deutscher Baukunst, Bildnerei und Malerei von der Einführung des Christenthums bis auf die neueste Zeit.* Vol. 2. Leipzig, 1856.

Frankfurter, Alfred. "Supplement to the Kress Collection." *ArtNews* 44 (February 1946), 26–29.

Freeden, Max H. von. *Riemenschneider-Bildnisse.* Stuttgart, 1951.

———. "Die Neuerwerbungen des Mainfränkischen Museums 1946–1956," and "Eine hl. Anna Selbdritt der Riemenschneider-Schule." *Mainfränkisches Jahrbuch für Geschichte und Kunst* 77 (1954), 1–65, 157–160.

———. "Die Grossostheimer Beweinung Christi. Ein unbekanntes Meisterwerk Riemenscheiders." *Weltkunst* 26, no. 6 (1965).

———. "Die Neuerwerbungen des Mainfränkischen Museums Würzburg 1966–1972." *Mainfränkisches Jahrbuch für Geschichte und Kunst* 96 (1973), 261–345.

———. *Tilmann Riemenschneider. Leben und Werk.* Munich, 1981.

Frenz, Karl Hans. *Der Schulkreis Niclaus Gerhaerts von Leiden am Mittel- und Oberrhein.* Freiburg im Breisgau, 1943.

Friedländer, Max J. "München. Ausstellung von Meisterwerken der Renaissance aus Privatbesitz." *Repertorium für Kunstwissenschaft* 24 (1901), 321–327. [Friedländer 1901a]

———. Review of Tönnies 1900. *Repertorium für Kunstwissenschaft* 24 (1901), 466–468. [Friedländer 1901b]

————, and Otto von Falke. *Die Kunstsammlung von Pannwitz.* Vol. 2. Munich, 1925.

Fründt, Edith, ed. *Bildwerke aus sieben Jahrhunderten.* Vol. 2. Staatliche Museen, Skulpturensammlung. Berlin, 1972.

Gaborit, Jean-René. *Le Louvre. La sculpture européenne.* Paris, 1994.

Germanisches Nationalmuseum. *Führer durch die Sammlungen.* Nuremberg, 1977.

Germanisches Nationalmuseum. *Schätze und Meilensteine deutscher Geschichte.* Nuremberg, 1997.

Gerstenberg, Kurt. *Tilman Riemenschneider.* Vienna, 1941; repr. Leipzig, 1955; repr. Munich, 1962.

Gillermann, Dorothy. "Gothic Sculpture in American Collections. The Checklist: 1. The New England Museums" (parts 2–3). *Gesta* (1981 and 1982).

Gross, Sibylle. *Hans Wydyz. Sein Oeuvre und die oberrheinische Bildschnitzkunst.* Hildesheim, Zurich, and New York, 1997.

Grossmann, Otto. "Eine Madonna von Riemenschneider?" *Hessen-Kunst, Kalender für alte und neue Kunst* 4 (1909), 21–32.

Haack, Friedrich. "Studien aus dem Germanischen Museum 1. Zu Riemenschneider." *Repertorium für Kunstwissenschaft* 29 (1906), 242–248.

Habicht, Victor Curt. "Die Hauptwerke im Roselius-Haus in Bremen." *Pantheon* 7 (1931), 106–111. [Habicht 1931a]

————. "Tilmann Riemenschneider und der Harz. Bemerkungen zur Lehrzeit und Wanderschaft." *Zeitschrift des Harz-Vereins für Geschichte und Altertumskunde* 64 (1931), 1–11. [Habicht 1931b]

————. "Tilmann Riemenschneiders Lehr- und Wanderjahre." *Niedersächsisches Jahrbuch für Landesgeschichte* 14 (1937), 1–34.

Haedecke, Hans-Ulrich. "Die Riemenschneider-Madonna im Kunstgewerbemuseum in Köln." *Museen der Stadt Köln, Bulletin* 2 (1961), 7.

Hampe, Theodor. "Die Neuerwerbung einer hl. Elisabeth von Tilmann Riemenschneider." *Anzeiger des Germanischen Nationalmuseums* 69 (1922–1923), 3–8.

Hasse, Max. *Lübeck St. Annen-Museum. Die sakralen Bildwerke des Mittelalters.* Lübeck, 1964.

Hefner-Alteneck, Jakob H. von. *Trachten, Kunstwerke und Geräthschaften des christlichen Mittelalters.* Vol. 7. 1886.

Hessig, Edith. *Die Kunst des Meisters E. S. und die Plastik der Spätgotik.* Berlin, 1935.

Homolka, I. *Gotická plastika in Slovenska.* Bratislava, 1972.

Hotz, Walter. "Die Grossostheimer Beweinung. Ein Frühwerk von Tilmann Riemenschneider." *Aschaffenburger Jahrbuch* 3 (1956), 217–226.

————. *Meister Mathis der Bildschnitzer. Die Plastik Grünewalds und seines Kreises.* Aschaffenburg, 1961.

Hubala, Erich. "Besprechung der Ausstellung Tilman Riemenschneider. Frühe Werke." *Das Münster* 35, no. 3 (1982), 226–231.

Jopek, Norbert. *Studien zur deutschen Alabasterplastik des 15. Jahrhunderts.* Manuskripte zur Kunstwissenschaft in der Wernerschen Verlagsgesellschaft. Vol. 21. Worms, 1988.

Josephi, Walter. *Die Werke plastischer Kunst.* Germanisches Nationalmuseum. Nuremberg, 1910.

Kahsnitz, Rainer. "Veit Stoss in Nürnberg, eine Nachlese zum Katalog und zur Ausstellung." *Anzeiger des Germanischen Nationalmuseums* (1984), 39–70.

————. *Tilman Riemenschneider. Zwei Figurengruppen unter dem Kreuz Christi.* Bayerisches Nationalmuseum. Munich, 1997.

————, and Peter Volk, eds. *Skulptur in Süddeutschland 1400–1770. Festschrift für Alfred Schädler.* Munich and Berlin, 1998.

Kalden, Iris. *Tilman Riemenschneider. Werkstattleiter in Würzburg.* Ammersbek bei Hamburg, 1990.

Kehrer, Hugo. *Die heiligen Drei Könige in der Legende und in der deutschen bildenden Kunst bis Albrecht Dürer.* Strasbourg, 1904.

————. *Die heiligen Drei Könige in Literatur und Kunst.* Leipzig, 1909.

Kepinski, Zdzistaw. *Veit Stoss.* Warsaw, 1981.

Klesse, Brigitte, and Hans-Ulrich Haedecke. *Die Sammlung Wilhelm Clemens.* Cologne, 1963.

Kobler, Friedrich. "Riemenschneider in Münnerstadt heute." *Kunstchronik* 35 (1982), 199–206.

Knapp, Fritz. *Tilmann Riemenschneider und Würzburg.* Paderborn, 1931.

————. *Riemenschneider.* Leipzig and Bielefeld, 1935.

Krohm, Hartmut, ed. *Zum Frühwerke Tilman Riemenschneiders. Eine Dokumentation, Staatliche Museen Preussischer Kulturbesitz, Skulpturengalerie.* Berlin, 1982.

———. "Eine Muttergottesfigur aus dem Stilkreis der Strassburger Münsterkanzel." In *Jahrbuch der Berliner Museen*, new series 31 (1989), 87–105.

———. "Der Schongauersche Bildgedankte des *Noli me Tangere* aus Münnerstadt. Druckgraphik und Bildgestalt des nichtpolychromierten Flügelaltars." In Krohm and Oellermann 1992, 84–102.

———, ed. *Meisterwerke mittelalterlicher Skulptur*. Berlin, 1996.

———. "Zuschreibungen an Niclaus Gerhaert von Leyden. Eine noch längst nicht abgeschlossene Diskussion." In Kahsnitz and Volk 1998, 109–128.

———, and Eike Oellermann. "Der ehemalige Münnerstädter Magdalenenaltar von Tilman Riemenschneider und seine Geschichte. Forschungsergebnisse zur monochromen Oberflächengestalt." *Zeitschrift des Deutschen Vereins für Kunstwissenschaft* 34 (1980), 16–99.

———, eds. *Flügelaltäre des späten Mittelalters*. Berlin, 1992.

Kuhn, Charles L. "Riemenschneider in the Harvard Collections." *The Art Bulletin* 56 (1974), 244–247.

Leisching, Julius. *Figurale Holzplastik*. Vol. 1. *Wiener Privatbesitz*. Vienna, 1908.

Liebmann, Michael J. *Die deutsche Plastik, 1350–1550*. Leipzig, 1982.

Lill, Georg, and Friedrich Karl Weysser. *Die Kunstdenkmäler von Unterfranken und Aschaffenburg*. Vol. 2. *Stadt und Bez. Amt Kitzingen*. Munich, 1911.

Lösch, Johann Christan Ernst. *Geschichte und Beschreibung der Kirche zu St. Jakob in Nürnberg nach ihrer Erneuerung im Jahr 1824/1825*. Nuremberg, 1825.

Lossnitzer, Max. *Veit Stoss. Die Herkunft seiner Kunst, seine Werke und sein Leben*. Leipzig, 1912.

Louvre. *Catalogue des sculptures*. Vol. 1. *Moyen Age et Renaissance*. Paris, 1922.

Lutze, Eberhard. "Die 'italienischen' Werke des Veit Stoss." *Pantheon* 19 (1937), 183–189.

———. *Veit Stoss*. Munich and Berlin, 1968.

Maek-Gérard, Michael. *Liebieghaus-Museum alter Plastik. Nachantike grossplastische Bildwerke*. Vol. 3. *Die Deutschsprachigen Länder, c. 1380–1530/1540*. Meslungen, 1985.

Maskell, Arthur. *Wood Sculpture*. London, 1931.

Meier, Michael. "Ein spätgotisches Wanddenkmal zu Basel und seine Stellung in der Kunst der Oberrheinlande." *Zeitschrift für Kunstgeschichte* 20 (1957), 287–295.

Metz, Peter, ed. *Bildwerke der christlichen Epoche von der Spätantike bis zum Klassizismus*. Staatliche Museen zu Berlin, Skulpturensammlung. Munich, 1966.

Meurer, Heribert. "Württembergisches Landesmuseum Stuttgart. Neuerwerbungen 1994. *Maria Cleophä und Alphäus*." *Jahrbuch der Staatlichen Kunstsammlungen in Baden-Württemberg* 23 (1995), 180.

Mezenceva, Earmian A. "Die Holzplastik 'Maria mit dem Kind' aus der Staatlichen Sammlung Ermitage und ihre stilistische Umgebung." *Forschungen und Berichte* 19 (1979), 57–60.

Middeldorf, Ulrich. *Sculptures from the Samuel H. Kress Collection*. London and New York, 1976.

Milliken, William M. "*St. Jerome and the Lion* by Tilman Riemenschneider." *The Bulletin of the Cleveland Museum of Art* 33, no. 10 (1946), 175–177.

Müller, Petro. *Die Antoniuskapelle zu Grosslangheim*. Schweinfurt, 1997.

Müller, Theodor. *Die Bildwerke in Holz, Ton und Stein von der Mitte des 15. bis gegen Mitte des 16. Jahrhunderts*. Bayerisches Nationalmuseum. Munich, 1959.

———. *Sculpture in the Netherlands, Germany, France, and Spain, 1400 to 1500*. The Pelican History of Art. Harmondsworth, England, 1966.

Muth, Hanswernfried. "Tilman Riemenschneiders Madonna im Rosenkranz in der Wallfahrtskirche 'Maria auf dem Kirchberg' bei Volkach." *Mainfränkisches Jahrbuch für Geschichte und Kunst* 77 (1954), 161–169.

———. "Eine Adam-Statuette von Tilman Riemenschneider." *Altfränkische Bilder und Wappenkalender* 80 (1981), 5.

———. *Tilman Riemenschneider. Die Werke des Bildschnitzers und Bildhauers, seiner Werkstatt und seines Umkreises*. Mainfränkisches Museum. Würzburg, 1982.

———, and Toni Schneiders. *Tilman Riemenschneider und seine Werke*. Würzburg, 1978; 2nd ed. 1982.

National Gallery of Art. *Paintings and Sculpture from the Samuel H. Kress Collection*. Washington, 1959.

National Gallery of Art. *Summary Catalogue of European Paintings and Sculpture*. Washington, 1965.

National Gallery of Art, Washington. New York, 1992.

Nicolaisen, Jan. "Die Verwendung der Kupferstiche Martin Schongauers in der Schnitzwerkstatt Tilmann Riemenschneiders." *Le Beau Martin. Actes du colloque de Colmar 1991*, 251–283. Colmar, 1991.

Nostitz, Charles E. von. "Two Unpolychromed Riemenschneiders at The Cloisters." *The Metropolitan Museum Journal* 10 (1975), 51–62.

Otto, Gertrud. *Ulmer Plastik der Spätgotik*. Reutlingen, 1927.

————. *Gregor Erhart*. Berlin, 1943.

Paatz, Walter. "Nicolaus Gerhaert von Leiden." *Heidelberger Jahrbücher* 3 (1959), 68–94.

————. *Süddeutsche Schnitzaltäre der Spätgotik*. Heidelberg, 1963.

Pilz, Kurt. *Die St. Jakobskirche in Nürnberg. Ihre Geschichte und ihr Kunstgewerbe*. Nuremberg, 1964.

Pinder, Wilhelm. *Die deutsche Plastik vom ausgehenden Mittelalter bis zum Ende der Renaissance*, part 2. Wildpark-Potsdam, 1929.

Pope-Hennessy, John. Review of Middeldorf 1976. *Apollo* 104 (July 1976), 70–72.

Rasmussen, Jörg. "Zum kleinplastischen Werk des Veit Stoss." *Pantheon* 34 (1976), 108–114.

————. "'…far stupire il mondo' Zur Verbreitung der Kunst des Veit Stoss." In *Veit Stoss. Die Vorträge des Nürnberger Symposions*, 107–122. Munich, 1985.

Recht, Roland. *Nicolas de Leyde et la sculpture à Strasbourg (1460–1525)*. Strasbourg, 1987.

Ring, Grete. "St. Jerome Extracting the Thorn from the Lion's Foot." *The Art Bulletin* 27 (1945), 188–194.

Ruppert, Ursula. *Studien zum Frühwerk Riemenschneiders. Datierung, Autorschaft, Eigenheit und Entwicklung des Stils*. Würzburg, 1992.

————. "Neue Forschungen: Studien zum Frühwerk Riemenschneiders: Datierung, Autorschaft, Eigenheit und Entwicklung des Stils." *Das Münster* 46 (1993), 253–255.

Schädler, Alfred. "Eine Strahlenkranzmadonna von Tilmann Riemenschneider im Bayerischen Nationalmuseum." *Pantheon* 33 (1975), 99–106.

————. "Die 'Dürer' Madonna der ehemaligen Sammlung Rothschild in Wien und Nicolaus Gerhaert." *Städel Jahrbuch* 10 (1983), 41–54.

————. "Zu Tilmann Riemenschneiders Kruzifixen." *Artibus et historiae* 12, no. 2 (1991), 37–51.

Schäfer, Karl. *Meisterwerke deutscher Bildschnitzerkunst im Germanischen Nationalmuseum zu Nürnberg*. Nuremberg, 1896.

————. *Die Sammlung W. Clemens*. Cologne, 1923.

Schestag, Franz. *Katalog der Kunstsammlung des Freiherren Anselm von Rothschild in Wien*. Vienna, 1866.

Schilling, R. "Ausstellung der Sammlung R. v. Passavant-Gontard im Städelschen Kunstinstitut." *Pantheon* 3 (1929), 183–189.

Schmitt, Otto, ed. *Reallexikon zur deutschen Kunstgeschichte*. Vol. 1. Stuttgart, 1937.

————, and Georg Swarzenski. *Meisterwerke der Bildhauerkunst in Frankfurter Privatbesitz*. Frankfurt, 1921.

Schmoll (also called Eisenwerth), Joseph Adolf. "Madonnen Nikolaus Gerhaerts von Leyden, seines Kreises und seiner Nachfolger." *Jahrbuch der Hamburger Kunstsammlungen* 3 (1958), 52–102.

Schneider, Ernst, ed. *Museum der Stadt Aschaffenburg*. Aschaffenburg, 1964.

————. "Zu den Spuren Riemenschneiders im Aschaffenburger Raum." *Aschaffenburger Jahrbuch* 13–14 (1990), 47–87.

Schrade, Hubert. *Tilmann Riemenschneider*. Heidelberg, 1927.

Sello, Gottfried. *Tilmann Riemenschneider*. Munich, 1983.

Simon, Holger. *Der Creglinger Marienaltar von Tilman Riemenschneider*. Berlin, 1998.

Söding, Ulrich. "Der Münnerstädter Altar von Tilman Riemenschneider." In Kahsnitz and Volk 1998, 129–156.

Sommer, Clemens. "Zur Anna-Selbdritt-Gruppe des Nicolaus Gerhaert von Leyden." *Berliner Museen. Berichte aus den Preussischen Kunstsammlungen* 48 (1927), 112–114.

Straus-Ernst, Luise. "Die Sammlung Clemens." *Zeitschrift für bildende Kunst* 56 (1921), 14–18.

Streit, Carl. *Tylmann Riemenschneider 1460–1531. Leben und Kunstwerke des fränkischen Bildschnitzers. Quellenmässig zusammengestellt und erläutert*. Berlin, 1888.

Swarzenski, Georg. "Die Sammlung Harry Fuld." *Kunstblatt* 2 (1918), 78–90.

————. "Deutsche Alabasterplastik des 15. Jahrhunderts." *Städel-Jahrbuch* 1 (1921), 167–213.

Taggart, Rossa, and George L. McKenna. *Handbook of the Collections.* Vol. 1. *Art of the Occident.* Nelson-Atkins Museum of Art. Kansas City, 1973.

Tiemann, Grete. *Beiträge zur Geschichte der mittelrheinischen Plastik um 1500.* Veröffentlichungen der pfälzischen Gesellschaft zur Förderung der Wissenschaft. Vol. 10. Speyer, 1930.

Tönnies, Eduard. *Leben und Werke des Würzburger Bildschnitzers Tilmann Riemenschneider 1468–1531.* Strasbourg, 1900.

Treutwein, Karl. "Weihnachtsdarstellungen in Riemenschneiders Werk." *Frankenland* 33 (1981), 263–265.

Trnek, Helmut. In *Kunsthistorisches Museum Wien. Führer durch die Sammlungen.* Vienna, 1988.

Vetter, Ewald Maria. "Tilman Riemenschneiders Münnerstädter Altar. Zum Verständnis des theologischen Gehalts." *Pantheon* 38 (1980), 359–376.

———. "Würzburg, Mainfränkisches Museum. Ausstellung: *Tilman Riemenschneider. Frühe Werke.*" *Pantheon* 40 (1982), 66–67.

———. "Tilman Riemenschneiders Adam und Eva und die Restaurierung der Marienkapelle in Würzburg." *Pantheon* 49 (1991), 74–87.

———, and Eike Oellermann. "Raphel und Tobias von Veit Stoss, ein Nachtrag zum Gedenkjahr 1983." *Pantheon* 42 (1984), 39–70.

Vikan, Gary. *Catalogue of the Sculpture in the Dumbarton Oaks Collection from the Ptolemaic Period to the Renaissance.* Washington, 1995.

Vitry, Paul. "Les accroissements du département des sculptures." *Revue de l'Art* 22 (1908), 205–217.

Vöge, Wilhelm. *Beschreibung der Bildwerke der christlichen Epochen.* Vol. 4. Staatliche Museen. Berlin, 1910.

———. "Jörg Syrlin der ältere und seine Bildwerke." In *Denkmäler deutscher Kunst.* Berlin, 1950.

Volk, Peter, et al. *Das Kunstgewerbemuseum der Stadt Köln.* Cologne, 1971.

Walker, John. *National Gallery of Art, Washington.* New York, 1976.

Ward, Roger, and Patricia Fidler. *The Nelson-Atkins Museum of Art: A Handbook of the Collection.* New York, 1993.

Weber, Anton. *Leben und Werke des Bildhauers Dill Riemenschneider.* Würzburg, 1884; rev. ed. 1888.

———. *Til Riemenschneider. Sein Leben und Wirken.* Regensburg, 1911.

Wertheimer, Otto. *Nicolaus Gerhaert. Seine Kunst und seine Wirkung.* Berlin, 1929.

Weskott, Hanne. *Die Darstellung der Tobiasgeschichte in der bildenden Kunst West-Europas.* Munich, 1975.

Wilm, Hubert. *Mittelalterliche Plastik im Germanischen Nationalmuseum zu Nürnberg.* Munich, 1922.

———. *Die gotische Holzfigur. Ihr Wesen und ihre Technik.* Leipzig, 1923; rev. ed. Stuttgart, 1944.

Winzinger, Franz. "Ein zerstörtes Hauptwerk Tilman Riemenschneiders." *Das Münster* 4 (1951), 129–137.

Wirtz, Juliane. "Zur Anna Selbdritt aus dem Umkreis Nicolaus Gerhaerts von Leiden im Bodemuseum." Master's thesis, Freie Universität, Berlin, 1994.

Wixom, William D. "Two Lindenwood Sculptures by Tilmann Riemenschneider." *The Bulletin of the Cleveland Museum of Art* 46, no. 9 (1959), 189–197.

———. "Medieval Sculpture at The Cloisters." *The Metropolitan Museum of Art Bulletin* 46 (1988), 3–64.

———. "Recent Acquisitions." *The Metropolitan Museum of Art Bulletin* 54 (Fall 1996), 21.

Young, Bonnie. *A Walk through The Cloisters.* New York, 1988.

Zeissner, Sebastian. "Dr. Kilian von Bibra." *Mainfränkisches Jahrbuch für Geschichte und Kunst* (1950), 78–121.

Zimmermann, Eva. *Badisches Landesmuseum Karlsruhe. Die mittelalterlichen Bildwerke.* Karlsruhe, 1985.

Italic page numbers refer to illustrations; boldface page numbers, to catalogue entries. T R refers to the "works" list under "Riemenschneider, Tilman."